Mergers, Acquisitions, and Corporate Restructurings

The Wiley Corporate F&A series provides information, tools, and insights to corporate professionals responsible for issues affecting the profitability of their company, from accounting and finance to internal controls and performance management.

Founded in 1807, John Wiley & Sons is the oldest independent publishing company in the United States. With offices in North America, Europe, Asia, and Australia, Wiley is globally committed to developing and marketing print and electronic products and services for our customers' professional and personal knowledge and understanding.

Mergers, Acquisitions, and Corporate Restructurings

Sixth Edition

PATRICK A. GAUGHAN

WILEY

Published by John Wiley & Sons, Inc., Hoboken, New Jersey.
The Fifth Edition was published by John Wiley & Sons, Inc. in 2011.
Published simultaneously in Canada.

For general information on our other products and services or for technical support, please contact our Customer Care Department within the United States at (800) 762-2974, outside the United States at (317) 572-3993 or fax (317) 572-4002.

Wiley publishes in a variety of print and electronic formats and by print-on-demand. Some material included with standard print versions of this book may not be included in e-books or in print-on-demand. If this book refers to media such as a CD or DVD that is not included in the version you purchased, you may download this material at http://booksupport.wiley.com. For more information about Wiley products, visit www.wiley.com.

Library of Congress Cataloging-in-Publication Data:

ISBN 978-1-118-99754-3 (Hardcover)
ISBN 978-1-119-06335-3 (ePDF)
ISBN 978-1-119-06336-0 (ePub)

Printed in the United States of America

10 9 8 7 6 5 4 3 2 1

Contents

PART IV: CORPORATE RESTRUCTURING

Preface

THE FIELD OF MERGERS and acquisitions has undergone tumultuous changes over the past 20 years. The 1990s witnessed the fifth merger wave—a merger wave that was truly international in scope. After a brief recessionary lull, the merger frenzy began once again and global megamergers began to fill the corporate landscape. This was derailed by the subprime crisis and the Great Recession. When the economic recovery was slow, so too was the rebound in M&A activity. However, by 2013 and 2014 M&As began to rebound more strongly.

Over the past quarter of a century we have noticed that merger waves have become longer and more frequent. The time periods between waves also has shrunken. When these trends are combined with the fact that M&A has rapidly spread across the modern world, we see that the field is increasingly becoming an ever more important part of the worlds of corporate finance and corporate strategy.

As the M&A field has evolved we see that many of the methods that applied to deals of prior years are still relevant, but new rules are also in effect. These principles consider the mistakes of prior periods along with the current economic and financial conditions. It is hoped that these new rules will make the mergers of the future sounder and more profitable than those of prior periods. However, while dealmakers have asserted that they will pursue such goals, we would be remiss if we did not point out that when deal volume picked up dramatically such intentions seemed to fall by the wayside and M&A mistakes started to occur. In fact, as with many other areas of finance, learning from past mistakes proves challenging. Lessons that are learned tend to be short-lived. The failures of the fourth merger wave were so pronounced that corporate decision makers loudly proclaimed that they would never enter into such foolish transactions. However, there is nothing like a stock market boom to render past lessons difficult to recall while bathing in the euphoria of rising equity values.

The focus of this book is decidedly pragmatic. We have attempted to write it in a manner that will be useful to both the business student and the practitioner. Since the world of M&A is clearly interdisciplinary, material from the fields of law and economics is presented along with corporate finance, which is the primary emphasis of the book. The practical skills of finance practitioners have been integrated with the research of the academic world of finance. In addition we have an expanded chapter devoted to the valuation of businesses, including the valuation of privately held firms. This is an important topic that usually is ignored by traditional finance references. Much of the finance literature tends to be divided into two camps: practitioners and academicians. Clearly, both groups have made valuable contributions to the field of M&As. This book attempts to interweave these contributions into one comprehensible format.

The increase in M&A activity has given rise to the growth of academic research in this area. In fact, M&A seems to generate more research than other areas of finance. This book attempts to synthesize some of the more important and relevant research studies and to present their results in a straightforward and pragmatic manner. Because of the voluminous research in the field, only the findings of the more important studies are highlighted. Issues such as shareholder wealth effects of antitakeover measures have important meanings to investors, who are concerned about how the defensive actions of corporations will affect the value of their investments. This is a good example of how the academic research literature has made important pragmatic contributions that have served to shed light on important policy issues. It is unfortunate that corporate decision makers are not sufficiently aware of the large body of pragmatic, high-quality research that exists in the field of M&A. One of the contributions we seek to make with this book is to render this body of pragmatic research readily available, understandable, and concisely presented. It is hoped then that practitioners can use it to learn the impacts of the deals of prior decision makers.

We have avoided incorporating theoretical research that has less relevance to those seeking a pragmatic treatment of M&As. However, some theoretical analyses, such as agency theory, can be helpful in explaining some of the incentives for managers to pursue management buyouts. Material from the field of portfolio theory can help explain some of the risk-reduction benefits that junk bond investors can derive through diversification. These more theoretical discussions, along with others, are presented because they have important relevance to the real world of M&As. The rapidly evolving nature of M&As requires constant updating. Every effort has been made to include recent developments occurring just before the publication date. We wish the reader an enjoyable and profitable trip through the world of M&As.

Patrick A. Gaughan

PART ONE

Background

CHAPTER ONE

Introduction

 ## RECENT M&A TRENDS

The pace of mergers and acquisitions (M&As) picked up in the early 2000s after a short hiatus in 2001. The economic slowdown and recession in the United States and elsewhere in 2001 brought an end to the record-setting fifth merger wave. This period featured an unprecedented volume of M&As. It followed on the heels of a prior record-setting merger wave—the fourth. This one in the 1990s, however, was very different from its counterpart in the previous decade. The fifth wave was truly an international one, and it featured a heightened volume of deals in Europe and, to some extent, Asia, in addition to the United States. The prior merger waves had been mainly a U.S. phenomenon. When the fourth merger wave ended with the 1990–1991 recession, many felt that it would be a long time before another merger wave like it would occur. However, after a relatively short recession and an initially slow recovery, the economy picked up speed in 1993, and by 1994 the world was on a path to another record-setting merger period. This wave would feature deals that would make the ones of the 1980s seem modest. There would be many megamergers and many cross-border deals involving U.S. buyers and sellers, but also many large deals not involving U.S. firms.

Figure 1.1 shows that both European and U.S. M&A volume began to rise in 2003 and by 2006–2007 had reached levels comparable to their peaks of the fifth wave. Similar trends were apparent in Europe. With such high deal volume huge megamergers were not unusual (see Table 1.1 and 1.2). However, by 2008 the effects of the global recession and the subprime crisis began to take hold. The U.S. recession, which began in

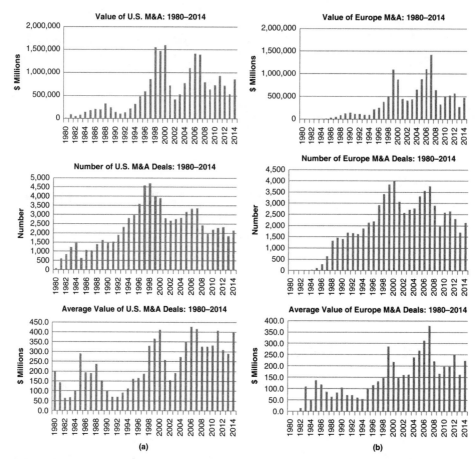

FIGURE 1.1 Value of M&As 1980–2014: (a) United States and (b) Europe. *Source*: Thomson Financial Securities Data, March 6, 2015.

January 2008, caused potential acquirers to reign in their acquisition-oriented expansion plans. Those bidders who were still inclined to go ahead with proposed deals found that their access to financing was sharply curtailed. Many bidders who had reached agreements with targets sought to renegotiate the deals or even back out altogether. Deals were canceled with increased frequency.

Deal volume in most regions of the world generally tended to follow the patterns in the United States and Europe. Australia, for example, exhibited such a pattern, with deal volume growing starting in 2003 but falling off in 2008 and 2009 for the same reason it fell off in the United States and Europe. The situation was somewhat different in China and Hong Kong. The value of deals in these economies has traditionally been well below the United States and Europe but had been steadily growing even in 2008, only to fall off sharply in 2009. China's economy has realized double-digit growth for a number of years and is now more than one-half of the size of the U.S. economy

TABLE 1.1 Top 10 Worldwide M&As by Value of Transaction

Date Announced	Date Effective	Value of Transaction ($ mil)	Target Name	Target Nation	Acquirer Name	Acquirer Nation
11/14/1999	6/19/2000	202,785.13	Mannesmann AG	Germany	Vodafone AirTouch PLC	United Kingdom
1/10/2000	1/12/2001	164,746.86	Time Warner	United States	America Online Inc	United States
9/2/2013	2/21/2014	130,298.32	Verizon Wireless Inc	United States	Verizon Communications Inc	United States
8/29/2007	3/28/2008	107,649.95	Philip Morris Intl Inc	Switzerland	Shareholders	Switzerland
4/25/2007	11/2/2007	98,189.19	ABN-AMRO Holding NV	Netherlands	RFS Holdings BV	Netherlands
6/19/1999	6/19/2000	89,167.72	Warner-Lambert Co	United States	Pfizer Inc	United States
12/1/1998	11/30/1999	78,945.79	Mobil Corp	United States	Exxon Corp	United States
1/17/2000	12/27/2000	75,960.85	SmithKline Beecham PLC	United Kingdom	Glaxo Wellcome PLC	United Kingdom
10/28/2004	8/9/2005	74,558.58	Shell Transport & Trading Co	United Kingdom	Royal Dutch Petroleum Co	Netherlands
3/5/2006	12/29/2006	72,671.00	BellSouth Corp	United States	AT&T Inc	United States

Source: Thomson Financial Securities Data, February 19, 2015.

TABLE 1.2 Top 10 European M&As by Value of Transaction

Date Announced	Date Effective	Value of Transaction ($ mil)	Target Name	Target Nation	Acquirer Name	Acquirer Nation
11/14/1999	06/19/2000	202,785.134	Mannesmann AG	Germany	Vodafone AirTouch PLC	United Kingdom
08/29/2007	03/28/2008	107,649.948	Philip Morris Intl Inc	Switzerland	Shareholders	Switzerland
04/25/2007	11/02/2007	98,189.193	ABN-AMRO Holding NV	Netherlands	RFS Holdings BV	Netherlands
01/17/2000	12/27/2000	75,960.847	SmithKline Beecham PLC	United Kingdom	Glaxo Wellcome PLC	United Kingdom
10/28/2004	08/09/2005	74,558.583	Shell Transport & Trading Co	United Kingdom	Royal Dutch Petroleum Co	Netherlands
02/25/2006	07/22/2008	60,856.454	Suez SA	France	Gaz de France SA	France
01/26/2004	08/20/2004	60,243.380	Aventis SA	France	Sanofi-Synthelabo SA	France
07/05/1999	03/27/2000	50,070.051	Elf Aquitaine	France	Total Fina SA	France
05/30/2000	08/22/2000	45,967.068	Orange PLC	United Kingdom	France Telecom SA	France
06/15/2014	01/26/2015	42,729.867	Covidien PLC	Ireland-Rep	Medtronic Inc	United States

Source: Thomson Financial Securities Data, February 19, 2015.

TABLE 1.3 Top 10 Asian M&A by Value of Transaction

Date Announced	Date Effective	Target Name	Target Nation	Acquirer Name	Acquirer Nation	Value of Transaction ($ mil)
03/26/2014	08/25/2014	CITIC Ltd	China	CITIC Pacific Ltd	Hong Kong	42,247.47
02/29/2000	08/17/2000	Cable & Wireless HKT	Hong Kong	Pacific Century CyberWorks Ltd	Hong Kong	37,442.15
10/04/2000	11/13/2000	Beijing Mobile, 6 others	China	China Telecom Hong Kong Ltd	Hong Kong	34,161.79
05/25/2008	10/15/2008	China Netcom Grp (HK) Corp Ltd	Hong Kong	China Unicom Ltd	Hong Kong	25,416.14
08/01/2012	12/31/2012	China Netcom Corp-3G Assets	China	China Telecom Corp Ltd	China	18,047.28
05/12/2008	11/17/2008	St George Bank Ltd	Australia	Westpac Banking Corp	Australia	17,932.98
04/11/2007	07/25/2007	SK Corp-Petrochemical Business	South Korea	Shareholders	South Korea	16,984.45
07/02/2007	11/23/2007	Coles Group Ltd	Australia	Wesfarmers Ltd	Australia	15,287.79
10/27/2006	07/16/2007	Rinker Group Ltd	Australia	Cemex SAB de CV	Mexico	14,247.73
02/11/2007	05/08/2007	Hutchison Essar Ltd	India	Vodafone Group PLC	United Kingdom	12,748.00

Source: Thomson Financial Securities Data, February 19, 2015.

(although on a purchasing power parity basis it is approximately the same size). However, there are many regulatory restrictions imposed on M&As in China that inhibit deal volume from rising to levels that would naturally occur in a less controlled environment. The Chinese regulatory authorities have taken measures to ensure that Chinese control of certain industries and companies is maintained even as the economy moves to a more free market status. This is why many of the larger Asian deals find their origins in Hong Kong (see Table 1.3).

In the rest of Asia, deal volume generally expanded starting in 2003 and declined with the global recession in 2008 and 2009. This was the case in India and South Korea

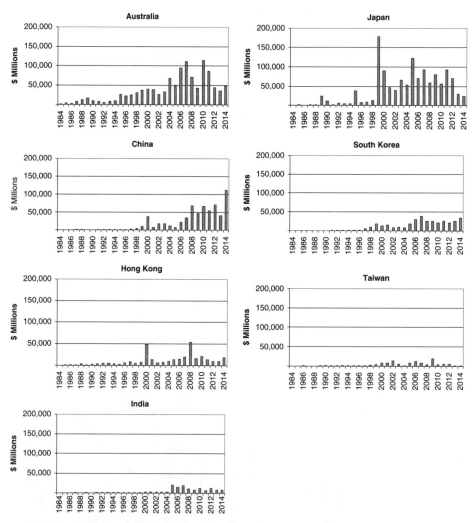

FIGURE 1.2 Value of M&A 1984–2014: By Nation. *Source*: Thomson Financial Securities Data, March 6, 2015.

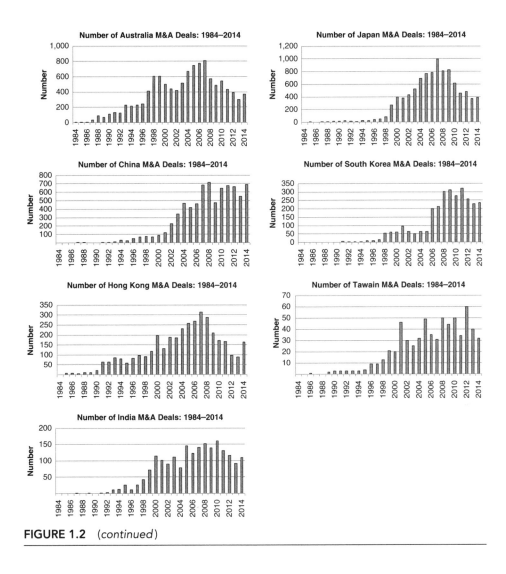

FIGURE 1.2 *(continued)*

(see Figure 1.2). In Japan, other factors help explain the trend in deal volume. Although Japan is the world's third largest national economy, it suffered a painful decade-long recession in the 1990s that has had lasting effects, some of which remain even today. The government has sought to deregulate the economy and take apart the myriad restrictive corporate interrelationships that had kept alive many businesses that otherwise would have failed. The country under Prime Minister Shinzo Abe and his Abenomics has tried various policies to stimulate the economy, but the nation suffers long-term problems, such as the aging of its population and the country's reluctance to allow immigrants to make up this shortfall.

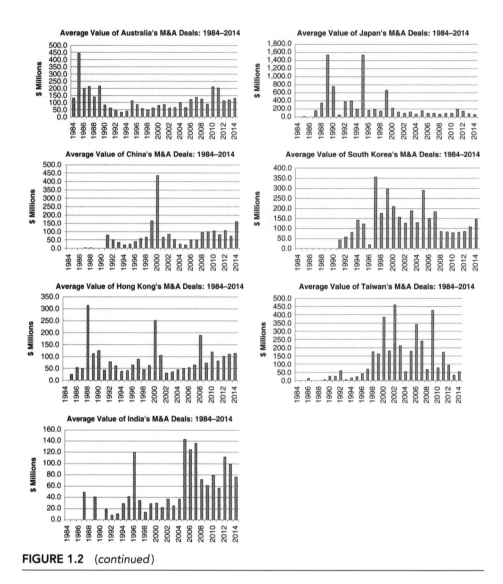

FIGURE 1.2 (continued)

VODAFONE TAKEOVER OF MANNESMANN: LARGEST TAKEOVER IN HISTORY

Vodafone Air Touch's takeover of Mannesmann, both telecom companies (and actually alliance partners), is noteworthy for several reasons in addition to the fact that it is the largest deal of all time (see Table 1.1). Vodafone was one of the world's largest mobile phone companies and grew significantly when it acquired Air Touch in 1999. This largest deal was an unsolicited hostile bid by a British company of a German firm. The takeover shocked the German corporate world because it was the first time a large German company had been taken over by a foreign company—and especially in this case, as the foreign company was housed in Britain and the two countries had fought two world wars against each other earlier in the century. Mannesmann was a large company with over 100,000 employees and had been in existence for over 100 years. It was originally a company that made seamless tubes but over the years had diversified into industries such as coal and steel. In its most recent history it had invested heavily in the telecommunications industry. Thus it was deeply engrained in the fabric of the German corporate world and economy.

It is ironic that Vodafone became more interested in Mannesmann after the latter took over British mobile phone operator Orange PLC. This came as a surprise to Vodafone as Orange was Vodafone's rival, being the third-largest mobile operator in Great Britain. It was also a surprise as Vodafone assumed that Mannesmann would pursue alliances with Vodafone, not move into direct competition with it by acquiring one of its leading rivals.[a]

Mannesmann tried to resist the Vodafone takeover, but the board ultimately agreed to the generous price paid. The Mannesmann board tried to get Vodafone to agree to maintain the Mannesmann name after the completion of the deal. It appeared that Vodafone would do so, but eventually they chose to go with the Vodafone name—something that made good sense in this age of globalization, as maintaining multiple names would inhibit common marketing efforts.

Up until the mid-1990s, Germany, like many European nations, had a limited market for corporate control. The country was characterized as having corporate governance institutions, which made hostile takeovers difficult to complete. However, a number of factors began to change starting in the second half of the 1990s and continued through the 2000s. First, the concentration of shares in the hands of parties such as banks, insurance companies, and governmental entities, which were reluctant to sell to hostile bidders, began to decline. In turn, the percentage of shares in the hands of more financially oriented parties, such as money managers, began to rise. Another factor that played a role in facilitating hostile deals is that banks had often played a defensive role for target management. They often held shares in the target and even maintained seats on the target's board and opposed hostile bidders while supporting management. One of the first signs of this change was apparent when WestLB bank supported Krupp in its takeover of Hoesch in 1991. In the case of Mannesmann, Deutsche Bank, which had been the company's bank since the late 1800s,[b] had a representative on Mannesmann's board but he played no meaningful role in resisting Vodafone's bid. Other parties who often played a defensive role, such as representatives of labor, who often sit on boards based on what is known as codetermination policy, also played little role in this takeover.

The position of target shareholders is key in Germany, as antitakeover measures such as poison pills (to be discussed at length in Chapter 5) are not as effective due to Germany's corporate law and the European Union (EU) Takeover Directive, which requires equal treatment of all shareholders. However, German takeover law includes exceptions to the strict neutrality provisions of the Takeover Directive, which gives the target's board more flexibility in taking defensive measures.

It is ironic that Vodafone was able to take over Mannesmann as the latter was much larger than Vodafone in terms of total employment and revenues. However, the market, which was at that time assigning unrealistic values to telecom

(*continued*)

(continued)

companies, valued Mannesmann in 1999 at a price/book ratio of 10.2 (from 1.4 in 1992), while Vodafone had a price/book ratio of 125.5 in 1999 (up from 7.7 in 1992).[c] This high valuation gave Vodafone "strong currency" with which to make a stock-for-stock bid that was difficult for Mannesmann to resist.

The takeover of Mannesmann was a shock to the German corporate world. Parties that were passive began to become more active in response to a popular outcry against any further takeover of German corporations. It was a key factor in steeling the German opposition to the EU Takeover Directive, which would have made such takeovers easier.

[a] Simi Kidia, "Vodafone Air Touch's Bid for Mannesmann," *Harvard Business School Case Study #9-201-096,* August 22, 2003.

[b] Martin Hopner and Gregory Jackson, "More In-Depth Discussion of the Mannesmann Takeover," *Max Planck Institut für Gesellschaftsforschung,* Cologne, Germany, January 2004.

[c] Martin Hopner and Gregory Jackson, "Revisiting the Mannesmann Takeover: How Markets for Corporate Control Emerge," *European Management Review* 3 (2006): 142–155.

The total volume of deals in South and Central America (see Figure 1.3 and Table 1.4) is small compared to the United States and Europe. However, in South America, M&A growth was in some years stronger than other regions. Argentina has continued to be plagued by a dysfunctional economy but the Brazilian economy and M&A grew for a while until it fell into recession.

In Central America the larger deals are attributable to Mexico. Mexico has been undergoing something of an economic resurgence, which has been boosted by recent attempts to deregulate major industries, such as petroleum and telecommunications, while fostering greater competition. It is too early to determine the outcome of these efforts, but they imply a higher volume of M&A in the future.

 TERMINOLOGY

A merger differs from a consolidation, which is a business combination whereby two or more companies join to form an entirely new company. All of the combining companies are dissolved and only the new entity continues to operate. One classic example of a consolidation occurred in 1986 when the computer manufacturers Burroughs and Sperry combined to form Unisys. A more recent example of a consolidation occurred in 2014 when Kinder Morgan consolidated its large oil and gas empire. It had Kinder Morgan, Inc., acquire Kinder Morgan Energy Part LP, Kinder Morgan Management LLC, and

TABLE 1.4 Top 5 Central American M&A by Value of Transaction, Top 5 South American M&A by Value of Transaction

Top Five Central American M&A by Value of Transaction

Date Effective	Value of Transaction ($mil)	Target Name	Target Nation	Acquirer Name	Acquirer Nation
01/19/2007	31,756.677	America Telecom SA de CV	Mexico	America Movil SA de CV	Mexico
06/04/2013	17,995.711	Crupo Modelo SAB de CV	Mexico	Anheuser-Busch Mexico Holding	Mexico
06/16/2010	17,807.347	Carso Global Telecom SAB de CV	Mexico	America Movil SA de CV	Mexico
06/10/2008	16,170.822	Telmex Internacional SAB de CV	Mexico	Shareholders	Mexico
02/07/2001	15,098.655	America Movil SA	Mexico	Shareholders	Mexico

Top Five South American M&A by Value of Transaction

Date Effective	Value of Transaction ($mil)	Target Name	Target Nation	Acquirer Name	Acquirer Nation
09/29/2010	42,877.032	Brazil-Oil & Gas Blocks	Brazil	Petro Brasileiro SA	Brazil
06/24/1999	13,151.700	YPF SA	Argentina	Repsol SA	Spain
05/08/2008	10,309.087	Bovespa Holding SA	Brazil	BM&F	Brazil
07/10/2000	10,213.310	Telecummunicacoes de Sao Paulo	Brazil	Telefonica SA	Spain
09/27/2010	9,742.793	Brasilcel NV	Brazil	Telefonica SA	Spain

Source: Thomson Financial Securities Data, February 19, 2015.

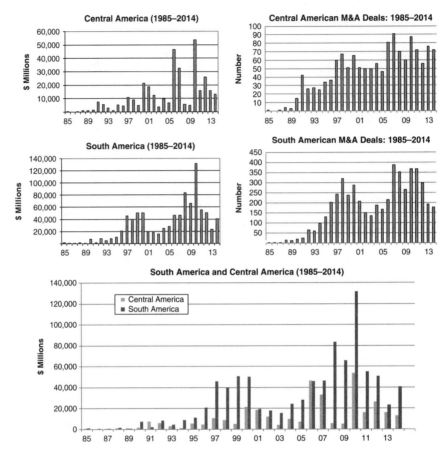

FIGURE 1.3 Central America and South America, 1985–2014. *Source*: Thomson Financial Securities Data, March 6, 2015.

El Paso Pipeline Partners LP. The acquired entities were master limited partnerships that provided certain tax benefits but that limited the ability of the overall business to grow and do larger M&As.

In a consolidation, the original companies cease to exist and their stockholders become stockholders in the new company. One way to look at the differences between a merger and a consolidation is that with a merger, A + B = A, where company B is merged into company A. In a consolidation, A + B = C, where C is an entirely new company. Despite the differences between them, the terms *merger* and *consolidation*, as is true of many of the terms in the M&A field, are sometimes used interchangeably. In general, when the combining firms are approximately the same size, the term *consolidation* applies; when the two firms differ significantly in size, *merger* is the more appropriate term. In practice, however, this distinction is often blurred, with the term *merger* being broadly applied to combinations that involve firms of both different and similar sizes.

VALUING A TRANSACTION

Throughout this book we cite various merger statistics on deal values. The method used by Mergerstat is the most common method relied on to value deals. Enterprise value is defined as the base equity price plus the value of the target's debt (including both short- and long-term) and preferred stock less its cash. The base equity price is the total price less the value of the debt. The buyer is defined as the company with the larger market capitalization or the company that is issuing shares to exchange for the other company's shares in a stock-for-stock transaction.

TYPES OF MERGERS

Mergers are often categorized as horizontal, vertical, or conglomerate. A horizontal merger occurs when two competitors combine. For example, in 1998, two petroleum companies, Exxon and Mobil, combined in a $78.9 billion megamerger. Another example was the 2009 megamerger that occurred when Pfizer acquired Wyeth for $68 billion. If a horizontal merger causes the combined firm to experience an increase in market power that will have anticompetitive effects, the merger may be opposed on antitrust grounds. In recent years, however, the U.S. government has been somewhat liberal in allowing many horizontal mergers to go unopposed. That stance, however, appeared to toughen slightly when new leadership was put in place at the Justice Department following the election of Barack Obama. In Europe the European Commission has traditionally been somewhat cautious when encountering mergers that may have anticompetitive effects.

Vertical mergers are combinations of companies that have a buyer-seller relationship. A good example is the U.S. eyeglasses industry. One company, an Italian manufacturer, Luxottica, expanded into the U.S. market through a series of acquisitions. It was able to acquire retailers such as Lenscrafters and Sunglasses Hut, as well as major brands such as Ray-Ban and Oakley. It is surprising to some that the company was allowed by regulators to assume the large vertical position it enjoys in the U.S. eyeglasses market.[1]

A conglomerate merger occurs when the companies are not competitors and do not have a buyer-seller relationship. One example would be Philip Morris, a tobacco company, acquiring General Foods in 1985 for $5.6 billion, Kraft in 1988 for $13.44 billion, and Nabisco in 2000 for $18.9 billion. Interestingly, Philip Morris, which later changed its name to Altria, had used the cash flows from its food and tobacco businesses to become less of a domestic tobacco company and more of a food business. This is because the U.S. tobacco industry has been declining at an average rate of 2% per year (in shipments), although the international tobacco business has not been experiencing such a decline. The company eventually concluded that the litigation problems of its U.S.

---

[1] Patrick A. Gaughan, *Maximizing Corporate Value through Mergers and Acquisitions: A Strategic Growth Guide* (Hoboken, NJ: John Wiley & Sons, 2013), 160–163.

tobacco unit, Philip Morris USA, were a drag on the stock price of the overall corporation and disassembled the conglomerate.

Another major example of a conglomerate is General Electric (GE). This company has done what many others have not been able to do successfully—manage a diverse portfolio of companies in a way that creates shareholder wealth (most of the time). GE is a serial acquirer and a highly successful one at that. As we will discuss in Chapter 4, the track record of diversifying and conglomerate acquisitions is not good. We will explore why a few companies have been able to do this while many others have not.

 ## MERGER CONSIDERATION

Mergers may be paid for in several ways. Transactions may use all cash, all securities, or a combination of cash and securities. Securities transactions may use the stock of the acquirer as well as other securities, such as debentures. The stock may be either common stock or preferred stock. They may be registered, meaning they are able to be freely traded on organized exchanges, or they may be restricted, meaning they cannot be offered for public sale, although private transactions among a limited number of buyers, such as institutional investors, are permissible.

If a bidder offers its stock in exchange for the target's shares, this offer may provide for either a fixed or floating exchange ratio. When the exchange ratio is floating, the bidder offers a dollar value of shares as opposed to a specific number of shares. The number of shares that is eventually purchased by the bidder is determined by dividing the value offered by the bidder's average stock price during a prespecified period. This period, called the *pricing period*, is usually some months after the deal is announced and before the closing of the transaction. The offer could also be defined in terms of a "collar," which provides for a maximum and minimum number of shares within the floating value agreement.

Stock transactions may offer the seller certain tax benefits that cash transactions do not provide. However, securities transactions require the parties to agree on not only the value of the securities purchased but also the value of those that are used for payment. This may create some uncertainty and may give cash an advantage over securities transactions from the seller's point of view. For large deals, all-cash compensation may mean that the bidder has to incur debt, which may carry with it unwanted, adverse risk consequences.

Merger agreements can have fixed compensation or they can allow for variable payments to the target. It is common in deals between smaller companies, or when a larger company acquires a smaller target, that the payment includes a contingent component. Such payments may include an "earn out" where part of the payments are based upon the performance of the target. The opposite type of variable compensation is one that includes *contingent value rights* (CVRs). The CVRs guarantee some future value if the acquirer's shares that were given in exchange for the target's shares fall below some agreed-upon threshold. One innovative use of CVRs was Viacom's 1994 offer for QVC, which provided for the sellers to receive the difference between Viacom's stock price at closing and $48. At the time of the offer Viacom's stock price was $40. If a seller believes that its stock is undervalued and will rise in value in the foreseeable future, it may offer a CVR as a way of guaranteeing this. Buyers may possess asymmetric information on the possible future value of their stock that sellers do not have. Chatterjee and Yan found that announcement period returns for offers that include CVR were higher than stock-only bids.[2]

Sometimes merger agreements include a *holdback provision*. While alternatives vary, such provisions in the merger agreement provide for some of the compensation to be withheld based upon the occurrence of certain events. For example, the buyer may deposit some of the compensation in an escrow account. If litigation or other specific adverse events occur, the payments may be returned to the buyer. If the events do not occur, the payments are released to the selling shareholders after a specific time period.

 ## MERGER PROFESSIONALS

When a company decides it wants to acquire or merge with another firm, it typically does so using the services of attorneys, accountants, and valuation experts. For smaller deals involving closely held companies, the selling firm may employ a business broker who may represent the seller in marketing the company. In larger deals involving publicly held companies, the sellers and the buyers may employ investment bankers. Investment bankers may provide a variety of services, including helping to select the appropriate target, valuing the target, advising on strategy, and raising the requisite financing to complete the transaction. Table 1.5 is a list of leading investment bankers and advisors.

Investment Bankers

The work that investment bankers do for clients is somewhat different based upon whether they are on the sell side or the buy side of a transaction. On the buy side they can assist their clients in developing a proposal that, in turn, contemplates a specific deal structure. They may handle initial communications with the seller and/or its representatives. In addition, they do due diligence and valuation so that they have a good sense of what the market value of the business is. Investment bankers may have done some of this work in advance if they happened to bring the deal to the buyer.

On the sell side investment bankers consult with the client and develop an acquisition memorandum that may be distributed to qualified potential buyers. The banker screens potential buyers so as to deal only with those who both are truly interested and

---

[2] Sris Chatterjee and An Yan, "Why Do Some Firms Pay with Contingent Value Rights," *Journal of Financial and Quantitative Analysis* 43, no. 4 (December 2008): 1001–1036.

TABLE 1.5 U.S. Financial Advisor Rankings, 2013

Rank	Financial Advisor	Total Deal Value ($ Billions)	Total Number of Deals
1	JPMorgan Chase & Co.	391.2	136
2	Goldman Sachs & Co.	379.7	174
3	Bank of America Merrill Lynch	372.1	130
4	Morgan Stanley	330.9	138
5	Barclays Plc	253.9	73
6	UBS AG	224.0	71
7	Deutsche Bank AG	157.3	85
8	Citigroup	148.2	105
9	Guggenheim Capital LLC	133.7	13
10	Lazard	133.5	99

Source: Mergerstat Review, 2014.

have the capability of completing a deal. Those who qualify then have to sign a confidentiality agreement prior to gaining access to key financial information about the seller. Once the field has been narrowed, the administrative details have to be worked out for who has access to the "data room" so the potential buyers can conduct their due diligence.

The investment banker often will handle communications with buyers and their investment bankers as buyers formulate offers. The bankers work with the seller to evaluate these proposals and select the most advantageous one.

Legal M&A Advisors

Given the complex legal environment that surrounds M&As, attorneys also play a key role in a successful acquisition process. Law firms may be even more important in hostile takeovers than in friendly acquisitions because part of the resistance of the target may come through legal maneuvering. Detailed filings with the Securities and Exchange Commission (SEC) may need to be completed under the guidance of legal experts. In both private and public M&As, there is a legal due diligence process that attorneys should be retained to perform. Table 1.6 shows the leading legal M&A advisors. Accountants also play an important role in M&As by conducting the accounting due diligence process. In addition, accountants perform various other functions, such as preparing pro forma financial statements based on scenarios put forward by management or other professionals. Still another group of professionals who provide important services in M&As are valuation experts. These individuals may be retained by either a bidder or a target to determine the value of a company. We will see in Chapter 14 that these values may vary, depending on the assumptions employed. Therefore, valuation experts may build a model that incorporates various assumptions, such as different revenue growth rates or costs, which may be eliminated after the deal. As these and other assumptions vary, the resulting value derived from the deal also may change.

TABLE 1.6 U.S. Legal Advisor Rankings, 2013

Rank	Legal Advisor	Total Deal Value ($ bil)	Total Number of Deals
1	Wachtell, Lipton, Rosen & Katz	285.6	47
2	Davis Polk & Wardwell LLP	281.8	79
3	Simpson Thatcher & Bartlett LLP	281.5	124
4	Weil, Gotshal & Manges LLP	272.7	98
5	Jones Day LP	207.7	191
6	Hogan Lovells	202.5	69
7	Slaughter & May Ltd.	195.8	15
8	Debeboise & Plimpton LLP	152.9	16
9	Sullivan & Cromwell LLP	145.5	64
10	Macfarlanes LLP	135.1	6

Source: *Mergerstat Review*, 2014.

AVIS: A VERY ACQUIRED COMPANY

Sometimes companies become targets of an M&A bid because the target seeks a company that is a good strategic fit. Other times the seller or its investment banker very effectively shops the company to buyers who did not necessarily have the target, or even a company like the target, in their plans. This is the history of the often-acquired rent-a-car company, Avis.

Avis was founded by Warren Avis in 1946. In 1962 the company was acquired by the M&A boutique investment bank Lazard Freres. Lazard then began a process where they sold and resold the company to multiple buyers. In 1965 they sold it to their conglomerate client ITT. When the conglomerate era came to an end, ITT sold Avis off to another conglomerate, Norton Simon. That company was then acquired by still another conglomerate, Esmark, which included different units, such as Swift & Co. Esmark was then taken over by Beatrice, which, in 1986, became a target of a leveraged buyout (LBO) by Kohlberg Kravis & Roberts (KKR).

KKR, burdened with LBO debt, then sold off Avis to Wesray, which was an investment firm that did some very successful private equity deals. Like the private equity firms of today, Wesray would acquire attractively priced targets and then sell them off for a profit—often shortly thereafter.

This deal was no exception. Wesray sold Avis to an employee stock ownership plan (ESOP) owned by the rent-a-car company's employees at a high profit just a little over a year after it took control of the company.

At one point General Motors (GM) took a stake in the company: For a period of time the major auto companies thought it was a good idea to vertically integrate by buying a car rental company. The combined employee-GM ownership lasted for about nine years until 1996, when the employees sold the company to HFS. Senior managers of Avis received in excess of $1 million each while the average employee received just under $30,000. One year later HFS took Avis public. However, Cendant, a company that was formed with the merger of HFS and CUC, initially owned

(continued)

(continued)

one-third of Avis. It later acquired the remaining two-thirds of the company. Avis was then a subsidiary within Cendant—part of the Avis Budget group, as Cendant also had acquired Budget Rent A Car. Cendant was a diversified company that owned many other subsidiaries, such as Century 21 Real Estate, Howard Johnson, Super 8 Motels, and Coldwell Banker. The market began to question the wisdom of having all of these separate entities within one corporate umbrella without any good synergistic reasons for their being together. In 2006 Cendant did what many diversified companies do when the market lowers its stock valuation and, in effect, it does not like the conglomerate structure—it broke the company up; in this case, into four units.

The Avis Budget Group began trading on the New York Stock Exchange in 2006 as CAR. Avis's curious life as a company that has been regularly bought and sold underscores the great ability of investment bankers to sell the company and thereby generate fees for their services. However, despite its continuous changing of owners, the company still thrives in the marketplace.

MERGER ARBITRAGE

Another group of professionals who can play an important role in takeovers is arbitragers. Generally, *arbitrage* refers to the buying of an asset in one market and selling it in another. Risk arbitragers look for price discrepancies between different markets for the same assets and seek to sell in the higher-priced market and buy in the lower one. Practitioners of these kinds of transactions try to do them simultaneously, thus locking in their gains without risk. With respect to M&A, arbitragers purchase stock of companies that may be taken over in the hope of getting a takeover premium when the deal closes. This is referred to as *risk arbitrage*, as purchasers of shares of targets cannot be certain the deal will be completed. They have evaluated the probability of completion and pursue deals with a sufficiently high probability.

The merger arbitrage business is fraught with risks. When markets turn down and the economy slows, deals are often canceled. This occurred in the late 1980s, when the stock market crashed in 1987 and the junk bond market declined dramatically. The junk bond market was the fuel for many of the debt-laden deals of that period. In addition, when merger waves end, deal volume dries up, lowering the total business available. It occurred again in 2007–2009, when the subprime crisis reduced credit availability to finance deals and also made bidders reconsider the prices they offered for target shares.

Some investment banks have arbitrage departments. However, if an investment bank is advising a client regarding the possible acquisition of a company, it is imperative that a "Chinese wall" between the arbitrage department and the advisors working directly with the client be constructed so that the arbitragers do not benefit from the information that the advisors have but that is not yet readily available to the market. To derive financial benefits from this type of inside information is a violation of securities laws.

The arbitrage business has greatly expanded over the past decade. Several active funds specialize in merger arbitrage. These funds may bet on many deals at the same time. They usually purchase the shares after a public announcement of the offer has been made. Under certain market conditions, shares in these funds can be an attractive investment because their returns may not be as closely correlated with the market as other investments. In market downturns, however, the risk profile of these investments can rise.

We will return to the discussion of merger arbitrage in Chapter 6.

LEVERAGED BUYOUTS AND THE PRIVATE EQUITY MARKET

In a leveraged buyout (LBO), a buyer uses debt to finance the acquisition of a company. The term is usually reserved, however, for acquisition of public companies where the acquired company becomes private. This is referred to as *going private* because all of the public equity is purchased, usually by a small group or a single buyer, and the company's shares are no longer traded in securities markets. One version of an LBO is a *management buyout*. In a management buyout, the buyer of a company, or a division of a company, is the manager of the entity.

Most LBOs are buyouts of small and medium-sized companies or divisions of large companies. However, what was then the largest transaction of all time, the 1989 $25.1 billion LBO of RJR Nabisco by Kohlberg Kravis & Roberts, shook the financial world. The leveraged buyout business declined after the fourth merger wave but rebounded in the fifth wave and then reached new highs in the 2000s (Figure 1.4). While LBOs were mainly a U.S. phenomenon in the 1980s, they became international in the 1990s and have remained that way since.

LBOs utilize a significant amount of debt along with an equity investment. Often this equity investment comes from investment pools created by private equity firms. These firms solicit investments from institutional investors. The monies are used to acquire equity positions in various companies. Sometimes these private equity buyers acquire entire companies, while in other instances they take equity positions in companies. The private equity business grew significantly between 2003 and 2007; however, when the global economy entered a recession in 2008 the business slowed markedly. Private equity activity declined then and buyers did fewer and smaller-sized deals. This business steadily rebounded during the years 2013–2014. We will discuss this further in Chapter 9.

CORPORATE RESTRUCTURING

The term *corporate restructuring* usually refers to asset sell-offs, such as divestitures. Companies that have acquired other firms or have developed other divisions through activities such as product extensions may decide that these divisions no longer fit into the company's plans. The desire to sell parts of a company may come from poor performance

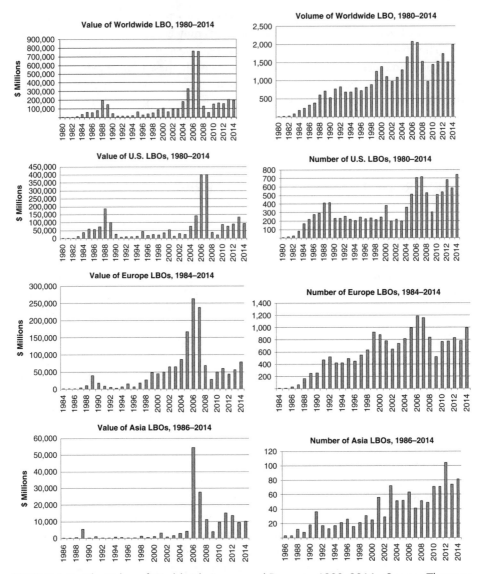

FIGURE 1.4 The Value of Worldwide Leveraged Buyouts, 1980–2014. *Source*: Thomson Financial Securities Data, February 19, 2015.

of a division, financial exigency, or a change in the strategic orientation of the company. For example, the company may decide to refocus on its core business and sell off non-core subsidiaries. This type of activity increased after the end of the third merger wave as many companies that engaged in diverse acquisition campaigns to build conglomerates began to question the advisability of these combinations. There are several forms of corporate sell-offs, with divestitures being only one kind. Spin and equity carve-outs are other ways that sell-offs can be accomplished. The relative benefits of each of these alternative means of selling off part of a company are discussed in Chapter 11.

MERGER NEGOTIATIONS

Most M&As are negotiated in a friendly environment. For buyer-initiated takeovers the process usually begins when the management of one firm contacts the target company's management, often through the investment bankers of each company. For seller-initiated deals the seller may hire an investment banker, who will contact prospective bidders. If the potential bidders sign a confidentiality agreement and agree to not make an unsolicited bid, they may receive nonpublic information. The seller and its investment banker may conduct an auction or may choose to negotiate with just one bidder to reach an agreeable price. Auctions can be constructed more formally, with specific bidding rules established by the seller, or they can be less formal.

The management of both the buyer and seller keep their respective boards of directors up to date on the progress of the negotiations because mergers usually require the boards' approval. Sometimes this process works smoothly and leads to a quick merger agreement. A good example of this was the 2009 $68 billion acquisition of Wyeth Corp. by Pfizer. In spite of the size of this deal, there was a quick meeting of the minds by management of these two firms and a friendly deal was agreed to relatively quickly. However, in some circumstances a quick deal may not be the best. AT&T's $48 billion acquisition of TCI is an example of a friendly deal where the buyer did not do its homework and the seller did a good job of accommodating the buyer's (AT&T's) desire to do a quick deal at a higher price. Speed may help ward off unwanted bidders, but it may work against a close scrutiny of the transaction.

Sometimes friendly negotiations may break down, leading to the termination of the bid or a hostile takeover. An example of a negotiated deal that failed and led to a hostile bid was the tender offer by Moore Corporation for Wallace Computer Services, Inc. Here negotiations between two archrivals in the business forms and printing business proceeded for five months before they were called off, leading to a $1.3 billion hostile bid. In 2003 Moore reached agreement to acquire Wallace and form Moore Wallace. One year later Moore Wallace merged with RR Donnelley.

In other instances a bid is opposed by the target right away and the transaction quickly becomes a hostile one. One classic example of a very hostile bid was the 2004 takeover battle between Oracle and PeopleSoft. This takeover contest was unusual due to its protracted length. The battle went on for approximately a year before PeopleSoft finally capitulated and accepted a higher Oracle bid.

Most merger agreements include a *material adverse change* clause. This clause may allow either party to withdraw from the deal if a major change in circumstances arises that would alter the value of the deal. This occurred in late 2005 when Johnson & Johnson (J&J) stated that it wanted to terminate its $25.4 billion purchase of Guidant Corporation after Guidant's problems with recalls of heart devices it marketed became more pronounced. J&J, which still felt the criticism that it had paid too much for its largest prior acquisition, Alza (acquired in 2001 for $12.3 billion), did not want to overpay for a company that might have unpredictable liabilities that would erode its value over time. J&J and Guidant exchanged legal threats but eventually seemed to agree on a lower value of $21.5 billion. J&J's strategy of using the material adverse change clause to get a better price backfired, as it opened the door for Boston Scientific to make an alternative offer and eventually outbid J&J for Guidant with a $27 billion final.

Auctions versus Private Negotiations

Many believe that auctions may result in higher takeover premiums. Boone and Mulherin analyzed the takeover process related to 377 completed and 23 withdrawn acquisitions that occurred in the 1990s.[3] Regarding the auctions in their sample, they found that on average 21 bidders were contacted and 7 eventually signed confidentiality and standstill agreements. In contrast, the private negotiated deals featured the seller dealing with a single bidder.

Boone and Mulherin found that more than half of deals involved auctions; the belief in the beneficial effects of auctions raised the question of why all deals are not made through auctions. One explanation may be agency costs. Boone and Mulherin analyzed this issue using an event study methodology, which compared the wealth effects to targets of auctions and negotiated transactions. Somewhat surprisingly they failed to find support for the agency theory. Their results failed to show much difference in the shareholder wealth effects of auctions compared to private negotiated transactions. This result has important policy implications as there has been some vocal pressure to require mandated auctions. The Boone and Mulherin results imply that this pressure may be misplaced.

Confidentiality Agreements

When two companies engage in negotiations the buyer often wants access to nonpublic information from the target, which may serve as the basis for an offer acceptable to the target. A typical agreement requires that the buyer, the recipient of the confidential information, not use the information for any purposes other than the friendly deal at issue. This excludes any other uses, including making a hostile bid. While these agreements are negotiable, their terms often are fairly standard.

Confidentiality agreements, sometimes also referred to as non-disclosure agreements (NDAs), usually cover not just information about the operations of the target, including intellectual property like trade secrets, but also information about the deal itself. The latter is important in instances where the target does not want the world to know it is secretly shopping itself. In addition, these agreements often include a standstill agreement, which limits actions the bidder can take, such as purchases of the target's shares. Standstill agreements often cover a period such as a year or more. We discuss them further in Chapter 5. However, it is useful to merely point out now that these agreements usually set a stock purchase ceiling below 5%, as purchases beyond that level may require a Schedule 13D disclosure (discussed in Chapter 3), which may serve to put the company in play.

---

[3] Audra L. Boone and J. Harold Mulherin, "How Are Firms Sold?" *Journal of Finance* 62, no. 20 (April 2007): 847–875.

In a recent Delaware Chancery Court decision, Chancellor Strine underscored that a confidentiality agreement does not automatically assume a standard agreement.[4] However, he also stated that the NDA may limit the ability of one party to use information covered by the NDA to take actions not allowed under the agreement, including a hostile bid.

Initial Agreement

When the parties have reached the stage where there are clear terms upon which the buyer is prepared to make an offer that it thinks the seller may accept, the buyer prepares a *term sheet*. This is a document that the buyer usually controls but that the seller may have input into. It may not be binding, but it is prepared so that the major terms of the deal are set forth in writing, thus reducing uncertainty as to the main aspects of the deal. The sale process involves investing significant time and monetary expenses, and the term sheet helps reduce the likelihood that parties will incur such expenses and be surprised that there was not prior agreement on what each thought were the major terms of the deal. At this point in the process, a great deal of due diligence work has to be done before a final agreement is reached. When the seller is conducting an auction for the firm, it may prepare a term sheet that can be circulated to potential buyers so they know what is needed to close the deal.

While the contents will vary, the typical term sheet identifies the buyer and seller, the purchase price and the factors that may cause that price to vary prior to closing (such as changes in the target's financial performance). It will also indicate the consideration the buyer will use (i.e., cash or stock) as well as who pays what expenses. While there are many other elements that can be added based on the unique circumstances of the deal, the term sheet should also include the major representations and warranties the parties are making.

The term sheet may be followed by a more detailed *letter of intent* (LOI). This letter delineates more of the detailed terms of the agreement. It may or may not be binding on the parties. LOIs vary in their detail. Some specify the purchase price, while others may only define a range or formula. It may also define various closing conditions, such as providing for the acquirer to have access to various records of the target. Other conditions, such as employment agreements for key employees, may also be noted. However, many merger partners enter into a merger agreement right away. So a LOI is something less than that, and it may reflect one of the parties not necessarily being prepared to enter into a formal merger agreement, For example, a private equity firm might sign a LOI when it does not yet have firm deal financing. This could alert investors, such as arbitragers, that the deal may possibly never be completed.

Disclosure of Merger Negotiations

Before 1988, it was not clear what obligations U.S. companies involved in merger negotiations had to disclose their activities. However, in 1988, in the landmark *Basic v. Levinson* decision, the U.S. Supreme Court made it clear that a denial that

---

[4] *Martin Marietta Materials, Inc. v. Vulcan Materials Co.*, C.A. 7102-CS (Del. Ch. May 4, 2012) (Strine, C.), May 4, 2012.

negotiations are taking place, when the opposite is the case, is improper.[5] Companies may not deceive the market by disseminating inaccurate or deceptive information, even when the discussions are preliminary and do not show much promise of coming to fruition. The Court's decision reversed earlier positions that had treated proposals or negotiations as being immaterial. The *Basic v. Levinson* decision does not go so far as to require companies to disclose all plans or internal proposals involving acquisitions. Negotiations between two potential merger partners, however, may not be denied. The exact timing of the disclosure is still not clear. Given the requirement to disclose, a company's hand may be forced by the pressure of market speculation. It is often difficult to confidentially continue such negotiations and planning for any length of time. Rather than let the information slowly leak, the company has an obligation to conduct an orderly disclosure once it is clear that confidentiality may be at risk or that prior statements the company has made are no longer accurate. In cases in which there is speculation that a takeover is being planned, significant market movements in stock prices of the companies involved—particularly the target—may occur. Such market movements may give rise to an inquiry from the exchange on which the company trades. Although exchanges have come under criticism for being somewhat lax about enforcing these types of rules, an insufficient response from the companies involved may give rise to disciplinary actions against the companies.

Deal Structure: Asset versus Entity Deals

The choice of doing an asset deal as opposed to a whole entity deal usually has to do with how much of the target is being sold. If the deal is for only part of the target's business, then usually an asset deal works best.

Asset Deals

One of the advantages for the acquirer of an asset deal is that the buyer does not have to accept all of the target's liabilities. This is the subject of negotiation between the parties. The seller will want the buyer to accept more liabilities and the buyer wants fewer liabilities. The benefit of limiting liability exposure is one reason a buyer may prefer an asset deal. Another benefit of an asset acquisition is that the buyer can pick and choose which assets it wants and not have to pay for assets that it is not interested in. All the assets acquired and liabilities incurred are listed in the *asset purchase agreement*.

Still other benefits of an asset deal are potential tax benefits. The buyer may be able to realize *asset basis step-up*. This can come from the buyer raising the value of the acquired assets to fair market value as opposed to the values they may have been carried at on the seller's balance sheet. Through such an increase in value the buyer can enjoy more depreciation in the future, which, in turn, may lower their taxable income and taxes paid.

---

[5] *Basic, Inc. v. Levinson*, 485 U.S. 224 (1988). The U.S. Supreme Court revisited this case in 2014 and addressed the case's reliance on the efficiency of markets in processing information. The Court declined to reverse *Basic* on this issue.

Sellers may prefer a whole entity deal. In an asset deal the seller may be left with assets it does not want. This is particularly true when the seller is selling most of its assets. Here they are left with liabilities that they would prefer getting rid of. In addition, the seller may possibly get hit with negative tax consequences due to potential taxes on the sale of the assets and then taxes on a distribution to the owners of the entity. Exceptions could be entities that are 80% owned subsidiaries, pass-through entities, or businesses that are LLPs or LLCs. Tax issues are very important in M&As. This is why much legal work is done in M&As not only by transactional lawyers but also by tax lawyers. Attorneys who are M&A tax specialists can be very important in doing deals, and this is a subspecialty of the law separate from transactional M&A law.

There are still more drawbacks to asset deals, in that the seller may have to secure *third-party consents* to the sale of the assets. This may be necessary if there are clauses in the financing agreements the target used to acquire the assets. It also could be the case if the seller has many contracts with *nonassignment* or *nontransfer clauses* associated with them. In order to do an asset deal the target needs to get approval from the relevant parties. The more of them there are, the more complicated the deal becomes. When these complications are significant, an asset deal becomes less practical, and if a deal is to be done it may have to be an entity transaction.

Entity Deals

There are two ways to do an entity deal—a stock transaction or a merger. When the target has a limited number of shareholders, it may be practical to do a stock deal as securing approval of the sale by the target's shareholders may not be that difficult. The fewer the number of shareholders, the more practical this may be. However, when dealing with a large public company with a large and widely distributed shareholder base, a merger is often the way to go.

Stock Entity Deals

In a stock entity deal, deals which are more common involving closely held companies, the buyer does not have to buy the assets and send the consideration to the target corporation as it would have done in an asset deal. Instead, the consideration is sent directly to the target's shareholders who sell all their shares to the buyer. One of the advantages of a stock deal is that there are no *conveyance issues*, such as what there might have been with an asset deal, where there may have been the aforementioned contractual restrictions on transfer of assets. With a stock deal, the assets stay with the entity and remain at the target, as opposed to the acquirer's level.

One other benefit that a stock deal has over a merger is that there are no *appraisal rights* with a stock deal. In a merger, shareholders who do not approve of the deal may want to go to court to pursue their appraisal rights and seek the difference between the value they received for their shares in the merger and what they believe is the true value of the shares. In recent years the volume of appraisal litigation in Delaware has risen.

This is, in part, due to the position the Delaware court has taken regarding the wide latitude it has in determining what a "fair value" is.[6]

One of the disadvantages of an entity deal is that the buyer may have to assume certain liabilities it may not want to have. One way a buyer can do a stock deal and not have to incur the potential adverse exposure to certain target liabilities it does not want is to have the seller indemnify it against this exposure. Here the buyer accepts the unwanted liabilities but gets the benefit of the seller's indemnification against this exposure. However, if the buyer has concerns about the long-term financial ability of the target to truly back up this indemnification, then it may pass on the stock deal.

Another disadvantage of a stock-entity deal is that all the target shareholders have to approve the deal. If some of them oppose the deal, it cannot be completed. When this is the case, then the companies have to pursue a merger. When the target is a large public corporation with many shareholders, this is the way to go.

Merger Entity Deals

Mergers, which are more common for publicly held companies, are partly a function of the relevant state laws, which can vary from state-to-state. Fortunately, as we will discuss in Chapter 3, more U.S. public corporations are incorporated in Delaware than any other state, so we can discuss legal issues with Delaware law in mind. However, there are many similarities between Delaware corporation laws and those of other states.

In merger laws certain terminology is commonly encountered. *Constituent corporations* are the two companies doing the deal. In a merger one company survives, called the *survivor*, and the other ceases to exist.

In a merger the surviving corporation succeeds to all of the liabilities of the nonsurviving company. If this is a concern to the buyer, then a simple merger structure is not the way to go. If there are assets that are unwanted by the buyer, then these can be spun out or sold off before the merger is completed.

In a merger the voting approval of the shareholders is needed. In Delaware the approval of a *majority* of the shareholders is required. This percentage can vary across states, and there can be cases where a corporation has enacted supermajority provisions in its bylaws. Unlike stock deals, shareholders who do not approve the deal can go to court to pursue their appraisal rights.

Forward Merger

The basic form of a merger is a *forward merger*, which is sometimes also called a *statutory merger*. Here the target merges directly in the purchaser corporation, and then the target disappears while the purchaser survives. The target shares are exchanged for cash or a combination of cash and securities. The purchaser assumes the target's liabilities, which is a drawback of this structure. However, given the assumption of these liabilities, there are usually no conveyance issues. Another drawback is that Delaware law treats forward mergers as though they were asset sales, so if the target has many contracts with third-party consents or nonassignment clauses, this may not be an advantageous

---

[6] *Huff Fund Investment Partnership v. CKx, Inc.*, C.A, No, 6844-VCG (Del Ch. Nov. 1, 2013).

route for the parties. Given the position of Delaware law on forward mergers, these deals look a lot like assets deals that are followed by a liquidation of the target, because the assets of the target move from the target to the buyer and the target disappears, while the deal consideration ends up with the target's shareholders.

A big negative of a basic forward merger is that the voting approval of the shareholders of both companies is needed. This can add an element of uncertainty to the deal. Another drawback is that the buyer directly assumes all of the target's liabilities, thereby exposing the buyer's assets to the target's liabilities. It is for these reasons that this deal structure is not that common. The solution is for the buyer to "drop down" a subsidiary and do a *subsidiary deal*. There are two types of subsidiary mergers—forward and reverse.

Forward Subsidiary Merger

This type of deal is sometimes called a forward triangular merger, given the structure shape shown in Figure 1.5. Instead of the target merging directly into the purchaser, the purchaser creates a merger subsidiary and the target merges directly into the subsidiary. There are a number of advantages of this structure. Firstly, there is no automatic vote required to approve the deal. In addition, the purchaser is not exposing its assets to the liabilities of the target. In this way the main purchaser corporation is insulated from this potential exposure.

As with much of finance, there are exceptions to the approval benefit. If the buyer issues 20% or more of its stock to finance the deal, the New York Stock Exchange and NASDAQ require approval of the purchaser's shareholders. There could also be concerns about litigants piercing the corporate veil and going directly after the purchaser corporation's assets.

Reverse Subsidiary Merger

Reverse subsidiary mergers, also called reverse triangular mergers (see Figure 1.6), improve upon the forward subsidiary merger by reversing the direction of the merger. The acquirer subsidiary pays the target's shareholders and receives the shares in the target in exchange. Here the subsidiary formed for the purposes of the deal merges directly into the target. The target corporation survives, and the subsidiary goes out of existence.

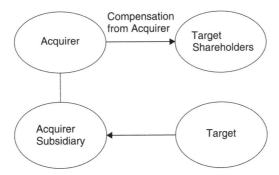

FIGURE 1.5 Forward Triangular Merger

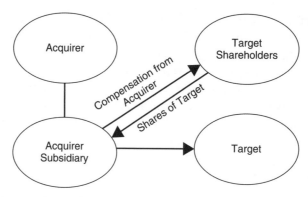

FIGURE 1.6 Reverse Triangular Merger

There are key advantages of this structure. One is that the assets of the target do not move anywhere. Therefore, there should be no problems with nonassignment or nonassignability clauses.

 MERGER AGREEMENT

Once the due diligence process has been completed, the law firms representing the parties prepare a detailed merger agreement. It is usually initiated by the buyer's law firm and is the subject of much back-and-forth negotiation. This document is usually long and complex—especially in billion-dollar deals involving public companies. However, some of the key components are sections that define the purchase price and consideration to be used. The agreement also includes all representations and warranties, what is expected of the seller and buyer prior to closing, the details of the closing (i.e., location and date), and what could cause a termination of the agreement. If the buyer incurs a penalty if it terminates, those termination fees are defined. Attached to the merger agreement is a whole host of supporting documents. These may include copies of resolutions by the seller's board of directors approving the deal as well as many other documents that are far too numerous to be listed here.

As noted earlier, the merger agreement may contain a material adverse event (MAE) or change clause that may allow the buyer to back out upon the occurrence of certain adverse events. Usually if the buyer opts out based on this clause, protracted litigation may ensue.

 MERGER APPROVAL PROCEDURES

In the United States, each state has a statute that authorizes M&As of corporations. The rules may be different for domestic and foreign corporations. Once the board of directors of each company reaches an agreement, they adopt a resolution approving the deal. This resolution should include the names of the companies involved in the deal and the name of the new company. The resolution should include the financial terms of the deal and other relevant information, such as the method that is to be used to convert securities of each company into securities of the surviving corporation. If there are any changes in the articles of incorporation, these should be referenced in the resolution.

At this point the deal is taken to the shareholders for approval. Friendly deals that are a product of a free negotiation process between the management of the two companies are typically approved by shareholders. Following shareholders approval, the merger plan must be submitted to the relevant state official, usually the secretary of state. The document that contains this plan is called the *articles for merger* or consolidation. Once the state official determines that the proper documentation has been received, it issues a certificate of merger or consolidation. SEC rules require a proxy solicitation to be accompanied by a Schedule 14A. Item 14 of this schedule sets forth the specific information that must be included in a proxy statement when there will be a vote for an approval of a merger, sale of substantial assets, or liquidation or dissolution of the corporation. For a merger, this information must include the terms and reasons for the transaction as well as a description of the accounting treatment and tax consequences of the deal. Financial statements and a statement regarding relevant state and federal regulatory compliance are required. Fairness opinions and other related documents must also be included. Following completion of a deal, the target/registrant must file a Form 15 with the SEC terminating the public registration of its securities.

Special Committees of the Board of Directors

The board of directors may choose to form a special committee of the board to evaluate the merger proposal. Directors who might personally benefit from the merger, such as when the buyout proposal contains provisions that management directors may potentially profit from the deal, should not be members of this committee. The more complex the transaction, the more likely it is that a committee will be appointed. This committee should seek legal counsel to guide it on legal issues, such as the fairness of the transaction, the business judgment rule, and numerous other legal issues. The committee, and the board in general, needs to make sure that it carefully considers all relevant aspects of the transaction. A court may later scrutinize the decision-making process, such as what occurred in the *Smith v. Van Gorkom* case (see Chapter 15).[7] In that case the court found the directors personally liable because it thought that the decision-making process was inadequate, even though the decision itself was apparently a good one for shareholders.

Fairness Opinions

It is common for the board to retain an outside valuation firm, such as an investment bank or a firm that specializes in valuations, to evaluate the transaction's terms and price. This firm may then render a fairness opinion, in which it may state that the offer is in a range that it determines to be accurate. This became even more important after the *Smith v. Van Gorkom* decision, which places directors under greater scrutiny. Directors

---

[7] *Smith v. Van Gorkom*, 488 A.2d 858, 3 EXC 112 (Del. 1985).

who rely on fairness opinions from an expert are protected under Delaware law from personal liability.[8] In an acquisition, the fairness opinion focuses on the financial fairness of the consideration paid by the buyer to the seller. In connection with a divestiture, the fairness opinion focuses on the fairness to the corporation as opposed to the stockholders of the company. Only if the shareholders directly receive the buyer's consideration will the fairness opinion focus on fairness to the holders of the seller's shares.

A fairness opinion could focus on fairness to the buyer in light of the amount it is paying. Like all valuations, fairness opinions are specific to a valuation date and the issuers of such opinions generally disclaim any responsibility to update them with the passage of time and the occurrence of other relevant events.[9]

It is important to note that fairness opinions tend to have a narrow financial focus and usually do not try to address the strategic merits of a given transaction. Writers of such opinions also try to avoid making recommendations to shareholders on how they should vote on the transactions. They also avoid considerations of many relevant aspects of a deal, such as lockup provisions, no-shop provisions, termination fees, and financing arrangements.

The cost of fairness opinions can vary, but it tends to be lower for smaller deals compared to larger ones. For deals valued under $5 billion, for example, the cost of a fairness opinion might be in the $500,000 range. For larger deals, however, costs can easily be several million dollars. The actual opinion itself may be somewhat terse and usually features a limited discussion of the underlying financial analysis. As part of the opinion that is rendered, the evaluator should state what was investigated and verified and what was not. The fees received and any potential conflicts of interest should also be revealed.

Voting Approval

Upon reaching agreeable terms and receiving board approval, the deal is taken before the shareholders for their approval, which is granted through a vote. The exact percentage necessary for stockholder approval depends on the articles of incorporation, which in turn are regulated by the prevailing state corporation laws. Following approval, each firm files the necessary documents with the state authorities in which each firm is incorporated. Once this step is completed and the compensation has changed hands, the deal is completed.

 DEAL CLOSING

The closing of a merger or acquisition often takes place well after the agreement has been reached. This is because many conditions have to be fulfilled prior to the eventual closing. Among them may be the formal approval by shareholders. In addition, the parties may also need to secure regulatory approvals from governmental authorities, such

---

[8] Delaware General Corporation Law Section 141(e).
[9] *In re Southern Peru Copper Corp. Shareholder Derivative Litigation*, C.A. No. 961-CS (Del. Ch. Oct 14, 2011).

as the Justice Department or Federal Trade Commission as well as regulators in other nations in the case of global firms. In many cases the final purchase price will be adjusted according to the formula specified in the agreement.

SHORT-FORM MERGER

A short-form merger may take place in situations in which the stockholder approval process is not necessary. Stockholder approval may be bypassed when the corporation's stock is concentrated in the hands of a small group, such as management, which is advocating the merger. Some state laws may allow this group to approve the transaction on its own without soliciting the approval of the other stockholders. The board of directors simply approves the merger by a resolution.

A short-form merger may occur only when the stockholdings of insiders are beyond a certain threshold stipulated in the prevailing state corporation laws. This percentage varies depending on the state in which the company is incorporated, but it usually is in the 90% to 95% range. Under Delaware law the short-form merger percentage is 90%.

A short-term merger may follow a tender offer as a second-step transaction, where shareholders who did not tender their shares to a bidder who acquired substantially all of the target's shares may be frozen out of their positions.

FREEZE-OUTS AND THE TREATMENT OF MINORITY SHAREHOLDERS

Typically, a majority of shareholders must provide their approval before a merger can be completed. A 51% margin is a common majority threshold. When this majority approves the deal, minority shareholders are required to tender their shares, even though they did not vote in favor of the deal. Minority shareholders are said to be frozen out of their positions. This majority approval requirement is designed to prevent a holdout problem, which may occur when a minority attempts to hold up the completion of a transaction unless they receive compensation over and above the acquisition stock price. This is not to say that dissenting shareholders are without rights. Those shareholders who believe that their shares are worth significantly more than what the terms of the merger are offering may go to court to pursue their shareholder appraisal rights. To successfully pursue these rights, dissenting shareholders must follow the proper procedures. Paramount among these procedures is the requirement that the dissenting shareholders object to the deal within the designated period of time. Then they may demand a cash settlement for the difference between the "fair value" of their shares and the compensation they actually received. Of course, corporations resist these maneuvers because the payment of cash for the value of shares will raise problems relating to the positions of other stockholders. Such suits are difficult for dissenting shareholders to win. Dissenting shareholders may file a suit only if the corporation does not file suit to have the fair value of the shares determined, after having been notified of the dissenting shareholders' objections. If there is a suit, the court may appoint an appraiser to assist in the determination of the fair value.

Following an M&A it is not unusual that months after the deal as many as 10% to 20% of shareholders still have not exchanged their frozen-out shares for compensation. For a fee, companies, such as Georgeson Securities Corporation, offer services paid by the shareholders, where they locate the shareholders and seek to have them exchange their shares.

REVERSE MERGERS

A reverse merger is a merger in which a private company may go public by merging with an already public company that often is inactive or a corporate shell. The combined company may then choose to issue securities and may not have to incur all of the costs and scrutiny that normally would be associated with an initial public offering. The private-turned-public company then has greatly enhanced liquidity for its equity. Another advantage is that the process can take place quickly and at lower costs than a traditional initial public offering (IPO). A reverse merger may take between two and three months to complete, whereas an IPO is a more involved process that may take many months longer.[10] Reverse mergers usually do not involve as much dilution as IPOs, which may involve investment bankers requiring the company to issue more shares than what it would prefer. In addition, reverse mergers are less dependent on the state of the IPO market. When the IPO market is weak, reverse mergers can still be viable. For these reasons there is usually a steady flow of reverse mergers, which explains why it is common to see in the financial media corporate "shells" advertised for sale to private companies seeking this avenue to go public.

The number of reverse mergers rose steadily from 2003 to 2008. Falloff in 2009 was relatively modest compared to the decline in the number of traditional M&As (see Figure 1.7). In terms of deal value, however, 2006 was the banner year and the value of these deals generally declined over the years 2008–2013.

For many companies, going public through a reverse merger may seem attractive, but it actually lacks some of the important benefits of a traditional IPO—benefits that make the financial and time costs of an IPO worthwhile. The traditional IPO allows the company going public to raise capital and usually provides an opportunity for the owners of the closely held company to liquidate their previously illiquid privately held shares. This does not automatically happen in a reverse merger. If the company wants to sell shares after the reverse merger, it still has to make a public offering, although it may be less complicated than an IPO. Being public after a reverse merger does not mean the shares of the combined company are really liquid. It all depends on how attractive the company is to the market and the condition of the market itself.

One advantage of doing a reverse merger is that it gives the company more liquid shares to use to purchase other target companies. Prospective targets might be reluctant

---

[10] Daniel Feldman, *Reverse Mergers* (New York: Bloomberg Press, 2009), 27–33.

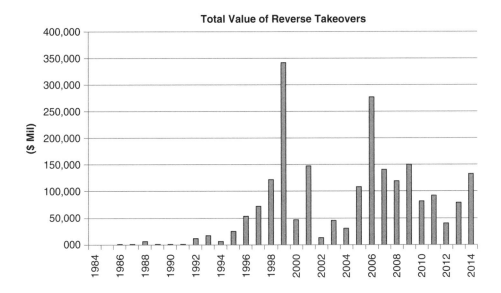

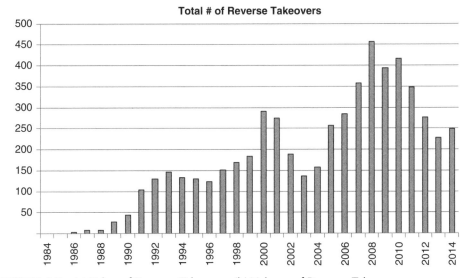

FIGURE 1.7 (a) Value of Reverse Takeovers (b) Volume of Reverse Takeovers.
Source: Thomson Financial Securities Data, March 6, 2015.

to accept illiquid shares from a privately held bidder. Shares from a public company for which there is an active market are often more appealing. Thus if the goal is to finance stock-for-stock acquisitions, a reverse merger may have some appeal.

Reverse mergers have often been associated with stock scams, as market manipulators have often merged private companies with little business activity into public shells and tried to "hype" up the stock to make short-term fraudulent gains. The SEC has tried to keep an eye out for these manipulators and limit such opportunities.

Special Purchase Acquisition Vehicles

Special purchase acquisition vehicles (SPACs) are companies that raise capital in an IPO where the funds are earmarked for acquisitions. They are sometimes also referred to as blank check companies or cash-shells. SPACs were very popular between 2006 and 2008, especially in 2008. The number of SPACs peaked in 2009 and declined in the years that followed (see Figure 1.8).

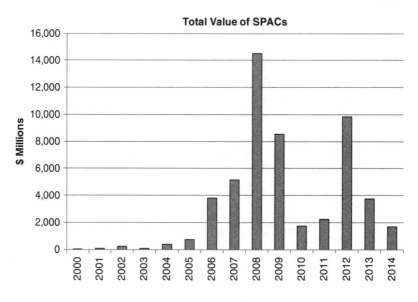

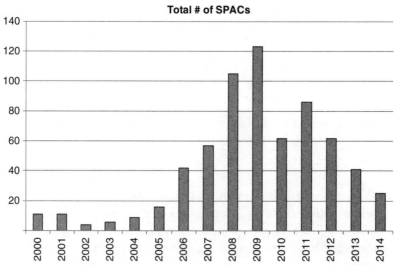

FIGURE 1.8 (a) Value of SPACs (b) Volume of SPACs. *Source*: Thomson Financial Securities Data, March 6, 2015.

Usually between 80% and 90% of the funds are placed in a trust that earns a rate of return while the company seeks to invest the monies in acquisitions. The remainder of the monies is used to pay expenses. Shareholders usually have the right to reject proposed deals. In addition, if the founders do not recommend a deal within a defined time period, such as 18 months, or complete a deal within 24 months, the monies are returned to investors less expenses plus a return earned in the capital. This contrasts with private equity investments, where shareholders do not have to approve specific deals.

Such investments can be risky for investors as it is possible that the company may not complete an acquisition. If that is the case, investors could get back less money than they originally invested. Even when the company does complete deals, they do not know in advance what targets will be acquired. During the period of time between the IPO and the completion of an acquisition, the funds raised are held in a trust fund and typically are invested in government securities.

The IPO offerings of SPACs are unique and differ in many ways from traditional IPOs. In addition to the differences in the nature of the company that we have discussed, they usually sell in units that include a share and one or two warrants, which usually detach from the shares and trade separately a couple of weeks after the IPO. Because the market for these shares can be illiquid, they often trade at a discount—similar to many closed-end funds. The post-IPO securities can be interesting investments as they represent shares in an entity that holds a known amount of cash but that trades at a value that may be less than this amount.

Founders of SPACs benefit by receiving a share, usually 20%, of the value of the acquisition. Normally, other than this ownership position, the founders of the SPAC do not receive any other remuneration. Their shares usually are locked up for a period, such as three years, after the IPO date.

In Chapter 4 we discuss the various factors that lead to a value-destroying M&A strategy. With SPACs, however, there is no strategy as investors are seeking to convert their liquid cash into an equity investment in an unknown company. Not surprisingly, in a study of 169 SPACs over the period 2003–2010, Jenkinson and Sousa found that over half of the deals immediately destroyed value.[11] They compared the per share value of the SPAC at the time of the deal with the per share trust value. They reasoned that if the market value is equal to or less than the trust value, the SPAC should be liquidated and the acquisition should not go forward.

In spite of the disappointing results of Jenkinson and Sousa, there is an explanation for SPAC's continued popularity. The investments are liquid and the shares have been sold to the market in the initial IPO. This compares favorably to private equity investments, which are not very liquid.

In spite of the fact that the market prices as of the acquisition approval date indicated *ex ante* that the deals would be value-destroying, more than half of the deals were nonetheless approved by investors. Jenkinson and Sousa found that investors who went

---

[11] Tim Jenkinson and Miguel Sousa, "Why SPAC Investors Should Listen to the Market," *Journal of Applied Finance* 21, no. 2 (September 2011): 38–57.

along with the recommendations of the SPAC founders in spite of a negative signal from the market suffered −39% cumulative returns within six months and −79% after one year. The fact that the founders recommended the deal is not surprising given that they derived their compensation by receiving 20% of the capital value of any acquisition. Therefore, they want the investors to approve an acquisition as that is how they get their money. The deal may cause investors to lose money, but it can still make the founders a significant return. In light of the poor performance of SPACs it is surprising that roughly three quarters of deals are approved by the SPAC investors.

 HOLDING COMPANIES

Rather than a merger or an acquisition, the acquiring company may choose to purchase only a portion of the target's stock and act as a holding company, which is a company that owns sufficient stock to have a controlling interest in the target. Holding companies trace their origins back to 1889, when the State of New Jersey became the first U.S. state to pass a law that allowed corporations to be formed for the express purpose of owning stock in other corporations. If an acquirer buys 100% of the target, the company is known as a wholly owned subsidiary. However, it is not necessary to own all of a company's stock to exert control over it. In fact, even a 51% interest may not be necessary to allow a buyer to control a target. For companies with a widely distributed equity base, effective working control can be established with as little as 10% to 20% of the outstanding common stock.

Advantages

Holding companies have certain advantages that may make this form of control transaction preferable to an outright acquisition:

- **Lower cost.** With a holding company structure, an acquirer may be able to attain control of a target for a much smaller investment than would be necessary in a 100% stock acquisition. Obviously, a smaller number of shares to be purchased permits a lower total purchase price to be set. In addition, because fewer shares are demanded in the market, there is less upward price pressure on the firm's stock and the cost per share may be lower. The acquirer may attempt to minimize the upward price pressure by gradually buying shares over an extended period of time.
- **No control premium.** Because 51% of the shares are not purchased, the full control premium that is normally associated with 51% to 100% stock acquisitions may not have to be paid.
- **Control with fractional ownership.** As noted, working control may be established with less than 51% of the target company's shares. This may allow the controlling company to exert certain influence over the target in a manner that will further the controlling company's objectives.

- **Approval not required.** To the extent that it is allowable under federal and state laws, a holding company may simply purchase shares in a target without having to solicit the approval of the target company's shareholders. As discussed in Chapter 3, this has become more difficult to accomplish because various laws make it difficult for the holding company to achieve such control if serious shareholder opposition exists.

Disadvantages

Holding companies also have disadvantages that make this type of transaction attractive only under certain circumstances:

- **Multiple taxation.** The holding company structure adds another layer to the corporate structure. Normally, stockholder income is subject to double taxation. Income is taxed at the corporate level, and some of the remaining income may then be distributed to stockholders in the form of dividends. Stockholders are then taxed individually on this dividend income. Holding companies receive dividend income from a company that has already been taxed at the corporate level. This income may then be taxed at the holding company level before it is distributed to stockholders. This amounts to triple taxation of corporate income. However, if the holding company owns 80% or more of a subsidiary's voting equity, the Internal Revenue Service allows filing of consolidated returns in which the dividends received from the parent company are not taxed. When the ownership interest is less than 80%, returns cannot be consolidated, but between 70% and 80% of the dividends are not subject to taxation.
- **Antitrust issues.** A holding company combination may face some of the same antitrust concerns with which an outright acquisition is faced. If the regulatory authorities do find the holding company structure anticompetitive, however, it is comparatively easy to require the holding company to divest itself of its holdings in the target. Given the ease with which this can be accomplished, the regulatory authorities may be quicker to require this compared with a more integrated corporate structure.
- **Lack of 100% ownership.** Although the fact that a holding company can be formed without a 100% share purchase may be a source of cost savings, it leaves the holding company with other outside shareholders who will have some controlling influence in the company. This may lead to disagreements over the direction of the company.

CHAPTER TWO

History of Mergers

N MUCH OF FINANCE there is very little attention paid to the history of the field. Rather, the focus is usually on the latest developments and innovations. This seems to be particularly the case in the United States, where there is less respect for that which is not new. It is not surprising, then, when we see that many of the mistakes and types of failed deals that occurred in earlier years tend to be repeated. The market seems to have a short memory, and we see that a pattern of flawed mergers and acquisitions (M&As) tends to reoccur. It is for this reason that we need to be aware of the history of the field. Such an awareness will help us identify the types of deals that have been problematic in the past.

There have been many interesting trends in recent M&A history. These include the fact that M&A has become a worldwide phenomenon as opposed to being mainly centered in the United States. Other trends include the rise of the emerging market acquirer, which has brought a very different type of bidder to the takeover scene. We devote special attention in this chapter to these important trends in recent M&A history.

 ## MERGER WAVES

Six periods of high merger activity, often called merger waves, have taken place in U.S. history. These periods are characterized by cyclic activity—that is, high levels of mergers followed by periods of relatively fewer deals. The first four waves occurred between 1897 and 1904, 1916 and 1929, 1965 and 1969, and 1984 and 1989. Merger activity declined at the end of the 1980s but resumed again in the early 1990s to begin the fifth merger wave. We also had a relatively short but intense merger period between 2003 and 2007.

WHAT CAUSES MERGER WAVES?

Research has shown that merger waves tend to be caused by a combination of economic, regulatory, and technological shocks.[1] The economic shock comes in the form of an economic expansion that motivates companies to expand to meet the rapidly growing aggregate demand in the economy. M&A is a faster form of expansion than internal, organic growth. Regulatory shocks can occur through the elimination of regulatory barriers that might have prevented corporate combinations. Examples include the changes in U.S. banking laws that prevented banks from crossing state lines or entering other industries. Technological shocks can come in many forms as technological change can bring about dramatic changes in existing industries and can even create new ones. Harford shows that these various shocks by themselves are generally not enough to bring about a merger wave.[2] He looked at industry waves, rather than the overall level of M&A activity, over the period 1981–2000. His research on 35 industry waves that occurred in this period shows that capital liquidity is also a necessary condition for a wave to take hold. His findings also indicate that misevaluation or market timing efforts by managers are not a cause of a wave, although they could be a cause in specific deals. The misevaluation findings, however, are contradicted by Rhodes-Kropf, Robinson, and Viswanathan, who found that misevaluation and valuation errors do motivate merger activity.[3] They measure these by comparing market to book ratios to true valuations. These authors do not say that valuation errors are the sole factor in explaining merger waves, but they say that they can play an important role that gains in prominence the greater the degree of misevaluation.

Rau and Stouraitis have analyzed a sample of 151,000 corporate transactions over the period 1980–2004, including a broader variety of different corporate events than just M&As. They have found that "corporate waves" seem to begin with new issue waves, first starting with seasoned equity offerings and then initial public offerings, followed by stock-financed M&A and later repurchase waves.[4] This finding supports the neoclassical efficiency hypothesis, which suggests that managers will pursue transactions when they perceive growth opportunities and will engage in repurchases when these opportunities fade.

FIRST WAVE, 1897–1904

The first merger wave occurred after the depression of 1883, peaked between 1898 and 1902, and ended in 1904 (Table 2.1). Although these mergers affected all major mining and manufacturing industries, certain industries clearly demonstrated a higher

---

[1] Mark Mitchell and J. H. Mulherin, "The Impact of Industry Shocks on Takeover and Restructuring Activity," *Journal of Financial Economics* 41, no. 2 (June 1996): 193–229.

[2] Jarrad Harford, "What Drives Merger Waves," *Journal of Financial Economics* 77, no. 3 (September 2005): 529–560.

[3] Matthew Rhodes-Kropf, David T. Robinson, and S. Viswanathan, "Valuation Waves and Merger Activity: The Empirical Evidence," *Journal of Financial Economics* 77, no. 3 (September 2005): 561–603.

[4] Panambur Raghavendra Rau and Aris Stouraitis, "Patterns in the Timing of Corporate Event Waves," *Journal of Financial and Quantitative Analysis* 46, no. 1 (February 2011): 209–246.

TABLE 2.1 First Wave, 1897–1904

Year	Number of Mergers
1897	69
1898	303
1899	1,208
1900	340
1901	423
1902	379
1903	142
1904	79

Source: Merrill Lynch Business Brokerage and Valuation, *Mergerstat Review*, 1989.

incidence of merger activity.[5] According to a National Bureau of Economic Research study by Professor Ralph Nelson, eight industries—primary metals, food products, petroleum products, chemicals, transportation equipment, fabricated metal products, machinery, and bituminous coal—experienced the greatest merger activity. These industries accounted for approximately two-thirds of all mergers during this period. The mergers of the first wave were predominantly horizontal combinations (Table 2.2). The many horizontal mergers and industry consolidations of this era often resulted in a near monopolistic market structure. For this reason, this merger period is known for its role in creating large monopolies. This period is also associated with the first billion-dollar megamerger when U.S. Steel was founded by J. P. Morgan, who combined Carnegie Steel, founded by Andrew Carnegie and run by Carnegie and Henry Clay Frick, with Federal Steel, which Morgan controlled. However, Morgan also added other steel companies, such as American Tin Plate, American Steel Hoop, American Steel Sheet, American Bridge, American Steel and Wire, International Mercantile Marine,

TABLE 2.2 Mergers by Types, 1895–1904

Type of Merger	Percentage (%)
Horizontal	78.3
Vertical	12
Horizontal and vertical	9.7
Total	100

Source: Neil Fligstein, *The Transformation of Corporate Control* (Cambridge, MA: Harvard University Press, 1990), 72.

---

[5] Ralph Nelson, *Merger Movements in American Industry: 1895–1956* (Princeton, NJ: Princeton University Press, 1959).

National Steel, National Tube, and Shelby Steel Tube. Combined under the corporate umbrella of U.S. Steel, the company controlled one-half of the U.S. steel industry.[6] The resulting steel giant merged 785 separate steel-making operations. At one time, U.S. Steel accounted for as much as 75% of U.S. steel-making capacity.

Besides U.S. Steel, some of today's great industrial giants originated in the first merger wave. These include DuPont, Standard Oil, General Electric, Eastman Kodak, American Tobacco (merged with Brown and Williamson in 1994, which in turn merged with RJ Reynolds in 2004), and Navistar International (formerly International Harvester but became Navistar in 1986 when it sold its agricultural business). While these companies are major corporations today with large market shares, some were truly dominant firms by the end of the first merger wave. For example, U.S. Steel was not the only corporation to dominate its market. American Tobacco enjoyed a 90% market share, and Standard Oil, owned by J. D. Rockefeller, commanded 85% of its market. In the first merger movement, there were 300 major combinations covering many industrial areas and controlling 40% of the nation's manufacturing capital. Nelson estimates that in excess of 3,000 companies disappeared during this period as a result of mergers.

By 1909, the 100 largest industrial corporations controlled nearly 18% of the assets of all industrial corporations. Even the enactment of the Sherman Antitrust Act (1890) did not impede this period of intense activity. The Justice Department was largely responsible for the limited impact of the Sherman Act. During the period of major consolidation of the early 1900s, the Justice Department, charged with enforcing the Act, was understaffed and unable to aggressively pursue antitrust enforcement. The agency's activities were directed more toward labor unions. Therefore, the pace of horizontal mergers and industry consolidations continued unabated without any meaningful antitrust restrictions.

By the end of the first great merger wave, a marked increase in the degree of concentration was evident in U.S. industry. The number of firms in some industries, such as the steel industry, declined dramatically, and in some sectors only one firm survived. It is ironic that monopolistic industries formed in light of the passage of the Sherman Act. However, in addition to the Justice Department's lack of resources, the courts initially were unwilling to literally interpret the antimonopoly provisions of the Act. For example, in 1895, the U.S. Supreme Court ruled that the American Sugar Refining Company was not a monopoly and did not restrain trade.[7] At this time, the Supreme Court was not concerned by the fact that the Sugar Trust controlled 98% of the sugar refining capacity in the United States. This favorable ruling gave the green light to companies such as DuPont, Eastman Kodak, General Electric, International Harvester, Standard Oil, and U.S. Steel to engage in M&As without being concerned about legal interference.[8] The courts initially saw the Sherman Act's focus to be on regulating stockholder trusts, in which investors would invest funds in a firm and entrust their stock certificates to directors, who would ensure that they received dividends for their "trust certificates."

---

[6] Ron Chernow, *The House of Morgan* (New York: Grove Press, 1990).

[7] Joseph R. Conlin, *The American Past* (Fort Worth, TX: Harcourt Press, 1997), 500.

[8] George Stigler, "Monopoly and Oligopoly by Merger," *American Economic Review* 40 (May 1950): 23–34.

With a misguided focus on trusts, the law was not applied to hinder the formation of monopolies in several industries in the first merger wave. The trusts were formed by dominant business leaders, such as J. P. Morgan of the House of Morgan and John D. Rockefeller of Standard Oil and National City Bank, as a response to the poor performance of many of the nation's businesses as they struggled with the weak economic climate. They saw the structure of many industries, which included many small and inefficient companies, as part of the reason for this poor performance. They reorganized failing companies in various industries by forcing shareholders to exchange their equity in troubled companies for trust certificates in a holding company that would control the business in question but also many other competitors. With such control, J. P. Morgan was able to rein in intense competition that he saw was rendering companies in many industries weak. In doing so he was able to give investors confidence in the soundness of companies for which he and others were seeking to market securities. His main initial focus was the railroad industry, which at that time accounted for the majority of stocks traded on the New York Stock Exchange. Being an industry with large demands for capital, railroad companies aggressively marketed stocks and bonds through investment bankers across the United States and Europe. However, railroad companies were prone to compete aggressively on rates and sought to drive each other to the brink of bankruptcy. Morgan hated such unrestrained competition and sought to reorganize this industry, and eventually others, using holding company trusts that would push aside aggressive competitor managers and replace them with those who would preside over a more orderly market. Morgan did not consider that consumers would suffer from these consolidations as his focus was on investors who would seek to benefit.

Trusts grew and came to dominate many industries. Among them were the American Cottonseed Oil Trust and the National Lead Trust, which dominated their respective industries. Morgan Bank, in turn, controlled First National Bank, the National Bank of Commerce, the First National Bank of Chicago, Liberty National Bank, Chase National Bank, Hanover National Bank, and the Astor National Bank.[9]

In addition to lax enforcement of federal antitrust laws, other legal reasons explain why the first merger wave thrived. For example, in some states, corporation laws were gradually relaxed. In particular, corporations became better able to secure capital, hold stock in other corporations, and expand their lines of business operations, thereby creating a fertile environment for firms to contemplate mergers. Greater access to capital made it easier for firms to raise the necessary financing to carry out an acquisition, and relaxed rules controlling the stockholdings of corporations allowed firms to acquire stock in other companies with the purpose of acquiring the companies.

Not all states liberalized corporate laws. As a result, the pace of M&As was greater in some states than in others. New Jersey, in which the passage of the New Jersey Holding Company Act of 1888 helped liberalize state corporation laws, was the leading state in M&As, followed by New York and Delaware. The law enabled holding company trusts to be formed and the State of New Jersey became a mecca for this corporate form.

---

[9] Nell Irvin Painter, *Standing at Armageddon: The United States, 1877–1919* (New York: Norton, 1987), 178–179.

This Act pressured other states to enact similar legislation rather than see firms move to reincorporate in New Jersey. Many firms, however, did choose to incorporate in New Jersey, which explains the wide variety of New Jersey firms that participated in the first merger wave. This trend declined dramatically by 1915, when the differences in state corporation laws became less significant.

The development of the U.S. transportation system was another of the major factors that initiated the first merger wave. Following the Civil War, the establishment of a major railway system helped create national rather than regional markets that firms could potentially serve. Transcontinental railroads, such as the Union Pacific–Central Pacific, which was completed in 1869, linked the western United States with the rest of the country. Many firms, no longer viewing market potential as being limited by narrowly defined market boundaries, expanded to take advantage of a now broader-based market. Companies now facing competition from distant rivals chose to merge with local competitors to maintain their market share. Changes in the national transportation system made supplying distant markets both easier and less expensive. The cost of rail freight transportation fell at an average rate of 3.7% per year from 1882 to 1900.[10] In the early 1900s, transportation costs increased very little despite a rising demand for transportation services. It is interesting to note that the ability of U.S. railroads to continue to cost-effectively ship goods in a global economy impressed Warren Buffett so much that in 2009 he bid $26.3 billion in cash and stock for the remainder of the Burlington Northern railroad that he did not already own. Burlington Northern is actually a product of 390 different railroad M&As over the period 1850–2000.

Several other structural changes helped firms service national markets. For example, the invention of the Bonsack continuous process cigarette machine enabled the American Tobacco Company to supply the nation's cigarette market with a relatively small number of machines.[11] As firms expanded, they exploited economies of scale in production and distribution. For example, the Standard Oil Trust controlled 40% of the world's oil production by using only three refineries. It eliminated unnecessary plants and thereby achieved greater efficiency.[12] A similar process of expansion in the pursuit of scale economies took place in many manufacturing industries in the U.S. economy during this time. Companies and their managers began to study the production process in an effort to enhance their ability to engage in ever-expanding mass production.[13] The expansion of the scale of business also required greater managerial skills and led to further specialization of management.

As mentioned, the first merger wave did not start until 1897, but the first great *takeover battle* began much earlier—in 1868. Although the term *takeover battle* is commonly used today to describe the sometimes acerbic conflicts among firms in takeovers,

---

[10] Ibid.

[11] Alfred D. Chandler, *The Visible Hand: The Managerial Revolution in American Business* (Cambridge, MA: Belknap Press, 1977), 249.

[12] Alfred D. Chandler, "The Coming of Oligopoly and Its Meaning for Antitrust," in *National Competition Policy: Historians' Perspective on Antitrust and Government Business Relationships in the United States* (Washington, DC: Federal Trade Commission, 1981), 72.

[13] Robert C. Puth, *American Economic History* (New York: Dryden Press, 1982), 254.

it can be more literally applied to the conflicts that occurred in early corporate mergers. One such takeover contest involved an attempt to take control of the Erie Railroad in 1868. The takeover attempt pitted Cornelius Vanderbilt against Daniel Drew, Jim Fisk, and Jay Gould. As one of their major takeover defenses, the defenders of the Erie Railroad issued themselves large quantities of stock, in what is known as a stock watering campaign, even though they lacked the authorization to do so.[14] At that time, because bribery of judges and elected officials was common, legal remedies for violating corporate laws were particularly weak. The battle for control of the railroad took a violent turn when the target corporation hired guards, equipped with firearms and cannons, to protect its headquarters. The takeover attempt ended when Vanderbilt abandoned his assault on the Erie Railroad and turned his attention to weaker targets.

In the late nineteenth century, as a result of such takeover contests, the public became increasingly concerned about unethical business practices. Corporate laws were not particularly effective during the 1890s. In response to many anti-railroad protests, Congress established the Interstate Commerce Commission in 1897. The Harrison, Cleveland, and McKinley administrations (1889–1901) were all very pro-business and filled the commission with supporters of the very railroads they were elected to regulate. Not until the passage of antitrust legislation in the late 1800s and early 1900s, and tougher securities laws after the Great Depression, did the legal system attain the necessary power to discourage unethical takeover tactics.

Lacking adequate legal restraints, the banking and business community adopted its own voluntary code of ethical behavior. This code was enforced by an unwritten agreement among investment bankers, who agreed to do business only with firms that adhered to their higher ethical standards. Today Great Britain relies on such a voluntary code. Although these informal standards did not preclude all improper activities in the pursuit of takeovers, they did set the stage for reasonable behavior during the first takeover wave.

Financial factors rather than legal restrictions forced the end of the first merger wave. First, the shipbuilding trust collapse in the early 1900s brought to the fore the dangers of fraudulent financing. Second, and most important, the stock market crash of 1904, followed by the banking Panic of 1907, closed many of the nation's banks and ultimately paved the way for the formation of the Federal Reserve System. As a result of a declining stock market and a weak banking system, the basic financial ingredients for fueling takeovers were absent. Without these, the first great takeover period came to a halt. Some economic historians have interpreted the many horizontal combinations that took place in the first wave as an attempt to achieve economies of scale. Through M&As, the expanding companies sought to increase their efficiency by lower per-unit costs. The fact that the majority of these mergers failed implies that these companies were not successful in their pursuit of enhanced efficiency. Under President Theodore Roosevelt, whose tenure in the executive office lasted from 1901 to 1909, the antitrust environment steadily became more stringent. Although he did not play a significant role

---

[14] T. J. Stiles, *The First Tycoon: The Epic Life of Cornelius Vanderbilt* (New York: Alfred A. Knopf, 2009) 456.

in bringing an end to the first wave, Roosevelt, who came to be known as the *trustbuster*, continued to try to exert pressure on anticompetitive activities.

The government was initially unsuccessful in its antitrust lawsuits, but toward the end of Roosevelt's term in office it began to realize more success in the courtrooms. The landmark Supreme Court decision in the 1904 Northern Securities case is an example of the government's greater success in bringing antitrust actions. Although President Roosevelt holds the reputation of being the trustbuster, it was his successor, William Howard Taft, who succeeded in breaking up some of the major trusts. It is ironic that many of the companies formed in the breakup of the large trusts became very large businesses. For example, Standard Oil was broken up into companies such as Standard Oil of New Jersey, which later became Exxon; Standard Oil of New York, which became Mobil and merged with Exxon in 1998; Standard Oil of California, which rebranded under the name Chevron, and acquired Gulf Oil in 1985, Texaco in 2001, and Unocal in 2005; and Standard Oil of Indiana, which became Amoco, and was acquired by BP in 1998. The mergers between some of the components of the old Standard Oil reflect the partial undoing of this breakup as the petroleum market has been global, and these descendants of J. D. Rockefeller's old company now face much international competition.

 ## SECOND WAVE, 1916–1929

George Stigler, the late Nobel prize–winning economist and former professor at the University of Chicago, contrasted the first and second merger waves as "merging for monopoly" versus "merging for oligopoly." During the second merger wave, several industries were consolidated. Rather than monopolies, the result was often an oligopolistic industry structure. The consolidation pattern established in the first merger period continued into the second period. During this second period, the U.S. economy continued to evolve and develop, primarily because of the post–World War I economic boom, which provided much investment capital for eagerly waiting securities markets. The availability of capital, which was fueled by favorable economic conditions and lax margin requirements, set the stage for the stock market crash of 1929.

The antitrust environment of the 1920s was stricter than the environment that had prevailed before the first merger wave. By 1910, Congress had become concerned about the abuses of the market and the power wielded by monopolies. It also had become clear that the Sherman Act was not an effective deterrent to monopoly. As a result, Congress passed the Clayton Act in 1914, a law that reinforced the antimonopoly provisions of the Sherman Act. (For a discussion of the Sherman and Clayton Acts, see Chapter 3.) As the economy and the banking system rebounded in the late 1900s, this antitrust law became a somewhat more important deterrent to monopoly. With a more stringent antitrust environment, the second merger wave produced fewer monopolies but more oligopolies and many vertical mergers. In addition, many companies in unrelated industries merged. This was the first large-scale formation of conglomerates. However, although these business combinations involved firms that did not directly produce the same products, they often had similar product lines.

Armed with the Clayton and Sherman Acts, the U.S. government was in a better position to engage in more effective antitrust enforcement than had occurred during the first merger wave. Nonetheless, its primary focus remained on cracking down on unfair business practices and preventing cartels or pools, as opposed to stopping anti-competitive mergers. At this time widespread price-fixing occurred in many industries, which was thought to be a more pressing threat to competition than mergers, which now were mainly vertical or conglomerate transactions. Just as in the first merger wave, the second merger period witnessed the formation of many prominent corporations that still operate today. These include General Motors, IBM, John Deere, and Union Carbide.

 THE 1940S

Before we proceed to a discussion of the third merger period, we will briefly examine the mergers of the 1940s. During this decade, larger firms acquired smaller, privately held companies for motives of tax relief. In this period of high estate taxes, the transfer of businesses within families was very expensive; thus, the incentive to sell out to other firms arose. These mergers did not result in increased concentration because most of them did not represent a significant percentage of the total industry's assets. Most of the family business combinations involved smaller companies.

The 1940s did not feature any major technological changes or dramatic development in the nation's infrastructure. Thus, the increase in the number of mergers was relatively small. Nonetheless, their numbers were still a concern to Congress, which reacted by passing the Celler-Kefauver Act in 1950. This law strengthened Section 7 of the Clayton Act. (For further details on the Clayton Act, see the following section and Chapter 3.)

 THIRD WAVE, 1965–1969

The third merger wave featured a historically high level of merger activity. This was brought about in part by a booming economy. During these years, often known as the conglomerate merger period, it was not uncommon for relatively smaller firms to target larger companies for acquisition. In contrast, during the two earlier waves, the majority of the target firms were significantly smaller than the acquiring firms. Peter Steiner reports that the "acquisition of companies with assets over $100 million, which averaged only 1.3 per year from 1948 to 1960, and 5 per year from 1961 to 1966, rose to 24 in 1967, 31 in 1968, 20 in 1969, 12 in 1970 before falling to 5 each year in 1971 and 1972."[15]

The number of M&As during the 1960s is shown in Figure 2.1. These data were compiled by W. T. Grimm and Company (now provided by Houlihan Lokey Howard & Zukin), which began recording M&A announcements on January 1, 1963. As noted, a

[15] Peter O. Steiner, *Mergers: Motives, Effects and Policies* (Ann Arbor: University of Michigan Press, 1975).

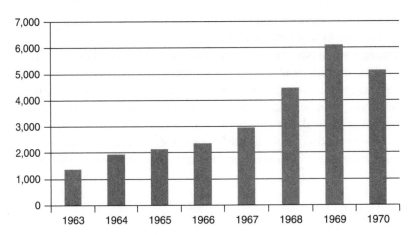

FIGURE 2.1 Third Merger Wave, Merger and Acquisition Announcements, 1963–1970. The Third Merger Wave Peaked in 1969. The Decline in the Stock Market, Coupled with Tax Reforms, Reduced the Incentive to Merge. *Source: Mergerstat Review*, 2014.

larger percentage of the M&As that took place in this period were conglomerate transactions. The Federal Trade Commission (FTC) reported that 80% of the mergers that took place in the 10-year period between 1965 and 1975 were conglomerate mergers.[16]

The conglomerates formed during this period were more than merely diversified in their product lines. The term *diversified firms* is generally applied to companies that have some subsidiaries in other industries but a majority of their production within one industry category. Unlike diversified firms, conglomerates conduct a large percentage of their business activities in different industries. Good examples are Ling-Temco-Vought (LTV), Litton Industries, and ITT. In the 1960s, ITT acquired such diverse businesses as Avis Rent A Car, Sheraton Hotels, Continental Baking, and other far-flung enterprises, such as restaurant chains, consumer credit agencies, home building companies, and airport parking firms. Although the third merger wave is associated with well-known conglomerate firms such as ITT and LTV, many corporations of varying sizes engaged in a diversification strategy. Many small and medium-sized firms also followed this fad and moved into areas outside their core business.

As firms with the necessary financial resources sought to expand, they faced tougher antitrust enforcement. The heightened antitrust atmosphere of the 1960s was an outgrowth of the Celler-Kefauver Act of 1950, which had strengthened the antimerger provisions of the Clayton Act of 1914. The Clayton Act made the acquisition of other firms' stock illegal when the acquisition resulted in a merger that significantly reduced the degree of competition within an industry. However, the law had an important loophole: It did not preclude the anticompetitive acquisition of a firm's assets. The Celler-Kefauver Act closed this loophole. Armed with tougher laws, the federal government adopted a stronger antitrust stance, coming down hard on

---

[16] Federal Trade Commission, *Statistical Report on Mergers and Acquisitions* (Washington, DC, 1977).

both horizontal and vertical mergers. Expansion-minded firms found that their only available alternative was to form conglomerates.

The more intense antitrust enforcement of horizontal mergers was partially motivated by the political environment of the 1960s. During this decade, Washington policymakers, emphasizing the potential for abuses of monopoly power, worked through the FTC and the Justice Department to curb corporate expansion, which created the potential for monopolistic abuses. Prime advocates of this tougher antitrust enforcement were Attorney General John Mitchell and Assistant Attorney General Richard McLaren, the main architect of the federal government's antitrust efforts during the 1960s. In his book *Managing*, Harold Geneen, then chief executive officer of ITT, has described the difficulty his company had in acquiring companies when McLaren was in office.[17] McLaren opposed conglomerate acquisitions based on his fears of "potential reciprocity." This would occur, for example, if ITT and its other subsidiaries gave Hartford Insurance, a company ITT acquired, a competitive edge over other insurance companies. ITT was forced to compromise its plans to add Hartford to its conglomerate empire. It was able to proceed with the acquisition only after agreeing to divest itself of other divisions with the same combined size of Hartford Insurance and to not acquire another large insurance company for 10 years without prior Justice Department approval. Years later the European Commission would voice similar arguments for opposing takeovers in the 2000s.

With the election of Richard M. Nixon toward the end of the decade, Washington policymakers advocated a freer market orientation. Nixon supported this policy through his four appointees to the U.S. Supreme Court, who espoused a broader interpretation of concepts such as market share. The tough antitrust enforcement of the Justice Department came to an end in 1972, as the Supreme Court failed to accept the Justice Department's interpretation of antitrust laws. For example, in some cases the Supreme Court began to use a broad international market view as opposed to a more narrow domestic or even regional market definition. Consequently, if as a result of a merger, a firm had a large percentage of the U.S. market or a region of the nation but a small percentage of the international market, it could be judged to lack significant monopolistic characteristics. By this time, however, the third merger wave had already come to an end.

Management Science and Conglomerates

The rapid growth of management science accelerated the conglomerate movement. Schools of management began to attain widespread acceptability among prominent schools of higher education, and the master of business administration degree became a valued credential for the corporate executive. Management science developed methodologies that facilitated organizational management and theoretically could be applied to a wide variety of organizations, including corporations, government, educational institutions, and even the military. As these management principles gained wider acceptance, graduates of this movement believed they possessed the broad-based skills necessary to manage a wide variety of organizational structures. Such managers reasonably believed that they could manage a corporate organization that spanned several

---

[17] Harold Geneen, *Managing* (New York: Avon, 1989), 228–229.

industry categories. The belief that the conglomerate could become a manageable and successful corporate entity started to become a reality.

Industry Concentration and the Conglomerate Wave

Because most of the mergers in the third wave involved the formation of conglomerates rather than vertical or horizontal mergers, they did not appreciably increase industrial concentration. For this reason, the degree of competition in different industries did not significantly change despite the large number of mergers. Some 6,000 mergers, entailing the disappearance of 25,000 firms, took place; nonetheless, competition, or market concentration, in the U.S. economy was not greatly reduced. This clearly contrasts with the first merger wave, which resulted in a dramatic increase in industry concentration in many industries.

Shareholder Wealth Effects of Diversification during the Conglomerate Wave

In Chapter 4 we critically examine diversification strategies and their impact on shareholder wealth. However, while we are discussing the conglomerate wave, it is useful to briefly address some research that has attempted to assess the impact of these types of deals on shareholder wealth. Henri Servaes analyzed a large sample of firms over the years 1961–1976.[18] He showed that over this time period, the average number of business segments in which firms operated increased from 1.74 in 1961 to 2.7 in 1976. He then examined the Q ratios (ratios of the market value of securities divided by the replacement value of assets) of the companies in his sample and found that diversified firms were valued at a discount—even during the third merger wave when such diversifying deals were so popular. He found, however, that this diversification discount declined over time. Servaes analyzed the assertion that insiders derive private benefits from managing a diversified firm, which may subject the firm to less risk although at a cost that may not be in shareholders' interests. If managers derive private benefits that come at a cost to shareholders (the discount), then this may explain why companies with higher insider ownership were focused when the discount was high but began to diversify when the discount declined. At least they did not pursue their private benefits when it was imposing a cost on shareholders.

Some research shows that the stock market response to diversifying acquisitions in the conglomerate was positive.[19] Matsusaka found that not only did the market respond positively, but also the response was clearly positive when bidders agreed to keep target management in place and negative when management was replaced as in disciplinary takeovers. While this may have been the case, this does not mean that the market's

---

[18] Henri Servaes, "The Value of Diversification during the Conglomerate Wave," *Journal of Finance* 51, no. 4 (September 1996): 1201–1225.
[19] John G. Matsusaka, "Takeover Motives during the Conglomerate Merger Wave," *RAND Journal of Economics* 24, no. 3 (Autumn 1993): 357–379.

response in this time period to these diversifying deals was correct. When one considers the track record of many of these deals, it is easy to conclude that they were flawed. Later research covering more recent time periods shows that the market may have learned this lesson, and such deals do not meet with a favorable response.

Price-Earnings Game and the Incentive to Merge

As mentioned previously, investment bankers did not finance most of the mergers in the 1960s, as they had in the two previous merger waves. Tight credit markets and high interest rates were the concomitants of the higher credit demands of an expanding economy. As the demand for loanable funds rose, both the price of these funds and interest rates increased. In addition, the booming stock market prices provided equity financing for many of the conglomerate takeovers.

The bull market of the 1960s bid stock prices higher and higher. The Dow Jones Industrial Average, which was 618 in 1960, rose to 906 in 1968. As their stock prices skyrocketed, investors were especially interested in growth stocks. Potential bidders soon learned that acquisitions, financed by stocks, could be an excellent "pain-free" way to raise earnings per share without incurring higher tax liabilities. Mergers financed through stock transactions may not be taxable. For this reason, stock-financed acquisitions had an advantage over cash transactions, which were subject to taxation.

Companies played the price-earnings ratio game to justify their expansionist activities. The *price-earnings ratio (P/E ratio)* is the ratio of the market price of a firm's stock divided by the earnings available to common stockholders on a per-share basis. The higher the P/E ratio, the more investors are willing to pay for a firm's stock given their expectations about the firm's future earnings. High P/E ratios for the majority of stocks in the market indicate widespread investor optimism; such was the case in the bull market of the 1960s. These high stock values helped finance the third merger wave. Mergers inspired by P/E ratio effects can be illustrated as follows.

Let us assume that the acquiring firm is larger than the target firm with which it is considering merging. In addition, assume that the larger firm has a P/E ratio of 25:1 and annual earnings of $1 million, with 1 million shares outstanding. Each share sells for $25. The target firm has a lower P/E ratio of 10:1 and annual earnings of $100,000, with 100,000 shares outstanding. This firm's stock sells for $10. The larger firm offers the smaller firm a premium on its stock to entice its stockholders to sell. This premium comes in the form of a stock-for-stock offer in which one share of the larger firm, worth $25, is offered for two shares of the smaller firm, worth a total of $20. The large firm issues 50,000 shares to finance the purchase.

This acquisition causes the earnings per share (EPS) of the higher P/E firm to rise. The EPS of the higher P/E firm has risen from $1.00 to $1.05. We can see the effect on the price of the larger firm's stock if we make the crucial assumption that its P/E ratio stays the same. This implies that the market will continue to value this firm's future earnings in a manner similar to the way it did before the acquisition. The validity of this type of assumption is examined in greater detail in Chapter 14.

Based on the assumption that the P/E ratio of the combined firm remains at 25, the stock price will rise to \$26.25 (25 × \$1.05). We can see that the larger firm can offer the smaller firm a significant premium while its EPS and stock price rise. This process can continue with other acquisitions, which also result in further increases in the acquiring company's stock price. This process will end if the market decides not to apply the same P/E ratio. A bull market such as occurred in the 1960s helps promote high P/E values. When the market falls, however, as it did at the end of the 1960s, this process is not feasible. The process of acquisitions, based on P/E effects, becomes increasingly untenable as a firm seeks to apply it to successively larger firms. The crucial assumption in creating the expectation that stock prices will rise is that the P/E ratio of the high P/E firm will apply to the combined entity. However, as the targets become larger and larger, the target becomes a more important percentage of the combined firm's earning power. After a company acquires several relatively lower P/E firms, the market becomes reluctant to apply the original higher P/E ratio. Therefore, it becomes more difficult to find target firms that will not decrease the acquirer's stock price. As the number of suitable acquisition candidates declines, the merger wave slows down. Therefore, a merger wave based on such "finance gimmickry" can last only a limited time period before it exhausts itself, as this one did.

With its bull market and the formation of huge conglomerates, the term *the go-go years* was applied to the 1960s.[20] When the stock market fell in 1969, it affected the pace of acquisitions by reducing P/E ratios. Figure 2.2 demonstrates how this decline affected some of the larger conglomerates.

Accounting Manipulations and the Incentive to Merge

Under accounting rules that prevailed at the time, acquirers had the opportunity to generate paper gains when they acquired companies that had assets on their books that were well below their market values. The gains were recorded when an acquirer sold off certain of these assets. To illustrate such an accounting manipulation, A. J. Briloff recounts how Gulf & Western generated earnings in 1967 by selling off the films of Paramount Pictures, which it had acquired in 1966.[21] The bulk of Paramount's assets were in the form of feature films, which it listed on its books at a value significantly less than their market value. In 1967, Gulf & Western sold 32 of the films of its Paramount subsidiary. This generated significant "income" for Gulf & Western in 1967, which succeeded in supporting Gulf & Western's stock price.

Some believe that these accounting manipulations made fire and casualty insurance companies popular takeover targets during this period.[22] Conglomerates found their large portfolios of undervalued assets to be particularly attractive in light of the impact of a subsequent sale of these assets on the conglomerate's future earnings. Even the very large Hartford Insurance Company, which had assets of nearly \$2 billion in

---

[20] John Brooks, *The Go-Go Years: The Drama and Crashing Finale of Wall Street's Bullish 60s* (New York: John Wiley & Sons, 1998).

[21] A. J. Briloff, "Accounting Practices and the Merger Movement," *Notre Dame Lawyer* 45, no. 4 (Summer 1970): 604–628.

[22] Steiner, *Mergers*, 116.

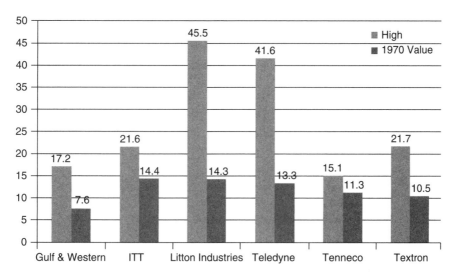

FIGURE 2.2 Third Merger Wave, Conglomerate P/E Ratios 1960, 1970. The End of the Third Merger Wave Was Signaled by the Dramatic Decline in the P/E Ratios of Some of That Era's Leading Conglomerates. *Source*: Peter O. Steiner, *Mergers: Motives, Effects and Policies* (Ann Arbor: University of Michigan Press, 1975), 104.

1968 (approximately $13.9 billion in 2014 dollars), had assets that were clearly under-valued. ITT capitalized on this undervaluation when it acquired Hartford Insurance.

Another artificial incentive that encouraged conglomerate acquisitions involved securities, such as convertible debentures, which were used to finance acquisitions. Acquiring firms would issue convertible debentures in exchange for common stock of the target firm. This allowed them to receive the short-term benefit of adding the target's earnings to its EPS valuation while putting off the eventual increase in the acquirer's shares outstanding.

Decline of the Third Merger Wave

The decline of the conglomerates may be first traced to the announcement by Litton Industries in 1968 that its quarterly earnings declined for the first time in 14 years.[23] Although Litton's earnings were still positive, the market turned sour on conglomerates, and the selling pressure on their stock prices increased.

In 1968, Attorney General Richard McLaren announced that he intended to crack down on the conglomerates, which he believed were an anticompetitive influence on the market. Various legal changes were implemented to limit the use of convertible debt to finance acquisitions. The 1969 Tax Reform Act required that convertible debt be treated as equity for EPS calculations while also restricting changes in the valuation of undervalued assets of targets. The conglomerate boom came to an end, and this helped collapse the stock market.

---

[23] Stanley H. Brown, *Ling: The Rise, Fall and Return of a Texas Titan* (New York: Atheneum, 1972), 166.

Performance of Conglomerates

Little evidence exists to support the advisability of many of the conglomerate acquisitions. Buyers often overpaid for the diverse companies they purchased. Many of the acquisitions were followed by poor financial performance. This is confirmed by the fact that 60% of the cross-industry acquisitions that occurred between 1970 and 1982 were sold or divested by 1989.

There is no conclusive explanation for why conglomerates failed. Economic theory, however, points out the productivity-enhancing effects of increased specialization. Indeed, this has been the history of capitalism since the Industrial Revolution. The conglomerate era represented a movement away from specialization. Managers of diverse enterprises often had little detailed knowledge of the specific industries that were under their control. This is particularly the case when compared with the management expertise and attention that are applied by managers who concentrate on one industry or even one segment of an industry. It is not surprising, therefore, that companies like Revlon, a firm that has an established track record of success in the cosmetics industry, saw its core cosmetics business suffer when it diversified into unrelated areas, such as health care.

 TRENDSETTING MERGERS OF THE 1970S

The number of M&A announcements in the 1970s fell dramatically, as shown in Figure 2.3. Even so, the decade played a major role in merger history. Several path-breaking mergers changed what was considered to be acceptable takeover behavior in the years to follow. The first of these mergers was the International Nickel Company (INCO) acquisition of ESB (formerly known as Electric Storage Battery Company).

INCO versus ESB

After the third merger wave, a historic merger paved the way for a type that would be pervasive in the fourth wave: the hostile takeover by major established companies.

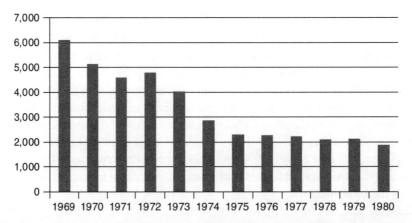

FIGURE 2.3   Merger and Acquisition Announcements, 1969–1980. *Source:* Mergerstat Review, 2014.

In 1974, Philadelphia-based ESB was the largest battery maker in the world, specializing in automobile batteries under the Willard and Exide brand names as well as other consumer batteries under the Ray-O-Vac brand name. Although the firm's profits had been rising, its stock price had fallen in response to a generally declining stock market. Several companies had expressed an interest in acquiring ESB, but all these efforts were rebuffed. On July 18, 1974, INCO announced a tender offer to acquire all outstanding shares of ESB for $28 per share, for a total of $157 million. The Toronto-based INCO controlled approximately 40% of the world's nickel market and was by far the largest firm in this industry. Competition in the nickel industry had increased in the previous 10 years while demand proved to be increasingly volatile. In an effort to smooth their cash flows, INCO sought an acquisition target that was less cyclical.

INCO ultimately selected ESB as the appropriate target for several reasons. As part of what INCO considered to be the "energy industry," ESB was attractive in light of the high oil prices that prevailed at that time. While it featured name brands, ESB was also not in the forefront of innovation and was losing ground to competitors, such as Eveready and Duracell.

Because the takeover was an unfriendly acquisition, INCO did not have the benefit of a detailed financial analysis using internal data. Before INCO acquired ESB, major reputable corporations did not participate in unfriendly takeovers; only smaller firms and less respected speculators engaged in such activity. If a major firm's takeover overtures were rebuffed, the acquisition was discontinued. Moreover, most large investment banks refused to finance hostile takeovers.

At this time, the level of competition that existed in investment banking was putting pressure on the profits of Morgan Stanley, INCO's investment banker. Although it was seeking additional sources of profits, Morgan Stanley was also concerned that by refusing to aid INCO in its bid for ESB, it might lose a long-term client. Morgan Stanley, long known as a conservative investment bank, reluctantly began to change posture as it saw its market share erode because of the increasingly aggressive advance of its rivals in the investment banking business. Underwriting, which had constituted 95% of its business until 1965, had become less profitable as other investment banks challenged the traditional relationships of the underwriting business by making competitive bids when securities were being underwritten.[24]

Many banks, seeking other areas of profitability, expanded their trading operations. By the 1980s, trading would displace underwriting as the investment bank's key profit center.[25] This situation would change once again toward the end of the 1980s as fees related to M&As became an increasingly important part of some investment banks' revenues.

---

[24] John Brooks, *The Takeover Game* (New York: Dutton, 1987), 4.

[25] Ken Auletta, *Greed and Glory on Wall Street: The Fall of the House of Lehman* (New York: Random House, 1986). Auletta provides a good discussion of how the traders, led by Lewis Glucksman, usurped the power of the investment bankers, led by Pete Peterson, and forced Peterson out of the firm. Peterson, however, went on to thrive as one of the founders of the very successful Blackstone private equity firm. For a good discussion of how Glucksman's protégé and successor, Richard Fuld, ended up leading Lehman Brothers right into the largest bankruptcy in history, see Lawrence G. McDonald and Patrick Robinson, *A Colossal Failure of Common Sense: The Insider Story of the Collapse of Lehman Brothers* (New York: Crown Business, 2009).

ESB found itself unprepared for a hostile takeover, given the novelty of this type of action. INCO gave it only a three-hour warning of its "take it or leave it." ESB had installed some antitakeover defenses, but they were ineffective. It sought help from the investment bank of Goldman Sachs, which tried to arrange a friendly takeover by United Aircraft, but by September 1974, INCO's hostile takeover of ESB was completed.[26] The takeover of ESB proved to be a poor investment, primarily because INCO, as a result of legal actions associated with antitrust considerations, was not given a free hand to manage the company. Not until 39 months after INCO had completed the acquisition did it attain the right to exercise free control over the company. Moreover, as noted previously, ESB's competitors were already aggressively marketing superior products. By 1981, ESB was reporting operating losses; INCO eventually sold it in four separate parts. INCO continued to be the world leader in the nickel business. Interestingly, it stepped into the role of white knight in 2006, when it made a bid for Canadian Falconbridge, a leading copper, nickel, and zinc producer, which was the target of an unwanted 2005 bid from the Swiss mining company Xstrata. This led to a long and complicated takeover battle involving several companies. Eventually, INCO was acquired for approximately $17 billion by the world's largest producer of iron ore, Brazilian company CVRD.

Although the ESB acquisition was not financially successful, it was precedent-setting. It set the stage for hostile takeovers by respected companies in the second half of the 1970s and through the fourth merger wave of the 1980s. This previously unacceptable action—the hostile takeover by a major industrial firm with the support of a leading investment banker—now gained legitimacy. The word *hostile* now became part of the vocabulary of M&As. "'ESB is aware that a hostile tender offer is being made by a foreign company for all of ESB's shares,' said F. J. Port, ESB's president. 'Hostile' thus entered the mergers and acquisitions lexicon."[27]

While the Inco-ESB deal was precedent setting in the U.S. market as it was the first hostile takeover by a major corporation and supported by a major investment bank, it was not the first hostile takeover. As we have already noted, such deals were attempted in the United States in the 1800s. In Europe, the first major hostile deal appears to be the 1956 takeover of British Aluminum by Reynolds Metal and Tube Investments. This deal, known as the "aluminum war," was engineered by the then up-and-coming investment bank S. G. Warburg.[28]

United Technologies versus Otis Elevator

As suggested previously, following INCO's hostile takeover of ESB, other major corporations began to consider unfriendly acquisitions. Firms and their chief executives who

---

[26] For an excellent discussion of this merger, see Jeff Madrick, *Taking America* (New York: Bantam Books, 1987), 1–59.

[27] "Hostility Breeds Contempt in Takeovers, 1974," *Wall Street Journal*, October 25, 1989.

[28] Niall Ferguson, *High Financier: The Lives and Times of Siegmund Warburg* (New York: Penguin Press, 2010), 183–199.

were inclined to be raiders but inhibited by censure from the business community now became unrestrained. United Technologies was one such firm.

In 1975, United Technologies had recently changed its name from United Aircraft through the efforts of its chairman, Harry Gray, and president, Edward Hennessy, who were transforming the company into a growing conglomerate. They were familiar with the INCO-ESB acquisition, having participated in the bidding war for ESB as the unsuccessful white knight that Goldman Sachs had solicited on ESB's behalf. Up until the bid for Otis, United had never participated in a hostile acquisition.

At that time the growth of the elevator manufacturing business was slowing down and its sales patterns were cyclical inasmuch as it was heavily dependent on the construction industry. Nonetheless, this target was extremely attractive. One-third of Otis's revenues came from servicing elevators, revenues that tend to be much more stable than those from elevator construction. That Otis was a well-managed company made it all the more appealing to United Technologies. Moreover, 60% of Otis's revenues were from international customers, a detail that fit well with United Technologies' plans to increase its international presence. By buying Otis Elevator, United could diversify internationally while buying an American firm and not assuming the normal risk that would be present with the acquisition of a foreign company.

United initially attempted friendly overtures toward Otis, which were not accepted. On October 15, 1975, United Technologies bid $42 per share for a controlling interest in Otis Elevator, an offer that precipitated a heated battle between the two firms. Otis sought the aid of a white knight, the Dana Corporation, an auto parts supplier, while filing several lawsuits to enjoin United from completing its takeover. A bidding war that ensued between United Technologies and the Dana Corporation ended with United winning with a bid of $44 per share. Unlike the INCO-ESB takeover, however, the takeover of Otis proved to be an excellent investment of United's excess cash. Otis went on to enjoy greater-than-expected success, particularly in international markets.

United's takeover of Otis was a ground-breaking acquisition; not only was it a hostile takeover by an established firm, but also it was a successful venture and Otis remains a valuable part of United today. This deal helped make hostile takeovers acceptable.

Colt Industries versus Garlock Industries

Colt Industries' takeover of Garlock Industries was yet another precedent-setting acquisition, moving hostile takeovers to a sharply higher level of hostility. The other two hostile takeovers by major firms had amounted to heated bidding wars but were mild in comparison to the aggressive tactics used in this takeover.

In 1964, the Fairbanks Whitney Company changed its name to Colt Industries, which was the firearms company it had acquired in 1955. During the 1970s, the company was almost totally restructured, with Chairman George Strichman and President David Margolis divesting the firm of many of its poorly performing businesses. The management wanted to use the cash from these sales to acquire higher-growth industrial businesses. As part of this acquisition program, in 1975, Colt initiated a hostile bid for Garlock Industries, which manufactured packing and sealing products. The deal was path-breaking due to the fact that Garlock fought back furiously and aggressively by using public relations as part of its defensive arsenal. Colt responded in kind and eventually acquired Garlock. This deal is notable for making hostile deals truly hostile. Such deals are commonplace today.

LING-TEMCO-VOUGHT: GROWTH OF A CONGLOMERATE[a]

Ling-Temco-Vought (LTV) Corporation was one of the leading conglomerates of the third merger wave. The company was led by James Joseph Ling—the Ling of Ling-Temco-Vought. The story of how he parlayed a $2,000 investment and a small electronics business into the fourteenth-largest industrial company in the United States is a fascinating one. Ling-Temco-Vought was a sprawling industrial corporation, which at its peak included such major enterprises as Jones & Laughlin Steel, the nation's sixth-largest steel company; Wilson & Co., a major meat packing and sporting goods company; Braniff Airways, an airline that serviced many domestic and international routes; Temco and Vought Aircraft, both suppliers of aircraft for the military; and several other companies. The company originated in a small Texas electrical contracting business that Jimmy Ling grew, through a pattern of diverse acquisitions, into one of the largest U.S. corporations. The original corporate entity, the Ling Electric Company, was started in 1947 with a modest investment of $2,000, which was used to buy war surplus electrical equipment and a used truck. By 1956, Ling Electronics had enjoyed steady growth and embarked on one of its first acquisitions by buying L. M. Electronics. Various other electronic and defense contractors were then acquired, including the American Microwave Corporation, the United Electronics Company, and the Calidyne Company. Acquisitions such as these—companies that lacked the requisite capital to expand—were financed by Ling through a combination of debt and stock in his company, which traded on the over-the-counter market.

By 1958, this master dealmaker sold an offering of convertible debentures in a private placement that was arranged by the Wall Street investment bank of White Weld & Company. This type of securities offering was particularly popular with the dealmakers of the third wave because it did not have an immediate adverse impact on earnings per share, thus leaving the company in a good position to play the "profits/earnings game." With its stock price trading in the $40s, Ling started the process of buying targets that were much bigger than the acquiring company with the 1958 stock-for-stock acquisition of Altec Companies, a manufacturer of sound systems.

After some other small acquisitions, Ling initiated his largest acquisition when he merged his company with the Texas Engineering and Manufacturing Company, Temco. This deal enabled Ling to accomplish a long-term goal when the merged company, Ling-Temco Electronics, became part of the Fortune 500. Shortly thereafter, Ling prevailed in a hostile takeover of the Vought Aircraft Company to form Ling-Temco-Vought.

Ling-Temco-Vought went through a period of lackluster financial performance, which forced Ling to restructure the company by selling off poorly performing divisions. In 1967, Ling successfully completed a tender offer for Wilson & Company, a firm twice the size of LTV. This deal vaulted LTV to number 38 on the Fortune 500 list. Wilson was composed of three subsidiaries: Wilson & Company, the meat-packing business; Wilson Sporting Goods; and the Wilson Pharmaceutical and Chemical Corporation. Traders sometimes referred to these divisions as "meatball, golf ball, and goof ball." The next step Ling took in assembling this massive conglomerate was to buy the Great America Corporation, which was a holding company with investments in a variety of businesses, such as Braniff Airlines and National Car Rental, as well as banks and insurance companies. Although few beneficial commonalities appeared to be associated with this acquisition, Ling was able to exploit several, such as the insurance companies' writing insurance for a variety of LTV units and employees.

After an unsuccessful takeover of the Youngstown Sheet and Tube Company, Ling set his sights on the fourth-largest steel producer in the United States, Jones & Laughlin Steel. Ling-Temco-Vought bought Jones & Laughlin in an $85 tender offer for a company with a preannouncement price of $50. This $425 million bid was the largest cash tender offer as of that date and represented a 70% premium for a company in a low-growth industry. Unfortunately, the takeover of Jones & Laughlin drew the ire of Assistant Attorney General Richard McLaren, who saw it as another anticompetitive conglomerate acquisition. The Justice Department filed an antitrust lawsuit, which was bad news for any defendant because the government won a very high percentage of such cases. The market seemed to concur with this legal assessment because the stock price declined after the announcement. Because of the lawsuit, LTV was prevented from playing an active role in the management of Jones & Laughlin and taking steps to turn around the poorly performing steel company that had just announced its worst earnings performance in a decade. With the addition of Jones & Laughlin, LTV now had two major components of its empire—Braniff Airlines being the other one—reporting sizable losses. A settlement of the lawsuit was reached in which LTV agreed to sell off Braniff and the Okonite Company, a cable and wire manufacturer.

Although LTV was able to achieve a favorable settlement, its stock suffered, partly as a result of the lawsuit, the poor performance of its subsidiaries, and the overall decline in the market. These factors gave rise to pressures from dissident shareholders and bondholders to remove Ling from control of LTV. Ling was not able to survive these pressures; he was demoted from his position as chief executive and eventually left LTV. The story of Jimmy Ling and the huge conglomerate that he built is one of a man who was ahead of his time. He was probably the most renowned of the great conglomerate builders of the third merger wave. Whereas the 1980s featured such raiders as Carl Icahn and Boone Pickens, Ling was joined in the third wave by other "conglomerators," such as Lawrence Tisch of Loews, Charles Bluhdorn of Gulf & Western, and Ben Heineman of Northwest Industries. Long before the 1980s, Ling had mastered the art of the LBO and hostile takeover. Unlike many of the raiders of the 1980s, however, Ling was opposed to trying to turn a quick profit on acquisitions by selling off assets. He bought companies with a more long-term strategy in mind, which, nonetheless, many criticized.

What was once LTV has undergone many changes since the 1960s. The company experienced financial troubles in the 1980s, as did many companies in the U.S. steel industry. It was acquired in 2002 by Wilber Ross, who rolled the company into the International Steel Group. This company was then sold by Ross to Mittal in 2004.

[a] For an excellent discussion of the history of this company during the conglomerate era, see Stanley H. Brown, *Ling: The Rise and Fall of a Texas Titan* (New York: Atheneum, 1972).

FOURTH WAVE, 1984–1989

The downward trend that characterized M&As in the 1970s through 1980 reversed sharply in 1981. Although the pace of mergers slowed again in 1982 as the economy weakened, a strong merger wave had taken hold by 1984. Figure 2.4 shows the number of M&A announcements for the period from 1970 to 2013. The unique characteristic of the fourth wave is the significant role of hostile mergers. As noted previously, hostile mergers had become an acceptable form of corporate expansion by the 1980s, and the corporate raid had gained status as a highly profitable speculative activity. Consequently, corporations and speculative partnerships played the takeover game as a means of enjoying very high profits in a short time. Whether takeovers are considered friendly or hostile generally is determined by the reaction of the target company's board of directors. If the board approves the takeover, it is considered friendly; if the board is opposed, the takeover is deemed hostile.

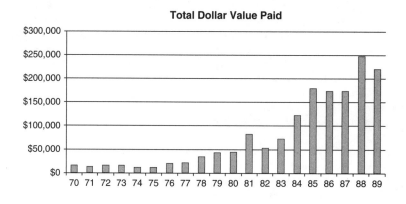

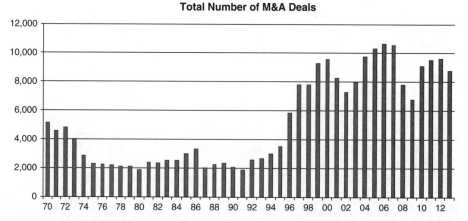

FIGURE 2.4   Net Merger and Acquisition Announcements 1970–2013. *Source: Mergerstat Review,* 2014.

Although the absolute number of hostile takeovers in the fourth merger wave was not high with respect to the total number of takeovers, the relative percentage of hostile takeovers in the total value of takeovers rose during the fourth wave.

The fourth merger period may also be distinguished from the other three waves by the size and prominence of the M&A targets. Some of the nation's largest firms became targets of acquisition during the 1980s. The fourth wave became the wave of the *megamerger*. The total dollar value paid in acquisitions rose sharply during this decade. Figure 2.5 shows how the average and median prices paid have risen since 1970. In addition to the rise in the dollar value of mergers, the average size of the typical transaction increased significantly. The number of $100 million transactions increased more than 23 times from 1974 to 1986. This was a major difference from the conglomerate era of the 1960s, in which the acquisition of small and medium-sized businesses predominated. The 1980s became the period of the billion-dollar M&As. The leading megamergers of the fourth wave are shown in Table 2.3.

M&A volume was clearly greater in certain industries. The oil industry, for example, experienced more than its share of mergers, which resulted in a greater degree of concentration within that industry. The oil and gas industry accounted for 21.6% of the total dollar value of M&As from 1981 to 1985. During the second half of the 1980s, drugs and medical equipment deals were the most common. One reason some industries experienced a disproportionate number of M&As as compared with other industries was deregulation. When the airline industry was deregulated, for example, airfares became subject to greater competition, causing the competitive position of some air carriers to deteriorate. The result was numerous acquisitions and a consolidation of this industry. The banking and petroleum industries experienced a similar pattern of competitively inspired M&As.

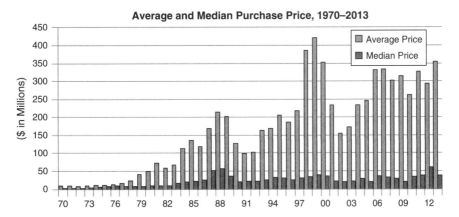

FIGURE 2.5 Average and Median Purchase Price, 1970–2013. *Source: Mergerstat Review*, 2014; Table 1-4.

TABLE 2.3 Ten Largest Acquisitions, 1981–1989

Year	Buyer	Target	Price ($ bil)	Price (2014 $)
1988	Kohlberg Kravis	RJR Nabisco	25.1	54.1
1984	Chevron	Gulf Oil	13.3	31.4
1988	Philip Morris	Kraft	13.1	28.3
1989	Bristol Myers	Squibb	12.5	26.2
1984	Texaco	Getty Oil	10.1	23.8
1981	DuPont	Conoco	8.0	22.6
1987	British Petroleum	Standard Oil of Ohio	7.8	16.9
1981	U.S. Steel	Marathon Oil	6.6	18.7
1988	Campeau	Federated Stores	6.5	14.0
1986	Kohlberg Kravis	Beatrice	6.2	13.8

Source: Wall Street Journal, November 1988. Reprinted by permission of the Wall Street Journal, copyright Dow Jones & Company, Inc. All rights reserved.

Role of the Corporate Raider

In the fourth wave, the term *corporate raider* made its appearance in the vernacular of corporate finance. The corporate raider's main source of income is the proceeds from takeover attempts. The word *attempt* is the curious part of this definition because the raider frequently earned handsome profits from acquisition attempts without ever taking ownership of the targeted corporation. The corporate raider Paul Bilzerian, for example, participated in numerous raids before his acquisition of the Singer Corporation in 1988. Although he earned significant profits from these raids, he did not complete a single major acquisition until Singer.

Many of the takeover attempts by raiders were ultimately designed to sell the target shares at a higher price than that which the raider originally paid. The ability of raiders to receive greenmail payments (or some of the target's valued assets) in exchange for the stock that the raider has already acquired made many hostile takeover attempts quite profitable. Even if a target refuses to participate in such transactions, the raider may succeed in putting the company "in play." When a target goes into play, the stock tends to be concentrated in the hands of arbitragers, who readily sell to the highest bidder. This process often results in a company eventually being taken over, although not necessarily by the original bidder.

Although arbitrage is a well-established practice, the role of arbitragers in the takeover process did not become highly refined until the fourth merger wave. Arbitragers such as the infamous Ivan Boesky gambled on the likelihood of a merger being consummated. They would buy the stock of the target in anticipation of a bid being made for the company.

Arbitragers became a very important part of the takeover process during the 1980s. Their involvement changed the strategy of takeovers. Moreover, the development of this "industry" helped facilitate the rising number of hostile takeovers that occurred in those years.

In the 2000s we do not have corporate raiders such as those attacked companies in the fourth merger wave. However, the modern version of these raiders are today's activist hedge funds which we discuss in Chapter 7.

Other Unique Characteristics of the Fourth Wave

The fourth merger wave featured several other interesting and unique characteristics. These features sharply differentiated this time from any other period in U.S. merger history.

Aggressive Role of Investment Bankers

The aggressiveness of investment bankers in pursuing M&As was crucial to the growth of the fourth wave. In turn, mergers were a great source of virtually risk-free advisory fees for investment bankers. The magnitude of these fees reached unprecedented proportions during this period. Merger specialists at both investment banks and law firms developed many innovative products and techniques designed to facilitate or prevent takeovers. They pressured both potential targets and acquirers into hiring them either to bring about or to prevent takeovers. Partially to help finance takeovers, the investment bank of Drexel Burnham Lambert pioneered the development and growth of the junk bond market. These previously lowly regarded securities became an important investment vehicle for financing many takeovers. Junk bond financing enabled expansionist firms and raiders to raise the requisite capital to contemplate acquisitions or raids on some of the more prominent corporations.

Increased Sophistication of Takeover Strategies

The fourth merger wave featured innovative acquisition techniques and investment vehicles. Offensive and defensive strategies became highly intricate. Potential targets set in place various preventative antitakeover measures to augment the active defenses they could deploy in the event that they received an unwanted bid. Bidders also had to respond with increasingly more creative takeover strategies to circumvent such defenses. These antitakeover strategies are discussed in detail in Chapter 5.

More Aggressive Use of Debt

Many of the megadeals of the 1980s were financed with large amounts of debt. This was one of the reasons small companies were able to make bids for comparatively larger targets. During this period the term *leveraged buyout* (LBO) became part of the vernacular of Wall Street. Through LBOs, debt may be used to take public companies private. It often was the company's own management that used this technique in *management buyouts*. Although public corporations had been brought private before the fourth wave, this type of transaction became much more prominent during the 1980s.

Legal and Political Strategies

During this period new conflicts arose between the federal and state governments. Besieged corporations increasingly looked to their state governments for protection against unwanted acquisition offers. They often were able to persuade local legislatures to pass antitakeover legislation, which brought the federal and state governments into direct conflict. Some representatives of the federal government, such as the Securities and Exchange Commission, believed that these laws were an infringement of interstate commerce. For their part, some state governments believed that such laws were based on their constitutionally granted state rights. Clearly, however, some state governments became protectors of indigenous corporations.

International Takeovers

Although most of the takeovers in the United States in the 1980s involved U.S. firms taking over other domestic companies, foreign bidders affected a significant percentage of takeovers, although nothing compared to what would take place in the fifth merger wave. An example of one of the international megadeals of the fourth wave was the 1987 acquisition of Standard Oil by British Petroleum for $7.8 billion. Many of the deals were motivated by non-U.S. companies seeking to expand into the larger and more stable U.S. market. In addition to the normal considerations that are involved in domestic acquisitions, foreign takeovers also introduce currency valuation issues. If the dollar falls against other currencies, as it did in the 1990s relative to many currencies, stock in U.S. corporations declines in value and the purchasing value of foreign currencies rises. A falling dollar may make U.S. acquisitions attractive investments for Japanese or European companies. The increased globalization of markets in the 1980s and 1990s brought foreign bidders to U.S. shores in increased numbers. Although U.S. companies may also engage in acquisitions in foreign markets, as many have, a falling dollar makes such acquisitions more expensive.

Role of Deregulation

Certain industries were deregulated during the 1980s. Mitchell and Mulherin analyzed a sample of 1,064 M&As and other restructurings over the period 1982–1989.[29] They found that in industries that had undergone significant federal deregulation, such as air transport, broadcasting, entertainment, natural gas, and trucking, this deregulation was found to be a significant causal factor. They also noticed that all industries did not respond to deregulation in the same way. For example, the response in broadcasting was quicker than in air transport.

Why the Fourth Merger Wave Ended

The fourth merger wave ended in 1989 as the long economic expansion of the 1980s came to an end and the economy went into a brief and relatively mild recession in 1990.

---

[29] Mark L. Mitchell and J. Harold Mulherin, "The Impact of Industry Shocks on Takeover and Restructuring Activity," *Journal of Financial Economics* 41, no. 2 (June 1996): 193–229.

The economic slowdown led to the unraveling of a number of the high-profile leveraged deals of the fourth wave. In addition to the overall slowdown in the economy, other factors that led to the end of the wave included the collapse of the junk bond market, which had provided the financing for many of the LBOs of the period.

FIFTH WAVE

Starting in 1992, the number of M&As once again began to increase (Figure 2.6). Large deals, some similar in size to those that occurred in the fourth merger wave, began to occur once again. At this time, the track record of many of the highly leveraged deals of the fourth wave, some of which were still in Chapter 11 bankruptcy, was quite apparent. Managers vowed they would not duplicate the mistakes of the 1980s and focused more on strategic deals that did not unduly rely on leverage. Short-term, purely financial plays were also avoided. This all seemed to go according to plan—at least for a while.

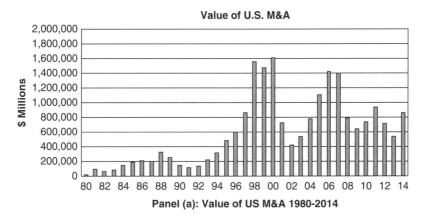

Panel (a): Value of US M&A 1980-2014

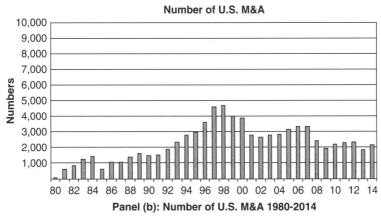

Panel (b): Number of U.S. M&A 1980-2014

FIGURE 2.6 U.S. M&A 1980–2014. *Source:* Thomson Securities Financial Data, March 6, 2015.

During the 1990s, the U.S. economy entered into its longest postwar expansion, and companies reacted to the increased aggregate demand by pursuing M&As, which are a faster way to grow than internal growth. At the same time, the stock market values of companies took off and various market indexes reached new highs (Figure 2.7).

While the expanding economy required that there be some adjustment in expected profitability, the high levels of the market became difficult to explain. We will revisit this issue a little later in this chapter.

Although the fifth merger wave featured many large megamergers, there were fewer hostile high-profile deals and more strategic mergers occurred. As the economy recovered from the 1990–1991 recession, companies began to seek to expand and mergers once again were seen as a quick and efficient manner in which to do that. Unlike the deals of the 1980s, however, the initial transactions of the 1990s emphasized strategy more than quick financial gains. These deals were not the debt-financed bust-up transactions of the fourth merger wave. Rather, they were financed through the increased use of equity, which resulted in less heavily leveraged combinations. Because the deals of the early 1990s did not rely on as much debt, there was not as much pressure to quickly sell off assets to pay down the debt and reduce the pressure of debt service. The deals that occurred were, at least initially, motivated by a specific strategy of the acquirer that could more readily be achieved by acquisitions and mergers than through internal expansion.

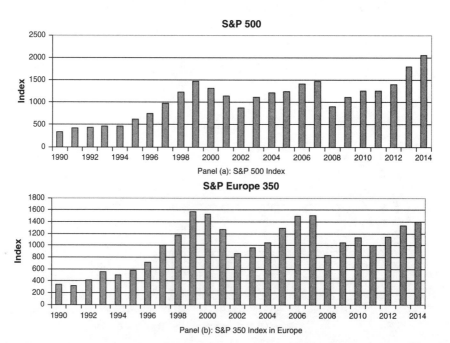

FIGURE 2.7 S&P Index in US and Europe. *Source*: Bloomberg, www.econstats.com/eqty/eqea_mi_1.htm (Panel a); http://us.spindices.com/indices/equity/sp-europe-350 (Panel b).

Industry Concentration during the Fifth Wave

Certain industries accounted for a disproportionate share of the total dollar volume of M&As in the United States during the fifth merger wave. In particular, banking and finance and communications and broadcasting accounted for 26.5% of all U.S. deals over the period 1993–2004. However, the percentage accounted for in these industries rose from a low of 7.5% in 1994 to a high of 41.9% of deals in 1999. This was caused by a combination of factors, including the continued impact of deregulation and consolidation of the banking industry, as well as the dramatic changes that were ongoing in telecom and Internet-related businesses. The fifth wave would have been different had it not been for the "inflating" yet short-lived impact of these sectors.

Fad of the Fifth Merger Wave: Roll-Ups and Consolidations of Industries

Each wave brought with it certain uniquely different transactions, and the fifth wave was no exception. In the mid-1990s, the market became enthralled with consolidating deals—what were called roll-ups. Here fragmented industries were consolidated through larger-scale acquisitions of companies that were called consolidators. Certain investment banks specialized in roll-ups; they were able to get financing and were issuing stock in these consolidated companies. Table 2.4 lists some of the more prominent consolidated companies. Roll-ups were concentrated in particular businesses, such as funeral printing, office products, and floral products.

The strategy behind roll-ups was to combine smaller companies into a national business and enjoy economies of scale while gaining the benefits of being able to market to national as opposed to regional clients. There may have been some theoretical benefits to these combinations, but the track record of many of these deals was abysmal. As with fads from prior M&A periods of frenzy, dealmakers, in this case firms that specialized in doing roll-ups, excelled for a period of time at convincing the market that there were realistic benefits to be derived from these deals. While some, such as

TABLE 2.4 Large Roll-Ups

Company Name	Industry
Metal USA	Metal service centers
Office Products USA	Office products
Floral USA	Florists
Fortress Group	Home building
U.S. Delivery Systems	Delivery
Comfort Systems USA	Air conditioning
Coach USA	Bus company
Waste Management	Waste removal
Republic Industries	Car dealerships

Coach USA, have survived, many others were successful only in generating fees for the dealmakers. Many of the consolidated entities went bankrupt, while others lost value and were sold to other companies. Roll-ups were a fad that became popular while the market of the 1990s was caught up in a wave of irrational exuberance and was looking for investment opportunities.

Fifth Merger Wave in Europe, Asia, and Central and South America

The fifth merger wave was truly an international merger wave. As Figure 2.6 shows, the dollar value and number of deals in the United States increased dramatically starting in 1996. In Europe, the fifth wave really took hold starting in 1998. By 1999, the value of deals in Europe was almost as large as that of deals in the United States. Within Europe, Great Britain accounted for the largest number of deals, followed by Germany and France. In Asia, merger value and volume also increased markedly starting in 1998. The volume of deals was significant throughout Asia, including not only Japan but all the major nations in Asia. Many of the Asian nations only recently have begun to restructure their tightly controlled economies, and this restructuring has given rise to many sell-offs and acquisitions.

As discussed in Chapter 1, while the size of the M&A market in Central and South America is much smaller than Asia, which is in turn smaller than Europe and the United States, a significant volume of deals also took place in this region. The forces of economic growth and the pursuit of globalization affected all economies as the companies sought to service global markets. Expansion efforts that take place in one part of the globe set in motion a process that, if unrestrained by artificial regulation, has ripple effects throughout the world. This was the case in the fifth merger wave.

Performance of Fifth Merger Wave Acquirers

When the fifth merger wave began to take hold, corporate managers steadfastly stated that they would not make the same mistakes that were made in the fourth merger wave. Many maintained they would not engage in short-term, financially oriented deals, but would focus only on long-term, strategic deals. In fact, there is evidence that managers pursued deals that had modest positive effects for shareholders. In a large sample of 12,023 transactions with values greater than $1 million over the period 1980–2001, Moeller, Schlingemann, and Stulz found that the deals done at the beginning of the fifth wave enhanced shareholder value.[30] However, between 1998 and 2001, acquiring firm shareholders lost a shocking $240 billion! (See Figure 2.8.) These losses dramatically contrast with the $8 billion that was lost during the entire 1980s (inflation-adjusted values). From a societal perspective, one might wonder, did the gains of target shareholders more than offset the losses of acquiring firm shareholders? The answer is they did not even come close. Bidder shareholder losses exceeded those of target shareholders by $134 billion. However, from the bidder shareholder's perspective, these "offsetting"

---

[30] Sara B. Moeller, Frederick P. Schlingemann, and René M. Stulz, "Wealth Destruction on a Massive Scale? A Study of Acquiring-Firm Returns in the Recent Merger Wave," *Journal of Finance* 60, no. 2 (April 2005): 757–783.

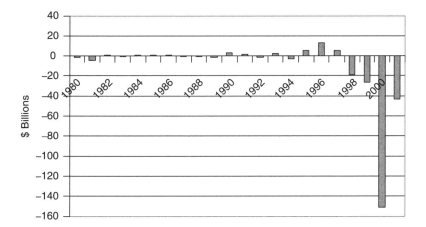

FIGURE 2.8 Yearly Aggregate Dollar Return of Acquiring Firm Shareholders, 1980–2001. *Source*: Moeller, Sara B., Frederik P. Schlingemann, and René M. Stulz. "Wealth destruction on a massive scale? A study of acquiring-firm returns in the recent merger wave." Journal of Finance, vol. 60, no. 2 (April 2005).

gains are irrelevant. To consider these gains would be like saying, "Let's pay this large premium for a given target and, sure, we will lose a large amount of money, but we will be giving target shareholders a large gain, at our expense, and from society's perspective, there may be a net gain on this deal."

The number of large losers is striking. Moeller and her colleagues found that there were 87 deals over the period 1998–2001 that lost $1 billion or more for shareholders. Why were the acquirer's losses in the fifth wave as large as they were? One explanation is that managers were more restrained at the beginning and the middle of the fifth wave. They wanted to avoid the mistakes of the prior merger period. However, as the stock market bubble took hold, the lofty stock valuation went to managers' heads. This is evidenced by the dramatically higher P/E ratios that prevailed during this period (Figure 2.9). Managers likely believed they were responsible for the high values their shares had risen to. These hubris-filled executives thought that these high valuations were the product of their managerial expertise rather than the fact that their company, and most of the market, was riding an irrational wave of overvaluation. When such executives proposed deals to their board, they now carried the weight of the management's team "success" record. It is hard for a board to tell a chief executive officer (CEO) his or her merger proposals are unsound when they come from the same CEO who claims responsibility for the highest valuations in the company's history.

Emerging Market Acquirers

A new type of acquirer became more prominent in the fifth merger wave and in the 2000s—the emerging market bidder. Many of these acquiring companies were built through acquisitions of privatized businesses and consolidations of relatively smaller competitors in these emerging markets. Some grew to a substantial size and have

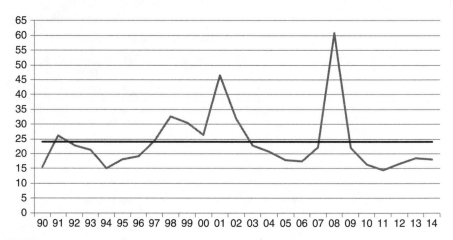

FIGURE 2.9 S&P 500 P/E Ratio: 1990–2014. *Source*: Standard & Poor's.

targeted large Western companies. One example of this is Mittal, which has used M&As across the world, many of them privatized steel businesses, to become the largest steel company in the world (Table 2.5). Its clout was felt throughout the world in 2006, when it made a successful hostile bid for the second largest steel company—Arcelor. Mittal is but one example of this trend. Another is the Dubai-based Ports World, which in 2006 took over the venerable Peninsular & Oriental Navigation Co. (P&O) in a $6.8 billion acquisition. Still another is the Mumbai-based Tata Group, then led by Ratan N. Tata. The company he created is an international conglomerate that includes not only one of the world's largest sellers of coffee and tea but also luxury hotels, soft drinks, and a telecommunications business. In October 2006, the company acquired the British-owned Corus Group, which made the Tata Group one of the largest steel companies in the world. Later in 2008 the Tata Group acquired the Range Rover and

TABLE 2.5 Largest Worldwide Steel Companies: 2004 and 2008 Production

Company	2004 Steel Production (millions of tons)		2008 Steel Production (millions of tons)
Mittal Steel	65	ArcelorMittal	101.6
Arcelor	52	Nippon Steel	37.5
Nippon Steel	34	Baosteel Group	35.4
JFE Steel	34	Hebei Steel Group	33.3
Posco	34	JFE	32.4
Baosteel	23	POSCO	31.7
U.S. Steel	23	Wuhan Steel Group	27.7

Sources: Mittal Steel, Paul Glader, "Mittal, Arcelor Clash on Strategy in Takeover Battle," Wall Street Journal, March 10, 2006, A2 and the World Steel Association.

Jaguar brands from the Ford Motor Company as that company fought to become a smaller, less diverse, and profitable enterprise.

The significance of the arrival of large bids from emerging market companies is that the M&A business has now become truly a worldwide phenomenon. While not that long ago most of the large bids came from U.S. bidders, the field has become truly globalized, with large, well-financed bidders coming from not only developed countries but also emerging markets. These emerging market companies have come to establish large worldwide market shares, making them highly credible bidders.

European Protectionism during the 2000s

Several European nations have difficulty allowing foreign bidders to acquire major national companies. In several instances European nations have stepped in to erect barriers to impede takeovers of national champions. For example, this was the case in 2006, when the French government arranged a hasty marriage between two French utilities, Suez SA and Gaz de France SA, as a way of fending off an unwanted bid from Italian utility Enel SpA. Spain also implemented a new takeover law to try to prevent German E.ON AG's takeover of Spanish utility Endesa SA. The European Commission ruled that Spain violated European merger rules by applying conditions that violated the spirit of these regulations. Many European countries want free markets to allow their own indigenous companies to expand beyond their own borders. At the same time they want the ability to prevent free market access when it comes to hostile bids by other nations. In several instances in the 2000s, nationalism has overpowered the pursuit of free markets.

 SIXTH MERGER WAVE

As with the four prior merger waves, the fifth wave came to an end when the economy turned down and entered a brief eight-month recession in 2001. An initially weak recovery took place after the recession ended. However, the economy was buoyed by the low interest rates initially established by the Federal Reserve as a response to the 9/11 economic shock that took place at the end of the 2001 recession. Many have criticized then chairman Alan Greenspan for holding rates low for so long. These low rates provided the fuel for a speculative bubble in real estate that became an international bubble as the international investment world developed an insatiable appetite for mortgage-backed securities and other debt securitizations. Industries tied to housing, such as construction, also thrived during the building boom that took place.

The low interest rates also gave a major boost to the private equity business. Leveraged acquisitions became less expensive for private equity buyers to do as the bulk of the financing costs was relatively low interest rate debt. The economy and the market were also thriving, so equity financing was also readily available. The rising market made it easier to be successful in the private equity business. Private equity firms found it easy to raise equity capital and equally easy to borrow money at extremely attractive rates.

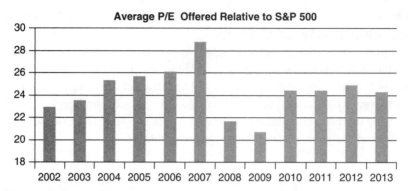

FIGURE 2.10 Average P/E Offered Relative to S&P 500. *Source: Mergerstat Review*, 2014.

They used this equity and debt capital to buy companies or divisions of companies and then waited for the rising market to push the values of the acquired entities up, at which point they sold them off at a profit. Since the bulk of the financing was low interest rate debt, they were able to generate high returns for the equity holders. This made private equity firms thrive, which, in turn, fueled the demand for M&A targets. As Figure 2.10 shows, the rising demand for targets resulted in higher offers, as reflected by the increase in the P/Es paid for targets. Thus, we had a relatively short but nonetheless intense M&A wave that came to a rapid end when the subprime crisis that started in 2007 cut off the access these firms had to cheap debt and eager equity investors.

Figure 2.11 compares the inflation-adjusted value of U.S. deals over the 25-year period during 1980–2013. Clearly, the value of deals in the sixth merger wave covering the four-year period 2004–2007 was comparable to the fifth wave and exceeded that of the fourth wave.

As with prior merger waves, this wave came to an end when the subprime crisis took hold and the economy entered a recession in 2008.

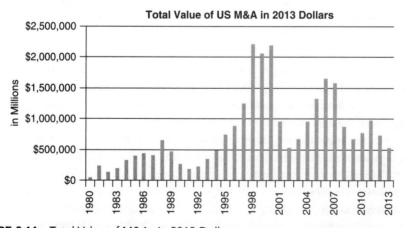

FIGURE 2.11 Total Value of M&As in 2013 Dollars.

CHAPTER THREE

Legal Framework

THIS CHAPTER FOCUSES MAINLY on the legal regulations governing mergers and acquisitions (M&As) in the United States. However, the rules for other countries are also discussed. It will be clear that there are many similarities in the takeover regulations of various countries, although there are some important differences.

The legal requirements governing M&As in the United States differ depending on whether a transaction is a friendly merger or a hostile deal. Within each of these categories the rules vary depending on whether the transactions are cash- or stock-financed. The regulatory framework of each of these alternatives is as follows:

- **Friendly merger—cash financed.** The bidder is required to file a proxy statement with the Securities and Exchange Commission (SEC) that describes the deal. Usually, the bidder has to file a preliminary statement first. If the SEC makes comments, the preliminary statement may be changed before it is finalized. The finalized proxy statement is then mailed to shareholders along with a proxy card that they fill out and return. Following this, the deal has to be approved at a shareholders' meeting, whereupon the deal can then be closed.
- **Friendly merger—stock financed.** This process is similar to a cash-financed merger except that the securities used to purchase target shares have to be registered. The bidder does this by filing a registration statement. Once this is approved, the combined registration/proxy statement can be sent to shareholders.
- **Hostile deal—cash tender offer.** The bidder initiates the tender offer by disseminating tender offer materials to target shareholders. Such offers have to be made pursuant to the requirements of the Williams Act. This law is discussed at length in

this chapter. However, unlike the friendly transactions just described, the SEC does not have an opportunity to comment on the materials that are sent to shareholders prior to their dissemination. The SEC may do so, however, during the minimum offer period, which will be described later in this chapter.

■ **Hostile deal—stock tender offer.** The bidder first needs to submit a registration statement and wait until it is declared effective prior to submitting tender offer materials to shareholders. The SEC may have comments on the preliminary registration statement that have to be resolved before the statement can be considered effective. Once this is done, the process proceeds similar to a cash tender offer.

LAWS GOVERNING MERGERS, ACQUISITIONS, AND TENDER OFFERS

Several laws regulate the field of M&As in the United States. These laws set forth the rules that govern the M&A process. Because target companies use some of these laws as a defensive tactic when contemplating a takeover, an acquiring firm must take careful note of legal considerations. The three main groups of laws are securities laws, state corporation laws, and antitrust laws.

Securities Laws

There are various securities laws that are important to the field of M&As. The more important parts of these laws are reviewed in this chapter, beginning with the filing of an 8K, followed by a detailed discussion of the Williams Act.

Filing of an 8K

The Securities Exchange Act of 1934 requires that an 8K filing must be made within 15 calendar days after the occurrence of certain specific events.[1] Such events include the acquisition and disposition of a significant amount of assets, including companies. The filing will include information such as the following:

- Description of the assets acquired or disposed of
- Nature and amount of consideration given or received
- Identity of the persons from whom the assets were acquired
- In the case of an acquisition, the source of the funds used to finance the purchase
- Financial statements of the business acquired

Acquisitions are determined to involve a significant amount of assets if the equity interest in the assets being acquired or the amount paid or received in an acquisition or disposition exceeds 10% of the total book assets of the registrant and its subsidiaries. This threshold can be important. For example, in the 1990s Tyco did many acquisitions

---

[1] www.sec.gov/about/forms/form8-k.pdf.

for which it did not file an 8K due to this filing threshold. However, it did so many acquisitions that the combination was easily in excess of this percentage. Moreover, as the company grew through its acquisition program, more and larger acquisitions were "going under the radar" as it became more difficult to readily see the true extent of Tyco's acquisition program.

Filing of an S-4

When a public company has to issue new stock to acquire a target, it must register these shares by filing a disclosure form with the SEC.[2] This usually is done through the filing of an S-4 form, which is slightly less detailed than the S-1 form that a company files when it first goes public. NYSE and NASDAQ rules, as well as most state corporation laws, require that when a company issues more than 20% of its outstanding shares to acquire a target, it must receive the approval of its shareholders. The S-4 provides a substantial amount of information for shareholders to review to learn about the purposes of the deal. For example, when Pfizer acquired Wyeth in 2009 in a cash- and stock-financed transaction, it filed a 351-page S-4.[3]

In most stock-for-stock transactions the acquirer and target will file a joint proxy statement/prospectus within the Form S-4. It will include the proxy statement that is sent to target shareholders for their approval. If the acquirer's shareholders have to approve the deal, they will also receive a proxy statement, which is included in the filing. All such filings are available on the SEC's website.[4] They must be submitted to the SEC 10 days prior to being mailed to shareholders. The written consent materials sent to shareholders must be received by them at least 20 calendar days prior to a shareholder meeting to approve the deal. If approved by shareholders, the merger is effective immediately after the filing of a Certificate of Merger in the state in which the target is incorporated. In a typical long-form merger, there is no issue of doing a back-end freeze-out as all target shares are converted into a right to receive the merger consideration.

The acquirer is restricted to a period of 48 to 72 hours after the announcement to make public statements about the transactions. After this time period a quiet period ensues until the S-4 becomes effective and is available to the public.

Williams Act

The Williams Act, which was passed in 1968, is one of the most important pieces of securities legislation in the field of M&A. It had a pronounced impact on merger activity in the 1970s and 1980s. Before its passage, tender offers were largely unregulated, a situation that was not a major concern before 1960 because few tender offers were made. In the 1960s, however, the tender offer became a more popular means of taking control of corporations and ousting an entrenched management. In tender offers that used securities as the consideration, the disclosure requirement of the Securities Act of 1933

---

[2] www.sec.gov/about/forms/forms-4.pdf.
[3] http://ccbn.tenkwizard.com/xml/download.php?form at=PDF&ipage=6232028.
[4] www.sec.gov.

provided some limited regulation. In cash offers, however, there was no such regulation. As a result, the SEC sought to fill this gap in the law, and Senator Harrison Williams, as chairman of the Senate Banking Committee, proposed legislation for that purpose in 1967. The bill won congressional approval in July 1968. The Williams Act provided an amendment to the Securities Exchange Act of 1934, a legal cornerstone of securities regulations. This act, together with the Securities Act of 1933, was inspired by the government's concern for greater regulation of securities markets. Both acts have helped eliminate some of the abuses that many believe contributed to the stock market crash of October 1929.

Specifically, these laws provide for greater disclosure of information by firms that issue securities to the public. For example, the Securities Act of 1933 requires the filing of a detailed disclosure statement when a company goes public. In addition, the Securities Exchange Act of 1934 proscribed certain activities of the securities industry, including wash sales and the churning of customer accounts. It also provided an enforcement agency, the SEC, which was established to enforce federal securities laws. In amending the Securities Exchange Act of 1934, the Williams Act added five new subsections to the law.

The Williams Act has four major objectives:

1. **To regulate tender offers.** Before the Williams Act was passed, stockholders of target companies often were stampeded into tendering their shares quickly to avoid receiving less advantageous terms.
2. **To provide procedures and disclosure requirements for acquisitions.** Through greater disclosure, stockholders could make more enlightened decisions regarding the value of a takeover offer. Disclosure would enable target shareholders to gain more complete knowledge of the potential acquiring company. In a stock-for-stock exchange, the target company stockholders would become stockholders in the acquiring firm. A proper valuation of the acquiring firm's shares depends on the availability of detailed financial data.
3. **To provide shareholders with time to make informed decisions regarding tender offers.** Even if the necessary information is available to target company stockholders, they still need time to analyze the data. The Williams Act allows them to make more informed decisions.
4. **To increase confidence in securities markets.** By increasing investor confidence, securities markets can attract more capital. Investors will be less worried about being placed in a position of incurring losses when making decisions based on limited information.

Section 13(d) of the Williams Act

Section 13(d) of the Williams Act provides an early warning system for stockholders and target management, alerting them to the possibility that a threat for control may soon occur. This section provides for disclosure of a buyer's stockholdings, whether they have come from open-market purchases, tender offers, or private purchases, when these holdings reach 5% of the target firm's total common stock outstanding. When the law was first passed, this threshold level was 10%; this percentage was later considered too high, and the more conservative 5% was adopted. The disclosure of the required information, pursuant to the rules of Section 13(d), is necessary even when there is no tender offer. The buyer who intends to take control of a corporation must disclose the required information following the attainment of a 5% holding in the target. The buyer makes this disclosure by filing a Schedule 13D. A filing may be necessary even though no one individual or firm actually owns 5% of another firm's stock. If a group of investors act in concert, under this law their combined stockholdings are considered as one group.

Schedule 13D

Section 13(d) provides for the filing of a Schedule 13D with the SEC and any exchange on which the issuer's stock is traded, as well as the issuer.[5] The SEC filing is done through the SEC database—EDGAR (Electronic Data Gathering and Retrieval).[6] The filing must be done within 10 days of acquiring 5% of the issuer's outstanding stock. Certain parties are exempt from this filing requirement, such as brokerage firms holding shares in street names or underwriters who happen to acquire shares for a limited period (up to 40 days).

Schedule 13D requires the disclosure of the following information:[7]

- The name and address of the issuing firm and the type of securities to be acquired. For example, a company may have more than one class of securities. In this instance, the acquiring firm must indicate the class of securities of which it has acquired at least 5%.
- Detailed information on the background of the individual filing the information, including any past criminal violations.
- The number of shares actually owned.
- The purpose of the transaction. At this point the acquiring firm must indicate whether it intends to take control of the company or is merely buying the securities for investment purposes.
- The source of the funds used to finance the acquisition of the firm's stock. The extent of the reliance on debt, for example, must be disclosed. This is important since if borrowed funds are used and have to be repaid, this could cause the eventual sale of the stock in the market, which may have an effect on the stock price. Written statements from financial institutions documenting the bidder's ability to procure the requisite financing may be required to be appended to the schedule.

In addition to the preceding, the bidder must disclose all transactions in the target's shares that occurred over the 60-day period prior to the offer.

---

[5] www.financialfilings.com/inc/pdf/sched13d.pdf.
[6] www.sec.gov/edgar.shtml.
[7] Bryon E. Fox and Eleanor M. Fox, *Corporate Acquisitions and Mergers*, 2nd ed. (New York: Matthew Bender, 1994).

Amendments Required under Section 13(d)(2)

Section 13(d)(2) requires the "prompt" filing, with the SEC and the exchanges, by the issuer when there has been a "material change," such as acquiring an additional 1%, in the facts that were set forth in Schedule 13D. As with much of the Williams Act, the wording is vague regarding what constitutes a material change or even the time period that is considered prompt. However, Rule 13d-2 does specify that an increase or decrease of 1% is considered material. The law is not specific on the time period for filing an amendment to the original 13D form, although a 10-day period may be acceptable.[8] However, for significant events a filing within one or two days may be expected.[9] Such significance could be found in the market's sensitivity and reliance on the new information as well as prior information disclosed in the original filing that now may be significantly different.

Remedies for Failure to Comply with Section 13(d)

If there is a perceived violation of Section 13(d), either shareholders or the target company may sue for damages. The courts are more mindful of the target's shareholders' rights under Section 13(d) than those of the target corporation itself because this section of the statute was designed for their benefit as opposed to protecting the interests of the target corporation. Courts have been more inclined to grant equitable relief, such as in the form of an injunction, as opposed to compensatory relief in the form of damages. They are more concerned about making sure the proper disclosure is provided to shareholders as opposed to standing in the way of an acquisition. In addition to the courts, the SEC may review the alleged violation of Section 13(d) and could see fit to pursue an enforcement action. Parties that are found guilty of violating Section 13(d) may face fines and possible disgorgement.

Derivatives

Generally the principle governing derivatives is that if the security holders do not have voting or dispositive power of the equity securities, then they do not have to file. If the acquisition of the derivatives was to avoid having to file a 13D, then a court may not looking kindly on the failure to file.

Schedule 13G

The SEC makes special provisions for those investors, usually institutional investors, who acquire 5% or more of a company's shares but who did not acquire more than 2% of those shares in the previous 12 months and who have no interest in taking control of the firm. Such investors are required to file the much less detailed Schedule 13G. Schedule 13G must be filed on February 14 of each year.[10] These shareowners are sometimes called 5% *beneficial owners*. Parties who own shares or who have "dispositive"

---

[8] Brent A. Olsen, *Publicly Traded Corporations, Governance, Operation and Regulation* (New York: Thompson-West, 2005), 14–19.

[9] Dennis Block, *Understanding Securities Laws 2013* (New York: Practising Law Institute, August 9, 2013), 13.

[10] If the ownership is greater than 10%, however, the filing must be made within 10 days after the end of the month in which the 10% interest was acquired.

power (power to dispose of the securities), which entitles them to vote the shares, have to file.

If the status of a 13G filer changes, such as they now want to try to influence the control of the company or even make a bid for it, they must file a 13D and must "sit out" for a "cooling off" period of 10 days. That is, they cannot take any actions, such as those that may have been described in the 13D filing, until the passage of 10 days.

Employee Stock Ownership Plans

The SEC may consider the trustee of an employee stock ownership plan to be a beneficial owner of the shares of stock in the plan. An employee stock ownership plan may have a trustee who is a bank advisor or an investment advisor. In making the determination of whether the trustee is the beneficial owner, the SEC would consider whether the trustee has discretionary authority to vote or dispose of the shares. If the trustee has such discretionary powers, there may be an obligation to file.

Section 14(d)

The Williams Act also provides for disclosure of various information in tender offers, principally through Section 14(d). Both Sections 13(d) and 14(d) apply only to equity securities registered with the SEC. These regulations apply to tender offers that, if successful, would result in the owner possessing 5% or more of a class of equity securities.

Schedule TO

Under the original wording of the law, disclosure came in the form of a Schedule 14D-1. A similar schedule, Schedule 13E-4, was filed for tender offers done by the issuer itself. Since both schedules related to tender offers, either by the issuer or a third party, the SEC decided in January 2000 to combine the schedule into one filing, which is now called a Schedule TO.

Schedule TO requires the bidder to disclose various information, such as the specific shares to be acquired, the identity and background of the bidder, the terms and purpose of the transaction, and the source of funds to be used. With the schedule the bidder has to include the last two years of its financial statements.

Commencement of the Offer

The time period of the tender offer may be crucially important in a contested takeover battle. Therefore, the date on which the offer is initially made is important. For cash tender offers, the tender offer will begin on 12:01 a.m. on the date that any one of the following occurs:

- Publication of the tender offer
- Advertisement of the tender offer (e.g., through an advertisement in the *Wall Street Journal*)
- Submittal of the tender offer materials to the target

Following an announcement of an offer, the bidder has five business days to disseminate the tender offer materials.

For exchange offers, the bidder has to adhere to the registration requirements of the Securities Act of 1933, and according to Rule 14d-5, the offer cannot commence until a complete registration statement has been filed with the SEC.

Nature of the Offer

It is important to understand that in tender offers, the agreement is between the bidder and the target shareholders. The bidder may possibly reach some agreement with the target corporation, but that entity is not necessarily part of the tender offer. The bidder makes an offer to the target's shareholders and gives them the means to accept the offer by giving them a letter of transmittal. When they send it back to the bidder (really its agent), then they have a contractual agreement that is subject to the terms of the offer.

Position of the Target Corporation

The target company must respond to the tender offer by filing a Schedule 14D-9 within 10 business days after the commencement date, indicating whether it recommends acceptance or rejection of the offer.[11] If the target contends that it maintains no position on the offer, it must state its reasons. In addition to filing with the SEC, the target must send copies of the Schedule 14D-9 to each of the organized exchanges on which the target's stock is traded. The target may not make public solicitations or recommendations to its shareholders until the 14D-9 has been filed with the SEC.

Time Periods of the Williams Act

Minimum Offer Period

According to the Williams Act, a tender offer must be kept open for a minimum of 20 business days, during which the acquiring firm must accept all shares that are tendered. However, it may not actually buy any of these shares until the end of the offer period. The minimum offer period was added to discourage shareholders from being pressured into tendering their shares rather than risk losing out on the offer. With a minimum time period, shareholders can take their time to consider this offer and compare the terms of the offer with those of other offers. The offering firm may get an extension on the 20-day offer period, if, for example, it believes there is a better chance of getting the shares it needs. The acquiring firm must purchase the shares tendered (at least on a pro rata basis) at the offer price unless the firm does not receive the total number of shares it requested in the terms of the tender offer. The acquirer may, however, still choose to purchase the tendered shares.

The tender offer may be worded to contain other escape clauses. For example, when antitrust considerations are an issue, the offer may be contingent on attaining the regulatory agencies' approval. Therefore, the offer might be so worded as to state that the bidder is not bound to buy if the Justice Department or the FTC objects to the merger.

Unlike some other countries, in the United States, while there is a minimum offer period there is no maximum offer period.

---

[11] www.jofish.net/Sched14D-9F.pdf.

Exchange Offers

When the offer is a stock-for-stock transaction, this is referred to as an exchange offer. The rules allow an exchange offer to commence after a registration statement for the shares being offered has been filed with the SEC. This is an "early" commencement as the offered is not yet "effective." In order to be able to do that, the bidder does the filing, disseminates a prospectus to all the security holders, and files the Schedule TO. However, no shares may be actually purchased until 20 business days after commencement.

Withdrawal Rights

Shareholders may withdraw their shares any time during the entire period the offer remains open. The goal of this rule is to allow shareholders sufficient time to evaluate the offer—or offers, in the case of multiple bids. However, under the new 14d-11 Rule the bidder may provide an optional three days after the expiration of the 20-day period to accept additional shares tendered, assuming the bidder promptly pays for the shares already tendered and gives the shareholders who tender during this 3-day period the same consideration and prompt payment.

Partial and Two-Tiered Tender Offers

A partial tender offer is one in which there is a bid for less than 100%, such as a bid for 51%, which usually affords the acquirer control of the target. Two-tiered tender offers are bids that provide one type of compensation for a first tier, such as the first 51%, and other compensation for the remaining shares. Courts have generally found these types of bids coercive and opposing the spirit of the Williams Act, as shareholders in the back end of the offer may find that their shares trade for less than before the bid. They may also be in constant fear that their stock positions will be frozen out. The Best Price Rule, which we discuss shortly, combined with similar state laws, as well as similar corporate charter amendments, has reduced the effectiveness of such coercive offers.

While these types of bids are not illegal in the United States, courts have found that targets may be freer to take aggressive defensive measures when faced with such offers.[12] This is different from the position of courts in the United Kingdom, which prevents a majority shareholder from freezing out minority shareholders.

Pro Rata Acceptance

In many instances tender offers are oversubscribed. For example, an offer to purchase 51% of a target company's stock may receive 80% of the total shares outstanding. Approximately five-eighths of each share submitted would be accepted if all 80% of the shares were tendered during the first 10 days of an offer to purchase 51% of the outstanding stock. If an additional 10% were submitted after the tenth calendar day of the offer, these shares would not be accepted unless the acquiring company decided to accept more shares than were stipulated in the 51% offer.

---

[12] *Unocal Corp. v. Mesa Petroleum*, 493 A.2d, 946, 956 (Del 1985).

Definition of a Tender Offer

The Williams Act is purposefully vague regarding the definition of a tender offer. Not surprisingly, this vagueness gave rise to litigation as tender offer participants chose to adopt the definition of a tender offer that was most favorable to them. In *Kennecott Copper Corporation v. Curtiss-Wright Corporation*, the court found that open market purchases without a deadline and for which no premium was offered did not constitute a tender offer.[13] However, in *Wellman v. Dickinson* the U.S. District Court for the Second Circuit set forth the *Eight Factor Test*.[14]

These factors are listed here and are revisited in Chapter 6:

1. There is active and widespread solicitation of public shareholders for shares of an issuer.
2. Solicitation is made for a substantial percentage of an issuer's stock.
3. Offer to purchase is made at a premium over the prevailing market price.
4. Terms of the offer are firm rather than negotiated.
5. Offer is contingent on the tender of a fixed number of shares and possibly specifying a maximum number of shares.
6. Offer is open for only a limited time period.
7. Offeree is subject to pressure to sell stock.
8. There are public announcements of a purchasing program that precede or are coincident with a rapid accumulation of shares.[15]

A transaction need not satisfy all eight factors in order to be considered a tender offer.

In *Hanson Trust PLC v. SCM Corp.*, the U.S. Court of Appeals for the Second Circuit recognized that the *Wellman* factors are relevant to determining whether certain actions by a bidder constitute a tender offer.[16] However, the court stopped short of saying that these factors are a "litmus test." Rather this court applied the "*totality of the circumstances test*" when it focused on whether offerees would be put at an informational disadvantage if official tender offer procedures were not followed. Other courts have put forward more basic tests. In a district court opinion in *S-G Securities, Inc. v. Fuqua Investment Co.*, the court concluded that a tender offer exists if the following occurs:[17]

- A bidder publicly announcing its intention to acquire a substantial block of a target's shares for the purpose of acquiring control of the company.
- A substantial accumulation of the target's stock by the bidder through open-market or privately negotiated purchases.

---

[13] *Kennecott Copper Corp. v. Curtiss-Wright Corp.*, 584 F.2d 1195 (CA2 1978).
[14] *Wellman v. Dickinson*, 475 F. Supp. (SD NY 1979), *aff'd* 632 F.2d 355 (CA2 1982), *cert. denied*, 460 U.S. 1069 (1983).
[15] This last factor was added after the *Wellman v. Dickinson* decision.
[16] *Hanson Trust PLC v. SCM Corp.*, 744 F.2d 47 (2d Cir. 1985).
[17] *S-G Securities, Inc. v. Fuqua Investment Co.*, 466 F. Supp. 1114 (D. Mass. 1978).

SUN OIL VERSUS BECTON DICKINSON

The Becton Dickinson Corporation is a medical products company that is located in Bergen County, New Jersey. The company was run for 25 years by Fairleigh S. Dickinson Jr. until 1974. He was the son of the founder of the company, Fairleigh Dickinson Sr., who also founded Fairleigh Dickinson University. Fairleigh Dickinson Jr. had turned over the day-to-day control to a management team headed by Wesley Howe and Marvin Ashe. As time passed, disagreements occurred between Fairleigh Dickinson Jr. and Howe and Ashe. For example, they disagreed on certain personnel decisions and on other strategic decisions, such as the acquisition of National Medical Care—a Boston-based medical care company. Fairleigh Dickinson Jr. opposed this particular acquisition because the equity offered for the purchase would dilute his shareholdings and his ownership percentage. The pattern of disagreements came to a head in a board of directors meeting in which Ashe and Howe called for the removal of Fairleigh Dickinson Jr. as chairman of the board of directors.

While the internecine conflicts were ongoing at Becton Dickinson, Sun Oil Inc., a Philadelphia-based corporation, was pursuing an expansion program that would help them diversify outside the petroleum industry. They were working with their investment banker, Salomon Brothers, to find suitable non-oil acquisition candidates. Given its position in its industry, they found Becton Dickinson an attractive takeover target. Salomon Brothers, the investment banker for both Sun Oil and Fairleigh Dickinson Jr., was more easily able to reach an understanding between the two parties, which provided for Fairleigh Dickinson Jr. to sell his 5% holdings in Becton Dickinson to Sun Oil at the appropriate time.

Sun Oil obtained commitments from 33 financial institutions to buy 20% of the outstanding shares of Becton Dickinson. On one day couriers were sent to these institutions to purchase these shares. Following the stock purchase, Sun Oil informed the New York Stock Exchange and Becton Dickinson of their actions. They did not file a 14D-1 but did file a 13D.

In a lawsuit that followed, the court ruled that Sun Oil had violated the Williams Act by not filing a 13D when it had reached its understanding with Fairleigh Dickinson Jr. to purchase his 5%.

Materials That Shareholders Receive

Shareholders receive an Offer to Purchase and a Letter of Transmittal. The Offer to Purchase sets forth the terms of the offer. Chief among these terms are the number of shares to be purchased, the offer price, and the length of time the offer will remain open. The Offer to Purchase may be many pages in length (e.g., 30 pages) and may contain much additional information for shareholders to consider, such as withdrawal rights, a discussion of tax considerations, and more details on the terms of the offer.

Method of Tendering Shares

Stockholders tender their shares through an intermediary, such as a commercial bank or trust company, which is referred to as the paying agent. As stockholders seek to participate in the tender offer, they submit their shares to the paying agent in exchange for cash or securities, in accordance with the terms of the offer. Attached to their shares must be a *letter of transmittal.*

The agent accumulates the shares but does not pay the stockholders until the offer expires. In the event that the offer is extended, the paying agent holds the shares until the new offer expires, unless instructed otherwise by the individual stockholders. The bidder may extend an undersubscribed tender. In fact, it is not unusual for an offer to be extended several times as the bidder tries to get enough shares to ensure control. If the bidder decides to extend the offer, it must announce the extension no later than 9:00 a.m. on the business day following the day on which the offer was to have expired. At that time the bidder must disclose the number of shares that have already been purchased. As noted, shareholders have the right to withdraw their shares at any time during the offer period. The fact that they originally tendered them in response to the offer does not limit their ability to change their mind or tender these same shares to a competing offer after they withdraw them.

Changes in the Tender Offer

The Williams Act allows a modification in the offer period if there is a material change in the terms of the offer. The length of the extension in the offer period depends on the significance of the change, which generally is considered a *new offer*. A new offer ensures the stockholders a 20-day period to consider the offer. A higher price might be considered such a significant change. A less significant change results in an *amended offer*, which provides for a 10-day minimum offer period. An increase in the number of shares to be purchased might be considered an amended offer.

Best Price Rule and Other Related Rules

Under Section 14(d)(7), if the bidder increases the consideration offered, the bidder must pay this increased consideration to all those who have already tendered their shares at the lower price. The goal of this section is to ensure that all tender shareholders are treated equally, regardless of the date within the offer period that they tender their shares. Under SEC Rule 14d-10, a bidder may offer more than one type of consideration. In such cases, however, selling stockholders have the right to select the type of consideration they want. More recently this rule was revised to allow management shareholders to receive extra compensation as long as that extra compensation was for services they would provide. A "safe harbor" compensation arrangement is also available to directors.

Bidder Purchases Outside of Tender Offer

The bidder may not purchase shares outside the tender offer on terms that are different from those of the tender offer. There may be exceptions to this rule if the SEC agrees to exempt the transactions based on its belief that the purchases are not manipulative, fraudulent, or deceptive. Such purchases, however, are permitted in the event that the tender offer concludes or is withdrawn.

Payment Following Completion of the Offer

The law provides that the tendered shares must be either paid for promptly after the offer is terminated or returned to the shareholders. This prompt payment may be frustrated by other regulatory requirements, such as the Hart-Scott-Rodino Act. The bidder may postpone payment if other regulatory approvals must still be obtained after the Williams Act offer period expires.

Mini-Tender Offers

Mini-tender offers are bids for less than 5% of a company's stock. Such offers are much less regulated as bidders, and are not required to comply with the disclosure requirements for larger tender offers. Investors who accept such offers need to know that they are not entitled to pro rata acceptance and do not have withdrawal rights. These offers may not contain a premium and may even be below the market price. Therefore, investors need to be wary of them.

Taking Control after a Successful Tender Offer

It is common that after a successful tender offer the target and the bidder agree that the bidder may elect a majority of the board of directors. This allows the bidder to take control of the board of directors without calling a meeting of the shareholders and soliciting their voting approval. After a successful tender offer for 50% or more of the target's shares, the so-called *minimum condition*, the outcome of such a vote is moot.

The process of using a tender offer to gain control of a target can be more difficult when there are antitakeover defenses that limit the ability of a bidder to appoint members to the board. If this is not the case, the board change may go smoothly. If the target agrees to the change in control of the board, it must communicate to the SEC and its shareholders information about the new directors similarly to how it would normally be disclosed if they were nominees in an election of directors.

Delisting the Target

Following a takeover and merger of a target into the bidder, a bidder/target may then file to have the target's shares delisted from the exchanges on which it was traded. A Form 25 then needs to be filed with and approved by the SEC.

Competing Tender Offers

An initial tender offer often attracts rival tender offers in takeover battles. Because the law was designed to give stockholders time to carefully consider all relevant alternatives, an extension of the offer period is possible when there is a competing offer. The Williams Act states that, in the event of a new tender offer, stockholders in the target company must have at least 10 business days to consider the new offer. In effect, this 10-day consideration period can extend the original offer period. Consider, for example, that we are 16 days into the first offer when a new bidder makes a tender offer for the target firm; then target shareholders have at least 10 days to decide on the original offer. As a result, the original offer period is extended. If, however, the new offer occurred on the fourth day of the first offer period, there would not be an extension of the original offer period.

Applicability of U.S. Tender Offer Rules to Takeovers of Non-U.S. Companies

The U.S. tender offer rules apply to U.S. companies when they make bids for the shares of foreign companies if the target's shares are registered in the United States. Exemptions may be had in cases where the foreign issuer's U.S. shareholders make up less than 10% of the total shares outstanding.

Tender Offers for Debt Securities

Technically, tender offers for straight debt securities (debt that is not convertible) have to conform to the antifraud provisions of securities laws that govern tender offers, including the minimum 20-day offer period and the requirement that offer periods be extended when the offer price changes. However, the SEC has issued "no-action" letters in which it has indicated that it will not enforce these laws in the case of straight debt tender offers. However, convertible debt securities are considered to be equity securities for the purpose of enforcing tender offer rules.

OTHER SPECIFIC TAKEOVER RULES IN THE UNITED STATES

There are other takeover rules that may be relevant to certain takeovers. For example, in the utility sector, there is the Public Utility Holding Company Act (PUHCA), passed in 1935, which imposed geographical limitations on utility mergers while also placing restrictions on utilities' investments in non-energy companies. This law was overseen by the SEC. However, the Energy Policy Act liberalized these outmoded rules. The Federal Energy Regulatory Commission was formed and took a role in reviewing utility deals.

Takeovers that are determined to be threats to U.S. national security can be halted by the president. Such deals are reviewed by the Committee on Foreign Investment in the United States (CFIUS), a 12-member interagency panel that includes the secretaries of state, defense, treasury, and commerce, which makes a recommendation to the president. This panel does not review all deals, and most dealmakers and their advisors, when they believe there may be a potential security issue, contact the committee so as not to have a problem after the fact. Potential opposition to deals related to CFIUS was a key factor in China's CNOOC Ltd. dropping its $18.5 billion all-cash offer for Unocal in August 2005 and for the Dubai-owned Ports World's amendment of its 2006 $6.8 billion offer for Britain's Peninsular and Oriental Steam Navigation Co., which held contracts to manage six U.S. ports.

Regulation of Proxy Solicitation

State corporation laws require annual shareholder meetings. In order to achieve a quorum, the company solicits proxies from shareholders. Bidders attempting to take over a company may also solicit proxies from shareholders. Section 14(a) of the Securities Exchange Act regulates these solicitations. As part of these regulations, a solicitor must file a proxy statement and a Schedule 14A, which must also be given to security holders. According to Rule 14a-6, proxy materials must be filed with the SEC 10 days before they are used. An exception exists for more noncontroversial events, such as annual meetings. However, in no case must the materials be used prior to being submitted. In light of the substantial mailing costs that security holders who have their own proposals may incur, the law requires the issuer to provide a supporting statement (up to 500 words), which is included with management proxy proposals. Only a very small percentage of such security holder solicitations are successful.

INTERNATIONAL SECURITIES LAWS RELATING TO TAKEOVERS

In this section we will highlight some of the different takeover laws that exist in countries other than the United States. A comprehensive discussion of these various laws is beyond the scope of this book. However, some of them are discussed to give the reader a flavor of their variety and also the extent to which many have provisions similar to U.S. takeover rules.

Global financial regulation has evolved substantially over the past quarter of a century. As many companies are becoming increasingly globalized, large variation in securities laws has become an impediment to growth. Fortunately, we have seen a trend toward common regulations across many nations. This is true with many forms of securities regulations, and M&As are no exception. There are still differences across nations, but more and more those differences have declined.

Europe

Great Britain

British takeover regulation is a form of self-regulation by the corporate sector and the securities industry. This regulation is based on the City Code of Takeovers and Mergers, a collection of standards and regulations on takeovers and mergers, and is enforced by the Panel on Takeovers and Mergers, which was established in 1968. This panel is composed of members of the Bank of England, London Stock Exchange members, and various other financial leaders. Its chief responsibility is to ensure that a level playing field exists—that is, that all investors have equal access to information on takeover offers. This contrasts with regulation in the U.S. which is effectively done by the courts of the state of Delaware through the development of its common or case law.

The Panel also attempts to prevent target firms from adopting antitakeover measures without prior shareholder approval. Some of the more important provisions of the British code are as follows:

- Investors acquiring 30% or more of a company's shares, having acquired *de facto control*, must bid for the remaining shares at the highest price paid for the shares already acquired. This is sometimes referred to as the "put up or shut up rule."

- Substantial partial offers for a target must gain the approval of the target and the panel.
- Antitakeover measures, such as supermajority provisions or the issuance of options to be given to friendly parties, must be approved by the target's shareholders.

The unique aspect of the British system is that compliance is voluntary; the panel's rulings are not binding by law. Its rulings are considered most influential, however, and are commonly adopted. If the panel detects a violation and lack of compliance with its rules by a party involved in a takeover, it may refer the matter to the Financial Services Authority (FSA), which is the main financial regulator in the United Kingdom. Mergers that may be anticompetitive may be referred to the Competition Commission.

Pursuant to Britain's Companies Act, buyers of 3% or more of a target's shares must notify the target within two days of acquiring that position. Rule 2.5 of this country's Share Acquisition Rules requires the bidder to make a public announcement of offers. In the case of hostile bids, the target must respond with its position within 14 days of the bid.[18]

The case law in the United Kingdom favors shareholders rights and is generally supportive of takeover bids. Antitakeover defenses that impede shareholder rights and that lack clear corporate purposes other than management entrenchment are frowned upon.[19] This includes defensive tools such as poison pills which are quite popular in the U.S. Staggered boards are also ineffective in the U K as shareholders have the right to remove directors at any time. This is why hostile bids may be more likely to succeed in the UK then in the U.S.[20]

European Union

The European Commission had sought one set of rules for all European nations, including the United Kingdom, rather than separate rules for each country that might be involved in cross-border deals. Such an accord was under discussion for almost two decades. Agreement on a joint takeover directive was finally reached after 15 years of debate and was made effective in May 2006. As of that date each EU member country had to implement the directive into its national laws. While the original form of the takeover directive included many shareholder rights provisions, it has been diluted by countries that want to give their indigenous companies a greater ability to oppose hostile takeovers from bidders from other countries—even if they are from EU member states. The main opposition to a common set of rules came from Germany and Sweden.

---

[18] Charles Mayo, "UK: England and Wales," in *Mergers and Acquisitions: 2005/06* (London: Practical Law, 2005–2006).
[19] Christin M. Forstinger, *Takeover Law in the EU and the USA* (The Hague, The Netherlands: Kluwer Law International, 2002), 71–72.
[20] John Armour and David A. Skeel, "Who Writes the Rules for Hostile Takeovers and Why? The Peculiar Divergence of U.S. and U.K. Takeover Regulation," *Georgetown Law Journal*, 95, 2007, 1727–1794.

In order to protect minority shareholders the directive contains a requirement to make a mandatory offer after a bidder purchases a certain number of shares. This bid must be made at an equitable price and must be submitted to shareholders with certain disclosures relating to the offer and bidder. Target shareholders must have no less than two weeks to evaluate the bid. The directive contains provisions to limit the use of poison pills and shares with multiple voting rights to oppose hostile bids. However, member states may choose to opt out of the provisions that they find not in their interests and substitute their own national rules. Their individual national rules are still relevant depending on the particular circumstances.

France

In France, takeover activity is more common than in most other nations in continental Europe. In France, bids are regulated by the Financial Markets Authority, and bidders, acting through financial representatives such as banks, must submit disclosures to this entity. Filings must be made within five trading days of crossing various shareholding thresholds, starting with 5% and moving up to two-thirds of outstanding shares.[21] Bidders acquiring additional shares must disclose their holdings on a daily basis. Offers for French companies are required to remain open for 25 trading days but not longer than 35 trading days. Bidders who do not take control of a target they have acquired shares in may voluntarily launch a bid for the remainder of the shares, but if the bidder acquires control in the target, a compulsory bid is required. France also has an antitakeover law, which provides protection to potential targets.

Germany

In general, Germany tends to be more supportive of management and more accepting of antitakeover defenses. This position is partly due to the shock of the takeover of Mannesmann by Vodafone. In Germany, as well as in the Netherlands, there is a system of worker codetermination, where it is common for a representative of management to sit on the board of directors and seek to exercise a worker claim to corporate profits. Also on the board may be representatives of banks who are major lenders to the company and who may look out for the interests of creditors.

Takeovers are regulated by several laws, including the Takeover Act. They are supervised by the Federal Office of Supervision of Financial Services (Bundesanstalt für Finanzdienstleistungsaufsicht or BaFin). In Germany, mandatory offers for the complete company are required when a bidder acquires a threshold number of shares. Offers must be kept open for 28 days but no more than 60 days. Targets must respond within two weeks of receiving the offer. Offers must be publicized in approved national newspapers. Hostile bids are not common in Germany due to the large cross holdings that have been assembled over many years, including major holdings by banks that tend to be supportive of management.

---

[21] Pierre Servan-Schreiber, Armand W. Grumberg, and Arash Attar, "France," in *Mergers and Acquisitions: 2005/06* (London: Practical Law, 2005–2006).

Ireland

Takeovers in Ireland are regulated by the Takeover Panel Act of 1997, which established the Takeover Panel that oversees takeovers.[22] Acquisitions of shares of 5% or more require a disclosure. Additional disclosure is required for purchase of 1% or more of a target's shares. In Ireland, there is a 21-day minimum offer period. In hostile bids the target must respond within 14 days.

Netherlands

In the Netherlands takeovers must be made pursuant to the Securities Act, which is enforced by the Authority for Financial Markets. Acquisitions of shareholdings at various thresholds, starting at 5%, require disclosure. Bids must be kept open for at least 20 days, but, in effect, rules make this period 23 days.[23] For hostile bids, the target's board must disclose its position four days prior to a shareholder meeting that may be called to address the bid.

Spain

In Spain, as in France, hostile bids are common. Bidders acquiring 5% or more of a target's stock must notify the National Securities Market Commission. This body then suspends the trading of the target's stock. The bidder must make a formal announcement of the bid, in at least two national newspapers and the commission's Official Gazette, within five days of making the offer.[24] Offers may be kept open for as long as four months.

Russia

In mid-2006, Russia adopted a broad takeover reform law. It provides for both a minority put option and minority squeeze-out. The law provides for mandatory tender offers within 35 days after crossing an odd mix of share thresholds of 30%, 50%, and 70%. It also requires bidders to attain antimonopoly approval before completing 100% stock acquisitions. Mandatory tender offers have minimum price requirements, with shareholders having an option to choose cash in the case of securities offers. The minimum price cannot be lower than the stock's price in the prior six-month trading period. Offers documents must be filed with the Russian Federal Service for the Financial Markets.

Competing offers must be submitted no less than 25 days prior to the expiration of the original bidder's offer. Such a competing offer may not feature a price lower than the original bidder's offer.

Canada

Takeover rules in Canada were revised in February 2008 to be more consistent with those of the United States. Filing requirements are similar to the Schedule TO that is filed

---

[22] John Given and Cian McCourt, "Ireland," in *Mergers and Acquisitions: 2005/06* (London: Practical Law, 2005–2006).

[23] Maarten Muller and Johan Kleyn, "The Netherlands," in *Mergers and Acquisitions: 2005/06* (London: Practical Law, 2005–2006).

[24] Francisco Pena and Fernando de las Cuevas, "Spain" in *Mergers and Acquisitions: 2005/06* (London: Practical Law, 2005–2006).

in the United States. However, there are some important differences in Canada. One such difference is the mandatory offer requirement when bidders acquire 20% or more of a target's shares. Like the United States and many other nations, Canada has regulations that allow the government to intervene to stop transactions larger than $250 million if the government believes that national security is threatened by the deal.

Asia

As noted in Chapters 1 and 2, the M&A business is rapidly evolving in many Asian markets. As these markets continue to restructure, their laws evolve to accommodate the volume of deals.

Japan

For many years there was little takeover activity in Japan and thus less focus on takeover regulation. For example, over the two-decade period between 1971 and 1990 there were only four tender offers.[25] However, as the Japanese economy faltered when its stock and real estate bubble collapsed and the nation entered a decade-long recession, the slow process of restructuring the Japanese corporate world began. As part of that process, takeovers became more common. The takeover market in Japan has been undergoing major changes in recent years. These changes have taken pace while some major takeover battles have occurred. One was the takeover battle between Mitsubishi Tokyo Financial Group, UFJ, and Sumitomo. Japanese courts have reached decisions similar to those of courts in the state of Delaware. In response to heightened takeover pressures, Japanese corporations have adopted various antitakeover defenses, including poison pills.

Tender offer regulations were first introduced in Japan in 1971. They were significantly revised in 1990 and again in 2006. Japanese takeover regulations are contained in the Securities and Exchange Law of Japan (SEL). Pursuant to this law, tender offers must be kept open for 20 calendar days but not more than 60. Mandatory tender offers are required in cases where purchasers acquire more than a third of the target's shares.

As in the United States, the target is required to file a response called the Opinion Report in 10 business days with the Kanto Local Finance Bureau. In this response the target can raise questions about the offer. The bidder, in turn, must then respond by filing a Report in Response to Questions within five business days. Bidders can increase their bid but not decrease it, and they are limited in their ability to withdraw an offer. They are also prevented from purchasing shares outside the tender offer. Shareholders, however, may withdraw their shares at any time during the offer period.

Tender offers commence after a public notice of the offer and an announcement that must be carried in two or more major newspapers. In addition, a Registration Statement has to be filed with the Kanto Local Finance Bureau on the announcement day. This Registration Statement contains information somewhat similar to a U.S. Schedule TO.

---

[25] Nobutoshi Yamanouchi, Ken Kiyohara, and Scott Jones, "Recent Revisions to Japanese Tender Offer Rules: Toward Transparency and Fairness," Jones Day internal publication, June 2007. www.jonesday.com/pubs/pubs-detail.aspx?pubID=72473925-1424-4665-9519-afc9ffa1b7c3&RSS=true.

The recent revisions of SEL impose additional management buyout requirements that try to ensure the fairness of the offer as well as limit conflicts of interest.

Effective 2007, Japan's Company Law allowed forward triangular mergers where a foreign company could acquire a Japanese target in a triangular merger using its own shares, as opposed to those of its Japanese subsidiary, which would typically have unregistered, nonpublicly traded shares.

Japanese securities rules also require that defenses should be disclosed when installed and that they should facilitate the enhancement of shareholder value. The defenses that are allowed include required share exchanges in which a bidder's acquired voting shares can be exchanged for nonvoting stock. Japanese rules also state that the level of defense should be related to the magnitude of the threat to shareholder value, which is somewhat akin to a U.S. Unocal Standard.

In enforcing takeover laws, Japanese courts have reached decisions somewhat similar to what one would expect to see in Delaware courts. These decisions allow for the use of antitakeover defenses but with an eye toward enhancing shareholder value and not in a way that would hurt shareholders and merely entrench management.

On the competition front, in 2004 Japan's Fair Trade Commission issued new merger guidelines that are somewhat similar to the antitrust rules enforced by the U.S. Justice Department. For example, these guidelines feature the use of quantitative measures, such as Herfindahl-Hirshmann indices, using similar thresholds to those employed in the United States.

South Korea

The South Korean Commercial Code contains a broad variety of laws governing South Korean companies, including those that relate to the incorporation of businesses but also takeover regulations and other control share transactions. Acquisitions by foreign buyers of South Korean companies traded on the South Korean Exchange are also governed by the Financial Investment Services and Capital Markets Act. In addition, antitrust issues are governed by the Monopoly Regulation and Fair Trade Act, which is enforced by the South Korean Fair Trade Commission.

Under South Korea's Securities Exchange Law, when a shareholder acquires a stock position of 5%, that shareholder is required to file a Public Ownership Report with this country's Financial Supervisory Commission within five business days of reaching that percentage holding. An additional report is required for further share purchases of 1% or more. The acquiring shareholder is subject to a cooling-off period, in which it must wait five days after acquiring the stock position before exercising the voting rights associated with the stock. As a result of an effort by Dubai-based Sovereign Asset Management Ltd. to remove the chairman of the South Korean refiner SK Corp, Korean laws were changed to now require holders of 5% or more to disclose their intentions if they are interested in pursuing changes in management.

South Korea's Securities Exchange Law requires that a tender offer statement be filed when such a bid is initiated. Target companies are not required to do a formal filing in response to a bid, but they can make such a statement if they choose to. Tender offer rules apply equally to offers from outside parties as well as self-tenders. Violators of these laws are subject to both administrative and criminal penalties.

There are restrictions on the ability of foreign investors to acquire companies in certain key industries, but these have been significantly relaxed in recent years. Many Korean companies are protected by rules that allow for large golden parachutes, as well as a requirement that two-thirds shareholder approval be received before changes in the board of directors can take place.

China

With the advent of communism in the 1950s in China, shareholding disappeared. China began the slow process of returning to some form of a free market economy in the 1980s. The Shanghai and Shenzhen Exchanges were founded in 1990, and all trading was expected to occur on these exchanges. Interim trading rules were established in 1993. This was followed by the Securities Law of China, which went into effect in July 1999. This law provided for acquisitions of public companies through agreement between the parties as well as through bids.

The Securities Law requires that owners of 5% or more of a public company's shares disclose this holding to the Chinese Securities Regulatory Commission (CRSC), the exchange on which the shares are traded, and to the issuing company within three days of acquiring this position. Once a 30% holding is achieved, the holder of the shares is prohibited from purchasing more shares unless it does a tender offer for the entire company. This is referred to as the mandatory bid rule. These rules were amended in the Takeover Code released in 2006, which allows for a partial tender offer that would be available to all shareholders. The acquiring shareholder, however, may request a waiver of the mandatory bid requirement from the CRSC.

The 2006 rules also governed the price that would be paid by bidders using a form of a fair price provision. Like other international jurisdictions, the consideration can be cash or securities, but if the securities are deemed illiquid, then the buyer must provide a cash alternative.

Acquisitions by Foreigners of Chinese Companies   In December 2005 new rules, called Administrative Measures for Strategic Investment by Foreign Investors in Listed Companies, were implemented that potentially reversed a long-term policy limiting the ability of foreign investors to acquire controlling positions in Chinese companies. Prior to this rule, foreign investors limited in their ability to acquire tradable Class A shares were often restricted to nontradable Class B shares, which are less appealing. The new rules opened up the Chinese market for foreign investors to purchase tradable shares. This, however, does not mean that the market is totally open and foreign investors have an unrestricted ability to acquire control over Chinese corporations. In fact, after opening the door for foreign investors to purchase tradable Class A shares, China adopted additional rules that require foreign buyers of Chinese assets to get Ministry of Commerce (MofCom) clearance before completing deals involving key industries and well-known Chinese brands. If U.S. readers find such restrictions inconsistent with their desire for open and free markets, they need to remember back to 2005 and the opposition to Chinese petroleum company CNOOC's bid for Unocal on "national security" grounds and realize that even countries that hold themselves out to be advocates of free markets may deviate from such a stance for political reasons.

In 2008 China finally passed its new antimonopoly law that had been 10 years in the making. The law is based upon aspects of U.S. and European competition laws, but it basically has provisions that seek to prevent dominance of markets by certain companies. It also has unique aspects, such as protecting the public interest and a "socialist market economy." The law also features protections for state-owned businesses and the monopoly positions they may have.

One of the first big bids for a Chinese company that was halted under the new rules was Coca Cola's 2009 $42.4 billion offer for the largest beverage company in China—Huiyuan. While for years China had been open to greenfield investments, this was a test of whether it was open to a highly respected international company acquiring a major Chinese firm. Clearly China was not.

China's entry as a "player" in the global M&A antitrust approval process has made the closing of global deals slower and more complicated. As of 2014 MofCom's Anti-Monopoly Bureau was reported to have about 20 case handlers, which is well below the staff assigned to such work in the United States and the EU.[26] However, given the newness of the 2008 antimonopoly law, its enforcement is a learning process for Chinese regulators. Part of the problem is that it seems, not unlike the EU, China may be using antimonopoly reviews to further the interest of Chinese companies. For example, it approved Glencore PLC's acquisition of Xstrata only in April 2013, which was a year after the Chinese authorities were notified of the deal and five months after the United States and the EU gave their approval. In order to get the Chinese approval, Glencore had to agree to sign a long-term contract to supply copper concentrate to Chinese customers at specified prices. This could not have been caused by antimonopoly concerns as the combined shares on the merged companies in those markets were not high.[27] Amazingly, the Bureau also required a divestiture of a copper mine in Peru, even though the combined entity does not own any copper facilities in China. Clearly, China is using the antitrust review process for more than protections against the use of monopoly power in the Chinese market.

An example of this occurred in 2014 when MofCom had a problem with the P3 alliance of three of the world's largest shipping companies: AP Meller-Maresk, CMA GCM SA, and Mediterranean Shipping Co. (MSC). Given the dependence of China on exports and shipping, it was concerned about the impact this alliance would have on shipping prices. However, this and other opposition to international deals signaled that China would play an important role in the global antitrust approval process. In response Maersk and MSC entered into a smaller-scale agreement—P2.

---

[26] Dominic Chopping and John D. Stoll, "China Puts Brake on Global Mergers," *Wall Street Journal*, April 1, 2014, C1–C2.
[27] Ibid.

Taiwan

Taiwan's main M&A law is the Business Mergers and Acquisitions Act, which was passed in 2002 and updated in 2004. Taiwan's takeover rules are set forth in the Tender Offer Rules for Public Issuance Companies. Tender offer rules have been in effect since 1995, but they have had little impact due to the paucity of such offers, which is in part due to the fact that many companies are controlled by large family shareholding positions. Revisions of these rules took effect in 2005. These rules require that bidders make a public announcement prior to initiating an offer. They also provide for greater disclosure in such tender offers. Under prior rules, target shareholders could withdraw shares for the entire offer period, but those withdrawal rights are now limited if the terms of the offer have been met during the offer period.

As with many countries in Asia, Taiwan has limitations on acquisitions by foreign investors, but it too has followed the trend to relax these restrictions. The competitive impact of M&As is evaluated by Taiwan's Fair Trade Commission.

India

Prior to the 1990s, takeovers in India were regulated by the Companies Act. However, this law proved insufficient to deal with the first Indian merger wave that took place in the 1980s. Up to that point, any bidders who acquired 25% or more of a company's shares were required to make a public offer to the shareholders of the company. Bidders circumvented this law by acquiring just under 25% but using the shareholding to control the target. The Indian financial and legal establishment recognized the insufficiency of their M&A rules, and a process of upgrading the regulations began to take place.

Today takeovers are regulated by the Takeover Code of 1997, which was amended with the Takeover Code of 2002. These rules are enforced by the Company Court and the Department of Company Affairs. For companies that are publicly traded, the Securities Exchange Board of India supervises the transaction.[28]

India's Takeover Code sets forth the rules governing takeovers. Bidders are required to retain an investment bank which, in turn, is required to inform the target company and the stock exchange about the level of the holding within two days after acquiring 5% or more of a company's shares. The disclosures contain information typical of such disclosures across the world. The information includes the offer price, identity of the acquirer, purpose of the acquisition, and plans for the target. Further announcements are required after acquiring 10% and 14% ownership. Offers have to remain open for 20 days. Mandatory offers are required after reaching the 10% threshold. The minimum offer price is the average of the highest and lowest price over a 26-week period or two weeks prior to the offer (whichever is the highest). There are also limitations of the ability of the bidder to withdraw an offer.

In India, companies have developed some of the various takeover defenses we see in the United States, such as poison pills and greenmail.

---

[28] Shardul Shroff, "India," in *Mergers and Acquisitions: 2005/06* (London: Practical Law, 2005–2006).

Australia

The Uniform Companies Code that was passed in 1961 provided regulations for takeovers. Various changes in the law were made since then, and they culminated with the Corporate Law Economic Reform Program (CLERP), which went into effect in March 2000 and amended the Corporations Law. CLERP law makes the Corporations and Securities Panel the sole entity responsible for ruling on various takeover-related disputes during the bid period. This transferred such responsibility from the courts to the panel.[29] The panel is the only entity that can initiate legal proceedings related to a takeover in the government. One of the benefits of having such a panel with its broad powers is that it resolves matters quickly—often reaching a decision within 24 hours.

The Act made compulsory takeovers necessary when a bidder purchased 75% of the value of a company's outstanding stock. Also, bids that seek to acquire 20% or more of a company's stock are allowed as long as they are followed by subsequent bids for the remaining stock of the company. The law also sets forth disclosure rules relating to bids while also requiring supplementary disclosures. Acquisitions of shares equal to or greater than 5% require disclosure of this holding. Bids must remain open for at least one month but no more than one year. In addition, the Act places limits on the use of certain antitakeover defenses and some, such as greenmail, are not allowed.

 ## U.S. STATE CORPORATION LAWS AND LEGAL PRINCIPLES

In this section we will review some major issues of U.S. state corporation laws and the legal principles underlying some of the court rulings that have interpreted these laws.

Business Judgment Rule

The *business judgment rule* is the standard by which directors of corporations are judged when they exercise their fiduciary duties in the course of an attempted takeover. Under this standard it is presumed that directors act in a manner that is consistent with their fiduciary obligations to shareholders. Thus, any party contesting this presumption must conclusively demonstrate a breach of fiduciary duties. If the plaintiff in a U.S. action against a company's directors establishes this, then the burden shifts to the directors to establish that the transaction was "entirely fair." Specific court decisions have highlighted certain relevant issues regarding how directors must act when employing antitakeover defenses. Through these decisions, standards such as the *Revlon duties* and the *Unocal standard* have been developed.

Under Delaware law, director's duties pursuant to the business judgment rule are that they should manage the affairs of the company by keeping three key duties in mind:

1. They have a duty of *loyalty*.
2. They have to demonstrate *care* for the interests of shareholders.

---

[29] Emma Armson, "The Australian Takeovers Panel: Commercial Body or Quasi-Court?" *Melbourne University Law Review* 28, no. 3 (December 1, 2004): 565–589.

3. They should carry out their duties in a manner that is in the *best interests* of the corporation and its shareholders.

In the context of M&A, the business judgment rule does not necessarily mean that the target's directors need to jump up and react emphatically to any bid that "comes down the pike." They should be informed about the value of their company and the specifics of the offer being presented. They do not have to go so far as to necessarily enter into an active negotiation with the bidder and go back and forth with the bidder on how the offer should be changed. On the other hand, they cannot simply close their eyes to the bid and be uninformed about its financial characteristics and what merits it may have for their shareholders.

Unocal Standard

In *Unocal v. Mesa Petroleum*, the Delaware Supreme Court reviewed the actions of the Unocal board of directors as they implemented an antitakeover strategy to thwart the unwanted tender offer by Mesa Petroleum, led by its colorful chief executive officer, T. Boone Pickens.[30] This strategy included a self-tender offer in which the target made a tender offer for itself in competition with the offer initiated by the bidder. In reaching its decision, the court noted its concern that directors may act in their own self-interest, such as in this case, in which they were allegedly favoring the self-tender as opposed to simply objectively searching for the best deal for shareholders. In such instances directors must demonstrate that they had reason to believe that there was a danger to the pursuit of a corporate policy that was in the best interest of shareholders. In addition, they must show that their actions were in the best interest of shareholders. Subsequent courts have refined the Unocal standard to feature a two-part responsibility:

1. **Reasonableness test.** The board must be able to clearly demonstrate that their actions were reasonable in relation to their perceived beliefs about the danger to their corporate policies. For example, an inadequate price is considered a danger to corporate policy.
2. **Proportionality test.** The board must also be able to demonstrate that their defensive actions were in proportion to the magnitude of the perceived danger to their policies.[31]

Once these standards are satisfied, the normal presumptions about director behavior under the business judgment rule apply. When a board receives an offer from an unwanted bidder and is determining whether to accept or reject it, the business judgment rule is the operative standard. However, when they move from rejection to taking active steps to fight off the bidder, then the Unocal Standard kicks in.

The standards of directors' fiduciary duty that we have in the United States sharply contrast with those of some other nations that have active takeover markets.

---

[30] *Unocal Corp. v. Mesa Petroleum Co.*, 493 A.2d 946 (Del. 1985).
[31] *Unitrin, Inc. v. American General Corp.*, 651 A.2d 1361 (Del. 1995) and *Moore Corp. v. Wallace Computer Services*, 907 F. Supp. 1545, 1556 (D. Del. 1995).

For example, the United Kingdom's self-regulatory system in effect precludes the development of a detailed case law on this issue, as such cases rarely reach the courts in the United Kingdom.

Revlon Duties

In *Revlon, Inc. v. MacAndrews and Forbes Holdings*, the Delaware Supreme Court ruled on what obligations a target board of directors have when faced with an offer for control of their company.[32] In this transaction, which is discussed further in Chapter 5 in the context of lockup options, the court ruled that certain antitakeover defenses that favored one bidder over another were invalid. The court determined that rather than promoting the auction process, which should result in maximizing shareholder wealth, these antitakeover defenses—a lockup option and a no-shop provision—inhibited rather than promoted the auction process. *Revlon duties* come into play when it is clear that the sale or breakup of the company is inevitable. At that time, directors have a responsibility to maximize the gains for their shareholders. That is, they have a responsibility to shift their focus away from actions that they normally would take to preserve the corporation and its strategy to actions that will result in the greatest gains for shareholders, such as making sure they get the highest bid possible for shareholders.

In reaching its decision rendering the lockup options and no-shop provisions invalid, the court did not go so far as to say that the use of defenses per se was invalid. The use of defenses that might favor one bidder over another could be consistent with the board's Revlon duties if they promoted the auction process by enabling one bidder to be more competitive with another bidder, thereby causing offer prices to rise. However, defenses that hinder the auction process are not valid. The court also did not go so far as to require target boards to solicit bids and actively shop the company. In failing to do so, the court chose not to narrowly circumscribe the actions that target boards can take. However, in its decision the court implied that directors should have a good reason for not considering an auction process.

Blasius Standard of Review

In 1988 the Delaware Chancery Court put forward the "compelling justification" standard which supported a target board's decision to take actions to limit a dissident shareholder's abilities to elect a majority of the board.[33] In combination with the *Unocal Standard* these decisions give significant power to a target's board which opens the door to potential abuse of power.[34]

The *Blasius* standard was clarified in later decisions in which the Delaware Chancery court noted that it would carefully scrutinize a board's decisions to ensure that shareholder's rights were upheld by a board's actions and that a board would

---

[32] *Revlon, Inc. v. MacAndrews & Forbes Holdings, Inc.*, 506 A.2d 173, CCH Fed. Sec. L. Rep. ¶ 92, 348 (Del. 1986).

[33] *Blasius Industries v. Atlas Corp.* 564 A. 2d 651 (Del. Ch. 1988)

[34] Bradley R. Aronstam, "The Interplay of *Blasius* and *Unocal* – A Compelling Problem Justifying the Call for Substantial Change, *Oregon Law Review*, 81 (1), (Symmer 2002) 429–476.

not abuse its discretion to disenfranchise shareholders. In the 2007 case of *Mercer v. Inter-Tel* the Delaware Chancery Court found that the board of directors had "compelling justification" to postpone a shareholder's meeting to prevent the defeat of a merger proposal.[35] However, the Delaware court's concern about an abuse of the *Unocal* and *Blasius* standards were underscored in other cases such as *Portnoy v. Cryo-Cell International* wherein the Delaware court noted that if shareholder's interests were thwarted by a board it would grant shareholders relief.[36]

STATE ANTITAKEOVER LAWS

Many non-Americans are confused and dismayed by the sometimes conflicting combination of federal laws and state laws that characterizes the U.S. legal system. Indeed, under current federal and state takeover laws, it is possible that conforming to some aspects of federal laws means violating certain state laws. The line of demarcation between federal takeover laws and their state counterparts has to do with the focus of each. Federal laws tend to be directed at securities regulation, tender offers, and antitrust considerations, whereas state laws govern corporate charters and their bylaws. Currently, a broad array of inconsistent state laws exists across the United States. Many of these laws were passed in response to pressure by particular corporations who found themselves the object of interest by potential acquirers. The usual scenario is that a local firm petitions the state legislature to pass an antitakeover law or amend the current one to make it more difficult for a local corporation to be taken over. The political pressure that is brought to bear on the state legislature comes in the form of allegations that a takeover by a "foreign raider" will mean a significant loss of jobs as well as other forms of community support, such as charitable donations by the local corporation.

The system of differing state laws is not unique to the United States. The EU has worked to have a common set of merger rules but has achieved approval of only a set of limited rules. Given that EU countries have the right to opt out of the new EU merger rules and then apply their own differing country-specific laws, the situation in the EU is in some respects somewhat analogous to what we have in the United States.

In the United States and the United Kingdom, laws emphasize the rights of shareholders (although more so in the U.K.), whereas in certain European countries, such as Austria, Germany, France, and Italy, the rights of creditors are emphasized more. In addition, shareholdings are less concentrated in the hands of families and insiders in the United States and the United Kingdom. To a certain extent this helps explain why the laws have evolved differently in these two nations. In addition, while there are many similarities in the securities markets and laws of the United States and the United Kingdom, there are significant differences. For example, many U.S. states allow management to engage in aggressive antitakeover defensive actions, while UK laws forbid management from engaging in such evasive actions without shareholder approval.

---

[35] *Mercier v. Inter-Tel*, 929 A. 2d 786 (Del Ch 2007).
[36] *Portnoy v. Cryo-Cell International*, 942 A. 2d, 43, (Del. Ch. 2008)

Genesis of State Antitakeover Laws in the United States

The first state to adopt an antitakeover law was Virginia in 1968, with many states following thereafter. These statutes typically required that disclosure materials be filed following the initiation of the bid. The problem with these "first-generation" state antitakeover laws was that they applied to firms that did only a small amount of business in that state. This seemed unfair to bidding corporations. Thus, the stage was set for a legal challenge.

Key Court Decisions Relating to Antitakeover Laws

Certain court decisions have defined the types of state antitakeover laws that are acceptable and those that are not. These decisions, which were recorded in the 1980s, are still relevant today.

Edgar v. MITE

The constitutionality of these first-generation antitakeover laws was successfully challenged in 1982, in the famous *Edgar v. MITE* decision.[37] In this decision the U.S. Supreme Court ruled that the Illinois Business Takeover Act was unconstitutional on the grounds that it violated the commerce clause of the U.S. Constitution. The Illinois law was extraterritorial in nature in that it permitted the state to block a nationwide tender offer for a state-affiliated target corporation if the bidder failed to comply with the disclosure laws of Illinois.

The challenge to the Illinois law caused states with similar laws to question their constitutionality and redevelop their provisions. The states still wanted to inhibit takeovers, which they thought were not in the best interest of the states, but now they had to adopt a different approach, which came in the form of the "second-generation" laws. The second-generation state antitakeover laws had a narrower focus than the first-generation laws. They tended to apply only to those firms that were incorporated within the state or that conducted a substantial part of their business activities within state boundaries. They were not directed at regulating disclosure in tender offers, as the first-generation laws were. Rather, they focused on issues of corporate governance, which traditionally are the domain of state corporation laws.

Dynamics v. CTS

The *Edgar v. MITE* decision delivered a severe blow to the first-generation laws. Many opponents of antitakeover legislation attacked the second-generation laws, which they believed were also unconstitutional. These legal actions resulted in the *Dynamics v. CTS* decision of April 1987.[38] In this case, the CTS Corporation used the Indiana law to fight off a takeover by the Dynamics Corporation. Dynamics challenged the law, contending

---

[37] *Edgar v. MITE Corporation*, 102 S. Ct. 2629 (1982). Prior to this decision, in 1978, the Fifth Circuit found these statutes objectionable in *Great Western United Corp. v. Kidwell*, 577 F. 2d 1256 (5th cir. 1978).
[38] *Dynamics Corporation of America v. CTS Corporation*, 637 F. Supp. 406 (N.D. Ill. 1986).

that it was unconstitutional. In *Dynamics v. CTS*, the U.S. Supreme Court ruled that the Indiana antitakeover law, which was a control share statute, was constitutional. This law allows stockholders to vote on whether a buyer of controlling interest can exercise his or her voting rights. The CTS decision gave the Supreme Court's approval to the second-generation state takeover laws. Since the April 1987 CTS decision, many states have adopted antitakeover laws. Today most states have some kind of law regulating takeovers.

Amanda Acquisition Corporation v. Universal Foods Corporation

In November 1989, the U.S. Supreme Court refused to hear a challenge to the Wisconsin antitakeover law.[39] The Court's unwillingness to hear this challenge further buttressed the legal viability of state antitakeover laws. The Wisconsin law requires a bidder who acquires 10% or more of a target company's stock to receive the approval of the other target shareholders or wait three years to complete the merger. The three-year waiting period makes heavily leveraged buyouts, which were typical of the fourth merger wave, prohibitively expensive.

The Supreme Court decision arose from a legal challenge by the Amanda Acquisition Corporation, which is a subsidiary of the Boston-based High Voltage Engineering Corporation. Amanda challenged the Wisconsin law that prevented it from proceeding with a tender offer for the Milwaukee-based Universal Foods Corporation. The directors of Universal Foods opposed the takeover and reacted by using what has been called the Just Say No defense. Amanda charged that the Wisconsin law was an interference with interstate commerce and was harmful to shareholders. The Supreme Court failed to agree and refused to hear the challenge to the law. The Court's position in this case reaffirms the *Dynamics v. CTS* decision that upheld the constitutionality of the Indiana antitakeover law in 1987.

Under Delaware law if the target board conducts a reasonable investigation and come to the good faith conclusion that an unsolicited bid is not in the best interests of its shareholders, it may simply Say No and not redeem a poison pill defense. For example, this was the case in *Moore Corp. v Wallace*, where Wallace's board contended that the results of its recent capital investments were just starting to bear fruit, and it did not even want to let shareholders tender their shares to Moore in what they considered to be an offer that did not reflect these investments. Thus, Wallace's board was able to successfully Just Say No to the "threat" Moore's offer represented.

Legality of Poison Pills In Chapter 5 we discuss poison pills, or what are called shareholder rights plans, in detail. As part of that material we discuss the various cases, such as *Moran v. Household International* and *Air Products v. Airgas*. However, the bottom lines of these Delaware decisions are that poison pills are a legitimate defense when they are used by diligent directors who perceive that an unwanted bid is not in the best interest of their shareholders.

---

[39] *Amanda Acquisition Corp. v. Universal Foods Corp.*, 877 F.2d 496 (7th Cir. 1989).

Components of Second-Generation Laws

Most second-generation laws incorporate some or all of the following provisions:

- Fair price provision
- Business combination provision
- Control share provision
- Cash-out statute

Fair Price Provision

A fair price provision requires that in a successful tender offer all shareholders who do not decide to sell will receive the same price as shareholders who do accept the offer. These provisions are designed to prevent the abuses that may occur in two-tiered tender offers. With two-tiered bids, a high price is offered to the first-tier tenders, whereas a lower price or less advantageous terms (e.g., securities of uncertain value instead of cash) are offered to the members of the second tier.

Business Combination Provision

This provision prevents business agreements between the target company and the bidding company for a certain time period. For example, the wording of a business combination provision may rule out the sales of the target's assets by the bidding company. These provisions are designed to prevent leveraged hostile acquisitions. When an acquiring company assumes a large amount of debt to finance a takeover, it may be relying on the sales of assets by the target to pay the high interest payments required by the debt. The law is designed to prevent the transformation of local firms, with a low-risk capital structure, into riskier leveraged companies.

Control Share Provision

Some states, such as Ohio, Michigan, and Pennsylvania, have control share statutes, while others, such as Delaware, do not. A control share provision requires that acquiring firms obtain prior approval of current target stockholders before the purchases are allowed. These provisions typically apply to stock purchases beyond a certain percentage of the outstanding stock. They are particularly effective if the current share ownership includes large blocks of stock that are held by groups of people who are generally supportive of management, such as employee stockholders.

Essentially control share statutes limit "creeping acquisitions" above a certain threshold, such as 20%. Once the threshold has been crossed, the control shareholder must get the approval of the other shares prior to exercising its votes associated with the shares it owns.

Bidders do not necessarily dislike control share statutes. In effect, they can serve as an early referendum on the possibility of a bid. In addition, shareholders often do not want to eliminate the possibility of getting a good takeover premium, so they may not vote against the bidder. If that is the result, then the bidder can use the vote to put pressure of the target's board by citing that shareholders support the bidder and not the board. So, ironically, the bidder may actually call for the vote.

Cash-Out Statute

This provision, like the fair price requirement, is designed to limit tender offers. It typically requires that if a bidder buys a certain percentage of stock in a target firm, the bidder is then required to purchase all the remaining outstanding shares at the same terms given to the initial purchase. This provision limits acquiring firms that lack the financial resources for a 100% stock acquisition. It also limits leveraged acquisitions because it may require the bidder to assume an even greater amount of debt with the associated high debt service. Bidders might therefore be discouraged because of their inability to obtain financing for a 100% purchase or simply because they do not believe their cash flow will service the increased debt.

Constituency Provisions

Some state laws (but not Delaware) also have constituency provisions, which allow the board to take into account the impact a deal may have on other relevant stakeholders, such as workers or the community. This is not a powerful tool in the face of an offer that is clearly in the financial interests of shareholders. However, it may give the board an additional, albeit secondary, point to raise after they assert that the offer is inadequate.

Delaware Antitakeover Law

The Delaware Antitakeover Law is probably the most important of all the state antitakeover laws because more corporations are incorporated in Delaware than in any other state. General Motors, Exxon Mobil, Walmart, and DuPont are among the 850,000 companies that have incorporated in Delaware. One-half of all publicly traded companies are incorporated there, along with 63% of the Fortune 500 companies.

There is a clear preference on the part of companies to incorporate in Delaware. It has often been assumed that the reason for the preference for Delaware is that it has a well-developed body of law and a sophisticated court system.[40] Delaware's court system utilizes very knowledgeable judges to decide corporate lawsuits, as opposed to juries.

Another explanation for the preference for Delaware is that Delaware's incorporation fees are cheaper than all but eight other states (although the $180,000 that Delaware charges may not be that significant for a Fortune 500 company). Still the fee difference is not significant enough to explain the preference for Delaware.[41] Another desirable characteristic of Delaware that contributes to its popularity is the fact that companies and their shareholders do not need to be a resident of the state to incorporate there. In addition, non-Delaware businesses do not have to pay Delaware corporate taxes even if they are incorporated in that state.

---

[40] Stephen J. Massey, "Chancellor Allen's Jurisprudence and the Theory of Corporate Law," *Delaware Journal of Corporate Law* 683, 702, no. 79 (1992).
[41] Jill E. Fisch, "The Peculiar Role of the Delaware Court in the Competition for Corporate Charters," Fordham University Law School, Research Paper 00–02, May 2000.

Delaware was relatively late in adopting an antitakeover law. Its law, which is similar to the Wisconsin law but less restrictive, was passed in 1988, but was made retroactive to December 23, 1987, the day before corporate raider Carl Icahn acquired 15% of Texaco Corporation. The law was passed in response to an intense lobbying effort by companies seeking to adopt a protective statute. They threatened that if such a protective statute was not passed, they would reincorporate in states that did have antitakeover laws. The fact that incorporation fees account for nearly 20% of the Delaware state budget underscored the importance of this threat.[42] The choice of the effective date testifies to the power of this lobbying effort. The law stipulates that an unwanted bidder who buys more than 15% of a target company's stock may not complete the takeover for three years except under the following conditions:[43]

 - If the buyer buys 85% or more of the target company's stock. This 85% figure may not include the stock held by directors or the stock held in employee stock ownership plans.
 - If two-thirds of the stockholders approve the acquisition.
 - If the board of directors and the stockholders decide to waive the antitakeover provisions of this law.

Being primarily a business combination statute (Section 203 of Delaware Corporation Law), the law is designed to limit takeovers financed by debt. Raiders who have financed their takeovers by large amounts of debt often need to sell off company assets and divisions to pay off the debt. The need to pay off the debt quickly becomes significant in the case of the billion-dollar takeover, as in the 1980s, when interest payments were as much as half a million dollars per day. Although the Delaware law might discourage some debt-financed takeovers, it is not very effective against cash offers. Moreover, even debt-financed offers at a very attractive price may be sufficiently appealing for stockholders to waive the antitakeover provisions of the law.

Why Do State Antitakeover Laws Get Passed?

Most state antitakeover laws get passed as a result of lobbying efforts of companies that are concerned about being taken over. For example, the Pennsylvania antitakeover law was passed partly as a result of the efforts of Armstrong World Industries of Lancaster, Pennsylvania, which was concerned about being taken over by the Belzberg family of Canada. Harcourt Brace Jovanovich and Gillette promoted the respective Florida and Massachusetts control share statutes. Burlington Industries promoted North Carolina's antitakeover law, whereas Dayton-Hudson and Boeing promoted antitakeover laws in Minnesota and Washington, respectively. Ironically, some indigenous companies are so aggressive in promoting such laws that they even draft the statute for lawmakers. The result is a patchwork of many different state laws across America.

---

[42] Robert A. G. Monks and Nell Minow, *Corporate Governance* (Cambridge, MA: Blackwell Business, 1995), 35.
[43] Section 203 of the Delaware General Corporation Law.

Wealth Effects of State Antitakeover Laws

In a study of 40 state antitakeover bills introduced between 1982 and 1987, Karpoff and Malatesta found a small but statistically significant decrease in stock prices of companies incorporated in the various states contemplating passage of such laws.[44] They even found that companies doing significant business in these states also suffered a decline in stock prices. Szewczyk and Tsetsekos found that Pennsylvania firms lost $4 billion during the time this state's antitakeover law was being considered and adopted.[45] It should be kept in mind, however, that these effects are short-term effects based on the reactions of traders in the market during that time period.

Comment and Schwert analyzed a large sample of takeovers in an effort to determine the impact of both the passage of state antitakeover laws and the adoption of poison pills.[46] They did not find that the laws significantly deterred takeovers. In fact, they found that the effects of the laws and poison pills served to enhance the bargaining power of targets, which, in turn, raised takeover premiums.

Bertrand and Mullainathan examined the possible effects of the passage of second-generation takeover laws on blue- and white-collar wages as well as the likelihood that management would build new plants and close older ones.[47] They found that after the passage of such laws both blue- and white-collar wages went up—especially white-collar wages. However, they found that these higher wages do not "pay for themselves," as operational efficiency was lower in the postpassage years, in which there was a decline in plant creation and destruction. The authors conclude that maybe the protection of the laws insulates entrenched managers to "live the quiet life," which may come at the expense of shareholders, although not of workers.

More recently, Giroud and Mueller analyzed the impact of the passage of 30 business combination statutes on the operating performance of companies in those states.[48] They found that operating performance deteriorated after the passage of these laws in industries that were not competitive, while this did not occur in competitive industries. In noncompetitive industries input costs, wages, and overhead increased. This implies that competition can help reduce "managerial slack." It was also noteworthy that they found that the market correctly anticipated these effects. Share prices tended to fall after the passage of the laws for companies in noncompetitive industries but not for companies in competitive industries.

---

[44] Johnathan M. Karpoff and Paul Malatesta, "The Wealth Effects of Second Generation State Takeover Legislation," *Journal of Financial Economics* 25, no. 2 (December 1989): 291–322.

[45] S. H. Szewczyk and G. P. Tsetsekos, "State Intervention in the Market for Corporate Control: The Case of Pennsylvania Senate Bill 1310," *Journal of Financial Economics* 31, no. 1 (February 1992): 3–23.

[46] Robert Comment and Richard Schwert, "Poison or Placebo? Evidence on the Deterrence and Wealth Effects of Modern Antitakeover Measures," *Journal of Financial Economics*, 39 (1995): 3–43.

[47] Marianne Bertrand and Sendhil Mullainathan, "Enjoying the Quiet Life? Corporate Governance and Managerial Preferences," *Journal of Political Economy* 111, no. 5 (October 2003): 1043–1075.

[48] Xavier Giroud and Holger M. Mueller, "Does Corporate Governance Matter in Competitive Industries?" *Journal of Financial Economics* 95, no. 3 (March 2010): 312–331.

Cost of Capital, Performance, and State Antitakeover Laws

From a theoretical perspective, there are several ways that the protections from the market for corporate control could affect the costs of capital and in particular the costs of debt. Takeovers may work to keep management "on their toes" and force them to generate better performance, lest the stock price slip and they become vulnerable to takeovers. In addition there can be a "coinsurance effect" whereby postacquisition companies are larger and possibly less risky. On the other hand, as we will discuss in Chapter 8, there could also be an increased leverage effect where the postacquisition company has more debt and bondholder wealth declines, although seller shareholders may have realized a premium. Qiu and Yu analyzed the costs of debt capital in relation to an exogenous shock—the passage of business combination statutes during the period 1985–1991.[49] They measured the costs of debt using the spread between comparable corporate debt and Treasury securities. They found that the passage of such laws resulted in a 28 basis point increase in the costs of debt. However, consistent with the research of Giroud and Mueller, they found that these effects were not present in competitive industries where, presumably, competitive pressures serve to lower managerial slack.[50] Giroud and Mueller examined company performance before and after the passage of business combination statutes and found that performance worsened in noncompetitive industries but had little effect in competitive ones.

TIME-WARNER–PARAMOUNT

In March 1989, Time Inc. entered into a merger agreement with Warner Communications Inc. The deal was a planned stock-for-stock exchange that would be put before the shareholders of both companies for their approval. Paramount Communications Inc. then entered the fray with a hostile tender offer for Time. This offer was structured by Paramount to be higher than the valuation that was inherent to the original Time-Warner agreement. Time then responded with a tender offer for Warner that featured a cash offer for 51% of Warner, followed by a second-step transaction using securities as consideration.

Paramount sued and contended that the original merger agreement between Time and Warner meant that there was an impending change in control, thereby bringing the Revlon duties of the directors into play. In *Paramount Communications, Inc. v. Time, Inc.*, the court rejected Paramount's argument that there would be a change in control.[a] The court was impressed by the fact that both companies were public and their shares were widely held. Based on such reasoning, the court concluded that this was not an acquisition in which one company was acquiring another but rather a strategic merger. Therefore, Revlon duties were not triggered, and the normal business judgment rule standard applied.

---

[49] Jaiping Qiu and Fan Yu, "The Market for Corporate Control and the Cost of Debt," *Journal of Financial Economics* 93, no. 3 (September 2009): 505–524.

[50] Xavier Giroud and Holger Mueller, "Does Corporate Governance Matter in Competitive Industries?" *Journal of Financial Economics* 95, no. 3 (March 2010): 312–331.

The significance of this decision is that the announcement of a strategic merger between two companies is not a signal that either of the companies is for sale. Therefore, the directors do not have to consider other offers as if there were an auction process. This implies that if there is an unwanted bid, the directors may consider the use of antitakeover measures to avoid the hostile bid while they go ahead with the strategic merger.

[a] *Paramount Communications, Inc. v. Time, Inc.,* 571 A.2d 1140 (Del. 1989).

 ## REGULATION OF INSIDER TRADING

The SEC rules specify remedies for shareholders who incur losses resulting from insider trading. Insiders are bound by SEC Rule 10b-5, which states that insiders must "disclose or abstain" from trading the firm's securities. The rule derives from an SEC response to a complaint filed in the 1940s that a company provided indications that earnings would be weak while it planned to announce much stronger performance and the company's president purchased shares while knowing the true earnings. It was not until two decades later that the SEC notified the market that it would bring civil claims under this little-known rule. However, it was not until the late 1970s that the rule was used by the SEC and federal prosecutors to bring criminal lawsuits.

Insider trading regulation was buttressed by the passage of the Insider Trading and Securities Fraud Enforcement Act of 1988. This law imposed maximum penalties of up to $1 million and up to 10 years in prison while also setting up a bounty program whereby informants could collect up to 10% of the insider's profits. It also established the possibility of top management's being liable for the insider trading of subordinates. In the wake of Enron, the Sarbanes-Oxley law increased the maximum penalty for insider trading to $5 million and a possible jail sentence of up to 20 years.

The 1988 law followed the passage of the Insider Trading Sanctions Act of 1984, which gave the SEC the power to seek treble damages for trading on inside information. This law provided a dual-pronged approach for regulators, who now could seek civil remedies in addition to the criminal alternatives that were available before the passage of the 1984 act. Illegal insider trading may occur, for example, if insiders, acting on information that is unavailable to other investors, sell the firm's securities before an announcement of poor performance. Other investors, unaware of the upcoming bad news, may pay a higher price for the firm's securities. The opposite might be the case if insiders bought the firm's stock or call options before the announcement of a bid from another firm. Stockholders might not have sold the shares to the insiders if they had known of the upcoming bid and its associated premium.

Who Are Insiders?

Insiders may be defined more broadly than the management of a company. They may include outsiders, such as attorneys, investment bankers, financial printers, or consultants, who can be considered "temporary insiders." Under Rule 10b-5, however, the U.S.

Supreme Court held that outside parties who trade profitably based on their acquired information did not have to disclose their inside information. This was the case in the 1980 *Chiarella v. United States*, in which a financial printer acquired information on an upcoming tender offer by reviewing documents in his print shop.[51] If an individual misappropriates confidential information on a merger or acquisition and uses it as the basis for trade, however, Rule 10b-5 will apply. The rule is applicable only to SEC enforcement proceedings or criminal actions, but not to civil actions under the Insider Trading Sanctions Act of 1984, which permits the recovery of treble damages on the profits earned or the loss avoided.

A classic example of illegal insider trading was the famous Texas Gulf Sulphur case. In 1963, Texas Gulf Sulphur discovered certain valuable mineral deposits, which it did not disclose for several months; actually, the firm publicly denied the discovery in a false press release. Meanwhile, officers and directors bought undervalued shares based on their inside information. The SEC successfully brought a suit against the insiders. The short swing profit rule prohibits any officer, director, or owner of 10% of a company's stock from a purchase and sale, or a sale and purchase, within a six-month period. Profits derived from these transactions must be paid to the issuer even if the transactions were not made on the basis of insider information.

Do Insider Trading Laws Effectively Deter Insider Trading?

One research study by Nejat Seyhun has questioned the effectiveness of laws in curbing insider trading.[52] In addition, Lisa Muelbroek empirically confirmed that stock price run-ups before takeover announcements do reflect insider trading.[53] Other research seems to indicate that such laws may have a significant deterrent effect. Jon Garfinkel examined insider trading around earnings announcements and found that after the passage of the Insider Trading and Securities Fraud Enforcement Act, insiders appeared to adjust the timing of their transactions so that the trades occurred after the release of the relevant information.[54] The fact that the laws and the enforcement activity do seem to have a positive effect does not negate the fact that insider trading seems to remain a part of merger and acquisition activity of public companies.

This conclusion was underscored in more recent research that examined trading in call and put options prior to M&A announcements. Augustin, Brenner, and Subrahmanyam found statistically significant abnormal trading volume in U.S. equity options over a 30-day period prior to M&A announcements.[55] The researchers examined the trading volume in equity options in days prior to M&A announcements compared to randomly selected days. Their sample consisted of 1,859 corporate transactions over

---

[51] *Chiarella v. United States*, 445 U.S. 222, 100 S. Ct. 1108, 63 L.Ed.2d, 348 (1980).

[52] Nejat H. Seyhun, "The Effectiveness of Insider Trading Regulations," *Journal of Law and Economics* 35 (1992): 149–182.

[53] Lisa Muelbroek, "An Empirical Analysis of Insider Trading," *Journal of Finance* 47, no. 5 (December 1992): 1661–1700.

[54] Jon A. Garfinkel, "New Evidence on the Effects of Federal Regulations on Insider Trading: The Insider Trading and Securities Fraud Enforcement Act," *Journal of Corporate Finance* 3, no. 2 (April 1997): 89–111.

[55] Patrick Augustin, Menachem Brenner, and Marti G. Subrahmanyam, "Informed Options Trading Prior to P&M Announcements: Insider Trading," 2014. As of the date of this writing this paper is not yet published.

the period 1996–2012. The fact that M&As should be unexpected would imply that there should not be a statistically significant difference in the trading volume. This was definitely not the case as the volume preceding M&A announcements was significantly greater. The fact that this occurred so often in their sample also implies that, while the SEC has made great efforts to publicize its insider trading enforcement actions in some high-profile cases, the evidence from these researchers implies that M&A-related insider trading is not only quite prevalent but also largely unpunished by the SEC. This is clearly the case in smaller M&As. It seems many traders are engaging in insider trading in M&As and getting away with it.

ANTITRUST LAWS

The ability to merge with or acquire other firms is limited by antitrust legislation. Various antitrust laws are designed to prevent firms from reducing competition through mergers. Many mergers are never attempted simply because of the likelihood of governmental intervention on antitrust grounds. Other mergers are halted when it becomes apparent that the government will likely oppose the merger.

The U.S. government has changed its stance on the antitrust ramifications of mergers several times since 1890. As noted previously, in recent years the government's attitude has been evolving toward a freer market view, which favors a more limited government role in the marketplace. Although many horizontal mergers were opposed during the 1980s, many others proceeded unopposed. This is in sharp contrast to the government's earlier position in the 1960s. During that period, mergers and acquisitions involving businesses only remotely similar to the acquiring firm's business were often opposed on antitrust grounds. This situation encouraged large numbers of conglomerate mergers, which generally were not opposed.

In addition to the enforcement agencies changing their stance on antitrust enforcement, changes in market conditions sometimes render deals that would have been objectionable in one time period acceptable in another. For example, in 1997 the Federal Trade Commission objected to a merger between Staples and Office Depot. Sixteen years later, in 2013, the market had changed greatly, with competitors such as Amazon, Walmart, and Costco selling office supplies and taking market share from the large office supply companies. Based upon this, the merger of the number-two company, Office Depot, and the number-three, Office Max, was allowed.

Sherman Antitrust Act of 1890

The Sherman Antitrust Act is the cornerstone of all U.S. antitrust laws. The first two sections of the law contain its most important provisions:

Section 1 This section prohibits all contracts, combinations, and conspiracies in restraint of trade.

Section 2 This section prohibits any attempts or conspiracies to monopolize a particular industry.

The Sherman Act made the formation of monopolies and other attempts to restrain trade unlawful and criminal offenses punishable under federal law. The government or the injured party can file suit under this law, and the court can then decide the appropriate punishment, which may range from an injunction to more severe penalties, including triple damages and imprisonment. The first two sections of the Sherman Act make it immediately clear that it is written broadly enough to cover almost all types of anticompetitive activities. Surprisingly, however, the first great merger wave took place following the passage of the law. This first merger wave, which took place between 1897 and 1904, was characterized by the formation of monopolies. The resulting increased concentration in many industries, combined with the formation of many powerful monopolies, revealed that the Act was not performing the functions its first two sections implied.

The apparent ineffectiveness of the Sherman Act was partly due to the law's wording. Specifically, it stated that all contracts that restrained trade were illegal. In its early interpretations, however, the court reasonably refused to enforce this part of the law on the basis that this implies that almost all contracts could be considered illegal. The court had difficulty finding an effective substitute. Court rulings such as the 1895 Supreme Court ruling that the American Sugar Refining Company was not a monopoly in restraint of trade made the law a dead letter for more than a decade after its passage. The lack of government resources also made it difficult for the government to enforce the law. While a dead letter under President McKinley, the law started to have more impact on the business community under the pressure of trustbusting President Theodore Roosevelt and his successor, William Howard Taft. In an effort to correct the deficiencies associated with the wording of the law and the lack of an enforcement agency, the government decided to make a more explicit statement of its antitrust position. This effort came with the passage of the Clayton Act.

Clayton Act of 1914

The goal of the Clayton Act was to strengthen the Sherman Act while also specifically proscribing certain business practices. The Clayton Act did not prohibit any activities that were not already illegal under a broad interpretation of the Sherman Act. The Clayton Act, however, clarified which business practices unfairly restrain trade and reduce competition. The bill did not address the problem of the lack of an enforcement agency charged with the specific responsibility for enforcing the antitrust laws.

Section 7 is particularly relevant to M&As: "No corporation shall *acquire* the whole or any part of the stock, or the whole or any part of the assets, of another corporation where in any *line of commerce* in any *section of the country* the effect of such an acquisition may be to substantially lessen competition or tend to create a *monopoly*."

Originally the Clayton Act focused only on the acquisition of stock. However, this loophole was closed in 1950 to also include asset acquisitions.

Federal Trade Commission Act of 1914

One weakness of the Sherman Act was that it did not give the government an effective enforcement agency to investigate and pursue antitrust violations. At that time the Justice Department did not possess the resources to be an effective antitrust deterrent. In an effort to address this problem, the Federal Trade Commission Act, which was passed in 1914, established the FTC. The FTC was charged with enforcing both the Federal Trade Commission Act and the Clayton Act. In particular, the FTC Act was passed with the intention of creating an enforcement arm for the Clayton Act. The main antitrust provision of the Act is Section 5, which prohibits unfair methods of competition. Although the FTC was given the power to initiate antitrust lawsuits, it was not given a role in the criminal enforcement of antitrust violations. The Act also broadened the range of illegal business activities beyond those mentioned in the Clayton Act.

Celler-Kefauver Act of 1950

Until the passage of the Celler-Kefauver Act companies used the "asset loophole" to effect acquisitions while not buying the target's stock. This loophole was eliminated by the passage of the Celler-Kefauver Act of 1950, which prohibited the acquisition of assets of a target firm when the effect was to lessen competition. The Celler-Kefauver Act also prohibited vertical mergers and conglomerate mergers when they were shown to reduce competition. The previous antitrust laws were aimed at horizontal mergers, which are combinations of firms producing the same product. The Celler-Kefauver Act set the stage for the aggressive antitrust enforcement of the 1960s.

Hart-Scott-Rodino Antitrust Improvements Act of 1976

Even though we went through two decades of vigorous antitrust enforcements in the United States, it was not until the passage of the Hart-Scott-Rodino Antitrust Improvements Act in 1976 (HSR) that the power of the two antitrust enforcement agencies, the Justice Department and the Federal Trade Commission, really increased. Prior to this law, the enforcement agencies did not have the power to require third parties, the competitors of the merging companies, to provide them with their private economic data. This led the enforcement agencies to drop many investigations due to the lack of hard economic data. As we will discuss, HSR gave the Justice Department the right to issue "Civil Investigative Demands" to the merging companies but also third parties to gather data prior to filing a complaint. In addition, it was not until the passage of HSR that the government could require the postponement of proposed M&As until the authorities gave their approval of the deal.

HSR requires that the Bureau of Competition of the FTC and the Antitrust Division of the Justice Department be given the opportunity to review proposed M&As in advance. According to the Act, an acquisition or merger may not be consummated until these authorities have reviewed the transaction. These two agencies must decide which of the two will investigate the particular transaction. The law prevents consummation of a merger until the end of the specified waiting periods. Therefore, failure to file in a timely manner may delay completion of the transaction.

HSR was passed to prevent the consummation of transactions that would ultimately be judged to be anticompetitive. Thus, the Justice Department would be able to avoid disassembling a company that had been formed in part through an anticompetitive merger or acquisition. This process is sometimes euphemistically referred to as "unscrambling" eggs.

The law became necessary because of the government's inability to halt transactions through the granting of injunctive relief while it attempted to rule on the competitive effects of the business combination. When injunctive relief was not obtainable, mandated divestiture, designed to restore competition, might not take place for many years after the original acquisition or merger. HSR was written to prevent these problems before they occurred. It added another layer of regulation and a waiting period for tender offers beyond what was already in place with the Williams Act. Whether antitrust approval actually slows down a tender offer depends on the actual length of time it takes to receive the antitrust green light.

Size Requirements for Filing

Small M&As are less likely to have anticompetitive effects, so the law established size thresholds for filing. These thresholds are divided into size-of-transaction and size-of-person levels. Failure to file can result in monetary penalties of $16,000 for each day the filing is late.

Size-of-Transaction

As of 2014 the size-of-transaction threshold is met if the buyer is acquiring voting securities or assets of $75.9 million or more. Deals above that level require a filing, and there is no HSR filing requirement for smaller deals. However, we also have the size-of-person threshold.

Size-of-Person Threshold

The size-of-person test is met if one party to a transaction has $151.7 million or more in sales or assets and the other has $15.2 million or more in sales and assets. However, all deals valued at $303.4 million or more have to be reported regardless of the size-of-person test.

It is important to note that the Justice Department and the Federal Trade Commission still have the authority under the Sherman Act and the Federal Trade Commission Act to challenge an M&A on antitrust grounds even if a filing is not required under HSR.

Deadlines for Filing

A bidder must file under the Hart-Scott-Rodino Act as soon as it announces a tender offer or any other offer. The target is then required to respond. This response comes in the form of the target's filing, which must take place 15 days after the bidder has filed.

Type of Information to Be Filed

The law requires the filing of a 15-page form, which can be downloaded from the Federal Trade Commission website.[56] Business data describing the business activities and

---

[56] www.ftc.gov/bc/hsr/hsrform.shtm.

revenues of the acquiring and the target firms' operations must be provided according to Standard Industrial Classification (SIC) codes. Most firms already have this information because it must be submitted to the U.S. Bureau of the Census. In addition, when filing, the acquiring firm must attach certain reports it may have compiled to analyze the competitive effects of this transaction.

This presents an interesting conflict. When a transaction is first being proposed within the acquiring firm, its proponents may tend to exaggerate its benefits. If this exaggeration comes in the form of presenting a higher market share than what might be more realistic, the firm's ability to attain antitrust approval may be hindered. For this reason, when the firm is preparing its premerger reports, it must keep the antitrust approval in mind.

The filing is not made public, although agencies may disclose some information if the deal has been publicly announced. Along with the necessary data the filing party must pay a fee, which is greater the larger the size of the transaction.

Filing Time Requirements

HSR provides for a 30-day waiting period unless the deal is a cash tender offer or bankruptcy sale, in which case the waiting period is 15 days. If either the Justice Department or the Federal Trade Commission determines that a closer inquiry is necessary, it may put forward a *second request* for information. This second request extends to a waiting period of 30 days, except for 10 days in the case of cash tender offers or bankruptcy sales.

Most filing companies request an early termination of the waiting period on the grounds that there clearly are no anticompetitive effects. Most of these requests are granted. However, some investigations can be lengthy. It was not until January 2010, one year after the proposed merger between Ticketmaster, one of the world's largest event ticketing companies, and Live Nation, the world's largest concert promoter, was announced, that the Justice Department finally give its approval. Christine Varney, then head of the Justice Department's antitrust division, refused to give approval until the companies agreed to a combination of divestitures and behavioral prohibitions. Ticketmaster had to agree to divest itself of one of its ticketing divisions. In addition, the combined company had to agree to 10 years of "antiretaliation provisions," which seek to prevent the company from abusing its increased power in the concert business.

Significance of Notice of Government Opposition

If the Justice Department files suit to block a proposed acquisition, that usually is the end of the deal. Even if the bidder and the target believe that they might ultimately prevail in the lawsuit, it may not be in either company's interest to become embroiled in a protracted legal battle with the government that may last years. Such was the case in 1995, when Microsoft dropped its bid for financial software maker Intuit. At that time this deal would have been the largest software acquisition in history, with Intuit's equity being valued in the range of $2.3 billion.

Federal Trade Commission Rules on Creeping Acquisitions

The FTC has set forth various rules that refine the Hart-Scott-Rodino Act. These rules address the creeping acquisition, which is a situation in which an acquirer eventually accumulates a total holding that may be anticompetitive but where the individual share acquisitions are not by themselves anticompetitive. They also eliminate the need for repeated filings for each share acquisition beyond the original one that may have required a filing. These rules indicate that a purchaser does not have to file for additional purchases if, during a five-year period after the expiration of the original filing requirement period, the total share purchase does not reach 25% of the outstanding shares of the issuer. If there are continued purchases after the 25% level that required an additional filing, the purchaser does not have to file again until the 50% threshold is reached.

FTC Rules for Second Requests and Speed of Takeover Completion

A second request is often dreaded by M&A participants as it means delays and significant increases in expenses. Such requests often require as many as a million pages of documents to be provided by the companies. In 2006, the FTC announced new rules that give companies the option to agree to extend the deadline for an FTC decision to 30 days after the company has certified it is in compliance with the FTC's data requests. In these circumstances, the FTC agrees to place certain limits, such as confining the data requested to two years and limiting the number of employees whose files can be searched to 35.

Exemptions to the Hart-Scott-Rodino Act

Certain acquisitions supervised by governmental agencies, as well as certain foreign acquisitions, are exempt from the requirements of the Hart-Scott-Rodino Act. The *investment exception* permits an individual to acquire up to 10% of an issuer's voting securities as long as the acquisition is solely for the purposes of investment. The investment exception is designed to exempt those buyers of securities who are passive investors and have no interest in control. It allows investors to buy a large dollar amount of voting securities in a particular company without having to adhere to the HSR filing requirement.

Another exception is the convertible securities exception. Securities that are convertible into voting securities are exempt from the filing requirements of the HSR, as are options and warrants. In addition to these exceptions, purchases by brokerage firms are also exempt, assuming that these purchases are not being made for the purpose of evading the law.

Enforcement of Antitrust Laws: Justice Department and Federal Trade Commission Interaction

Both the Justice Department and the FTC share the responsibility for enforcing U.S. antitrust laws. When the Justice Department brings a suit, it is heard in federal court, whereas when the FTC initiates an action, it is heard before an administrative law judge at the FTC and the decision is reviewed by the commissioners of the FTC. If a defendant wants to appeal an FTC decision, it may bring an action in federal court. Both the Justice Department and the FTC may take steps to halt objectionable behavior by firms. The Justice Department may try to get an injunction, whereas the FTC may issue a cease and desist order. Criminal actions are reserved for the Justice Department, which may seek fines or even imprisonment for the violators as well as the costs of bringing the action. Readers should not infer that government agencies are the sole parties who may bring an antitrust action. Individuals and companies may also initiate such actions. Indeed, it is ironic that such private actions constitute a significant percentage of the total antitrust proceedings in the United States.[57]

REQUIRED DIVESTITURES AS PART OF THE ANTITRUST APPROVAL PROCESS: GLAXO-SMITHKLINE MERGER

Rather than prevent a merger, antitrust regulatory authorities may approve a deal subject to the companies' divesting of certain business units. One example of this was the qualified permission that the FTC gave Glaxo Wellcome PLC in December 2000 to acquire SmithKline Beecham PLC. The permission was given only on the condition that the companies would sell six businesses to rival drug companies. Glaxo and SmithKline agreed to sell their antiemetic drug, Kytril, to F. Hoffman LaRoche.[a] It also sold the U.S. marketing and distribution rights for an antibiotic (ceftazidime) to Abbott Laboratories, while selling the world rights to certain antiviral drugs to Novartis Pharma AG. In cases such as this, the companies have to determine whether the costs of selling valued units and product rights to rivals, which will make the rivals only more formidable competitors, are more than offset by the gains from the merger. In this instance, Glaxo-SmithKline clearly decided that the gains outweighed the costs. It is noteworthy that this is another cost of the deal—one that may not necessarily be known at the time the parties enter into an agreement. It is very much dependent on the actions of the antitrust regulatory authorities, which in turn are only partially predictable.

[a] Janet Seiberg, "Glaxo-Smith Kline's $73 B Merger Wins FTC Approval," *Daily Deal*, December 19, 2001, 10.

 ## MEASURING CONCENTRATION AND DEFINING MARKET SHARE

A key factor that courts have relied on in deciding antitrust cases has been the market share of the alleged violator of antitrust laws and the degree of concentration in the industry. The Justice Department's method of measuring market share and

---

[57] Lawrence White, *Private Antitrust Litigation: New Evidence, New Learning* (Cambridge, MA: MIT Press, 1989).

concentration has varied over the years. The varying standards have been set forth in various merger guidelines.

The 1968 Justice Department Merger Guidelines

In 1968, the Justice Department issued merger guidelines that set forth the types of mergers that the government would oppose. They were largely unchanged until 1982. Through these guidelines, which were used to help interpret the Sherman Act and the Clayton Act, the Justice Department presented its definitions, in terms of specific market share percentages, of highly concentrated and less highly concentrated industries. These guidelines are based upon the general concept that increased market concentration will likely reduce competition.

The guidelines used concentration ratios, which are the market shares of the top four or top eight firms in the industry. Under the 1968 guidelines, an industry was considered to be highly concentrated if the four largest firms held at least 75% of the total market. The 1968 guidelines set forth various share thresholds for acquiring and acquired companies that would drive regulatory attentions. By today's standards these share thresholds are small.

The 1982 Justice Department Guidelines

The limitations of such a rigid antitrust policy began to be felt in the 1970s; a policy that allowed more flexibility was clearly needed. Such a policy was instituted in 1982 through the work of William Baxter, head of the antitrust division of the Justice Department. Baxter was both a lawyer and an economist. Using his economics training, he introduced certain quantitative measures into the antitrust enforcement process, making it more mechanistic, predictable, and consistent with prevailing economic theory. Chief among these measures was the *Herfindahl-Hirschman (HH) index* to American antitrust policy.[58] The HH index is the sum of the squares of the market shares of each firm in the industry.

$$HH = \sum_{i}^{n} s_i^2$$

where s_i is the market share of the *i*th firm.

Using this index rather than simple market shares of the top four or top eight firms in the industry provides a more precise measure of the impact of increased concentration that would be brought on by a merger of two competitors. It is important to note, however, that when using the HH index (or even concentration ratios), the assumption that each of the merged firms would maintain their market shares needs to be carefully examined. The postmerger combined market share needs to be considered even when this may be difficult.

---

[58] Lawrence J. White, "Economics and Economists in Merger Antitrust Enforcement," in Patrick A. Gaughan and Robert Thornton, eds., *Developments in Litigation Economics* (Amsterdam: Elsevier/JAI, 2005), 205–216.

Properties of the HH Index

The Herfindahl-Hirschman index possesses certain properties that make it a better measure of merger-related market concentration than simple concentration ratios:

- The index increases with the number of firms in the industry.
- The index sums the squares of the firms in the industry. In doing so, it weights larger firms more heavily than smaller firms. Squaring a larger number will have a disproportionately greater impact on the index than squaring a smaller number. Moreover, a merger that increases the size differences between firms will result in a larger increase in the index than would have been reflected using simple concentration ratios.
- Because larger firms have greater impact on the index, the index can provide useful results even if there is incomplete information on the size of the smaller firms in the industry.

  In evaluating market concentration the following thresholds apply:

- Postmerger HH less than 1,000: *Unconcentrated market*. This is unlikely to cause an antitrust challenge unless there are other anticompetitive effects.
- Postmerger HH between 1,000 and 1,800: *Moderately concentrated market*. If a merger increases the HH index by less than 100 points, this is unlikely to be a problem, but if it raises the index by more than 100 points, there may be concentration-related antitrust concerns.
- Postmerger HH above 1,800: *Highly concentrated market*. If a merger raises the index only by less than 50 points, this is unlikely to be objectionable. Increases of greater than 50 points "raise significant antitrust concerns."

Example of the HH Index

Consider an industry composed of eight firms, each of which has a 12.5% market share. The Herfindahl-Hirschman index then is equal to:

$$HH = \sum_{i=1}^{8} Si^2 = 8(12.5)^2 = 1,250$$

If two of these equal-sized firms merge, the index is computed to be:

$$HH = 625 + 937.5 = 1,562.5$$

1984 Justice Department Guidelines

On June 14, 1984, the Justice Department again revised its merger guidelines in an attempt to further refine its antitrust enforcement policies. The department recognized that its prior guidelines, including the more accurate HH index, were too mechanistic and inflexible. In an attempt to enhance the flexibility of its policies, the department allowed the consideration of *qualitative* information in addition to the quantitative measures it had been employing. This qualitative information would include factors such as the efficiency of firms in the industry, the financial viability of potential merger candidates, and the ability of U.S. firms to compete in foreign markets.

The 1984 merger guidelines also introduced the 5% test. This test requires the Justice Department to make a judgment on the effects of a potential 5% increase in the price of each product of each merging firm. This test is based on the assumption that there may be an increase in market power resulting from the merger. If so, the merged firms may have the ability to increase prices. The test attempts to examine the potential effects of this increase on competitors and consumers.

One macroeconomic measure that provides an indication of the responsiveness of consumers and competitors is the concept of *elasticity*. The price elasticity of demand provides an indication of the consumers' responsiveness to a change in the price of a product. It is measured as follows:

- e > 1 *Demand is elastic.* The percentage change in quantity is more than the percentage change in price.
- e = 1 *Unitary elasticity.* The percentage change in quantity is equal to the percentage change in price.
- e < 1 *Inelastic demand.* The percentage change in quality is less than the percentage change in price.

If demand is inelastic over the 5% price change range, this implies greater market power for the merged firms; if, however, demand is elastic, consumers are not as adversely affected by the merger.

The 1982 and 1984 merger guidelines recognized the possibility of efficiency-enhancing benefits from mergers. Although they do not have the force of law, the 1968 merger guidelines were found to warrant some legal consideration.

The 1992 Merger Guidelines

The current position of the Justice Department and the FTC is set forth in the jointly issued 1992 merger guidelines, which were revised in 1997. They are similar to the 1984 guidelines in that they also recognize potential efficiency-enhancing benefits of mergers. However, these guidelines indicate that a merger will be challenged if there are anticompetitive effects, such as through price increases, even when there are demonstrable efficiency benefits. Clearly, mergers that lead to an anticompetitive increase in market powers will be challenged.

The 1992 guidelines provide a clarification of the definition of the relevant market, which often is a crucial issue of an antitrust lawsuit. They state that a market is the smallest group of products or geographic area where a monopoly could raise prices by a certain amount, such as by 5%. Like the 1984 guidelines, they also use the HH index to measure the competitive effects of a merger.

The 1992 guidelines set forth a five-step process that the enforcement authorities follow:

1. **Market Definition and Concentration**: Assess whether the merger significantly increases concentration. This involves a definition of the relevant market, which may be an issue of dispute.
2. **Competitive Effects**: Assess any potential anticompetitive effects of the deal.
3. **Entry**: Assess whether the potential anticompetitive effects could be mitigated by entry into the market by competitors. The existence of barriers to entry needs to be determined.
4. **Efficiencies**: Determine if there could be certain offsetting efficiency gains that may result from the deal and that could offset the negative impact of the anticompetitive effects.
5. **Failing Firm Defense**: Determine whether either party would fail or exit the market but for the merger. These possible negative effects are then weighed against the potential anticompetitive effects. The 1997 revisions highlight the antitrust authorities' willingness to consider the net antitrust effects of a merger. Adverse anticompetitive effects may be offset by positive efficiency benefits. The merger participants need to be able to demonstrate that the benefits are directly related to the merger. It is recognized that such benefits may be difficult to quantify in advance of the deal, but their demonstration may not be vague or speculative. Practically, the merger-specific efficiencies offset only minor anticompetitive effects, not major ones.

The 1997 revision of the 1992 guidelines emphasized how merger-specific efficiencies might allow companies to better compete and could possibly be translated into lower prices for consumers. These efficiencies can be achieved only through the merger and are measurable or *cognizable*.

One of the major contributions of the 2010 merger guidelines was that the Justice Department made clear what was generally known by participants in this marketplace—that the Justice Department did not really follow the mechanistic, step-by-step process implied by the 1992 guidelines. Rather, it focused more broadly on competitive effects and the analysis and research that would need to be done to make these effects clear. Thus these guidelines brought closer together actual practice with the letter of the prior guidelines.

In 2011 the Antitrust Division of the Justice Department issued a *Guide to Merger Remedies*, which emphasized that proposed remedies for mergers must ensure that competition will be preserved and the deal participants must make sure that the remedies have a beneficial impact on consumers and not market participants.

 ## EUROPEAN COMPETITION POLICY

In December 1989, the European Union adopted what is referred to as the *merger regulation*. This policy went into effect in September 1990 but was later amended.

The regulation focused on mergers, but also joint ventures, that have an impact on the degree of competition beyond one nation's borders. Under the regulation, mergers with significant revenues must receive European Commission (EC) approval. Unlike the U.S. system, in which antitrust regulators must go to court to block a merger, the EC's regulatory system is not dependent on the courts.

In its revised 2004 merger regulations, the EC established its M&A policy as follows:

> A concentration that would sufficiently impede competition, in the common market or a substantial part of it, in particular as a result of the creation, or *strengthening of a dominant position, shall be declared incomparable with the Common Market.*

The later EC M&A regulations are broader than the prior version in that while they mention market dominance, this is now merely an example of an anticompetitive condition.[59] As part of its analysis the EC first defines the market and then looks to determine the market power before and after the deals. As part of this determination, factors such as barriers to entry are taken into account. Once this analysis is done, the EC does a further analysis of the competitive effects of the deal.

The EC utilizes its own horizontal merger guidelines, which start off with postdeal market shares greater than 50% giving rise to concerns, while shares below 25%–30% tend not to raise such concerns. The EC is also less likely to raise concerns when HH indexes are below 1, 000, or when they are below 2,000 but the postdeal delta is low (such as between 150 and 250).

Transactions that the EC finds particularly objectionable may be brought to the European Court of Justice.

U.S. companies that do significant business in Europe must secure European Union approval in addition to the approval by U.S. antitrust authorities. Sometimes this can be a time-consuming process. For example, the European Union pursued a six-month investigation into Oracle Corporation's $7.4 billion takeover of Sun Microsystems Inc. prior to approving the deal in January 2010.

Although the instances in which the U.S. antitrust authorities and their European counterparts disagree on the competitive effects of M&As receive much attention, most of the time they agree on the effects.[60] One prominent example where they disagreed was the proposed $40 billion General Electric–Honeywell merger. The European opposition to the GE–Honeywell deal, a merger that was not opposed in the United States, raised many eyebrows as some felt the European Union was using its competition policy to insulate European companies from competition with larger U.S. rivals. Others concluded that the decision was the product of an inadequate analysis on the part of the EC.[61] This conflict led to a round of discussions to make the competition policies in both

---

[59] Mats A. Bergman, Malcolm B. Coate, Maria Jakobsson, and Shawn W. Ulrick, "Comparing Merger Policies in the European Union and the United States, " *Review of Industrial Organization* 36, no. 4 (June 2010): 305–331.
[60] François Lévêque, "Le Contrôle des Concentrations en Europe et aux États-Unis: Lequel Est le Plus Sévère?" *Concurrences* 2 (2005): 20–23.
[61] Eleanor Morgan and Steven McGuire, "Transatlantic Divergence: GE–Honeywell and the EU's Merger Policy," *Journal of European Public Policy* 11, no. 1 (2004): 39–56.

markets more consistent. Under the leadership of then antitrust chief Mario Monti, a former Italian economics professor, the EC antitrust regulators, based in Brussels, used an economic doctrine known as *collective dominance* when reviewing the impact that mergers may have on the level of competition within the EU. This refers to the ability of a group of companies to dominate a particular market. In the EU market shares below 40% could draw an enforcement action whereas much higher thresholds, such as 60%, may apply in the U.S.

While European regulators have framed their opposition to certain M&As as a way of limited monopoly power and helping consumer welfare, others are more cynical about their motives. Aktas, deBodt, and Roll analyzed a sample of 290 proposed acquisitions that were examined by the European regulators during the 1990s.[62] They found the greater the adverse impact on European rivals resulting from deals by foreign companies, the more likely that regulators would move to oppose the M&A.

EU Merger Control Procedures

The European Commission sets certain deal sizes, or "turnover thresholds," above which a deal will be reviewed by the EU. Size is defined in terms of both worldwide and EU business volume. The EC requires that it be notified before a merger is completed. It has preprepared templates that merger partners complete. Many deals do not get much EC scrutiny, but if the deal results in 15% combined horizontal market shares or 25% in vertical markets, the EC does an investigation. The investigation process starts with Phase I, which is usually completed in 25 business days. Ninety percent of all cases are *cleared* in Phase I. The remaining 10% have attracted competition concerns, and these are addressed in Phase II.

In Phase II the deal participants are expected to put forward or agree to remedies that will *guarantee continued competition*. Phase II is usually completed in 90 business days, although the EC can add another 15 days to this time limit. If the EC agrees to the remedies, then it appoints a trustee who will oversee the implementation of the remedies to make sure that they are enacted. For example, the EC agreed to allow the acquisition of EMI's recorded music business by Universal Music Group in 2012 only after the divestment of certain assets.[63] This is an example of what are known as *structural remedies*. At the end of Phase II the EC will indicate that the deal is either unconditionally clear or will be approved if remedies are implemented, or it is prohibited. All EC decisions are subject to a review by the General Court and potentially by the Court of Justice.

The EU adopted new rules effective January 2014, according to which companies can submit a shortened version of Form CO: the parties could submit initial information showing that they do not believe the deal raises antitrust concerns and thereby seek EU approval.

---

[62] Nihat Aktas, Eric deBodt, and Richard Roll, "Is European M&A Regulation Protectionist?" *Economic Journal* 117, no. 522 (July 2007): 1096–1121.
[63] Joshua R. Wueller, "Merging of Majors: Applying the Failing Firm Doctrine in the Recorded Music Industry," *Brooklyn Journal of Corporate, Financial and Commercial Law*, January 1, 2013.

CHAPTER FOUR

Merger Strategy

THIS CHAPTER FOCUSES ON the strategic motives and determinants of mergers and acquisitions (M&As). It begins with a discussion of two of the most often cited motives for M&As—faster growth and synergy. Also discussed are the relative benefits of horizontal, vertical, and diversifying mergers as well as other motives, such as the pursuit of economies of scale.

 ## GROWTH

One of the most fundamental motives for M&As is growth. Companies seeking to expand are faced with a choice between internal or organic growth and growth through M&As. Internal growth may be a slow and uncertain process. Growth through M&As may be much more rapid, although it brings with it its own uncertainties. Companies may grow within their own industry or they may expand outside their business category. Expansion outside one's industry means diversification. Because diversification has been a controversial topic in finance, it is discussed separately later in this chapter. In this section we focus on growth within a company's own industry.

If a company seeks to expand within its own industry, it may conclude that internal growth is not an acceptable means. For example, if a company has a window of opportunity that will remain open for only a limited period of time, slow internal growth may not suffice. As the company grows slowly through internal expansion, competitors may respond quickly and take market share. Advantages that a company may have can dissipate over time or be whittled away by the actions of competitors. The only solution may be to acquire another company that has established offices and facilities, management, and other resources, in place. There are many opportunities that must be acted on immediately lest they disappear. It could be that a company has developed a new product or process and has a time advantage over competitors. Even if it is possible to patent the product or process, this does not prevent competitors from possibly developing a competing product or process that does not violate the patent. Another example would be if a company developed a new merchandising concept. Being first to develop the concept provides a certain limited time advantage. If not properly taken advantage of, it may slip by and become an opportunity for larger competitors with greater resources.

JOHNSON & JOHNSON: GROWTH THROUGH ACQUISITIONS STRATEGY

Johnson & Johnson is a manufacturer and marketer of a wide range of health care products. Over the period 1995–2014, the company engineered over 70 significant acquisitions as part of its growth through acquisitions strategy (see Table A). The company is an assemblage of multiple acquisitions leading to a corporate structure that includes in excess of 200 subsidiaries.

TABLE A   Johnson & Johnson's Growth through Acquisitions Strategy: Selected Deals during 1994–2014

Company Acquired	Primary Focus	Date	Size in $ Billions
Synthes	Trauma devices	2011	21.3
Pfizer Consumer Healthcare	Consumer healthcare	2006	16.6
Alza	Drug delivery	2001	12.3
Centocor	Immune-related diseases	1999	6.3
Depuy	Orthopedic devices	1998	3.6
Scios	Cardiovascular diseases	2003	2.4
Crucell	Bio-tech	2011	2.3
Cordis	Vascular diseases	1996	1.8
Alios BioPharma	Viral therapies	2014	1.8
Inverness Med. Tech.	Diabetes self-management	2001	1.4
Mentor Corporation	Medical products	2008	1.1
Aragon Pharmaceuticals	Prostate cancer treatment	2013	1.0
Cougar Biotechnology	Cancer drug development	2009	1.0
Neutrogena	Skin and hair care	1994	0.9
Acclarent	Medical products	2009	0.8
Micrus	Stroke devices	2010	0.5
Omrix Biopharmaceuticals	Biosurgery products	2008	0.4
Closure	Topical wounds	2005	0.4
Peninsula Pharmaceuticals	Life-threatening infections	2005	0.3

This strategy is similar to that pursued by companies in other rapidly changing, innovation-filled industries, such as the computer software industry. Rather than internally trying to be on the forefront of every major area of innovation, Johnson & Johnson, a company that generated $71 billion in revenues in 2013, has sought to pursue those companies who have developed successful products. In doing so, they sought not to waste time with unsuccessful internal development attempts and went after only those products and companies that have demonstrated success. However, the company has to pay a premium for such deals. This strategy has sometimes simply meant that Johnson & Johnson would buy its competitors rather than try to surpass them using internal growth. For example, in 1996 it acquired Cordis in the medical stent business for $1.8 billion. When this deal failed to place it in the lead in this market segment, Johnson & Johnson resorted to M&A again with its $25.4 billion (initial) bid for market leader Guidant. This acquisition would have been the largest deal in Johnson & Johnson's long history of M&A. However, it lowered its bid when Guidant's litigation liabilities became known, and then was outbid by Boston Scientific. In 2006 following the collapse of the Guidant deal, the cash-rich Johnson & Johnson acquired Pfizer's consumer products division for $16 billion.

The acquisition of Pfizer's consumer products business expanded J&J's presence in the comsumer products segment. J&J's consumer revenues rose from $9 billion prior to the acquisition to $15.8 billion by 2009. However, revenues in this segment remained flat and by the end of 2013 were $14.7 billion (Figure A). At the same time sales of drugs and medical devices continued to grow. Pre-tax profit margins on drugs rose from 28.5% in 2009 to 32.6% by 2013. The acquisition of Pfizer's consumer products business gave J&J significant "top line" growth but helped to lower overall corporate margins as consumer products have lower margins (Figure B).

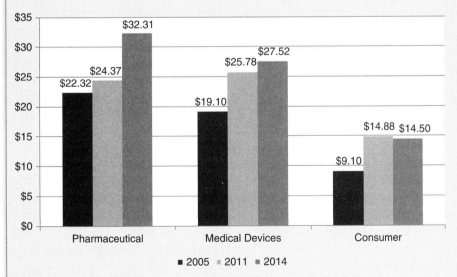

FIGURE A Johnson & Johnson Sales by Segment (in billions of dollars)

(continued)

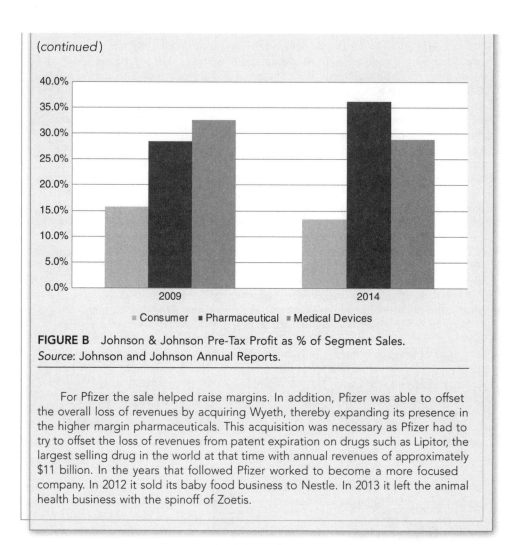

(continued)

FIGURE B Johnson & Johnson Pre-Tax Profit as % of Segment Sales.
Source: Johnson and Johnson Annual Reports.

For Pfizer the sale helped raise margins. In addition, Pfizer was able to offset the overall loss of revenues by acquiring Wyeth, thereby expanding its presence in the higher margin pharmaceuticals. This acquisition was necessary as Pfizer had to try to offset the loss of revenues from patent expiration on drugs such as Lipitor, the largest selling drug in the world at that time with annual revenues of approximately $11 billion. In the years that followed Pfizer worked to become a more focused company. In 2012 it sold its baby food business to Nestle. In 2013 it left the animal health business with the spinoff of Zoetis.

Another example of using M&As to facilitate growth is when a company wants to expand to another geographic region. It could be that the company's market is in one part of the country, but it wants to expand into other regions. Alternatively, perhaps it is already a national company but seeks to tap the markets of other nations, such as a U.S. firm wanting to expand into Europe. In many instances, it may be quicker and less risky to expand geographically through acquisitions than through internal development. This may be particularly true of international expansion, where many characteristics are needed to be successful in a new geographic market. The company needs to know all of the nuances of the new market, recruit new personnel, and circumvent many other hurdles, such as language and custom barriers. Internal expansion may be much slower and difficult. Mergers, acquisitions, joint ventures, and strategic alliances may be the fastest and lowest-risk alternatives.

Achieving Growth in a Slow-Growth Industry through Acquisitions

Corporate managers are under constant pressure to demonstrate successful growth. This is particularly true when the company and the industry have achieved growth in the past. However, when the demand for an industry's products and services slows, it becomes more difficult to continue to grow. When this happens, managers often look to M&A as a way to jump-start growth. It often is hoped that acquisitions will lead not only to revenue growth but also to improved profitability through synergistic gains. Unfortunately, it is much easier to generate sales growth by simply adding the revenues of acquisition targets than it is to improve the profitability of the overall enterprise. In fact, one can argue that although acquisitions bring with them the possibility of synergistic gains, they also impose greater demands on management, which now runs an even larger enterprise. Management needs to make sure that the greater size in terms of revenues has brought with it commensurate profits and returns for shareholders. If not, then the growth through M&A strategy has not improved shareholders' positions and investors would have been better off if management had resigned themselves to being a slower-growth company.

FLAVOR AND FRAGRANCE INDUSTRY: USING ACQUISITIONS TO ACHIEVE GROWTH IN A SLOW-GROWTH INDUSTRY (IFF'S ACQUISITION OF BUSH BOAKE ALLEN)

The growth in the flavor and fragrance industry slowed significantly in the 1990s. Companies in this industry sold products to manufacturers and marketers of various other products. As the demand for the end users' products slowed, the demand for intermediate products, such as flavors, also slowed. Food manufacturers rely on various suppliers, including flavor developers, to come up with new or improved products. The frozen food business is a case in point.

With the advent of the microwave oven, this business grew dramatically. However, when the proliferation of this innovation reached its peak, the growth in the frozen food business also slowed. Companies that sold to frozen food manufacturers experienced the impact of this slowing demand in the form of a slower demand for their products and increased pressure placed on them by manufacturers for price concessions that would enable the manufacturers to improve their own margins. Faced with the prospect of slow growth, International Flavors and Fragrances (IFF), one of the largest companies in this industry, acquired competitor Bush Boake Allen, which was about one-third the size of IFF. On the surface, however, the acquisition of Bush Boake Allen increased the size of IFF by one-third, giving at least the appearance of significant growth in this slow-growth industry.

Is Growth or Increased Return the More Appropriate Goal?

It is virtually assumed without question that a major goal for a company's management and board is to achieve growth. However, managers need to make sure that the growth is one that will generate good returns for shareholders. Too often management may be able to continue to generate acceptable returns by keeping a company at a given size, but instead choose to pursue aggressive growth.[1] Boards need to critically examine the expected profitability of the revenue derived from growth and determine if the growth is worth the cost. Consider the case of Hewlett-Packard in the post-Fiorina era. Having made a highly questionable $19 billion mega-acquisition of Compaq in 2002 (Compaq itself had acquired Tandem Computers in 1997 and Digital Equipment in 1998), Hewlett-Packard found itself managing several business segments in which it was a leader in only one—printers. In 2009 the company had revenues in excess of $114 billion. If, as an example, its goal was to grow at 10% per year, it would have to generate approximately $11 billion in new revenues each year. In effect, it would have to create another large company's worth of revenues each year to satisfy management's growth goals. When we consider the fact that much of its business comes from the highly competitive personal computer market with its weak margins coupled with steady product price *deflation*, such growth can be a challenge.

In the years after Fiorina's departure the company continued with its pattern of failed acquisitions. In 2008, with Mark Hurd at the helm, HP acquired EDS, which was followed by a write-down of $8 billion. In 2011, with Leo Apotheker as CEO, HP acquired Autonomy for $10 billion, which was followed by a charge of $8.8 billion. While it may not have as long a track record of M&A failures as AT&T, HP seems to be working hard to catch AT&T for the position of "world leader" in M&A failures.[2]

International Growth and Cross-Border Acquisitions

Companies that have successful products in one national market may see cross-border acquisitions as a way of achieving greater revenues and profits. Rather than seek potentially diminishing returns by pursuing further growth within their own nation, companies may use cross-border deals as an advantageous way of tapping another market. A cross-border deal may enable an acquirer to utilize the country-specific know-how of the target, including its indigenous staff and distribution network. The key question, as it is with every acquisition, is whether the risk-adjusted return from the deal is greater than what can be achieved with the next best use of the invested capital.

With the advent of the European Common Market, cross-country barriers have been reduced. This has given rise to a spate of cross-border deals in Europe. Certain Asian markets continue to be resistant to foreign acquirers (although there are signs that this is

---

[1] Andrew Campbell and Robert Park, *The Growth Gamble* (London: Nicholas Brealey International, 2005).
[2] Patrick A. Gaughan, *Maximizing Corporate Value through Mergers and Acquisitions: A Strategic Growth Guide* (Hoboken, NJ: John Wiley & Sons, 2013), 314–315.

changing); thus, the volume of cross-border deals in this region is probably significantly less than what it will be in the future, if and when these artificial market restrictions become more relaxed.

Cross border deals present some basic and obvious challenges that domestic deals lack. A business model that may work well in a home country can fail for unexpected reasons in another nation. A recent example of this was Target's failed expansion into Canada. The giant retailer believed the fact that Canadian visitors to the U.S. liked to shop at Target was a signal that expansion into neighboring Canada would be fruitful. This proved not to be the case. In 2015 Target decided to close its 133 Canadian stores just two years after this failed expansion strategy.

Language differences can also pose a challenge not just in the initial negotiations but also in post-deal integration.[3] In addition, even though new geographic markets may present opportunites for revenue and profit growth, physical distances can also increase managerial demands.

As with all types of acquisitions, we need to consider the market reactions to international M&As and compare them to intracountry deals. Doukas and Travlos found that, unlike many domestic acquisitions, acquirers enjoyed positive (although not statistically significant) returns when they acquired targets in countries in which they did not previously have operations. Interestingly, the returns were negative (although also not statistically significant) when the acquirers already had operations in these foreign countries.[4] When the company is already in the market, and presumably has already exploited some of the gains that can be realized, then investors may be less sanguine about the gains that may be realized through an increased presence in this same region.

Another study compared the shareholder wealth effects of acquisitions of U.S. firms by non-U.S. bidders and the opposite—acquisitions of non-U.S. companies by U.S. bidders. Cakici, Hessel, and Tandon analyzed the shareholder wealth effects from 195 acquisitions, over the period 1983–1992, of non-U.S. companies that bought U.S. targets.[5] They then compared these effects to a sample of 112 deals in which U.S. companies acquired non-U.S. firms. The non-U.S. acquirers generated statistically significant returns of just under 2% over a 10-day window, whereas the U.S. acquirers realized the negative returns that we often generally see from acquisitions.

Still another research study by Markides and Oyon, using a sample of 236 deals, compared acquisitions by U.S. firms of European (189) versus Canadian targets (47). They found positive announcement effects for acquisitions of continental European

---

[3] Kenneth Ahern, Danielle Daminelli and Cesare Fracassi, "Lost if Translation? The Effect of Cultural Values on Mergers Around the World," *Journal of Financial Economics*, (2012).

[4] John Doukas and Nicholas G. Travlos, "The Effect of Corporate Multinationalism on Shareholders' Wealth," *Journal of Finance* 43, no. 5 (December 1988): 1161–1175.

[5] Nusret Cakici, Chris Hessel, and Kishore Tandon, "Foreign Acquisitions in the United States: Effect on Shareholder Wealth of Foreign Acquiring Firms," *Journal of Banking & Finance* 20, no. 2 (March 1996): 307–329.

targets but not for acquisitions of British or Canadian target firms.[6] These negative shareholder wealth effects for acquisitions of Canadian firms were also found by Eckbo and Thorburn, who considered 390 deals involving Canadian companies over the period 1962–1983.[7]

The fact that acquisitions of non-U.S. targets by U.S. companies may be riskier than deals involving all-U.S. targets is underscored by a large sample study by Moeller and Schlingemann.[8] They analyzed 4,430 deals over the period 1985–1992. They found that U.S. bidders who pursued cross-border deals realized lower returns than acquisitions where the bidders chose U.S. targets.

Currency-Related Effects

Exchange rates can play an important role in international takeovers. When the currency of a bidder appreciates relative to that of a target, a buyer holding the more highly valued currency may be able to afford a higher premium, which the target may have difficulty passing up. In analyzing a large sample of 56,978 cross border M&As covering the period 1990–2007, Erel, Liao, and Wesibach confirmed the important role that exchange rates play in M&As.[9] In their sample they found that countries whose currencies appreciated were more likely to have acquirers and countries whose currency decreciated were more likely to have targets. Lin, Officer, and Shen analyzed a sample of 12,131 cross border M&As over the period 1996–2012 and found that not only do acquirers from countries with appreciating currencies realize higher announcement period returns than those not affected by such currency changes, but also that this positive effect, which was present at the time of the announcement and also in the post-merger period, was greater the better the corporate governance of the acquirer.[10]

INTERNATIONAL GROWTH AND THE HOTEL INDUSTRY

In January 2006, the Hilton Hotels Corp. announced a $5.7 billion offer to purchase the international hotel business unit owned by Hilton Group PLC. This acquisition offer came with a touch of irony as the two businesses were one prior to 1964,

---

[6] Constantinos Markides and Daniel Oyon, "International Acquisitions: Do They Create Value for Shareholders?" *European Management Journal* 16, no. 2 (April 1998): 125–135.

[7] Epsen Eckbo and K. S. Thorburn, "Gains to Bidder Firms Revisited: Domestic and Foreign Acquisitions in Canada," *Journal of Financial and Quantitative Analysis* 35, no. 1 (March 2000): 1–25.

[8] Sara B. Moeller and Frederick P. Schlingemann, "Global Diversification and Bidder Gains: A Comparison between Cross-Border and Domestic Acquisitions," *Journal of Banking and Finance* 29, no. 3 (March 2005): 533–564.

[9] Isil Erel, Rose C. Liao and Michael S. Wiesbach, "Determinants of Cross-Border Mergers and Acquisitions," *Journal of Finance*, 67 (3) June 2012, 1045–1082.

[10] Chen Lin, Micah S. Officer and Beibei Shen, "Currency Appreciation Shocks and Shareholder Wealth Creation in Cross-Border Mergers and Acquisitions," paper presented at American Finance Association Annual Meeting, 2015.

when Hilton parted ways with its international hotel business. The move to expand outside the United States came partly in response to the international expansion efforts of two of Hilton's main rivals—Marriott International Inc. and Starwood Hotels and Resorts Worldwide Inc.

The combination united the hotels operating under the Hilton name and allows Hilton to offer an international network of properties across the globe. The chain traces its roots to Conrad Hilton in 1919, when he bought his first hotel. The company was split in 1964 and as part of that division the two units agreed not to compete with one another. However, market opportunities in the 1960s were very different from those of the 2000s. The current world market is much more globalized. Hotel businesses that can offer a true global network can leverage their customer base in one market to generate sales in another. For example, some American travelers familiar with the Hilton brand and seeking comparable services when abroad might more likely stay at a Hilton property than another that they were unfamiliar with.

In 2007 Hilton Hotels was acquired by the Blackstone private equity firm in a $26 billion dollar LBO. The price was expensive and it refected a purchase at the top of the market. When the global economy turned down and the U.S. entered the Great Recession, the Hilton pricey acquisition looked questionable. However, after a shaky initial period where Blackstone had to infuse more equity capital into the hotel chain, the business increased its efficiency while also expanding its revenue base. It added over 200,000 new rooms to increase its total rooms to 700,000.[a] Over the period 2009–2014 Hilton's operating profits increased significantly (Figure A).

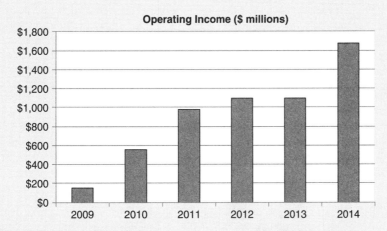

FIGURE A Hilton's Operating Income (in millions): 2009–2014. *Source*: Hilton Worldwide 2014 Annual Report.

---

[a] William Cohan, "Blackstone's $26 Billion Hilton Deal: The Best Levreraged Buyout Ever", *Fortune*, September 11, 2014.

INTERNATIONAL DIVERSIFICATION IN THE AUTOMOBILE INDUSTRY

Over the past two decades, many of the major automobile companies have engaged in a pattern of cross-border acquisitions as they have sought to exploit markets outside of their own borders. Indeed this form of expansion has been going on much longer than the past couple of decades. However, when the pace of M&As from two of the largest merger waves took hold, the automobile industry responded like so many others and pursued its own deals.

As we look back on many of these deals, we see that many were major disappointments. Probably the most notable flop was Daimler's 1998 takeover of Chrysler. Chrysler was profitable at the time it was acquired by Daimler, but the market was changing around that time, and following the deal, sales of many of its profitable cars and SUVs declined as consumer tastes changed. Led by its hubris-filled CEO, Jurgen Schrempp, Daimler Chrysler was reluctant to admit the deal was a failure even as it generated staggering losses.[a] The distracted Daimler worked to fix the problems at Chrysler, which it did, but only at the expense of "taking its eye off the ball" at Mercedes, its highly successful luxury brand.[b] Quality problems began to emerge in various Mercedes autos, such as the E and M class sedans, and Mercedes began to lose ground to its chief rival—BMW. Indeed, Daimler's losing deal with Chrysler was not its only flop. Its investment in Mitsubishi was also fraught with problems.

Daimler was not the only auto company to lose from its international deals. General Motors pursued a number of international acquisitions as it sought to expand its presence throughout the world. Many of these were major losers. Perhaps the most embarrassing for GM was its investment in Fiat, which gave the troubled Italian automaker the right to require GM to pay $2 billion to Fiat if GM wanted to end their alliance. As Fiat's financial problems mounted, GM was forced to pay $2 billion at a time when it was experiencing many other financial problems.[c] In addition, other GM global deals were troubled. Its investments in the Russian auto market were fraught with difficulties.

Ford experienced its share of M&A woes. It acquired targets in Europe so as to expand its presence in that market while also providing the number-two U.S. auto maker with luxury brands, such as Jaguar. While Jaguar is a world-renowned brand and, along with Land Rover, served as a key component in Ford's Premier Auto Group, it failed to generate profits for Ford. At a time when Ford labored under burdensome union agreements and intense foreign competition in its main market, the United States, it was forced to continually invest in its failed acquisition, Jaguar, which regularly lost money for Ford. The company finally parted ways with Jaguar and Land Rover in 2008 when it sold the car businesses to Tata Motors for $2.3 billion. When one considers that Ford paid $2.5 billion for Jaguar in 1989 and $2.75 billion to BMW for Land Rover in 2000 (BMW was never able to make Land Rover profitable), these deals were clear failures. However, while Tata Motors struggled with the introduction of the long-awaited Nano, which was not well received by the Indian middle-class market it hoped to appeal to, Jaguar and Land Rover sales were a bright spot for Tata. Since the acquisitions of Jaguar and Land Rover, Tata Motors enjoyed significant increases in revenues and EBITDA. Thus the "early returns" seems to show promise for Tata's international auto expansion strategy. This is clear from the figures below:

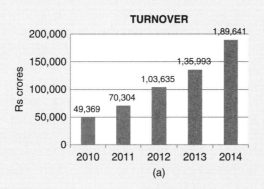

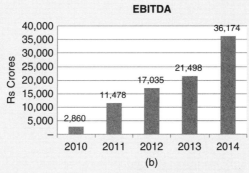

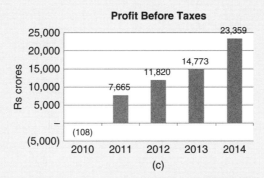

FIGURE A (A) Jaguar Land Rover Group's Turnover, (B) EBITDA, and (C) Profit BeforeTaxes (In Rs Crores)

---

[a] Bill Vlasic and Bradley A. Stertz, *Taken for a Ride: How Mercedes-Benz Drove Off with Chrysler* (New York: William Morrow, 2000).

[b] Patrick Gaughan, *Mergers: What Can Go Wrong and How to Prevent It* (Hoboken, NJ: John Wiley & Sons, 2004), 306–316.

[c] "G.M. Warned of a Cut in Debt Rating," *New York Times*, February 15, 2005, late ed., C2.

 SYNERGY

The term *synergy* is often associated with the physical sciences rather than with economics or finance. It refers to the type of reaction that occurs when two substances or factors combine to produce a greater effect together than that which the sum of the tywo operating independently could account for. For example, a synergistic reaction occurs in chemistry when two chemicals combine to produce a more potent total reaction than the sum of their separate effects. Simply stated, synergy refers to the phenomenon of 2 + 2 = 5. In mergers this translates into the ability of a corporate combination to be more profitable than the individual parts of the firms that were combined.

The anticipated existence of synergistic benefits allows firms to incur the expenses of the acquisition process and still be able to afford to give target shareholders a premium for their shares. Synergy may allow the combined firm to appear to have a positive *net acquisition value* (NAV).

$$NAV = V_{AB} - [V_A + V_B] - P - E \qquad (4.1)$$

where:

V_{AB} = is the combined value of the two firms,
V_A = the value of A,
V_B = the value of B,
P = the premium paid for B, and
E = the expenses of the acquisition process.

Reorganizing equation 4.1, we get:

$$NAV = [V_{AB} - (V_A + V_B)] - (P + E) \qquad (4.2)$$

The term in the brackets is the synergistic effect. This effect must be greater than the sum of P + E to justify going forward with the merger. If the bracketed term is not greater than the sum of P + E, the bidding firm will have overpaid for the target. What are to be considered synergistic effects? Some researchers view synergy broadly and include the elimination of inefficient management by installing the more capable management of the acquiring firm.[11] Although it is reasonable to define synergy in this manner, this chapter defines the term more narrowly and treats management-induced gains separately. This approach is consistent with the more common uses of the term *synergy*.[12]

The two main types of synergy are operating synergy and financial synergy. *Operating synergy* comes in two forms: revenue enhancements and cost reductions. These

---

[11] Paul Asquith, "Merger Bids, Uncertainty and Stockholder Returns," *Journal of Financial Economics* 11, nos. 1–4 (April 1983): 51–83, and Michael Bradley, Anand Desai, and E. Han Kim, "The Rationale behind Interfirm Tender Offers: Information or Synergy?" *Journal of Financial Economics* 11, nos. 1–4 (April 1983): 183–206.
[12] Michael Jensen and Richard Ruback, "The Market for Corporate Control: The Scientific Evidence," *Journal of Financial Economics* 11, nos. 1–4 (April 1983): 5–50.

revenue enhancements and efficiency gains or operating economies may be derived in horizontal or vertical mergers. *Financial synergy* refers to the possibility that the cost of capital may be lowered by combining one or more companies.

ALLEGIS: SYNERGY THAT NEVER MATERIALIZED

The case of the Allegis Corporation is a classic example of synergistic benefits that had every reason to occur but failed to materialize. The concept of Allegis was the brainchild of CEO Richard Ferris, who rose through the ranks of United Airlines.

Ferris's dream was to form a diversified travel services company that would be able to provide customers with a complete package of air travel, hotel, and car rental services. Accordingly, United Airlines paid $587 million for Hertz Rent A Car to RCA in June 1986—a price that was considered a premium. In addition to buying Pan American Airways' Pacific routes, Ferris bought the Hilton International hotel chain from the Transworld Corporation for $980 million. The Hilton International purchase on March 31, 1987, was also considered expensive.

United Airlines had already acquired the Westin International hotel chain in 1970 for only $52 million. On February 18, 1987, United Airlines changed its name to Allegis Corporation. Allegis's strategy was to offer customers "one-stop" travel shopping. With one telephone call they could book their air travel, hotel reservations, and car rental within the same corporate umbrella. Allegis hoped to weave the network together through a combination of cross-discounts, bonus miles, and other promotional savings and the introduction of a new computer system called Easy Saver. Through Easy Saver, customers could check prices and book reservations through the Allegis network. All travel services could be charged on an Allegis credit card. Travel agents using United Airlines' Apollo computer reservation system, the largest in the airline industry, would pull up Allegis's air, hotel, and car services before any other competitor's products.

Despite the concept's appeal to United's management, customers and the market failed to respond. At a time when the stock market was providing handsome returns to investors, the Allegis stock price fell; in February 1987, its stock price was in the low- to mid-$50 range. The market did respond, however, when Coniston Partners, a New York investment firm, accumulated a 13% stake in the travel company. Coniston planned to sell off the various parts of the Allegis travel network and distribute the proceeds to the stockholders. On April 1, 1987, Allegis announced a large recapitalization plan proposal that would have resulted in the company's assuming $3 billion worth of additional debt to finance a $60 special dividend. The recapitalization plan was intended to support the stock price while instilling stockholder support for Allegis and away from the Coniston proposal. The United Airlines Pilots Union followed up Allegis's recapitalization plan proposal with its own offer to buy the airline and sell off the nonairline parts.

The pressure on CEO Ferris continued to mount, leading to a pivotal board of directors meeting. According to Chairman of the Board Charles Luce, the board, watching the company's stock rise, "thought the market was saying that Allegis was worth more broken up and that the current strategy should be abandoned."

(continued)

(continued)

Although the outside directors had supported Ferris during the company's acquisition program, they now decided that Ferris was an obstacle to restructuring the
company. "There comes a point," said Luce, "when no board can impose its own
beliefs over the opposition of the people who elected it." Ferris was replaced by
Frank A. Olsen, chairman of Allegis's Hertz subsidiary.[a]

Allegis is one of many examples of management wanting to create a "one-stop
shop" for consumers that the market failed to embrace. Sears's diversifying acquisitions (see "Sears: A Failed Diversification Strategy") and Citicorp's related acquisitions are other examples of such failures. Boards that should know better seem to be
too passive and allow managers to waste resources on these failed empire-building
efforts.

[a] Arthur Fleisher Jr., Geoffrey C. Hazard Jr., and Miriam Z. Klipper, *Board Games: The Changing
Shape of Corporate America* (Boston: Little, Brown, 1988), 192.

OPERATING SYNERGY

Operating synergy can come from gains that enhance revenues or those that lower costs.
Of the two, revenue enhancements can be the more difficult to achieve. Such gains are
easier for deal proponents to talk about than to achieve.

Revenue-Enhancing Operating Synergy

As we have noted, revenue enhancing synergies can be difficult to achieve. One survey
by McKinsey estimated that 70% of mergers failed to achieve their expected revenue
synergies.[13]

Revenue-enhancing synergies can come from various sources:

- Pricing power
- Combination of functional strengths
- Growth from faster-growth markets or new markets

A combination of two companies may lead to *greater pricing power* or purchasing
power. This will normally be possible only if the two companies are in the same business.
Whether this will be achievable depends on the degree of competition in the industry and
relevant geographic markets as well as the size of the merger partners. With respect to
pricing power, if the combination leads to a more oligopolistic market structure, this *may*
be possible. On the other hand, if large pricing gains are achievable through increased
concentration, the deal may not get regulatory approval.

Research on the source of gains from horizontal mergers has found that gains
associated with such deals can be attributed to efficiency improvements, not increased

[13] Scott A. Christofferson, Robert S. McNish, and Diane L. Sims, "Where Mergers Go Wrong," *McKinsey Quarterly* 2 (2004): 92–99.

market power.[14] These studies examined the stock market response reactions, or lack of a response, by competitors, customers, and suppliers.

Another potential source of merger revenue enhancement can be the *combination of functional strengths*. Perhaps one company has strong R&D or production abilities, while the other has great marketing and distribution. Each merger partner could be bringing important capabilities "to the table"—one that the other lacks. Many good examples of this have occurred in the pharmaceutical industry through combinations between drug companies with good R&D, something the industry has been struggling to improve, and large pharmaceutical companies with great manufacturing capacity and quality control (very important in this industry) but also global marketing and distribution capabilities.

In mature markets, Japan, and Europe, corporate growth has slowed and companies have to work harder and harder to achieve meaningful growth. This sometimes means that large companies have to invest greater amounts to increase market share or sometimes to merely maintain what they have. However, such companies may be able to achieve important increases in growth by moving into more rapidly growing markets, such as those in the emerging world. When many companies are struggling to expand their mature markets and reaching rapidly diminishing returns, the fastest way to realize meaningful growth can be to enter *higher-growth new markets*.

Revenue-Related "Dissynergies"

Not only may M&A-related increases in revenues be difficult to achieve, but also M&A-related losses in revenues may be difficult to prevent. Customers of the target may not want to stay with the larger company. However, when the bidder paid a premium for the target, the profitability of its total revenues were likely used to compute the total price. If revenues are lost, this can make the deal a loser. This is why simplistic projections of deal gains must be carefully examined.

Cost-Reducing Operating Synergies

Merger planners tend to look for cost-reducing synergies as the main source of operating synergies. These cost reductions may come as a result of *economies of scale*—decreases in per-unit costs that result from an increase in the size or scale of a company's operations.

Manufacturing firms, especially capital-intensive ones, typically operate at high per-unit costs for low levels of output. This is because the fixed costs of operating their manufacturing facilities are spread out over relatively low levels of output. As the output levels rise, the per-unit costs decline. This is sometimes referred to as *spreading overhead*. Some of the other sources of these gains arise from increased specialization of labor and management and the more efficient use of capital equipment, which might

---

[14] C. Edward Fee and Shawn Thomas, "Source of Gains in Horizontal Acquisitions: Evidence from Consumer, Supplier and Rival Firms", *Journal of Financial Economics*, 74, 2004, 423–460; and H. Sahhrur, " Industry Structure and Horizontal Takeovers: Analysis of Wealth Effects of Rivals, Suppliers and Corporate Customers," *Journal of Financial Economics*, 76, 2005, 61–98.

not be possible at low output levels. This phenomenon continues for a certain range of output, after which per-unit costs may rise as the firm experiences diseconomies of scale. Diseconomies of scale may arise as the firm experiences higher costs and other problems associated with coordinating a larger-scale operation. The extent to which diseconomies of scale exist is a topic of dispute for many economists. Some economists cite as evidence the continued growth of large multinational companies, such as Exxon and General Electric. These firms have exhibited extended periods of growth while still paying stockholders an acceptable return on equity.[15] Others contend that such firms would be able to provide stockholders a higher rate of return if they were smaller, more efficient companies.

PFIZER'S PURSUIT OF COST ECONOMIES IN ITS WYETH ACQUISITION

In 2010 Pfizer began the process of integrating Wyeth into Pfizer. One of the key elements of that process was cost cutting at the combined company's facilities, which would ultimately yield significant synergies. This included closing eight manufacturing sites in Ireland, Puerto Rico, and the United States.[a] It also was able to implement large workforce reductions.

At the end of 2008 Pfizer had over 80,000 employees and Wyeth had under 50,000, with the combined amount being just under 130,000. By the end of 2013 Pfizer had 77,000 workers. More than 50,000 employees were eliminated at the combined company. Some were though layoffs, and others occurred due to restructurings. For example, Pfizer sold Capsugel to KKR for $2.4 billion in cash, and with it Pfizer shed just under 3,000 workers. It then sold off its lower-margin nutrition business to Nestle for $11.9 billion. This unit accounted for over 5,000 jobs. It also spun off its animal health business, Zoetis, and in doing so reduced its workforce by another 10,000.

The acquisition of Wyeth gave Pfizer a number of blockbuster drugs, such as Enbrel and Prevnar, to help offset the loss of Lipitor sales as a result of the end of its patent protection. It also allowed the company to consolidate its R&D efforts that were focused on some of the same illnesses.

Pfizer knew its industry and knew a good amount about Wyeth's business. It had a good idea prior to the merger that it would be able to eliminate many costs, including redundant workers, at Wyeth. It also had a good basis to believe that the revenue stream it was acquiring would remain stable after the merger. This made Wyeth more profitable for Pfizer than Wyeth was as a stand-alone company, which needed all of those redundant costs to operate. This allowed Pfizer to make an attractive offer to Wyeth's shareholders, which they accepted.

[a] "Pfizer Global Manufacturing Announces Plans to Reconfigure Its Global Plant Network," Pfizer Press Release, May 18, 2010.

---

[15] Even though it sported a long and impressive performance record, GE paid a heavy price for its foray into financial services when the subprime crisis took hold in 2007–2008.

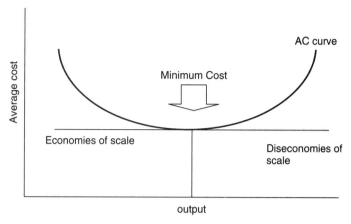

FIGURE 4.1 Economies and Diseconomies of Scale

Figure 4.1, which depicts scale economies and diseconomies, shows that an optimal output level occurs when per-unit costs are at a minimum. This implies that an expansion through the horizontal acquisition of a competitor may increase the size of the acquiring firm's operation and lower per-unit costs.

CONSOLIDATION IN THE CRUISE INDUSTRY AND THE PURSUIT OF ECONOMIES AND OTHER SYNERGIES

Several examples of mergers and acquisitions (M&As) motivated by the pursuit of scale economies have occurred in the cruise industry, which has undergone a series of consolidating M&As. Examples include the 1989 acquisition of Sitmar Cruises by Princess Cruises and the 1994 merger between Radisson Diamond Cruises and Seven Seas Cruises, which enabled the combined cruise lines to offer an expanded product line in the form of more ships, beds, and itineraries while lowering per-bed costs. The cruise industry has learned that a sales force of a given size can service a greater number of ships and itineraries. As cruise lines combine, they find that they do not need to maintain the same size of administrative facilities and sales forces. For example, each cruise line has its own network of district sales managers who call on travel agencies within an area. When one cruise line buys another, one company's sales force may be able to service the combined itineraries of both groups of ships. This enables the acquiring company to purchase the target's projected revenues with less than the target's historical cost structure.

Another example of scale economies related to these cruise mergers is the use of marketing expenditures. Partly because of the size of their fleets the large U.S. cruise lines such as Carnival, Royal Caribbean, and NCL can conduct national

(continued)

(*continued*)

television advertising campaigns. Such campaigns are cost-prohibitive for smaller cruise lines.

Carnival was particularly effective at using M&As to create a full-service cruise line. Originally a low-priced, mass-market cruise line, it has become the largest company in the industry through a broad acquisition program. Its acquisitions include Princess Cruises, Holland American, Seaborne, Winstar, and Costa Cruises. These acquisitions constitute the full range of price points in the industry. Carnival is a lower-priced, mass-market product, while Seaborne is at the opposite end of the price spectrum and offers five-star cruising. Businesses often find it challenging to be everything to all consumers, but Carnival does it well by keeping each cruise line within the overall company a separate and distinct cruise experience for customers.

There is empirical support spanning a long time period for the assertion that M&As are used to achieve operating economies. For example, Lichtenberg and Siegel detected improvements in the efficiency of plants that had undergone ownership changes.[16] In fact, they found that those plants that had performed the worst were the ones that were most likely to experience an ownership change. There is also more recent research that supports these findings. Shahrur examined the returns that occurred around the announcement of 463 horizontal mergers and tender offers over the period 1987–1999. He noticed positive combined bidder/target returns and interpreted these findings to imply that the market saw the deals as efficiency-enhancing.[17] These results are also consistent with the stock market reactions (positive return of 3.06% over a three-day window) detected in Fee and Thomas's analysis of a large sample of 554 horizontal deals over the period 1980–1997.[18]

It should not, however, be concluded that simply because some evidence exists that mergers are associated with operating economies, mergers are the best way to achieve such economies. That proposition is not supported by economic research.

Another concept that is closely related to and sometimes confused with economies of scale is *economies of scope*, which is the ability of a firm to utilize one set of inputs to provide a broader range of products and services. A good example of scope economies arises in the banking industry. In the banking industry, scope economies may be as important as economies of scale in explaining M&As.[19] The pursuit of these economies is one of the factors behind the consolidation within the banking industry that occurred in the fifth merger wave.

---

[16] Frank Lichtenberg and Donald Siegel, "Productivity and Changes in Ownership of Manufacturing Plants," *Brookings Papers on Economic Activity* 3 (1987): 643–683.

[17] Husayn Shahrur, "Industry Structure and Horizontal Takeovers: Analysis of Wealth Effects on Rivals, Suppliers and Corporate Customers," *Journal of Financial Economics* 76, no. 1 (April 2005): 61–98.

[18] C. Edward Fee and Shawn Thomas, "Sources of Gains in Horizontal Mergers: Evidence from Customer, Supplier, and Rival Firms," *Journal of Financial Economics* 74 (December 2004): 423–460.

[19] Loretta J. Mester, "Efficient Product of Financial Services: Scale and Scope Economies," Review, *Federal Reserve Bank of Philadelphia* (January/February 1987): 15–25.

Cost Improvements Through Gains in Purchasing Power

If a combination of two companies yields enhanced purchasing power, this can lead to meaningful reductions in costs. Examples of this can be seen in InBev's acquisition of Anheuser Busch and, to some extent, Mittal's consolidation of steel producers. One benefit of purchasing power enhancement is that it may be less likely to draw the attention of regulators than combinations that will have more apparent effects on consumers.

To test whether horizontal combinations can result on purchasing power improvements Bhattacharyya and Nain analyzed a large sample of deals over the period 1984–2003. They sought to test the impact of horizontal mergers on supplier industries through the impact these deals had on the profits and prices of these companies.[20] They found that horizontal deals reduced the profitability of dependent suppliers and reduced their selling prices over a three-year period following the merger. They also found that supplier industries that were more concentrated prior to the downstream merger experienced greater price declines. This implies that perhaps the merger was designed to achieve what John Galbraith called "countervailing power."[21] More recent research has also found evidence of increased buying power even in conglomerate acquisitions. Green, Kini, and Shenoy analyzed a sample of 785 conglomerate acquisitions over the period 1986–2010.[22] They found evidence of increased buying power over common supplier industries that were supplying inputs to both acquirers and targets.

WACHOVIA: SUCCESSFUL PURSUIT OF SCOPE ECONOMIES IN 2005 FOLLOWED BY A DISASTROUS PURSUIT OF SIZE IN 2006

As discussed, over the past 20 years, the bank we now know as Wachovia grew from a medium-sized bank to the fifth largest bank in the United States. By 2005, Wachovia commanded a huge base of depositors but not the product line width of some of its large competitors. With its large depositor base, Wachovia had a great amount of capital to lend but not enough business opportunities, such as consumer loans, to lend these monies out. In 2000, the Charlotte, North Carolina–based bank sold off its credit card and mortgage divisions due to their poor performance. It used the monies from the sale of these business units to help finance Wachovia's $13.6 billion merger with First Union in 2001. However, it still needed to be able to offer customers services that other major banks offered—credit cards and mortgages.

(continued)

---

[20] Sugato Bhattacharyya and Amrita Nain, "Horizontal Acquisitions and Buying Power: A Product Market Analysis," *Journal of Financial Economics*, 99, 2011, 97–115.

[21] John K. Galbraith, *American Capitalism: The Concept of Countervailing Power* (Boston: Houghton Mifflin) 1952.

[22] Daniel Greene, Omesh Kini and Jaideep Shenoy, "Buyer Power in Conglomerate Acquisitions." Paper presented at the American Finance Association Annual Meetings, 2015.

(continued)

In order to do that, Wachovia entered into agreements with MBNA for credit cards and Countrywide Financial Corp. for mortgages.

In late 2005, Wachovia elected not to renew its five-year agreement with MBNA and started to offer credit cards directly. In September 2005, Wachovia decided to use M&A to accelerate its returns to the consumer finance business by buying Westcorp Inc. for $3.9 billion (Westcorp has a significant auto lending business). This acquisition quickly made Wachovia the ninth largest auto lender in the United States—a position more consistent with its overall size in the market. At the same time, Wachovia also internally expanded its own mortgage lending business while acquiring AmNet, a small West Coast mortgage company, for $83 million.[a] Through a combination of internal development and M&A, Wachovia quickly was able to achieve economies of scope.

The acquisition of Westcorp is a relatively modest deal when compared to the bold acquisition of MBNA, the largest credit card issuer in the United States, by Bank of America in June 2005 for $35 billion. While Wachovia had pursued some negotiations for MBNA, a company that it was familiar and therefore somewhat comfortable with, the price tag of this deal was more than Wachovia wanted to pay for a business that is much riskier than traditional banking. Up to that point Wachovia had acquired a number of smaller companies. In doing so, it acquired the expertise it needed in specialized areas, such as Westcorp's skills in auto lending, while not risking the capital needed to do a megadeal. With these moves, Wachovia had achieved a broader product line without all of the risk that Bank of America assumed with its MBNA deal.[b] However, Wachovia's CEO changed his strategy in 2006 when Wachovia acquired Golden West Financial, the parent company of thrift World Savings, for $25.5 billion. Golden West was the largest issuer of subprime mortgages in the West and Southwest. It boasted a 285-branch network spanning 10 states. Its owners, Marian and Herb Sandler, who bought Golden West in 1964 for $4 million, smiled when they sold the bank at the top of the market to Wachovia, whose CEO referred to Golden West as his "crown jewel." His pursuit of size through M&A proved to be the bank's undoing. He was eventually fired, and Wachovia was sold to Wells Fargo in 2008 for $15 billion. Wachovia's failed M&A strategy carries many lessons. Relatively smaller, strategic deals can fuel profitable growth and steady expansion. However, the aggressive pursuit of size through M&A is fraught with peril.

[a] David Enrich, "Wachovia Re-Enters the Consumer Finance," *Wall Street Journal*, December 14, 2005, B3B.
[b] Exposure to credit card losses would come back to haunt Bank of America in 2010.

Synergy and Acquisition Premiums

In Chapter 15 we discuss the concept of acquisition premiums, which typically are paid in control share acquisitions. This premium is a value in excess of the market value of a company that is paid for the right to control and proportionately enjoy the profits of the business. Bidders often cite anticipated synergy as the reason for the payment of a premium. Given the track record of some acquisitions that have not turned out as anticipated, the market sometimes questions the reasonableness of this synergy, especially when it is used as the justification for an unusually high premium. Synergy requires that the bidder receive gains, such as in the form of performance improvements, that offset the premium.[23] It is hoped that these gains will be realized in the years following the transaction. In order for the premium payment (P) to make sense, the present value of these synergistic gains (SG) must exceed this amount. This relationship is expressed as follows:

$$P < [SG_1/(1+r) + SG_2/(1+r)^2 + \ldots + SG_n/(1+r)^n] \qquad (4.3)$$

where

r risk-adjusted discount rate
n number of periods

One of the complicating factors in rationalizing the payment of a significant premium is that the premium is usually paid up front, with the gains coming over the course of time. The further into the future these gains are realized, the lower their present value. In addition, the higher the discount rate that is used to convert the synergistic gains to present value, the more difficult it is to justify a high premium. If the bidder also anticipates that there will be a significant initial period before the gains begin manifesting themselves, such as when the bidder is trying to merge the two corporate cultures, this pushes the start of the gains further into the future. If a bidder is using a high discount rate and/or does not expect gains to materialize for an extended period of time, it is hard to justify a high premium. Moreover, the higher the premium, the more pressure the combined company is under to realize a high rate of growth in future synergistic gains.

The best situation is when the business is able to realize both revenue enhancement and cost reduction. When a bidder has paid a significant premium, it implicitly assumes more pressure to realize greater revenue enhancement and more cost reductions. The higher the premium, the more of both that is needed.

Throughout the process, the bidder needs to be aware of the actual and anticipated response of competitors. Enhanced revenues may come at the expense of competitors' revenues. It may not be realistic to assume that they will stand still and watch a competitor improve its position at their expense through acquisitions. When a company can demonstrate such performance improvements through M&As, competitors may respond with their own acquisition programs. Once again, the myriad different responses may be somewhat difficult to model, but they, nonetheless, need to be carefully considered. Although it has already been mentioned, it is so important that it is worth mentioning again how easy it is to build a financial model that shows whatever result one wants to see. Assumptions can be built into the valuation models that are developed in Chapter 15 to show both revenue enhancement and cost reductions. As the merged business takes steps to realize the theorized financial gains, it may discover that the financial model building process was the easiest part, whereas working through all the other steps necessary to realize the actual gains proves to be the most difficult task.

---

[23] See Mark L. Sirower, *The Synergy Trap* (New York: Free Press, 1997), 44–81.

Financial Synergy

Financial synergy refers to the impact of a corporate merger or acquisition on the costs of capital to the acquiring firm or the merging partners. Depending on the extent to which financial synergy exists in corporate combinations, the costs of capital may be lowered. Whether the benefits of such financial synergy are really reasonable, however, is a matter of dispute among corporate finance theorists.

As noted, the combination of two firms may reduce risk if the firms' cash flow streams are not perfectly correlated. If the acquisition or merger lowers the volatility of the cash flows, suppliers of capital may consider the firm less risky. The risk of bankruptcy would presumably be less, given the fact that wide swings up and down in the combined firm's cash flows would be less likely.

Higgins and Schall explain this effect in terms of *debt coinsurance*.[24] If the correlation of the income streams of two firms is less than perfectly positively correlated, the bankruptcy risk associated with the combination of the two firms may be reduced. Under certain circumstances one of the firms could experience conditions that force it into bankruptcy. It is difficult to know in advance which one of two possible firms could succumb to this fate. In the event that one of the firms fails, creditors may suffer a loss. If the two firms were combined in advance of financial problems, however, the cash flows of the solvent firm that are in excess of its debt service needs would cushion the decline in the other firm's cash flows. The offsetting earnings of the firm in good condition might be sufficient to prevent the combined firm from falling into bankruptcy and causing creditors to suffer losses.

The problem with the debt-coinsurance effect is that the benefits accrue to debtholders at the expense of equity holders. Debtholders gain by holding debt in a less risky firm. Higgins and Schall observe that these gains come at the expense of stockholders, who lose in the acquisition. These researchers assume that the total returns that can be provided by the combined firm are constant (R_T). If more of these returns are provided to bondholders (R_B), they must come at the expense of stockholders (R_S):

$$R_T = R_S + R_B \qquad (4.4)$$

In other words, Higgins and Schall maintain that the debt-coinsurance effect does not create any new value but merely redistributes gains among the providers of capital to the firm. There is no general agreement on this result. Lewellen, for example, has concluded that stockholders gain from these types of combinations.[25] Other research, however, fails to indicate that the debt-related motives are more relevant for conglomerate acquisitions than for nonconglomerate acquisitions.[26] Studies have shown the existence of a coinsurance effect in bank mergers. Penas and Unal examined 66 bank mergers and looked at the effects of these deals on 282 bonds.[27] They found positive

---

[24] Robert C. Higgins and Lawrence C. Schall, "Corporate Bankruptcy and Conglomerate Mergers," *Journal of Finance* 30, no. 1 (March 1975): 93–113.

[25] Wilbur G. Lewellen, "A Pure Rationale for the Conglomerate Merger," *Journal of Finance* 26, no. 2 (May 1971): 521–545.

[26] Pieter T. Elgers and John J. Clark, "Merger Types and Shareholder Returns: Additional Evidence," *Financial Management* 9, no. 2 (Summer 1980): 66–72.

[27] Maria Fabiana Penas and Haluk Unal, "Gains in Bank Mergers: Evidence from the Bond Markets," *Journal of Financial Economics* 74, no. 1 (October 2004): 149–179.

bond returns for both targets (4.3%) as well as acquiring banks (1.2%). One explanation that may play a role is that larger banks may be "too big to fail," as regulators would not want to allow a larger bank to fail outright and would step in to provide assistance.

Billet, King, and Mauer examined the wealth effects for target and acquirer returns in the 1980s and 1990s.[28] They found that target company bonds that were less than investment grade prior to the deal earned significantly positive announcement period returns. In contrast, acquiring company bonds earned negative announcement period returns. They also found that these announcement period returns were greater in the 1990s compared to the 1980s. These results support the coinsurance effect.

Higgins and Schall show that the stockholders' losses may be offset by issuing new debt after the merger. The stockholders may then gain through the tax savings on the debt interest payments. Galai and Masulis have demonstrated this result.[29] The additional debt would increase the debt-equity ratio of the postmerger firm to a level that stockholders must have found desirable, or at least acceptable, before the merger. With the higher debt-equity ratio, the firm becomes a higher risk–higher return investment.

As noted previously, a company may experience economies of scale through acquisitions. These economies are usually thought to come from production cost decreases, attained by operating at higher capacity levels or through a reduced sales force or a shared distribution system. As a result of acquisitions, *financial* economies of scale may be possible in the form of lower flotation and transaction costs.[30]

In financial markets, a larger company has certain advantages that may lower the firm's cost of capital. It enjoys better access to financial markets, and it tends to experience lower costs of raising capital, presumably because it is considered to be less risky than a smaller firm. Therefore, the costs of borrowing by issuing bonds are lower because a larger firm would probably be able to issue bonds offering a lower interest rate than a smaller company. For many years this was one of the benefits that GE bestowed upon many of its acquired companies. Thus larger companies may provide targets access to an *internal capital market*.[31] This is supported by research which has showed that diversified companies, which tend to be larger than undiversified firms, have better credit quality and better access to capital markets.[32]

Another, more basic way financial synergy can work is when a company with large financial resources and cash holdings but a paucity of high-return projects acquires a "cash-strapped" target with certain high-return projects that it is not capable of funding. Such deals can be a "win-win" for both firms.

---

[28] Matthew T. Billet, Tao-Hsien Dolly King, and David C. Mauer, "Bondholder Wealth Effects in Mergers and Acquisitions," *Journal of Finance* 59, no. 1 (February 2004): 107–135.

[29] Dan Galai and Ronald W. Masulis, "The Option Pricing Model and the Risk Factor of Stock," *Journal of Financial Economics* 3, no. 1/2 (January/March 1976): 53–81.

[30] Haim Levy and Marshall Sarnat, "Diversification, Portfolio Analysis and the Uneasy Case for Conglomerate Mergers," *Journal of Finance* 25, no. 4 (September 1970): 795–802.

[31] Matthew Billet and David Mauer, "Cross Subsidies, External Financial Constraints, and the Contribution of the Internal Capital Market to Firm Value," *Review of Financial Studies*, 16, 2003, 1167–1201 and Murillo Campello, "Internal Capital Markets in Financial Conglomerates: Evidence from Small Bank Responses to Monetary Policy," *Journal of Finance*, 57, 2002, 2773–2805.

[32] Valentin Dimitrov, "Corporate Diversification and Capital Constraints: Real Effects Across the Business Cycle," *Review of Financial Studies*, 19, 2006, 1465–1498.

DIVERSIFICATION

Diversification means growing outside a company's current industry category. This motive played a major role in the acquisitions and mergers that took place in the third merger wave—the conglomerate era. Many of the firms that grew into conglomerates in the 1960s were disassembled through various spin-offs and divestitures in the 1970s and 1980s. This process of *deconglomerization* raises serious doubts as to the value of diversification based on expansion.

Although many companies have regretted their attempts at diversification, others can claim to have gained significantly. Up until recently, one such firm was General Electric (GE). Contrary to what its name implies, for many years now GE has been no longer merely an electronics-oriented company. Through a pattern of acquisitions and divestitures, the firm has become a diversified conglomerate, with operations in insurance, financial services, television stations, plastics, medical equipment, and so on.

During the 1980s and 1990s, at a time when the firm was acquiring and divesting various companies, earnings rose significantly. The market responded favorably to these diversified acquisitions by following the rising pattern of earnings.

Diversification and the Acquisition of Leading Industry Positions

Part of the reasoning behind GE's successful diversification strategy has been the types of companies it has acquired. General Electric sought to acquire leading positions in the various industries in which it owned businesses. Leading is usually interpreted as the first or second rank according to market shares. It is believed by acquirers like GE that the number-one or number-two position provides a more dominant position, which affords advantages over the smaller competitors. These advantages can manifest themselves in a number of ways, including broader consumer awareness in the marketplace as leading positions in distribution. Corporations in the secondary ranks, such as numbers four or five, may sometimes be at such a disadvantage that it is difficult for them to generate rewarding returns. Companies within the overall company framework that do not hold a leading position, and do not have reasonable prospects of cost-effectively acquiring such a position, become candidates for divestiture. The released resources derived from such a divestiture can then be reinvested in other companies to exploit the benefits of their dominant position or used to acquire leading companies in other industries.

GE: WHAT TO DO WHEN YOU CAN'T ACHIEVE A LEADING POSITION

While the General Electric Company has enjoyed great success with acquisitions in many different industries, it has experienced significant difficulty turning a profit in the insurance industry. This was underscored in November 2005, when General Electric (GE) announced that it would sell its reinsurance business to Swiss Re for $8.5 billion. GE's chief executive officer at that time, Jeffrey Immelt, successor to the well-known Jack Welch, indicated that the insurance business was "a tough strategic fit for GE." That business had lost over $700 million in the five years prior to the sale and had required the infusion of $3.2 billion more of GE capital. However, even with the strong financial support of GE, its reinsurance business could not move up in industry rankings relative to leaders Munich Re, Swiss Re, and General Re. GE found the reinsurance business to be volatile and a high demander of capital.

This sale to Swiss Re, which then had combined total revenues of $34 billion, allowed it to overtake Munich Re, which had 2004 sales of just under $29 billion. These two companies are clearly the market leaders as their sales are more than double their nearest rivals, General Re ($10.6 billion) and Hanover Re ($10.1 billion). GE, which marketed its reinsurance business under the name GE Insurance Solutions, had $8.2 billion in total 2004 sales.

For GE this was an admission of failure by a very successful company. GE cut its losses and sold the reinsurance business to another company that was better at it. GE has done this before when an acquisition had failed to achieve expected goals. For example, in 1982, it sold off its Trane air conditioning business, which, with its 10% market share, was an "also-ran" by GE standards and was more trouble than it was worth.[a] In many ways this is a sign of good management, as managers need to know when to cut their losses and focus on areas in which they can achieve greater returns, rather than continue with a failing business just to avoid having to admit mistakes to shareholders. Given the volume of deals that GE does, all of them are not going to be a success. The key is to quickly recognize and admit mistakes and refocus on the winners.

While in some instances GE was quick to recognize poor performance and risk potential, this was not the case in its treatment of its GE Capital unit. For a period the company enjoyed high profits from GE Capital as that unit was able to access cheap capital from the commercial paper and bond market, which it used to engage in aggressive lending. The unit built up a large portfolio of property loans, credit card debt, and other loan investments. When capital markets reversed in the subprime crisis, GE found itself dangerously exposed. The company lost its prized AAA rating and began to shrink its GE Capital division.

[a] Patrick A. Gaughan, *Mergers: What Can Go Wrong and How to Prevent It* (Hoboken, NJ: John Wiley & Sons, 2004), 51–52.

CITIBANK: FINANCIAL SUPERMARKET THE MARKET DID NOT WANT

The recent subprime crisis has underscored the concern about financial institutions that are too big to fail. Banking mergers and acquisitions (M&As) result in larger financial institutions that impose risks on the whole financial system. When a medium-sized financial institution fails, the exposure to the rest of the system is limited. When a large financial institution fails, perhaps one that is large as a result

(continued)

(continued)

of a program of many M&As, the impact of its failure can be far-reaching. When we have several such types of institutions taking similar risks, such as risk directly or indirectly related to mortgage-backed securities, then the exposure of the banking system is greatly magnified. In addition, when banks such as Citigroup become so large and diversified, the demands on management become much greater. When Sandy Weil created the Citigroup financial conglomerate based on a failed growth strategy, and then handed off the management of the giant bank to Charles Prince, an attorney by training and a man poorly equipped to understand and manage such a complex financial institution, it was only a matter of time before problems would manifest themselves. This was exacerbated when one of its directors, the politically savvy Robert Rubin, encouraged the bank to take more risks as a way to elevate its returns. This is just what the bank did, and the rest is history.

Regulators were asleep at the wheel while Weill built a superbank based on a strategy that made little sense. Laws designed to limit the growth of banks into nonbanking businesses were disassembled to allow aggressive growth and risk taking. Regulators were even more asleep when they allowed such an institution to take on so much leverage and invest in risky assets, jeopardizing depositors' assets.

There are many lessons to be learned from Citigroup's failed growth through M&A strategy. However, the history of M&A tells us that such lessons tend to be quickly forgotten.

Diversification to Enter More Profitable Industries

One reason management may opt for diversified expansion is its desire to enter industries that are more profitable than the acquiring firm's current industry. It could be that the parent company's industry has reached the mature stage or that the competitive pressures within that industry preclude the possibility of raising prices to a level where extranormal profits can be enjoyed.

One problem that some firms may encounter when they seek to expand by entering industries that offer better profit opportunities is the lack of an assurance that those profit opportunities will persist for an extended time in the future. Industries that are profitable now may not be as profitable in the future. Competitive pressures serve to bring about a movement toward a long-term equalization of rates of return across industries. Clearly, this does not mean that the rates of return in all industries at any moment in time are equal. The forces of competition that move industries to have equal returns are offset by opposing forces, such as industrial development, that cause industries to have varying rates of return. Those above-average-return industries that do not have imposing barriers to entry will experience declining returns until they reach the cross-industry average.

Economic theory implies that in the long run only industries that are difficult to enter will have above-average returns. This implies that a diversification program to enter more profitable industries will not be successful in the long run. The expanding firm may not be able to enter those industries that exhibit persistently above-average returns because of barriers that prevent entry, and may be able to enter only the industries with low barriers. When entering the low-barrier industry, the expanding company will probably be forced to compete against other entrants who were attracted by temporarily above-average returns and low barriers. The increased number of competitors will drive down returns and cause the expansion strategy to fail.

MONTANA POWER: FAILED CORPORATE TRANSFORMATION

The story of Montana Power is one of a company that existed for decades as a stable but slow-growth power utility. During the 1990s, its management began the process of transforming it into a telecommunications company. The end result was a disaster.

Montana Power was founded in 1912. It moved into oil and gas in the 1930s and then expanded into coal in the 1950s. Its initial entry into the telecommunications business began in the 1980s, when it took advantage of the breakup of AT&T. It slowly began to expand its position in the telecommunications business by laying more fiber and building more of its own network.

In February 2001, the company eventually sold off its "boring" power utility business for $1.3 billion and invested the proceeds into a high-flying telecommunications business called Touch America. The energy distribution business was sold to NorthWestern Corporation for $612 million in cash plus the assumption of $488 million in debt.[a] The monies from the sale were invested in Touch America's telecom business. In August 2000, PanCanadian Petroleum Ltd. agreed to purchase Montana Power's oil and gas business for $475 million.[b] This acquisition increased PanCanadian's oil field capacity by providing it with properties in Alberta, Montana, and Colorado. It was indicated by PanCanadian that the accrued fields had reserves of 550 billion cubic feet of gas and 20 million barrels of crude oil. In the summer of 2000, Touch America then entered into a deal to buy Quest's in-region long-distance network, which regulatory constraints forced Quest to divest pursuant to an agreement related to its acquisition of U.S. West—one of the seven superregionals that were formed in the breakup of AT&T. This $200 million deal gave Touch America long-distance operations in 14 states with sales of approximately $300 million in revenues and 250,000 customers.[c]

After the sell-off of the power utility business, Montana Power changed its name to Touch America Holdings Inc. The company was traded on the New York Stock Exchange. For a while it was highly touted by the market and the industry.[d] Touch America started off as a growing, largely debt-free company in a growing industry. Initially, it seemed that the combination of rapid growth without debt pressures made Touch America highly desirable. However, all was not well in the telecom sector and Touch America's fate declined with the industry. While its 2001 results were impressive, in the second and third quarters of 2002 the company generated losses of $32.3 million and $20.9 million. This occurred even though revenues increased. At the time Touch America sold off its utility business, its stock was as high as $65 per share. By the third quarter of 2003, the stock had fallen to $0.53 per share and was delisted.[e]

(continued)

(continued)

Like many companies in the telecom sector, Touch America had invested heavily in network expansion and fiber laying throughout the 1990s and early 2000s. Billions of dollars were spent on laying fiber-optic cable as telecom and nontelecom companies expanded. The result is that 360 networks held over 87,000 miles of fiber-optic cable, linking urban areas in North America, Asia, and South America.[f] Touch America was one such company. The overcapacity in the industry fueled increased competition and declining margins. Only the more savvy companies would survive, and newcomer Touch America was not one of them. Touch America finally filed for Chapter 11 bankruptcy protection on June 19, 2003, but assets were eventually put up for sale despite the objections of various creditors.

[a] "Montana Power and Northwestern in $612 Million Deal," *New York Times*, October 3, 2000.
[b] "PanCanadian Will Acquire Oil and Gas Assets," *New York Times*, August 29, 2000.
[c] "Unit of Montana Power Is Buying Quest Phone Business," *New York Times*, March 17, 2000.
[d] Steve Skobel, "Rising Starts," *Telecom Business*, July 1, 2001.
[e] Matt Gouras, "Touch America Trading Suspended: Company Made Disastrous Move into Telecommunications," Associated Press Newswires, March 29, 2003.
[f] Lucy I. Vento, "Who Will Profit from the U.S. Fiber Network Glut?" *Business Communications Review*, September 1, 2001.

Positive Evidence of Benefits of Conglomerates

Many studies question the risk-reduction benefits of conglomerates. However, some studies cast the wealth effects of conglomerates in a better light. For example, one study by Elger and Clark has shown that returns to stockholders in conglomerate acquisitions are greater than in nonconglomerate acquisitions.[33]

The study, which examined 337 mergers between 1957 and 1975, found that conglomerate mergers provided superior gains relative to nonconglomerate mergers. The researchers reported these gains for both buyer and seller firms, with substantial gains registered by stockholders of seller firms and moderate gains for buying company stockholders. This finding was supported by later research by Wansley, Lane, and Yang. They focused on 52 nonconglomerate and 151 conglomerate mergers. It was also found, however, that returns to shareholders were larger in horizontal and vertical acquisitions than in conglomerate acquisitions.[34]

---

[33] Peter T. Elgers and John J. Clark, "Merger Types and Shareholder Returns: Additional Evidence," *Financial Management* 9, no. 2 (Summer 1980): 66–72.
[34] James Wansley, William Lane, and Ho Yang, "Abnormal Returns to Acquired Firms by Type of Acquisition and Method of Payment," *Financial Management* 12, no. 3 (Autumn 1983) 16–22.

Is There a Diversification Discount?

Using the aforementioned large sample drawn from the 1960s, Henri Servaes compared the Tobin's qs of diversified firms to those that were not diversified. He found no evidence that diversification increased corporate values. On the contrary, he found that the Tobin's qs for diversified firms were significantly lower than those for multisegment companies. Other research has found that the diversification discount was not restricted to the conglomerate era. A study conducted by Berger and Ofek, using a large sample of firms over the 1986–1991 sample period, found that diversification resulted in a loss of firm value that averaged between 13% and 15%.[35] This study estimated the imputed value of a diversified firm's segments as if they were separate firms. The results found that the loss of firm value was not affected by firm size but was less when the diversification occurred within related industries. The loss of firm value results were buttressed by the fact that the diversified segments showed lower operating profitability than single-line businesses. The results also showed that diversified firms overinvested in the diversified segments more than single-line businesses. This implies that overinvestment may be a partial cause of the loss of value associated with diversification.

Value-reducing effects of diversification were detected by Lang and Stulz.[36] Using a large sample of companies (in excess of 1,000), Lang and Stulz found that greater corporate diversification in the 1980s was inversely related to the Tobin's q of these firms. Like Berger and Ofek, when these findings are combined with those of Lang and Stulz, we see that diversification often lowers firm values. This conclusion, however, is not universally accepted by finance researchers. Villalonga believes that the diversification discount is merely an artifact of the data used by these researchers.[37] He states that the data used by these researchers were artificially restricted by the Financial Accounting Standards Board definition of segments as well as requirements that only segments that constitute 10% or more of a company's business are required to be reported. Using a data source that is not affected by this problem, Villalonga finds a diversification premium, as opposed to a discount. As we will discuss further, this is issue is a complicated one and it is hard to draw broad generalizations about diversification which universally apply.

Focus Hypothesis

Other studies have tackled the problem differently. Comment and Jarrell analyzed a sample of exchange-listed firms from 1978 to 1989. They found that increased corporate focus or specialization was consistent with shareholder wealth maximization.[38] They

---

[35] Philip Berger and Eli Ofek, "Diversification Effect on Firm Value," *Journal of Financial Economics*, 37 (1), January 1995, 39–65.

[36] Larry Lang and Rene Stulz, "Tobin's q, Corporate Diversification and Firm Performance," *Journal of Political Economy* 102, no. 6 (December 1994): 1248–1280.

[37] Belen Villalonga, "Diversification Discount or Premium? New Evidence from the Business Information Tracking Series," *Journal of Finance* 59, no. 2 (April 2004): 479–506.

[38] Robert Comment and Gregg Jarrell, "Corporate Focus and Stock Returns," *Journal of Financial Economics* 37, no. 1 (January 1995): 67–87.

concluded that the commonly cited benefits of diversification, economies of scope, go unrealized and that the access to greater internal capital does not appear to affect the diversified firm's propensity to pursue external capital. One "benefit" of diversification that was found was that diversified firms tend to be targets of hostile takeovers less frequently than their less diversified counterparts. Nonetheless, diversified firms were more active participants, as both buyers and sellers, in the market for corporate control.

Some studies have explored the issue of which firms are the most likely to diversify. These studies have shown the poorer performing firms are more likely to diversify than their better performing counterparts.[39] One would think that if this is true, it is motivated by managers of relatively poorly performing companies trying to enter industries that generate higher returns. Critics of the diversification discount point to this research as saying that the studies that find such a discount are not controlling for endogenous factors stemming from poorly performing firms doing the acquisitions and possibly extending their poor management to the diversified entities they acquire. However, studies that have attempted to control for these endogenous factors also find a diversification discount.[40]

TYPES OF FOCUS INCREASES

A study by Dasilas and Leventi analyzed the types of focus-increasing spin-offs that had the greatest positive shareholder wealth effects.[41] Their research compared spin-offs that increased industrial focus with those that increased geographical focus. Spin-offs that increased industrial focus generated positive shareholder wealth effects, while those that increased geographical focus did not. In addition, the positive market response to increases in industrial focus was greater for U.S. spin-offs than it was for European deals.

FOCUS INCREASING ASSET SALES INCREASE FIRM VALUES

When companies notice their market values are below the values that would result from determining the estimated market value of all their major business units as stand-alone entities, they may look to asset sales to raise their equity price. John and Ofek used several accounting measures of performance, such as operating margins and return on assets, to determine if a company performance improved after it sold off assets.[42] They

[39] Jose M. Campa and Simi Kedia, "Is There a Diversification Discount?" *Journal of Finance* 57 (2002): 1731–1762; and David Hyland, "Why Firms Diversify: An Empirical Examination," Working Paper, University of Texas, Arlington, 1999.

[40] Owen A. Lamont and Christopher Polk, "Does Diversification Destroy Value? Evidence from Industry Shocks," *Journal of Financial Economics* 63, no. 1 (January 2002): 51–77.

[41] Apostolos Dasilas and Stergios Leventi, "Wealth Effects and Operating Performance of Spin-Offs: International Evidence" (Working Paper, International Hellenic University, Greece, 2010).

[42] Kose John and Eli Ofek, "Asset Sales and Increase in Focus," *Journal of Financial Economics* 37, no. 1 (January 1995): 105–126.

compared 321 divestitures that resulted in greater focus with ones that did not. They found that only those firms in their sample that had greater focus after the assets sales showed improved performance. Those that sold assets but did not have an increase in focus failed to show improved performance. Thus, their conclusion is that it is the focus-enhancing effects of the divestitures, not just the simple act of a divestiture, that are the source of the value gains. These value gains can then serve to undo the diversification discount.

EXPLANATION FOR THE DIVERSIFICATION DISCOUNT

On the surface, we may be led to simply conclude that diversification itself destroys value. We can easily think of some very logical explanations for this destruction process. Perhaps it is the greater managerial demands of a diverse and less focused enterprise that limit the potential of diverse companies. Perhaps it is simply wasteful managers who pursue diverse M&As for their own self-interests. For example, the larger diversified company might compensate its senior managers much better and allow them to believe they were great *empire builders*. However, could it also be the greater analytical demands such enterprises present for market analysts who may be inclined to assign them lower valuations compared to more focused business?

Many analysts specialize in a type of business. For example, in its heyday, Altria was followed by tobacco analysts, who covered the Philip Morris part of the business, but also food analysts, who covered the Kraft side. Investors had to put the two together when assessing the investment prospects of the overall entity. The problem was even more challenging when Altria owned Miller beer and beer industry analysts had to chime in with their thoughts about this relatively weaker business.

An interesting study by Lamont and Polk of a large sample of 2,390 diverse firms, covering the 19-year period of 1979 through 1997, raises some questions regarding a simple explanation for value destruction of diverse companies.[43] Among their various findings was that companies with discounts have *higher* subsequent returns than companies that trade at a premium! Could it be that the market is incorrectly assigning discounts that turn out to be wrongfully assigned when the diverse firms end up generating higher returns than what the discounts implied?

The Lamont and Polk story does not eliminate the challenges to diversified firms. Their analysis focused on just returns; there are many other measures, such as profitability, capital expenditures, and other fundamental measures, that may give support for the traditional explanations of the diversification discount, such as irrational managers, productivity, corporate waste, and so on. However, for adherents of behavioral finance, whose ranks have been rapidly growing, one additional explanation for the diversification discount may be that the market irrationally undervalues diverse companies. At a minimum, the Lamont and Polk research sheds light on the complexity of the *diversification puzzle*.

---

[43] Owen Lamont and Christopher Polk, "The Diversification Discount: Cash Flows versus Returns," *Journal of Finance* 56, no. 5 (October 2001): 1693–1721.

Related versus Unrelated Diversification

Diversification does not mean conglomerization. That is, it is possible to diversify into fields that are related to the buyer's business. An example of a related diversification occurred in 1994, when Merck purchased Medco. Merck is one of the largest pharmaceutical companies in the world, and Medco is the largest marketer of pharmaceuticals in the United States. The two businesses are different in that one company is a manufacturer and the other company is a distributor. Nonetheless, the two companies are both in the broadly defined pharmaceutical industry, and each has a greater knowledge of the other's business than an outside firm would have. In addition, there may be a more reliable expectation of economies of scale and scope in related diversifications because a buyer may be better able to leverage its current resources and expertise if it stays closer to its current business activities. However, while these two companies were leaders in their respective segments of the drug industry, their combination did not yield synergistic benefits. Merck assumed that in the world of managed care, owning a company such as Medco would provide it competitive advantages. Indeed, shortly after the Merck-Medco merger in 1994, some of Merck's competitors thought the same, as Roche acquired Syntex Corp. for $5.3 billion and Eli Lilly bought PCS Health Systems for $4.1 billion. Unfortunately, relatedness was not enough to ensure success, and Merck and Medco had to later undo the deal after concluding that they did not understand the regulatory environment that would not allow Medco to influence the usage by physicians and consumers of its drugs. This eliminated certain synergistic benefits.

It is not always clear when another business is related in a meaningful way. One example put forward by Young and Morck is the 3M Corp.[44] 3M is well known for its brand of Scotch tape. However, the company also extends this success to marketing of other related products, such as Post-it notes as well as other tape products. This company was able to extend its brand name to other products whose manufacturing and marketing have some commonalities with its main business activities.

The track record of related acquisitions is significantly better than that of unrelated acquisitions. Morck, Shleifer, and Vishny found that the market punished shareholders in companies that engaged in unrelated acquisitions, whereas shareholders in companies that made related acquisitions did significantly better.[45] Their study of 326 acquisitions between 1975 and 1987 presented a more favorable picture of this type of diversification. Rather, a particular form of diversification, unrelated diversification, showed poor results. They measured relatedness by determining if the two firms had at least one of their top three lines of business in the same Standard Industrial Classification (SIC) code. Not all the research on related diversification shows the same results. For example, the result found by Agrawal, Jaffe, and Mandelker was the opposite of the result

---

[44] Bernard Young and Randall Morck, "When Synergy Creates Real Value," in *Mastering Strategy* (Upper Saddle River, NJ: Financial Times Press, 1999).

[45] Randall Morck, Andrei Shleifer, and Robert Vishny, "Do Managerial Objectives Drive Bad Acquisitions?" *Journal of Finance* 45, no. 1 (March 1990): 31–48.

of Morck, Shleifer, and Vishny. Their result showed that unrelated acquisitions outperformed related acquisitions.[46] The market performance of diversified firms is discussed later in this chapter.

Atkas, de Bodt, and Roll showed that for companies and CEOs who engage in multiple acquisitions, the average time between deals was greater for related deals.[47] One reasonable explanation for this is that related targets present the potential of more synergistic gains and thereby are more likely to bring about an auction process that may consume more time and generate higher premiums for their shareholders.

LVMH: IS LUXURY RELATED?

If the track record of related diversifications is better than unrelated, then how do we define *related*? This is not that obvious and, unfortunately, is open to interpretation. If it is misinterpreted, it can result in losses for shareholders. One such example was LVMH's fifth merger wave expansion strategy. LVMH, which stands for Louis Vuitton, Moet, and Hennessy, led by its flamboyant chief executive officer (CEO), Bernard Arnault, seems to see any connection to luxury to be related. The Paris-based company went on an acquisition binge that focused on a wide variety of companies that marketed products or services to upper-end customers. This led them to acquire such major brand names as Chaumet jewelry, Dom Perignon (part of Moet), Fendi, Givenchy, Donna Karan, Loewe leather goods, Sephora, TAG Heuer, Thomas Pink shirts, and Veuve Cliquot champagne. The company has become a clearinghouse for luxury products, but the combination of various acquired companies has provided few, if any, synergies. Many of the acquired businesses, such as Fendi and Donna Karan, while major international brands, generated few profits. In November 1999, LVMH stretched the luxury-related connection by buying fine art auctioneer Phillips de Pury & Luxembourg for $115 million. However, in doing so, Arnault violated several rules of merger success. First, he acquired a company that was a distant third behind Sotheby's and Christie's. Second, he stretched the definition of related so far that there were no possible synergies. Finally he acquired a company that needed a large cash infusion with little potential for it to be recouped. As with many other failed deals, CEO Arnault went unchecked by his directors, and shareholders paid the price. LVMH eventually admitted this failure and sold off the art auctioneering company at a loss. Clearly, defining *related* as any luxury good or service was a faulty strategy. Relatedness is a subjective concept; the more narrow the definition, the more likely the deal will be successful.

The LVMH that we see today seems to have stood the test of time even though its strategy raises some questions. As Figure A shows, it is quite diversified within the so-called luxury market. It also is quite diversified internationally (see Figure B). Its global strength and reputation helped it successfully expand into markets such as Asia.

(continued)

---

[46] Anup Agrawal, Jeffrey F. Jaffe, and Geherson N. Mandelker, "The Post-Merger Performance of Acquiring Firms: A Reexamination of an Anomaly," *Journal of Finance 47*, no. 4 (September 1992): 1605–1671.

[47] Nihat Atkas, Eric de Bodt, and Richard Roll, "The Elapsed Time between Acquisitions," unpublished working paper, March 2008.

(continued)

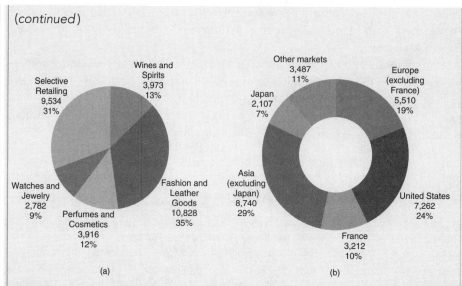

(a)   (b)

FIGURE (A) 2014 LVMH Revenue by business group and (B) Revenue by geographic region (in millions of Euros). *Source*: Consolidated Financial Statements of LVMH Group, December 31, 2014.

One of the benefits of being a large international luxury conglomerate has been the ability to grow by taking advantage of all available global alternatives. We see in Figures C and D that while the global recession slowed LVMH's revenue and profit growth in 2009, the company recovered impressively. Thus while we can question the company's strategy of being a luxury conglomerate that combines various dissimilar products, such as liquor, jewelry and fashion goods, the financial performance does, nonetheless, show some benefits.

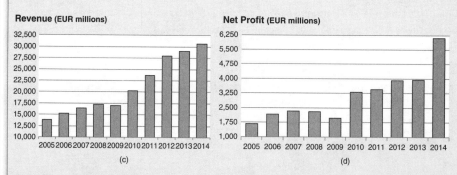

(c)   (d)

FIGURE (C) LVMH Revenue (in millions of Euros). (D) Net Profit (in millions of Euros). *Source*: Consolidated Financial Statements of LVMH Group, December 31, 2014.

DO DIVERSIFIED OR FOCUSED FIRMS DO BETTER ACQUISITIONS?

We have examined the benefits and costs of a diversified, as opposed to more focused brsiness structure. However, a separate question is which typed of companies, diversified or focused, are better at M&A. Cihan and Tice analyzed a large sample of 1,810 deals over the period 1981–2010.[48] They found that diversified firms had 1.5% higher announcement returns than single segment bidders. They then went on try to find the source of the higher value for diversified acquriers. They conducted a regression analysis in which post-merger performance measures reflecting profitability and costs were regressed against bidder's diversification status and pre-merger performance. They found, for example, "that SG&A is 1.8% to 2.6% lower for firms with diversified acquirers than for firms with focused acquirers."[49] The combined companies where the bidder was diversified had higher profit margins and lower costs. These results imply that diversified acquirers are better able to implement postdeal efficiency improvements compared to more focused bidders.

 ## OTHER ECONOMIC MOTIVES

In addition to economies of scale and diversification benefits, there are two other economic motives for M&As: horizontal integration and vertical integration. *Horizontal integration* refers to the increase in market share and market power that results from acquisitions and mergers of rivals. *Vertical integration* refers to the merger or acquisition of companies that have a buyer-seller relationship.

Horizontal Integration

Combinations that result in an increase in market share may have a significant impact on the combined firm's market power. Whether market power actually increases depends on the size of the merging firms and the level of competition in the industry. Economic theory categorizes industries within two extreme forms of market structure. On one side of this spectrum is pure competition, which is a market that is characterized by numerous buyers and sellers, perfect information, and homogeneous, undifferentiated products. Given these conditions, each seller is a price taker with no ability to influence market price. On the other end of the industry spectrum is monopoly, which is an industry with one seller. The monopolist has the ability to select the price-output combination that maximizes profits. Of course, the monopolist is not guaranteed a profit simply because it is insulated from direct competitive pressures. The monopolist may or may not earn a profit, depending on the magnitude of its costs relative to revenues

---

[48] Mehmet Cihan and Sheri Tice, "Do Diversified or Focused Firms Make Better Acquisitions," Paper Presented at the American Finance Associations Annual Meetings, 2015.
[49] Ibid

at the optimal "profit-maximizing" price-output combination. Within these two ends of the industry structure spectrum is monopolistic competition, which features many sellers of a somewhat differentiated product. Closer to monopoly, however, is oligopoly, in which there are a few (i.e., 3 to 12) sellers of a differentiated product. Horizontal integration involves a movement from the competitive end of the spectrum toward the monopoly end.

HORIZONTAL INTEGRATION: MOBIL MERGER WITH EXXON

In December 1998, Exxon announced that it was merging with the Mobil Oil Company. The $82 billion merger created the world's largest oil company. Both companies were vertically integrated with substantial oil reserves and a broad retail network. In spite of their substantial size, the companies were able to convince regulators that the new oil behemoth would not stifle competition.

One of the difficulties in a merger between companies the size of these two firms is the postmerger integration. To achieve the synergistic gains predicted to the media at the time of the deal, two companies must be able to successfully integrate their varied resources. At the time of the Exxon-Mobil deal the companies predicted merger savings on the order of $3.8 billion. In what was a little unusual for such megamergers, less than two years later the combined Exxon Mobil announced that merger savings would be approximately 20% higher—$4.6 billion. The success of this deal, along with concerns that they would be left at a competitive disadvantage, led several of their competitors to do their own deals (see Table A).

TABLE A Revenue of Merger Companies in the Oil Industry as of 2009

	Revenue of Merger Companies in the Oil Industry		
	Revenue	Oil Reserves	Gas Reserves
Company	($ billions)	(million barrels)	(billions cubic feet)
Exxon-Mobil	$310.6	7,744	32,610
Royal Dutch Shell	278.2	3,776	40,895
BP-Amoco	246.1	5,492	41,130
Chevron-Texaco	171.6	7,087	22,140

With the greatly increased size of the combined Exxon Mobil entity, the deal set off a series of horizontal combinations in the industry. One of the measures of economic power in the industry is the ownership of reserves. This led British Petroleum (BP) to buy the Atlantic Richfield Company (ARCO) in 1999 for $26.8 billion. In the next year Chevron bought Texaco for $36 billion, expanding its oil supplies, for which it enjoyed significant profits at the end of the decade as oil prices rose sharply. Even with these combinations, Exxon Mobil still led the industry by a wide margin. The success of this deal was underscored when in 2009 Exxon Mobil announced the highest annual profits of any corporation in history. The company's

2008 annual profits were $45.2 billion on sales of $459 billion, making it the largest company in the United States (Number 2 in 2014). However, in recent years, such as 2011–2013 Exxon revenues have been declining from $467 million to $420 million. Profits also have been declining from $42 billion in 2011 to $33 billion in 2014. Indeed the figure below confirm that crucial role that oil prices play in Exxon's profitability.

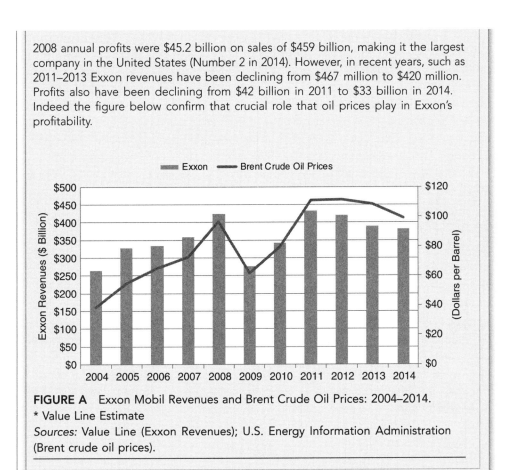

FIGURE A Exxon Mobil Revenues and Brent Crude Oil Prices: 2004–2014.
* Value Line Estimate
Sources: Value Line (Exxon Revenues); U.S. Energy Information Administration (Brent crude oil prices).

Market Power

Market power, which is sometimes referred to as monopoly power, is defined as the ability to set and maintain price above competitive levels. Because in the long run sellers in a competitive industry earn only a normal return and do not earn "economic rent," competitive firms set price equal to marginal cost. Market power refers to the ability to set price in excess of marginal cost. Abba Lerner developed what has been known as the *Lerner index,* which measures the magnitude of the difference between price and marginal cost relative to price. Simply having a positive difference between price and marginal cost, however, does not guarantee profits, because fixed costs could be sufficiently high that the firm generates losses.

$$\text{Lerner index} = P - MC/P \tag{4.5}$$

where:

P = price, and
MC = marginal cost.

There are three sources of market power: product differentiation, barriers to entry, and market share. Through horizontal integration, a company is able to increase its market share. It could be the case that even with a substantial increase in market share, the lack of significant product differentiation or barriers to entry could prevent a firm from being able to raise its price significantly above marginal cost. If an industry does not possess imposing barriers to entry, raising price above marginal cost may only attract new competitors who will drive price down toward marginal costs. Even in industries that have become more concentrated, there may be a substantial amount of competition. In addition, if prices and profits rise too high, new entrants may enter such contestable markets quickly, raising the degree of competition.

Empirical Evidence on M&As and Market Power

Research in this area has approached the question of whether M&As increase market power using two broad methodologies. One focuses on the stock price effects of rivals of the merged companies whereas other studies focused on product prices. If a merger results increased market power for the combined company, we would expect a positive stock price effect for the bidder. Indeed, if the industry became more concentrated after the combination and competitors also benefited from greater market power, we would expect their stock prices to rise as well. Unfortunately, just focusing on stock price effects does not enable us to discern if the cause of the positive response was due to greater market power, or increased efficiency, or both. Thus, stock price studies alone will not allow us to conclude that a positive equity market response was due to the greater market power.

Early studies by Stillman and also by Eckbo found that rival firms received either zero or some positive stock market responses to horizontal merger announcements.[50] The Stillman and also the Eckbo study sample periods were ones that featured more aggressive antitrust enforcement than in the years that followed. Schumann analyzed a sample of 37 merger proposals that were challenged by the FTC over the years 1981–1987.[51] While the time period and the level of antitrust enforcement was very different in the Schumann sample compared to the Stillman and Eckbo study periods, the results were similar. Schumann detected a statistically significant positive stock price effect around the announcement of the deal but no effect in response to the filing of the antitrust complaint. Once again, the market power collusive hypothesis was not supported. A later study by Eckbo expanded the time period and number of horizontal merger proposals and actually found a negative stock market response—which clearly provides no support for the market power hypothesis.[52]

[50] Robert S. Stillman, "Examining Antitrust Policy Towards Horizontal Mergers," *Journal of Financial Economics* 11, no. 1 (April 1983): 225–240; and B. Espen Eckbo, "Horizontal Mergers, Collusion and Stockholder Wealth," *Journal of Financial Economics* 11, no. 1 (April 1983): 241–273; and B. Epsen Eckbo, "Horizontal Mergers, Collusion and Stockholder Wealth," *Journal of Financial Economics* 11, no. 1 (April 1983): 241–273.
[51] Laurence Schumann, "Patterns of Abnormal Returns and the Competitive Effects of Horizontal Mergers," *Review of Industrial Organization* 8, 1993, 679–696.
[52] B. Espen Eckbo, "Mergers and Market Concentration Doctrine: Evidence from the Capital Markets," *Journal of Business*, 58, 1985, 325=349.

Some studies focused upon specific industries, and their findings were similar to the broad-based studies of Stillman and Eckbo. Becher, Mulherin, and Walking, which found negative industry wealth effects when analyzing horizontal mergers in the electric utility industry.[53] Akdogu detected similar effects when he studied the telecommunications industry.[54]

Several other studies examined the effects in markets outside of the United States. These studies found negative stock price effects for rivals. For example, using a U.S.-Canadian sample, Eckbo found such negative industry wealth effects on rivals following horizontal merger announcements.[55] In a sample drawn from the European Union, Aktas, de Bodt, and Roll also found negative abnormal returns when analyzing a sample of horizontal mergers, several of which were challenged on antitrust grounds.[56]

When we consider the variety of studies that are broad-based, industry-specific, and international in their perspective, it seems clear that there is little support for the view that firms merge to collude and achieve monopoly power. This does not mean that this never occurs. It simply means that in general this is not the case.

Other research went on to focus on the role of consumers and suppliers. First focusing on rival firms, both Fee and Thomas and also Shahrur reported positive shareholder wealth effects around the merger announcements. Fee and Thomas analyzed a sample of 554 horizontal transactions over the period 1980–1997.[57] They used accounting rules that require reporting of data on customers, which comprise 10% of more of a given public company's sales. They also traced the sales of suppliers. The question they were addressing was what was the source of the positive stock market response? Both Fee and Thomas as well as Shahrur determined that price increases for customers were not the source of the positive stock market responses. However, when focusing on suppliers the results were different. Both Fee and Thomas and and Sharhur did find evidence of losses to suppliers, which implies the positive shareholder wealth effects may come from some monopsonist buying power. Fee and Thomas, who analyzed a sample of 463 horizontal mergers and tender offers over the period 1987–1999, went on to explore further the source of the supplier losses. They found that the losses came from the termination of the supply relationship. When the relationship remained intact, suppliers did not incur losses. In other words, if the M&A causes the supplier to "lose the account," they will incur losses—a very common sense outcome.

Structural Remedies and Horizontal Mergers

Companies pursuing horizontal M&As may encounter antitrust concerns from regulators which may require them to implement structural remedies such as the sale

[53] David Becher, J. Harold Mulherin, and Ralph A. Walking, "Industry Shocks and Merger Activity: An Analysis of U.S. Public Utilities," Drexel University working paper, 2008.

[54] Evrim Akdogu, "Gaining a Competitive Edge through Acquisitions: Evidence from the Telecommunications Industry," *Journal of Corporate Finance* 15, no. 1 (February 2009): 99–112.

[55] B. Espen Eckbo, "Mergers and the Value of Antitrust Deterrence," *Journal of Finance* 47 (1992): 1005–1029.

[56] Nihat Atkas, Eric de Bodt, and Richard Roll, "Was European M&A Regulation Protectionist?", *Economic Journal* 117, no. 522 (July 2007): 1096–1121.

[57] C. Edward Fee and Shawn Thomas, "Sources of Gains in Horizontal Takeovers: Evidence from Customer, Supplier, and Rival Firms," *Journal of Financial Economics* 74, no. 3 (December 2004): 423–460.

of specific units. Nain and Qian analyzed a sample of 1,153 horizontal mergers over the period 1980–2010.[58] They found that post-merger increase in product prices was smaller when the deal was accompanied by divestitures as opposed to not having to dispose of assets. This limit on price inceases was greater when the buyer of the assets was outside the industry of the merged companies. These results seem to confirm that structure remidies, such as asset sales, do limit market power.

Horizontal Integration, Consolidation, and Roll-Up Acquisition Programs

The 1990s featured a consolidation within certain industries. Many of these deals involved larger companies buying smaller rivals in a series of acquisitions. The acquired companies were then combined into an ever-growing larger company. Such deals are sometimes referred to as *roll-up acquisitions*.

The market of the 1990s liked roll-ups, although not as much as they were enamored with Internet companies. The typical market that was attractive to consolidators was one that featured many relatively smaller competitors in an industry that was fragmented and unconcentrated. Many of the targets in such industries, such as those in the bus transportation or the funeral home business, were closely held. The owners lacked liquidity, and being acquired by a large public company enabled them to convert their illiquid closely held shares into a more liquid asset. Consolidators were able to convince the market that the large-scale acquisition of these smaller targets would enable the combined company to realize scale economies while also enhancing sales through a greater ability to service national clients. The scale economies were supposed to have many sources, including increased buying power that a national company would have compared to a small regional firm. A whole host of roll-up companies were formed in the United States during the fifth wave, with names such as Coach USA, Metals USA, and Floral USA.

For many of the privately held sellers, the dream of liquidity combined with an attractive premium proved to be a nightmare. This was the case in the funeral home industry, where big consolidators like Service Corp. and Leowen encountered financial problems; Leowen eventually had to file for Chapter 11 bankruptcy protection. Many consolidators were good at only one thing—doing deals. They were not good managers, and it took the market a long time to come to this realization.

Serial Acquirers and Corporate Acquisitions Programs

Roll-up acquisitions are a form of serial acquisitions. With roll-ups companies in fragmented industries are combined by dealmakers to form larger, typically national, companies. Serial acquirers engage in an acquisition program that may not involve consolidation. Cisco is one example of a successful serial acquirer. Oracle has also used a pattern of M&A to greatly expand its position in its industry. While these companies may be able

---

[58] Amrita Nain and Yiming Qian, "The Role of Divestitures in Horizontal Mergers: Evidence from Product and Stock Markets," Paper Presented at the American Finance Association Annual Meetings 2015.

to cite M&As as a source of some of their success, the track record of serial acquirers is not that favorable. Indeed Aktas, de Bodt, and Roll show that returns to acquiring firms and their CEOs are declining as a function of the number of the deals they do.[59]

WORLDCOM

One classic example of a consolidation acquisition program is the acquisitions of WorldCom, formerly LDDS, over the second half of the 1980s and the 1990s. WorldCom, based in Jackson, Mississippi, was formed through a series of more than 40 acquisitions, culminating in the $37 billion acquisition of MCI in 1998. Many of these deals were acquisitions of regional long-distance telecommunication resellers, who added more minutes to WorldCom's market clout while bringing a regionally based sales force to service the acquired market. It is ironic that WorldCom was a telecommunications business owned by ITT that was later acquired by LDDS. ITT was a conglomerate that underwent a series of downsizing transactions (see Chapter 10), whereas LDDS went on to grow horizontally to become the second leading long-distance company in the U.S. market. In paying a high price for MCI, which enabled it to outbid British Telecom, WorldCom asserted that it would realize significant cost savings from combining these two long-distance companies.

WorldCom is a classic example of a company run by a chief executive officer (Bernie Ebbers) who was a good dealmaker but a bad manager. The company's board was asleep at the wheel and allowed its CEO to pursue deals when the company was already of a sufficient size. They also allowed him to continue to run the company when he was clearly out of his element. He continued to pursue deals, but the company became so large that meaningful deals, such as the proposed acquisition of Sprint, were halted by antitrust regulators. It has been alleged that management resorted to illegal means to try to manufacture profits that it could not otherwise achieve. The end result of this acquisition program was an inefficient company that spiraled into the largest bankruptcy of all time.

Further support was provided by Ismail, who studied 16,221 takeovers over the years 1985–2004 and found that single acquirers, companies who pursue only one acquisition, outperformed multiple acquirers by 1.66%.[60]

Many of the roll-up deals of the 1990s fell into bankruptcy when the market euphoria and economic expansion of that period came to an end. Some, such as Coach USA, a company put together by consolidator Simon Harter, were sold to other buyers. Others, such as Wayne Huizinga's Waste Management and Blockbuster Video, and Jonathan Ledecky's Cort Business Services, survived the collapse of the roll-ups. Still others, such as Westinghouse, thrived.

---

[59] Nihat Atkas, Eric de Bodt, and Richard Roll, "Learning, Hubris and Corporate Serial Acquisitions," *Journal of Corporate Finance* 15, no. 5 (December 2009): 543–561.
[60] Ahmad Ismail, "Which Acquirers Gain More, Single or Multiple? Recent Evidence from the USA Market," *Global Finance Journal* 19 (2008): 72–84.

Vertical Integration

Vertical integration involves the acquisition of firms that are closer to the source of supply or to the ultimate consumer. An example of a movement toward the source of supply was Chevron's acquisition of Gulf Oil in 1984. Chevron bought Gulf primarily to augment its reserves, a motive termed *backward integration*. In the same year, Mobil bought Superior Oil for similar reasons. Mobil was strong in refining and marketing but low on reserves, whereas Superior had large oil and gas reserves but lacked refining and marketing operations. An example of *forward integration* would be if a firm with large reserves bought another company that had a strong marketing and retailing capability.

MERCK'S ACQUISITION OF MEDCO: AN EXAMINATION OF VERTICAL INTEGRATION AND COPYCAT M&A

In July 1993, Merck & Co., the largest pharmaceutical company in the world at that time, acquired Medco Containment Services for $6.6 billion. Medco was the largest prescription benefits management company. With the drug industry experiencing the effects of managed care, pharmaceutical companies had to adapt to new means of distribution. Merck realized that the decisions of what treatments and what drugs should be used in patients' care were increasingly being influenced by the managed care environment rather than by physicians. In the world of managed care, it was no longer sufficient to market just to physicians. The successful pharmaceutical companies of the future would be companies that were able to adapt to the changed distribution system.

This vertical integration move by Merck was not lost on its rival drug companies. Shortly after the Medco acquisition, other drug companies began their own acquisitions so as not to leave Merck with better channels to the ultimate consumer. Toward that end, in 1994, Eli Lilly bought PCS Health Systems for $4.1 billion, while Roche Holdings bought Syntex Corp. for $5.3 billion. This is an example of copycat acquisitions, as Merck's competitors instinctively reacted to a perceived competitive advantage that Merck may have achieved. Copycat acquisitions are very common. The automobile industry did the same with its forward and backward vertical integration strategies as well as its international expansion programs. All of these have yielded questionable results for many of these companies.

Merck and its copycat competitors, however, did not do their homework. Regulatory concerns arose regarding Merck possibly unduly influencing consumers' prescription alternatives through Medco. Merck was forced to eventually undo this acquisition.

Another example of forward integration took place in the securities industry when Shearson Lehman Brothers bought E. F. Hutton. Shearson was attracted by E. F. Hutton's strong network of retail brokers. This vertical combination was motivated by a movement toward the consumer. It is also an example of a previously vertically integrated firm that wanted to expand its access to the consumer. Before the merger, Shearson Lehman had a large network of retail brokers. After the merger, however, it acquired a retail capacity to rival all competitors, including Merrill Lynch. Although this strategy of combining seemingly complementary and closely related businesses appeared to make sense, it also was later undone and the firms were sold off.

Motives for Vertical Integration

A firm might consider vertically integrating for several reasons. As seen in the case of the Mobil–Superior Oil combination, companies may vertically integrate to be assured of a *dependable source of supply*. Dependability may be determined not just in terms of supply availability but also through quality maintenance and timely delivery considerations. Having timely access to supplies helps companies to provide their own products on a reliable basis. In addition, as companies pursue *just-in-time* inventory management, they may take advantage of a vertically integrated corporate structure to lower inventory costs.

It is popularly believed that when a company acquires a supplier, it is obtaining a cost advantage over its rivals. The thinking is that it will not have to pay the profit to suppliers that it was previously paying when it was buying the inputs from independent suppliers. This raises the question: What is the appropriate *internal transfer price?* It is the price carried on the company's books when it acquires its supplies or inputs from a supplier that it now controls and may be a subsidiary. If the price for these inputs is less than the prevailing market price, the parent company will appear to be more profitable than it really is. The reason is that the lower costs and higher profits for the parent company come at the cost of lower profitability for the subsidiary. This is a paper transfer, however, and does not result in increased value to the combined firm.

Although the establishment of an accurate transfer price helps dismiss the illusion that supplies derived from a newly acquired supplier come at a lower cost, there may be other cost savings from acquiring a supplier. These savings may come in the form of lower *transactions costs*.[61] By acquiring a supplier and establishing a long-term source of supply at prearranged costs, the acquiring firm may avoid potential disruptions that might occur when agreements with independent suppliers end. When the buyer owns the supplier, it may be better able to predict future supply costs and avoid the uncertainty that normally is associated with renegotiation of supply agreements.

Still another reason for vertical integration could arise from the need to have *specialized inputs*. These may be custom-designed materials or machinery that might have little or no market value other than to the buyer. The buyer may then be at the mercy of these companies if they choose not to provide the products. It may be difficult to switch to other suppliers if there are fixed costs associated with the initial manufacture of the materials. Other suppliers may be unwilling to produce the specialized products unless the buyer compensates for the initial costs or enters a long-term supply agreement that

---

[61] Dennis Carlton and Jeffrey Perloff, *Modern Industrial Organization*, 2nd ed. (New York: HarperCollins, 1994), 502.

allows the supplier to amortize the up-front costs. One way to eliminate this problem is to acquire the supplier. The buyer can then have access to these specialized inputs and be in an even better position to oversee the maintenance of the company's own standards of manufacturing. In Chapter 13, however, we will explore whether some of these goals can be better accomplished through lower costs, joint ventures, or strategic alliances.

Another interesting example of vertical integration occurs in the marketing of automobiles. Automobile manufacturers have long realized that they may need to provide potential buyers with financial assistance, in the form of less expensive and more readily available credit, to sell more cars. For this reason, General Motors (GM) formed General Motors Acceptance Corporation (GMAC). General Motors Acceptance Corporation, now Ally Financial, Inc., provides low-cost credit to many car buyers who might not be able to get the financing necessary to buy a new car. Companies such as GMAC were able to sell commercial paper at money market rates and use the difference between these rates and the financing rates it charges to car buyers to help sell cars while making profits on financing. However, in the 2000s, automakers needed to try to maintain market share to keep their costly plants and labor force generating revenues and were forced into costly financing programs that competitors, such as Toyota, avoided.

VERTICAL INTEGRATION IN THE AUTOMOBILE INDUSTRY

For a period of time all of the U.S. automakers were vertically integrated, both backward and forward, in one form or another. General Motors, the number-one auto company in the world for many years, owned its own supplier, Delphi, which is the largest parts supplier in the automobile business. GM spun off this entity in 1999. Ford was in the auto supply business for many years, going back to the decision of Henry Ford to create his own parts supplier and avoid reliance on other suppliers, such as those controlled by the Dodge brothers. Ford spun off this entity in 2000 when it formed Visteon. Unfortunately, due to the tight hold the United Auto Workers (UAW) had on these two companies, they could not sever their financial obligations to the workers at these companies. Ford was forced to take back many of Visteon's employees in 2005. When Delphi filed for bankruptcy, it reminded GM that it must honor obligations to its workers.

There are many suppliers of parts, and by buying a large percentage of their parts from their own captive suppliers, both Ford and GM, in effect, were purchasing parts at higher prices than what they would otherwise pay if they were dealing with suppliers who did not have the same burdensome labor agreements with the UAW. Both Ford and GM, and other automakers, pressure their suppliers to be very competitive in their prices. The combination of intensely competitive pricing, combined with high labor costs, did not make this an attractive business for Ford and GM.

At one time, Chrysler, Ford, and GM all were vertically integrated forward through their purchases of car rental companies. In 1989, Chrysler bought Thrifty Rent-A-Car, which in turn bought Snappy Rent-A-Car in 1990. In addition, Chrysler solidified its presence in the car rental business by buying Dollar Rent-A-Car in 1990.

Lee Iacocca termed the combination a "natural alliance." However, what was natural in 1990 became unnatural just a few years later.

Similarly, in 1988, GM acquired a 45% interest in National Car Rental. The company also owned an interest in Avis—the number-two company in the industry. Ford acquired Hertz, the number-one company in the car rental industry, in 1987 from Allegis for $1.3 billion.

The automakers thought that the purchase of the larger buyers of their cars, car rental companies, would lock in demand for their products. In addition, the entry of these automakers into the car rental business is an example of "copycat" acquisitions as one auto manufacturer did not want to let another one gain market share at its expense. Market share has always been a major focus in the auto industry as the industry has a huge investment in capital in its plants as well as relatively fixed obligations to workers that are not flexible due to the pressures from the UAW. These burdensome agreements with the UAW caused the companies to lose market share to non-U.S. manufacturers, such as Toyota and Honda, who built nonunion plants in the United States that enjoyed major cost advantages over their U.S. rivals.

Unfortunately for the U.S. automakers, the sales gained from deals with the car rental industry were not very profitable. Car rental companies, being large buyers, purchase at attractive prices and require the manufacturers to buy back these autos after a period such as one year, so that they can maintain a relatively modern fleet of vehicles. The terms of these sales were not good for U.S. car companies because they used such sales, along with heavily discounted promotional sales and rebate offers, to try to offset their shrinking market shares. Foreign automakers, such as Toyota, Nissan, and Honda, steered clear of this part of the market and focused on gaining market share while maintaining profitability.

As U.S. automakers began to rethink the benefits of forward vertical integration, they began to extricate themselves from the car rental business. GM took a $300 million charge related to National Car Rental and had to write down the goodwill on its balance sheet stemming from National. In 1995, it sold National to Lobeck for $1.3 billion. In 1997, Chrysler did an equity carve-out of its car rental business for $387.5 million. Finally, in 2005, Ford sold off Hertz to a private equity group. Ironically, Hertz was a profitable business, valued at approximately $15 billion. However, at that time Ford was losing money and market share and had to sell off this asset to try to consolidate its business.

By the mid-2000s, the U.S. automakers had reversed many of their vertical integration efforts (to the extent the UAW agreement allowed them to). Clearly, their moves to vertically integrate were not a success.

 ## HUBRIS HYPOTHESIS OF TAKEOVERS

An interesting hypothesis regarding takeover motives was proposed by Roll.[62] He considered the role that hubris, or the pride of the managers in the acquiring firm, may play in explaining takeovers. The hubris hypothesis implies that managers seek to acquire

[62] Richard Roll, "The Hubris Hypothesis of Corporate Takeovers," *Journal of Business* 59, no. 2 (April 1986): 197–216.

firms for their own personal motives and that the pure economic gains to the acquiring firm are not the sole motivation or even the primary motivation in the acquisition.

Roll and others have researched this hypothesis to explain why managers might pay a premium for a firm that the market has already correctly valued. Managers, they claim, have superimposed their own valuation over that of an objectively determined market valuation.[63] Their position is that the pride of management allows them to believe that their valuation is superior to that of the market. Implicit in this theory is an underlying conviction that the market is efficient and can provide the best indicator of the value of a firm. Many would dispute this point. As evidence, there is a wide body of research studies that we review in the following section.

Empirical Evidence

A large body of research covering a quarter of a century has lent support to the hubris hypothesis as an explanation for many takeovers. Early research sought to see if the announcements of deals caused the target's price to rise, the acquirer's to fall, and the combination of the two to result in a net negative effect. Various studies lend support for some or all of these effects.

Early Research

A number of studies show that the acquiring firm's announcement of the takeover results in a decline in the value of the acquirer's stock. Dodd found statistically significant negative returns to the acquirer following the announcement of the planned takeover.[64] Other studies have demonstrated similar findings.[65] Not all studies support this conclusion, however. Paul Asquith failed to find a consistent pattern of declining stock prices following the announcement of a takeover.[66]

There is more widespread agreement on the positive price effects for target stockholders who have been found to experience wealth gains following takeovers. Bradley, Desai, and Kim show that tender offers result in gains for target firm stockholders.[67] Admittedly, the hostile nature of tender offers should produce greater changes in the stock price than friendly takeover offers. Most studies, however, show that target stockholders gain following both friendly and hostile takeover bids. Varaiya showed that bidders tend to overpay.[68]

---

[63] Patrick A. Gaughan, *Mergers: What Can Go Wrong and How to Prevent It* (Hoboken, NJ: John Wiley & Sons, 2005) 75–82.

[64] Peter Dodd, "Merger Proposals, Management Discretion and Stockholder Wealth," *Journal of Financial Economics* 8, no. 2 (June 1980): 105–137.

[65] Carol E. Eger, "An Empirical Test of the Redistribution Effect of Mergers," *Journal of Financial and Quantitative Analysis* 18, no. 4 (December 1983): 547–572.

[66] Paul Asquith, "Merger Bids, Uncertainty and Stockholder Returns," *Journal of Financial Economics* 11, no. 1 (April 1983): 51–83.

[67] Michael Bradley, Anand Desai, and E. Han Kim, "The Rationale behind Interfirm Tender Offers: Information or Synergy?" *Journal of Financial Economics* 11, no. 1 (April 1983): 183–206.

[68] Nikhil P. Varaiya, "Winners Curse Hypothesis and Corporate Takeovers," *Managerial and Decision Economics* 9, no. 3 (September 1988): 209–219.

In a study that examined the relationship between the bid premium and the combined market values of the bidder and the target, it was found that the premium paid by bidders was too high relative to the value of the target to the acquirer. The research on the combined effect of the upward movement of the target's stock and the downward movement of the acquirer's stock does not seem to provide strong support for the hubris hypothesis. Malatesta examined the combined effects and found that "the evidence indicates that the long-run sequence of events culminating in merger has no net impact on combined shareholder wealth."[69] It could be countered, however, that Malatesta's failure to find positive combined returns does support the hubris hypothesis.

Later Research

More recent research lends support to the hubris hypothesis by approaching the problem differently.[70] Using a sample of 106 large acquisitions, Hayward and Hambrick found CEO hubris positively associated with the size of premiums paid. Hubris was measured by variables such as the company's recent performance and CEO self-importance (as reflected by media praise and compensation relative to the second-highest paid executive). The study also considered independent variables, such as CEO inexperience, as measured by years in that position, along with board vigilance, as measured by the number of inside directors versus outside directors (see Figure 4.2).

Other studies provide support for the hubris hypothesis for takeover of U.S. firms by foreign corporations. Using shareholder wealth effect responses similar to those theorized by Roll, in a sample of 100 cross-border deals over the period 1981 to 1990, Seth,

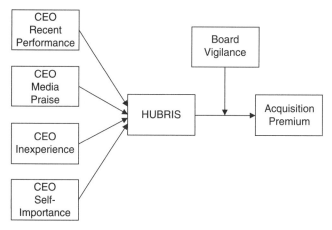

FIGURE 4.2 Model of CEO Hubris and Acquisition Premiums. *Source*: Mathew L. A. Hayward and Donald C. Hambrick, "Explaining Premiums Paid for Large Acquisitions: Evidence of CEO Hubris," unpublished manuscript, July 1995.

---

[69] Paul Malatesta, "Wealth Effects of Merger Activity," *Journal of Financial Economics* 11, no. 1 (April 1983): 178–179.
[70] Mathew L. A. Hayward and Donald C. Hambrick, "Explaining Premiums Paid for Large Acquisitions: Evidence of CEO Hubris," *Administrative Sciences Quarterly*, 42 (1997): 103–127.

Song, and Pettit found that hubris played an important role in these deals.[71] Other factors, such as synergy and managerialism, also played a role. Managerialism is somewhat similar to hubris, in that both may involve overpaying for a target. In managerialism, however, the bidder's management knowingly overpays so as to pursue their own gains, even though it comes at the expense of their shareholders—to whom they have a fiduciary obligation.

Malmendier and Tate investigated the role that overconfidence played in deals done by 394 large companies.[72] They measured overconfidence by the tendency of CEOs to overinvest in the stock of their own companies and their statements in the media. They found that the likelihood of doing acquisitions was 65% higher for the overconfident group of CEOs in their sample. They also determined that overconfident CEOs were more likely to make lower-quality, value-destroying acquisitions. Billet and Qian further researched the role of overconfidence by examining the acquisition history of 2,487 CEOs and 3,795 deals over the years 1980–2002.[73] CEOs who had a positive experience with acquisitions were more likely to pursue other acquisitions. These CEOs' net purchases of their company's own stock were greater prior to the subsequent deals than they were prior to the first deals. The researchers interpret this result as these CEOs being overconfident and attributing the success of the original deal to their own managerial abilities and superior insight.

Aktas, de Bodt, and Roll showed that overconfident and hubris-filled CEOs tend to do deals more rapidly and there is less time between their deals.[74] They also noted there was a "learning effect," in which CEOs who had done more deals in the past tended to act faster and have less time between their deals. This learning effect has been supported by other research by these same authors.[75] The research of Aktas et al., as well as other studies, has shown that the cumulative abnormal returns of serial acquirers decline as a function of the number of acquisitions they do. Some interpret this as an indicator of hubris as the CEOs continue to pursue deals that generate decreasing returns to shareholders. Others opine that the declining returns could merely be a function of less productive opportunities available in the marketplace. While this is a possible causal explanation, it still seems that the hubris-filled CEOs should refrain from continuing an acquisition program when the returns fall below some specific targeted return.

---

[71] Anju Seth, Kean P. Song, and Richardson Pettit, "Synergy, Managerialism or Hubris? An Empirical Examination of Motives of Foreign Acquisitions of U.S. Firms," *Journal of International Business Studies* 31, no. 3 (3rd Quarter, 2000): 387–405.

[72] Ulrike Malmendier and Geoffrey Tate, "Who Makes Acquisitions? CEO Overconfidence and the Market's Reaction, *Journal of Financial Economics* 89, no. 1 (July 2008): 20–43.

[73] Matthew T. Billet and Yiming Qian, "Are Overconfident CEOs Born or Made? Evidence of Self-Attribution Bias from Frequent Acquirers," *Management Science* 54, no. 6 (June 2008): 1037–1051.

[74] Nihat Aktas, Eric de Bodt, and Richard Roll, "The Elapsed Time between Deals," UCLA Anderson School of Management working paper, March 2008.

[75] Nihat Aktas, Eric de Bodt, and Richard Roll, "Learning, Hubris and Corporate Serial Acquisitions," *Journal of Corporate Finance* 15, no. 5 (December 2009): 543–561.

DO MANAGERIAL AGENDAS DRIVE M&A?

Managers have their own personal agendas, and these may differ from that of the company. For managers, and CEOs in particular, it may be to extend their stay in their positions and to continue to receive what in the United States are bountiful compensations and perks. This monetary compensation is on top of the psychic income they receive from being "the Big Cheese."

Morck, Shleifer, and Vishny analyzed 326 acquisitions over the period 1975 to 1987.[76] They found that bad deals were driven by the objectives of the managers doing the deals. They found that three types of acquisitions caused lower and usually negative announcement period returns. These were: diversifying M&As, acquiring a rapidly growing target, and acquiring a company when the managers have a poor performance track record prior to the deals. Their findings about diversification are further evidence that such a strategy is questionable. However, their results related to rapidly growing targets probably reflect the fact that it is hard to "buy growth," and when you do, you will likely be forced to overpay. We saw this in Chapter 3.

Their findings related to bad managerial track records are also quite intuitive. If you are bad at running the business you have, adding to it and thereby increasing the managerial demands will only worsen managerial performance. Perhaps managers are good at managing a specific type of focused business. Allowing them to foray into areas beyond their knowledge base may be a prescription for disaster. On the other hand, senior management at companies that have been historically diverse, such as GE, is in the business of managing very diverse enterprises. These management abilities are their skill set. In effect, this is what they do.

VIVENDI AND MESSIER'S HUBRIS: ANOTHER FAILED CORPORATE TRANSFORMATION

Vivendi Universal SA (Vivendi) is a colorful case study involving a stodgy French water utility run by a chief executive officer (CEO) who wanted to be a high-flying leader of an international media company. He eventually transformed this water utility into a media giant. The only problem was that he sacrificed shareholders' interests to do so. Shareholders picked up the tab for his grandiose dreams, and when they failed he walked away with too much of their money in his pockets and in the pockets of others he brought in to help with his schemes.

Vivendi's roots come from being a 100-year-old water utility that was housed in an entity eventually called Vivendi Environment SA. When the division was sold off

(continued)

---

[76] Randall Morck, Andrei Shleifer, and Robert W. Vishny, "Do Managerial Objectives Drive Bad Acquisitions?" *Journal of Finance* 45, no. 1 (March 1990): 31–48.

(*continued*)

as part of the bust-up of the company, it raised 2.5 billion euros. This was a relatively small amount compared to the losses that Messier's media empire would generate.

If Vivendi's financial performance had been good, no one would have questioned the apparent lack of synergy between Vivendi's water and entertainment industry assets. Unfortunately, the combination of the two produced very poor results. The company lost 23 billion euros in 2002, which followed a 13.6 billion euro loss in 2001. This was the largest corporate loss in French history. Vivendi cannot be proud that its 2002 23.6 billion euro loss narrowly passed the prior record of 23 billion euros that was held by French Telecom. As the situation worsened in 2002, major shareholders pushed for action—they were just a few years too late.

CEO Messier was not satisfied with being the CEO of a water utility. Messier had a dealmaker's background. He was formerly an investment banker at Lazard LLC, where he spent six years of his business career. If you put an investment banker at the helm of a water utility, odds are that he is going to engage in *investment banker–like activities*. Messier, originally a utility CEO, became an entertainment CEO by engaging in major acquisitions of entertainment companies.

One of Messier's big deals was to buy Seagram Universal in 2000. This sale gave the Bronfmans, major shareholders in Seagram, 88.9 million shares in Vivendi, which constituted 8.9% of the company.[a] This acquisition marked Vivendi's major foray into the media industry by buying a company that itself was a combination between the liquor and soft drinks company, Seagram, and the Universal movie studios. It is quite ironic that Messier would buy Seagram Universal as this company was formed by the acquisition engineered by young Edgar Bronfman when he took a leadership position at Seagram. He used the assets and cash flows of the Seagram family business to finance its venture into the entertainment sector. This deal went through its own rocky period as the movie business proved to be not as exciting to Seagram's shareholders as it was to the young Mr. Bronfman.

Messier's acquisition plans did not stop with Seagram Universal. He then bought Canal Plus—a pay-cable French TV network, who also owned shares in British Sky Broadcasting. He then purchased Barry Diller's USA Networks in December 2001 for $10.3 billion, only to see its value drop, like many other Messier purchases. The deal brought together the Universal Studios Group with the entertainment assets of the USA Networks to form what they called Vivendi Universal Entertainment. As with so many other acquisitions, Vivendi stated that it hoped to realize significant synergies that would improve content, ratings, and subscriber fees.[b]

Messier paid 12.5 billion euros for Canal Plus, even though there were significant limitations on the ability of any buyer to make significant changes at the European cable company to make the programming more profitable. Canal Plus was not profitable and had approximately 2.8 billion euros of debt.[c] Messier also bought a 44% stake in Cegetal—a French phone company that owned 80% of SFR, France's second biggest mobile phone operator. In addition, the company purchased Houghton Mifflin, a book publisher, for $2.2 billion, which included $500 million in debt. Vivendi also owned an equipment division that held U.S. Filter Corporation.

In the midst of his acquisition binge, Messier, the CEO of this water/worldwide media company, moved to New York in September 2001. To say that Messier was filled with hubris seems to be an understatement. He himself concedes that this may be a normal characteristic of a CEO. In his book he stated, "Don't ask a CEO to be modest. The costume does not fit him. A strong ego, not to say an outsized one, is more becoming, although each has its way of wearing." We would have to say that when this ego leads the company down the path of billions in losses, it can be very draining on the value of investors' portfolios. Messier loved the limelight—especially the lights of New York—much to the chagrin of his French management and shareholders.

When Vivendi began to rack up huge losses, shareholders and creditors began to call for an end of the acquisition binge and the ouster of its colorful CEO. After a new, supposedly more conservative management team of Chairman Jean-Rene Fourtou and CEO Bernard Levy were put in place, the company began the slow and costly process of disassembling the media and utility conglomerate that the hubris-filled Messier had built. They sold four Gulfstream corporate jets, a castle outside Paris, and a publishing company.[d] The new management returned the company to profitability while enjoying stable growth in revenues. In 2009 the company announced it was selling its 20% stake in NBC Universal and would use some of the billions it received to pursue "bolt-on" acquisitions. They started the M&A process again and acquired Brazil telecom company GVT for $1.87 billion. In 2011 it acquired the recorded music division of EMI for $1.87 billion. Finally, the board had enough and Levy was forced to step down. The sell-offs then resumed, and in 2013 Vivendi sold its interest in Activism Blizzard for $13.2 billion.

[a] "The Bronfman Family Feels Messier's Pain," *New York Times*, April 25, 2002.

[b] Vivendi Universal press release, December 17, 2001.

[c] "Messier's Mess," *Economist*, June 6, 2002.

[d] Max Colchester, "Vivendi to Rebuild with New Cash," *Wall Street Journal*, December 16, 2009, B1.

Winner's Curse Hypothesis of Takeovers

The concept of the winner's curse was first put forward by three engineers at Atlantic Richfield who discussed auctions for oil drilling rights and the challenges of bidding for assets whose true value is difficult to estimate.[77] The winner of these bidding contests can then be cursed by putting forward a winning bid that exceeds the value of the assets. Richard Thaler has demonstrated how the winner's curse could work in a variety of contexts, including mergers and acquisitions.[78]

The winner's curse of takeovers is the ironic hypothesis that states that bidders who overestimate the value of a target will most likely win a contest. This is due to the fact that they will be more inclined to overpay and outbid rivals who more accurately value the target. This result is not specific to takeovers but is the natural result of any bidding contest.[79] One of the more public forums where this regularly occurs is the free agent markets of sports such as baseball and basketball.[80] In a study of 800 acquisitions from

[77] E. C. Capen, R. V. Clapp, and W. M. Campbell, "Competitive Bidding in High-Risk Situations," *Journal of Petroleum Technology* 23 (June 1971): 641–653.

[78] Richard Thaler, *The Winner's Curse: Paradoxes and Anomalies of Economic Life* (Princeton: Princeton University Press, 1994).

[79] Max Baserman and William Samuelson, "I Won the Auction but I Don't Win the Prize," *Journal of Conflict Resolution* 27, no. 4 (December 1983): 618–634.

[80] James Cassing and Richard Douglas, "Implication of the Auction Mechanism in Baseball's Free Agent Draft," *Southern Economic Journal* 47, no. 1 (July 1980): 110–121.

1974 to 1983, Varaiya showed that on average the winning bid in takeover contests significantly overstated the capital market's estimate of any takeover gains by as much as 67%.[81] He measured overpayment as the difference between the winning bid premium and the highest bid possible before the market responded negatively to the bid. This study provides support for the existence of the winner's curse, which in turn also supports the hubris hypothesis.

Do Bad Bidders Become Good Targets?

Given that many acquisitions have failed to live up to expectations, the question arises: Does the market punish companies that make bad acquisitions? Using a sample of 1,158 companies, Mitchell and Lehn examined their control transactions from 1980 to 1988.[82] They determined that companies that make acquisitions that cause their equity to lose value are increasingly likely to become takeover targets. That is, they found that "the likelihood of becoming a takeover target is significantly and inversely related to the abnormal stock price performance with the firm's acquisitions."[83] Their analysis shows that takeovers may be both a problem and a solution. Takeovers that reduce market value may be bad deals, assuming the market correctly assesses them, and this is a problem. The deals market, however, may take care of the problem through another takeover of the "bad bidder." The Mitchell and Lehn analysis also implies that just looking at the returns to acquirers, which research has shown may be zero or slightly negative, obscures the picture because it aggregates good deals and bad deals. When the negative market impact of bad deals is taken into account, it becomes clear that good acquisitions should have a positive impact on share values, whereas bad deals should cause the stock price of these acquirers to lag behind the market.

Fortunately there is some evidence that the corporate governance process may eventually address the poor performance of the "bad acquirer" CEOs. In an analysis of 390 firms over the period 1990–1998 Lehn and Zhao found an inverse relationship between the returns of acquiring firms and the likelihood that the CEOs would be fired.[84]

Executive Compensation and Corporate Acquisition Decisions

One theory of acquisitions that is closely related to the hubris hypothesis is the theory that managers of companies acquire other companies to increase their size, which in turn allows them to enjoy higher compensation and benefits.[85] Khorana and Zenner

---

[81] Nikhil Varaiya, "The Winner's Curse Hypothesis and Corporate Takeovers," *Managerial and Decision Economics* 9, no. 3 (September 1988): 209–219.

[82] Mark L. Mitchell and Kenneth Lehn, "Do Bad Bidders Become Good Targets?" *Journal of Political Economy* 98, no. 2 (April 1990): 372–398.

[83] Ibid., 393.

[84] Kenneth Lehn and Mengxin Zhao, "CEO Turnover after Acquisitions: Do Bad Bidders Get Fired?" *Journal of Finance* 61, no. 4 (August 2006): 1759–1811.

[85] William Baumol, *Business Behavior, Value and Growth*, 2nd ed. (New York: Macmillan, 1959).

analyzed the role that executive compensation played in the corporate acquisition decisions of 51 firms that made 84 acquisitions between 1982 and 1986.[86] For companies that engaged in acquisitions, they found a positive relationship between firm size and executive compensation but not for those that did not. However, when they separated good acquisitions from bad acquisitions, they found that good acquisitions increased compensation, whereas bad deals did not have a positive effect on compensation. When the fact that bad deals may result in departures from the firm is taken into account, there is even a negative relationship between bad acquisitions and executive compensation.

More recent evidence from the fifth merger wave provides evidence that CEOs receive compensation for doing deals. Grinstein and Hribar conducted a study using a database of 327 large deals drawn from the period 1993 to 1999.[87] In examining proxy statements that identified the components of CEO compensation, they found that in 39% of the cases the board of directors' compensation committee cited completing deals as one of the reasons why the compensation was at the level it was.

 ## OTHER MOTIVES

Improved Management

Some takeovers are motivated by a belief that the acquiring firm's management can better manage the target's resources. The bidder may believe that its management skills are such that the value of the target would rise under its control. This leads the acquirer to pay a value for the target in excess of the target's current stock price.

The improved management argument may have particular validity in cases of large companies making offers for smaller, growing companies. The smaller companies, often led by entrepreneurs, may offer a unique product or service that has sold well and facilitated the rapid growth of the target.

The growing enterprise may find that it needs to oversee a much larger distribution network and may have to adopt a very different marketing philosophy. Many of the decisions that a larger firm has to make require a different set of managerial skills from those that resulted in the dramatic growth of the smaller company. The lack of managerial expertise may be a stumbling block in the growing company and may limit its ability to compete in the broader marketplace. These managerial resources are an asset that the larger firm can offer the target.

Little significant empirical research has been conducted on the importance of the improved management motive. The difficulty is determining which takeovers are motivated solely by this factor, because improved management usually is just one of several factors in the acquirer's decision to make a bid. It is difficult to isolate improved management and to explain its role in the bidding process. The argument that takeover offers

[86] Ajay Khorana and Marc Zenner, "Executive Compensation of Large Acquirers in the 1980s," *Journal of Corporate Finance* 4, no. 3 (September 1998): 209–240.
[87] Yaniv Grinstein and Paul Hribar, "CEO Compensation and Incentives: Evidence from M&A Bonuses," *Journal of Financial Economics* 73, no. 1 (July 2004): 119–143.

by large companies for smaller, growing companies are motivated in part by managerial gains may be reasonable.

For large public firms, a takeover may be the most cost-efficient way to bring about a management change. Proxy contests may enable dissident stockholders to oust the incumbent management, whom they may consider incompetent. One problem with this process is that corporate democracy is not very egalitarian. It is costly to use a proxy fight to replace an incumbent management team. The process is biased in favor of management, who may also occupy seats on the board of directors. It is therefore difficult to win a proxy battle. The proxy process is explained in detail in Chapter 6.

Improved Research and Development

Research and development (R&D) is critically important to the future growth of many companies, particularly pharmaceutical companies. This was one of the reasons for the consolidation that occurred in the pharmaceutical industry in the fifth merger wave. For example, the $73 billion megamerger between Glaxo Wellcome and SmithKline Beecham in 1999, which formed the largest company in that industry at that time, merged the R&D budgets of two companies. This was estimated to equal an annual total of $4 billion, which was, at that time, more than double the R&D budgets of some of their larger rivals, such as Pfizer and Merck. In response, other companies began to look for their own merger targets so as to remain competitive in pharmaceutical R&D. This helps explain the successful 2000 acquisition by Pfizer of Warner-Lambert. Not only did this deal give Pfizer enhanced R&D, but also it filled up its drug pipeline, including the addition of the largest-selling drug in the world—Lipitor.

The drug development and approval process is a slow one, oftentimes taking over 10 years. It is also quite expensive, with a blockbuster drug (a drug with annual sales in excess of $1 billion) costing as much as $1 billion to develop. The Federal Drug Administration approves relatively few drugs per year, making the problem of drugs coming off patent protection a challenging issue for large drug companies. The drug discovery process has evolved over time, with the role of biotech research being very important. This helps explain why in 2009 Pfizer acquired Wyeth. Wyeth had a number of blockbuster drugs that it marketed. In addition, it had a promising "biologic" research program investigating treatments for important illnesses, such as Alzheimer's, schizophrenia, and antibiotic-resistant bacterial infections, to name a few.

MERCK: INTERNAL DEVELOPMENT OR M&A—THE PURSUIT OF NEW DRUGS

During the fifth merger wave, widespread consolidation took place in the pharmaceutical industry. One of the motives for such deals was the mounting cost of the research and development (R&D) needed to come up with new drugs. Such factors help explain the megamergers that took place between Glaxo Wellcome and SmithKline Beecham in 1999 and the merger between Pfizer and Warner-Lambert in 2000. However, not all the industry leaders decided that merging was the best way to enhance product development.

One prominent example is the internal development program that was pursued by Merck as an alternative to M&As. Part of the problem continually facing pharmaceutical companies is that patents, which allow developers to recoup the substantial costs of drug development, eventually expire, subjecting the company to competition with generic "knockoffs." For example, two of Merck's big sellers were Vasotec, an antihypertensive drug that was scheduled to come off patent protection in August 2000, and Mevacor, an anticholesterol drug that would lose patent protection in December 2001.[a] Amid the consolidation going on in its industry in the fifth wave, Merck was left with the choice to continue to use internal resources to come up with replacement drugs or to engage in expensive acquisitions to replace the drugs about to come off patent protection. Merck decided to go it alone. Using internal R&D it came up with a number of promising replacement drugs, such as the anti-inflammatory cyclooxygenase-2 (COX-2) inhibitor—Vioxx.

For a while Merck's decision not to acquire R&D externally raised many questions. Merck had enjoyed impressive revenue growth in the 1980s, but this growth slowed in the first half of the 1990s. By the beginning of 2001, Merck was again among the industry leaders in revenue growth and profitability while maintaining its independence. This growth was stunted in 2005–2006 when it encountered a massive wave of Vioxx-related lawsuits.

However, in 2009 Merck departed from its internal growth strategy when it agreed to acquire rival Schering-Plough Corp. for $41 billion. Part of the reason for this was that the internal development process stopped bearing fruit and some of its leading products, such as asthma treatment Singulair, which had global sales of $4.3 billion in 2008, were coming off patent protection. If Merck kept pursuing internal development it may have had to accept being a significantly smaller pharmaceutical company. In the years after the Schering deal Merck continued to pursue M&A as a way of offsetting an industry-wide lack of R&D productivity. In 2011 it acquired Inspire Pharmaceuticals and in 2014 it acquired Inenix Pharmaceuticals for $3.85 billion and antibiotics maker Cubist Pharmaceuticals for $7.5 billion. Part of the funds for these deals came from the of Merck's consumer business to Bayer for $14.2 billion. The result of this process is that Merck is a more focused company with a more productive drug pipeline.

[a] Gardiner Harris, "With Big Drugs Dying, Merck Didn't Merge—It Found New Ones," *Wall Street Journal*, January 10, 2001.

While drug companies used M&A as a means to make up for blockbuster drugs that were coming off patent protection, the track record of M&A as a means to greatly enhance R&D has not been impressive. In the pharmaceutical industry M&A has been more successful in creating large global sales and distribution organizations and wringing out cost savings from the consolidation of acquired targets. Even with respect to R&D, drug companies recognized that there were great redundancies in the separate R&D departments that different drug firms maintained. Merck was able to benefit from this in 2010 by closing 16 such sites following its 2009 acquisition of Schering. Nonetheless, while the large drug firms' key need is productive R&D, the large bureaucratic structures created by megamergers have not been fertile environments for development of new blockbuster drugs.

Improved Distribution

Companies that make a product but do not have direct access to consumers need to develop channels to ensure that their product reaches the ultimate consumer in a profitable manner. Vertical mergers between manufacturers and distributors or retailers often give competitor manufacturers cause for concern in that they worry about being cut off from distribution channels. Locking in dependable distribution channels can be critical to a firm's success.

PEPSI: UNDO SELL-OFF TO IMPROVE DISTRIBUTION

In 1999, in a robust equity market, PepsiCo Inc. spun off in an initial public offering (IPO) its lower-margin bottling business. PepsiCo's stock had been weak for years even in the bull market, and it was hoped this move would help lift its stock price. The company also used the IPO proceeds to lower its risk profile by paying down debt. This move is what many similar businesses have done as they have discovered that distribution is capital- and labor-intensive and not where the profitability of the business lies—or so it seemed at the time. Following those transactions, two large bottling firms became independent public companies on which PepsiCo depended for its distribution.

By the late 2000s PepsiCo had a change of heart and regretted losing control over its distribution. It had retained minority stakes in the two bottlers but could not control the strategy of these companies, which deviated from Pepsi's.

In recent years, as the U.S. consumer became increasingly health-conscious, soft drink sales weakened. Pepsi wanted to promote more sales of water and enhanced water products. The bottlers wanted access to Gatorade, which Pepsi owned but which is manufactured through a different process than what the bottlers use to make soda and which is distributed through a more traditional warehouse system. In addition, the bottlers began to distribute Crush soda, made by the Pepsi rival Dr. Pepper Snapple Group. As a result, the former Pepsi distribution system became a distribution channel for Pepsi's competition. All this was too much for Pepsi to take and in August 2009, it reached an agreement to reacquire the bottlers for $7.8 billion.

Tax Motives

Whether tax motives are an important determinant of M&As has been a much-debated topic in finance. Certain studies have concluded that acquisitions may be an effective means to secure tax benefits. Gilson, Scholes, and Wolfson have set forth the theoretical framework demonstrating the relationship between such gains and

M&As.[88] They assert that for a certain small fraction of mergers, tax motives could have played a significant role. Hayn, however, has empirically analyzed this relationship and has found that "potential tax benefits stemming from net operating loss carry forwards and unused tax credits positively affect announcement-period returns of firms involving tax-free acquisitions, and capital gains and the step-up in the acquired assets' basis affect returns of firms involved in taxable acquisitions."[89] Moreover, whether the transaction can be structured as a tax-free exchange may be a prime determining factor in whether to go forward with a deal. Sellers sometimes require tax-free status as a prerequisite of approving a deal.

In 2014 a number of deals drew attention for the impact that tax motives played in the merger decision. These were called *redomicile* deals. They were driven by differing tax rates in the countries involved. For example, AbbVie acquired Shite PLC and in doing so established its new headquarters in the UK. Reports have indicated that this move would lower the company's tax rate, which was 22% in 2013, to 13% in 2016.[90] The United States has one of the highest corporate tax rates of all major countries, and the U.S. Congress does not have the political willpower to change the rates to bring them more in line with other modern countries. This has caused many companies to maintain large cash balances outside of the United States and be reluctant to repatriate these monies. In order for the deal to qualify for redomicile status it has to meet certain conditions, such as a minimum threshold of shares offered. However, the U.S. government has cracked down on these deals and instituted new rules which may them harder to do.

SEARS: A FAILED DIVERSIFICATION STRATEGY

In 1992, Sears, Roebuck and Co. announced that it was divesting its financial services operations and was going to refocus on the retail operations for which it is world-famous. This ended the company's expensive and aggressive foray into the financial services business. The overall company was first formed in 1886 by Alvah Roebuck and Richard Sears. At the turn of the century it created a financial division that handled credit it extended to its customers. In the 1930s, it formed an insurance division, Allstate, which offered automobile insurance. In the 1950s, the company formed Sears Roebuck Acceptance Corporation, which handled short-term financial management activities for the company.

Around this time the company also began offering its own credit card. Therefore, financial services were nothing new to Sears. However, these activities were

(continued)

---

[88] Ronald Gilson, Myron S. Scholes, and Mark A. Wolfson, "Taxation and the Dynamics of Corporate Control: The Uncertain Case for Tax-Motivated Acquisitions," in John Coffee, Louis Lowenstein, and Susan Rose Ackerman, eds., *Knights, Raiders and Targets* (New York: Oxford University Press, 1988), 273–299.

[89] Carla Hayn, "Tax Attributes as Determinants of Shareholder Gains in Corporate Acquisitions," *Journal of Financial Economics* 23, no. 1 (June 1989): 121–153.

[90] Hester Plimridge and Peter Loftus, "AbbVie Clinches Takeover of Shire," *Wall Street Journal*, July 19–20, 2014, B1.

(continued)

complementary to the overall retail operations of the company, except for perhaps Allstate's insurance sales and its later expansion into mutual fund activities and the purchase of California Financial Corporation, a large savings and loan.

Major Expansion into Financial Services

In the late 1970s, the management of Sears was disappointed with the weak performance of the company's retail business. It was losing ground to Walmart, a company that had steadily grown at the expense of traditional rivals such as Sears. Rather than try to fix the problem, management decided that they would not be able to achieve their desired return in the retail business and that the way to achieve their financial goals was to expand into a supposedly more lucrative business—financial services. In 1981, Sears bought Coldwell Banker & Co. for approximately $175 million in stock and cash and Dean Witter Reynolds Inc. for a little over $600 million in stock and cash. In making these acquisitions, Sears's management believed it had acquired leaders in their respective fields. Coldwell Banker was the largest real estate brokerage firm in the United States, whereas Dean Witter was one of the larger stock brokerage firms.

Anticipated Synergy: Cross-Selling to Each Other's Customers

Sears's management believed that there would be great cross-selling opportunities for the respective units that were now under the Sears umbrella. Sears was reported to have had over 25 million credit card holders. Each was considered a potential customer for the securities and real estate sales. The synergistic gains would materialize as soon as the cross-selling would take place. Unfortunately, as with many mergers that were based in part on such cross-selling hopes, the different divisions were not successful in achieving these overly optimistic goals.

Anticipated Synergy: Selling Financial Services through Retail Stores

Sears was thwarted from going so far into financial services that it operated like a bank. Based on the success of its other financial services efforts, perhaps these regulatory strictures prevented the company from investing even more resources in an unsuccessful area than it already had. Nonetheless, Sears tried to market its financial services through financial services centers that it operated in more than 300 of its retail stores. These centers failed to become profitable. This strategy of selling houses and stocks at places usually reserved for lawn mowers and washing machines hurt the company's ability to keep pace with rivals that specialized in more targeted endeavors.

Corporate Governance: A Management-Dominated Board and an Institutional Investor Revolt

Gillan, Kensinger, and Martin chronicled the battle between the CEO of Sears, Edward Brennan, and institutional investors, championed by Robert Monks of the LENS fund.[a] Management held almost a majority of the board, while board members also held positions on each other's boards, creating a very chummy atmosphere. Insiders chaired important board committees. Gillan and colleagues concluded that Sears was a "firm lacking management accountability." While the market began to seriously question Sears's diversification strategy, management and the board initially circled the wagons and tried to aggressively oppose external dissent. Eventually, in 1991, the number of insiders was reduced to only one.

Market Reaction and Shareholder Returns

The market often is skeptical of claimed synergies when deals are announced. Investors often express this skepticism by showing little reaction or by selling pressure, which may cause the stock price of a bidder to fall after the announcement of a proposed merger. With Sears, however, this was not the case. The market responded positively to the diversifying acquisitions made by Sears. The market eventually caught on, and the stock price, relative to that of its industry peers, weakened. There is a lesson here that although securities markets may be somewhat (certainly not perfectly) efficient in the long run, they can efficiently react in the wrong direction. Efficiency merely states that the market reacts quickly to news such as a merger. This does not mean that the reaction is correct or rational but merely that it occurs quickly. Gillan and colleagues measured the shareholder returns of Sears relative to the market and the industry. They found that a $100 investment in Sears on January 1, 1981, would be worth $746, whereas a similar investment in a hypothetical portfolio designed to mimic the composition of businesses within Sears would have been worth $1,256. Clearly, shareholders who invested in Sears incurred a significant opportunity cost.

[a] Stuart Gillan, John W. Kensinger, and John Martin, "Value Creation and Corporate Diversification," *Journal of Financial Economics* 56, no. 1 (January 2000): 103–137.

PART TWO

Hostile Takeovers

CHAPTER FIVE

Antitakeover Measures

ANTITAKEOVER MEASURES HAVE EVOLVED greatly over the past quarter of a century. Corporate takeovers reached new levels of hostility during the 1980s. This heightened bellicosity was accompanied by many innovations in the art of corporate takeovers. Although hostile takeover tactics advanced, methods of corporate defense were initially slower to develop. As a result of the increased application of financial resources by threatened corporations, however, antitakeover defenses became quite elaborate and more difficult to penetrate. By the end of the 1980s, the art of antitakeover defenses became very sophisticated. Major investment banks organized teams of defense specialists, who worked with managements of larger corporations to erect formidable defenses that might counter the increasingly aggressive raiders of the fourth merger wave. After installing the various defenses, teams of investment bankers, along with their law firm counterparts, stood ready to be dispatched in the heat of battle to advise the target's management on the proper actions to take to thwart the bidder. By the 1990s, most large U.S. corporations had in place some form of antitakeover defense. The array of antitakeover defenses can be divided into two categories: preventative and active measures. Preventative measures are designed to reduce the likelihood of a financially successful hostile takeover, whereas active measures are employed after a hostile bid has been attempted.

This chapter describes the more frequently used antitakeover defenses. The impact of these measures on shareholder wealth, a controversial topic, is explored in detail. Opponents of these measures contend that they entrench management and reduce the value of stockholders' investment. They see the activities of raiders, or their more modern version, activist hedge funds, as an element that seeks to keep management "honest." They contend that managers who feel threatened by raiders will manage the firm more effectively, which will in turn result in higher stock values. Proponents of the use of antitakeover defenses argue, however, that these measures prevent the actions of the hostile raiders who have no long-term interest in the value of the corporation but merely are speculators seeking to extract a short-term gain while sacrificing the future of the company, which may have taken decades to build. Thus, proponents are not reluctant to take actions that will reduce the rights of such short-term shareholders because they are not equal, in their eyes, to long-term shareholders and other *stakeholders*, such as employees and local communities. The evidence on shareholder wealth effects does not, however, provide a consensus, leaving the issue somewhat unresolved. Some studies purport clear adverse shareholder wealth effects, whereas others fail to detect an adverse impact on the shareholders' position. This chapter includes the results of most of the major studies in this field so that readers can make an independent judgment.

 ## MANAGEMENT ENTRENCHMENT HYPOTHESIS VERSUS STOCKHOLDER INTERESTS HYPOTHESIS

The *management entrenchment hypothesis* proposes that nonparticipating stockholders experience reduced wealth when management takes actions to deter attempts to take control of the corporation. This theory asserts that managers of a corporation seek to maintain their positions through the use of active and preventative corporate defenses. According to this view, stockholder wealth declines in response to a reevaluation of this firm's stock by the market.

The *shareholder interests hypothesis*, sometimes also referred to as the convergence of interests hypothesis, implies that stockholder wealth rises when management takes actions to prevent changes in control. The fact that management does not need to devote resources to preventing takeover attempts is considered a cost savings. Such cost savings might come in the form of management time efficiencies savings, reduced expenditures in proxy fights, and a smaller investor relations department. The shareholder interests hypothesis can also be extended to show that antitakeover defenses can be used to maximize shareholder value through the bidding process. Management can assert that it will not withdraw the defenses unless it receives an offer that is in the shareholders' interests.

The shareholder wealth effects of various antitakeover measures, both preventative and active, are examined with an eye on the implications of the validity of these two competing hypotheses. If the installation of a given antitakeover defense results in a decline in shareholder wealth, this event lends some support to the management entrenchment hypothesis. If, however, shareholder wealth rises after the implementation of such a defense, the shareholder interests hypothesis gains credence. Morck, Shleifer, and Vishny examined the validity of these two competing hypotheses separate from a consideration of antitakeover defenses.[1] They considered the entrenchment of managers along with several other relevant factors, such as management's tenure with the company, personality, and status as a founder, and other factors such as the presence of a large outside shareholder or an active group of outside directors. The study

[1] R. Morck, A. Shleifer, and R. W. Vishny, "Management Ownership and Market Valuation: An Empirical Analysis," *Journal of Financial Economics* 20, no. 1/2 (January/March 1988): 293–315.

examined the relationship between Tobin's q—the market value of all of a company's securities divided by the replacement costs of all assets—as the dependent variable and the shareholdings of the board of directors in a sample of 371 of the Fortune 500 firms in 1980. They found that Tobin's q rises as ownership stakes rise. The positive relationship was not uniform in that it applied to ownership percentages between 0% and 5% as well as to those above 25%, whereas a negative relationship applied for those between 5% and 25%. The positive relationship for all ownership percentages, except the 5% to 25% range, provides some support for the shareholder interests hypothesis, because higher ownership percentages imply greater entrenchment, which in turn was shown to be associated with higher values of securities except the intermediate range of 5% to 25%. The conflicting results for the intermediate 5% to 25% range notwithstanding, Morck, Shleifer, and Vishny have provided some weak support for the shareholder interest hypothesis. More recent support comes from a study by Straska and Waller that showed that companies with low bargaining power can improve their position and shareholders' potential gains by adopting antitakeover measures.[2]

RIGHTS OF TARGETS BOARDS TO RESIST: UNITED STATES COMPARED TO THE REST OF THE WORLD

U.S. laws give the boards of directors of U.S. companies much leeway in resisting hostile bids and taking an array of evasive actions. Under U.S. laws boards can offer such resistance as part of what they see as their fiduciary responsibilities. This is different than how such actions are viewed in other regions, such as Great Britain, the Euro Zone, and Canada. In these jurisdictions the laws are more shareholder rights–oriented and boards are much more limited in the defensive actions they can take. Here the laws tend to favor offers being made directly to shareholders and letting them decide. In the United States the laws allow directors to exercise their own judgment about what is best for shareholders. When boards are too close to entrenched managers, this can work against shareholders' interests.

PREVENTATIVE ANTITAKEOVER MEASURES

Preventative antitakeover measures have become common in corporate America. Most Fortune 500 companies have considered and developed a plan of defense in the event that the company becomes the target of a hostile bid. One of the key actions a potential target can take is to enhance its preparedness. This means having a defensive strategy already designed and a defense team selected. This includes an outside law firm, investment bankers, proxy solicitors, and a public relations firm. Ideally, this group should meet, perhaps even once a year, and outline the strategy they will deploy in the event of an unwanted bid. This strategy should be revisited based upon changes in the M&A arena as well as other changes, such as industry M&A trends.

---

[2] Miroslava Straska and Gregory Waller, "Do Antitakeover Provisions Harm Shareholders?" *Journal of Corporate Finance* 16, no. 4 (September 2010): 487–497.

The potential target will want to prepare what is sometimes referred to as a "Corporate Profile." This document may outline the company's potential vulnerability and will suggest a strategy for how hostile bids may be dealt with. It will describe the relevant corporate bylaws and charter provisions. This is a very important part of a company's takeover preparedness as takeover battles can be surprisingly swift and a potential target needs to have its defensive strategy well thought out in advance. In fact, there are companies that assess the takeover vulnerability of public firms and market this information.

Early Warnings Systems: Monitoring Shareholding and Trading Patterns

One of the first steps in developing a preventative antitakeover defense is to analyze the distribution of share ownership of the company. Certain groups of shareholders, such as employees, tend to be loyal to the company and probably will vote against a hostile bidder. Institutional investors usually invest in the security to earn a target return and may eagerly take advantage of favorable pricing and terms of a hostile offer. If a company is concerned about being a target of a hostile bid, it may closely monitor the trading of its shares. A sudden and unexpected increase in trading volume may signal the presence of a bidder who is trying to accumulate shares before having to announce its intentions. Such an announcement will usually cause the stock price to rise, so it is in a bidder's interest to accumulate as many shares as possible before an announcement.

Types of Preventative Antitakeover Measures

In effect, the installation of preventative measures is an exercise in wall building. Higher and more resistant walls need to be continually designed and installed because the raiders, and their investment banking and legal advisors, devote their energies to designing ways of scaling these defenses. These defenses are sometimes referred to as shark repellants.

Among the preventative measures that are discussed in this chapter are the following:

- **Poison pills.** These are securities issued by a potential target to make the firm less valuable in the eyes of a hostile bidder. There are two general types of poison pills: flip-over and flip-in. They can be an effective defense that has to be taken seriously by any hostile bidder. In fact, they can be so effective that shareholders' rights activists have pressured many companies to remove them.
- **Corporate charter amendments.** The target corporation may enact various amendments in its corporate charter that will make it more difficult for a hostile acquirer to bring about a change in managerial control of the target. Some of the amendments that are discussed are supermajority provisions, staggered boards, fair price provisions, and dual capitalizations.

First-Generation Poison Pills: Preferred Stock Plans

Poison pills were invented by the famous takeover lawyer Martin Lipton, who used them in 1982 to defend El Paso Electric against General American Oil and again in 1983 during the Brown Foreman versus Lenox takeover contest. Brown Foreman was the fourth largest distiller in the United States, marketing such name brands as Jack Daniels whiskey, Martel cognac, and Korbel champagne, and generating annual sales of $900 million. Lenox was a major producer of china. Lenox's shares were trading at approximately $60 per share on the New York Stock Exchange. Brown Foreman believed that Lenox's stock was undervalued and offered $87 a share for each share of Lenox. This price was more than 20 times the previous year's per share earnings of $4.13. Such an attractive offer is very difficult to defeat. Lipton suggested that Lenox offer each common stockholder a dividend of preferred shares that would be convertible into 40 shares of Brown Foreman stock if Brown Foreman took over Lenox. These convertible shares would be an effective antitakeover device because, if converted, they would seriously dilute the Brown family's 60% share ownership position.

The type of poison pill Lenox used to fend off Brown Foreman is referred to as a *preferred stock plan*. Although they may keep a hostile bidder at bay, these first-generation poison pills had certain disadvantages. First, the issuer could redeem them only after an extended period of time, which might be in excess of 10 years. Another major disadvantage is that they had an immediate adverse impact on the balance sheet. This is because when an analyst computes the leverage of a company, the preferred stock may be added to the long-term debt, thus making the company more heavily leveraged and therefore riskier in the eyes of investors after the implementation of the preferred stock plan.

In recent years Brown Forman has pursued acquisitions that make much more strategic sense. In 2000, it bought 45% of Finland's Finlandia Vodka and bought the remaining 55% in 2004. In 2006, it purchased the Chambord brand (the main component of Kir Royale cocktails) from French liquor firm Charles Jacquin et Cie, and in 2007 it bought Mexican liquor company Tequila Herradura and in 2011 acquired the Maximus vodka brand.

Second-Generation Poison Pills: Flip-Over Rights

Poison pills did not become popular until late 1985, when their developer, Martin Lipton, perfected them. The new pills did not involve the issuance of preferred stock so that, by being easier to use, the pills would be more effective. They would also eliminate any adverse impact that an issue of preferred stock might have on the balance sheet as analysts often treat it as a fixed income security.

The perfected pills came in the form of rights offerings that allowed the holders to buy stock in the acquiring firm at a low price. Rights are a form of call option issued by the corporation, entitling the holders to purchase a certain amount of stock for a particular price during a specified time period. The rights certificates used in modern poison pills are distributed to shareholders as a dividend and become activated after a triggering event. A typical triggering event could be one of the following:

- An acquisition of 20% of the outstanding stock by any individual, partnership, or corporation.
- A tender offer for 30% or more of the target corporation's outstanding stock.

Flip-over poison pills seemed to be a potent defense until they were effectively overcome in the 1985 takeover of the Crown Zellerbach Corporation by the Anglo-French financier Sir James Goldsmith. Goldsmith acquired more than 50% of Crown Zellerbach's share to gain control of the company and its forest assets, which he coveted. However, he avoided acquiring control of the target, thus avoiding the flip-over pill Crown Zellerbach had in place. The flip-over pill was designed to prevent 100% acquisitions, which Goldsmith avoided doing. Ironically, the pill made it difficult for Crown Zellerbach to seek out a white knight and its stock price suffered. This improved Goldsmith's bargaining position, and he was able to negotiate a favorable total acquisition, followed by a sale of Crown Zellerbach's assets, including the Camus Mill, which he sold to the James River Corporation.[3]

After the use of poison pills was upheld in the courts, large corporations rushed to adopt their own poison pill defenses. In the 1990s, poison pill defenses were commonplace (see Figure 5.1).

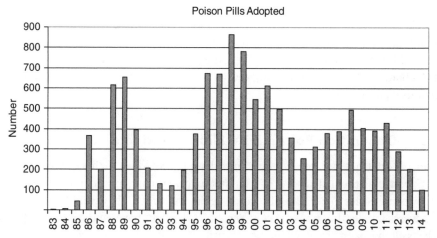

FIGURE 5.1 Poison Pill Adopted: 1983–2014. *Source*: Thomson Financial Securities Data, March 6, 2015.

---

[3] In 1997 James River and Fort Howard Corporations merged to form the Fort James Corporation, which then became the largest tissue producer in the United States. In 2000 the Camus Mill was sold to Georgia Pacific Corp.

Third-Generation Poison Pills: Flip-In Poison Pills

Flip-over poison pills have the drawback that they are effective only if the bidder acquires 100% of the target; they are not effective in preventing the acquisition of a controlling but less than 100% interest in the target. Given that most acquirers want to obtain 100% of the target's stock so as to have unrestricted access to the target's resources, flip-over provisions may prevent many, but not all, control transactions. Flip-in poison pills were an innovation designed to deal with the problem of a bidder who was not trying to purchase 100% of the target. With the flip-over provisions, a bidder could avoid the impact of the pill simply by not buying all of the target's outstanding stock.

Flip-in provisions allow holders of rights to acquire stock in the target, as opposed to *flip-over* rights, which allow holders to acquire stock in the acquirer. The flip-in rights were designed to dilute the target company regardless of whether the bidder merged the target into his company. They can be effective in dealing with raiders who seek to acquire a controlling influence in a target while not acquiring majority control. The raider does not receive the benefits of the rights, while other shareholders do. Thus the presence of flip-in rights makes such controlling acquisitions very expensive.

A flip-over plan may also contain flip-in provisions, thus combining the advantages of a flip-over plan, which is used against a 100% hostile acquisition, with a flip-in plan, which is used against a control share acquisition that is not a 100% share acquisition.

Back-End Plans

Another variant on the poison pill theme are *back-end plans*, also known as *note purchase rights plans*. The first back-end plan was developed in 1984. Under a back-end plan, shareholders receive a rights dividend, which gives shareholders the ability to exchange this right along with a share of stock for cash or senior securities that are equal in value to a specific "back-end" price stipulated by the issuer's board of directors. These rights may be exercised after the acquirer purchases shares in excess of a specific percentage of the target's outstanding shares. The back-end price is set above the market price, so back-end plans establish a minimum price for a takeover. The board of directors, however, must in good faith set a reasonable price.

Back-end plans were used to try to limit the effectiveness of two-tiered tender offers. In fact, the name *back-end* refers to the back end of a two-tiered offer. However, given that two-tiered offers are considered coercive and in conflict with the Williams Act, they are now less relevant.

Voting Plans

Voting plans were first developed in 1985. They are designed to prevent any outside entity from obtaining voting control of the company. Under these plans the company issues a dividend of preferred stock. If any outside entity acquires a substantial percentage of the company's stock, holders of preferred stock become entitled to supervoting rights. This prevents the larger block holder, presumably the hostile bidder, from obtaining voting control of the target. The legality of these plans has been successfully challenged in court. Therefore, they are not very commonly used.

Mechanics of Issuing Poison Pills

Poison pills are issued by distributing to common stockholders a *dividend* of one right for each share of stock they own. Rights holders receive the right to purchase one share of stock during the exercise period, which is typically 10 years in length. The rights are initially redeemable and trade with the common stock but are not initially exercisable. Rights plans are usually authorized by the board of directors without shareholder approval. However, shareholder rights entities have pressured companies whose boards adopt them to secure shareholder approval within a reasonable time period, such as a year.

Until the occurrence of the first triggering event, such as a bidder's announcement of intentions to purchase 15% or 20% of the issuer stock (without board approval) or to make an offer for 30% of its shares, the rights trade with the common shares and no separate rights certificates are issued. The bidder does not get to enjoy the benefits of the rights.

Once this triggering event occurs, however, the rights detach and become exercisable. At that time rights certificates are mailed to shareholders. However, the exercise price of these rights is set so high that they really have no value as it would not make any sense to exercise them. However, the second trigger occurs when the bidder closes on the purchase of the target's shares. The rights now convey upon the holder the right to purchase shares at "50% off" prices.

As noted previously, the issuer may redeem the rights after the first trigger for a nominal amount, such as $0.02 per right, if it decides that it is advantageous. For example, if the issuer receives a bid that it finds desirable, the existence of the rights may be an impediment to an advantageous deal and the issuer may want to remove them. However, once the second trigger has occurred, the rights are no longer redeemable by the board.[4]

Simple Example of Poison Pill Mechanics

Let us consider a very simplistic example of the mechanics of flip-in poison pills. Assume that Corporation A makes a bid for Company B and the target has a poison pill. Let us further assume that the pill has an exercise price (Pe) of $60, while the target's stock price (Ps) is $10. Then the number of shares that can be purchased are as follows:

Pe = $60 and Ps = $10, so the number of shares that can be purchased are

Pe/(Ps/2) = $60/($10/2) = $60/5 = 12 shares.

It is important to note that when the board sets the exercise price, often with the assistance of a valuation firm, it is not putting forward an appropriate transaction value of acquisition price. It tries to consider the long-term value of the stock over the life of

---

[4] R. Matthew Garms, "Shareholder By-Law Amendments and the Poison Pill: The Market for Corporate Control and Economic Efficiency," *Journal of Corporation Law* 24, no. 2 (Winter 1994): 436.

the plan. Often a range of three to five times the current value of the stock may be a norm, but it can be higher for growth companies and lower for mature firms. So our example is of a firm that may be more growth-oriented.

Let us also assume that there are 1,000 shares outstanding (SO) prior to the bid and that the bidder has purchased 200 of them, so the remaining 800 shares are not in the hands of the bidder. Then the poison pill allows each of these 800 shares to be used to purchase 12 new shares, for a total of 9,600 shares. If all of the warrants are exercised, then the total shares outstanding will be 1,000 + 9,600 =10,600 shares.

In this simplistic analysis the value of the target's equity prior to the exercise of the warrants was $10 × 1,000 shares or $10,000. The exercising of the warrants adds to this equity in the amount of $60 × 800 shares or $48,000. At this point total equity capital is $10,000 + $48,000 or $58,000. There are 10,600 shares outstanding so the per share equity value is $58,000/10,600 or $5.47.

The loss of the value of the shares to the control shareholder is as follows:

$$(\$10.00 - \$5.47) = 0.453 \text{ or } 45.3\%$$

The loss of the value of the shares does not fully capture the control shareholder's total loss. In addition to losing a significant portion of the value of its shares, the control shareholder has also lost a very significant amount of its control in the target company. After the warrants are exercised, we have 10,600 shares outstanding. Prior to the exercise of the warrants, the control shareholder owned 20% of the company (200/1,000). After the warrants are exercised, this "control" shareholder now owns 1.89% of the firm (200/10,600).

Poison Pills and Shareholder Approval

Directors can quickly authorize a poison pill defense without formally requesting shareholder approval. For many years such defenses were in place for 10 years before they came up for renewal. In effect, they were "Not For Sale" signs on corporations. However, shareholder rights advocates, such as Institutional Shareholders Services (ISS), opposed such indiscriminate implementation of poison pills. They recognized that, properly used, they can enhance shareholder value. Their concern, however, was that they could also be used to entrench managers. Therefore, they tend to oppose pills that are in place for more than a year without shareholders providing their approval.

A *chewable pill* allows for a shareholder vote on whether a particular takeover bid would be covered by the company's poison pill. This helps prevent pills from being used to entrench managers.

Another alternative is a "TIDE" (three-year independent director evaluation) plan. This is where the poison pill plan contains a provision requiring that the company's independent directors review the plan every three years to see if it still is serving the interests of shareholders. If they decide that the plan is no longer in shareholders' interest, the plan may also provide them with the ability to rescind it.

Blank Check Preferred Stock

Although a board of directors may have authority to issue rights, its ability to issue shares is dictated by the corporate charter. For this reason, boards may amend the articles of incorporation so as to create and reserve a certain amount of preferred stock that can be issued in the event that the rights become exercisable.[5] This prevents the board from having to solicit shareholder approval to amend the charter to allow for the issuance of shares to satisfy the rights. Such a request for shareholder approval would be tantamount to a referendum on the poison pill itself. It would also mean additional delay and uncertainty and would effectively weaken the poison pill defense. Typically the board has the right to determine voting, dividend, and conversion rights of such shares.

Blank check preferred stock can also be used in conjunction with a white squire defense. Here a board can quickly issue shares to a friendly party, such as an employee stock ownership plan or an outside investor not interested in control. Shareholder rights groups, such as ISS, are not supportive of blank check preferred rights if they are used as an antitakeover defense.

Dead Hand, Slow Hand, and No Hand Provisions

Poison pills can be deactivated by the target's board of directors. Bidders can try to use this feature to offset the poison pill by initiating a tender offer that is contingent on the removal of the pill. The higher the premium offered, the more pressure on the board to remove the pill defense. Dead hand provisions give the power to redeem the poison pill to the directors who were on the target's board of directors when the pill was adopted or who were appointed by such directors. Even if these directors are ousted, they retain the voting power to control the pill's redemption. Courts in several states have not been receptive to dead hand provisions.[6] For example, dead hand provisions have been ruled invalid in Delaware.[7]

Slow hand provisions place a limit on the time period when only prior directors can redeem the pill. Limitation periods are typically 180 days.[8] Some states, such as Pennsylvania, but not Delaware, allow slow hand provisions. No hand provisions limit the period for redemption to a certain time frame.

Shadow Pill

A bidder cannot simply look at a target company and conclude from the fact that it may not have a poison pill in place that it will not have to face such a defense. Targets may simply adopt a pill after a bid has taken place. For large companies, this can be done in a single day at a board of directors meeting during which the members approve the pill.[9] This is a fact that bidders should be aware of when weighing a target's defenses.

---

[5] Arthur Fleischer Jr., and Alexander Sussman, *Takeover Defense*, 5th ed. (New York: Aspen, 1995), 5–105.

[6] *Carmody v. Toll Bros., Inc.*, 723 A. 2d 1180 (Del Ch. 1988).

[7] *Quickturn Design Systems v. Mentor Graphic Corp.*, 721 A.2d 1281 (Del. 1999).

[8] *Special Study for Corporate Counsel on Poison Pills*, William A. Hancock, ed. (Chesterfield, OH: Business Laws, 2002), 101.010.

[9] John C. Coates, "Takeover Defense in the Shadow of the Pill: A Critique of the Scientific Evidence," *Texas Law Review* 79, no. 2 (December 2000).

Legality of Poison Pills

In a November 1985 ruling in the Delaware Supreme Court, the court upheld the legality of Household International's use of a poison pill. At that time Household owned various businesses, including Household Finance, Von's Grocery, and National Car Rental. The board sought to prevent a takeover by one of its largest shareholders and member of Household's board—John Moran. He argued that this use of a pill was discriminatory as it was unfairly directed at him and his bid. However, the Delaware court's position in *Moran v. Household International* was that the pills did not necessarily keep bidders away; rather, they gave target corporations the opportunity to seek higher bids.[10]

The Delaware court has not supported poison pills when they are used to preempt the auction process. This was also the court's position in the Pantry Pride bid for Revlon, where the court found that Revlon's use of its poison pill preempted the auction process in favoring Forstmann Little's offer while halting Pantry Pride's bid.[11] Similarly, in 1988, British publisher Robert Maxwell successfully challenged the publisher Macmillan's poison pill defense. A Delaware court ruled that Macmillan's poison pill defense unfairly discriminated against Maxwell's offer for the New York publishing firm. The court concluded that poison pills should be used to promote an auction. In the court's view, Macmillan's pill prevented an effective auction. Also in 1988, a Delaware court reached a similar decision when it ruled that Interco's poison pill unfairly favored Interco's own recapitalization plan while discriminating against the Rales tender offer.

In 2014 activist hedge fund manager David Leob, and his fund Third Point, challenged a particularly aggressive use of a poison pill by the famed auction house Sotheby's. Sotheby's adopted a poison pill that limited Loeb's holdings to 10% before incurring the adverse effects of the company's poison pill defense but allowed other passive investors to hold up to 20% without being affected by the pill. Leob sued on the grounds that this was clearly unfair. The question before the Delaware Court of Chancery was whether a company can use a poison pill defense that targets activist hedge funds. In a ruling issued on May 2, 2014, Judge Donald Parson ruled companies could use poison pills in this manner.

While U.S. courts have often supported the use of poison pills when they do not preempt the auction process, other nations that place greater emphasis on shareholder rights have not viewed them so kindly. For example, the United Kingdom and the European Union have not been supportive of poison pills.

Net Operating Loss (NOL) Poison Pills

A company's poor financial performance can actually provide value by allowing the owner of these NOLs to offset other income in the future and lower its tax obligations. NOLs are tax losses that can be used to offset profits two years past and up to 20 years forward. However, the IRS has placed limitations on their use in cases of stock ownership changes. The IRS defines ownership changes as 50% or more of the shares

---

[10] *Moran v. Household International, Inc.*, 500 A. 2d 1346 (Del. 1985).
[11] *Revlon, Inc. v. MacAndrews & Forbes Holdings, Inc.*, 506 A.2d 173 (Del. 1986).

changing ownership over a three-year period. However, the only shareholders whom the IRS focuses on (for this 50% change in ownership) are those who have obtained 5% or more of the outstanding stock over a three-year period. Thus the NOLs have a lower share threshold.

In *Selectica, Inc. v. Versata, Inc.* the Delaware court applied the *Unocal* standard when it concluded that it was legitimate for a company to use its pill—in this case one that had a low 4.99% trigger threshold—to protect its NOLs.[12]

This decision was interesting in that the court did not have a problem with the fact that the value of the NOLs was not clearly established. This case was also interesting in that it is one of the rare instances where a bidder actually triggered a pill.

As we have noted, an NOL pill typically has a lower threshold, usually 4.99%, and it contains provisions for the event that one or more 5% shareholders increase their position over a three-year period. The lower trigger threshold effectively means that target board approval is required in order for 5% or more shareholders to increase their ownership.

Poison Pills and Proxy Fights

While a poison pill may make a hostile bid such as a tender offer prohibitively expensive unless it is deactivated, it does not prevent a proxy contest. This creates an opportunity for activists seeking control of the board of directors, which, in turn, can lead to deactivating the poison pill. We will return to this issue later in this chapter after we discuss classified boards.

Number of Poison Pill Plans

The number of companies reporting poison pills has declined in recent years. Shark Repellent reported that 12% of the S&P 1500 had poison pills, while less than 8% of the S&P 500 had such plans. This is not surprising given how quickly such a plan can be put in place. Many companies have "ready to go" plans "on the shelf," which can be put in place once a takeover threat appears.

Impact of Poison Pills on Stock Prices

Several studies have examined the impact of poison pill provisions on stock prices. Early studies, such as one by Malatesta and Walking that considered what effect the announcement of the adoption of a poison pill had on 132 firms between 1982 and 1986, found that poison pill defense reduced shareholder wealth.[13] Malatesta and Walking found that poison pill defenses appeared to reduce stockholder wealth and that, on average, the firms that announced poison pill defenses generated small, but statistically significant, abnormal negative stock returns (−0.915%) during a two-day

---

[12] *Selectica, Inc. v. Versata Enters.*, 2010 Del Ch. LEXIS, 39, (Del. Ch. 2010), and *Unocal Corp. v. Mesa Petroleum Corp.*, 493 A. 2d 946 (Del 1985).

[13] Paul H. Malatesta and Ralph A. Walking, "Poison Pills Securities: Stockholder Wealth, Profitability and Ownership Structure," *Journal of Financial Economics* 20, no. 1/2 (January/March 1988): 347–376.

window around the announcement date. When these firms abandoned their poison pill plans, they showed abnormal positive returns.

Malatesta and Walking's results provide some support for the managerial entrenchment hypothesis in that the firms adopting the pills tended to have below-average financial performance. They also found that, on average, the managerial ownership percentage was significantly less for firms that adopted poison pills compared with industry averages. This supports the management entrenchment hypothesis. The findings of Malatesta and Walking were supported by other early studies, such as one by Michael Ryngaert of 380 firms that had adopted poison pill defenses between 1982 and 1986.[14] Ryngaert found statistically significant stock price declines from firms that adopted pill defenses and that were perceived as takeover targets. Ryngaert also analyzed the impact on the target firm's stock of legal challenges to the pill defense. He noted negative excess stock returns in 15 of 18 promanagement court decisions (upholding the legality of the pill) and positive excess returns in 6 of 11 proacquirer decisions (invalidating the pill). Ryngaert's research also touched on the effectiveness of poison pills as an antitakeover defense. He found that hostile bids are more likely to be defeated by firms that have a poison pill in place. Thirty-one percent of the pill-protected firms remained independent after receiving unsolicited bids, compared with 15.78% for a control group of non-pill-protected firms that also received unsolicited bids. Moreover, in 51.8% of the unsolicited bids, pill-protected firms received increased bids, which Ryngaert attributes to the presence of the pill defense. This finding is consistent with other research, such as the Georgeson study that is discussed next.

Later and more comprehensive research by Comment and Schwert indicated that poison pills do not necessarily harm shareholders.[15] They find this is the case based upon the impact of poison pill on takeover premiums. We will discuss the impact of pills on premiums shortly.

ORACLE HELD AT BAY BY PEOPLESOFT'S POISON PILL

In June 2003, the second-largest U.S. software maker (behind Microsoft), Oracle Corp., initiated a $7.7 billion hostile bid for rival and third-largest PeopleSoft Inc. Both firms market "back-office" software that is used for supply management as well as other accounting functions. Lawrence Ellison, Oracle's very aggressive chief executive officer (CEO), doggedly pursued PeopleSoft, which brandished its powerful poison pill defense to keep Ellison at bay. The takeover battle went on for approximately a year and a half, during which PeopleSoft was able to prevent Oracle from completing its takeover due to the strength of its poison pill.

(continued)

---

[14] Michael Ryngaert, "The Effects of Poison Pill Securities on Stockholder Wealth," *Journal of Financial Economics* 20, no. 1/2 (January/March 1988): 377–417.

[15] Robert Comment and G. William Schwert, "Poison or Placebo: Evidence on the Deterrence and Wealth Effects of Modern Antitakeover Measures," *Journal of Financial Economics* 39, no. 1 (September 1995): 3–43.

(continued)

PeopleSoft's board rejected Oracle's offer as inadequate and refused to remove the poison pill. Oracle then pursued litigation in Delaware to force PeopleSoft to dismantle this defense. Over the course of the takeover contest Oracle increased its offer from an initial share offer price of $19 to $26, lowered it to $21, and then raised it back up to $24. PeopleSoft also used a novel defense when it offered its customers, in the event of a hostile takeover by Oracle, a rebate of up to five times the license fee they paid for their PeopleSoft software. PeopleSoft defended this defense by saying that the hostile bid made it difficult for PeopleSoft to generate sales: Customers were worried that if they purchased PeopleSoft software it would be discontinued by Oracle in the event of a takeover, as Oracle had its own competing products and no incentive to continue the rival software. Ironically, Oracle really wanted PeopleSoft's customer base, not its products or even many of its employees.

The takeover contest became very hostile, with the management of the companies launching personal attacks against each other. PeopleSoft's management called Ellison the "Darth Vader" of the industry. PeopleSoft's own board eventually got so fed up with this way of handling the contest that it asked the company's CEO, Craig Conway, to step down.

The battle went on for approximately a year and a half, but eventually PeopleSoft succumbed in January 2005. One week later Oracle began sending layoff notices to thousands of PeopleSoft's employees. While the poison pill did not help these employees directly, PeopleSoft's shareholders benefited by the higher $10.3 billion takeover price. Employees indirectly benefited as the prolonged contest allowed many of them to make alternative employment plans. This takeover contest featured an effective use of a poison pill defense and also showed just how useful it can be in increasing shareholder value. However, while it underscored the effectiveness of poison pills, it also showed that even a poison pill will not necessarily hold off a determined bidder who is willing to pay higher and higher prices.

Impact of Poison Pills on Takeover Premiums

Two often-cited studies concerning the impact of poison pills on takeover premiums were conducted by Georgeson and Company, a large proxy solicitation firm. In a study released in March 1988, the firm showed that companies protected by poison pills received 69% higher premiums in takeover contests than unprotected companies. The study compared the premiums paid to pill-protected companies with those paid to companies without pill protection. Protected corporations in the Georgeson sample received premiums that were 78.5% above where the company's stock was trading six months before the contest. Unprotected corporations received premiums that were 56.7% higher. The firm did a later study in November 1997, analyzing transactions from 1992 to 1996. The results were similar, although the difference between premiums was less. Premiums paid to pill-protected companies averaged eight percentage points, or 26%, higher than those without pill protection. The difference was greater for small capitalization companies than for large capitalization companies.

The positive impact of poison pills on takeover premiums that was found in both Georgeson studies has also been confirmed by academic research. Comment and Schwert also found that poison pills are associated with higher takeover premiums.[16] More generally, Varaiya found that antitakeover measures were one of the determinants of takeover premiums.[17] For companies that are taken over, target shareholders may receive higher premiums. However, in those instances where the pill prevents a takeover, shareholders lose the opportunity to get the premium.

Poison Pills and the Auction Process

The fact that poison pills result in high takeover premiums has been supported by other research on the relationship between poison pills and the auction process.[18] One of the reasons poison pills result in higher premiums is that they facilitate the auction process. Bradley, Desai, and Kim have shown that auctions result in an added takeover premium of 11.4%,[19] whereas Comment and Schwert found added premiums equal to 13%. Poison pill defenses are often circumvented when the bidder increases its bid or makes an attractive all-cash offer. All-cash offers have been associated with 12.9% higher premiums.[20] In the face of increased prices brought about by an auction that may have been combined with more attractive compensation, such as an all-cash offer, target boards are often pressured to deactivate the poison pill.

Conclusion of Research on Shareholder Wealth Effects of Poison Pills

The consensus of the research is that the implementation of poison pill defenses tends to be associated with negative, although not large, excess returns to the target's stock. We must remember, however, that these studies focus on a narrow time period around the date when the adoption of the pill plan is announced. Pill-protected firms that ultimately are *acquired* may receive higher returns as a result of the pill defense. These higher premiums were not reflected in this body of research which focuses on short term returns around the announcement date of the poison pill defense.

Poison Puts

Poison puts are a unique variation on the poison pill theme. They involve an issuance of bonds that contain a *put option* exercisable only in the event that an unfriendly takeover occurs. A put option allows the holder to sell a particular security to another individual or firm during a certain time period and for a specific price. The issuing firm hopes that

---

[16] Comment and Schwert, "Poison or Placebo."

[17] Nikhil P. Varaiya, "Determinants of Premiums in Acquisition Transactions," *Managerial and Decision Economics* 8, no. 3 (September 1987): 175–184.

[18] Comment and Schwert, "Poison or Placebo."

[19] Michael Bradley, Anand Desai, and E. Han Kim, "Synergistic Gains from Corporate Acquisitions and Their Division between the Shareholders of the Target and Acquiring Firms," *Journal of Financial Economics* 21, no. 1 (May 1988): 3–40.

[20] Yen-Sheng Huang and Ralph A. Walking, "Target Abnormal Returns Associated with Acquisition Announcements: Payment, Acquisition Form, and Managerial Resistance," *Journal of Financial Economics* 19, no. 2 (December 1987): 329–349.

the holders' cashing of the bonds, which creates large cash demands for the merged firm, will make the takeover prospect most unattractive. If the acquiring firm can convince bondholders, however, not to redeem their bonds, these bond sales may be avoided. In addition, if the bonds are offered at higher than prevailing interest rates, the likelihood of redemption will not be as high.

Recent Trends in Poison Pill Adoptions

As we discuss at length in Chapter 13, corporate governance has been the focus of much attention over the past 10 years. Shareholder rights advocates and activist investors, such as hedge funds, have put increasing pressure on companies to scale back their anti-takeover defenses. Since poison pills are considered the strongest defense, there has been pressure on many companies to not renew plans that typically have a 10-year life. This is shown in Figures 5.1 and 5.2. Many companies have chosen to not renew plans that may have been put in place in the prior decade and adopt a new plan only if a threat appears. These are referred to as *in play* adoptions. For example, companies that may be the target of activist investors, such as hedge funds, which may be seeking to take advantage of net operating loss carry forwards, can protect shareholders' interests by quickly adopting a poison pill. However, companies that seek to maximize shareholder value may not want to adopt a poison pill lest it reduce the probability of being acquired at a good premium. This concern has brought down the total number of poison pill plans in place at large capitalization companies.[21]

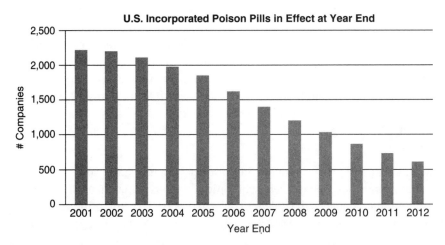

FIGURE 5.2   U.S. Incorporated Poison Pills in Effect at Year End.   *Source*: FactSet Shark Repellent, www.sharkrepellent.net.

---

[21] www.sharkrepellent.net.

Corporate Boards and Poison Pills

The board of directors of a company has the power to deactivate the poison pill defense. Therefore, if a bidder can change the target's board, it can get around the poison pill. So while the poison pill is a powerful defense, if the bidder believes that it can, perhaps through activism and the proxy process, replace the target's board, the poison pill will look less formidable. If, however, the target can include another defense we will discuss shortly, a staggered board, a defense that makes it more difficult to change an entire board, then this combination can be a quite powerful defense. However, perhaps the greatest pressure a bidder can exert on the target's board is a high-premium, all-cash offer.

Corporate Charter Amendments

Before discussing corporate charter amendments in detail it is useful to differentiate between a *corporate charter* and the corporation's *bylaws*. The bylaws are usually established by the board of directors, and they set forth important rules for how the company will operate. For example, they will indicate when directors meet and when and where the corporation's annual shareholders' meeting will be. They may also specify what corporate officer and director positions exist and how directors may be replaced. A corporate charter, sometimes also called the articles of incorporation, is a more fundamental document that sets forth the company's purpose and the different classes of shares it may have. Usually a shareholder vote is required to change the articles of incorporation. More major changes in how a company operates may have to be set forth in the corporate charter and not the bylaws. From an M&A perspective, an action such as staggering the board of directors, which we will discuss shortly, needs to be in the corporate charter. In order to get it in the charter it needs shareholder approval. If this is not in the corporate charter prior to a hostile bid, it is unlikely shareholders will approve it.

Changes in the corporate charter are common antitakeover devices. The extent to which they may be implemented depends on state laws, which vary among states. Corporate charter changes generally require shareholder approval. The majority of antitakeover charter amendments are approved. Only in extreme cases of poor management performance do stockholders actively resist antitakeover amendments. This is partly because management is generally much more organized in its lobbying efforts than those shareholders who may oppose the proposed charter changes. Another important reason that shareholders tend to approve these amendments is that the majority of shareholders in large U.S. corporations are institutions, which have in the past been known to side with management. Some evidence suggests that this tendency is starting to change. Moreover, institutions as a whole are not unified in their support of management.

Brickley, Lease, and Smith point out that certain types of institutional investors, such as banks, insurance companies, and trusts, are more likely to vote in favor of management's proposals than other institutions, such as mutual funds, public pension funds, endowments, and foundations.[22] They believe that the latter category of investors is more independent of management in that they do not generally derive income from the lines of business controlled by management. When the charter amendment proposal clearly reduces shareholder wealth, institutions in general are more clearly found to be in opposition to the amendment.

The process of proxy approval of shareholder amendments is discussed in Chapter 6. A later study by Brickley, Lease, and Smith explored the circumstances under which managers are more constrained by the voting process.[23] They found that although there is a high rate of passage of proposals put forward by management, managers tend to make such proposals only when they are highly likely to pass. In addition, in a study of 670 antitakeover corporate charter amendments involving 414 firms, they showed that managers are more constrained by voting when the following conditions apply: (1) small companies with more concentrated ownership, (2) companies that have large outside blockholders, (3) when information about possible adverse shareholder wealth effects has attracted media attention, and (4) companies that have stringent voting rules.

We will examine the shareholder wealth effects of the various specific types of amendments. However, research on amendments in general points to negative effects following their passage.[24] When we explore the wealth effects of specific amendments, we will see that they tend to differ and various factors, such as the strength of the specific defense, tend to determine whether there are significant impacts.

Some of the more common antitakeover corporate charter changes are as follows:

- Staggered terms of the board of directors
- Supermajority provisions
- Fair price provisions
- Dual capitalizations

Staggered Board Amendments

A normal direct election process provides for each director to come up for election at the company's annual meeting. When a board is staggered or classified, only a certain percentage, such as one-third, will come up for election during any one year, so that each director is elected approximately once every three years.[25] Staggered boards require shareholder approval before they can be implemented.

Staggered or classified boards are a controversial antitakeover defense. While in the early 2000s the majority of U.S. public companies had staggered boards, also called classified boards, the majority of companies now have declassified or unitary boards. The

---

[22] James A. Brickley, Ronald C. Lease, and Clifford W. Smith, "Ownership Structure and Voting on Antitakeover Amendments," *Journal of Financial Economics* 20 (January/March 1988): 267–291.

[23] James A. Brickley, Ronald C. Lease, and Clifford W. Smith, "Corporate Voting: Evidence from Corporate Charter Amendment Proposals," *Journal of Corporate Finance* 1, no. 1 (March 1994): 5–31.

[24] James Mahoney and Joseph Mahoney, "An Empirical Investigation of the Effect of Corporate Charter Antitakeover Amendments on Shareholder Wealth," *Strategic Management Journal* 14, no. 1 (January 1993): 17–31.

[25] Under most state laws the maximum number of classes of directors is three.

staggered board defense varies the terms of the board of directors so that only a few, such as one-third, of the directors may be elected during any given year. This may be important in a takeover battle because the incumbent board may be made up of members who are sympathetic to current management. Indeed, boards may also contain members of management. When a bidder has already bought majority control, the staggered board may prevent him from electing managers who will pursue the bidder's goals for the corporation, such as the sale of assets to pay down the debt incurred in the acquisition process. In a proxy contest staggered boards require insurgents to win more than one proxy fight at two successive shareholder meetings to gain control of the target. This can create much uncertainty as a lot can happen over the one- to two-year period that is needed to gain control of a staggered board.

The trend toward declassification of boards has partially been in response to pressure by shareholder rights activists. Indeed, a significant amount of this pressure came from the Harvard Shareholder Rights Project which was started these efforts in the 2010 proxy season. This project works with institutional investors such as pension funds to initiate proxy proposals to pressure companies declassify their boards. It claims that 98 boards of S&P 500 and Fortune 500 companies were declassified as a result of these efforts during the 2012–2014 proxy seasons. However, the Project has attracted more than its share of criticism.[26]

Companies, such as Chesapeake Energy Corp., Hewlett-Packard and Verizon have declassified their boards in response to outside pressure. This trend is much more pronounced at larger, S&P 500 firms, than at smaller public companies. While over half S&P500 had classified boards in 2000, this percentage fell below 20% by the end of 2013 (see Figure 5.3). At smaller public companies, however, such as those in the S&P Small Cap 600, the number of firms with classified boards is just under one-half (see Figure 5.3).

Under Delaware law, classified directors cannot be removed before their term expires. Nonclassified board members, however, can be removed by majority voting from the shareholders. Like many other corporate charter amendments, staggered boards are not a sufficiently powerful defense to stop a determined bidder; rather, they are usually one of a collection of defenses that together can make a takeover difficult and costly to complete. In addition, in recent years shareholders are much more reluctant to approve a staggered board, especially if the proposal comes after a hostile bid has been launched.

As we have noted in our discussion of poison pills, the combination of a poison pill and a staggered board can be a powerful defensive combination since one way to deactivate the poison pill is to change the target's board and get a new board who will eliminate the pill. When a staggered board imposes long delays to change the board, the poison pill defense becomes more powerful.

---

[26] Daniel M. Gallagher and Joseph A. Grunfest, "Did Harvard Violate Federal Securities Law? The Campaign Against Classified Boards of Directors," Rock Center for Corporate Governance, Working Paper No 199, December 2014 and Martin Lipton, Theodore Mirvis, Daniel Neff and David Katz, "Harvard's Shareholder Rights Project is Wrong," Wachtell, Lipton, Rosen and Katz, March 12, 2012.

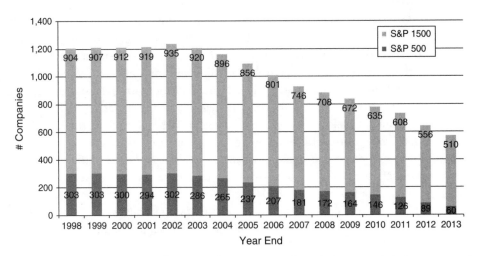

FIGURE 5.3 S&P1500 Classified Boards at Year End (includes non-U.S. incorporated companies). *Source*: FactSet SharkRepellent, www.sharkrepellent.net.

A potentially less powerful staggered board is one with no limitations on the size of the board. Here a controlling shareholder could win an election and replace one-third of the board but also could increase the size of the board and place his own representatives in these new board positions. In doing so, he could have a majority of the board votes. This is sometimes referred to as a *leaky staggered board*. A company's corporate charter should set forth the rules for how the board size is determined. If, however, this issue is addressed only in the corporate bylaws, then a controlling shareholder may be able to amend these bylaws to allow for the board size to increase. Potential target companies need to make sure the corporate charter includes such rules, as well as prohibitions on the removal of directors for any reason other than valid cause. Under Delaware law it is assumed that a classified board may have its board members removed only for cause if the charter is silent on this.

Recent Trends in Activism and Takeover Defenses

Up until recent years structural defenses, such as a combination poison pill and a staggered board gave the management of a target significant leverage over hostile bidders. This still is the case today. However, in recent years the threat's to targets are not coming as much from bidders seeking to take over the company but from activists. We will discuss the activities of activist hedge funds in detail in Chapter 7. However, some comments are in order as they relate to takeover defense and activists.

Activists may acquire a significant holding in the target but not necessarily one to activate a poison pill. They also may work with other large institutional shareholders to pressure the board to make changes such as not only declassifying the board but putting the activist's representatives on the board. While an activist may not be interested in acquiring the target, it may want the target to be sold to another bidder. The actions of activists have reduced the level of comfort that potential target boards had in the power of their takeover defenses.

Staggered Board Research

The impact of staggered boards on shareholder wealth has been the subject of research for over 20 years. Some early studies, such as the one conducted by DeAngelo and Rice, seemed to find some evidence of negative shareholder wealth effect. They studied a sample of 100 different firms, of which 53 had a staggered board.[27] However, their sample included other forms of antitakeover amendments, although staggered boards made up a significant percentage of the amendments considered. These results were also tempered by low statistical significance. Other early research by Ruback failed to find a statistically significant relationship between a negative stock price effect and staggered board provisions.[28] His research showed a negative 1% decline in stock prices resulting from passage of staggered board provisions; these results were not statistically significant.

A later study by Bhagat and Jefferis considered 344 companies that adopted classified boards along with other defenses.[29] They did not find evidence of significant shareholder wealth effects following the adoption of several defenses, including staggered boards. However, once again, this study did not exclusively focus on staggered boards alone but rather a grouping of various different preventative antitakeover defenses.

Research by Bebchuk and Cohen found a negative relationship between firm value, as measured by Tobin's q, and the implementation of a staggered board.[30] They focused on the period between 1995 and 2002. This study implies that staggered boards lower firm values. Other recent empirical research has reached similar conclusions.[31] In fact, Olubunmi Faleye, analyzing a large sample of over 2,000 companies with classified boards, found that companies with classified boards underperform those without such boards and that such companies are less likely to fire their CEO for poor performance. This research lends support to the view that classified boards entrench management. Like much of M&A research, there is some inconsistent evidence that shows a less clear view. Cremers, Litov and Sepe analyzed a large data set covering the period 1978–2011 and did indeed find that, from a cross sectional perspective, companies with staggered boards do have lower values as reflected by the Tobin's q values.[32] However, from a time series perspective this is not the case. That is, looking at the impact of a staggered board on q values over time, they find that adopting a staggered board increases certain

---

[27] Harry DeAngelo and Eugene Rice, "Antitakeover Charter Amendments and Stockholder Wealth," *Journal of Financial Economics* 11, no. 1–4 (April 1983): 329–360.

[28] Richard Ruback, "An Overview of Takeover Defenses," in Alan J. Auerbach, ed., *Mergers and Acquisitions* (Chicago: National Bureau of Economic Research, University of Chicago Press, 1987), 49–67.

[29] Sanjai Bhagat and Richard H. Jefferis, "Voting Power in the Proxy Process: The Case of Antitakeover Charter Amendments," *Journal of Financial Economics* 30, no. 1 (November 1991): 193–225.

[30] Lucian A. Bebchuk and Alma Cohen, "The Costs of Entrenched Boards," *Journal of Financial Economics* 78, no. 2 (November 2005): 409–432.

[31] Olubunmi Faleye, "Classified Boards and Long-Term Valuation Creation," *Journal of Financial Economics* 83 (2005): 501–529.

[32] K. J. Cremers, Lubomir Litov and Simone Sepe, "Staggered Boards and Firm Value, Revisited," unpublished paper.

company's q values and de-staggering lowers them. They interpret these results as reflecting a company's commitment to long term values and that staggered boards may help prevent short term oriented attacks on firms with a more long term orientation—such as those that have significant R&D investments.

Supermajority Provisions

A corporation's charter dictates the number of voting shares needed to amend the corporate charter or to approve important issues such as mergers. Other transactions that may require stockholder approval are corporate liquidation, lease of important assets, sale of the company, or transactions with interested parties or substantial shareholders. The definition of a substantial shareholder may vary, but it most often means a stockholder with more than 5%–10% of the company's outstanding shares.

A supermajority provision provides for a higher than majority vote to approve a merger—typically 80% or two-thirds approval. The more extreme versions of these provisions require a 95% majority. Supermajority provisions may be drafted to require a higher percentage if the size of the bidder's shareholding is larger. They are more effective when management, or other groups that tend to be very supportive of management on issues such as mergers, holds a sufficient amount of stock to make approval of a merger more difficult. For example, if management and an employee stock ownership plan (ESOP) hold 22% of the outstanding stock and the corporation's charter requires 80% approval for mergers, it will be very difficult to complete a merger if the 22% do not approve.

Supermajority provisions generally contain escape clauses, sometimes called *board out clauses*, which allow the corporation to waive or cancel the supermajority provision. The most common escape clause provides that the supermajority provisions do not affect mergers that are approved by the board of directors or mergers with a subsidiary. Most of these escape clauses are carefully worded so that the members of the board of directors who are interested parties may not vote with the rest of the board on related issues. An example of the interested party qualification would be the raider who holds 12% of a target company's stock, which has allowed the raider to command one or more seats on the board of directors. The escape clause would prevent this raider from exercising his votes on issues of approving a merger offer.

Supermajority provisions are most frequently used in conjunction with other antitakeover corporate charter changes. Corporations commonly enact supermajority provisions along with or after they have put other antitakeover charter amendments into place. If the supermajority provisions require a supermajority to amend the corporate charter, it is more difficult for a raider to erase the other antitakeover provisions once the supermajority provision is in place. Supermajority provisions are more effective against partial offers. Offers for 100% of the target tend to negate the effects of most supermajority provisions. Exceptions may occur when certain groups loyal to the target hold a percentage greater than the difference between 100% and the supermajority threshold.

Legality of Supermajority Provisions

The courts have upheld the legality of supermajority provisions when these provisions have been adopted *pursuant to shareholder approval*. For example, in *Seibert v. Gulton Industries Inc.*, the court upheld a supermajority provision requiring 80% voting approval to approve a takeover by a 5% shareholder.[33] The provision required the supermajority approval before the bidder reached the 5% threshold. The courts have pointed out the obvious fact that shareholders themselves adopted the supermajority provisions and clearly possess the ability to "unadopt" them if they so choose.

Supermajority Provision Shareholder Wealth Effects

Early research on the shareholder wealth effects of antitakeover amendments, many of which included supermajority provisions, found some initial negative effects around the announcement of their implementation. DeAngelo and Rice[34] and Linn and McConnell[35] both conducted studies in 1983 and failed to find significant negative price effects for the various antitakeover amendments considered. These results are somewhat contradicted, however, by Jarrell and Poulsen, who point out that these other studies considered only the earlier versions of supermajority provisions, which do not include an escape clause.[36] They found that the later supermajority provisions, which included such escape clauses, were associated with a statistically significant negative 5% return. However, those supermajority provisions without escape clauses did not show significant negative returns.

In 1987, a study shed light on the effectiveness of classified boards and supermajority provisions. Pound examined two samples of 100 firms each; one group had supermajority provisions and classified boards, whereas the control group had neither. His results showed that the frequency of takeovers was 28% for the group with the antitakeover amendments in place but 38% for the nonprotected control group.[37] These findings were also supported in a study by Ambrose and Megginson, who found that companies with supermajority amendments were insignificantly less likely to be the target of a takeover bid.[38]

---

[33] *Seibert v. Gulton Industries, Inc.*, No. 5631.5 Del. J. Corp. L. 514 (Del. Ch. June 21, 1974), *aff'd without opinion* 414 A.2d 822 (Del. 1980).

[34] Harry DeAngelo and Eugene Rice, "Antitakeover Charter Amendments and Stockholder Wealth," *Journal of Financial Economics* 11, nos. 1–4 (April 1983): 329–360.

[35] Scott C. Linn and John J. McConnell, "An Empirical Investigation of the Impact of Antitakeover Amendments on Common Stock Prices," *Journal of Financial Economics* 11, nos. 1–4 (April 1983): 361–399.

[36] Gregg A. Jarrell and Annette B. Poulsen, "Shark Repellents and Stock Prices: The Effects of Antitakeover Amendments since 1980," *Journal of Financial Economics* 19, no. 1 (September 1987): 127–168.

[37] John Pound, "The Effectiveness of Antitakeover Amendments on Takeover Activity," *Journal of Law and Economics* 30, no. 2 (October 1987): 353–367.

[38] Brent W. Ambrose and William L. Megginson, "The Role of Asset Structure, Ownership Structure and Takeover Defenses in Determining Acquisition Likelihood," *Journal of Financial and Quantitative Analysis* 27, no. 4 (December 1992): 575–589.

Fair Price Provisions

A fair price provision is a modification of a corporation's charter that requires the acquirer to pay minority shareholders at least a fair market price for the company's stock. This may be stated in the form of a certain price or in terms of the company's price-earnings (P/E) ratio. That is, it may be expressed as a multiple of the company's earnings per share. The P/E multiple chosen is usually derived from the firm's historical P/E ratio or is based on a combination of the firm's and the industry's P/E ratio. Fair price provisions are usually activated when a bidder makes an offer. When the fair price provision is expressed in terms of a specific price, it usually states that stockholders must receive at least the maximum price paid by the acquirer when he or she bought the holdings.

Many state corporation laws already include fair price provisions. Fair price amendments to a corporation's charter augment the fair price provisions of the state's laws. In states in which fair price provisions exist, corporate fair price provisions usually provide for higher prices for stockholders in merger offers. The target corporation may waive most fair price provisions.

Fair price provisions are most useful when the target firm is the object of a two-tiered tender offer. The requirement for the bidder to pay a minimum fair price helps negate the pressure a two-tiered offer tries to impose. However, as we have already noted, two-tiered offers are no longer as important to takeovers. This is why fair price provisions are not as popular today. Given that fair price provisions are a relatively weak antitakeover defense, it is not surprising that research on their shareholder wealth effects does not reveal major effects following implementation.

Shareholder Wealth Effects of Fair Price Provisions

Research on the impact of fair price provisions on stockholder wealth has thus far failed to show a significant relationship between fair price amendments and stock prices. Jarrell and Poulsen reported a small but statistically insignificant (negative) −0.65% change in stock prices in response to the implementation of fair price amendments.[39] This means that although they found the expected sign (negative), their results were not sufficiently robust to state confidently that there is any relationship between the fair price provisions and stock prices.

Dual Capitalization

Dual capitalization is a restructuring of equity into two classes of stock with different voting rights. This equity restructuring can take place only with shareholder approval. There are various reasons to have more than one class of stock other than to prevent a hostile takeover. For example, General Motors (GM) used its Class E shares to segregate the performance and compensation of shareholders of its EDS division. GM also had Class H shares for its Hughes Aircraft division. General Motors has long since parted ways with

---

[39] Gregg A. Jarrell and Annette B. Poulsen, "Shark Repellents and Stock Prices: The Effects of Antitakeover Amendments since 1980," *Journal of Financial Economics* 19, no. 1 (September 1987): 127–168.

these diversifications. Another example of a dual classification is the Ford Motor Company, which has both Class A and Class B shares, with the Class B shares having 16.561 votes per share as opposed to Class A shares, which have one vote per share. The greater voting rights of the Class B shares allow those shareholders to command 40% of the voting power in the company even though they own only 2% of the total shares issued.

From an antitakeover perspective, however, the purpose of dual capitalization is to give greater voting power to a group of stockholders who might be sympathetic to management's view. Management often increases its voting power directly in a dual capitalization by acquiring stock with greater voting rights. A typical dual capitalization involves the issuance of another class of stock that has superior voting rights to the current outstanding stock. The stock with the superior voting rights might have 10 or 100 votes for each share of stock. This stock is usually distributed by the issuance of superior voting rights stock to all stockholders. Stockholders are then given the right to exchange this stock for ordinary stock. Most stockholders choose to exchange the super-voting rights stock for ordinary stock because the super stock usually lacks marketability or pays low dividends. However, management, who may also be shareholders, may not exchange its supervoting rights stock for ordinary stock. This results in management increasing its voting control of the corporation.

Why Do Dual Class Recapitalizations Get Approved?

Companies must first receive the approval of shareholders before they can create a dual class recapitalization. However, if the end result of such recapitalizations is to concentrate voting power in the hands of a small group who usually are insiders, one may wonder why shareholders would willingly agree to such equity structures. The answer is straightforward—shareholders seek the financial gain from the higher dividends and may not value control that highly. Research also shows that companies that pursue dual class recapitalizations seem to do better in some ways (not as well in others) than another group of firms—leveraged buyout (LBO) firms, which also change their capital structure while increasing control in the hands of management. Lehn, Netter, and Poulsen showed that, for the firms in the sample, which covered the period 1977–1987, dual class firms spent more on capital expenditures although LBO firms showed better financial performance.[40] However, this compares companies with dual classifications and companies that have undergone an LBO as opposed to companies that have not done either.

Shareholder Wealth Effects of Dual Capitalizations

Jarrell and Poulsen examined 94 firms that recapitalized with dual classes of stock that had different voting rights between 1976 and 1987.[41] Forty of the firms were listed on the New York Stock Exchange, with 26 on the American Stock Exchange and 31 traded over the counter. The study found significant abnormal negative returns equal to 0.82%

---

[40] Kenneth Lehn, Jeffrey Netter, and Anne Poulsen, "Consolidating Corporate Control: Dual Class Recapitalizations versus Leveraged Buyouts," *Journal of Financial Economics* (October 1990): 557–580.
[41] Gregg Jarrell and Annette Poulsen, "Dual Class Recapitalizations as Antitakeover Mechanisms," *Journal of Financial Economics* 20, nos. 1–2 (January/March 1988): 129–152.

for a narrow time period around the announcement of the dual capitalization. Jarrell and Poulsen also reported that the greatest negative effects were observed for firms that had high concentrations of stock held by insiders (30%–50% insider holdings). Dual capitalization will be more effective in consolidating control in the hands of management when management already owns a significant percentage of the firm's stock. The fact that negative returns were higher when management already held more shares implies that when management entrenchment was more likely (which in turn implies that the potential for a successful bid was lower), the market responded by devaluing the shares.

Shum, Davidson, and Glascock found that, although the implementation of dual capitalizations may not generate significant shareholder wealth effects, when their implementation causes the original shareholders to lose control without receiving compensation in return, there are negative effects.[42] Bacon, Cornett, and Davidson found out that how the market reacted to dual capitalizations depended on how many independent directors were on the board.[43] When independent directors dominated, the market response was positive. This implies that the market believes that if a largely independent board approved the dual capitalizations, then the defense furthered shareholders' interests and did not entrench management. When corporate governance is discussed in Chapter 12, we will see that shareholder wealth is enhanced when boards are dominated by independent directors.

More recent research has not cast dual classifications in a favorable light. As we will also discuss in Chapter 13, Masulis, Wang, and Xie analyzed a large sample of 503 dual class companies over the period 1995–2003. They found that the greater the divergence between insider voting rights and cash flow rights, the more likely shareholder wealth will decline.[44] In addition, as this divergence increases, CEO compensation rises and the propensity to pursue value-destroying M&As grows. They also found that the productivity of capital investments was less at dual classification. This led them to reach the intuitive result that dual classification facilitates management entrenchment and enables managers to engage in empire-building and value-destroying M&As.

Antigreenmail Provisions

Antigreenmail charter amendments restrict the ability of a target corporation to pay greenmail to a potential hostile bidder. Some amendments allow the payment if shareholders extend their approval. Other variations allow for the payment of some ceiling amount, such as the market price. In the case of a takeover battle, which generally causes stock prices to rise, this may still provide a hostile shareholder a profit from his activities. Greenmail is discussed later in this chapter with active antitakeover defenses.

---

[42] Connie M. Shum, Wallace N. Davidson III, and John L. Glascock, "Voting Rights and the Market's Reaction to Dual Class Common Stock," *Financial Review* 32, no. 2 (1995): 275–288.

[43] Curtis J. Bacon, Marcia M. Cornett, and Wallace N. Davidson III, "The Board of Directors and Dual Class Recapitalizations," *Financial Management* 26, no. 3 (1997): 5–22.

[44] Ronald M. Masulis, Cong Wang, and Fei Xie, "Agency Problems at Dual Classification Companies," *Journal of Finance* 64, no. 4 (August 2009): 1697–1727.

Restrictions on Ability to Call an Election

Unless there are specific restrictions in the corporate charter, most states require corporations to call a special shareholder meeting if a certain percentage of the shareholders request it. Such meetings may be used as a forum whereby insurgents try to gain control of the company. At shareholder meetings, takeover defenses such as poison pills may be dismantled. These meetings may also be used to promote proxy fights. Given the opportunities for bidders that shareholder meetings present, companies may try to amend the charter to limit the ability to call meetings. Some of the more extreme restrictions limit the ability to call a meeting to the board of directors or only if a certain high percentage of the shareholders request it. In addition, there may be limitations imposed on the types of issues that may be raised at the shareholder meeting.

Antitakeover Amendments and Managerial Ownership Research

McWilliams conducted a study on the impact of managerial share ownership and the shareholder wealth effects of antitakeover amendments.[45] She examined 763 amendments that were adopted by 325 New York Stock Exchange and American Stock Exchange firms. McWilliams's research was partially motivated by a desire to explain why several earlier research studies failed to find a statistically significant share price response with the adoption of antitrust amendments. These earlier studies did not consider managerial share ownership, which varies by firm.

McWilliams's results show a negative relationship between managerial share ownership and the adoption of antitakeover amendment proposals (with the exception of fair price provisions). The stock price reaction to amendment proposals was positive when managerial share ownership was near zero and became negative as these ownership percentages rose. She concludes that the market is interpreting these proposals as lowering the likelihood of a takeover when proposed by companies that have high managerial share ownership.

Golden Shares

The origin of the term *golden shares* first arose in the 1980s when Great Britain privatized certain companies. Golden shares were used in the privatization of British Aerospace and British Telecom.

With the privatization of many state-owned companies, some governments are reluctant to totally embrace the free market ownership of these enterprises. In Europe and Asia some governments resorted to holding golden shares, which are shares owned by the government that give the government certain control, such as in the form of significant voting rights, over the companies once they are privatized. Governments have claimed that this is necessary, particularly when they see there are strategic interests at stake and they fear those interests would be compromised if some outside shareholders gained control of the businesses. An alternative to actual shares are laws that are passed to limit the number of shares or votes any one outside shareholder can control.

---

[45] Victoria McWilliams, "Managerial Share Ownership and the Stock Price Effects of Antitakeover Amendment Proposals," *Journal of Finance* 45, no. 5 (December 1990): 1627–1640.

The British government's golden shareholding in BAA, the British airport authority, was declared illegal by European courts based on the position that such shares limit the free movement of capital in Europe. There were similar rulings regarding the Spanish government's holdings in Endesa, Repsol, and Telefonica.

CHANGING THE STATE OF INCORPORATION

Because different U.S. states have antitakeover laws that vary in degrees of protection, a company may choose to relocate its legal corporate home so it is protected by another state's laws that have stronger antitakeover provisions. This is usually accomplished by a company creating a subsidiary in the new state and then merging the parent into the subsidiary. Reincorporating in another state that has stronger antitakeover laws, however, will not ensure a firm's independence. For example, Singer moved its state of incorporation from Connecticut to New Jersey, a state that has a strong antitakeover law. The move did not prevent Singer from ultimately being taken over by raider Paul Bilzerian in 1988. Nonetheless, reincorporating may make a takeover more difficult for the raider. This stronger bargaining position may help the target get a better price for the shareholders.

Shareholder Wealth Effects of Reincorporation

Netter and Poulsen examined the shareholder wealth effects of reincorporation announcements for 36 firms in 1986 and 1987.[46] They divided their sample into two groups: 19 firms that reincorporated from California and the remaining 17 firms. They point out that California is a shareholder rights state whose corporation laws protect shareholder interests. Among the rights provided are mandatory cumulative voting, a prohibition against classified boards, and other shareholder rights, such as the ability to remove directors without cause or to call special meetings. Netter and Poulsen reasoned that if there were stock price effects, they would be greater in reincorporations from California to Delaware. Their results failed to reveal any shareholder wealth effects either from the 36 reincorporations in their sample or from the California subsample. On the basis of their study, we may conclude that the greater flexibility provided to management by incorporating in Delaware will not reduce shareholder wealth.

ACTIVE ANTITAKEOVER DEFENSES

Installing the various preventative antitakeover defenses will not guarantee a company's independence. It may, however, make the takeover more difficult and costly. Some bidders may decide to bypass a well-defended target in favor of other firms that have not

---

[46] Jeffrey Netter and Annette Poulsen, "State Corporation Laws and Shareholders: The Recent Experience," *Financial Management* 18, no. 3 (Autumn 1989): 29–40.

installed formidable defenses. Nonetheless, even those firms that have deployed a wide array of preventative antitakeover defenses may still need to actively resist raiders when they become targets of a hostile bid. The second half of this chapter describes some of the various actions a target may take after it receives an unwanted bid or learns that it is about to be the target of such a bid. The target may become aware of this in several ways, such as through the results of its stock watch or market surveillance programs or through required public filings, such as a Hart-Scott-Rodino filing.

The following actions are discussed in the second half of this chapter:

- **Greenmail.** Share repurchases of the bidder's stock at a premium.
- **Standstill agreements.** These agreements usually accompany a greenmail payment. Here the bidder agrees not to buy additional shares in exchange for a fee.
- **White knight.** The target may seek a friendly bidder, or white knight, as an alternative to the hostile acquirer.
- **White squire.** The target may place shares or assets in the hands of a friendly firm or investor. These entities are referred to as white squires.
- **Capital structure changes.** Targets may take various actions that will alter the company's capital structure. Through a *recapitalization*, the firm can assume more debt while it pays shareholders a larger dividend. The target can also simply assume more debt without using the proceeds to pay shareholders a dividend. Both alternatives make the firm more heavily leveraged and less valuable to the bidder. Targets may also alter the capital structure by changing the total number of shares outstanding. This may be done through a new offering of stock, placement of shares in the hands of a white squire, or an ESOP. Instead of issuing more shares, some targets buy back shares to ensure they are not purchased by the hostile bidder.
- **Litigation.** Targets commonly sue the bidder, and the bidder often responds with a countersuit. It is unusual to see a takeover battle that does not feature litigation as one of the tools used by either side.
- **Pac-Man defense.** One of the more extreme defenses occurs when the target makes a counteroffer for the bidder. This is one of the more colorful takeover defenses, although it is seldom used.

The coverage of these active antitakeover defenses is similar to the coverage of the preventative measures. The use of each action is described, along with the research on its shareholder wealth effects. Bear in mind that a target may choose to use several of these defenses together as opposed to selecting merely one. It is difficult, therefore, for research studies to isolate the shareholder wealth effects of any specific defense. In addition, some of the research, using different data sets drawn from different time periods with varying market conditions, reaches conflicting conclusions. As the market changes and adapts to the various defenses, their effectiveness—and therefore their impact on stock prices—also varies. These problems were also apparent in the research studies on the preventative measures.

Greenmail

The term *greenmail* refers to the payment of a substantial premium for a significant shareholder's stock in return for the stockholder's agreement that he will not initiate a bid for control of the company. Greenmail is a form of *targeted share repurchases*, which is a general term that is more broadly applied to also include other purchases of stock from specific groups of stockholders who may not ever contemplate a raid on the company.

One of the earlier reported instances of greenmail occurred in July 1979, when Carl Icahn bought 9.9% of Saxon Industries stock for approximately $7.21 per share. Saxon repurchased Icahn's shares for $10.50 per share on February 13, 1980.[47] This stock buyback helped launch Icahn on a career as a successful corporate raider and years later as an "activist hedge fund manager." Icahn was not the first greenmailer, however. That distinction may belong to Charles Bluhdorn, chairman of Gulf & Western Industries, "who was an early practitioner when Cannon Mills in 1976 bought back a Gulf & Western holding."[48] While many of the corporate raiders from the fourth merger wave have left the mergers and acquisitions (M&A) business, Icahn has actually risen in prominence and has become the leader of large hedge funds in the 2000s. Greenmail brought significant profits to those who were able to successfully pursue the practice. The Bass Brothers were said to have earned $400 million on the Texaco-Getty deal, whereas Icahn reportedly received $6.6 million for his stake in American Can, $9.7 million for Owens Illinois, $8.5 million for Dan River Mills, and $19 million for Gulf & Western.[49] Saul Steinberg's 1984 attempted takeover of Disney earned him not only an impressive payout of $325 million for his share holdings but also another $28 million for his expenses.

Legality of Differential Payments to Large-Block Shareholders

The courts have ruled that differential payments to large-block shareholders are legal as long as they are made for valid business reasons.[50] However, the term *valid business reasons* is so broad that it gives management considerable latitude to take actions that may favor management more than stockholders. Managers may claim that to fulfill their plans for the corporation's future growth, they need to prevent a takeover of the corporation by any entity that would possibly change the company's direction.

The interpretation of legitimate business purposes may involve a difference in business philosophies between the incumbent management and a bidder. It may also simply be that managers are seeking to preserve the continuity of their business strategies. Although some managers think that the court's broad views on this matter may serve to entrench management, others see the court's position as one that helps preserve management's ability to conduct long-term strategic planning. Many corporate managers believe that the court's position allows them to enact the necessary defenses to fend off

---

[47] "Icahn Gets Green as Others Envy Him," *Wall Street Journal*, November 13, 1989, B1.
[48] Ibid.
[49] John Brooks, *Takeover* (New York: Dutton, 1987), 186.
[50] Charles M. Nathan and Marilyn Sobel, "Corporate Stock Repurchases in the Context of Unsolicited Takeover Bids," *Business Lawyer* (July 1980): 1545–1566.

takeovers by hostile bidders who might acquire the corporation simply to sell off assets and achieve short-term returns. Considerable debate surrounds the issue of short-term versus long-term motives of corporate bidders.

The legality of greenmail itself was upheld in a legal challenge in the Texaco greenmail payment to the Bass Brothers. The Delaware Chancery Court found that the 1984 payment of $1.3 billion, which was a 3% premium, to the Bass Brothers was a reasonable price to pay for eliminating the potentially disruptive effects that the Bass Group might have posed for Texaco in the future.[51] The Delaware Chancery Court's approval of the greenmail payment and dismissal of a shareholder class action suit were upheld by the Delaware Supreme Court. The important decision clearly established a precedent for the legality of greenmail in the all-important Delaware court system. However, other states, such as California, have not been as supportive of the practice of greenmail. The board of Disney was sued by shareholders who objected to the company's alleged greenmail payments to Steinberg. The court issued an injunction, and when the case was finally settled in 1989, both Steinberg's Reliance Corp. and Disney itself had to pay damages.

Shareholder Wealth Effects of Greenmail

One of the early leading studies on the effects of greenmail payments on stockholder wealth was conducted by Bradley and Wakeman. Their study considered 86 repurchases from insiders or individuals who were unaffiliated with the firms from 1974 to 1980. The Bradley and Wakeman study showed that privately negotiated purchases of a single block of stock from stockholders who were unaffiliated with the company reduced the wealth of nonparticipating stockholders.[52] Repurchases from insiders, however, were associated with increases in shareholder wealth. Bradley and Wakeman's research therefore supports the management entrenchment hypothesis. In revealing that stockholders lose money as a result of targeted share repurchases from outsiders, the study implies that these targeted share repurchases are not in the stockholders' best interest. It further implies that, by engaging in these repurchases, management is doing stockholders a disservice. Other research, such as a study by Dann and DeAngelo that is discussed further in the context of standstill agreements, also found negative shareholder wealth effects for nonparticipating shareholders when the company announced target share repurchases.[53]

In 1986, Wayne Mikkelson and Richard Ruback analyzed 111 repurchases and found that only 5% occurred after the announcement of a takeover attempt.[54] One-third of the repurchases took place after less overt attempts to change control, such

---

[51] *Good v. Texaco, Inc.*, No. 7501 (Del. Ch. February 19, 1985), *aff'd sub nom. Polk v. Good*, 507 A.2d 531 (Del. 1986).

[52] Michael Bradley and L. MacDonald Wakeman, "The Wealth Effects of Targeted Share Repurchases," *Journal of Financial Economics* 11, nos. 1–4 (April 1983): 301–328.

[53] Larry Dann and Harry DeAngelo, "Standstill Agreements, Privately Negotiated Stock Repurchases, and the Market for Corporate Control," *Journal of Financial Economics* 11, nos. 1–4 (April 1983): 275–300.

[54] Wayne Mikkelson and Richard Ruback, "Targeted Share Repurchases and Common Stock Returns," *Rand Journal of Economics* 22, no. 4 (Winter 1991): 554–561.

as formulation of preliminary plans for acquisitions or proxy fights. Almost two-thirds of the repurchases occurred without any overt indication of an impending takeover. It is interesting that the Mikkelson and Ruback study showed that the downward impact of the targeted share repurchases was more than offset by the stock price *increases* caused by purchasing the stock. Mikkelson and Ruback found a combined overall impact on stock prices of 17%! Their study supports the stockholder interests hypothesis in that it finds that the target share repurchases actually benefit incumbent stockholders. It therefore conflicts with the Bradley and Wakeman results and so has added more fuel to this debate. Mikkelson and Ruback's analysis also showed that the payment of greenmail was not associated with a lower probability of a change in control. They showed that the frequency of control changes following targeted share repurchases was three times higher than a control sample of firms that did not engage in such repurchases.

More recent research, using data derived from targeted share repurchases from 1974 to 1983, failed to provide support for the management entrenchment hypothesis.[55] Bhagat and Jefferis found that the performance of firms that pay greenmail was no worse than the performance of firms in a control group that did not engage in greenmail payments. This does not support the view that firms that engage in greenmail are poor performers who are seeking shelter from the normal market processes that might bring about a change in management. The differences between these results and those of Bradley and Wakeman are mainly attributable to different samples considered.

Ang and Tucker found that managers who pay greenmail are often let go by the corporations in the years that follow the repurchase.[56] They find that the likelihood of this occurring is directly related to the magnitude of the premium they pay to the selling shareholders.

Corporate Finance of Share Repurchases

It is important to note that share repurchases are a common occurrence and usually take place for reasons having nothing to do with takeovers or threats of M&As. Companies may use share repurchases as a way of providing a return to shareholders. In this sense they are an alternative to dividends. Companies with excess cash may choose to pay a higher dividend or issue a special one-time dividend. Another alternative would be to purchase shares at a price that will be attractive to shareholders. Kahle examined over 700 repurchases during the first half of the 1990s.[57] She found that companies that had higher cash flow to asset ratios were more likely to do share repurchases as opposed to increasing their dividends. Interestingly, she noted that companies often do not repurchase all of the shares they announce they intend to. Grinstein and Michaely, in their study of 79,000 firm years over the period 1980–1996, noticed that firms that

[55] Sanjai Bhagat and Richard H. Jefferis, "The Causes and Consequences of Takeover Defense: Evidence from Greenmail," *Journal of Corporate Finance* 1, no. 2 (August 1994): 201–231.

[56] James S. Ang and Allen R. Tucker, "The Shareholder Effects of Corporate Greenmail," *Journal of Financial Research* 11, no. 4 (1988): 265–280.

[57] Kathleen Kahle, "When a Buyback Isn't a Buyback: Open Market Repurchases and Employee Options," *Journal of Financial Economics* 63, no. 2 (February 2002): 235–261.

have done repurchases were more likely to do such repurchases in the future as opposed to dividend increases.[58]

Research studies have attempted to determine the primary reason why companies engage in share repurchases. One study by Bena, Nagar, Skinner, and Wong found a relationship between the dilutive effects of issuances of stock options by Standard & Poor's (S&P) 500 companies and the propensity of companies to repurchase shares.[59] Fenn and Liang, in their study of over 1,100 companies during the 1990s, found a similar relationship between repurchases and the issuance of employee stock options.[60]

From an accounting perspective, repurchased shares are recorded at their cost. They are reflected in the financial statements through a reduction of total stockholder equity. Treasury shares may be "retired," resulting in a subsequent reduction of the common stock and paid-in capital accounts, or they may be reissued. Any difference in the reissuance proceeds from the cost of those treasury shares results in an adjustment to paid-in capital.

Decline of Greenmail

For a variety of reasons, greenmail has become uncommon. For one, the pace of hostile takeover activity has declined dramatically in the 1990s, thus reducing the need to engage in greenmail payments. In addition, federal tax laws imposed a 50% tax penalty on gains derived from greenmail payments. Under this law, greenmail is defined as consideration paid to anyone who makes or threatens to make a tender offer for a public corporation. In order for the payment to be considered greenmail, the offer must not be available to all shareholders. Furthermore, although various legal decisions have upheld the legality of greenmail, defendants in greenmail-inspired lawsuits have been sufficiently uncertain of the outcome to be willing to pay large settlements. For example, in 1989, Disney and Saul Steinberg were reported to have paid $45 million to settle a lawsuit with shareholders, prompted by an alleged greenmail payment in 1984 that included a $59.7 premium.[61] Donald Trump was reported to have paid $6.5 million to settle a lawsuit involving an alleged greenmail payment that included an $18 million premium. In addition, companies have adopted antigreenmail amendments to their corporate charters that limit the company's ability to pay greenmail. Research has shown that such amendments are usually adopted as part of a package of different antitakeover amendments.[62] While some research has found that antitakeover amendments may have negative shareholder wealth effects, Eckbo showed that in a subsample of a larger study he did on antitakeover amendments in general, the passage of antigreenmail amendments was associated with a positive

[58] Yaniv Grinstein and Roni Michaely, "Institutional Holdings and Payout Policy," *Journal of Finance* 60, no. 3 (June 2005): 1389–1426.

[59] Daniel Bena, Venky Nagar, Douglas Skinner, and M. H. Wong, "Employee Stock Options, EPS Dilution and Share Repurchases," *Journal of Accounting and Economics* 36, no. 1–3 (December 2003): 51–90.

[60] George Fenn and Nellie Liang, "Corporate Payout Policy and Managerial Stock Incentives," *Journal of Financial Economics* 60, no. 1 (April 2001): 45–72.

[61] Sanjai Bhagat and Richard H. Jefferis, "The Causes and Consequences of Takeover Defense: Evidence from Greenmail," *Journal of Corporate Finance* 1, no. 2 (August 1994): 201–231.

[62] Sanjai Bhagat and Richard H. Jefferis, "Voting Power in the Proxy Process: The Case of Antitakeover Charter Amendments," *Journal of Financial Economics* 30, no. 1 (November 1991): 193–225.

market response.[63] The combined effects of the declining volume of hostile takeovers, tax penalties, antigreenmail charter amendments, and fear of litigation costs have caused greenmail to virtually disappear from the 1990s takeover scene.

Evolution of the Greenmailer

We really do not have greenmail like we had in the fourth merger wave, as the greenmailer has evolved into a new form of activist shareholder and is practicing his art somewhat differently. We now have hedge funds, which assume significant stock positions in corporations and, instead of seeking to be bought out at a premium lest they launch a hostile takeover, these activist investors are taking a different tack in the 2000s. Rather than demand greenmail, raiders turned activists hedge fund managers, such as Carl Icahn, demand changes which will increase the value of their, and other shareholders, equity holdings. We discuss this phenomenon in detail in Chapter 7.

Standstill Agreements

A standstill agreement occurs when the target corporation reaches a contractual agreement with a potential acquirer whereby the would-be acquirer agrees not to increase its holdings in the target during a particular time period. This has been found to be legal under Delaware law.[64] Such an agreement takes place when the acquiring firm has established sufficient stockholdings to be able to pose a threat to mount a takeover battle for the target. Many standstill agreements are accompanied by the target's agreement to give the acquirer the right of first refusal in the event that the acquirer decides to sell the shares it currently owns. This agreement is designed to prevent these shares from falling into the hands of another bidder who would force the target to pay them standstill compensation or, even worse, attempt to take over the target. Another version of a standstill agreement occurs when the acquirer agrees not to increase its holdings beyond a certain percentage. In other words, the target establishes a ceiling above which the acquirer may not increase its holdings. The acquiring firm agrees to these various restrictions for a fee. Like greenmail, standstill agreements may provide compensation for an acquirer not to threaten to take control of the target. In fact, standstill agreements often accompany greenmail. However, while greenmail is not normally a part of the current M&A world, standstill agreements are often featured in normal M&A negotiations.

Standstill agreements usually have a time limit on them, such as one year. In that case the control shareholder agrees not to increase his holdings and/or make a bid for a year. It is usually the case, though, that the control shareholder can privately approach the target and ask if it would be acceptable to make a bid for the company—perhaps at more attractive terms than what the shareholder first had in mind at the time he entered into the standstill. Courts would look negatively at the bidder if he chose to go public with his offer in violation of the standstill agreement, as then the "cat is out of the bag" and the company might thereby be put in play by a bidder who agreed to a standstill.

---

[63] Espen Eckbo, "Valuation Effects of Antigreenmail Prohibitions," *Journal of Financial and Quantitative Analysis* 25, no. 4 (December 1990): 491–505.
[64] *Alliance Gaming Corp. v. Bally Gaming International, Inc.*, 1995 W.L 523453 (Del. Ch. 1995).

The stock purchases threshold is usually less than 5% and often is 2% to 3%. The 5% ceiling is due to the Williams Act disclosure requirements, which may require the potential buyer to indicate its interest in buying the target. This disclosure may then put the company in play, which the target may want to avoid.

The parties to a standstill agreement may agree on a "Fall Away" clause, which essentially says that if another party makes a bid or the company is put in play then the initial party who agreed to the standstill can be released from it.

Don't Ask, Don't Waive Standstills

"Don't Ask, Don't Waive" standstill agreements include the typical provision of traditional standstill agreements but also include a provision that prohibits the potential bidder from submitting even a private proposal to the board.

Boards may even be prohibited by such agreements from seeking information on bids outside of the auction process. These are sometimes referred to as "No Talk" provisions. Such agreements state that the bidder may not ask, even privately, for the board to waive the standstill.

This may seem to be not in the interests of target shareholders, but some courts, including Delaware, have recognized that there are benefits to shareholders when board can control a bidding process in furtherance of the Revlon duties. Boards want bids submitted as part of that auction process and not one at a time in a piecemeal fashion.

In spite of courts, including Delaware, being enamored with the Revlon auction process, they have also recognized that Don't Ask, Don't Waive and No Talk provisions may leave the target's board in an informational vacuum, which may not be in the interest of its shareholders. The Delaware Chancery Court in *Phelps Dodge Corp. v. Cyprus Amax Minerals Company* found the No Talk provision of a merger agreement is not in shareholders' interests.[65] In addition, in the *Complete Genomics* case Vice Chancellor J. Travis Laster found the Don't Ask Don't Waive portion of the merger agreement between BGI-Shenzhen and Complete Genomics Inc. to be problematic and chose not to enforce it, although he found the rest of the standstill agreement acceptable.[66] However, as reflected by Chancellor Strine's position on the *In Re* Ancestry.com case, there is no *per se* rule against such provisions in Delaware.[67]

One of the problems with restrictions such as Don't Ask, Don't Waive agreements is if they are focused on one bidder and serves to impede, rather than facilitate, the bidding process. If this is the case, courts will have problems with them.

Shareholder Wealth Effects of Standstill Agreements

Standstill agreements usually accompany greenmail payments, so it is hard to separate their effects from each other when conducting research studies. Nonetheless, an early study by Dann and DeAngelo examined 81 standstill agreements between 1977

---

[65] *Phelps Dodge Corp. v. Cyprus Amax Minerals Co.*, 1999 Del. Ch. LEXIS 202 (Del. Ch. Sept. 27, 1999).
[66] *In re Complete Genomics, Inc. S'holders Litig.*, C.A. No. 7888-VCL (Del. Ch. Nov. 27, 2012).
[67] *In re Ancestry.com Inc. S'holder Litig.*, C.A. No. 7988-CS (Del. Ch. Dec. 17, 2012) .

and 1980.[68] They found that standstill agreements and negotiated stock purchases at a premium were associated with negative average returns to nonparticipating stockholders. On average, stock prices fell 4%. The Dann and DeAngelo study supports the management entrenchment hypothesis and, as such, is inconsistent with the stockholder interests hypothesis with respect to nonparticipating stockholders.

The Mikkelson and Ruback study considered the impact of greenmail payments that were accompanied by standstill agreements.[69] They found that when negative returns were associated with targeted share repurchases, they were much greater when these purchases were accompanied by standstill agreements. We may therefore conclude that these two antitakeover devices often, but certainly not always, tend to have a complementary negative impact on stock prices that is greater than the negative effect we would expect if just one of them were implemented.

White Knights

When a corporation is the target of an unwanted bid or the threat of a bid from a potential acquirer, it may seek the aid of a *white knight*—that is, another company that would be a more acceptable suitor for the target. The white knight will then make an offer to buy all or part of the target company on more favorable terms than those of the original bidder. These favorable terms may be a higher price, but management may also look for a white knight that will promise not to disassemble the target or lay off management or other employees. It is sometimes difficult to find a willing bidder who will agree to such restrictive terms. The target often has to bargain for the best deal possible to stay out of the first bidder's hands. The incumbent managers of the target maintain control by reaching an agreement with the white knight to allow them to retain their current positions. They may also do so by selling the white knight certain assets and keeping control of the remainder of the target. A target company may find a white knight through its own industry contacts or through the assistance of an investment banker who will survey potential suitors. The potential white knight might request favorable terms or other consideration as an inducement to enter the fray. However, if this consideration is given only to the white knight and not to the hostile bidder, and if it is so significant an advantage that it could cause the hostile bidder to withdraw, the deal with the white knight may be a violation of the target's Revlon duties.

Takeover Tactics and Shareholder Concentration: United States Compared with Europe

In the United States the majority of equity of U.S. companies is held by institutional investors, although individuals do own a significant number of total shares outstanding. In Great Britain the majority of equity is held by institutions. While institutions as a whole own the majority of equity in general, particular institutions tend not to own large

---

[68] Dann and DeAngelo, "Standstill Agreements."

[69] Wayne Mikkelson and Richard Ruback, "Targeted Share Repurchases and Common Stock Returns," Working Paper No. 1707–86, Massachusetts Institute of Technology, Sloan School of Management, June 1986.

percentages of specific companies. This is quite different from continental Europe, where even public companies have high concentrations of shares in the hands of specific groups or individuals. Franks and Mayer have noted that 80% of the largest public companies in Germany and France have a single shareholder who owns at least 25%.[70] The shareholder concentration is usually in the hands of a single individual or family or another corporation. More than half of the companies they studied have a single largest shareholder. Often this corporate shareholding is in the form of pyramids, where one company owns shares in another company, which in turn owns shareholders in another, and so on. In addition, many large companies in continental Europe are private and are not traded on public markets. Franks and Mayer have also noted that in Austria, Belgium, Germany, and Italy a single shareholder, individual, or group of investors controls more than 50% of voting rights. In 50% of Dutch, Spanish, and Swedish companies, more than 43.5%, 34.5%, and 34.9%, respectively, of votes are controlled by a single shareholder. Fifty-seven percent of the 250 largest companies that trade on the Paris exchange have been reported to be family-controlled in the late 1990s.[71] In contrast, the median blockholder in the United Kingdom controls only 9.9% of votes, and in the United States the median size of blockholding of companies quoted on NASDAQ and the New York Stock Exchange is just above the disclosure level of 5% (8.5% and 5.4%). Franks and Mayer's analysis also reviewed the holdings of the second- and third-largest shareholders. They concluded that share ownership is much more concentrated in continental Europe than it is in Great Britain and the United States.

The relevance of this to takeovers is that public appeals to shareholders, appeals that are much more common in the United States in the form of tender offers, are less successful in continental Europe due to the dominating presence of specific major shareholders. It is difficult to implement a hostile takeover when large blocks are in the hands of controlling shareholders unless they want to sell. The concentration of shares is an additional problem that a hostile bidder may face in Europe that usually would not be as much of a factor in the United States.

Shareholder Wealth Effects of White Knight Bids

Research results show that white knight bids are often not in the best interests of bidding firm shareholders. One study of 100 white knights over a 10-year period between 1978 and 1987 showed that white knight shareholders incurred losses in shareholder wealth.[72] These results are consistent with prior research. The explanation for these negative shareholder wealth effects is that such bids are not part of a planned strategic acquisition and do not yield net benefits for the acquiring firm's shareholders. In addition, the white knights are bidders in a contested auction environment, where prices tend to be higher than nonauction acquisitions.

[70] J. Franks and C. Mayer, "Ownership and Control," in H. Siebert, ed., *Trends in Business Organization: Do Participation and Cooperation Increase Competitiveness?* (London: Coronet Books, 1995).

[71] Peter Gumbel, "Putting on Heirs: A New Generation Is Leading Europe's Biggest Family Firms toward New Profits—and Risks," *Time*, March 24, 2003.

[72] Ajeyo Banerjee and James E. Owers, "Wealth Reduction in White Knight Bids," *Financial Management* 21, no. 3 (Autumn 1992): 48–57.

Research has shown that competition has a negative effect on shareholder wealth of bidding firms.[73] This negative effect is even greater for subsequent bidders.

T. BOONE PICKENS AND MESA PETROLEUM VERSUS CITIES SERVICE—MULTIPLE WHITE KNIGHTS

Just as the fourth merger wave was about to take hold, T. Boone Pickens was involved in a few classic takeover battles. One such contest was Pickens's bid for the Cities Service Oil Company. In June 1982, Pickens, the CEO of Mesa Petroleum, made a bid for the Cities Service Oil Company. Although not part of the Seven Sisters, the seven largest oil companies in the United States at that time, Cities Service was approximately 20 times as large as Mesa Petroleum. Mesa had been carrying an investment in Cities Service since 1979 and had chosen this time to make a bid for the larger oil company. Pickens thought that Cities Service possessed valuable assets but was badly managed. Cities Service is a case study of what was wrong with Big Oil's management. Based in Tulsa, Oklahoma, Cities Service was a large company. By 1982, it ranked thirty-eighth in the Fortune 500 companies and was the nineteenth-largest oil company in the country. It was unusually sluggish, even by the less-demanding standards of the oil industry, and had been for 50 years. Its refineries and chemical plants were losers, and although it had 307 million barrels of oil and 3.1 trillion cubic feet of gas reserves, it had been depleting its gas reserves for at least 10 years. Although it had leases on 10 million acres, it was finding practically no new oil and gas. Cities Service's problems were hidden by its cash flow, which continued in tandem with the Organization of Petroleum Exporting Countries (OPEC) price increases. The stock, however, reflecting management's record, sold at approximately a third of the value of its underlying assets. The management did not understand the problem or did not care; either condition is terminal.[a]

Mesa Petroleum made a $50-per-share bid for Cities Service. Cities Service responded with a Pac-Man defense in which it made a $17-per-share bid for the smaller Mesa Petroleum. The Cities Service offer was not a serious one because Mesa's stock had been trading at $16.75 before the Cities offer, which therefore did not contain a premium. Cities Service asked Gulf Oil to be its white knight. Pickens, a critic of the major oil companies, was equally critical of Gulf Oil. Gulf made a $63-per-share bid for Cities Service. Cities saw Gulf as a similar type of oil company and one that would be much friendlier to Cities management than Mesa. At that time Gulf was the third-largest oil company in the United States. Cities accepted Gulf's bid. Mesa ended up selling its shares back to Cities for $55 per share, which resulted in an $11-per-share profit for Mesa, or a total of $40 million. However, Gulf had second thoughts about the Cities acquisition: Gulf would have taken on a significant amount of debt if it had gone through with the merger. In addition, Gulf was concerned that the Federal Trade Commission might challenge the merger on antitrust grounds. Much to Cities Service's surprise and chagrin, Gulf dropped its offer for Cities. Cities Service stock dropped to $30 a share following the announcement of Gulf's pullout. Cities Service management was highly critical

---

[73] Bradley and Wakeman. "Wealth Effects."

of Gulf and stated that its action was reprehensible. Cities Service then had to look for another white knight. Occidental Petroleum, led by the well-known Armand Hammer, made an initial offer of $50 per share in cash for the first 49% of Cities stock and securities of somewhat uncertain value for the remaining shares. Cities rejected this bid as inadequate, and Occidental upped its offer to $55 in cash for the front end and better-quality securities for the back end. Cities Service then agreed to sell out to its second white knight.

[a] T. Boone Pickens, *Boone* (Boston: Houghton Mifflin, 1987), 150.

White Squire Defense

The white squire defense is similar to the white knight defense. In the white squire defense, however, the target company seeks to implement a strategy that will preserve the target company's independence. A *white squire* is a firm that consents to purchase a large block of the target company's stock. The stock selected often is convertible preferred stock. The convertible preferred shares may be already approved through a blank check preferred stock amendment of the company's charter. The target may need to receive the approval of shareholders even if the shares are blank check preferred stock. The New York Stock Exchange, for example, requires that shareholder approval be received if such shares are issued to officers or directors or if the number issued equals 20% of the company's shares outstanding. The white squire is typically not interested in acquiring control of the target. From the target's viewpoint, the appeal is that a large amount of the voting stock in the target will be placed in the hands of a company or investor who will not sell out to a hostile bidder. The deal may be structured so that the shares given to the white squire may not be tendered to the hostile bidder. Sometimes, however, a potential white squire is given incentives to go ahead with the transaction, such as a seat on the board. Other possible incentives could be a favorable price on the shares or a promise of generous dividends. In an effort to insure that the white squire does not become hostile, the white squire may have to agree in advance to vote with the target and not against it.

A classic example of a white squire defense was Carter Hawley Hale's (CHH's) sale of convertible preferred stock to the General Cinema Corporation in 1984. The stock sold to General Cinema had voting power equal to 22% of CHH's outstanding votes. CHH believed this was necessary to prevent a takeover by the Limited Corporation in 1984. CHH accompanied this white squire defense with a stock repurchase program that increased the voting power of General Cinema's stock to 33% of CHH's voting shares.

Merger Agreement Provisions

Targets may seek to enter into agreements with friendly parties, such as white knights, that provide these parties with certain benefits that give them an incentive to participate in the merger process. These incentives, which may come in the form of lockup options, topping fees, or bust-up fees, may work to the target's benefit by making a takeover by a hostile bidder more difficult and expensive.

Lockup Transactions

A lockup transaction is similar to a white squire defense. In the case of lockups, the target is selling assets to another party instead of stock. Sometimes the term *lockup transaction* is also used more generally to refer to the sale of assets as well as the sale of stock to a friendly third party. In a lockup transaction, the target company sells assets to a third party and thus tries to make the target less attractive to the bidder. The target often sells those assets it judges the acquirer wants most. This may also come in the form of *lockup options*, which are options to buy certain assets or stock in the event of a change in control. These options may be written so that they become effective even if a bidder acquires less than 51% of the target.

In some instances, lockup options have been held to be invalid. The court's position has been that, in limiting the desirability of the target to the original bidder, lockup options may effectively preempt the bargaining process that might result during the 20-day waiting period for tender offers required by the Williams Act. An example of such an invalid option was Marathon Oil's option that it gave to U.S. Steel in 1981 to buy its Yates Oil Field at a fixed price in an attempt to avoid a takeover by Mobil Oil Corporation. This option would be exercisable in the event that Marathon was taken over. It would have an important impact on future bidding contests because it was one of Marathon's most valued assets. The court invalidated this option on the grounds that it violated the spirit of the Williams Act. An appeals court later affirmed this ruling. U.S. Steel ended up acquiring Marathon Oil when Mobil's bid was stopped on antitrust grounds.

In 1994 the Delaware Supreme Court invalidated Viacom's lockup option to purchase 24 million shares of Paramount Communications treasury stock at a negotiated, preacquisition price if QVC acquired Paramount.[74] The option would have enabled Viacom to sell the shares to QVC, thereby increasing QVC's price.

REVLON VERSUS PANTRY PRIDE

In 1985, Ronald Perelman, chief executive officer of Pantry Pride, made an offer for Revlon Inc. MacAndrews and Forbes Holdings, the parent company of Pantry Pride, had built a diversified company with acquisitions between 1978 and 1984 that included a jewelry company, a cigar company, a candy manufacturer, and Pantry Pride—the supermarket chain. Charles Revson had built Revlon into one of the nation's largest cosmetics companies. Revson's successor, Michael Bergerac, a former head of the conglomerate ITT and protégé of Harold Geneen, expanded Revlon considerably through large acquisitions in the health care field. In terms of its revenues, Bergerac's Revlon was more of a health care company than a cosmetics

---

[74] *Paramount Communications, Inc. v. QVC Network, Inc.*, 637 A.2d. (Del. 1994).

company. In terms of assets, Revlon was approximately five times the size of Pantry Pride.

Revlon's acquisition strategy had not fared well for Bergerac, and Revlon's earnings had been declining. Perelman decided to make a bid for Revlon, his goal being to sell off the health care components and keep the well-known cosmetics business. Pantry Pride made a cash tender of $53 a share. It financed its offer for the significantly larger Revlon by borrowing $2.1 billion. Revlon's board of directors had approved a leveraged buyout (LBO) plan by Forstmann Little at $56 cash per share. When Pantry Pride increased its offer to $56.25, Revlon was able to get Forstmann Little to increase its offer to $57.25 by giving Forstmann Little a lockup option to purchase two Revlon divisions for $525 million. This was reported by Revlon's investment banker to be $75 million below these divisions' actual value.[a] This option would be activated if a bidder acquired 40% of Revlon's shares.

Delaware's Chancery Court ruled that in agreeing to this lockup agreement, the board of directors had breached its fiduciary responsibility. The court believed that this option effectively ended the bidding process and gave an unfair advantage to Forstmann Little's LBO. However, in its ruling, the court did not declare lockup options illegal. It stated that the options may play a constructive role in the bargaining process and thus increase bids and shareholder wealth.

[a] Dennis Block, Nancy Barton, and Stephen Radin, *Business Judgment Rule* (Englewood Cliffs, NJ: Prentice-Hall, 1988), 101.

The prevailing wisdom is that lockup options are used by management to entrench themselves. This surely is the case in some instances. However, in a study of 2,067 deals over the period from 1988 to 1995, of which 8% had lockup options, Birch found that announcement returns for targets were higher when lockup options were present, whereas acquirer returns were lower.[75] This implies that, on average, target shareholders may benefit from such arrangements.

Although the J. P. Stevens and West Point–Pepperell decision outlined the legally legitimate uses of lockup agreements, a subsequent decision in the Delaware Supreme Court further underscored the illegitimate uses of these agreements. The court ruled that a lockup agreement between Macmillan Inc. and Kohlberg Kravis & Roberts (KKR), which allowed KKR to buy certain valuable Macmillan assets even if the agreement between KKR and Macmillan fell through, was merely designed to end the auction process and to preempt bidding, which would maximize the value of stockholder wealth. The court stated that a lockup could be used only if it maximized stockholder wealth. In this case, the lockup was used to drive away an unwanted suitor, Maxwell Communications Corporation. The court's position remains that a lockup may be used only to promote, not inhibit, the auction process.[76]

---

[75] Timothy R. Birch, "Locking Out Rival Bidders: The Use of Lockup Options in Corporate Mergers," *Journal of Financial Economics* 60, no. 1 (April 2001): 103–141.
[76] Delaware High Court Rules a Company Can't Use 'Lockup' Just to Stop a Suitor," *Wall Street Journal*, May 8, 1989.

Termination, Breakup, and Topping Fees

Termination or breakup fees as well as topping fees can occur when a target agrees to compensate a bidder if the target company is taken over by a company other than the initial bidder. These fees, which typically range between 2% and 3% of purchase price, may help compensate the bidder for its deal costs in case the transaction falls through. Sometimes they are used to encourage a bidder who may be reluctant to engage in a costly bidding process with an uncertain outcome. They are somewhat of a disincentive for a raider because they are liabilities of the target and, therefore, are a cost that will have to be assumed if its takeover is successful. That is why we discuss them in this chapter, although they really should not be considered antitakeover defenses in the sense of other formidable defenses, such as poison pills. The fact that termination fees are a disincentive to the bidding process is the reason that when they are set too high, say over 5%, courts do not view them favorably as they become too preclusive.

The largest termination fee of all time was the $4 billion paid by AT&T in 2011 in connection with its failed acquisition of T-Mobile.[77] The deal failed when antitrust authorities opposed the deal. Given the concentrated nature of the mobile phone industry, and all the expensive advisors and managers AT&T had working for it, it is amazing that AT&T once again blundered in its M&As.[78]

Termination fees have become quite common. In the fourth merger wave termination fees were relatively uncommon. However, by the late 1990s, two-thirds of the M&A bids featured termination fee clauses.[79] One view of these fees is that they deter bids and therefore help entrench managers. Another view is that they give the target leverage that allows it to extract higher bids from acquirers. Micah Officer analyzed a sample of 2,511 merger bids and tender offers over the period 1988 to 2000. He found an average termination fee of just $35.24 million, although the median was just $8 million.[80] The mean termination fee was 5.87% of the equity being acquired. He found an average increased premium of 4% when the bids featured termination fees. The finding of higher premiums was supported by a study by Bates and Lemmon, who analyzed a sample of 3,307 deals and found that takeover premiums for firms with termination fees were 3.1% higher.[81] They also found that bids with termination fee clauses had a higher probability of completion.

For deals in which the bidder's advisors, such as investment banks and law firms, may be retained on a success-oriented basis, they may contract with the bidder to receive some part of the termination fee if the deal does not go through.

---

[77] T-Mobile has asserted that the fee is valued at closer to $6 billion. Michael J. De La Merced, "T-Mobile and AT&T: What's $2 Billion among Friends," Deal Book, *New York Times*, December 20, 2011.

[78] Patrick A. Gaughan, *Maximizing Corporate Growth through Mergers and Acquisitions: A Strategic Growth Guide* (Hoboken, NJ: John Wiley & Sons, 2013), 319–321.

[79] Micah S. Officer, "Termination Fees in Mergers and Acquisitions," *Journal of Financial Economics* 69, no. 3 (September 2003): 431–468.

[80] Ibid.

[81] Thomas W. Bates and Mitchell L. Lemmon, "Breaking Up Is Hard to Do? An Analysis of Termination Fee Provisions and Merger Outcomes," *Journal of Financial Economics* 69, no. 3 (September 2003): 469–504.

Termination fees can be a source of capital to finance an expansion strategy. In 2015 the Irish drug company Shire used the $1.6 billion termination fee it received AbbVie as a result of the fact that AbbVie cancelled its tax inversion motivated merger with Shire when the U.S. changed the rules on the treatment of such deals. Shire then used the termination fee to help finance a $5.2 billion acquisition of New Jersey based NPS Pharmaceuticals.

Reverse termination fees allow the buyer to walk away from a deal after a merger agreement has been reached through the payment of a fee to the seller. These clauses became popular in 2005, mainly for private equity deals, as they enhanced the financing out clause, which would allow the private equity buyer to walk away if it could not get the necessary financing. This was the case in 2007 when private equity firm Cerberus agreed to pay a reverse termination fee to United Rentals (but only after an intense legal battle). Reverse termination fees are usually between 3% and 5% of the deal's value.

Termination Fees and the Bidding Process

One view of termination fees is that they may inhibit the takeover process and limit auction, thereby entrenching management. Another view is that such fees are a normal part of the successful takeover process and do not really limit legitimate bidders. In analyzing the bidding process Boone and Mulherin point out that only part of the process is public—the part that follows a public announcement.[82] However, this is often preceded by a nonpublic process that features bidding by potentially more than one bidder. Thus prior research based upon public auctions reflects only part of the whole process. As Figure 5.4 shows, the private component may start with initial discussions that are followed by the signing of confidentiality and standstill agreements. Negotiations will follow, and they, in turn, are often followed by the signing of a termination agreement. Somewhere around this time is a public announcement that may give rise to other bidders and possibly an auction. The auction, however, will reflect only part of the

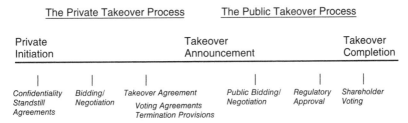

FIGURE 5.4 Timeline of the Takeover Process. *Source*: Adapted from Audra L. Boone and J. Harold Mulherin, "Do Termination Provisions Truncate the Takeover Bidding Process?" *Review of Financial Studies* 20, no. 2 (March 2007): 461–489.

---

[82] Audra Boone and J. Harold Mulherin, "Do Termination Provisions Truncate the Takeover Process," *Review of Financial Studies* 20, no. 2 (2002): 461–489.

bidding for the company. Boone and Mulherin confirmed this in an analysis of takeovers over the years 1989–1999. They analyzed SEC filings of companies that were taken over, which revealed the presence of other bids prior to any termination fee agreements.

No-Shop and Go-Shop Provisions

No-shop provisions are agreements that may be part of an overall acquisition agreement or letter of intent in which the seller agrees not to solicit or enter into negotiations to sell to other buyers. Targets may try to reach such an agreement with a white knight and use the existence of the no-shop provision as the reason they cannot negotiate with a hostile bidder.

This was done by Paramount Communications when it was trying to avoid a hostile takeover by QVC. As in this case, the courts tend to not look kindly on these provisions because they often have the effect of inhibiting the auction process. Although the court was highly critical of the no-shop provision in the Paramount-QVC takeover contest, it is not illegal under Delaware law.

In order to reduce the probability of a lawsuit from shareholders who may oppose a deal, sometimes merger agreements contain go-shop provisions. These provisions require a target who may want to accept an overture from a bidder to also attempt to seek a better offer. After such legitimate attempts to do so, the merger partners are in a better position to defend the terms of their deal to target shareholders.

One criticism of go-shop provisions is that they often allow only a relatively short window for the target to find a better deal. For example, in 2014 Media General reached an agreement to acquire LIN Media for $1.6 billion in cash and stock. The merger agreement provided for a one-month go-shop period wherein LIN Media would open its books to qualified potential buyers to see if it could achieve a better deal. If a new buyer emerged, then the agreement provided for that buyer to pay a 1.625% breakup fee on the $1.6 billion, which equated to $26 million. Defendants of a short period such as one month say it is difficult to suspend the operations of two companies for longer than that while they await the outcome of the merger. In addition, in a narrow industry such as the TV media business of Media General and LIN, there is a limited number of buyers who, presumably, all know the industry and the parties involved.

Capital Structure Changes

A target corporation may initiate various changes in its capital structure in an attempt to ward off a hostile bidder. These defensive capital structure changes are used in four main ways:

1. Recapitalize
2. Assume more debt:
   a. Bonds
   b. Bank loan

3. Issue more shares:
   a. General issue
   b. White squire
   c. Employee stock option plan
4. Buy back shares:
   a. Self-tender
   b. Open market purchases
   c. Targeted share repurchases

Recapitalize

In the late 1980s, recapitalization became a more popular, albeit drastic, antitakeover defense. After a recapitalization, the corporation is in dramatically different financial condition than it was before it. A recapitalization plan often involves paying a superdividend to stockholders, which is usually financed through assumption of considerable debt. For this reason, these plans are sometimes known as *leveraged recapitalizations*. When a company is recapitalized, it substitutes most of its equity for debt while paying stockholders a large dividend. In addition to the stock dividend, stockholders may receive a stock certificate called a *stub*, which represents their new share of ownership in the company.

In a recapitalization, total financial leverage usually rises dramatically. Studies have shown that, on average, total debt to total capitalization ratios increase from 20% to 70%.[83]

Recapitalization as an antitakeover defense was pioneered in 1985 by the Multimedia Corporation with the assistance of the investment bank of Goldman Sachs. Multimedia, a Greenville, South Carolina, broadcasting company, initiated a recapitalization plan after the original founding family members received unsolicited bids for the company in response to their LBO offer. In addition to a cash payout, Multimedia stockholders saw the value of their stub increase from an original value of $8.31 to $52.25 within two years.[84] The success of the Multimedia deal led to several other recapitalizations, such as FMC Corp., Colt Industries, and Owens Corning, several of which were completed in the following two years.

One attraction of a recapitalization plan is that it allows a corporation to act as its own white knight. Many companies in similar situations would either seek an outside entity to serve as a white knight or attempt an LBO. The recapitalization plan is an alternative to both. In addition, the large increase in the company's debt makes the firm less attractive to subsequent bidders. A recapitalization may defeat a hostile bid

---

[83] Atul Gupta and Leonard Rosenthal, "Ownership Structure, Leverage and Firm Value: The Case of Leveraged Recapitalizations," *Financial Management* 20 (Autumn 1991): 69–83, and Punett Handa and A. R. Radhakrishnan, "An Empirical Investigation of Leveraged Recapitalizations with Case Payout as a Takeover Defense," *Financial Management* 20 (Autumn 1991): 38–68.

[84] "The New Way to Halt Raiders," *New York Times*, May 29, 1988, D4.

because stockholders receive a value for their shares that usually is significantly in excess of historical stock prices. This amount is designed to be superior to the offer from the hostile bidder.

Another feature of recapitalization that is most attractive to the target company's management is that it may give management a greater voting control in the target following the recapitalization. The target company may issue several shares of common stock to an ESOP.[85] It may also create other security options that may give management enhanced voting power. Other stockholders, however, will receive only one share in the recapitalized company (the stub) as well as whatever combination of debt and cash has been offered. The company is required to make sure that all nonmanagement stockholders receive at least a comparable monetary value for their common stockholdings as did management. After the recapitalization the concentration of shares in the hands of insiders tends to significantly increase.

Many recapitalizations may require stockholder approval before they can be implemented, depending on the prevailing state laws and the corporation's own charter. When presenting a recapitalization plan to stockholders, corporations often seek approval for a variety of other antitakeover measures that are proposed as part of a joint antitakeover plan. Some of the other measures discussed previously, such as fair price provisions or staggered boards, might be included here.

In addition to possible restrictions in the company charter and state laws, companies may be limited from using the recapitalization defense by restrictive covenants in prior debt agreements. The corporation enters into these legal agreements when it borrows from a bank or from investors through the issuance of corporate bonds. Such agreements place limitations on the firm's future options so as to provide greater assurance for the lenders that the debt will be repaid. The language of these restrictive covenants might prevent the company from taking on additional debt, which might increase the probability that the company could be forced into receivership.

Comparison between Recapitalization Plans and LBOs

There are a number of similarities between LBOs and recapitalization plans, including the following:

- **Tax advantages of debt.** In a recapitalization plan, the firm assumes a considerable amount of debt and thereby substitutes tax-deductible interest payments for taxable dividend payments. Dividend payments are often suspended following the payout of a larger initial dividend. The effect of an LBO is similar. Firms going private in an LBO assume considerable debt to finance the LBO. This has the effect of sheltering operating income for the time period in which the debt is being paid.

---

[85] Ralph C. Ferrara, Meredith M. Brown, and John Hall, *Takeovers: Attack and Survival* (Salem, NC: Butterworth, 1987), 425.

- **Concentration of ownership in management's hands.** In an LBO, management usually receives a percentage of ownership as part of the LBO process. When the debt is repaid, this ownership position may become quite valuable, even after warrants held by debtholders are exercised. In a recapitalization plan, management often receives new shares instead of the cash payout that stockholders receive. Managers of firms involved in defensive recapitalization prefer this arrangement because the concentration of ownership in their hands helps prevent a takeover.

Kleinman points out that in view of the similarities between LBOs and recapitalizations, it is not surprising that good LBO and recapitalization candidates have much in common, such as the following:

- A stable earnings stream that can be used to service debt.
- Low pre-LBO or prerecapitalization plan debt levels. A low level of debt on the balance sheet gives the firm greater ability to assume more debt.
- A strong market position.
- A product line that is not vulnerable to a high risk of obsolescence.
- A business that does not need high levels of research and development or capital expenditures.
- The high debt service may not allow for such investments.
- A high borrowing capacity as reflected by the collateral value of the firm's assets.
- Assets and/or divisions that can be readily sold to help pay the debt.
- Experienced management with a proven track record, an important characteristic because the added pressure of the high debt service does not leave a high margin for error.[86]

Use of Recapitalization Plans Protected by Poison Pills

The recapitalization plan is the company's own offer, which is presented to stockholders as an alternative to a hostile raider's offer. Before 1988, companies used poison pills to try to counteract the bidder's tender offer while presenting their own unencumbered recapitalization plan. In November 1988, a Delaware Chancery Court struck down the combined use of these defenses.[87] In a case involving a challenge to the use by Interco of a recapitalization plan and a poison pill in opposition to a hostile bid from the Rales Brothers, the court ruled that both offers should be presented on an equal footing to shareholders as opposed to having the poison pill directed at the tender offer while not affecting the company's own recapitalization plan offer.

---

[86] Robert Kleinman, "The Shareholder Gains from Leveraged Cash Outs," *Journal of Applied Corporate Finance* 1, no. 1 (Spring 1998): 47–48.
[87] "Interco Defense against Rales Is Struck Down," *Wall Street Journal*, November 2, 1988, 83.

Shareholder Wealth Effects of Recapitalization Plans

The shareholder wealth effects of recapitalization plans differ depending on the reason for the recapitalization. If it is a recapitalization that is done for reasons other than to defend against a takeover, such as to change the company's capital structure to increase stockholder return, the shareholder wealth effects tend to be positive. For example, Handa and Radhakrishnan found that for the 42 recapitalizations that they studied, shareholder returns were 23% for the period between 60 and 15 days prior to the event, with some other days of positive returns before day 0 for the group of firms in their sample that were actual takeover targets.[88] For firms that were not actual takeover targets there was no run-up in prices and some days of negative returns before the recapitalization. Gupta and Rosenthal found similar positive returns for the period leading up to the announcement of the recapitalization (26.7%) for firms that were in play and lower but positive returns (15.1%) for those that were not in play.[89] These results are somewhat intuitive. Defensive recapitalizations usually generate a substantial amount of cash that can be used as an alternative to the offer from the hostile bidder. These shareholder wealth effects, however, are initial stock market reactions. Whether the recapitalization is good for the long-term welfare of the corporation is another issue. Dennis and David found that 31% of the 29 recapitalizations that they studied that did leveraged recapitalizations encountered subsequent financial distress.[90] Nine either filed Chapter 11 or had to restructure claims out of court. They attributed many of these problems to industry-wide troubles, as well as poor proceeds from asset sales. This was the case, for example, in the Interco recapitalization, which we discuss in a separate case study. Interco believed it would generate greater proceeds from asset sales, which could be used to pay down debt. These overly optimistic assessments were not shared by the market.

Assume More Debt

Although the assumption of more debt occurs in a recapitalization plan, the firm can also directly add debt without resorting to the implementation of recapitalization to prevent a takeover. A low level of debt relative to equity can make a company vulnerable to a takeover. A hostile bidder can utilize the target's borrowing capacity to help finance the acquisition of the target. Although some may interpret a low level of debt to be beneficial to the corporation, by lowering its risk, it can also increase the company's vulnerability to a takeover. However, additional debt can make the target riskier because of the higher debt service relative to the target's cash flow. This is something of a *scorched earth defense* because preventing the acquisition by assuming additional debt may result in the target's future bankruptcy.

---

[88] Handa and Radhakrishnan, "Empirical Investigation."

[89] Atul Gupta and Leonard Rosenthal, "Ownership Structure, Leverage and Firm Value: The Case of Leveraged Recapitalizations," *Financial Management* 20 (Autumn 1991): 69–83.

[90] David J. Dennis and Diane K. David, "Causes of Financial Distress Following Leveraged Recapitalizations," *Journal of Financial Economics* 37, no. 2 (February 1995): 129–157.

INTERCO: THE PROBLEMS WITH RECAPITALIZATION

Interco's recapitalization plan and the company's subsequent financial problems is a highly instructive case study. It highlights the problems not only of too much leverage but also of overoptimistic projections that often underlie both takeover and recapitalization failures.

In the fall of 1988, St. Louis–based Interco, a diverse manufacturer of well-known products, such as London Fog rainwear, Converse shoes, and Ethan Allan and Broyhill furniture, found itself the object of a hostile bid from the Rales Brothers. Steven and Michael Rales, relatively little-known investors from Washington, DC, had offered $74 per share in a $2.73 billion all-cash tender offer. Interco responded with a recapitalization plan defense. This defense was coupled with a poison pill, however. As is explained elsewhere in this chapter, the use of a poison pill to shield a recapitalization plan was found to be illegal by a Delaware Chancery Court. Nonetheless, the recapitalization plan proved sufficient to counter the Rales Brothers' offer. Although the recapitalization plan ensured Interco's independence, it did so at a drastic price. The plan, in part developed by merger strategists Bruce Wasserstein and Joseph Perella, increased Interco's debt service obligations beyond the firm's ability to pay. The result was a cash flow crisis that culminated in the firm's eventual default on June 15, 1990. Holders of junk bonds issued in the recapitalization process eventually had to accept equity in exchange for their bonds to avoid further losses that would result from bankruptcy.[a]

The expected success of the Interco recapitalization plan was contingent on the accuracy of the forecasts developed for asset sales and revenues from the company's operations. This plan, labeled Project Imperial, was reported by the *Wall Street Journal* to have been developed by "a few number crunching financial people with very little oversight from top officials at either Interco or Wasserstein-Perella."[b] The *Journal* reported that 10-year projections of cash flows and earnings were made by a team of financial analysts, one of whom was only one-and-a-half years out of college, without the benefit of much basic research. Several scenarios were considered, but the worst case showed a 20% annual return following the recapitalization.

The firm of Wasserstein-Perella earned $5.5 million for its work in the antitakeover defense of Interco. The plan it developed called for the sale of divisions such as the Ethan Allen furniture chain for approximately $500 million. However, the eventual sale price proved to be only $388 million. The Central Hardware division was valued at $312 million in the recapitalization plan but brought only $245 million when it was sold. Record annual profits of $70 million were forecasted for divisions such as Converse shoes, whereas fiscal 1990 profits proved to be only $11 million. Given the volatile and competitive nature of the athletic shoe industry (particularly at that time when there were more competitors that engaged in aggressive competition), the continual generation of increasing profit levels would be a most difficult task for any company in this industry (Figure A).

(*continued*)

(*continued*)

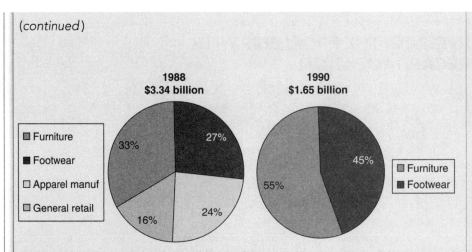

FIGURE A Interco's Recapitalization Problems. *Source*: George Anders and Francine Schwadel, "Wall Streeters Helped Interco Defeat Raiders—But at a Heavy Price," *Wall Street Journal*, July 11, 1990, A7. Reprinted by permission of the *Wall Street Journal*, copyright © 1990 Dow Jones & Company Inc. All rights reserved worldwide.

The fate of the Interco recapitalization plan is symbolic of much of what went wrong in the world of leveraged mergers during the late 1980s. Seemingly sophisticated financial analysis could be developed to make risky leveraged deals appear attractive. For those deals that fell into bankruptcy, the accuracy valuation analysis was questioned.[c]

[a] Michael Quint, "Interco Pact Includes Conversion of Bonds to Stock," *New York Times*, August 1, 1990, D22.
[b] George Anders and Francine Schwadel, "Wall Streeters Helped Interco Defeat Raiders—But at a Heavy Price," *Wall Street Journal*, July 11, 1990, 1.
[c] Data for this case were drawn from research by George Anders and Francine Schwadel of the *Wall Street Journal*.

The target can acquire the additional debt in two ways: It can borrow directly from a bank or other lender, or it can issue bonds. If the target has to wait for SEC approval for the bonds to be issued, it might be taken over before the debt issuance is completed. Companies with this defense in mind can prepare for it by obtaining prior SEC approval to issue bonds and taking advantage of SEC Rule 415, which is called the *shelf registration rule*. This rule allows the corporation to register with the SEC all those securities offerings it intends to make within the upcoming two years.

Issue More Shares

Another antitakeover option available to the target company is to issue more shares. Issuing more shares changes the company's capital structure because it increases equity while maintaining the current level of debt. By issuing more shares, the target company makes it more difficult and costly to acquire a majority of the stock in the target. The notion of increasing the number of shares to make it more difficult for a raider to obtain control has been around for some time. Matthew Josephson, in his book *The Robber Barons*, points out how this tactic was used to prevent Cornelius Vanderbilt from obtaining control of the Erie Railroad: "This explains how the 'Erie Gang' or the Erie Lackawanna Railroad successfully prevented the New York Central Railroad, a precursor to today's Conrail, and Cornelius Vanderbilt from taking control of Erie. Every time Vanderbilt came close to getting a majority, Erie would issue more shares."[91] On the negative side, issuing more shares dilutes stockholder equity. It is reasonable to expect the company's stock price to decline in the face of this stock issuance. This downward movement in the company's stock price is the market's reflection of the costs of this issuance. In the presence of these clear costs to stockholders, many states specifically require that corporations receive adequate compensation in return for the newly issued shares. When the shares are issued and not given to a particular group or company, they are called a general issue. However, because these shares might fall into hostile bidders' hands, the target often issues these shares directly into friendly hands. Such is the case in a white squire defense, where the target both increases the number of shares necessary to obtain control and makes sure that these newly issued shares will not fall into the hostile bidder's hands.

As an example of a defensive share issuance, in 1999, Gucci, which was incorporated in the Netherlands (for tax reasons) but operated out of Italy, issued more shares as a defense against a hostile bid from LVMH. Gucci sold a 40% stake in the company to Francois Pinault, the owner of French retail giant Pinault-Printemps. This led to a two-year acerbic battle between LVMH and its chief executive officer, Bernard Arnault, and Pinault, who at one time each sued the other for libel. The two eventually reached a settlement in 2001 that enabled Pinault to become a white knight for Gucci while LVMH earned gains on the stake it had accumulated in Gucci. In 2004 Pinault-Printemps-Redoute made an offer to buy out the minority shareholders and take the company private. In 2013 the company renamed itself Kering.

Share Issuance and ESOPs

Another option that the target may consider is to issue stock to an employee stock ownership plan (ESOP). To make it easy for the ESOP to purchase these shares, the ESOP may borrow using the corporation's guarantee. The company may also make tax-deductible contributions into the ESOP that may then be used to repay the loan. In using ESOPs as a defensive tactic, the target must make sure that the price paid by the ESOP for the

---

[91] Matthew Josephson, *The Robber Barons* (New York: Harcourt Brace, 1931).

target's securities is fair. If the company pays too high a price, the transaction could be judged improper according to the federal employee benefit laws. If the ESOP is allowed to buy the shares at too low a price, directors could be charged with violating their fiduciary duties to non-ESOP shareholders. Employee stock ownership plans are discussed in greater detail in Chapter 9.

In light of the passage of the Delaware antitakeover law, leveraged bust-up acquisitions can be impeded by placing 15% of a firm's outstanding shares in an ESOP. In December 1989, Chevron Corporation, to prevent a takeover by cash-rich Penzoil Corporation, issued 14.1 million shares to create an ESOP. Chevron borrowed $1 billion to repurchase the newly issued shares.[92] Before the issuance of these shares, employees had held 11% of Chevron's outstanding shares through a profit-sharing program. In an effort to offset the dilution effects of the share issuance, having perceived that the takeover threat had passed, Chevron announced a program of stock repurchases in 1990.

Chevron survived this takeover threat and grew into one of the larger companies in the oil industry. This was accomplished partly through its $35 billion acquisition of Texaco in November 2000.

SHAMROCK HOLDINGS INC. VERSUS POLAROID CORPORATION

In 1988, when Polaroid was the target of an unwanted takeover offer from Shamrock Holdings Inc., it used the employee stock ownership plan (ESOP) stock issuance defense. Shamrock Holdings Inc. was a Burbank, California, television and radio company owned by the Roy Disney family. It bought 6.9% of Polaroid and expressed interest in acquiring control of the company. Polaroid created an ESOP for the purpose of avoiding this takeover. It then placed 10 million newly issued shares, which constituted 14% of the outstanding stock of Polaroid, into the ESOP.

Polaroid considered this an effective defense because the ESOP would likely exercise its voting power to oppose an acquisition by Shamrock and to maintain current management. Polaroid, a Delaware-based corporation, had its defense bolstered by the ESOP stock issuance inasmuch as a bidder must buy 85% of a Delaware-incorporated target to be able to take control and sell off assets (see Chapter 3). With the ESOP stock issuance, only 86% of the outstanding stock remained in public hands.

Polaroid would go on to have a troubled history. The camera company fell behind the leading-edge companies in this industry and had to file for Chapter 11 bankruptcy protection in 2001. In 2005 it was acquired by one of its licensees, Petters Group Worldwide, for $426 million.

---

[92] "Chevron Purchasing Shares to Replace Stock Used for ESOP," *Wall Street Journal*, February 13, 1990, A.5.

Buy Back Shares

Another way to prevent a takeover is for the target to buy back its own shares. Such share repurchases can have several advantages for a target corporation:

- Share repurchases can divert shares away from a hostile bidder. Once the target has acquired certain shares, these shares are no longer available for the bidder to purchase.
- Share repurchases can also divert shares away from the hands of arbitragers. Arbitragers can be of great assistance to a hostile bidder because they acquire shares with the explicit purpose of earning high returns by selling them to the highest bidder. This is often the hostile acquiring corporation. By preventing some of the target's shares from falling into the hostile bidder's hands, the target can make the acquisition process more difficult.
- The acquisition of the target's own shares can allow the corporation to use up its own resources. The bidder can use these resources to finance the target's own acquisition. For example, if the target uses some of its excess cash reserves to acquire its own shares, the acquirer cannot use this cash to pay off some of the debt incurred in the acquisition.
- Similar reasoning can be applied to share repurchases by the target, which are financed through debt. By borrowing, the target is using up its own borrowing capacity, which could have been used to finance some of the acquisition. This can be effective in deterring bids by raiders who are relying on the heavy use of leverage.
- The acquisition of shares can be a necessary first step in implementing a white squire defense. If the target has enough SEC-authorized shares available, it must first acquire them through share repurchases.

Federal securities laws limit the ability of a target to repurchase its own shares after it has become the recipient of a target offer. These laws require the target to file with the SEC and to provide certain disclosures, including the number of shares to be repurchased, the purpose of the transaction, and the source of funding. Although share repurchases have several clear advantages for a target corporation, they are not without drawbacks. Share repurchases may be an instinctive first reaction by an embattled target CEO who is striving to maintain the company's independence. By repurchasing the company's shares, however, the CEO is withdrawing outstanding shares from the market. With fewer shares outstanding, it may be easier for the acquirer to obtain control because the bidder has to buy a smaller number of shares to acquire 51% of the target.

One solution to this dilemma is to use targeted share repurchases. This strategy takes shares out of the hands of those who would most likely sell them to the hostile bidder. If, at the same time, these shares are placed in friendly hands, the strategy can be successful. When CHH combined a buyback of 17.5 million shares in 1984 with a sale of stock to General Cinema Corporation, it was implementing a similar strategy to prevent The Limited from obtaining control of CHH.

General Cinema was able to help CHH to survive two hostile takeover attempts by The Limited in 1984 and 1986. It could not help the company, which used an aggressive acquisition program to build itself into the sixth-largest department store chain in the United States, to avoid bankruptcy. CHH had acquired such venerable names as Bergdorf Goodman, Thalhimer, Walden Books, and the Wanamaker chains. They were able to show higher and higher acquired revenues but not profits. When its results flagged it began to sell off assets. It separated one business unit, the Neiman Marcus Group, which contained Neiman Marcus and Bergdorf Goodman. As part of its reward for assisting CHH, General Cinema became the controlling shareholder of the Neiman Marcus Group when CHH filed for Chapter 11 and was eventually liquidated. The failure of this company, which was a major force in the Southern California market, is summed up by the following saying that was heard on Wall Street and in the media during the waning days of the company—"God gave them Southern California and they blew it." This failed merger strategy is one of many examples of companies that enjoyed significant success in their own markets but that incurred large losses by pursuing losing M&As.

Implementing a Share Repurchase Program

A target can implement a share repurchase plan in three ways:

1. General nontargeted purchases
2. Targeted share repurchases
3. Self-tender offer

General nontargeted purchases simply buy back a certain number of shares without regard to their ownership. Targeted share repurchases, however, are designed to take shares out of the hands of stockholders who may sell their shares to the hostile bidder. A self-tender occurs when the target makes a tender offer for its own securities. Regulations governing self-tenders are different from those that apply to tender offers by an outside party. Self-tenders are regulated by Section 13 of the Securities and Exchange Act of 1934. A company engaging in a self-tender has two main sets of filing requirements. According to Rule 13e-1, the target may not buy its own securities following a tender offer by a hostile bidder unless it first files with the SEC and announces its intentions. The target firm must disclose the following:

- Name and class of securities.
- Identity of purchaser.
- Markets and exchanges that will be used for the purchases.
- Purpose of the repurchase.
- Intended disposition of the repurchased shares.

The target corporation is also bound by Rule 14d-9, which requires that the company file a Schedule 14D-9 with the SEC within 10 days of the commencement of the tender offer. The 14D-9 filing, which is also required in the case of a hostile bid, requires management to indicate its position on the self-tender.

Discriminatory Self-Tenders: Unocal versus Mesa

In February 1985, T. Boone Pickens announced a bid from his investor group, Mesa Partners II, for Unocal Corporation.[93] Mesa had just purchased 8% of the larger Los Angeles–based oil company. Pickens's company, Mesa Petroleum, was flush with cash from successful prior offers for Gulf and Phillips Petroleum. Pickens made $800 million on his bid for Gulf and $90 million on the offer for Phillips.[94] Pickens has stated that these gains were not greenmail, based on his long-held position of refusing to accept a higher payment for his shares unless other shareholders could participate in the buyout by the target. Pickens increased the pressure on Phillips by increasing his holdings to 13% of Unocal's outstanding shares. He found Unocal an attractive target because of its low debt level and significant size (revenues of $11.5 billion). Mesa increased its credibility by amassing a war chest of $4 billion in financing through the help of its investment banker, Drexel Burnham Lambert. In April 1985, Pickens bid for just over 50% of Unocal at $54 per share. Unocal, led by Chairman Fred Hartley, responded with a discriminatory self-tender offer for 29% of Unocal's outstanding shares. Hartley wanted to defeat the Pickens bid but did not want to give his foe greenmail. His self-tender offer therefore contained a provision that Mesa Partners II could not participate in Unocal's offer. Pickens appealed to the Delaware Chancery Court to rule on what he believed was a clearly unfair offer by Unocal. The Delaware Chancery Court agreed that Unocal's offer was illegal, a ruling that was later reversed by the Delaware Supreme Court. The Delaware Supreme Court concluded on May 17, 1985, that Unocal's offer was within the board of directors' rights according to the business judgment rule. The court found that Mesa's offer was a "grossly inadequate two-tiered coercive tender offer coupled with the threat of greenmail." The higher court held that Unocal's response to this type of offer was within its rights as provided by the business judgment rule. The Delaware Supreme Court ruling forced Pickens to capitulate; he agreed to a standstill agreement. Ironically, this ruling led to the SEC's review of discriminatory self-tenders, which eventually resulted in a change in tender offer rules making such discriminatory self-tenders illegal.

The *Unocal* decision has become a standard guide for directors in the use of antitakeover measures. In applying *Unocal*, courts now look to see if the defensive measures being used are proportional to the threat perceived. Recall from Chapter 3 that while coercive and inconsistent with the spirit of the Williams Act, such offers are not illegal in the United States. This is while courts allow more aggressive defensive measures when targets are faced with such coercive offers. In a later decision clarifying this, the Delaware Supreme Court noted that the defensive response must not be "draconian" and must be within a "range of reasonableness."[95] In this decision, the Delaware Supreme Court noted that in applying *Unocal*, a court must go through a two-step process. The first step is to determine if the defensive measures go so far as to be coercive or preclusive and halt a takeover contest that might otherwise be in shareholders' interests. The second step is to see if the defensive measures taken are

---

[93] *Unocal v. Mesa*, 493 A.2d 949 (Del. 1985).
[94] Jeff Madrick, *Taking America* (New York: Bantam, 1987), 282.
[95] *Unitrin, Inc. v. American General Corp.*, 651 A. 2d 1361, 1388 (Del 1995).

reasonable in light of the perceived threat. In the case of Unitrin's response to American General's hostile bid, the Delaware Supreme Court found that the first prong of the test was satisfied, but it took issue with Unitrin's repurchase program, although it was not troubled by its poison pill or bylaw change requiring advance notice of an offer.

Corporate Restructuring as a Takeover Defense

Corporate restructuring is another of the more drastic antitakeover defenses. It may involve selling off major parts of the target or even engaging in major acquisitions. Defensive restructuring has been criticized as a case of "Do unto yourself as others would do unto you." Given the anticipated criticism, management usually employs this defense only as a last resort.

Defensive corporate restructuring can be both a preventative defense and an active antitakeover defense. If a firm believes it may become a takeover target, it may restructure to prevent this occurrence. Restructurings also occur in the midst of a takeover battle when the target feels that only drastic actions will prevent a takeover.

It is often difficult for an incumbent management to justify restructuring to prevent an acquisition because management must take considerable liberty with stockholders' resources. Management should be able to convince stockholders, however, that such drastic changes in the nature of the target's business and the rejection of the bidder's proposed premium are both in their best interests.

Defensive restructuring may take the following forms:

- Take the corporation private in an LBO.
- Sell off valued assets.
- Acquire other companies.
- Liquidate the company.

Going private is often the reaction of a management that does not want to give up control of the corporation. Going private and LBOs are discussed in detail in Chapter 8. They can be justified from the stockholders' point of view when they result in higher premiums than rival bids. However, if the buyers in the going-private transaction are managing directors, the offer price must be one that is clearly fair. Fairness may be judged as a significant premium that is higher than the premium offered by other bidders.

The sale of valued assets to prevent a takeover is a highly controversial defensive action. The idea is that the target will sell off the assets the acquirer wants, and so the target will become less desirable in the eyes of the hostile bidder. As a result, the bidder may withdraw its offer. This is essentially a lockup transaction. Stockholders have often strongly opposed these actions and have sometimes successfully sued to prevent their completion. If, however, the target can establish that it received fair and reasonable value for the assets and that their loss did not lower the overall value of the firm after taking into account the receipt of the proceeds from the sale, the target may be on firmer legal ground.

A target may acquire another company to prevent its own takeover for several reasons. First, it may seek to create an antitrust conflict for the acquirer. This will then involve the acquisition of a company in one of the bidder's main lines of business. This tactic was somewhat more effective when the Justice Department exercised stricter antitrust enforcement. However, even if there is a reasonable likelihood that the takeover will be opposed on antitrust grounds, this defense can be deactivated by the sale of the acquired business following the acquirer's acquisition of the target. In its filings with the Justice Department and the Federal Trade Commission (FTC), the acquirer can clearly state its intentions to sell the target's new acquisitions. This may result in an approval of the acquisition pending the acquirer's ability to sell off the necessary parts of the target. A classic case of acquisitions designed to ward off bidders by creating antitrust conflicts occurred when Marshall Field and Company made a series of acquisitions in 1980 in areas where potential bidders were present. These acquisitions were motivated not by any economic factor but only to keep Marshall Field independent. The result was a financially weaker Marshall Field and Company. The company was eventually acquired by Target Corp., which later sold it to May Department Stores in 2004 for $3.24 billion.

A target might want to acquire another concern to reduce its appeal in the eyes of the acquirer. If the target is a highly profitable, streamlined company, this state of financial well-being may be quickly changed by acquiring less profitable businesses in areas in which the acquirer does not want to be. If these acquisitions involve the assumption of greater debt, this increased leverage may also make the target less appealing.

One final restructuring option available for the target company is liquidation. In liquidation the target sells all of its assets and uses the proceeds to pay a liquidating dividend to stockholders. The payment of the dividend is restricted by a variety of legal constraints that protect the rights of the firm's creditors. Therefore, the liquidating dividend needs to be calculated after financial adjustments have been made to take into account outstanding obligations that have to be satisfied. In the best interests of stockholders, this dividend payment must exceed the offer of the hostile bidder. This may be possible, however, in instances in which the target believes that, perhaps because of inordinately low securities market prices, the premium above market price offered by the bidder is below that of the liquidation value of the company.

Litigation as an Antitakeover Defense

Litigation is one of the more common antitakeover defenses. In the early stages of the hostile takeover era (the mid-1970s), it was an effective means of preventing a takeover. However, its power in this area has somewhat diminished. Today litigation is only one of an array of defensive actions a target will take in hopes of preventing a takeover. Lipton and Steinberger cite four goals of antitakeover-related litigation:

1. To choose a more favorable forum.
2. To preclude the raider from taking the initiative and suing first.
3. To delay the bidder while the target pursues a white knight.
4. To provide a psychological lift to the target's management.[96]

---

[96] Martin Lipton and Erica H. Steinberger, *Takeovers and Freezeouts* (New York: Law Journal Seminar Press, 1987), 6–144.

One of the first legal maneuvers the target might try is to request that a court grant an injunction that will prevent the takeover process from continuing. Such an injunction coupled with a restraining order might bar the hostile bidder from purchasing additional stock until the bidder can satisfy the court that the target's charges are without merit.

The temporary halting of a takeover can delay the acquisition, giving the target time to mount more effective defenses. The additional time can also allow the target to seek a white knight. Litigation and the grant of injunctive relief may provide the necessary time to allow a bidding process to develop. Other bidders will now have time to properly consider the benefits of making an offer for the target. The bidding process should result in higher offers for the target. Another major benefit of litigation is to give the bidder time to raise the offer price. The target might indirectly give the bidder the impression that if the offer price and terms were improved, it would drop the litigation. The more common forms of defensive litigation are as follows:

- **Antitrust.** This type of litigation was more effective during the 1960s and 1970s, when the U.S. Justice Department practiced stricter enforcement of the antitrust laws. However, given the Department's pro-business stance over the past two decades, it has become much more difficult to establish an antitrust violation. In 2005, the EU instituted new rule changes that allow, if not encourage, companies to take their antitrust complaints to local national courts instead of before the understaffed EU. This may open the door for greater use of private antitrust litigation in Europe.
- **Inadequate disclosure.** This type of lawsuit often contends that the bidder has not provided complete and full disclosure as required under the Williams Act. The target might argue that, in not providing full and complete disclosure, the acquirer has either not given stockholders adequate information or has provided information that presents an inaccurate picture of the acquirer or the acquirer's intention. The target in these types of lawsuits commonly maintains that the bidder did not convincingly state how it would raise the requisite capital to complete the purchase of all the stock that was bid for. The bidder usually contends that the disclosure is more than adequate or agrees to supplement his or her filings.
- **Fraud.** This is a more serious charge and is more difficult to prove. Except in more extreme circumstances, it cannot be relied on to play a major role in the target's defense.

Litigation Research

In a 1985 study of attempted and completed takeovers that involved litigation between 1962 and 1980, Jarrell found that litigation occurred in one-third of all tender offers.[97]

---

[97] Gregg Jarrell, "Wealth Effects of Litigating by Targets: Do Interests Diverge in a Merge?" *Journal of Law and Economics* 28, no. 1 (April 1985): 151–177.

As noted previously, litigation may be beneficial for target shareholders even when it does not result in the acquirer's retraction of the bid. Litigation may result in a bid being delayed or force the bidder to raise his offer.

Jarrell found that 62% of the offers that had litigation had competing bids, whereas only 11% of those that did not have litigation had competing offers. He also found that, although it seems reasonable that litigation would cause bidders to raise their offer price to encourage the target to drop the litigation and avoid the legal expenses (as well as the possibility that the bid might be permanently halted), there was no evidence of a significant price effect. On average, a stock price decline took place when litigation was initiated. This decline occurred both for firms that were eventually acquired and for those that remained independent. However, unacquired stock returns fell 23.4%, whereas acquired returns declined slightly more than 21%.

Jarrell also found that when an auction for the firm resulted following the initiation of litigation, there was an additional 17% premium above the first offer relative to nonauctioned firms. When litigation results in the bidder's withdrawing its offer, however, target company stockholders suffer major losses. They incur both the loss of a premium, which averaged 32% for Jarrell's sample of firms, as well as the costs of litigation. We can conclude that litigation may bring benefits for targets, but if the bid is withdrawn, it may also result in significant losses for target stockholders.

Pac-Man Defense

The *Pac-Man defense*, so named after the popular video game in which characters try to eat each other before they are eaten themselves, is one of the more colorful defenses employed by target companies. It occurs when the target makes an offer to buy the raider in response to the raider's bid for the target. Because of its extreme nature, this defense is considered a "doomsday machine." One of the more famous uses of this defense came when the Martin Marietta Corporation made an offer to buy Bendix following Bendix's unwanted $43 tender offer for Martin Marietta in the summer of 1982.

The Pac-Man defense is often threatened but it is seldom used. Before the Bendix–Martin Marietta takeover battle, two companies had used it in a vain effort to maintain their independence. In 1982, NLT Corporation ended up merging with its bidder—American General Corporation. As stated earlier, Cities Service tried the Pac-Man defense in response to T. Boone Pickens's bid from Mesa Petroleum. Although the defense halted Mesa's bid and helped to convince Mesa to accept greenmail, Cities Service was nonetheless put in play and ended up selling out to Occidental Petroleum.

In another early use of the Pac-Man defense, Houston Natural Gas Corporation (which later became Enron Corporation) used a 1984 bid for the raider to try to fend off the Coastal Corporation. It was not successful because Houston Natural Gas sold off nearly half its assets to maintain its independence. The Heublein Corporation, however, threatened to use the Pac-Man defense when it was confronted by General Cinema Corporation and was able to scare away General Cinema.

There have been a limited number of successful uses of the Pac-Man defense. In 1988 E-II Holdings, a diverse group of consumer product companies formed from the spin-off of 15 companies after the LBO of Beatrice, made an offer for American Brands—also a collection of various name brand consumer products. This use of the Pac-Man defense was successful in that the original E-II offer elicited a Pac-Man bid from American Brands, which was what E-II's CEO, Donald Kelly, was seeking.

In 1999 there was another successful use of the Pac-Man defense when Chesapeake Corporation made a responding bid for Shorewood Corporation, which had launched a hostile bid for Chesapeake. The combination of the Pac-Man offer along with a very aggressive legal defense enabled Chesapeake to stay independent while, as a result of Chesapeake's tender offer, Shorewood was ultimately acquired by a third party. In that same year Elf Aquitaine used the Pac-Mac defense to acquire Total Fina. The two large oil and chemical companies fought a hostile battle after Total Fina made an unwanted bid for Elf Aquitaine, which wanted to remain independent. Elf Aquitaine, once owned by the French government, was warned by the government not to seek a white knight that would be a non-French company. It saw a Pac-Man bid for Total Fina as its only option. This did not allow it to acquire its hostile rival but did get shareholders an improved $52.8 billion bid.

The Pac-Man defense remains rarely used but reappeared in 2014 in the hostile takeover battle between two men's clothing chains. When Jos A. Bank Clothier initiated a hostile bid for larger rival Men's Warehouse, the target responded with its own bid for Jos. A. Bank. That Pac-Man bid proved successful.

"Just Say No"

In the most basic form of antitakeover defense, the target refuses to be taken over, simply hiding behind its poison pills and other defenses and stating that it will not deactivate them and will not bring the offer before the shareholders. In the *just say no* defense, the target may refuse to take any measures, even providing more cash to shareholders, by stating that it has more optimistic plans for the future of the company.

The Universal Foods Corporation, a manufacturer of products such as French fries and cheese, used the just say no defense in 1989, when it turned down an offer from the High Voltage Engineering Corporation. When High Voltage Engineering offered $38 per share, Universal responded that its investment banker, Goldman Sachs, had determined that this offer was inadequate. Universal's board of directors decided that profits were rising and that this was not the time to sell the company. Martin Lipton, the originator of the just say no defense, advised his client, Universal Foods, to reject the offer and not take any other action. Universal compromised by raising its dividend from 18 cents per share to 22 cents. The company's defense, especially its poison pill, was challenged in court. In March 1989, a federal court judge in Wisconsin ruled that if the company's executives believed that the offer was inadequate, they were in a position to determine an accurate value for the company.

Just Say No Reconciled with Revlon Duties

The just say no defense allows directors to reject a bid as inadequate or not in the company's long-term interests without putting the company up for sale in an auction. The just say no defense is a post-Revlon concept that target company directors often rally toward when confronted with an unwanted takeover bid. A leading case in support of this concept is *Paramount Communications v. Time.*[98] In this attempted takeover, Time Inc.'s directors rejected Paramount's bid in favor of Warner Communications Inc. It may be the case that this finding will be relevant only in situations where a target corporation has a well-developed long-term strategy that it is pursuing, as with the merger with Warner, and that other target corporations that lack such a long-term strategy involving an alternative merger would not fit the *Paramount v. Time* decision.[99] If future decisions determine that is the case, then target directors may not be able to liberally apply the just say no defense.

The just say no defense may be challenged by higher offers that will counter the board of directors' position that the future value of the company is worth more to stockholders than the offer price. There will always be some price that will leave the board of directors with no choice but to approve the offer.

 INFORMATION CONTENT OF TAKEOVER RESISTANCE

Throughout this chapter we have reviewed a variety of antitakeover defenses and have analyzed the shareholder wealth effects of several of these defenses. Looking at defenses more globally, Pound has studied the information content of takeover bids and the resistance of the target to the takeover.[100] Pound used consensus earnings forecasts as a proxy for the market's expected value of the targets as stand-alone entities. The effect of different types of takeover contests and defenses on the market's value of the target was assessed by considering whether the consensus changed. These tests were conducted for three samples: targets of friendly bids, targets of hostile bids that were ultimately acquired, and targets of hostile bids that remained independent. Pound observed that the consensus forecasts were unchanged after the initial takeover bid. He therefore concluded that the bids themselves do not convey important information. The unchanged forecasts also imply that the bid did not reveal to the marketplace a previously undiscovered case of undervaluation.

Pound found the resistance to a takeover to be associated with a downward revision of the average earnings forecasts of approximately 10%. This was the case both for firms that were acquired and for those that remained independent. Pound concluded that the market interprets the resistance as a negative signal about future performance.

---

[98] *Paramount Communications, Inc. v Time, Inc.*, 571 A. 2d 1140 (Del. 1989).
[99] Brent A. Olson, *Publicly Traded Corporations: Governance & Regulations* (New York: Thompson West, 2005).
[100] John Pound, "The Information Effects of Takeover Bids and Resistance," *Journal of Financial Economics* 22, no. 2 (December 1988): 207–227.

BENDIX VERSUS MARTIN MARIETTA

One of the most colorful takeover battles in U.S. economic history was the contest between the Bendix Corporation and the Martin Marietta Corporation. Bendix was led by its chairman, William Agee, who got his training in acquisitions while chief financial officer of Boise Cascade Corporation. Boise Cascade was a forest products company that transformed itself into a conglomerate through diverse acquisitions in the 1960s. Agee joined Bendix in 1972 as executive vice president, reporting to Michael Blumenthal, who left to become secretary of the treasury in the Carter Administration. At the age of 38 years, Agee was named chairman of the company, which had two main lines of business, auto products, such as ignition systems and brakes, and aviation products for the defense industry.

In August 1982, after an aborted takeover attempt of RCA, Agee began his bid for Martin Marietta, a company that was an established presence in the defense industry, particularly in aerospace products, such as missile systems. Bendix made a $43 tender offer for 45% of Martin Marietta (Bendix already had just under 5% of Martin Marietta), which was previously selling for $33 per share. Martin Marietta rejected the offer and initiated its own $75-per-share tender offer for Bendix, which had been previously selling for $50 per share.

Although Bendix, a Delaware corporation, bid for Martin Marietta first, Martin Marietta was incorporated in Maryland and that state's corporation laws required any bidder to give the target 10 days' notice before calling an election of the board of directors. This gave Martin Marietta an apparent advantage over Bendix because Martin Marietta could complete its tender offer for Bendix, following the necessary 20-day Williams Act waiting period that affected both offers, change Bendix's board of directors, and call off Bendix's tender offer before Bendix could do the same at Martin Marietta. Arthur Fleischer, of the firm Fried, Frank, Harris, Shriver, and Jacobson, had advised Agee that Bendix's corporate charter's election rules should be amended to remove this advantage, but that was never done.

Each firm engaged in various defenses, including litigation. Bendix adopted golden parachutes; Martin Marietta searched for a white knight. They found a gray knight, Harry Gray, chairman of United Technologies Corporation, who agreed to make a backup tender offer for Martin Marietta if its offer for Bendix failed.

Agee counted on the 23% of the company's stock that was held in an employee stock ownership plan (ESOP) that was managed by Citibank's trustee. Martin Marietta's tender offer was two-tiered, with better consideration being offered for the first tier. Citibank concluded that its fiduciary responsibilities were with the financial well-being of the ESOP shareholders and not based on any other loyalty to Bendix. Many of the employees, however, did not agree with this assessment.

Although Agee may have believed that he could have reached agreement with Martin Marietta to drop its offer, Martin Marietta could not count on United Technologies to simply walk away, so it went ahead with its bid for Bendix and raised the offer price. The absurdity of the deal was that it looked as if both companies would end up buying each other, with each company being debt-laden after the transaction.

Bendix contacted Edward Hennessy, then chairman of Allied Signal, to be its white knight. Hennessy bid for Bendix and won control of the company. He then reached agreement with Thomas Pownall, CEO of Martin Marietta, to exchange shares. Martin Marietta remained independent but highly leveraged. Hennessy ended up with valuable Bendix assets.

6

Takeover Tactics

F ROM A TARGET'S PERSPECTIVE, hostile bids are offers that the target publicly refuses to accept. In this chapter we focus on the options hostile bidders can use to complete a takeover of an unwilling target.

The fourth merger wave is considered by some the era of the hostile takeover; however, even during that period most takeovers were friendly deals. By the time we reached the fifth merger wave of the 1990s, the percentage of friendly deals increased even more. For example, using one data set Andrade Stafford and Mitchell found that 14% of deals were unfriendly in the 1980s, but that percentage fell to only 4% in the 1990s.[1] In the 2000s friendly deals are still much more common. Nonetheless, hostile deals are still important and actually can be interesting if not even entertaining.

This chapter analyzes the evolution of takeover tactics over the past quarter of a century and discusses how they are currently used and their relative effectiveness. It will become apparent that these tactics have evolved and changed substantially over time.

The takeover options for the hostile bidder are fewer in number compared with the broad variety of defenses that targets implement in advance of and during a hostile bid. The bidder is typically left with the choice of three main tactics: a bear hug, a tender offer, and a proxy fight. Each tactic has its strengths and weaknesses. In addition, each may be implemented in varying manners to increase the likelihood of success. The options and their shareholder wealth effects are the focus of this chapter.

Of the main takeover tactics, bear hugs are the least aggressive and often occur at the beginning of a hostile takeover. When the target is not strongly opposed to a takeover, a bear hug may be sufficient. However, for a determined and firmly entrenched target,

---

[1] George Andrade, Mark Mitchell, and George Stafford, "New Evidence and Perspectives on Mergers," *Journal of Economic Perspectives* 15, no. 2 (Spring, 2001): 106.

it is unlikely that a bear hug will be sufficient to complete the takeover. However, a bear hug may be a precursor to an eventual tender offer.

We also discuss tender offers. The rules governing such offers in the United States were already discussed in Chapter 3. In this chapter we will focus on the tactical elements of tender offers.

Another takeover tactic covered in this chapter is proxy fights. In this chapter we discuss not only the tactical aspects of proxy fights but also the relevant rules and regulations and shareholder wealth effects.

PRELIMINARY TAKEOVER STEPS

Casual Pass

Before initiating hostile actions, the bidder may attempt some informal overture to the management of the target. This is sometimes referred to as a casual pass. It may come from a member of the bidder's management or from one of its representatives, such as its investment banker. In fact, an approach from the bidder's bankers is often the least threatening. If the approach, however, comes from the bidder's senior management, then the bidder should have a well-thought-out plan to put forward at that time. When the bidder's senior management is making the approach, it will usually prefer a meeting as opposed to a telephone conference. The meeting allows a more detailed discussion, and the bidder can present an offer letter at that time.

A casual pass may be used if the bidder is unsure of the target's response. If the target has been the subject of other hostile bids that it has spurned, or if the target has publicly stated its desire to remain independent, this step may provide few benefits. In fact, it can work against the bidder because it provides the target with advance warning of the bidder's interest. In most takeover battles, the target tries to buy more time while the bidder seeks to force the battle to a quick conclusion. Managers of potential target companies are often advised by their attorneys to not engage in loose discussions that could be misconstrued as an expression of interest. They are often told to unequivocally state that the target wants to remain independent.

Establishing a Toehold

An initial step that is often pursued before using the various takeover tactics that are at the disposal of a hostile bidder is to begin an initial accumulation of the target's shares. In doing so, the bidder seeks to establish a toehold from which to launch its hostile bid. One of the advantages of such share purchases is that if the market is unaware of its actions, the bidder may be able to avoid the payment of a premium for the shares that form the toehold. This may lower the average cost of the acquisition. In addition, it may provide the bidder with some of the same rights that other shareholders have, thus establishing a fiduciary duty, which the board would now have in its dual role as the hostile bidder and as the target shareholder. This is why target defenses that relate to share acquisitions are exclusionary and usually leave out the accumulator/hostile bidder. This is often a subject of litigation between the company and the bidder. In addition, if a rival bidder acquires the target, the initial bidder may receive a premium on its toehold position, thereby providing it with potentially significant gains. Various researchers have showed that bidders with toeholds have a higher probability of acquiring the target.[2]

In light of the benefits just discussed, it is surprising that toeholds are not more prevalent. Researchers have categorized toeholds into two groups: short-term toeholds, which were purchased less than six months from an offer date; and long-term toeholds, which were purchased more than six months from the offer date. Betton, Eckbo, and Thornburn found a toehold frequency of 13%, with short-term toeholds of only 2%![3] There are costs that offset many of the benefits of toeholds; otherwise, most bids would have toeholds.

Pursuant to the requirements of Sec 13(d) of the Williams Act, bidders have to disclose their holdings by filing a Schedule 13D within 10 days after acquiring 5% of a target's stock. This disclosure can convey a competitive advantage to rival bidders and could possibly weaken the bidder's bargaining position relative to the target. There may also be additional required disclosure to antitrust agencies related to Hart-Scott-Rodino.

Another significant cost could be share price declines if the bid is not successful. The stock price may fall after it becomes clear that the bid is withdrawn. This may cause the bidder to incur a loss on its toehold acquisition. Still another cost is that the target's management, especially targets with entrenched managers, may not respond well to the existence of a toehold and may conclude that the bidder's offer is hostile in nature. This may make meaningful merger negotiations problematic, and with that the likelihood of receiving a termination fee if the target is ultimately sold to another bidder may be significantly lower.

Interestingly, Betton, Eckbo, and Thorburn found the distribution of their large sample to be bimodal.[4] That is, many bidders chose to forgo any toehold due to concerns about the costs, while others may amass large toeholds, such as 25%. Not surprisingly, hostile bids tend to more likely be associated with toeholds compared to friendly offers. Betton, Eckbo, and Thorburn report that 11% of friendly initial bidders in their sample had a toehold, whereas 50% of hostile bidders had toeholds.[5]

Information Asymmetry

One of the difficulties hostile bidders have is that they have to construct an offer without the benefit of information from the target that often is available in friendly deals. The bidder has to determine which of the target's assets might be lost after the target

---

[2] Ralph Walking, "Predicting Tender Offer Success: A Logistic Analysis," *Journal of Financial and Quantitative Analysis* 20, no. 4 (December 1985): 461–478; Robert H. Jennings and M. A Mazzeo, "Competing Bids, Target Management Resistance and the Structure of Bids," *Review of Financial Studies* 6, no. 4 (Winter 1993): 883–910; and Sandra Betton and B. Espen Eckbo, "Toeholds, Bid Jumps and Expected Payoff in Takeovers," *Review of Financial Studies* 13, no. 4 (Winter 2000): 841–882.

[3] Sandra Betton, B. Espen Eckbo, and Karin Thornburn, "Merger Negotiations and the Toehold Puzzle," *Journal of Financial Economics* 91 (2007): 158–178.

[4] Ibid.

[5] Sandra Betton, B. Espen Eckbo, and Karin Thorburn, "Corporate Takeovers," in B. Espen Eckbo, ed., *Handbook of Corporate Finance: Empirical Corporate Finance*, col. 2 (Amsterdam: North Holland, 2008), 336.

is acquired. For example, if the target has important contracts that might be lost if the target is acquired, this could lower its value and result in a lower bid. Such *value leakage* can be a real cause of concern. Therefore, it is very important that the bidder do diligent research and gain access to all relevant public information that can help create an enlightened offer.

Takeover Contest Process

When a bidder and target seek to pursue a friendly deal, they sign a merger agreement. However, the target's board of directors is required to still consider other bids as a way making sure they maximize shareholder wealth. This is referred to as the *fiduciary out* clause that is part of merger agreements.

Figure 6.1 shows the three common outcomes that can occur after an initial bid. The target may accept the offer, and no other bidders may enter the fray. The target can also choose to reject the offer, and either there will be other offers or no other bidder may materialize. If a rival bidder makes an offer, then several outcomes are possible. The target can reject all offers, or either the initial bidder or a rival bidder wins the takeover contest. Betton, Eckbo, and Thorburn analyzed 35,727 takeover contests over the period 1980–2005.[6] Eighty-one percent were merger bids, while 12.6% were tender offers and 6.2% were control-block trades.

A bidder has to consider the responses of not just the target but also other bidders. In an analysis of thousands of bids over the period 1980–2002 Betton, Eckbo, and Thorburn found that the initial bidder was successful two-thirds of the time.[7] This

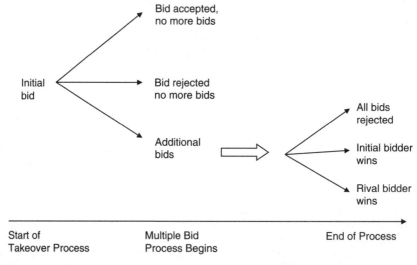

FIGURE 6.1   Takeover Process

[6] Sandra Betton and B. Espen Eckbo, "Toeholds, Bid Jumps and the Expected Payoff in Takeovers." *Review of Financial Studies*, 13, (2000), 841–882.
[7] Op cit

probability is significantly lower when the bidder contacts the target to negotiate a merger as opposed to being more assertive and making a strong tender offer. When a rival bidder enters the fray, the rival prevails over the initial bidder twice as often as the initial bidder does.[8] So a key for the initial bidder is to structure its first bid so that it will preempt other bidders while not overpaying. This can be termed the *optimal bid*. Once an auction occurs, then all bidders have to try to avoid paying the winner's curse. This is why they need to be very careful in crafting bid jumps—particularly if they put forward a rich initial bid.

Bid Jumps

As we have noted, a target's board has an obligation to consider other offers. If the initial bid is followed by one or more bids from other firms, we have an auction process. Betton and Eckbo found the time between the first and second bids to be 15 days in their sample.[9] It was somewhat longer in the later study by Betton, Eckbo, and Thorburn—40 days.[10]

Betton and Eckbo found that when a new bidder had a toehold, the approximate size of that toehold was similar to that of the initial bidder. To them this implied that the second bidder amassed its toehold to offer any advantages the initial bidder's toehold gave it.

Betton and Eckbo as well as Betton, Eckbo, and Thorburn found that the premium offer by single bidders was somewhat higher than the premium offered by an initial bidder in a takeover contest involving multiple bidders. One interpretation of this difference is a desire by the single bidder to preempt other bidders by making a strong offer they might not want to match and also making an offer that would impress the target's board and shareholders.[11] One should not put too much weight into this conclusion, and the differences between the single bidder premium and that of the initial bidder in a contest were not all that great.

One of the more interesting findings of Betton and Eckbo was the magnitude of bid jumps that are the differences in offer price between succeeding bids. They found an average bid jump of 10% for a second bid compared to the initial bid. This translated into a 31% increase in the premium. They also found a 14% increase from the initial bid to the final bid, which resulted in a 65% increase in the premium.

Bear Hugs

A bidder will sometimes try to pressure the management of the target before initiating a tender offer. This may be done by contacting the board of directors with an expression of interest in acquiring the target and the implied intent to go directly to stockholders with

---

[8] B. Espen Eckbo, "Bidding Strategies and Takeover Premiums," *Journal of Corporate Finance* 15, no. 1 (February 2009): 149–178.

[9] Sandra Betton and B. Espen Eckbo, "Toeholds, Bid Jumps, and Expected Payoffs in Takeovers." *Review of Financial Studies* 13, no. 4 (Winter 2000): 841–882.

[10] Betton, Eckbo, and Thorburn, "Merger Negotiations and the Toehold Puzzle." *Journal of Financial Economics*, 91, (2009), 158–178.

[11] Michael J. Fishman, "A Theory of Preemptive Takeover Bidding," *RAND Journal of Economics* 19 (1988): 88–101.

a tender offer if these overtures are not favorably received. This strategy—known as the *bear hug*—may also be accompanied by a public announcement of the bidder's intent to make a tender offer.

There are two kinds of bear hugs. A *teddy bear hug* is one that does not include a price or specific deal terms. It is also not meant to be made public. This kind of an overture is much less threatening than a normal bear hug, which often does include a price and is meant to be made public.

The bear hug forces the target's board to take a public position on the possible takeover by this bidder. Such offers carry with them the implication that if it is not favorably received, it will be immediately followed by a tender offer directly to shareholders. A bear hug also puts pressure on the board of directors because it must be considered lest the board be regarded as having violated its fiduciary duties.

Once a bear hug becomes public, arbitragers typically accumulate the target's stock. Depending on the companies involved, they may even want to sell the bidder's shares short based on the fact that when bidders make takeover offers, the bidder's shares may decline after the announcement. The accumulation of shares by arbitragers may make large share block purchases easier for the initiator of the bear hug or any other bidder. This often puts the company in play, which makes continued independence more difficult.

A stronger version of the standard bear hug occurs when one bidder offers a specific price in order to, among other reasons, establish a range for damages in possible stockholder lawsuits that might follow the target management's rejection of the bid. This tactic increases the pressure on the target's board, which might be the object of the lawsuits. The typical response of an unreceptive target board is to acquire a fairness opinion from an investment bank that will say that the offer is inadequate. This gives the board of directors a "legitimate" reason to reject the offer. If the bidder makes a public announcement while engaging in a bear hug, the bidder is bound to file pursuant to Rule 14d-2 of the Williams Act and is required to disseminate tender offer materials or abandon the offer within five days. If the target discloses the offer, the bidder is not required to file.

From a strategic point of view, if the bidder sees a realistic possibility of a negotiated transaction, the bear hug may be an attractive alternative to a tender offer. It is a less expensive and less time-consuming way to conduct a "hostile" acquisition. It may also reduce the adverse consequences that sometimes are associated with hostile deals, such as the loss of key target employees and a deterioration of employee morale following the acquisition. If the target strongly opposes the acquisition, however, the bear hug may be unsuccessful, leaving the bidder to pursue other methods, such as a tender offer.

Bidders who are reluctant to engage in a costly tender offer begin to use the bear hug as an initial, less expensive takeover tool. The advantage is that the pressure placed on the target's board of directors may be sufficient to complete the takeover.

Stock Price Runups and Markups

It is not unusual to see a target's stock price increase in advance of an eventual offer by an initial bidder. There are various explanations for such a runup, including rumors that a company might be a target as well as formal statements made in SEC 13(d) filings.

The question that researchers have focused on was whether this runup reflected an anticipated premium that would be paid if the company was eventually acquired by some bidder. It would have to a probability adjusted amount that reflected the discounted present value of the premium times the probability that the deal would be completed. If this is the case, though, then the market has a specific "pre-rumor" premium, and as of the runup some of this is already incorporated into the stock price. If that is the case, then the eventual premium offered would be less than what would have been offered if there was no runup. However, as Schwert has pointed out, the runup phenomena means that the premium is as set forth as in equation 6.1.[12]

$$\text{Premium} = \text{Runup} + \text{Markup} \qquad (6.1)$$

When the runup reflects the market increased valuation of the target, perhaps based upon new information, including the interest of more investors in the target, the combination of the runup and markup could result in a higher premium than what would have occurred. In an effort to empirically measure the component of a takeover premium that was caused by the runup, Schwert estimated the following relationship:

$$\text{Premium}_i = \alpha + \beta \, \text{Runup}_i + u_i \qquad (6.2)$$

He found that β (remember not beta from CAPM) was statistically significant (t value of 2.88) and equal to 1.13, which means for every dollar of a runup the takeover premium increased by $1.13.[13] The runup increases the premium.

The question that arises is whether the runup lowers the markup and whether there is some substitution going on between runup and the eventual offer markup. This question was addressed by Betton, Eckbo, and Thorburn, who estimated the following relationship:[14]

$$\text{Markup}_i = \alpha' + \beta' \, \text{Runup}_i + \varepsilon X_i + u_i \qquad (6.3)$$

They found that the runup was strongly statistically significant (t = −15.44) and that the sign of β was negative, indicating a trade-off between the runup and the markup (X is a set of target and bidder characteristics). Specifically they found that β' was −0.18. So this means that the runup causes the premium to rise but the markup is lower than what it would be if there was no runup. The combined effect is an initial offer price effect of $0.82.

Betton, Eckbo, and Thorburn also found that the runup was greater when the bidder purchased a target toehold during the runup period. Therefore, they shed light on another cost of establishing a toehold, which helps explain why toehold purchases have declined over time. A depiction of the runup developed by Betton, Eckbo, and Thornburn is shown in Figure 6.2.

---

[12] George W. Schwert, "Markup Pricing in Mergers and Acquisitions," *Journal of Corporate Finance* 10 (2004): 683–701.
[13] George W. Schwert, "Markup Pricing in Mergers and Acquisitions," *Journal of Financial Economics* 41 (1996): 153–196.
[14] Sandra Betton, B. Espen Eckbo, Rex Thompson, and Karin S. Thorburn, "Markup Pricing Revisited," Working Paper Tuck School of Business, Dartmouth University, 2008.

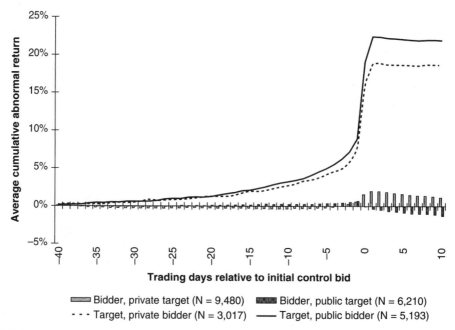

FIGURE 6.2 Runup and Announcement Period Returns. *Source*: Sandra Betton, B. Espen Eckbo and Karin Thornburn, "Corporate Takeovers" in *Handbook of Corporate Finance*, 2008, Vol. 2, (Amsterdam: North Holland), p. 367.

Bypass Offers

Before we begin our discussions of tender offers, it is useful to discuss which types of targets are more likely to receive bypass offers. A bypass offer is one that is unsolicited and that was not preceded by negotiations or discussions between the managements of the two companies. Bange and Mazzeo found that targets whose CEO was also the chair of the board were more likely to receive bypass offers.[15] This could be because the bidder believed that management was entrenched and more likely to oppose the offer. They also found that offers made to targets that had largely independent boards were less likely to be successful and, surprisingly, the initial offer premium is likely to be lower than their less independent counterparts.

Bange and Mazzeo did find that bypass offers were more likely to be successful and also featured greater gains for target shareholders. This supports the intuitive conclusion that a bidder, often using the services of a mergers and acquisitions (M&A) consultant such as an investment banker, can usually get a good sense of whether a target is going to be receptive to an offer, along with what type of offer will be needed for a deal to be completed.

---

[15] Mary Bange and Michael Mazzeo, "Board Composition, Board Effectiveness and the Opposed Composition of Takeover Bids," *Review of Financial Studies* 17, no. 4 (2004): 1185–1215.

TENDER OFFERS

Because the Williams Act is the key piece of federal legislation that regulates tender offers, it is ironic that the law does not even define the term. Instead, it has been left to the courts to formulate an exact definition. This ambiguity has naturally led to some confusion regarding what constitutes a tender offer. In some instances, bidders, believing that their actions were not a tender offer, have failed to follow the rules and procedures of the Williams Act. This occurred in the landmark case discussed in Chapter 3 involving the bid by Sun Oil Inc. for the Becton Dickinson Company. In late 1977, Sun Oil structured a deal with Fairleigh S. Dickinson, founder of the New Jersey private college of the same name, to purchase shares that Fairleigh Dickinson, his family, and other related parties held. Because the company did not file the proper disclosure statements at the time this agreement was reached, the court ruled that it had violated the Williams Act under the definition of a group as offered by the law. In deciding the case, the federal district court ruled that the establishment of an agreement between Dickinson and Sun Oil to sell shares to Sun and to have Dickinson become chairman of Becton Dickinson following its acquisition by Sun Oil warranted a disclosure filing. In arriving at its decision, the court established a definition of a tender offer, naming eight factors that are characteristic of a tender offer.[16] These factors, which were covered in Chapter 3, are listed in Table 6.1.

The eighth point was not relevant to the *Wellman v. Dickinson* case and was not discussed in this ruling. It is derived from an earlier ruling. Not all eight factors must be present for an offer to be judged a tender offer. The court did not want the eight factors to constitute an automatic litmus test for tender offers. Rather, in deciding whether the

TABLE 6.1 Tender Offer Eight-Factor Test

1. Active and widespread solicitation of public shareholders for the shares of an issuer
2. Solicitation made for the substantial percentage of an issuer's stock
3. Offer to purchase made a premium over the prevailing market price
4. Terms of the offer firm rather than negotiated
5. Offer contingent on the tender of a fixed number of shares, often subject to a fixed maximum number to be purchased
6. Offer open only a limited period of time
7. Offeree subject to pressure to sell his stock
8. Public announcements of a purchasing program concerning the target company precede or accompany rapid accumulation of larger amounts of the target company's securities

Source: Larry D. Soderquist, *Understanding Securities Laws* (New York: Practicing Law Institute, 1987), 236.

---

[16] *Wellman v. Dickinson*, 475 F. Supp. 783 (SD NY 1979).

circumstances of a given stock purchase constitute a tender offer, the eight factors are considered together, along with any other relevant factors.

Tender Offer—A Two-Step Transaction

A tender offer that is used to acquire a target is typically a two-step transaction. In the first step the acquirer seeks to buy a stipulated number of shares—at least the minimum stipulated in the offer. If this gives the acquirer control, then the buyer will usually follow with a second step, a back-end or close-out transaction to acquire the remaining shares. If the buyer acquires a very large percentage of the target's shares, it may be able to simply freeze out or close out the remaining shareholders automatically via what is called a *short form merger*.

Top-Up Option

If the buyer gets the minimum it sought in the tender offer, often just over 50%, it may request that the target give it a *"top up" option*, which would allow the buyer to buy sufficient newly issued shares to allow the buyer to cross the threshold to do a short-form merger (i.e., 90%) and acquire the target. New York Stock Exchange and NASDAQ have rules and limitations on the number of shares a company can issue without gaining shareholder approval.

Short-Form Merger

In a short-form merger, if the buyer acquires a minimum threshold dictated by relevant state law, usually 90%, it may simply close out the remaining shareholders, who then receive the compensation the acquirer paid to the other shareholders, and the buyer is not required to solicit the voting approval of those remaining shareholders. The buyer only needs to file an *articles of merger* with the secretary of state of incorporation.

Long-Form Merger

One alternative to a tender offer is a *long-form merger* where the acquirer seeks 100% ownership in a one-step transaction through which it wins shareholder voting approval of the takeover and sale of shares. This involves the bidder issuing a detailed proxy statement that must be preapproved by the SEC and then mailed to the target's shareholders. In a tender offer, however, the tender offer materials do not have to be pre-approved by the SEC prior to mailing to shareholders.

Once the target shareholders receive the materials, a vote on the deal ensues. It is important to bear in mind that if the tender provides the acquirer with a majority of the votes of the target—voting control—then the outcome of the vote is not in doubt. However, the longer process results in a delay in the acquisition timeline. In 2013 a new Delaware rule (sec 251h) eliminated the need for a time consuming voting approval if certain conditions are met including the bidder clearly holding voting control.

If a bidder is unsure of the success of the top-up option, it may proceed on a dual track, where it pursues both the top-up option and share purchases, while also proceeding with a long-form merger in case the former is not successful.

Time Periods: Tender Offer versus Long-Form Merger

A tender offer is more complex but potentially quicker than a long-form merger. Through a tender offer a bidder may be able to acquire control in 20 to 40 business days. In a long-form merger, control may not be achieved until, say, two to four months. One of the many reasons that a tender offer is quicker is that voting approval of the target shareholders is not needed. They approve by selling their shares to the bidder.

Open Market Purchases

The courts have generally found that open market purchases do not by themselves represent a tender offer. Generally, they do require that the purchaser file a Schedule TO. One version of open market purchases is a *creeping tender offer*, which is the process of gradually acquiring shares in the market or through private transactions. Although under certain circumstances these purchases may require a Schedule TO filing, the courts generally do not regard such purchases as a legal tender offer. Courts have repeatedly found that the purchase of stock from sophisticated institutional investors is not under the domain of the Williams Act.[17] However, the courts have maintained that a publicly announced intention to acquire control of a company followed by a rapid accumulation of that firm's stock is a tender offer.[18]

Reason for Using a Tender Offer

A company usually resorts to a tender offer when a friendly negotiated transaction does not appear to be a viable alternative. In using a tender offer, the bidder may be able to circumvent management and the target's board and obtain control even when the target's board opposes the takeover. The costs associated with a tender offer, such as legal filing fees as well as publicity and publication costs, make the tender offer a more expensive alternative than a negotiated deal. The initiation of a tender offer often means that the company will be taken over, although not necessarily by the firm that initiated the tender offer. The tender offer may put the company in play, which may cause it to be taken over by another firm that may seek to enter the bidding contest for the target. The auction process may significantly increase the cost of using a tender offer. It also tends to increase the returns enjoyed by target shareholders.

The tender offer can have the advantage of speed in that it is *theoretically* possible to complete a cash tender offer in 20 business days. Practically, there are defenses, such as the poison pill or right plan, that the target may deploy to derail and slow down the tender offer. Practically, once a poison pill has been deployed, the tender offer is temporarily stymied and the bidder must then pursue a proxy contest to change the board, which, in turn, can allow the tender offer to proceed.

A tender offer also shows the target's shareholders and its board the resolve the bidder has to complete a deal. It also can serve as a device for showing the intentions of

---

[17] *Stromfeld v. Great Atlantic & Pacific Tea Company*, 484 F. Supp. 1264 (SD NY 1980), aff'd 6464 F.2d 563 (2nd Cir. 1980), and *Kennecott Cooper Corp. v. Curtiss Wright Corp.*, 584 F.2d 1195 (2d Cir. 1978).
[18] *S-G Securities, Inc. v. Fuqua Investment Company*, 466 F. Supp. 1114 (D. Mass. 1978).

the target's shareholders. This is important as when the offer is made public the composition of the target's shareholder base often changes, with long-term shareholders often selling out to short-term investors, who are eager to receive a takeover premium. Such short-term shareholders may be reluctant to support entrenched target managers who oppose any sale of the company.

Success Rate of Tender Offers

Most offers are not contested (see Figure 6.3). Based on experience in the years from 1990 to 2013, the success rate of total contested tender offers for publicly traded companies was 58% on a weighted average basis.[19] The targets that were not acquired by a bidder either went to a white knight or remained independent. White knights accounted for a significant percentage of the instances in which targets fought off the original hostile bidder. Bidders have to take into account the fact that approximately half of the contested deals will be unsuccessful from their perspective when they launch a hostile bid. We have to also keep in mind that in this discussion we are defining success as being able to ultimately take over the target that is resisting the offer. We are not defining success as an eventual takeover and a deal that is also a financial success based on years of profitable, posttakeover performance. If this were done, the success rate would be lower.

Regulatory Considerations and Choice of a Tender Offer

When the target is in an industry that is highly regulated, then the deal closing may be held up until regulatory approval is secured. Practically, this could mean that the tender offer could be open for a long time period, such as nine months. A lot can happen in that

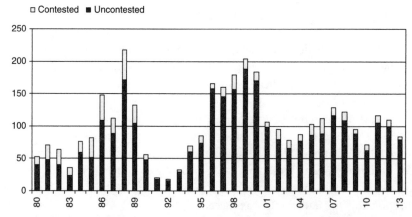

FIGURE 6.3 Tender Offers, 1980–2013: Contested versus Uncontested. *Source: Mergerstat Review,* 1998 and 2014.

---

[19] *Mergerstat Review,* 2013.

long a time period, such as a new bidder coming on the scene, which may make the tender offer a less attractive way to complete a takeover.

Cash versus Securities Tender Offers

The firm that is initiating a tender offer may go with an all-cash tender offer or may use securities as part or all of the consideration used for the offer. Securities, such as the bidder's own shares, may be more attractive to some of the target stockholders because under certain circumstances the transaction may be considered tax-free. When the bidder uses its own shares, this is sometimes referred to as an *exchange offer*.

The bidding firm may create a more flexible structure for target shareholders by using a double-barreled offer, which is an offer in which the target shareholders are given the option of receiving cash or securities in exchange for their shares. If securities are used in the transaction, they must be registered with the Securities and Exchange Commission (SEC) under the Securities Act of 1933. The securities must also be issued in compliance with the relevant state's blue sky laws, which regulate the issuance and transfer of securities.

The SEC review process may also slow down the tender offer. The acquiring firm is encumbered by the waiting periods of the Williams Act and the Hart-Scott-Rodino Act (see Chapter 3). The use of securities may add another waiting period while the firm awaits the SEC review. The SEC's Division of Corporate Finance has designed a system of selective review whereby it responds to repeat issuers more expeditiously. This system permits only a brief review of firms that may have already gone through a thorough review process for prior issues of securities. In these cases, the securities registration and review process may present few or no additional delays beyond the Williams Act and Hart-Scott-Rodino waiting periods.

Research on hostile bids show that cash is more likely to be offered as a means of payment in hostile offers. This is an intuitive result not only because of the aforementioned time-related advantages of cash offers over securities bids, but also because cash deals may be more appealing to target shareholders, even though they may bring with them adverse tax consequences.

10-Day Window of the Williams Act—13D

As noted in Chapter 3, the Williams Act requires that purchasers of 5% of the outstanding shares of a company's stock register with the SEC within 10 days by filing a Schedule 13D. The filing of this schedule notifies the market of the purchaser's intentions and alerts stockholders to an impending tender offer. It is in the bidder's interest to purchase shares as quickly as possible during the 10-day period after the acquirer reaches the 5% threshold. If the bidder is able to purchase securities during this period, the stock price may be lower than it would be following the notification to the market of the bidder's intentions. The filing gives the stockholders notice that a bidder may be about to make a bid. This implies a dramatic increase in the demand for the securities and makes them more valuable. Stockholders will demand a higher price to part with their stock, knowing that an upcoming bid and its associated premium may be forthcoming. The 10-day window gives the bidder an opportunity to purchase a larger amount of stock without having to pay the postfiling premium—assuming, however, that rumors have not already anticipated the content of the filing. It is difficult to purchase large amounts of stock and keep the identity of the purchaser secret.

The 10-day window may be turned into a 12-day window if the initial purchases are made on a Wednesday. This would require the purchaser to file on a Saturday. The SEC usually allows the purchaser to file on the next business day, which would be two days later, on Monday.

Response of the Target Management

SEC Rule 14e-2(a) requires that the target issues its response to the bid no later than 10 business days after the offer commenced. This response is done through the filing of a Schedule 14D-9. In its response the target basically has four options:

1. Recommend acceptance
2. Recommend rejection
3. State that it has no opinion and is neutral
4. State that it cannot take a position on the bid

In evaluating its response, the target's board has to keep in mind that its stockholders often view tender offers as a favorable development because they tend to bring high offer premiums. Nonetheless, the appropriate response of the target company's management is not always clear. If resistance will increase shareholder returns, then this may be a more appropriate course of action. Such resistance might be used as leverage to try to get the bidder to increase its offer. This assumes, however, that the company believes that an increased offer is more advantageous than the gains that shareholders could realize if the company remained independent.

By resisting the bid, the target may be able to force the bidder to raise its offer. The target may also be able to attract other bidders to start an auction process. We have seen that the winners of such auctions are often afflicted with the winner's curse, which inures to the target shareholders' advantage. Multiple bidders usually translate into higher premiums and somewhat greater leverage for the target.

One risk that the target bears when it resists the bid is that the bid may be withdrawn. If the premium offered reflects a value that is in excess of that which could be realized for shareholders by keeping the company independent, then resistance reduces value. Each takeover contest is different, and different circumstances apply. If the target's independence presents lower value for its own shareholders, but synergistic gains mean that the target is much more valuable when combined with the bidder, then it would seem that there should be a basis for a sale at a premium that is attractive for target shareholders.

When evaluating the level of resistance, target managers need to assess their options well in advance of an actual bid. If the target's board and management believe that the company would be an attractive target, they may install defenses in advance of any bid so that the company cannot be acquired at values less than what they believe the company is worth. The installation of such defenses conveys information to the market that the target may not be receptive to a hostile offer. If the target has already fought off prior hostile bids, this is also additional information for the market. It is difficult for any target board and management team to take the position that no offer, no matter how high, would be acceptable. However, there are cases where managers may not explicitly say the company would never be for sale at any price, but where their intentions seem to convey that view. Obviously, this is not in shareholders' interests.

Creation of a Tender Offer Team

The bidding firm assembles its team of essential players and coordinates its actions throughout the tender offer process. The team may be composed of the following members outside the corporation's own management and in-house counsel:

- *Investment bank.* The investment bank will play a key role in providing the requisite financing and advisory services through the tender offer. The investment bank may provide bridge financing, which allows the bidder to "buy now and pay later." It also may ultimately finance the bid by issuing securities such as junk bonds or through securing loan agreements. The investment bank's merger expertise is most important in cases of actively fought hostile acquisitions in which the target employs more sophisticated defensive maneuvers.
- *Legal advisors.* Attorneys who are knowledgeable in the tactics and defenses employed to evade tender offers may be an invaluable source of advice, both legal and strategic, for the bidder. Starting in the 1990s, a larger number of law firms began to play prominent roles in merger and acquisition advising in the United States. This differed from the 1980s, when two law firms dominated this market.
- *Information agent.* The information agent is typically one of the major proxy soliciting firms. The information agent is responsible for forwarding tender offer materials to stockholders. Proxy firms may also actively solicit the participation of stockholders in tender offers by means of a telephone and mail campaign.
- *Depository bank.* The depository bank handles the receipt of the tender offers and the payment for the shares tendered. The bank makes sure that shares have been properly tendered. An ongoing tabulation is kept for the bidder, allowing the probability of success to be determined throughout the tender offer.
- *Forwarding agent.* The bidder may decide to retain a forwarding agent in addition to the depository bank. The forwarding agent enhances the resources of the depository bank and transmits tenders received to the depository bank. A forwarding agent is particularly useful when there is a concentration of shares in a given area that is not well serviced by the depository bank.

Two-Tiered Tender Offers

A two-tiered tender offer is sometimes referred to as a *front end–loaded* tender offer. It provides superior compensation, such as cash or stock, for a first-step purchase, and is followed by inferior compensation, such as subordinated debentures, which often have a less certain value, for the second tier or the *back end* of the transaction. The two-tiered offer process normally starts with an actual offer combined with a notice of an intention to complete a back-end freeze-out transaction. The technique is often designed to exert pressure on stockholders who are concerned that they may become part of a second tier and that they may receive inferior compensation if they do not tender early enough to become part of the first tier. If sufficient shares are tendered in the first tier and if the merger or acquisition is approved, the remaining shareholders can be "frozen out" of their positions and may have to tender their shares for the inferior compensation. The compensation for the two tiers may be broken down into a first-tier, all-cash offer at a higher price for 51% of the target and a second-tier offer at a lower price that may provide noncash compensation, such as debentures. The noncash compensation in the form of debentures is often considered inferior when its value is less clear and less exact relative to cash consideration. The two-tiered pricing strategy is often considered coercive to stockholders because it attempts to stampede them into becoming part of the first tier.

The coercion of two-tiered bids invokes a *prisoner's dilemma* type of problem for target shareholders. They could all find the compensation of the front-tier offer to be undesirable but fear being caught in the back-end tier, so they rush to tender their shares.

Regulation of Two-Tiered Tender Offers

Those who oppose the two-tiered bid maintain that it is too coercive and unfair to shareholders in the second tier, who are entitled to equal treatment under the Williams Act. Two-tiered offers may be coercive in that shareholders in the front end receive better compensation than back-end shareholders. Although courts have ruled that two-tiered tender offers are not illegal *per se*, calls for horizontal equity—equal treatment for all shareholders—gave rise to changes in state corporation laws. In many states these statutes have been amended to try to bring about equitable treatment for all tendering shareholders. These amendments included fair price provisions and redemption rights.

Regulation of two-tiered offers has occurred through formal laws but also informally through market forces. For example, fair price provisions that were introduced to corporate charters required that all shareholders, even those in the second tier, receive a fair price. This price may be equal to the prices paid to the first-tier shareholders. In addition, redemption rights may allow shareholders to redeem their shares at a price similar to the price paid to the first tier. Jarrell and Poulsen have reported a dramatic rise in the adoption of fair price provisions in corporate charters in response to the increased use of front end–loaded offers.[20] They found that 354 adoptions of fair price amendments took place between 1983 and 1984, which is in sharp contrast to the total of 38 amendments passed between 1979 and 1982. Jarrell and Poulsen attribute this increase to the greater incidence of two-tiered bids in the early 1980s. These corporate charter amendments, begun in earnest in the 1980s, however, combined with the passage of specific state laws, have limited the effectiveness of two-tiered bids. Indeed, while the Williams

---

[20] Greg Jarrell and Annette Poulsen, "Shark Repellents and Stock Prices: The Effects of Antitakeover Amendments since 1980," *Journal of Financial Economics* 19, no. 1 (September 1987): 127–168.

Act allows two-tiered tender offers, the regulation of such potentially coercive tactics has been limited by state laws. In particular, the Delaware Supreme Court has maintained a consistent opposition to takeovers it determines are coercive. It has done so by allowing some aggressive antitakeover measures taken by target boards.[21]

Market forces also have dealt with what some consider to be the negative, coercive aspects of two-tiered bids. Competitive bidders can take advantage of the inferior compensation given to back-end shareholders to offer a more attractive any-and-all tender offer. Not surprisingly, in their analysis of 210 tender offers, Comment and Jarrell found that not only were two-tiered bids relatively rare in their sample but also that shareholders fared as well in any-and-all offers as they did in two-tiered bids.[22] That is, they found "average total premiums actually received by shareholders differ insignificantly in executed two-tiered and any-and-all tender offers."[23]

In Europe, tender offer regulations are somewhat similar to the United States but may impose additional restrictions on the bidder. For example, in England, a bidder who owns 30% or more of a company's voting outstanding shares must make an offer for all of the remaining shares at the highest price it paid to acquire its stock position. This renders partial bids and two-tiered offers ineffective. Bidders who acquire 51% of the outstanding shares cannot require a freeze-out of minority shareholders, as is possible in the United States.

Empirical Evidence on the Effects of Tender Offers

One of the early studies that comprehensively focused on the shareholder wealth effects of tender offers was conducted by Asquith as an outgrowth of his doctoral dissertation at the University of Chicago.[24] Asquith examined 211 successful and 91 unsuccessful merger bids between 1962 and 1976 and considered the impact of the bids on daily excess returns to stockholders in the affected companies. Daily excess returns reflect stock returns that are in excess of that which would be expected by the stock's risk level as measured by its Beta. Beta is a measure of systematic or diversifiable risk. This concept is covered in most corporate finance textbooks and is discussed in Chapter 14.

Asquith's results indicate a strong positive cumulative excess return for targets of successful bids when considering a 60-day window before and after the offer. It is interesting that the market was efficient in anticipating the offer, as reflected by the fact that most of the nearly 20% cumulative excess return was reached before the announcement date (press day). Unsuccessful targets lose most of their almost 10% gains by the end of the 60-day period after the announcement.

According to Asquith, acquiring firms in successful bids experience relatively small gains that persist 60 days after the takeover. Those potential acquirers in unsuccessful takeovers display a 25% cumulative excess return 60 days after the attempted takeover.

---

[21] *Unocal Corp. v. Mesa Petroleum, Inc.*, 493 A. 2d, (Del 1985), 946–956.

[22] Robert Comment and Gregg Jarrell, "Two-Tier and Negotiated Tender Offers," *Journal of Financial Economics* 19, no. 2 (December 1987): 283–310.

[23] Ibid., 285.

[24] Paul Asquith, "Merger Bids and Stock Returns," *Journal of Financial Economics* 11, no. 1–4 (April 1983): 51–83.

The Asquith study was published over three decades ago. However, its basic findings regarding the wealth effects of tender offers on bidders still are somewhat relevant to today's M&A market. Later research, such as that of Loughran and Vijh as well as by Rau and Vermaelen, has shown that these initial responses may not always be indicative of the long-term performance of the bidder.[25] One explanation for the positive initial stock market response is that bidders and the market may perceive tender offer targets to be undervalued and thus good buys. Perhaps these targets are companies that have been poorly managed and do not trade at prices consistent with their potential values. However, we have seen that over time, the performance of these bidders for these companies tends to erode. Indeed, Rau and Vermaelen have identified one group of bidders in particular who tend to do progressively poorly over time. These are what they refer to as *glamour* firms. They define glamour firms to be firms with low book-to-market ratios. The low book-to-market ratios imply that the market may be keen on these firms and they may trade at "popular" values, but these values are not reflected in the book value of their assets. They theorize that managers of such glamour companies, perhaps afflicted by hubris enhanced by the glamour status, may overestimate their ability to manage the target. Figure 6.4 shows the book-to-market rankings of glamour and value acquirers relative to broad market averages. The figure shows that glamour acquirers lose their glamour status following acquisitions, as reflected by the rising trend in the upper panel of this figure.

Wealth Effects of Unsuccessful Tender Offers

Although the premium associated with a successful bid may increase the target shareholder's wealth, the question exists whether the increase in the target's shares caused by the announcement of a bid persists when the bid fails. An early study by Bradley, Desai, and Kim analyzed the returns to stockholders by firms that either received or made *unsuccessful* control-oriented tender offers between 1963 and 1980.[26] They defined a control-oriented tender offer as one in which the bidding firm holds less than 70% of the target's shares and is attempting to increase its holdings by at least 15%. They considered a total of 697 tender offers. This study measured the impact of the tender offers by examining the cumulative abnormal returns to both the target and the bidding firm. *Abnormal returns* are those that cannot be fully explained by market movements. Returns are defined using the market model in equation 6.4:

$$R_{it} = \alpha_i + \beta_{mt}R_{mit} + \varepsilon_{it} \tag{6.4}$$

[25] Tim Loughran and Anand Vijh, "Do Long-Term Shareholders Benefit from Corporate Acquisitions?" *Journal of Finance* 52, no. 5 (December 1997): 1765–1790; and P. Raghavendra Rau and Theo Vermaelen, "Glamour, Value and the Post-Acquisition Performance of Acquiring Firms," *Journal of Financial Economics* 49, no. 2 (August 1998): 223–253.

[26] Michael Bradley, Anand Desai, and E. Han Kim, "The Rationale behind Interfirm Tender Offers: Information or Synergy," *Journal of Financial Economics* 11 (April 1983): 183–206.

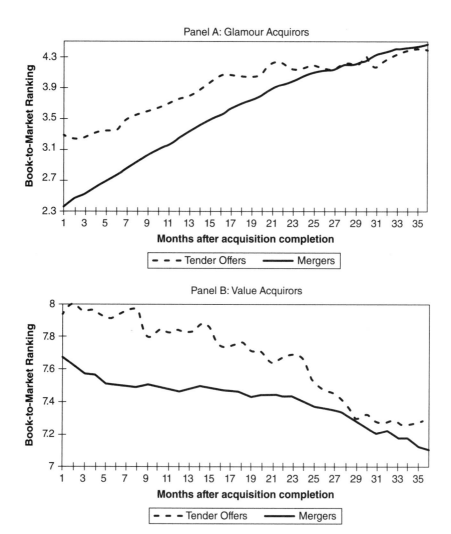

FIGURE 6.4 Evolution of Glamour and Value Status Acquirers in Mergers and Tender Offers. *Source*: P. Raghavendra Rau and Theo Vermaelen, "Glamour, Value and the Post-Acquisition Performance of Acquiring Firms," *Journal of Financial Economics* 49 (1998): 232.

where:

R_{it} is the cumulative dividend monthly stock return for the ith firm in month t;

R_{mit} is the return on an equally weighted market portfolio month t relative to the announcement of offer;

∞, β are the regression parameters; and

ε_{it} is a stochastic error term with a mean of zero.

Abnormal returns for firm i and month t are defined as follows:

$$AR_{it} = R_{it} - \alpha_i - \beta_{mt}R_{mit} \qquad (6.5)$$

These abnormal returns can then be summed for a defined time period to arrive at cumulative abnormal returns (CARs). CARs are used as a guide to abnormal effects in a wide variety of M&A event studies.

One goal of the study was to ascertain whether there were permanent wealth effects from tender offers on the target firm and the acquiring firm. These effects are discussed separately in the following sections.

Target

The results show that target shareholders realize positive abnormal returns surrounding the month of the announcement of the tender offer. They found that the cumulative abnormal returns reflected a positive response which did not go away in the event that the bid was rejected. [27] In their total sample of unsuccessful tender offers, 76.8% of the firms were taken over and 23.2% were not. A review of Figure 6.5 shows that this positive effect is the case for those that are eventually taken over, whereas it is very different for those that are not taken over.

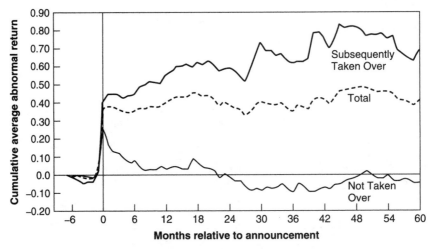

FIGURE 6.5 Cumulative Abnormal Returns to Unsuccessful Target Firms—Total Sample, and "Subsequently Taken Over" and "Not Taken Over" Subsamples in the Period 1963–1980. *Source*: Michael Bradley, Anand Desai, and E. Han Kim, "The Rationale behind Interfirm Tender Offers: Information or Strategy," *Journal of Financial Economics* 11 (April 1983): 192.

---

[27] Eugene Fama and Michael Jensen, "Separation of Ownership and Control," *Journal of Law and Economics* 26, no. 2 (June 1983): 301–325.

Bidder

The Bradley study reveals interesting results regarding the impact of tender offers on acquiring firms. As Figure 6.6 shows, the cumulative abnormal returns for bidding firms remain nonnegative when the target is independent and there is no change in control. When the target is acquired by another bidder and the bidder in question loses the tender offer, the value of the bidding firm falls significantly. Bradley and colleagues interpret this effect as the market's perception that the bidding firm has lost an opportunity to acquire a valuable resource. This effect is sometimes caused by competitors acquiring resources that will provide a competitive advantage over the firm that lost the bid.

The Bradley et al. study traced the time frame for the wealth effects on unsuccessful bidders and found that, for their sample of tender offers between 1963 and 1980, the average gap between the announcement of the unsuccessful bid and the subsequent successful tender offer was 60.6 days. Almost all the decline in the value of a portfolio of successful bidding firms had occurred by day 21. The value of the portfolio declined 2.84% by day 21.

Tender Offer Premiums and Director Independence

Independent directors are those who are not employees and who do not have any other relationship with the corporation. Finance theorists have long contended that the more

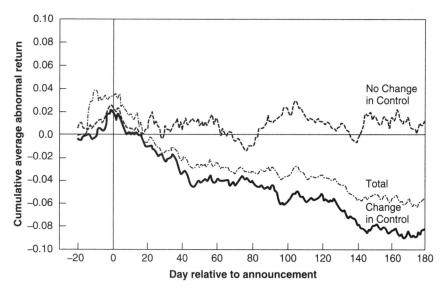

FIGURE 6.6 Cumulative Abnormal Returns to Unsuccessful Target Firms—Total Sample, and "No Change in Control" and "Change in Control" Subsamples in the Period 1963–1980. *Source:* Michael Bradley, Anand Desai, and E. Han Kim, "The Rationale behind Interfirm Tender Offers: Information or Strategy," *Journal of Financial Economics* 11 (April 1983): 200.

independent a board is, the greater the return to shareholders.[28] Cotter, Shivdasani, and Zenner studied 169 tender offers between 1989 and 1992.[29] Their results supported Fama and Jensen's hypothesis. They found that targets of tender offers experience shareholder gains that are 20% higher when the board is independent compared with less independent tender offer targets. They also found that bid premium revisions were also higher when the board was more independent. These findings suggest that independent directors are more active supporters of shareholder value than nonindependent directors. Cotter and colleagues extended their research to determine the source of the increased shareholder gains. Their results suggest that the higher target gains come at the expense of returns to bidder shareholders. This conclusion is consistent with other studies that we discuss throughout this book.

Takeover Premiums and Shareholders' Investment Horizons

Over time, shares have been increasingly controlled by institutional investors. However, such investors can have different investment horizons, with some being more short-term oriented and others having a longer investment horizon and average holding period. Theoretically, short-term investors, such as some mutual funds, may have less incentive to monitor management compared to longer-term investors, such as those who control shares in employee benefit plans. Short-term investors may also have less incentive to hold out for a higher takeover premium.

Using a sample of 3,814 takeover events over the period 1980–1999, Gaspar, Massa, and Matos found that targets whose shareholders own their shares for an average of less than four months received 3% lower takeover premiums compared to shareholders with longer investment horizons.[30] They also found that "short-term shareholder" companies had worse returns around the takeover announcement while also exhibiting lower long-term returns. These results lend support to the proposition that the more that the shareholder base is composed of short-term shareholders, the more leeway management has to pursue their own personal benefits at the expense of shareholders' gains—a view that has been discussed by other researchers.[31]

From a tactical perspective this research has several important ramifications for bidders (and targets). Target companies that have more short-term shareholders may be less expensive to acquire. They also may put forward less resistance and their management may be more willing to trade personal benefits in exchange for lower premiums for shareholders. This partly explains why investment bankers and merger advisory firms representing bidders do a shareholder analysis prior to launching a bid.

It is important to note that the findings we have discussed are generalizations that, while they have intuitive appeal and are consistent with research findings, may apply in

---

[28] James Cotter, Anil Shivdasani, and Marc Zenner, "Do Independent Directors Enhance Target Shareholder Wealth during Tender Offers?" *Journal of Financial Economics* 43, no. 2 (February 1997): 195–218.

[29] Ibid.

[30] Jose-Miguel Gaspar, Massimo Massa, and Pedro Matos, "Shareholder Investment Horizons and the Market for Corporate Control," *Journal of Financial Economics* 76, no. 1 (April 2005): 135–165.

[31] J. Hartzell, E. Ofek, and D. Yermack, "What's in It for Me? Personal Benefits Obtained by CEOs Whose Firms Get Acquired," *Review of Financial Studies* 17, no. 1 (Spring 2004): 37–61.

some cases and not in others. These finds also are drawn from a time period that precedes the proliferation of activist hedge funds.

Do CEOs Trade Premium for Power?

CEOs who do not want to lose their positions in control of the target may be willing to accept a lower premium for shareholders in exchange for positions of influence in the combined company. Julie Wolf analyzed a sample of 53 mergers of equals over the period 1991–1999.[32] She found that target shareholder returns were negatively correlated to target representation on the combined company's board. That is, when the merger agreement provided for target management or directors to receive a directorship in the combined company, they may have been less likely to negotiate for a higher premium for their shareholders.

Are "Bad Bidders" More Likely to Become Targets?

The impact of poor acquisitions was discussed in Chapter 4 in the context of conglomerate or diversification mergers that performed poorly. It was also discussed in Chapter 2 in the context of the acquisitions that occurred in the third merger wave. The issue of how a firm is affected by a poor acquisition is of interest to stockholders in the bidding firm as they consider whether they should favor a certain acquisition.

In 1988, Mitchell and Lehn analyzed the effects of poor acquisitions on acquiring firms.[33] They found that the probability of becoming a takeover target was inversely related to the cumulative average returns associated with the firm's acquisitions. They used a logistic regression, which is an econometric technique in which the dependent variable may vary between 0 and 1. In this case, the 0 or 1 represents the probability of whether a firm became a target. Some studies of the impact of acquisitions on acquiring firms show a zero or negative impact, while providing clear benefits for the target firm. Mitchell and Lehn contend that the market differentiates between good and bad acquiring firms. Although they found returns to acquirers to be approximately zero, they observed that subsamples of good acquirers outperformed acquiring firms that pursued failed acquisition strategies, or what Mitchell and Lehn refer to as bad bidders. For example, as shown in Figure 6.7, acquiring firms that did not subsequently become targets themselves showed clearly positive returns over a 60-day window around the acquisition announcement. Acquiring firms that became targets of either friendly or hostile acquisitions showed clearly negative returns. In other words, acquisitions by companies that become targets, especially hostile targets, cause the acquiring company's stock price to fall, whereas acquisition by companies that do not become targets results in an increase in the acquiring firm's stock price.

Mitchell and Lehn's explanation for the returns depicted in Figure 6.6 is twofold. Acquiring companies that become targets make acquisitions that the market expects

[32] Julie Wolf, "Do CEOs in Mergers Trade Power for Premium? Evidence from Mergers of Equals," *Journal of Law, Economics and Organization* 20, no. 1 (Spring 2004): 60–101.
[33] Mark L. Mitchell and Kenneth Lehn, "Do Bad Bidders Become Good Targets?" *Journal of Applied Corporate Finance* 3, no. 2 (Summer 1990): 60–69.

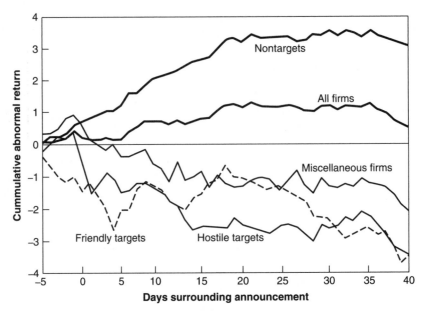

FIGURE 6.7 Stock Price Reaction to Acquisition Announcements, 1982–1986.
Source: Mark L. Mitchell and Kenneth Lehn, "Do Bad Bidders Become Good Targets?"
Journal of Applied Corporate Finance 3, no. 2 (Summer 1990): 60–69.

will reduce the combined profitability of these companies. That is, the market is saying that this is a bad acquisition. The second possible explanation for this phenomenon is that the acquiring company is overpaying for the target. It could be that at some lower price the acquisition would be a better one.

The authors of this study went on to trace the relationship between the acquisitions and subsequent divestitures. They found a statistically significantly negative stock price response (average of 24%) to acquisitions that were subsequently divested. For acquisitions that were not divested, they found a small, not statistically significant, positive stock price response (average of 1.9%). The import of this result is that it seems that at the time of the acquisition announcement, the market is making a prediction regarding which acquisitions are good and which are bad. Mitchell and Lehn's analysis suggests that the market is an efficient predictor of the success of acquisitions.

ADVANTAGES OF TENDER OFFERS OVER OPEN MARKET PURCHASES

Open market purchases may at first seem to provide many advantages over tender offers. For example, they do not involve the complicated legal requirements and costs associated with tender offers. (The bidder must be concerned that the open market purchases will be legally interpreted as a tender offer.) The costs of a tender offer may be far higher than the brokerage fees incurred in attempting to take control through open market purchases of the target's stock. As noted previously, Smiley estimated that the total cost of tender offers averaged approximately 13% of the post–tender offer market price of the target's shares.[34]

Open market purchases also have clear drawbacks that are not associated with tender offers. A bidder who purchases shares in the open market is not guaranteed that he will be able to accumulate sufficient shares to acquire clear control. If 51% clear control is not achieved, the bidder may become stuck in an undesirable minority position. One advantage of a tender offer is that the bidder is not bound to purchase the tendered shares unless the desired number of shares has been tendered. The bidder who becomes mired in a minority position faces the following alternatives:

- *Do a tender offer for additional shares.* In this case, the bidder incurs the tender offer expenses in addition to the costs of the open market purchasing program.
- *Begin a proxy fight.* This is another costly means of acquiring control, but the bidder, after having already acquired a large voting position, is now in a stronger position to launch a proxy fight.
- *Sell the minority stock position.* These sales would place significant downward pressure on the stock price and may result in significant losses.

Large-scale open-market purchases are also difficult to keep secret. Market participants regard the stock purchases as a signal that a bidder may be attempting to make a raid on the target. This may then change the shape of the target's supply curve for its stock by making it more vertical above some price.[35] This can make a street sweep effective but expensive. Other shareholders may also have the idea that a higher price may be forthcoming and may be reluctant to sell unless a very attractive offer is made. This threshold price may be quickly reached as the available supply of shares on the market, which may be relatively small compared with the total shares outstanding, becomes exhausted. As stockholders come to believe that a bid may be forthcoming, they have an incentive to *hold out* for a higher premium. The holdout problem does not exist in tender offers because the bidder is not obligated to purchase any shares unless the amount requested has been tendered. If the requested amount has not been tendered at the end of the expiration date of the offer, the bidder may cancel the offer or extend it.

A street sweep may be more effective when a bidder is able to locate large blocks of stock in the hands of a small group of investors. In cases in which there have been offers for the company or speculation about impending offers, stock often becomes concentrated in the hands of arbitragers. Although these investors are often eager to sell, they will often do so only at a high price. The existence of large blocks of stock in the hands of *arbitragers* may enable a bidder to amass a significant percentage of the target's stock, perhaps enough to gain effective control of the company, but only if the bidder is

---

[34] Robert Smiley, "Tender Offers, Transactions Costs and the Theory of the Firm," *Review of Economics and Statistics* 58, no. 1 (February 1976): 22–32.

[35] Lloyd R. Cohen, "Why Tender Offers? The Efficient Markets Hypothesis, the Supply of Stock and Signaling," *Journal of Legal Studies* 19, no. 1 (January 1990): 113–143.

willing to pay a possibly painful price. Often the cost will make this method of acquisition prohibitively expensive.

Arbitragers and Takeover Tactics

Theoretical risk-less arbitrage can occur when two identical assets are bought/sold at different prices. The opportunity for a risk-less profit can occur if the investor sells a higher-priced asset while simultaneously buying the identical asset at a lower price. Such investment activity may facilitate the "law of one price," where the buying of investors raises the price of the lower-priced asset while the selling activity does the opposite. However, this is not the type of arbitrage that occurs in M&A.

Risk arbitragers are firms that accumulate shares of companies that are targeted for acquisitions. Their investment strategy is basically a gamble that a given transaction will close. If a given deal is completed, arbitragers will profit from the difference between the purchase price and the takeover price. The arbitrageur may also hedge its investment by selling the acquirer's stock short. In fact, the short sale is really what makes the transaction arbitrage rather than simple speculation that a merger will close. The most famous, or really infamous, arbitrageur was Ivan Boesky, who in the 1980s was the most well-known practitioner of this craft. However, while he claimed the success he enjoyed from merger arbitrage came from his ability to judge the dealmakers themselves, he really purchased insider information from investment bankers, such as Martin Siegel of Kidder Peabody.

Arbitragers may provide a service or benefit to target shareholders as they can sell their shares soon after an offer is made and in doing so eliminate their risk that the deal will not be completed. That deal completion risk is then transferred to the arbitragers.[36]

Arbitrageurs and Target Vulnerability

From a bidder's perspective, if many "long-term" target shareholders sell out to "short-term" arbitrageurs, this is a positive development. Arbitrageurs will assess the bid and the vulnerability of the target. If they believe the bid is credible and the prospect of success is good, they may buy the stock with an eye toward realizing a premium from the acquisition. This then makes the company more vulnerable. If, however, the arbitrageurs are not convinced the deal will go through, perhaps through concern about the bidder and also the resolve and defensive capabilities of the target, they may hold off on buying shares lest they get stuck without a profitability investment exit strategy. Thus it is in the interest of the bidder and the target to convince arbitragers of the strength of their respective positions.

Arbitrageurs can act quickly. In fact, if they are convinced the bid is credible, it is in their interest to act quickly before the price rises. Therefore, if only a relatively small percentage of the target's shares, such as 5%–10%, is sold to arbitrageurs at the start of the bid, then this is a good sign for the target and bad for the bidder. However, if a large

---

[36] Malcolm Baker and Serkan Savasoglu, "Limited Arbitrage in Mergers and Acquisitions," *Journal of Financial Economics* 64 (2002): 91–115.

percentage of the target's shares is acquired by arbitrageurs, things look much more promising from the bidder's perspective.

Computing Arbitrage Returns

A simple expression of a risk arbitrageur's annualized return (RAR) is shown in equation 6.6:

$$RAR = GSS/I \times (365/IP) \tag{6.6}$$

where:

RAR = risk arbitrage return
GSS = gross stock spread
I = investment by arbitrager
IP = investment period (days between investment and closing date)

The gross stock spread is shown in equation 6.7:

$$GSS = OP - MP \tag{6.7}$$

where:

OP = offer price
MP = market price

As an example, assume that Company A makes a $50-per-share offer for Company B, which now trades at $45 per share. The gross stock spread is $5. Also assume that the deal is expected to close in 90 days. If the deal closes, then the risk arbitrager's return would be as follows:

$$RAR = (\$50 - \$45)/\$45 \times (365/90)$$

$$= 0.451 \text{ or } 45.1\%$$

This is an impressive *annualized* return. Practitioners in this area wish the reality of this business were as lucrative and simple as the preceding example. In effect, the annualization process assumes reinvestment at that rate. In addition, it closes its eyes to all the risks, which can lead to significant losses.

Arbitragers have to consider a variety of risk factors when they evaluate takeovers that they are gambling will be completed. A host of different factors can halt a deal. These include the defensive actions of the target but also regulatory factors, such as gaining antitrust approval. As we discussed in Chapter 3, for companies that have a significant international business, such as in Europe as well as in the United States, they must get antitrust approval of both the U.S. and the EU antitrust authorities. In addition, some deals may take a number of months before they close. The arbitrager's gain comes from the premium that will be received if the deal is completed. For deals that take an extended time to complete, arbitragers have to also consider dividends that will be paid on the shares during the waiting period.

In spite of a surge in M&A volume in 2014, event driven hedge funds, funds which make bets on M&As as well as other events, on average did poorly. Some funds which invested in tax inversions deals (discussed in Chapter 16), such as AbbVie's proposed merger with Shire, lost hundreds of millions of dollars. This underscores the risks inherent in M&A investing.

Simple Example of Risk Arbitrage in M&A

Let's assume that the Target has been trading at $19 (Pt = $19) and that the Acquirer has been trading in the range of $15 prior to the Acquirer's announcement of an exchange offer for the Target. The Acquirer offered two of its shares for one of the target. Based upon the nice premium relative to the announcement price ($30 − $19 = $11), it was not surprising that the target's shares rose sharply to $24 on the announcement, while the Acquirer's shares fell to $13.

Let's further assume an Arbitrageur buys 100 shares of the Target for $24 per shares. If the Arbitrageur were to simply hold these shares until a possible closing, that really would not be arbitrage as arbitrage requires the simultaneous buying and selling of the same asset at different prices. So let's also assume that the Arbitrageur sells 200 shares short at $13 per share (200 because that is what will be ultimately exchanged for the 100 target shares if the deal goes through). The profit of the Arbitrageur is as follows:

Buy 100 Shares Target @ $24 p/share	($2,400)
Sell 200 Shares Acquirer @ $13 p/share	$2,600
Profit	$200

If the deal eventually closes as planned, in 150 days the Arbitrageur will receive 200 shares of the Acquirer, which will offset the 200 shares it sold short, thus closing out the position, as the shares in the long position that were received were used to deliver shares to the counterparty in the short transaction. At that point the Arbitrageur has neither a long or a short position but a profit of $200. The arbitrageur's annualized return then is as follows:

$$\$200/\$2,400 \times 365/150 = 0.202 \text{ or } 20.2\%$$

This is a very impressive return due to the assumptions we built into the example. The annualization process is used to create an annual return, which can be used to compare the rate from this investment activity with other investment activities. However, it would be naive to believe that this return over that 150-day period could necessarily be duplicated. We also conveniently closed our eyes to the possibility that the deal might not have closed and that the Arbitrageur would be stuck with the shares of the Target that might sell at a lower price than what was paid for them; the Arbitrageur would still have to make good on its obligations to the counterparty on the share sale, having not gotten the 200 shares of the Acquirer since the deal did not close.

The example was also simplistic in that it assumed that there was no dividend income received from the long position nor were there any dividend-related obligations related to the short position. If both companies paid dividends over the investment period, this would provide both dividend income on the long position and an obligation for the Arbitrageur to pay the dividend on the short position.

It also assumed that the Arbitrageur could not earn any interest income by depositing the monies received from the short sale with a brokerage firm that was also willing to pay the Arbitrager an interest income. However, brokerage firms often are reluctant to pay interest on short sales.

In our example we also assume that the shares offered were fixed and there was not a "collar agreement." We will discuss collar agreements in Chapter 15, but for now let us note that such an agreement provides that the shares offered could go up or down, depending on the performance of the Acquirer's shares in the marketplace. Such an agreement reduces the risk for the target's shareholders, although it makes our return calculation more uncertain.

Arbitrage Returns Research

Research has shown that arbitragers often enjoy attractive returns. For example, Dukes, Frohlich, and Ma found average daily returns of 0.5%, which translated to holding period returns of 25%.[37] Their average arbitrage holding period was 52 days. Later research by Jindra and Walkling examined the arbitrage spreads in 362 *cash* tender offers over the period 1981 through 1995.[38] They found that the average spread was 2%. They also found that the spreads were greater when the takeover contest was longer and were smaller in hostile deals. They found that monthly return based upon the difference in the stock price one day after a bid was announced and the day the bid was resolved was 2%. This translated to returns in excess of 25%. Karolyi and Shannon analyzed 37 bids for 37 Canadian takeovers in 1997.[39] They found an average abnormal return from an arbitrage strategy was 5% on an average 57-day investment period.

From the bidder's perspective, the fact that shares become concentrated into the hands of arbitragers is a positive development. These shareholders have no loyalty to the target and actually want the deal to be completed. The greater their holdings, the more the bidder can count on being able to readily purchase the necessary shares to complete the deal.

Hsieh and Walkling analyzed the role that arbitragers played in takeover contests and their outcomes. They analyzed 608 takeover bids during the period 1992–1999.[40]

---

[37] William Dukes, Cheryl Frohlich, and Christopher Ma, "Risk Arbitrage in Tender Offers: Handsome Rewards—And Not for Insiders Only," *Journal of Portfolio Management* 18, no. 4 (Summer 1992): 47–55.

[38] Jan Jindra and Ralph Walkling, "Speculation Spreads and Markup Pricing of Proposed Acquisitions," *Journal of Corporate Finance* 10, no. 4 (September 2004): 495–526.

[39] Andrew G. Karolyi and John Shannon, "Where's the Risk in Risk Arbitrage," *Canadian Investment Review* 12 (1999): 11–18.

[40] Jim Hsieh and Ralph A. Walkling, "Determinants and Implications of Arbitrage Holdings in Acquisitions," *Journal of Financial Economics* 77, no. 3 (September 2005): 605–648.

They found that the holdings by arbitragers increased in bids that were more likely to be successful. They also found that the changes in the holdings of arbitragers were positively correlated with the probability of the success of bids and their premiums. They were also correlated with the likelihood of a later bid in instances where the initial bid was cancelled.

These studies present a rosy picture of the arbitrage business. However, the risk of large losses can be significant. The main cause of such losses is unexpected deal failure.[41]

Arbitrage and Price Movements around M&A Announcements

Research has shown that the stock price of acquirers tends to decline, especially those that use stock to finance bids, around the date of an announcement of an offer. Sometimes that decline can be so significant that it can cause the bidder to cancel its bid. This happened in 2014 when 21st Century Fox cancelled its $80 billion bid for Time Warner Inc., in part due to the negative market reactions but also due to the strong opposition from Time Warner.

Mitchell, Pulvino, and Stafford analyzed 2,130 mergers over the period 1994–2000 and found out that in stock-financed bids approximately one-half of this downward effect was caused by the short-selling actions of arbitragers.[42] Arbitragers will buy the target's shares, which puts upward price pressure on the target's stock, while often selling that bidder's shares in an effort to lock in a specific gain. One of the interesting results of their research was that they found these price effects were relatively short-lived.

Corporate Communications and Price Movements around M&A Announcements

Financial research has confirmed what the market has long known—media reports influence market trading and securities process.[43] This is why companies invest considerable sums in corporate communications. Ahern and Sosyura analyzed the media coverage involving 507 mergers over the years 2000–2008.[44] They found that bidders who used equity to finance their M&As originated significantly more news stories during the confidential merger negotiation period, which is prior to a public announcement of a bid. Not only did the number of stories about the bidders increase, but also the tone was more positive and there were fewer negative stories. Ahern and Sosyura were able to show that these stories, which were typically a function of public relations efforts by the bidders, paid off for these companies as they tended to cause the bidder's stock price to rise, thereby lowering the cost of the M&As.

---

[41] Malcolm Baker and Serkan Savasoglu, "Limited Arbitrage in Mergers and Acquisitions," *Journal of Financial Economics* 64, no. 1 (April 2002): 91–115.

[42] Mark Mitchell, Todd Pulvino, and Erik Stafford, "Price Pressure around Mergers," *Journal of Finance* 59, no. 1 (February 2004): 31–63.

[43] Joseph Engelberg and Christopher A. Parsons, "The Causal Impact of Media in Financial Markets," *Journal of Finance* 66, no. 1 (February 2011): 67–97.

[44] Kenneth R. Ahern and Denis Sosyura, "Who Writes the News? Corporate Press Releases during Merger Negotiations," *Journal of Finance* 69, no. 1 (February 2014): 241–291.

PROXY FIGHTS

A *proxy fight* is an attempt by a single shareholder or a group of shareholders to take control or bring about other changes in a company through the use of the proxy mechanism of corporate voting. Proxy contests are political processes in which incumbents and insurgents compete for shareholder votes through a variety of means, including mailings, newspaper advertisements, and telephone solicitations. In a proxy fight, a bidder may attempt to use his voting rights and garner support from other shareholders to oust the incumbent board and/or management. As noted, various federal and state regulations have limited the effectiveness of certain types of tender offers. However, courts have been reluctant to side with directors who seek to limit shareholders' use of the proxy contest process.

It is useful to define some terms prior to continuing our discussion of proxy fights. A *proxy* is a document, usually a card, that authorizes one individual to act on behalf of another. The proxy card contains certain required and brief information regarding the specific solicitation being made. The matter at issue is identified, and boxes are provided for shareholders to designate their approval, disapproval, or abstention of each of the matters highlighted on the card.

In a proxy fight *proxy statements* are issued. These are documents that provide relevant information about a solicitation of shareholders that is being made. The proxy statements contain more background information that is being put forward by the solicitor to gain the support of the shareholders.

Regulation of Proxy Contests

The SEC regulates proxy contests, and its staff monitors the process to ensure that the participants comply with proxy regulations. Proxy solicitations are made pursuant to Section 14(a) of the 1934 Act and require that any solicitation be accompanied by the information set forth in Schedule 14A. All materials that are used to influence the outcome of the contest must be submitted to the SEC examiners 10 calendar days in advance of any distribution of proxy materials. This includes newspaper announcements, materials being mailed to shareholders, and press releases. If the examiners find some of these materials objectionable, they may require that the information be reworded or include additional disclosure. If there are revisions of the proxy statements that constitute a significant change in a prior proxy filing, a new 10-day period applies.

The writing in proxy fight proposals tends to be much more direct and heated than what one normally finds in securities filings. The SEC allows this as a way for both parties to get their message across to shareholders. Under Rule 14a-7 the corporation is required to provide its shareholder list to the dissidents so that they can communicate directly to shareholders.

Proxys & M&A

SEC rules require a proxy solicitation to be accompanied by a Schedule 14A. Item 14 of this schedule sets forth the specific information that must be included in a proxy statement when there will be a vote for an approval of a merger, sale of substantial assets, or liquidation or dissolution of the corporation. For a merger, this information must include the terms and reasons for the transaction, as well as a description of the accounting treatment and tax consequences of the deal. Financial statements and a statement regarding relevant state and federal regulatory compliance are required. Fairness opinions and other related documents also must be included. Preliminary proxy statements related to mergers can be filed on a confidential basis, assuming they are marked "Confidential, for Use of the Commission Only."

Proxys and Insurgents

Rule 14a-8 provides shareholders with a mechanism to have their proposals included in the company's (the issuer's) own proxy statement. This is a very cost-effective way of getting their message to the shareholders. In order to qualify for this treatment, the shareholders in question must hold at least $2,000 in market value or 1% of the issuer's voting shares for at least one year. They also can submit only one proposal a year.

In an effort to strike back against the use of proxy fights by insurgents, companies sometimes petition the SEC to have it issue a *no action letter*. A no action letter disallows a shareholder proposal. The SEC is empowered to do this under Section 14(a) 8 of the Securities and Exchange Act. Such a letter may be issued if it can be demonstrated that the proposal is clearly not in the interests of other shareholders, serves only the personal interests of its proponent, or is designed to redress a personal claim of grievance of the shareholder.

Insurgents or nonmanagement activists must file a Schedule DFAN14A. This is a form covering nonmanagement proxy solicitations not supported by the registrant (the company). In this filing the insurgent indicates its investment position on the target and the specific action it is considering taking. These activist filings sometimes contain entertaining reading. For example, in one such filing Carl Icahn included an "open letter to shareholders of eBay" wherein he railed against management and the company's CEO and what he called the "Skype affair" in which he alleged that the company sold off Skype at too low a price in a transaction that featured certain alleged conflicts he found unacceptable.[45]

Shareholder Nominations of Board

SEC rules have changed with respect to the ability of shareholders to have their nominees put on the ballot. Rule 14a-8 allows shareholders to put their nominees on an issuer's board through a two-year, two-step process. The first step is that the shareholder submits a proposal to adopt "customized proxy access." The second step would occur in the next year, when the shareholders would use the proxy access process to put forward their own board nominees.

---

[45] Press release issued by Carl Icahn, February 24, 2014.

Proxy Fight Data

The number of proxy fights increased significantly over the period 2005–2013 (Figure 6.8). The rise in proxy contests over this period can be partly explained by the number of aggressive activist hedge funds that have been using the proxy contest mechanism to bring about changes in undervalued companies that will raise the value of shares they have purchased. To understand how such investors and others use proxy contests to bring about changes in targets, and sometimes take total control of a target, we need a basic understanding of the workings of the corporate election process.

Different Types of Proxy Contests

Typically, there are two main forms of proxy contests:

1. **Contests for seats on the board of directors.** An insurgent group of stockholders may use this means to replace management. If the opposing slate of directors is elected, it may then use its authority to remove management and replace them with a new management team. In recent years we have seen insurgents who believe they may lack the power to unseat directors try to organize a campaign to have shareholders withhold their votes as a way of recording their disapproval.

2. **Contests about management proposals.** These proposals can be control proposals relating to a merger or acquisition. Management may oppose the merger, and the insurgent group of stockholders may be in favor. Other relevant proposals might be the passage of antitakeover amendments in the company's charter. Management might be in favor, whereas the insurgent group might be opposed, believing that its opposition will cause the stock price to fall and/or reduce the likelihood of a takeover.

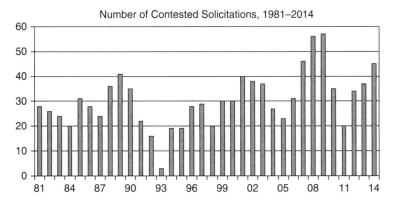

FIGURE 6.8 Number of Contested Solicitations, 1981–2014. *Source*: 2014 Annual Corporate Governance Review, Georgeson Inc.

Proxy Contests: From the Insurgents' Viewpoint

In a proxy contest, an insurgent group attempts to wrest control of the target by gathering enough supporting votes to replace the current board with board members of the group's choosing. The following characteristics increase the likelihood that a proxy fight will be successful:

- *Insufficient voting support.* Management normally can count on a certain percentage of votes to support its position. Some of these votes might be through management's own stockholdings. As we have noted, management can usually count on the voting support of brokers who have not received specific instructions from shareholders. Without a strong block of clear support for management among the voting shareholders, management and the incumbent board may be vulnerable to a proxy fight.
- *Poor operating performance.* The worse the firm's recent track record, the more likely it is that other stockholders will vote for a change in control. Stockholders in a firm that has a track record of declining earnings and a poor dividend record are more likely to support an insurgent group advocating changes in the way the firm is managed.
- *Sound alternative operating plan.* The insurgents must be able to propose changes that other stockholders believe will reverse the downward direction of the firm. These changes might come in the form of asset sales, with the proceeds paid to stockholders by means of higher dividends. Another possibility could be a plan that provides for the removal of antitakeover barriers and a receptive approach to outside offers for the sale of the firm.

Dead Shares Problem

Insurgents' shareholders involved in a proxy process can find it a challenging experience with many of the advantages in the hands of management. For an insurgent to effect a specific corporate action using a proxy contest, it must secure a majority of the votes (if not a supermajority, in cases where the company has such a defense in place). The insurgent may run into the problem of "dead shares." All shares that are not delivered by shareholders are, in effect, votes against the insurgent's plan. The more apathetic the target's shareholders or the more shareholders who have sold their shares without the underlying proxy after the record date, the more difficult it will be for the insurgent to secure the requisite majority approval.

Target Size and Proxy Fight Success

It is often easier and less expensive for insurgents in corporations that have a smaller market capitalization to control a sufficient number of shares to be able to influence, if not control, the outcome of a proxy fight. For larger corporations, this can be more difficult. An example would be Time Warner (formerly AOL Time Warner), which as of January 2006 had a market capitalization in excess of $83 billion. To control even 10% of the outstanding shares of this company requires approximately $8 billion. In 2005 and 2006, Carl Icahn and certain other institutional investors amassed Time Warner shareholding in excess of 3% of total shares outstanding. Icahn and Steve Case, the former AOL CEO, both lobbied Time Warner not to do more deals, such as a combination or venture with Google, but to seriously consider breaking the company up into several units. It is ironic that Case, one of the major movers of the original AOL Time Warner combination, would years later lobby the market to break up the combination that he helped to form. In early 2006, Icahn ended his proxy battle without getting Time Warner to agree to break up the company, but his strong pressure did cause management to agree to many of his proposals. However, clearly the size of the total market capitalization of Time Warner helped insulate management from even as determined a foe as Icahn.

Companies with larger market capitalizations are more insulated from proxy fight threats than smaller companies, where an insurgent, such as a hedge fund, can control a much larger percentage of shares while still not concentrating too much of its capital in this one investment. Given that this is the case, management does not have to be as responsive to pressures of insurgents.

Concentration of Shares and Proxy Fight Success

A key element that often has a great impact on the success of a proxy fight is the distribution of shares. If, for example, several activist hedge funds have amassed significant equity positions in a vulnerable target, then an insurgent/activist may have a lot of leverage. If, however, employees or certain institutional investors who may be supportive of management have large positions, it may be an uphill battle for the insurgent. Given the importance of the distribution of shares, the insurgent will hire firms that specialize in this work to advise them of the likelihood of winning an outright proxy fight. Usually, however, the activist is able to achieve many of its goals without having to go ahead with an actual proxy fight. Even the threat of an all-out battle will be enough to get valuable concessions that may increase the value of the shares the activist purchased and will serve as a mechanism for the activist to exit with a good return.

Effectiveness of Shareholder Activism

In 1989, Pound conducted a study of the effectiveness of shareholder activism by examining various countersolicitations by shareholders who opposed management's antitakeover proposals. Pound analyzed a sample of 16 countersolicitation proxy fights by shareholder groups that occurred in the 1980s. He reported the following results:[46]

- Countersolicitations were unsuccessful more often than they were successful. Dissidents in Pound's sample were successful only 25% of the time.
- When shareholders approved the contested provisions, the net-of-market share values of the company dropped an average of 6%. The range of stock price reactions was between 23% and 230%. Pound found that when the amendments were defeated, stock prices rose.

---

[46] John Pound, "Shareholder Activism and Share Values," *Journal of Law and Economics* (October 1989): 357–379; also in Patrick A. Gaughan, ed., *Readings in Mergers and Acquisitions* (Boston: Basil Blackwell, 1994), 235–254.

- The majority of the countersolicitations that Pound examined were preceded by a direct attempt to take control. In 8 of 16 countersolicitations in his sample, the dissidents had made an outright offer to take control of the company. In another seven cases, the dissidents had purchased a large stake in the firm. In only 1 of the 16 cases was there no attempt to take control.

Pound's study took place before the rise of the modern-day activist hedge funds. At that time such funds may have been more of a corporate raider. The modern activist hedge fund aggressively and actively uses the proxy process more than its prior corporate raider counterparts. Nonetheless, the Pound findings are largely still applicable.

Costs of a Proxy Fight

A proxy fight may be a less expensive alternative to a tender offer. Tender offers are costly because they offer to buy up to 100% of the outstanding stock at a premium that may be as high as 50%. In a tender offer, the bidder usually has certain stockholdings that may be sold off in the event the tender offer is unsuccessful. The bidder may take a loss unless there is an available buyer, such as a rival bidder or the target corporation. The stock sales, however, may be a way for the bidder to recapture some of the costs of the tender offer. Although a proxy fight does not involve the large capital outlays that tender offers require, it is not without significant costs. The losers in a proxy fight do not have a way to recapture their losses. If the proxy fight is unsuccessful, the costs of the proxy battle are usually not recoverable. In a minority of circumstances, however, the insurgents may recover their costs from the corporation.

The cost of conducting a proxy fight includes professional fees for the services of proxy solicitors, investment bankers, and attorneys. Other costs include efforts to communicate with shareholders and seek to have them vote in favor of the insurgent or activist. In addition, proxy fights often feature litigation, and this can add to the uncertainty and the costs of the contest. It is ironic that the insurgent/activist has to pay its own costs yet the company uses corporate resources to oppose the insurgent/activist, even though they may be one of the largest shareholders in the company.

Role of Proxy Advisory Firms

Institutions, such as pension funds, mutual funds, endowments, and insurance companies, are required by Department of Labor regulations to vote their shares. However, these institutional investors own shares in many companies and the asset managers are not in a position to closely monitor the corporate governance, or even sometimes the financial performance, of all the companies they own stock in. They may have hundreds of proxy proposals brought to them in a given year as shareholders in a diverse group of companies. They are not set up to deal with these issues, and there is little economic incentive for them to change the way they operate to properly address them. This has given rise to a business known as proxy advisors.

There are two main proxy advisors—Institutional Shareholder Services (ISS) and Glass Lewis and Co. The "industry" is basically a duopoly, and often the recommendations of these firms are blindly accepted by institutions. A question arises of whether this works to the benefit of shareholders. It is not clear that it really does.

Current rules require only that institutional investors vote their shares and be able to show that their votes are not conflicted. They can do this, however, by merely adopting the recommendations of proxy advisors. However, it is not clear that this works in shareholders' interests. Moreover, it is also not clear that the proxy advisory firms have the resources and staffing to properly research all the companies they issue recommendations on.

When one considers all the institutions that use the two proxy advisors firms, it is clear that they wield great influence on billions of dollars of equity. Yet the reality is that they actually own no shares of the companies they issue recommendations on. Is this appropriate? Is there a better system? If the business was more competitive, as opposed to being a duopoly, there might be a little more assurance that the market would ensure the quality of the work of these firms.

There is also another concern regarding ISS, which issues recommendation to institutions on the corporate governance of companies while also selling corporate governance consulting services to some of the companies it monitors. Isn't this a conflict of interest? Do companies that hire ISS for corporate governance consulting get unbiased recommendations or do their recommendations favor their institutional clients?[47]

The SEC issues guidance that presses advisory firms to disclose conflicts. However, not only is there need to disclose such conflicts but also there is a general concern that these firms exercise too much influence on corporate governance. It is also important to bear in mind that while the recommendations issued by proxy firms carry weight, it is often the case that their recommendation are not followed. The larger investment managers use information provided by such firms as only one input in their overall decision-making process.

How Does the Market View the Recommendations of Proxy Advisory Firms?

Does the market place a lot of weight on the recommendations of the two major proxy advisory companies? Larcker, McCall, and Ormazabal tested this using stock option repricing proposals that would change (lower) the strike price of option holders, typically managers, for their benefit.[48] They looked at 272 stock option reprising proposals over the period December 2004 through December 2009. These executive compensation-like proposals are required by the SEC to be brought to shareholder vote. Larker et al. tried to discern how much weight the market placed on ISS recommendations by looking at the stock returns of companies that followed the ISS or Glass Lewis restrictive recommendations. They found that the more companies followed the ISS or Glass Lewis recommendations, the lower their market value was. That is, companies that followed the recommendations had lower market reactions than those that did not. They also

---

[47] ISS itself was acquired in March 2014 by private equity firm Vestar Capital Partners. Glass Lewis is owned by the Ontario Teachers' Pension Plan Board.

[48] David F. Larcker, Allan L. McCall, and Gaizka Ormazabal, "Proxy Advisory Firms and Stock Option Repricing." *Journal of Accounting and Economics* 56, Nos. 2–3 (2013): 149–169.

had lower operating performance and higher employee turnover. They conclude that "proxy advisory firm recommendations were not value increasing for shareholders."

Threshold for Bringing Proposals to Shareholders

Companies typically hold their annual meetings in April. Thus, this part of the year is sometimes referred to as proxy season. Companies send out a proxy statement to shareholders prior to the meeting. These statements delineate issues that will be addressed, and perhaps voted on, at the shareholder meeting. They include the election of directors. In the United States all public companies have to file their proxy statements with the SEC. As time has passed and the Internet has become a successful communication medium, the SEC, under its *Notice and Access Rule*, has allowed public companies and mutual funds to make the proxy materials available on a public website as opposed to having to do expensive printing and mailings. The companies can send out a *Notice of Internet Availability of Proxy Materials* instead of the more expensive complete proxy package that used to be required.

The communication and distribution of the proxy materials are often "subcontracted" to a company that specializes in this work. In the United States the leader in this field is Broadridge Financial Solutions.

In 2013 there were more than 800 proxy proposals submitted to public companies. These proxy proposals focus on a variety of issues, such as executive compensation, the capital structure and dividend payments of the company, and governance and operations of the board. The shareholders submitting these proposals will request that the company includes them in communications to shareholders and that they be brought to a vote at the next shareholder meeting.

Currently, shareholders who have a $2,000 investment in a company have the right to make a proxy request of the company, which the company has to expend resources to respond to. Some believe that these requests, which by measurement cost a minimum of $50,000 each to respond to, are a waste of corporate resources—especially since 93% of the shareholder proposals that came to a vote at Fortune 250 companies in 2013 were denied.[49] On the other hand, many U.S. companies, particularly on issues such as executive compensation, have stonewalled shareholders and have even resisted reasonable requests to allow shareholders, the owners of the company, to vote on whether the compensation of managers is appropriate or excessive.

The $2,000 threshold is probably old and outdated. A higher threshold is probably reasonable—especially in light of the obvious fact that if a shareholder is going to be successful in opposing management and the current board, it should have the resources to fund a successful proxy fight, and this will make financial sense only if they have a significant investment in the company.

Shareholder Wealth Effects of Proxy Contests

Early Research

Dodd and Warner conducted a study of 96 proxy contests for seats on the boards of directors of companies on the New York Stock Exchange and the American Stock

---

[49] Edward Knight, "The SEC's Corporate Proxy Rules Need a Rewrite," *New York Times*, March 27, 2014, A17.

Exchange.[50] Their research revealed a number of interesting findings on the impact of proxy contests on the value of stockholders' investments in these firms. They showed that a positive stock price effect is associated with proxy contests. In a 40-day period before and including the announcement of the proxy contest, a positive, abnormal stock price performance of 0.105 was registered. Based on these results, Dodd and Warner concluded that proxy contests result in an increase in value inasmuch as they help facilitate the transfer of resources to more valuable uses.

The positive wealth effects of the Dodd and Warner study were confirmed in later research by DeAngelo and DeAngelo.[51] In a study of 60 proxy contests for board seats, they found an average abnormal shareholder wealth increase equal to 4.85% in a two-day window around the announcement of the dissident activity, whereas an 18.76% increase was associated with a 40-day window, which is the same time period as that of the Dodd and Warner study. DeAngelo and DeAngelo traced the source of the shareholder gains to cases in which the dissident activity led to the sale or liquidation of the company.

DeAngelo and DeAngelo attempted to trace the source of the shareholder gains by monitoring the firm for three years after the proxy fights. Fewer than 20% of the companies remained independent and under the same management three years later. At many of the companies, the CEO or president had resigned. In addition, at 15 of the 60 firms they studied, the companies were either sold or liquidated. They actually concluded that many of the gains from proxy fights were related to merger and acquisition activity. The proxy contests may have caused some of these firms to eventually sell the company, which in turn caused shareholders to realize a takeover premium. This is discussed further later in this chapter.

Later Research

A study by Borstadt and Swirlein analyzed 142 companies that traded on the New York and American Stock Exchanges over the period from 1962 to 1986.[52] They learned that dissidents were successful 42% of the time. They determined that shareholders realized just over an 11% rate of return during the contest period. These positive shareholder wealth effects are consistent with the bulk of research in this area, although one study, by Ikenberry and Lakonishok, found negative effects.[53]

More recent research further confirmed the positive shareholder wealth effect of prior studies. In a large study of 270 proxy contests that occurred between 1979 and 1994, Mulherin and Poulsen found that proxy contests help create shareholder value.[54] They traced most of the gains to the acquisition of the firms that occurred

---

[50] Peter Dodd and Jerrold Warner, "On Corporate Government: A Study of Proxy Contests," *Journal of Financial Economics* 11, nos. 1–4 (April 1983): 401–438.

[51] 52. Harry DeAngeleo and Linda DeAngeleo, "The Role of Proxy Contests in the Governance of Publicly Held Companies," *Journal of Financial Economics*, 23, June 1989, 29–60.

[52] Lisa Borstadt and T. J. Swirlein, "The Efficient Monitoring of Proxy Contests: An Empirical Analysis of Post-Contest Control Changes and Firm Performance," *Journal of Financial Management* 21 (Autumn 1992): 22–34.

[53] David Ikenberry and Josef Lakonishok, "Corporate Governance through the Proxy Contest: Evidence and Implications," *Journal of Business* 66 (July 1993): 405–433.

[54] J. Harold Mulherin and Annette B. Poulsen, "Proxy Contests and Corporate Change: Implications for Shareholder Wealth," *Journal of Financial Economics* 47 (1998): 279–313.

around the contest period. Gains were even found, however, when the company was not acquired, if that firm experienced management turnover. They found that the new management tended to engage in restructuring, which also created shareholder value. Either way, the proxy contest helped remove poorly performing managers, thus raising shareholder value.

In a study of 96 proxy contests involving merger votes over the period 2000–2006, Yair Listokin found that dissident victories increased shareholder value.[55] However, when management prevailed, shareholder value suffered. These findings are quite intuitive.

Hedge Fund Activists and the Success Rate of Proxy Contests

In Chapter 7 we discuss the rising importance of activist hedge funds who have become the new corporate raiders. However, it is useful at this point to note that with the rapid growth in assets of management by these funds, there has been a corresponding increase in the number of activist campaigns. In addition, though, activists have become more skilled at conducting these campaigns than their predecessors who in the past were better known by the term insurgents. Even recent academic research does not fully capture the impact of these activists. However, over the years 2012–2014 the success rate of proxy fights has risen sharply to 73% in 2014 (Figure 6.9).

Value of Shareholders' Votes

The value of shareholders' votes was also examined in the Dodd and Warner study. They attempted to test the hypothesis originally proposed by Manne, which stated

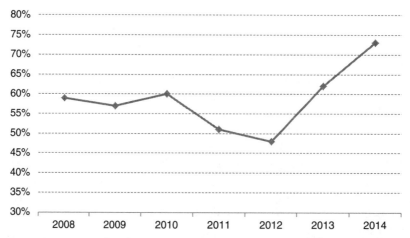

FIGURE 6.9 Success Rate of Proxy Contests. *Source:* FactSet SharkWatch; Wall Street Journal, 1/2/15, page B2.

---

[55] Yair Listokin, "Corporate Voting versus Market Price Setting," *American Law and Economics Review* 11, no. 2 (2009): 608–635.

that a positive stock price effect in proxy fights is associated with the increased value of the votes held by shareholders.[56] This value is perceived by participants in the contest who lobby for the support of shareholders. If their efforts are responsible for some of the increased value of shares, the value should decline after the record date. Shares purchased after the record date may be voted only under restricted and limited circumstances. For the 42 contests in which they had the specific record date, Dodd and Warner found negative results, which seem to support the Manne vote-value hypothesis.

Nature of the Dissidents and Dissident Campaigns

Research shows that the dissidents are often former managers of the target or those who have prior experience in the target's line of business. The Dodd and Warner study found that only a minority of the proxy contests involved a battle between an outside entity and the target corporation. Almost half of the contests were waged between former insiders who left the company following a policy dispute or other disagreement. DeAngelo and DeAngelo found that in almost 50% of the contests in their sample, the dissident leader had prior experience in the target's line of business. In almost one-third of the cases, the dissident leader was at one time employed by the target company.

Long-Term Effects of Proxy Contests

The DeAngelo and DeAngelo study found that dissidents prevailed in one-third of the contests in their sample, whereas another one-third of the companies had changes in top management within three years of the contest, with most of these changes occurring in the first year. In addition, they found that only 20% of the sample firms remained independent, publicly held companies run by the same management team that was in place before the proxy fight. In fact, one-quarter of the companies were either sold or liquidated shortly after the contest.

One of the conclusions of the DeAngelo and DeAngelo study is that once a proxy contest starts, it is more than likely that the company will not remain the same but will undergo some significant changes. It is common that proxy contests result in changes in the managerial structure of the company.

What Determines the Choice of a Tender Offer versus a Proxy Fight?

A study by Sridharan and Reinganum attempted to determine why in some cases a tender offer occurs and in other cases a proxy fight results.[57] They analyzed a sample of 79 tender offers and 38 proxy contests. They found that proxy contests tend to occur more frequently in cases in which the company's performance has been poor as measured by its stock market performance and return on assets. Proxy fights, however, tended to be

[56] Henry Manne, "The Higher Criticism of the Corporation," *Columbia Law Review* 62 (1962): 399–432.
[57] Una Sridharan and M.R. Reinganum, "Determinants of the Choice of Hostile Takeover Mechanism: An Empirical Analysis of Takeovers and Proxy Contests," *Financial Management* 24 (Spring 1995): 57–67.

associated with managerial inefficiency. The capital structure also seemed to be a causal factor as less highly leveraged companies more often were tender offer targets. They theorized that with more equity in the capital structure, there are more shares that may be acquired. In general they found that proxy fight targets are less profitable than targets of tender offers. The poor performance of companies that are the target of proxy fights gives the insurgents a more compelling argument for changing management and enacting other changes.

The poor performance of proxy fight targets was also confirmed by Ikenberry and Lakonishok, who found in a sample of 97 election contests "negative abnormal returns and deteriorating operating performance prior to the announcement of the proxy contest."[58]

Combination of a Proxy Fight and a Tender Offer

A proxy fight may be an effective ancillary tool when coupled with a tender offer. The hostile bidder may use the proxy fight to effect the approval of a shareholder proposal that would dismantle the target's antitakeover defenses. For example, a bidder could use a proxy fight to have the target dismantle its poison pill or other antitakeover defenses. This would then be followed by a more effective tender offer. Another option available to the bidder and/or insurgent is to have the target agree to elect not to be bound by the prevailing state antitakeover laws.

Still another benefit of combining a proxy contest with a tender offer could be for the bidder to use the proxy process to try to replace target directors who oppose the bid. A proxy contest can also be used to replace the target board and have the new directors redeem a poison pill that may be inhibiting a bidder's tender offer. A new board also could initiate the process to have the company exempted from a target's state antitakeover laws.

Disciplinary Effects of Proxy Fights

We have already discussed research such as the work of John Pound who showed how proxy contests tend to bring about changes in target companies after the contest. A study by Vyacheslav Fos of proxy contests over the period 1994–2008 showed that when the likelihood of a proxy contest increases companies implement various changes such as increasing leverage, dividends and CEO turnover and decreasing R&D and capital expenditures[59]. He showed that these changes can actually reduce the likelihood of a proxy contest.

---

[58] Ikenberry and Lakonishok, "Corporate Governance," 405.
[59] Vyacheslav Fos, "The Disciplinary Effects of Proxy Contests," University of Illinois Working Paper, January 2013.

CHAPTER SEVEN

Hedge Funds as Activist Investors

H EDGE FUNDS WERE DEVELOPED as an alternative to open-end investment funds or mutual funds. Managers of hedge funds do not make *public* solicitations for capital to investors in general and as such do not face the public reporting requirements that their mutual fund counterparts do. Since hedge funds do not face as great reporting requirements, investors have more limited access to return data.

Hedge funds grew dramatically during the strong economy that prevailed over the period 2003–2007 (see Figs. 7.1a and 7.1b). The number of hedge funds grew roughly doubled over period 2001–2007 where they peaked at 9,550 funds. Hedge fund assets grew similarly and reached 1.87 trillion in 2007. The subprime crisis and the Great Recession caused the industry to shrink and many of the "weaker players" left the business. However, fueled by large amounts of institutional capital to invest, growth resumed in 2009 and by 2011 both the number of funds and total assets under management surpassed their 2007 levels. This growth accelerated over the years 2012–2014.

Within the hedge fund category, however, we have two subgroups that are relevant to M&A. One is the risk arbitrage hedge funds, which we have already discussed. The other that we will now focus on is the activist hedge funds. These are funds that specialize in acquiring positions in targets that may be undervalued or that have other characteristics that make them vulnerable to activists. Sometimes this vulnerability is based upon poor performance. Other times it could be that the company's past performance left it with high levels of liquid assets that the activists may want the company to use to return cash to shareholders in the form of a stock buyback. This was the case in 2014 when Carl Icahn pressured Apple into using its cash to fund a more rapid stock buyback program than what it had planned. He did get the company to buy back $14 billion in stock within a two-week period. While this was not as much as he planned, he did not

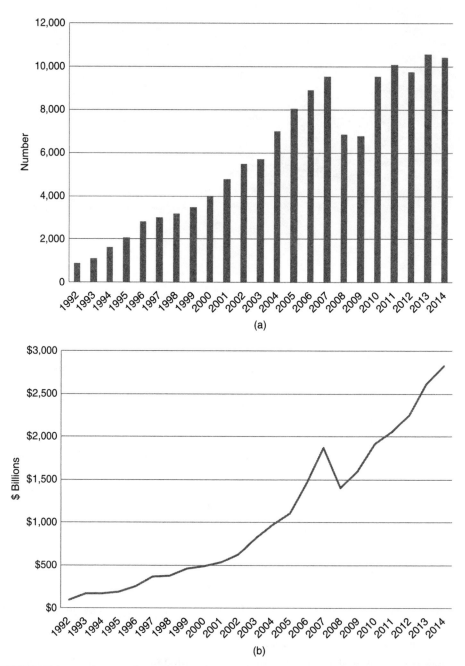

FIGURE 7.1　Hedge Fund Number and Assets. *Sources*: Hennessee Group, 1992–2007 data; Hedge Fund Research Press Releases (2008–2014 data); HFR Global Hedge Fund Industry Reports—Press Releases.

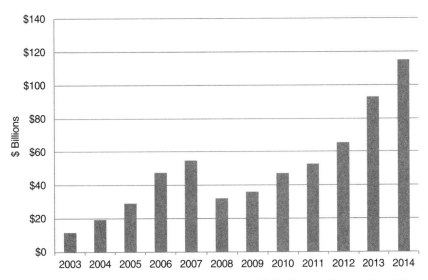

FIGURE 7.2 Activists Assets under Management (AUM). *Source*: Hedge Fund Research.

totally succeed due to the fact that he took on a huge target that already was pursuing a buyback program. In addition, Apple's institutional shareholders failed to rally around the activist, and ISS also failed to endorse Icahn's initiative.

Activism hedge funds performed well in the postrecession period and showed better performance than many other investments. As Figure 7.2 shows, this led to dramatic growth in the number of activist fund assets under management (AUM) by these funds.

The rapidly rising amount of assets under management by activist funds, which reached $115 billion in 2014, is naturally related to an marked increase in the number of activist campaigns (see Figure 7.3). There were 343 activist campaigns in 2014, which was a significant increase over the prior year.

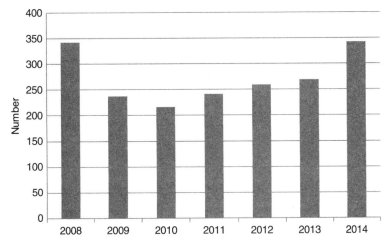

FIGURE 7.3 Number of U.S. Activist Campaigns. *Source*: FactSet SharkWatch; Wall Street Journal, 1/2/15, page B2.

MACROECONOMIC FOUNDATIONS OF THE GROWTH OF ACTIVIST FUNDS

We have noted that the number of activist funds as well as total AUM of these funds has grown dramatically. We have also pointed out this is partly due to the favorable returns these funds have generated in recent years. However, underlying these returns have been various deterministic macroeconomic factors that have created a favorable environment for such returns to be realized. We discuss these ahead.

Improved Macroeconomy

The 18-month-long Great Recession between January 2008 and June 2009 was one of the most severe downturns we have had since the Great Depression. It was totally unlike the relatively mild eight-month U.S. recessions we had in 1990–1991 and 2001. However, unlike other deep recessions we had in 1973–1974 and 1982–1983, the recovery from the Great Recession was quite anemic, particularly with respect to the labor market, which is inextricably linked to consumer spending. Since 2009 growth has picked up and the economy has gained momentum (see Figures 7.4a and 7.4b). This was the case even as Europe was plagued by the Sovereign Debt Crisis and there was weakness for a time in Asia. The growth in the U.S. economy helped stimulate a rebound in equity markets. Interestingly, this created opportunities for activists seeking poor performers.

Market Performance of Stock Market Laggards

When the subprime crisis and Great Recession took hold, the stock market turned down. The rebound in the economy had led to a momentum building recovery that continued to gain strength until it experienced a correction. However, as with all bull markets, not all companies get to participate. In fact, when the market is rising and taking most companies with it, laggards stand out even more. Figure 7.5 shows how dramatic this

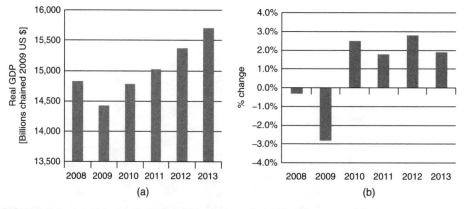

FIGURE 7.4 (a) U.S. Real GDP 2008–2013 and (b) % Chg in Real GDP. *Source:* U.S. Department of Commerce, Bureau of Economic Analysis, February 28, 2014.

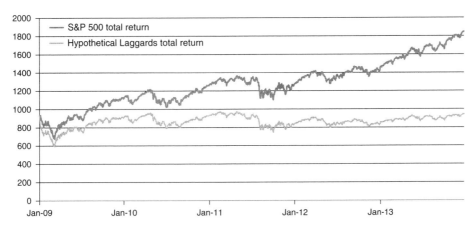

FIGURE 7.5 S&P 500 and S&P Laggards Total Return; 2009–2013. *Source*: Adapted from J. P. Morgan's presentation, "Considerations for Shareholder Activism," September 2013.

difference has been. Between 2009 and 2013 the total returns of the S&P 500 were approximately 100%, while the laggards barely generated a much lower return for their shareholders. Activists can feast on such poor performers. When the returns of the better performers are so high, there is no place for the laggards to hide.

Corporate Deleveraging and Cash Balances

The subprime crisis, Great Recession, and the initially weak buy momentum-gaining recovery that followed brought about major changes in U.S. corporate balance sheets. Both corporations and consumers were shocked by the financial crisis, and both went through a period of deleveraging. Reinhart and Rogoff have showed that these financial crises and their related downturns resulted in deleveraging, which lengthened the weak position recession period.[1]

Companies sought to be more financially prudent while they worried about when the economy and their sales would recover to prerecession growth rates. This manifested itself in aggressively deleveraging, which began in 2009. While the Federal Reserve lowered rates to record levels, the demand for new loans remained weak. New corporate borrowings were often mere refinancings as companies sought to take advantage of incredibly low rates to replace high interest rate debt with low-rate obligations. In addition, risk-averse companies began to stockpile cash and were reluctant to put these funds to use. Investment opportunities, including M&A, did not seem nearly as attractive in the postrecession world as they did in the boom years of 2004–2007.

While deleveraging and booming cash balances resulted in healthier corporate balance sheets, this actually served to make these companies more vulnerable to activists. Rather than be praised for the fiscal prudence, activists challenged some

---

[1] Carmen M. Reinhart and Kenneth Rogoff, *This Time Is Different: Eight Centuries of Financial* (Princeton, NJ: Princeton University Press, 2009).

of these cash rich-low debt companies to pay out some of their cash to shareholders rather than use the funds for other investments such as M&As which may have an uncertain outcome.

Leading Activist Hedge Funds and Institutional Investors

Figure 7.6 lists some of the major activist hedge funds. The top part of the figure shows some of the leading names that have been in the "activist business" for some time and are often in the media. These include Carl Icahn, David Einhorn, and Bill Ackman, as well as Nelson Peltz. The bottom part of the figure, however, shows some other entrants into this business.

While we are well aware of the role of the aforementioned activist investors, who have established funds just for this purpose, institutional investors are starting to engage in more activism. Institutions such as CalPERS and Calsters have become more active in this market. Funds have gone so far as to establish internal groups to address activism issues as they have recognized activist funds have at times generated good returns and that it might pay for them to deviate from the traditional buy and hold investment strategy. Sometimes these institutional investors may interact with the activists in such a way that they will mutually support and benefit from the activism.

FIGURE 7.6 Leading Activists

The activists tend to vary in their approach to activism. Some are very aggressive and public in their approach and may launch an attack at a company, following it up with a media blitz to put maximum pressure on the target's management and board. Others may announce their ownership of shares and what they demand from the company but then may pursue a more toned-down, behind-the-scenes battle for the changes they are looking for.

It is important to bear in mind that these activists are really short-term value investors. In a sense both they and the target's management and board have common interests in that both want the company's stock price to go up. Where they differ is how quickly they want to bring this about and by what means. For example, the activists may want the company to be put up for sale immediately, while management may even agree that an eventual sale is a good idea but they may not think this is the right time.

Changing Nature of the Targets of Activists

Traditionally, activists tended to target smaller companies. This is because a large, well-financed activist fund can acquire a large percentage of a smaller target's shares and basically "bully" the target board and management to get it to do its bidding. However, powerful activists, such as Carl Icahn's fund, had trouble with larger companies where they could invest billions in the target's stock yet still hold only less than 5% of its shares. This was the case in his attack on AOL Time Warner. However, while he was not successful in replacing the management, he was able to get a positive return on his investment in the company.

The activist landscape changed in the years 2012–2014, and companies as large and successful as Microsoft and Apple found themselves the target of activists. This is quite significant as it shows that no company is invulnerable and all have to be on guard for attacks by increasingly aggressive activists. This can be a good thing or a bad thing. It can be good as it pressures managers to run the company for the benefit of shareholders as measured by a good return on their equity. It pressures them not to amass assets such as large cash holdings without presenting shareholders a guide for how these monies are better off staying in the hands of the company rather than being distributed to shareholders in the form of a buyback or a special dividend. It can be bad, though, when companies are prevented from pursuing a viable long-term plan due to the short-term pressures of activists.

Part of the reason for activists pursuing larger targets is that with larger funds and much greater AUMs, larger targets are needed to produce more significant returns. Even if larger targets are more challenging for the activists, the larger AUMs demand that bigger prey be pursued.

Activists and "Short-Termism"

Activists are short-term investors. They acquire a position in a company and usually have a near-term exit strategy. They want to pressure the company to take actions that will cause the stock price to rise and enable them to exit the investment at a profit. Critics have contended that this can pressure a public company to manage the company to meet the near-term goals of the activist while sacrificing the long-term profitability and growth of the company. Activists will say that it is current management that has in the past sacrificed the true long-term growth and profitability of the company and that this mismanagement has created an opportunity for the activist, who is seeking to correct this problem. This continues to be a topic of debate with both sides presenting arguments that, depending on the particular circumstances, may have some merit.

Activist Campaigns for Board Seats

As we have discussed, activist hedge funds have grown significantly in recent years. Concomitant with that growth has been increasingly aggressive activist tactics—especially as they relate to influence on the target's board. Not that long ago an activist investor would acquire shares in the target and then try to pressure the target to put one or two of its representatives on the board. The thinking was that with a representative or two on the board the activist would be able to directly monitor the board's activities and deliberations but also have its voice and views heard at each board meeting. Even with only one or two representatives, funds such as Relational Investors have been able to bring about major changes in some companies.

Over time, however, activists began to demand more. Some were not satisfied by a voice on the board; they wanted multiple representatives on the board. Often there were calls for three of four representatives to be placed on the board. This sometimes grew even further to calls for control of the board. When an activist is so bold that it wants to take control of the target's board, that board knows it is in for a real fight. The activist also knows that there is a good likelihood that its plans for the company will be taken seriously. Oftentimes this means that there will be a serious negotiation followed by some agreement or settlement between the activist and the target.

The type of people nominated to boards by activists can vary. They often are people on the payroll of the fund, including possibly the head of the fund. They also could be industry experts or people who have been employed in the industry for some time. Sometimes, the activist has in mind having these specific people assume active management positions at the company if their activism is successful.

There is often a give and take in the board placement process. For example, the activist may propose three candidates that might include the portfolio manager of the fund and two outside industry people. The company may come back and say they accept the two outside people but they do not accept the internal fund representative. This then can be the subject of a negotiation process and will be a function of the relative bargaining positions of the two parties.

Super Aggressive Activist Hedge Fund: Starboard Value versus Darden Restaurants

When one thinks of aggressive activist hedge fund managers the names of Carl Icahn and Bill Ackman come to mind. However, if we think about the most aggressive activist contest, perhaps the leadership position goes to Jeff Smith and his Starboard Value fund. In 2014, and with less than 10% of the stock in Darden, Smith was able to take

100% control of Darden's board. This is even more notable when one considers that Darden actually had a competent and well-informed board. They were also advised by leading investment banks, such as Morgan Stanley and Goldman Sachs as the well known law firm Wachtell Lipton.

Darden is a Fortune 500 company that owned certain well-known restaurant chains such as Red Lobster, Olive Garden, and Longhorn Steakhouse as well as Capital Grill and Yardhouse. Darden was originally part of the food giant General Mills but was spun off as part of General Mills' increased focus strategy. In addition, the company owned a significant amount of real estate. In 2013 Darden was singled out by another hedge funds, Barrington Capital, which came up with a restructuring plan that called for the separation of slow-growing chains such as Olive Garden and Red Lobster and focusing on faster growth and higher margin chains like Capital Grille and Yardhouse. The plan also called for putting the real estate holdings into a real estate investment trust (REIT) which could provide shareholders with cash flow and tax benefits.

After it left General Mills, Darden was a real growth story but that growth slowed in 2012 at a time the economy was actually picking up steam and competitors were starting to register some good growth. The performance of some of the older chains like Red Lobster and Olive Garden, which appealed to lower middle class and middle class consumers, were hard hit by a U.S recovery that increased corporate profitability while real wages in the U.S. were flat. As Barrington and Darden battled for who had the best solution to the problem, Smith and Starboard pounced on the vulnerable Darden. Some imply that Smith's aggression was a "chance to burnish his brand as an activist investor."[2]

Darden's board's position was that they had studied these issues long before Barrington or Starboard came on the scene and that their ideas were not novel. The hedge funds, however, would say that if that was the case, the fact that the board did not take more aggressive action earlier made it even worse.

Darden, which recognized that the poorly performing Red Lobster chain was a glaring problem, retained Goldman Sachs to conduct an auction. This was made more difficult by the hedge funds opposing the sale and calling for shareholder approval before it could be completed. This reduced the interest of some potential buyers. Darden postponed the annual meeting and enacted bylaw changes to make calling a sooner annual meeting more difficult. Starboard used this action to enlist the support of large institutional investors such as Starboard's largest shareholder, Capital Research and Management. In fact, this is one of the unique aspects of this control contest. Normally, institutional investors are somewhat passive and often side with management. Here Starboard was able to enlist the support of the institutional investors.

Darden reached a deal to sell Red Lobster, and it felt it was getting a good price in light of the chain's poor financial performance. Starboard opposed the sale, claiming the price was too low. The board was hamstrung in its ability to publicly argue for the sale as to do so effectively would require them to discuss how bad Red Lobster had been doing.

---

[2] William D. Cohan, "Starboard Value's Jeff Smith: The Investor CEOs Fear the Most," *Fortune*, December 3, 2014.

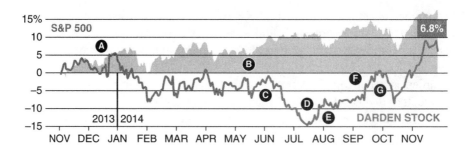

Ⓐ DEC 19, 2013
Smith begins a major accumulation of Darden shares and calls the company "deeply undervalued."

Ⓑ MAY 16, 2014
Darden's board vote to sell Red Lobster for $2.1 billion.

Ⓒ MAY 22, 2014
Smith says Starboard will begin a campaign to remove the Darden board.

Ⓓ JUL 24, 2014
Starboard sues Darden seeking confidential documents related to Red Lobster sale.

Ⓔ JUL 28, 2014
Darden CEO Otis announces he will resign.

Ⓕ SEP 11, 2014
Smith releases a 300-page PowerPoint that criticizes the quality of Olive Garden's pasta and breadsticks.

Ⓖ OCT 10, 2014
Darden shareholders vote to replace all 12 directors with Smith's nominees.

FIGURE A Anatomy of An Ativist Campaign. *Graphic Source*: S&P Capital IQ/Analee Kasudia. Appeared on Fortune, 12/3/2014; *"Starboard Value's Jeff Smith: The investor CEOs fear most,"* by William D. Cohan.

Smith and Starboard initiated a proxy fight to remove Darden's board. ISS and Glass Lewis supported Starboard (See figure A for a time line). In retrospect, Darden's board, while quite qualified, probably did a poor job communicating with its larger shareholders. Smith, on the other, did an excellent job.

Smith won the battle of the directors and replaced the entire board with himself and his hand-picked representatives. This raises certain governance issues. Normally, boards should include outsiders who are unaffiliated with management along with insiders. It does not always work out that way but that is the goal. What Starboard and Smith have done is filled all the seats on the board with their own representatives.

Staggered Boards and Activist Contests for Board Seats

In Chapter 5 we noted that when coupled with a poison pill, the combination can be a powerful antitakeover defense. However, staggered boards, or even poison pills, are not that relevant in activist battles where the activist is looking to accomplish its goals by replacing just a few members of the board. If this can be done, then majority control of the board, something that would normally be made difficult by the staggered board, may not prevent the activist from accomplishing its goals. In addition, outside pressures have forced many companies to abandon their staggered boards. (See Figure 7.7.)

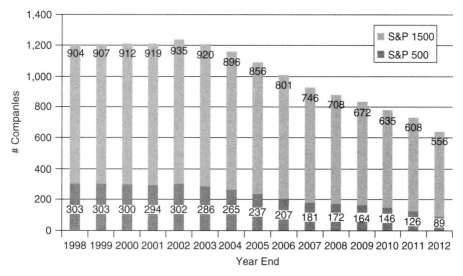

FIGURE 7.7 S&P 1500 Classified Boards at Year End (includes non-U.S. incorporated companies). *Source:* FactSet SharkRepellent, www.sharkrepellent.net.

 ## HEDGE FUNDS AS ACQUIRERS

As hedge funds began to feel the pressures from competitors to generate high returns, they started to look to takeovers—previously the exclusive fund territory of private equity funds. Investors took notice when Edward Lampert, through his hedge fund ESL Investments, did a blockbuster takeover of Kmart in January 2000. Lampert took over Kmart as it was emerging from Chapter 11 bankruptcy protection. In 2004, he then pursued an $11.5 billion merger between Kmart and Sears to form a retail giant that could try to compete on a more even basis with market leader Walmart; however, this did not work that well. Nelson Peltz and his Trian hedge fund were able to leverage his position as an activist shareholder to acquire Wendy's and add the company to his fast-food investments, which included Arby's.

Hedge Funds Team Up with Hostile Bidders

The continually evolving takeover business moved dramatically in another direction in 2014 when hedge fund activist William Ackman, and his Pershing Square fund, teamed up with Valeant Pharmaceuticals to make a $45.6 billion unsolicited bid for Allergan. Ackman brought special capabilities to the deal, including not just financing but also skills developed from being a highly successful activist over many years. They combined to purchase a 9.7% as a toehold in Allergan. As discussed in Chapter 6, the value of this position could fall if the bid does not succeed and another bidder does not buy Allergan. However, if the deal is not successful and another bidder acquires Allergan, the acquisition premium paid could provide handsome gains on the equity position in Allergan.

Over the period of February 2014 through April 10, Ackman and Valeant acquired a 4.99% stake in Allergan, mainly through the purchase of Allergan call options. The bulk of the capital was advanced by Pershing Square and not Valeant, which put up only less than $100 million. Once they crossed the 5% threshold, they had to file a Schedule 13D within 10 days. During that 10-day window Ackman and Valeant acquired another 4.7% stake in Allergan.

Ackman's innovative bid for Allergan was ultimately not successful. Actavis, formerly the generic drug maker Watson Pharmaceuticals, outbid Allegan and Valient with a $66 billion cash and stock offer. While Ackman did not win the bidding contest, he did win financially as Allergan's largest shareholder. The Activis bid was expensive which meant a good return on Ackman's holding. For Activis this deal was one of several it did in recent years. It acquired Forest Labsoratories in February 2014 for $28.4 billion. In 2013 it acquired Warner Chilcott for $5.9 billion, and in 2012 it acquired the Iceland drug maker Actavis for $5.9 billion and assumed the more well known name Actavis. The Allergan deal moved Actavis into the ranks of the top 10 drug companies in the world. While Valeant, a company built through M&A, lost out on this deal, in 2015 it acquired Salix Pharmaceuticals for $10.4 billion.

Hedge Funds as Sources of M&A Debt Financing

Hedge funds have pursued many different investment areas as they seek to find attractive returns for the capital they have been able to easily raise in recent years. One area they have focused on has been the debt of distressed companies. However, in recent years they have become involved in debt financing of M&As. Commercial banks often originate M&A debt financing that they syndicate to hedge funds that assume what usually is second lien debt. The addition of this source of debt financing from hedge funds has augmented the total capital that is available for M&A financing.

Impact of Hedge Funds on M&A Activity

The influence of activist hedge funds on M&A activity is complex. As we have noted, activist hedge funds usually have a short-term investment horizon and often seek to realize relatively short gains from their share positions. A common scenario is that one or more hedge funds acquire a share position in a company they may believe is undervalued or that has assets that could be sold or otherwise restructured. They may seek a short-term return through actions such as forcing the sale of the company. This then may contribute to an increase in M&A volume. It would be a similar result if the activists pressured the company to sell off certain assets to release unrealized values. Here again the acquirer's transaction helped increase overall M&A volume. However, if the target of the activist's interest wanted to pursue a strategic merger that would pay gains in the long run, the hedge fund might oppose the deal as it is looking for a short-term payoff. In this instance this opposition might lead to a lower overall level of M&A. Thus, we see the impact of activists on overall M&A volume is complex and not obvious.

When the M&A market is weak, the activist funds may have to pursue a strategy other than pushing the company to sell itself. This has led some of them to be more like financial engineers or operational activists. The financial engineering activist is perhaps too strong a term as many of these activists merely want the company to do basic things, such as use cash on the balance sheet to buy back shares. This is hardly financial engineering in the advanced MBA sense. The operational activist may get more deeply involved in the company's operational performance and may want to have the company run differently. This requires more time and study of the business and the industry. Such funds may employ industry consultants to help them with these tasks. They also may focus on certain industries and have former workers in their industries working full-time at the fund.

Activist Hedge Funds and Shareholder Wealth Effects

It is not unusual that when activist hedge funds announce they have accumulated an equity position in a company, it can have an uplifting effect on its stock price. For example, when well-known activist Carl Icahn announces a stock position in a company at which he intends to become an activist, the stock undergoes what some have euphemistically referred to as the "Icahn Lift."

Researchers have quantified this general phenomenon. For example, in an analysis of filings over the period 2001–2006, Brav, Jiang, Thomas, and Partnoy found that the announcement of hedge fund activism was associated with 7% abnormal returns over a short window around that announcement date.[3] Other researchers have similar findings.

In a study of 197 hedge funds over the period 1998–2005 Christopher Clifford analyzed the shareholder wealth effects of their activist blockholdings.[4] He was able to discern which holdings were a passivist or activist through a review of the fund's Schedule 13D filings with the SEC. Clifford found that companies that were targeted by activists realized higher excess stock returns. He found that firms targeted by activists experienced a 3.39% cumulative excess return around the announcement date. The firms the activists targeted also showed improved operating performance as measured by their return on assets. He traced many of these improvements to the divestiture of underperforming assets.

Klein and Zur confirmed the findings of other researchers who had found positive shareholder wealth effects of activist hedge funds accumulating stock positions in companies.[5] However, they expanded the scope of the research on this issue by comparing the market effects of activist hedge fund share accumulations with those of what they called entrepreneurial activists. This group consisted of individuals or asset managers acting on their behalf, private equity firms, and venture capitalists. They are considered activists if the purpose of their share accumulations is to bring about change in the company that will raise the stock prices and provide them with a profit from their investment

[3] Alon Brav, Wei Jiang, Randall S. Thomas, and Frank Partnoy, "Hedge Fund Activism, Corporate Governance and Firm Performance," *Journal of Finance* 63, no. 4 (August 2008): 1729–1775.
[4] Christopher P. Clifford, "Value Creation or Destruction? Hedge Funds as Shareholder Activists," *Journal of Corporate Finance* 14, no. 4 (September 2008): 323–336.
[5] April Klein and Emanuel Zur, "Entrepreneurial Shareholder Activist: Hedge Funds and Other Private Investors," *Journal of Finance* 64 (2009): 187–229.

as a result of their activism. Both samples were drawn from the 2003–2005 time period and were of a similar size: 151 hedge funds and 154 entrepreneurial activists. They found similarities and disparities in the market reactions to these two types of activists. While both were associated with positive abnormal stock returns, hedge funds showed 10.2% returns while the entrepreneurial group was associated with a 5.1% return. For both, the returns did not dissipate over time. In fact, they found that hedge funds' abnormal returns one year later were 11.4% and 17.8% for the other group.

Klein and Zur found that both groups were often successful in getting the target companies to do their bidding. Hedge funds had a 60% success rate, while the entrepreneurial group was successful 65% of the time.

One other very interesting finding of Klein and Zur was that the two groups of activists seemed to target different types of companies. Hedge funds tended to target companies that were in better financial conditions than did the entrepreneurial activists. Hedge funds seemed to seek out companies that had higher cash resources, and then they tried to pressure them into buying back shares and make other changes, like lowering senior executive compensation and increasing dividends. The entrepreneurial activists tended to focus more on the company's strategy. Often this was associated with changes in research and development and capital expenditures in the year after they began their activism.

Klein and Zur found that the way each group achieved its goals was through the use of the proxy process. However, they did not necessarily do so by actually having a proxy fight. Rather, they tended to use the threat of a proxy fight as their main tool to achieve their different goals.

Greenwood and Schor delved further into the source of these positive shareholder wealth effects.[6] They did this through the analysis of a large sample of companies that filed Schedule 13Ds over the years 1993–2006. They then cross-referenced this sample to the 13F filings, which are made by institutions (see Chapter 3). This led to a large sample that included many passive investors, which had to be deleted. They examined DFAN14A filings, which are filings made with the SEC by those investors considering pursuing a proxy fight. Lastly, they analyzed the shareholder wealth effects of the whole sample and subsamples that included those that were acquired and those that were not.

Greenwood and Schor found announcement period returns of greater than 5% for those companies that were eventually acquired. This is roughly double what the returns were for those companies that experienced other outcomes.

Hedge Fund Activism and Firm Performance

Hedge funds usually do not seek to take over a company in which they assume an equity position. They seek to realize an attractive return through their agitation so as to get the target company to make meaningful changes that will uplift the stock price. Brav, Jiang, Partnoy, and Thomas analyzed the market's reactions to announcements of activist hedge funds assuming positions in companies.[7] As we have already noted, they

---

[6] Robin Greenwood and Michael Schor, "Investor Activism and Takeovers," *Journal of Financial Economics* 92, no. 3 (June 2009): 362–375.
[7] Brav, Jiang, Partnoy, and Thomas, "Hedge Fund Activism."

used filings over the period 2001–2006, and they found an average abnormal return equal to 7%. They noticed that the performance of the companies improved after being targeted by hedge funds. They also noticed greater CEO turnover and increased use of pay for performance. Their research seems to imply that hedge funds can be a useful check on overly powerful CEOs who may fail to bring about stock price growth. This is a result that should be kept in mind when this topic is revisited in Chapter 13.

Bebchuk, Brav, and Jiang analyzed 2,040 activist interventions over the period 1994–2007.[8] They found that operating performance tended to improve after the activist interventions. They focused on performance measures, such as return on asset and Tobin's Qs.[9] In addition, they found that these performance improvements were not offset by falloffs somewhat later, which could have implied that they were just temporary and perhaps a function of accounting manipulation (see Figure 7.8).

Still additional evidence of the performance improving effect of hedge funds can be found in the work of Benjamin Solarz, who analyzed 718 hedge fund investments; he discerned from reading the funds' 13D filing that 393 were activist and 325 were passive investments.[10] As with other researchers, he concluded that the funds were activist if they indicated in their filings that they sought specific action, such as board seats, or wanted to pursue a proxy fight.

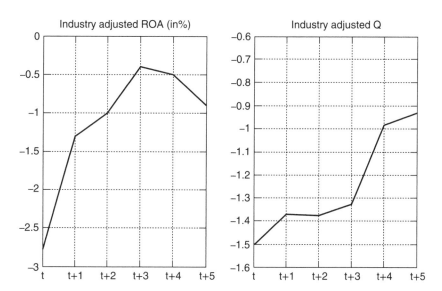

FIGURE 7.8 The Evolution of ROA and Q over the Period. *Source:* Lucian A. Bebchuk, Alon Brav, and Wei Jiang, "The Long-Term Effects of Hedge Fund Activism," Columbia Business School Research Paper No. 13–66, July 9, 2013.

---

[8] Lucian A. Bebchuk, Alon Brav, and Wei Jiang, "The Long-Term Effects of Shareholder Activism," Columbia University Working Paper no 13.66, July 9, 2013.
[9] As a reminder, Tobin's Q is named after the Yale, Nobel Prize–winning economist James Tobin. It measures the ability of a company to use its assets, measured at book value, to create market values in the equity market.
[10] Benjamin Solarz, "Hedge Fund Investments: Stock Picking in Disguise," *Michigan Journal of Business* 3, no. 1 (January 2010): 101–160.

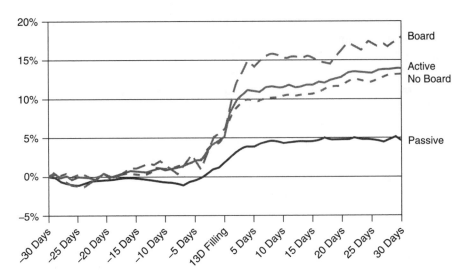

FIGURE 7.9 In the Short Run, Active Investments Outperform Passive. *Source*: Benjamin Solarz, "Stock Picking in Disguise? New Evidence That Hedge Fund Activism Adds Value," *Michigan Journal of Business* 3, no. 1 (January 2010): 101–160.

Firstly, as shown in Figure 7.9, activist funds, especially those that sought board seats (213 of the 393 activist investments) showed very clear short-term, excess returns that were significantly greater than passive investments.

Solarz also measured the performance of the companies that had active and passive hedge fund investors. For example, he found that after a two-year period there were improvements in the company's return on assets for the active group and declines in the passive group. He also found that shareholders gained through increases in leverage (although some might say this increases the company's risk) and a greater dividend payout ratio.

Hedge Fund Activism and Buyout Premiums: Hedge Funds versus Private Equity Firms

In Chapter 8 we cover leveraged buyouts, and in Chapter 9 we focus on private equity firms, which are often buyout sponsors. However, since activist hedge funds have an impact on these buyouts, we will discuss their role in this chapter.

There have been a number of cases where activist hedge funds have opposed takeover bids by private equity firms on the grounds that the bids included an insufficient takeover premium. The goal of a private equity buyer is to acquire the target at as low a cost as possible and to be able to sell it at a later date at a significantly higher price. Normally, target shareholders are not in a position to bargain for a higher premium and rely on boards to act in their best interests. However, when the ranks of the target's shareholders include an activist hedge fund that holds a significant block of stock, and may even have one or more seats on the board, the game changes and usually not for the better for the private equity buyer.

Huang analyzed a sample of 237 buyout proposals for U.S. public targets over the period 1990–2007.[11] He found that a one standard deviation increase in the fraction of equity of the target that is held by hedge funds prior to a buyout announcement was associated with a 3.6% increase in the buyout premium. He also found that the number of shares held by other types of institutional investors, such as mutual funds or pension funds, did not have any impact on buyout premiums. Huang also found that this premium uplifting effect was greater for management buyouts than outside initiated buyouts. It also was stronger for club deals—deals where more than one buyout firm companies to make a joint bid—than solo buyout offers.

Communications among Activist Shareholders

In recent years it is not unusual to see activists communicate their views and plans to other activist funds. That is, they may "tip each other off" on their views, either bullish or bearish on particular companies. These communications may precede their share accumulations or short sales. One concern is whether these are communications of legitimate investment research and strategies or efforts at stock manipulation. The magnitude of some of the activist market moves can help make them self-fulfilling prophecies.

An analysis conducted by the *Wall Street Journal* looked at the market movements of specific stocks 10 days *prior* to bullish and bearish announcements by activists. In an analysis of 975 bullish announcements by lead activist investors in 2007, they found that stocks rose an average of 3.2% over the 10-day period before the announcements (see Figure 7.10). Similarly, in an analysis of 43 bearish announcements by lead activists, they found the stocks declined 3.8% in the 10-day period after the announcements (see Figure 7.11).

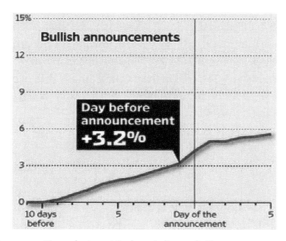

FIGURE 7.10 Average Cumulative Market-Adjusted Returns around Bullish Activist Announcements. *Source*: S&P Capital IQ data; *Wall Street Journal*, March 27, 2014, A14.

---

[11] Jiekun Huang, "Hedge Funds and Shareholder Wealth Gains in Leveraged Buyouts," working paper, University of Illinois at Urbana-Champaign, May 2010.

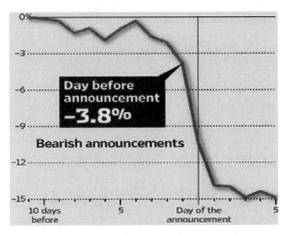

FIGURE 7.11 Average Cumulative Market-Adjusted Returns around Bearish Activist Announcements. *Source*: S&P Capital IQ data; *Wall Street Journal*, March 27, 2014, A14.

This is an issue being examined by the Securities Exchange Commission. The current laws on insider trading do not prohibit communications among investors of their views on companies. It can get a little more complicated if the investors work together in a manner that could be considered a "group," which could trigger a disclosure requirement at an earlier date than what would have been required without such communications.

In light of the fact that activist investors can have such a significant influence in the market, should regulators reexamine the sharing of information on companies among activists? One activist simply telling another about his strong views on a company and its market valuation can provide great insight into his investment plans, even if the plan themselves are not disclosed in detail. Should this be treated as inside information? Clearly it is not inside information the way it is defined in the current law (even though the law in this area actually does not clearly define inside information). However, does such sharing of insights give selected activists such an advantage over other investors that it tilts the playing field too far in their favor? This issue will be examined in more detail by regulators in the future.

PART THREE

Going-Private Transactions and Leveraged Buyouts

CHAPTER EIGHT

Going-Private Transactions and Leveraged Buyouts

A LEVERAGED BUYOUT (LBO) is a financing technique used by a variety of entities, including the management of a corporation or outside groups, such as other corporations, partnerships, individuals, or investment groups. Specifically, it is the use of debt to purchase the stock of a corporation, and it frequently involves taking a public company private. Its popularity is affected by factors such as the level of interest rates and the availability of debt financing. The low interest rates that prevailed during the years 2004–2007 helped explain why so many large LBOs occurred in that period. The lack of debt financing in the years of 2008–2009, at a time when interest rates were low, helps explain the big falloff in the number of deals in those years. In the economic recovery that occurred during 2010–2014 debt financing became increasingly available due to the large amounts of liquidity provided by expansionary monetary policy, but lenders were cautious and would not fund all of the types of deals that they did before the subprime crisis.

 TERMINOLOGY

There is much overlap in LBOs and going-private transactions. A *going-private deal* is where a public company is taken private. Such a transaction is financed with some debt and some equity. When the bulk of the financing comes from debt, this deal can also be referred to as an LBO. When a company sells a business unit, or even the entire company, to a management group, this type of deal is referred to as a management buyout (MBO). Many of these transactions involve a public company divesting a division, and in doing so they sell it to the unit's management as opposed to an outside party. Sometimes they are also referred to as unit management buyouts. When managers rely mainly on borrowed capital to finance the deal, it may also be referred to as a leveraged buyout. Thus we see there is significant overlap in the terms that may be used to describe these transactions.

 ## HISTORICAL TRENDS IN LBOS

Early Origins of LBOs

While the actual term *leveraged buyout* came into popular use in the 1980s, the concept of a debt-financed transaction in which a public company goes private has been around for a much longer period. One notable example was the LBO of the Ford Motor Company. In 1919, Henry Ford and his son Edsel, being displeased with having to answer to shareholders who differed with the founder of the auto company on issues such as dividend policy, borrowed what was considered an astronomical sum at that time to take the world's largest automobile company private. The Fords purchased the company's shares that they did not own for $106 million (approximately 1.76 billion in 2014 $), of which $75 million was borrowed from a collection of East Coast banks, such as Chase Securities of New York, Old Colony Trust, and Bond & Goodwin.[1] The Fords wanted to be free to manufacture and sell their Model Ts at ever-decreasing prices, which would come from reinvesting profits in the company as opposed to distributing them to shareholders. Shareholders such as the Dodge brothers were happy to cash out their positions in the auto giant as they were using their capital to expand their own auto company to compete with Ford, making higher-priced cars. Investors wanted higher profits that could be facilitated by higher prices, but Henry Ford was consumed by making the automobile affordable and attainable for the average American, and he needed continually lower prices to bring this about.

It is interesting to note that some of the problems that befell the LBOs of the fourth merger wave also affected Ford. When the U.S. economy turned down in the years 1920–1921, Ford incurred a cash crunch, and many worried it would not be able to service the huge debt load it had taken on in the buyout. Ford responded with a temporary halt in production, followed by layoffs and other cost-cutting measures. However, Ford had alternatives at its disposal that most companies do not have. Rather than have to head, hat in hand, to the East Coast bankers whom he despised, Henry Ford exercised rights in his agreements with Ford dealers and shipped them the mounting inventory of cars, even though they did not necessarily need them. This required the dealers to pay for them, and the dealers all across the United States headed out for financing, giving the Ford Motor Company the cash infusion it needed. Ironically, Ford got access to the needed cash by its dealers taking out many loans, as opposed to Ford seeking distressed financing.

Trends in LBOs: 1970s

The number of large LBOs increased dramatically in the 1980s, but they first began to occur with some frequency in the 1970s as an outgrowth of the 1960s bull market.

---

[1] Douglas Brinkley, *Wheels for the World* (New York: Penguin, 2003), 241–242.

Many private corporations took advantage of the high stock prices and chose this time to go public, thereby allowing many entrepreneurs to enjoy windfall gains. Even though some of these firms were not high-quality, their stock was quickly absorbed by the growing bull market. When the stock market turned down in the 1970s, the prices of some lower-quality companies fell dramatically. The bulk of this falloff in prices occurred between 1972 and 1974, when the Dow Jones Industrial Average fell from 1036 in 1972 to 578 in 1974. In 1974, the average price-earnings (P/E) ratio was six, which is considered low.

When the opportunity presented itself, managers of some of the companies that went public in the 1960s chose to take their companies private in the 1970s and 1980s. In addition, many conglomerates that had been built up in the 1960s through large-scale acquisitions began to become partially disassembled through sell-offs, a process that is called *deconglomeration*. Part of this process took place through the sale of divisions of conglomerates through LBOs. This process was ongoing through the 1980s and is partially responsible for the rising trend in divestitures that occurred during that period.

Around this time newly formed LBO firms, such as Kohlberg Kravis & Roberts (formed in 1976), Thomas Lee Partners (formed in 1974), and Forstmann Little (formed in 1978), created investment pools to benefit from finding undervalued assets and firms and using debt capital to finance their profitable acquisitions. These firms then became known as LBO firms. As time passed many other firms would join them in this activity, although the firms would later be known as private equity firms as opposed to LBO firms.

Trends in LBOs: 1980s–2000s

The value and number of worldwide LBOs increased dramatically starting in the early 1980s and peaked by the end of the decade (Figures 8.1a and 8.1b). By the mid-1980s, larger companies were starting to become the target of LBOs; the average LBO transaction increased from $39.42 million in 1981 to $137.45 million in 1987. Although LBOs attracted much attention in the 1980s, they were still small in both number and dollar value compared with mergers. For example, in 1987 there were 3,701 mergers but only 259 LBOs. Leveraged buyouts accounted for only 7% of the total number of transactions. In terms of total value, LBOs accounted for a higher percentage of the total value of transactions. In 1987, LBOs made up 21.3% of the total value of transactions, which shows that the typical LBO tends to have a larger dollar value than the typical merger. Some felt that the LBO structures were so efficient that they would start to replace the typical public corporation.[2] That prediction turned out to be very incorrect.

Figure 8.1 shows that the dollar value of LBOs fell dramatically in 1990 and 1991. This decrease coincided with the decline in the junk bond market that started in late 1988 and the 1990–1991 recession that followed a few years later.

The LBO business of the 1980s was a very different business than the one that followed over the period 1990–2014. In the fourth merger wave of the 1980s, a period that has been associated with large LBOs and many colorful hostile takeovers, however, there were a more limited number of sponsors or LBO dealmakers and also providers of

[2] Michael Jensen, "Eclipse of the Public Corporation," *Harvard Business Review* 67, no. 5 (1989): 61–74.

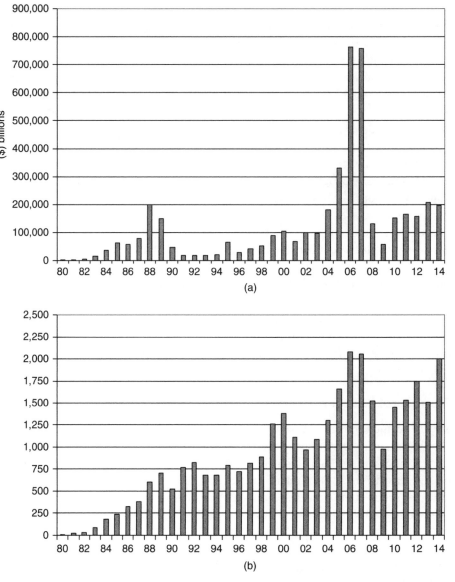

FIGURE 8.1 (a) Value of worldwide LBOs, 1980–2014. *Source*: Thomson Financial Securities Data, February 19, 2015.
(b) Number of worldwide LBOs, 1980–2014. *Source*: Thomson Financial Securities Data, March 6, 2015.

debt financing. The sponsors built their business on many personal contacts and were able to aggressively pursue deals using very high leverage percentages—sometimes 85% or 90%. With such high leverage, even small increases in the value of the company could result in high returns. These increases were brought about not by managerial acumen of the LBO dealmakers but by the rising market combined with the high leverage.

Many things changed since the 1980s. Providers of debt financing began to require much higher equity participations, in part due to many high-profile failures of debt-laden LBOs. In addition, as basic microeconomics predicts, the high returns and surprisingly minor barriers to entry attracted many competitors. The barriers to entry were really the access to capital, which proved not that challenging given the very large a number of pension funds and endowments aggressively seeking diverse investments in the hopes of achieving higher returns. They provided the equity capital, and then access to bank financing and public debt markets provided the rest. Employees at some of the original LBO firms went out to start their own firms, and the industry quickly grew exponentially.

Once again, consistent with basic microeconomic theory, competition grew and returns fell. Cao and Lerner have reported that while the average buyout firm formed between 1980 and 1985 generated an impressive 47% internal rate of return, those funds established between 1986 and 1999 earned less than 10%.[3] Amazingly, the poor returns did not stunt the fund-raising activity of LBO dealmakers.

The value, and especially the number of worldwide LBOs, increased significantly as we moved through the fifth merger wave. This effect was so pronounced that, by 1998, the number of LBOs reached an all-time high. However, in 1999, the number of deals increased approximately 50% over 1998, while in 2000 the number increased again. Even though the number of deals in 2000 was approximately double the 1980 level, the total value was only half. This is because the deals of the fifth merger wave were not the mega-LBOs of the fourth wave but smaller and more numerous.

The number and value of worldwide LBOs fell off dramatically in the 2001–2002 period. This is not surprising as these years coincided with a recession and an initially weak recovery. By 2004, however, LBO volume (along with merger-and-acquisition volume) rose significantly. This dramatic growth continued through 2007. The four-year period 2004–2007 proved to be the most robust LBO period in history. Not only were more LBOs being done, but also the average size of deals grew. The magnitude of the LBO boom that took place between 2004 and 2007 can be seen in Table 8.1, which shows that 7 of the 10 largest deals in history took place in 2006–2007.

The reason for this LBO boom can be found in the combination of a very robust economy, with a rising stock market and a housing-market bubble, along with low interest rates, which made the cost of debt financing for debt-laden LBOs unusually inexpensive. Equity and debt capital was very readily available, and in many instances there was more capital to do transactions than there were good deals to pursue. We will discuss later in this chapter the key role that private equity firms played in LBO growth during this period. This all came to a rapid halt when the subprime crisis took hold and the global economy entered a recession in 2008. While interest rates stayed low due to the stimulative monetary policy pursued by most central banks, credit availability dramatically shrank.

---

[3] Jerry Cao and Josh Lerner, "The Performance of Reverse Leveraged Buyouts," *Journal of Financial Economics* 91, no. 2 (February 2009): 139–157.

TABLE 8.1 Largest Worldwide LBOs

Date Announced	Target Name	Acquirer Name	Rank Value of Deal ($ mil)
06/30/2007	BCE Inc	Investor Group	51,182
11/19/2006	Equity Office Properties Trust	Blackstone Group LP	40,657
07/24/2006	HCA Inc	Hercules Acquisition Corp	32,919
11/16/1988	RJR Nabisco Inc	Investor Group	32,518
02/26/2007	TXU Corp	TXU Corp SPV	32,105
10/20/1988	RJR Nabisco Inc	Investor Group	31,144
10/24/1988	RJR Nabisco Inc	Kohlberg Kravis Roberts & Co	30,599
10/02/2006	Harrah's Entertainment Inc	Investor Group	27,888
11/16/2006	Clear Channel Commun Inc	BT Triple Crown Co Inc	25,874
04/02/2007	First Data Corp	Kohlberg Kravis Roberts & Co	25,670

Source: Thomson Financial Securities Data, March 6, 2015.

LBO deal making fell to a near term low in 2009 and, while it rebounded in the years that followed, it remained below the heady levels of 2004–2007.

RJR NABISCO: ONE OF THE LARGEST LBOS OF ALL TIME

Until 2006 the RJR Nabisco leveraged buyout was the largest LBO of all time and featured so many colorful characters that it was the subject of a feature film—*Barbarians at the Gate*—which in turn was based on a best-selling book of the same name. The company was a product of a merger between the RJ Reynolds tobacco company and the Nabisco food company.

There were several financial characteristics that made RJR Nabisco an attractive candidate for an LBO. Its cash flows, especially those from its tobacco business, were steady and predictable. The cash flows from both businesses did not vary appreciably with the ups and downs of the business cycles of the economy. In addition, neither business required major capital expenditures, thus allowing room for cash flows to be absorbed with interest obligations. RJR also had another characteristic that made it appealing to LBO dealmakers—it had a low debt level. This meant it had unused debt capacity.

RJR Nabisco had not been performing well prior to the buyout. Its return on assets had been falling while its ability to turn over its inventory had been declining. However, its tobacco and food businesses featured many well-recognized brands. The tobacco business product line included the Camel and Winston brands. Its food business featured many products that are household staples and well recognized across the world. The combination of many well-recognized products gave the company a high breakup value that Smith Barney estimated to be in the

$85–$92-per-share range compared with the $56 stock price just prior to the initial buyout offer.[a]

The initial offer for the company came from a management group led by CEO Ross Johnson. It was a lowball $75-per-share offer that the board of directors, which was very close and even beholden to Johnson, was embarrassed by. Johnson faced the conflict of interest of being a fiduciary for shareholders, charged with the responsibility of maximizing shareholder value, while also being in the position of a bidder trying to acquire the company for the best price possible. The low offer by Ross Johnson, who was backed by Shearson Lehman Hutton and Salomon Brothers, attracted other bidders, who quickly saw an undervalued company and responded with their own offers (see Figure A).

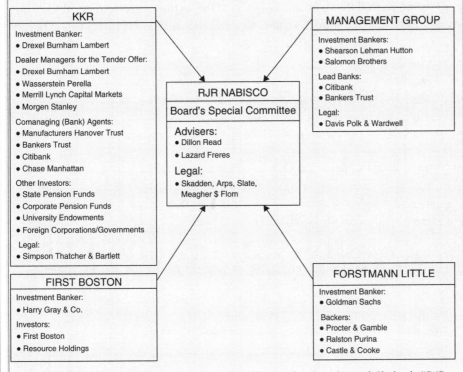

FIGURE A The Bidding Groups. *Source*: Allen Michael and Israel Shaked, "RJR Nabisco: A Case Study of a Complex Leveraged Buyout," *Financial Analysts Journal* (September/October 1991): 23.

After a series of bidding rounds, the board of directors selected Kohlberg Kravis & Roberts' (KKR) offer. One unusual aspect of the board's decision-making process is that it took into account a variety of factors beyond just the absolute price. These factors included a promise to keep the company intact and to still have some public share ownership. The Johnson group's offer included plans to sell off assets and use the proceeds to pay down debt. The board also was concerned by the conflict

(*continued*)

(continued)

of interests surrounding the Johnson initial low bid. KKR won the bidding contest, but the acquisition did not prove to be a financial success. In some ways the case is an example of the winner's curse, as KKR's returns were not impressive.

[a] Allen Michel and Israel Shaked, "RJR Nabisco: A Case Study of a Complex Leveraged Buyout," *Financial Analysts Journal* (September/October 1991): 15–27.

Globalization of LBOs

Figure 8.2 shows that the value and number of LBOs in the United States peaked during the years 2006–2007. Figure 8.3 shows that while there were very few LBOs in Europe

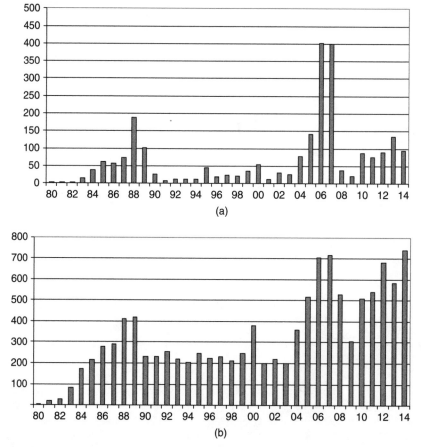

FIGURE 8.2 (a) Value of U.S. LBOs and (b) Number of U.S. LBOs. *Source*: Thomson Financial Securities Data, January 20, 2015.

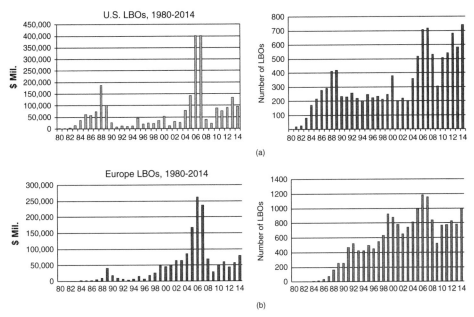

FIGURE 8.3 (a) U.S. LBOs, 1980–2014 and (b) Europe LBOs, 1980–2014.
Source: Thomson Financial Securities Data, January 20, 2015.

in the 1980s, the volume of these deals increased dramatically in the late 1990s. In fact, starting in 2001 through 2005, the value of European LBOs exceeded the value of U.S. LBOs. In addition, by 2005 the number of LBOs in Europe was roughly double the number that occurred in the United States. In addition, as Figure 8.4 shows, in many years the average value of European LBOs was below that of the United States, indicating that more LBOs were completed in Europe but, on average, they were somewhat smaller than the LBOs that took place in the United States. However, in 2006–2007, while LBO deal value rose sharply in Europe, the growth was even more dramatic in the United States. We have noted that 7 of the 10 largest LBOs of all time took place in 2006–2007 (see Table 8.1). These were all U.S. deals (see Table 8.2a). Table 8.2b shows that there certainly were a number of mega-LBOs in Europe over the period of 2005–2007, but some of the LBOs that took place in the United States were significantly larger.

MANAGEMENT BUYOUTS

As we have noted, an MBO is a type of LBO that occurs when the management of a company decides it wants to take its publicly held company, or a division of the company, private.[4] We have also noted that many MBOs are deals where a unit of a public company is purchased by managers of that division. Both the dollar volume and number

---

[4] Robert L. Kieschnick, "Management Buyouts of Public Corporations: An Analysis of Prior Characteristics," in Yakov Amihud, ed., *Leveraged Management Buyouts* (Homewood, IL: Dow Jones Irwin, 1989), 35–38.

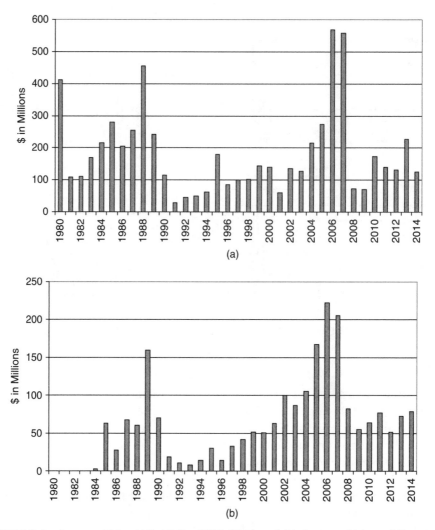

FIGURE 8.4 Average Value U.S. LBOs, 1980–2014 and (b) Average Value of European LBOs, 1980–2014. *Source*: Thomson Financial Securities Data, January 20, 2015.

of unit MBOs have risen sharply over the past 10 years (see Figure 8.5 for value of U.S. MBOs). Some of the same trends that are apparent in the total LBO data are also apparent in the management buyout data. Both the number and dollar value of MBOs fell off sharply after the fourth merger wave ended but recovered as we moved into the fifth wave. However, the dollar value of MBOs never returned to the levels witnessed in the fourth wave, while the number of these did come close to the mid-1980 levels by 2003.

The managers in an MBO may invest some of their own capital in the deal, but often other equity capital is provided by investors while the bulk of the funds are borrowed. The deal will often involve a sponsor working with the management group. The sponsor typically provides capital and access to its relationship with investment banks, which will work to raise the debt capital.

TABLE 8.2 (a) 10 Largest U.S. LBOs and (b) 10 Largest European LBOs

Date Announced	Target Name	Acquirer Name	Rank Value of Deal ($ mil)	Status
11/19/2006	Equity Office Properties Trust	Blackstone Group LP	40,656.911	Completed
07/24/2006	HCA Inc	Hercules Acquisition Corp	32,918.951	Completed
11/16/1988	RJR Nabisco Inc	Investor Group	32,517.840	Completed
02/26/2007	TXU Corp	TXU Corp SPV	32,105.382	Completed
10/20/1988	RJR Nabisco Inc	Investor Group	31,144.060	Completed
10/24/1988	RJR Nabisco Inc	Kohlberg Kravis Roberts & Co	30,598.780	Completed
10/02/2006	Harrah's Entertainment Inc	Investor Group	27,888.108	Completed
11/16/2006	Clear Channel Commun Inc	BT Triple Crown Co Inc	25,874.014	Completed
04/02/2007	First Data Corp	Kohlberg Kravis Roberts & Co	25,669.687	Completed
04/16/2007	SLM Corp	Investor Group	25,537.352	Completed

(a)

Date Announced	Target Name	Acquirer Name	Rank Value of Deal ($ mil)	Status
04/20/2007	Alliance Boots PLC	Investor Group	21,812.207	Completed
02/08/2006	BAA PLC	Airport Dvlp & Invest Ltd	21,810.571	Completed
07/11/1989	BAT Industries PLC	Hoylake Investments PLC	20,813.393	Completed
04/07/2007	J Sainsbury PLC	Investor Group	19,818.714	Completed
03/09/2007	Alliance Boots PLC	AB Acquisitions Ltd	19,604.189	Completed
05/04/2007	Altadis SA	CVC Capital Partners Ltd	17,620.073	Completed
10/16/2006	Thames Water PLC	Kemble Water Ltd	14,888.800	Completed
05/26/2005	Wind Telecomunicazioni SpA	Weather Investment Srl	12,799.342	Completed
11/30/2005	TDC A/S	Nordic Telephone Co Hldg ApS	10,618.375	Completed
01/16/2006	VNU NV	Valcon Acquisition BV	9,624.499	Completed

(b)

Source: Thomson Financial Securities Data, March 6, 2015.

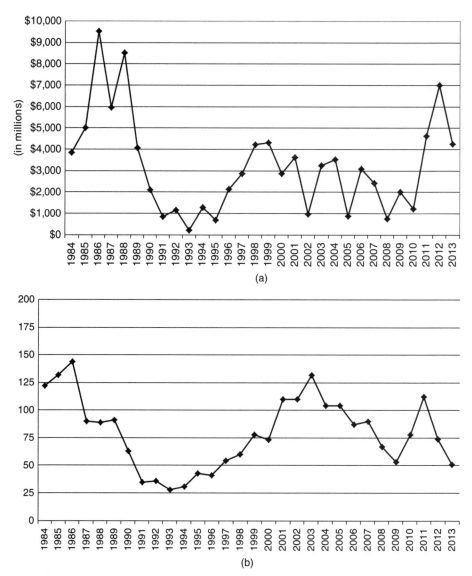

FIGURE 8.5 (a) Dollar Value of Unit Management Buyouts, 1984–2013 and (b) Number of Unit Management Buyouts, 1984–2013. *Source: Mergerstat Review*, 1992, 1998, and 2014.

The purchased entity then becomes a separate company with its own shareholders, board of directors, and management team. While the buying group is insiders in an MBO, and outsiders in an LBO, the process is otherwise not that different. Presumably, however, the buying group in an MBO has better access to information about the company's potential profitability than an outside buying group has. This is one factor that may give an MBO a greater likelihood of success than an LBO. Better information may not be enough. If the parent company is seeking to sell the division because of poor performance, it could be that this poor performance is attributable to management. An MBO leaves the company still in the hands of the same managers, whereas in an LBO the new owners may install their own managers. These new managers may be less tied to prior employees and other assets and may be more willing to implement the changes necessary to turn the company into a profitable entity.

When companies divest divisions, they normally sell them to outside parties. Only a small percentage of the time do they sell them to managers. For example, between 1996 and 2005, only 3.2% of all divestitures were unit MBOs. Nonetheless, the numbers are still significant. In 2004, the total dollar value of unit MBOs was $3.5 billion with the average size of a deal being $33.9 million. By M&A standards, these are comparatively smaller transactions.

KINDER MORGAN

In May 2006 the upper management of pipeline company Kinder Morgan, led by Richard Kinder, announced a $13.5 billion buyout. At that time this deal was the largest management buyout in history. Management proposed to contribute just under $3 billion of the total acquisition price. This equity contribution was augmented by a $4.5 billion investment by a group of private-equity investors led by Goldman Sachs Capital Partners and the Carlyle Group. The buyers planned to assume over $14.5 billion in debt, giving the deal an enterprise value of over $22 billion. Kinder Morgan was formed in late 1996 by a collection of assets that were disposed of by Enron for approximately $40 million. It is ironic that these assets rose markedly in value while Enron collapsed. The increase in the company's value is principally due to its successful acquisition program, initiated in 1999.

The diverging fates of Kinder Morgan and Enron were partly attributable to the strategies the two companies pursued. While Enron was a pipeline company, it became a risky energy-trading enterprise. Kinder Morgan, a Houston-based company founded in 1927 as K N Energy, conversely stayed in the pipeline business and steadily grew within this industry. With its acquisitions, it became an increasingly larger player in the less risky segment of the industry. Its steady performance also lowered its risk profile, which enabled management to attract private equity investors.

  CONFLICTS OF INTEREST IN MANAGEMENT BUYOUTS

A clear conflict of interest may exist in an MBO. Managers are responsible for running the corporation to maximize the value of stockholders' investment and provide them with the highest return possible. These same managers take on a very different role when they are required to present an offer to stockholders to buy the company. We have seen that this was the case when the management of RJR Nabisco presented an offer to stockholders to take Nabisco private in an MBO. This offer was quickly superseded by a competing offer from KKR as well as other responding offers from management.[5] If management truly was attempting to maximize the value of stockholders' investments, why did it choose to advocate an offer that it knew was clearly not in the stockholders' best interests? Many researchers believe that managers cannot serve in this dual, and sometimes conflicting, role as agent for both the buyer and the seller.

Another concern and potential conflict involves "earnings management" prior to an MBO. Managers who are interested in buying the company from the shareholders could have an incentive to take steps to lower reported profitability so as to pay less for the acquisition. Indeed, in their analysis of 175 management buyouts over the period 1981–1988, Perry and Williams found evidence that discretionary accruals were manipulated in the predicted direction in the year prior to the public announcement of the MBO.[6] Perry and Williams developed a control sample wherein matched firms for each bought-out company were selected. Accruals such as increases in depreciation expenses or decreases in noncash working capital were found to be associated with reduction in income in the MBO group. These results give us cause for concern and extra vigilance.

One proposed solution to these conflicts is neutralized voting, whereby the proponents of a deal do not participate in the approval process. If the proponents are stockholders, their votes would not be included in the approval process. They may have to participate in the voting process because under some state laws a quorum may not be possible without their participation if they hold a certain number of shares.[7] The appointment of an independent financial advisor to render a fairness opinion is a common second step in this process, which is meant to help reduce the conflicts of interest. Even if these precautionary measures are adopted, certain practical considerations may limit their effectiveness. Although those members of the board of directors who may profit from the LBO may not vote for its approval, other members of the board may have a close relationship to them and consider themselves obligated to support the deal. Lawsuits by stockholders suing directors for breach of fiduciary duty have placed limits on this tendency. Fairness opinions put forward by investment bankers who have done much business with management or who may have a financial interest in the deal may be of questionable value.

Although these steps are an important attempt to try to reduce some of the conflicts inherent in the MBO process, they do not address the issue of the manager being both the buyer's and the seller's agent. One solution that has been proposed is to have mandated auctions of corporations presented with an MBO.[8]

---

[5] Bryan Burrough and John Helyar, *Barbarians at the Gate: The Fall of RJR Nabisco* (New York: Harper & Row, 1990).

[6] Susan E. Perry and Thomas H. Williams, "Earnings Management Preceding Management Buyout Offers," *Journal of Accounting and Economics* 18 (1994): 157–179.

[7] Arthur M. Borden, *Going Private* (New York: Law Journal Seminar Press, 1987), 1–6.

[8] Louis Lowenstein, *What's Wrong with Wall Street?* (Reading, MA: Addison-Wesley, 1987), 184.

U.S. COURTS' POSITION ON LEVERAGED BUYOUT CONFLICTS

According to current case law, directors are not allowed to favor their own bid over another bid once the bidding process has begun. The prohibition on an unfair bidding process was set forth by a number of important court decisions. In *Revlon, Inc. v. MacAndrews & Forbes Holdings, Inc.*, the Delaware Supreme Court ruled that Revlon's directors breached their fiduciary duty in granting a lockup option to white knight Forstmann Little & Co.[9] The court ruled that this constituted an unfair bidding process that favored Forstmann Little & Co. over hostile bidder Pantry Pride.

In *Hanson Trust PLC v. SCM Corporation*, the Second Circuit Court took a similar position on the use of lockup options to favor an LBO by Merrill Lynch instead of a hostile bid by Hanson Trust PLC.[10] Hanson Trust had initially made a tender offer for SCM at $60 per share. In response to Merrill Lynch's LBO offer at $70 per share, Hanson Trust upped its bid to $72. The court ruled that SCM gave preferential treatment to Merrill Lynch by granting lockup options on two SCM divisions to Merrill Lynch.

In *Edelman v. Fruehauf*, the circuit court concluded that the board of directors had decided to make a deal with management and did not properly consider other bids, such as the all-cash tender offer by Asher Edelman.[11] The court held that the Fruehauf board of directors did not conduct a fair auction for the company.[12] Although the prior decisions establish a precedent that an auction for a firm must be conducted fairly, the courts stop short of spelling out the rules for conducting or ending the bidding process. These decisions fall within the purview of the business judgment rule. The law is also unclear regarding when or even if an auction is required. The formation of an independent directors' committee may facilitate the auction process.[13] This process is often used when management has proposed a buyout. When faced with a management proposal to take the firm private, the board of directors will usually respond by creating a special committee of independent, nonmanagement directors to ensure that shareholders receive fair, if not maximal, value for their investment. The committee may then decide to have its own valuation formulated, hire independent counsel, and conduct an auction.

Postbuyout Managerial Ownership

Even when management, as opposed to an outside group, is the buyer of a business unit, other equity is provided by outsiders, so management may not be in control of the postbuyout business. It depends on how much equity capital is needed and how much capital the managers have and are willing to invest in the deal. Using a sample of 76 management buyouts over the period of 1980–1986, Kaplan compared the median prebuyout

---

[9] *Revlon, Inc. v. MacAndrews & Forbes Holdings, Inc.*, 506 A.2d. 173 (Del. Sup. 1986).

[10] *Hanson Trust PLC v. SCM Corporation*, 781 F.2d 264 (2d Cir. 1986).

[11] *Edelman v. Fruehauf*, 798 F.2d 882, 886–87 (6th Cir. 1986).

[12] Lawrence Lederman and Barry A. Bryer, "Representing a Public Company in a Leveraged Transaction," in Yakov Amihud, ed., *Leveraged Management Buyouts* (Homewood, IL: Dow Jones Irwin, 1989), 111–174.

[13] Joseph Grunfest, "Management Buyouts and Leveraged Buyouts: Are the Critics Right?" in Yakov Amihud, ed., *Leveraged Management Buyouts* (Homewood, IL: Dow Jones Irwin, 1989), 241–261.

and postbuyout share ownership percentages of the CEOs and all management.[14] He found these percentages rose from 1.4% and 5.9% to 6.4% and 22.6%, respectively. Management ownership more than tripled after the buyout. Theoretically, given their much higher ownership interests, the managers should be better motivated to ensure that the company moves closer to profit-maximizing efficiency levels.

Going-Private Premiums and P/Es Offered

Table 8.3 and Figure 8.6 compare the median premiums for going-private deals and M&As. A couple of trends are immediately apparent. We see that premiums for both going-private deals and M&As vary over time. For going-private deals, premiums tend to be higher in merger waves than in periods of lower deal volume, whereas M&A premiums have tended to remain stable and have even risen somewhat over time. We also see in the 1980s and 1990s average premium for a going-private transaction was significantly lower than a merger or acquisition. This changed when we got into the 2000s; during those years the premiums were comparable.

TABLE 8.3 Going Private and M&A Premiums in the United States (1984–2014)

	Going Private (%)	M&A (%)
1980s	27.6	30.5
1990s	23.8	31.3
2000–2009	32.8	31.9
2010–2014	31.6	33.6
Total	28.7	31.7

Source: Mergerstat Review, 1992, 1998, and 2015.

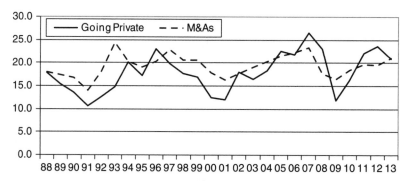

FIGURE 8.6 Going-Private and M&A Median P/Es Offered in the United States.
Source: Mergerstat Review, 1992, 1998, and 2014.

---

[14] Steven Kaplan, "The Effects of Management Buyouts on Operating Performance and Value," *Journal of Financial Economics* 24, no. 2 (1989): 217–254.

When we compare premiums for these recent years, it is useful to note that studies focusing on earlier years found higher premiums. For example, an early study by DeAngelo, DeAngelo, and Rice reviewed 72 MBOs during the period 1973–1980 and found relatively average premiums equal to 56%.[15] Other research on buyouts from the 1980s also showed relatively high premiums. For example, Kaplan and Stein found median premiums equal to 43%.[16] More recent research by Jerry Cao, focusing on a large sample of 5,305 M&As, of which 844 were LBOs, covering the years 1995–2007, has showed a diminishing pattern of declining premiums.[17] Cao's results showed LBO premiums were lower than M&As—consistent with the Mergerstat data discussed earlier. They are also consistent with research by Guo, Hotchkiss, and Song which found the average premium in 192 LBOs over the period 1990-2006 was 29.2%.[18]

In terms of P/Es offered, the values are similar for both going-private transactions and M&As. Buyers in going-private transactions have tended to pay lower premiums than buyers in M&As (Table 8.2). In addition, Figure 8.6 shows that in relation to earnings per share, the price that is paid in going-private deals often is less than in M&As.

Sources of LBO Gains

In Chapter 4 we reviewed some of the various reasons why companies pay premiums and incur some of the expenses of mergers. They pursue these deals for reasons such as enhancing their growth and realizing synergistic gains, as well as other reasons. Many of these reasons, such as synergies, may not be relevant as for LBOs and MBOs. In MBOs, for example, the company, at least initially, stays independent and does not have the opportunity to combine with another entity and realize synergistic gains. Then what is the source of the gains that allows the acquirer to pay a premium and also incur the financing charges associated with the increased leverage? Research points to several potential sources of these gains, which are discussed in the following sections.

Efficiency Gains

There are several areas in which efficiency gains can manifest themselves in an LBO. The first has to do with agency problems.[19] We discuss agency problems in several places in this text. They arise when the true owners of the company, shareholders, have to elect directors to oversee their interests.[20] These directors select managers who have a fiduciary responsibility to run the company in a manner that will maximize shareholder wealth. However, managers are human and they may pursue their own agendas

---

[15] Harry DeAngelo, Lina DeAngelo, and Eugene Rice, "Going Private: Minority Freezouts and Shareholder Wealth," *Journal of Law and Economics*, 27 no. 2 (October 1984): 367–402.

[16] Steven Kaplan and Jeremy Stein, "The Evolution of Buyout Pricing and Financial Structure in the 1980s," *Quarterly Journal of Economics*, 108, 1993, 313–357.

[17] Jerry X. Cao, "An Empirical Study of LBOs and Takeover Premium," Boston College Working Paper, 2008.

[18] Shourun Guo, Edith S. Hotchkiss, and Weihong Song, "Do Buyouts (Still) Create Value," *Journal of Finance* 66, no. 2 (April 2011): 479–517.

[19] Eugene Fama, "Agency Problems and the Theory of the Firm," *Journal of Political Economy* 7, no. 2 (April 1980): 288–307.

[20] Michael Jensen and William Meckling, "Theory of the Firm: Managerial Behavior, Agency Costs and Ownership Structure," *Journal of Financial Economics* 3, no. 4 (October 1976): 305–360.

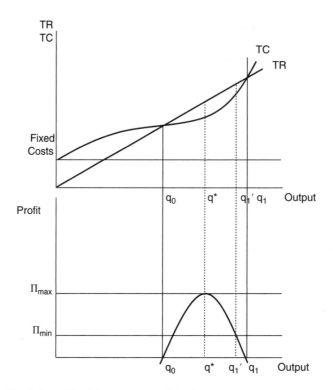

FIGURE 8.7 Total Cost, Total Revenues, and Profit Functions

and seek to further their own gains at shareholder expense. In doing so, they may not manage the company in a manner that will maximize profits. Managers may know that if they generate an acceptable return, such as π_{min} in Figure 8.7, it would be difficult for shareholders to mount a successful proxy fight and demand their ouster. π_{min} could be the average rate of return in the industry. Given that information on potential profitability is asymmetric and management is in a much better position to assess this than shareholders or even the board of directors, managers may know that π_{max} is possible.

This gap between potential profitability, π_{max} and π_{min}, is depicted in Figure 8.7. This is the theoretical gain from eliminating unnecessary costs and selling the output level where marginal revenue equals marginal costs. Managers may be following a different agenda, such as seeking to make the company larger than it optimally should be, so as to maximize their compensation, because it is well known that larger companies pay higher compensation to management.[21]

Boards try to install performance-based compensation systems to better align management and shareholder goals.[22] These are far from perfect. In the 1990s, more option- and stock-based incentives were touted as a partial solution to the managerial

---

[21] Dennis Mueller, "A Theory of Conglomerate Mergers," *Quarterly Journal of Economics* 83, no. 4 (November 1969): 643–659.

[22] Eugene Fama and Michael Jensen, "Separation of Ownership and Control," *Journal of Law and Economics* 26, no. 2 (June 1983): 301–325.

compensation problem. However, as a result of the various accounting scandals that occurred over the period 1998-2002, such as WorldCom, Enron, and Adelphia, critics cited such compensation schemes as one of the main problems. Managers pursued illegal means to try to raise stock prices, which in turn would provide them more stock-based compensation. In the wake of the subprime crisis it was clear that much of the oversized compensation of executives at large financial institutions that turned in abysmal performance included large equity grants. Clearly, installing stock-based incentives in the compensation package is not the total solution to eliminating the agency problem at public companies.

Managers who have a good sense of the difference between π_{max} and π_{min} may believe that this difference is sufficiently large to more than offset the costs of doing the deal and paying the service on the debt. This was certainly the case when Ross Johnson pursued his MBO proposal for RJR Nabisco. Unfortunately, his lowball offer so shocked his very friendly board that they looked to other offers, an auction ensued, and the company ended up being sold to KKR for a much higher price that eliminated many of the gains Johnson foresaw.

There is some evidence that efficiency gains really do occur in buyouts. For example, Harris, Siegel, and Wright examined productivity of 36,000 UK manufacturing plants.[23] They compared those that underwent an MBO with those that did not. They found clear increases in efficiency as reflected in output/labor ratios as well as other measures of factor productivity. They also noted that the MBO companies were less efficient than the non-MBO group prior to the buyouts. So these were companies where the potential for gain in the form of increased efficiencies was greater than for those that did not undergo a buyout.

TXU: HUGE BUYOUT BUST

The 2007 buyout of TXU Corporation was one of the largest of all time and it would become the biggest LBO bust of all time. The resulting bankruptcy case became the eighth largest in U.S. history. The buyout was a club deal involving such major private equity firms as KKR, TPG, and the buyout unit of Goldman Sachs. Other major private equity firms, such as the Apollo Group and Blackstone, purchased large amounts of Energy Future Holdings debt which was the name that the company assumed after the buyout.

There are several lessons in the TXU LBO failure. Firstly, it underscores how heady market conditions can blur the vision of seasoned dealmakers. Many deals looked good in 2006 and 2007, especially to those who can't see that what goes up too high often comes down. When the market is at a peak, many businesses look great. What these major firms should be "bringing to the table" is the ability to be able to predict how conditions would differ if there was a major change in

(continued)

---

[23] Richard Harris, Donald Siegel, and David Wright, "Assessing the Impact of Management Buyouts on Economic Efficiency: Plant-Level Evidence from the United Kingdom," *Review of Economics and Statistics* 87, no. 1 (February 2005): 148–153.

(*continued*)

the market. This was especially need in this case when the LBO candidate is in a commodity business.

This leads us to the second major flaw. Companies in volatile businesses, such as commodity oriented firms, tend not to make good LBO candidates. An LBO leaves the company with relatively high amounts of debt which require steady debt service. For TXU the company had almost $40 billion in debt. However, when natural gas prices fell in 2011, it lost almost $2 billion. The deal may have looked good when the economy was strong in 2007. However, debt-laden companies, which are susceptible to commodity prices swings, are not likely to survive a major downturn such as what we had in the Great Recession and the weak recovery that followed. It is amazing that such major private firms, which make a living doing buyouts, could not anticipate this. This was a criticism leveled at the industry in the late 1980s and early 1990s when it went by the name LBO firms. Many of these debt-laden LBOs of that era went bust, and the industry switched names to the more appealing private equity moniker. While name switching may have worked for marketing the industry, it did little for TXU and its investors.

Tax Benefits

When a company increases its degree of financial leverage—that is, increases the amount of debt relative to equity in its capital structure—it substitutes lower-cost debt capital for equity capital and its weighted average cost of capital usually declines. In general, even on a pretax basis, debt has lower costs than equity. That is, normally, equity requires the investors to bear greater risk, and investors require a higher rate of return before they assume this higher risk. In addition, interest payments on debt are tax-deductible, thereby lowering the after-tax cost of debt capital.

$$k_d^{at} = (1 - t)k_d^{bt} \qquad (8.1)$$

where:

k_d^{at} = after-tax cost of debt
t = the company's tax rate
k_d^{bt} = before-tax cost of debt

It is important to remember that when a company undergoes an LBO, the costs of both debt and equity capital generally increases. This is due to the fact that it takes on much more debt, which increases the risk profile of the company. It has more fixed obligations, which increases the probability that it may not be able to service such obligations as they come due. The market responds to this higher risk by requiring a greater risk premium for both debt and equity. Nonetheless, its overall costs of capital, especially after taking into account the tax deductibility of the interest payments, may be lower. This, then, is a benefit of doing the deal and provides some basis for paying a premium to the equity holders. The question is, how significant are these tax benefits?

The tax benefits from doing deals, and LBOs in particular, have changed over time as a function of new tax laws. Tax benefits put into law in 1981 allowed for aggressive accelerated depreciation. When this is combined with asset step-ups that are also allowed, they provide significant incentives to do leveraged deals. This helps explain some of the LBOs that took place in the fourth merger wave. However, the Tax Reform Act of 1986 eliminated many of these benefits.

A study by Kaplan attempted to quantify the tax benefits that post buyout firms enjoy.[24] He found that the interest deductions from the debt were almost 30% greater than the premium paid to the selling shareholders. The gains, however, mainly went to selling shareholders and not to the owners of the postbuyout company. "A comparison of the excess returns earned by pre buyout and post buyout investors to several measures of tax benefits is consistent with pre buyout shareholders receiving most of the potential tax benefits. The returns to post buyout investors are not related to the tax benefits created by the buyout. This is consistent with a market for corporate control that forces the buyout companies to pay public stockholders tax benefits that are ex-post predictable and obtainable by other bidders."[25]

Kaplan showed that the tax benefits of LBOs are largely predictable and are incorporated in the premium that pre-LBO stockholders receive. This implies that the post-LBO investors need to find other sources of value such as efficiency gains.

Cash Flow versus Asset-Based LBOs

As stated previously, LBOs are acquisitions that are financed primarily with debt. They are usually cash transactions in which the cash is borrowed by the acquiring firm. Much of the debt may be secured by the assets of the corporation being taken private. This section provides an overview of the LBO process. The financing of these deals is discussed in greater detail later in this chapter.

The target company's assets are often used to provide collateral for the debt that is going to be incurred to finance the acquisition. Thus, the collateral value of these assets needs to be assessed. This type of lending is often called *asset-based lending*. Firms with assets that have a high collateral value can more easily obtain such loans; thus, LBOs are often easier to conduct in capital-intensive industries—firms that usually have more assets that may be used as collateral than noncapital-intensive firms. It is not surprising, therefore, that Waite and Fridson found that LBO activity during the period they studied was more predominant in manufacturing than in nonmanufacturing industries.[26] Still, LBOs can also be done for firms that do not have an abundance of assets that may be used as collateral. Service industries are one example. They tend not to have as many physical assets with high-asset values that can be used as collateral for loans, but they may still be good LBO candidates if their cash flows are high enough. The high cash flows, as opposed to physical assets, provide the protection for lenders.

---

[24] Steven Kaplan, "Management Buyouts: Evidence on Taxes as a Source of Value," *Journal of Finance* 44, no. 3 (July 1989): 611–632.
[25] Steven Kaplan, "Management Buyouts," University of Chicago Working Paper no. 245, 44.
[26] Steven Waite and Martin Fridson, "The Credit Quality of Leveraged Buyouts," *High Performance* (New York: Morgan Stanley, 1989).

If the borrower defaults, however, the lenders may not have as many physical assets that can be sold in liquidation. Debt capital providers hope that the cash flows will be so reliable that they will never face a liquidation situation. They also are aware that even physical assets can be adversely affected by downturns of a company if they are industry- or even economy-wide downturns.

Cash-flow or unsecured LBOs, as they are sometimes called, tend to have a more long-term focus, with a maturity of 10 to 15 years. In contrast, secured or asset-based LBOs might have a financing maturity of only up to five years. Cash-flow LBOs allow firms that are not in capital-intensive industries to be LBO candidates. This is most important in the U.S. economy because the United States has become a more service-oriented economy. Many service industries, such as advertising, lack significant physical assets relative to their total revenue but have large cash flows.

Since cash-flow LBOs are generally considered riskier for lenders, they expect to receive a higher return for assuming the additional risk. This higher return may come from a higher interest rate as well as an *equity kicker*. This equity interest often comes in the form of warrants or direct shares in the target. The percentage of ownership may be as little as 10% or as high as 80% of the companies' shares. The percentage is higher when the lender perceives greater risk.

The fact that the loan is not collateralized does not mean that the lenders are not protected by the firm's assets. Unsecured lenders are entitled to receive the proceeds of the sale of the secured assets after full payment has been made to the secured lenders.

FINANCING FOR LEVERAGED BUYOUTS

Two general categories of debt are used in LBOs—secured and unsecured debt—and they are often used together. Secured debt, which is sometimes called *asset-based lending*, may contain two subcategories of debt: senior debt and intermediate-term debt. In some smaller buyouts these two categories are considered one. In larger deals there may be several layers of secured debt, which vary according to the term of the debt and the types of assets used as security. Unsecured debt, which is sometimes known as *subordinated debt* and *junior subordinated debt*, lacks the protection of secured debt, but generally carries a higher return to offset this additional risk. To the debt financing is added an equity investment. The percentage of the total financing that the equity component constitutes varies depending on market conditions, but it tends to be in the 20% to 40% range.

In an LBO the dealmaker, often called a sponsor, will work with providers of financing—investment banks. Investment banks will conduct due diligence on the proposed deal, and if confident it meets the criteria of the banks they work with, they will present the deal to them. The lead investment bank may conduct a presentation for the various prospective lenders wherein it shows its analysis and the reasons why lenders should feel secure providing capital to finance the deal. A similar *road show*-type process may be conducted to develop interest in an offering of high-yield bonds that may be part of the overall deal financing structure. Such road shows are often preceded by the distribution of a preliminary offering memorandum related to the bond offering.

Before this memorandum can become final, it will usually need SEC approval; otherwise, the bonds cannot be publicly offered.

If the banks agree to provide debt capital to the deal, they will often first provide a *commitment letter*, which sets forth the terms of the loans. Sometimes banks will hold some of the debt in their own portfolio while seeking commitments from other financing sources as they syndicate the rest of the debt.

Debt capital comes from two main sources. Banker lenders may provide revolving loans or amortizing term loans. These banks will include commercial banks, savings and loan associations, and finance companies. Longer-term debt commitments typically come from institutional investors, such as insurance companies, pension funds, and hedge funds. These dividing lines are not strictly defined, so we can see one group providing different types of capital in different deals (or even the same one).

Part of the debt capital may come from a bond issuance. This may require the investment bank to provide a *bridge loan* to close the time gap between when all the funds are needed to close a deal and when the bonds can be sold in the market.

LBO Debt Financing

There are two broad categories of LBO debt financing—senior debt and intermediate-term debt. The exact mix of the various sources of debt vary across deals but Table 8.4 shows a typical LBO structure.

Senior Debt

Senior debt consists of loans secured by liens on particular assets of the company. The collateral, which provides the downside risk protection required by lenders, includes physical assets, such as land, plants, and equipment. The term of this debt can be five years or more. Senior debt comes in various forms, which vary according to the nature of the target's business and the type of collateral it can provide.

Senior debt may constitute between 25% and 50% of the total financing of an LBO. The interest rate tends to be in the range of prime plus 2% to 3%. Typical sources of this secured financing are commercial and investment banks as well as other institutional investors, such as insurance companies, mutual funds, and finance companies. A typical

TABLE 8.4 LBO Capital Structure

Offering	Percentage of Transaction	Interest Rate	Sources
Senior debt	50%–60%	7%–10%	Commercial banks, credit companies, insurance companies
Subordinated debt	20%–30%	10%–20%	Public market (junk bonds), insurance companies, LBO/mezzanine funds
Equity	20%–30%	25%–40%	Management, LBO funds, subordinated debt holders, investment banks

term is between 5 and 10 years. While bank debt tends to be the least costly form of debt, it often comes with *maintenance covenants*, which impose financial restrictions on the target over the life of the loan.

Bank debt is usually priced above some variable base market rate, such as LIBOR or the prime rate. How much higher depends on the credit worthiness of the borrower.

Other Senior Debt Revolving Credit

In an LBO the company will typically have access to revolving credit, which may be secured by short-term assets, such as inventory and accounts receivable. The company may pay a variable that is pegged to some base rate, such as the prime rate in the prime plus a certain percentage. Revolving credit can be repaid but also "reborrowed" as agreed upon with the lender. This form of credit is often used to deal with seasonal credit needs, and how relevant it is depends on the nature of the business.

The sponsor may arrange a revolving credit line with a bank, which, in turn, may syndicate it with other banks. Such credit lines usually require the borrower to pay a commitment fee for access to the credit even if it is unused. If it is used, then the borrower pays the interest rate as well. The revolving credit line is usually secured by some specific assets and often has a term such as five years.

Asset-Based Lending (ABL)

If the business being acquired in the LBO has a high volume of current assets, such as inventories or receivables, the sponsor may be able to secure an ABL debt facility, which is secured by the relevant current assets. Usually this security provides a first lien on the current assets, and maybe if other noncurrent assets are used, the lien may be a second one. Lending with such facilities is a function of the allowable "borrowing base," which may define which assets are eligible. For example, older receivables or out-of-date inventories might not be eligible. In addition, the lending percentage will usually be less than the borrowing base to allow some protection cushion for the lender. ABL lending facilities are usually five years in length.

Term Loans

Term loans are another form of secured credit. They can be investment grade or non-investment grade. The latter group is referred to as *leveraged loans*. Unlike a revolving loan facility, which can be paid down but also reborrowed, term loans usually have a fixed amortization schedule and are to be paid over a set loan period. Once payments are made, they cannot be reborrowed.

An LBO may feature different forms of term loans with some having more rapid repayment of the principal than others. Those that have more rapid repayment, sometimes called Term A loans, will tend to have lower interest rates (all other things constant) than those that have more minimal principal repayment obligations—sometimes called Term B loans. Term B loans are often marketed to institutional investors and tend to be larger than Term A debt.

Subordinated Debt

The extent to which a debt is subordinated is set forth in subordination provisions of the credit agreement or bond indenture contract. Subordination refers to the fact that more senior creditors need to have their obligations satisfied before payment can be made to the subordinated creditors.

Subordinated debt, sometimes also referred to as intermediate-term debt, is usually subordinate to senior debt. The term is usually longer than the senior debt and may range between 6 to 10 years. Given that it is subordinate to the senior debt, it is riskier for the lenders so they charge a higher rate, which may be in the prime plus 4% to 7% range. A variety of investors may provide such financing, including pension funds, insurance companies, and finance companies, as well as mutual funds and hedge funds. The terms tend to vary and may include some equity-linked features, such as warrants.

High-Yield Bonds

A major source of subordinated debt is high-yield or junk bonds. These are bonds that have a rating of BB or worse from Standard & Poors (Ba from Moodys). We devote a chapter to junk bonds, so we will discuss them only in a limited way in this chapter.

High-yield bonds used in LBOs tend to have maturities of between 7 and 10 years. The coupon rate of high-yield bonds is usually pegged to Treasuries and includes an additional risk premium that is a function of the credit worthiness of the issuer.

High-yield bonds may include call protections, which may limit the ability of the issuer to prepay the debt. If the issuer does so, it may have to pay a *call premium*, which usually declines over the life of the bond. The specific amount of the premium is usually set forth in *call schedules* included in the indenture contract.

These bonds may feature *protective covenants*; however, they tend to be less restrictive than the covenants included in bank debt agreements. These covenants usually require that the borrowers maintain a certain financial condition over the life of the loan. While bank debt protective covenants tend to be more restrictive than high-yield bond covenants, an exception is *covenant-lite* bank debt in the *leveraged loan market*. These covenants are more like high-yield bond covenants than typical bank debt.

Bridge Loans

In order for an LBO to close, the sponsor needs to have all of the necessary funds available at the time of the closing. Sometimes the debt financing process can be a little fluid and uncertain, but the sponsor and the seller both need to know the funds will be there at closing. To alleviate this uncertainty, the sponsor's investment bank might agree to provide a bridge loan if necessary to eliminate this uncertainty. The investment bank receives a commitment for making this capital available if needed. Usually both parties, the sponsor and the investment bank, hope that it will never be needed.

Vertical Strips

It is not unusual for investors to provide financing through more than one of the foregoing categories. Although some institutional investors, such as insurance companies, have tended to be unsecured investors, they often participate in more than one type of LBO financing. This type of financing is sometimes referred to as *vertical strips*. In a vertical strip, investors may participate in several layers of financing within the same deal. For example, they may hold some secured debt and more than one form of unsecured debt as well as some equity.

Standard Debt Paydown Strategy

As heralded by its proponents, an LBO involves a company taking on a substantial amount of debt, but that debt should get paid down over a period such as five years, using cash flows from operations and possibly asset sales (see Figure 8.8). For example, Kaplan found that companies taken private in management buyouts paid down roughly 25% of their debt in the first two years after the deal.[27]

Standard Debt Paydown with Increased Enterprise Value

In Chapter 15 we discuss the computation of enterprise value. For now we will simply say it is the value of the debt and the equity of the target. Figure 8.8 basically assumed that there was no increase in enterprise value over the five-year period prior to exit from the investment. However, deal sponsors seek to also gain from increasing the value of the target and perhaps receiving a higher multiple as of the exit. Such a situation is depicted in Figure 8.9. For simplicity's sake we assume that the increase in equity is realized only in year five, although the increase in value would reasonably be expected to have risen over the prior years, even though it is only in the year of the exit that it is specifically known.

Leveraged Buyout Financial Analysis

The various participants in a leveraged buyout have to conduct their own financial analysis. This includes providers of debt financing as well as the sponsor. Fortunately, various

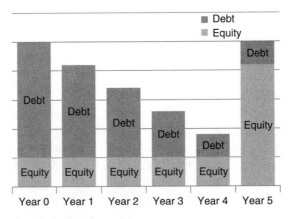

FIGURE 8.8 Standard Debt Paydown Strategy

---

[27] Steven Kaplan, "Management Buyouts: Evidence on Taxes as a Source of Value," *Journal of Finance* 41 (1989): 611–632.

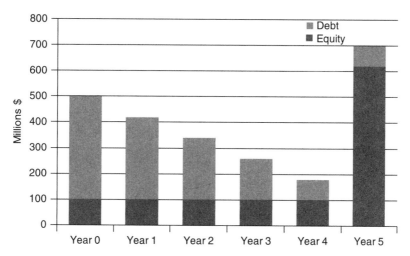

FIGURE 8.9 Standard Debt Paydown with Increase in Enterprise Value

Excel spreadsheet models exist so one does not need to "reinvent the wheel." In addition, Rosenbaum and Pearl's second edition of *Investment Banking* features very detailed M&A spreadsheet models, including ones for an LBO.[28] Thus, we will discuss only some basic concepts here.

Internal Rate of Return on LBOs

LBO dealmakers look to a commonly cited measure of financial performance that is a mainstay in the capital budgeting section of most financial analysis books and courses—internal rate of return. A version of the relevant relationship is shown in Equation 8.2. The left side of the equation features the equity investment, and the right side features various numerators which reflect the net cash flows generated by the target companies. These cash flows may reflect additional equity investments (negative amounts) and/or dividends received (positive amounts). In the example we assume that the sponsor will be able to exit the investment and hopefully sell the target at a higher equity value that what it paid for it.

Given that the left-hand side outlay is known (and negative) and the cash flows set forth in the numerators are projected, we have one unknown, r, the internal rate of return. It is the rate that when solved for will bring about the equality shown in the equation. Fortunately, we can use the built-in IRR function in Excel to solve for this rate.

$$CF_0 = \frac{CF_1}{(1+r)} + \frac{CF_2}{(1+r)^2} + \dots + \frac{CF_5}{(1+r)^5} \tag{8.2}$$

---

[28] Joshua Rosenbaum, Joshua Pearl, Joseph R. Perella, and Joshua Harris. *Investment Banking: Valuation, Leveraged Buyouts, and Mergers & Acquisitions.* Second edition, University edition. (Hoboken, N.J.: John Wiley & Sons), 2013.

CF_0 = equity investment

$CF_1 \ldots CF_4$ = annual cash flows that reflect any additional equity investments but also any dividends paid out

CF_5 = a combination of any additional equity, dividends, but mainly the exit proceeds

r = internal rate of return

An example showing these calculations is depicted next. Notice the relatively large value of $1.4 billion in year 5, which reflects the exit proceeds, which are well in excess of the equity investment in year 0 of $600 million. When we calculate IRR, we get 23%. As a rule of thumb LBO sponsors seek to get an IRR that is greater than 20%.

Internal Rate of Return Analysis of an LBO (mil $)

Year	0	1	2	3	4	5
Cash flows	−600	0	40	60	80	1,400
IRR		23.0%				

Desirable Characteristics of Secured Leveraged Buyout Candidates

There are certain characteristics that lenders look for in a prospective LBO candidate. Some of the more commonly cited features are discussed here.

- *Stable cash flows.* One of the most important characteristics of LBO candidates is the existence of regular cash flows as determined by examining the pattern of historical cash flows for the company. The more erratic the historical cash flows, the greater the perceived risk in the deal. Even in cases in which the average cash flows exceed the loan payments by a comfortable margin, the existence of high variability may worry a lender. Dependable cash flows alone are not sufficient to guarantee the success of an LBO.

  Example: Southland Corp. The financial difficulties of the Southland Corporation after its $4.9 billion buyout in 1987 is a classic example. The founders of the company, the Thompson family, took the company private out of concerns about a hostile takeover. The company's main business was the cash cow 7–Eleven convenience chain. Southland's problems emerged when some of the 7–Eleven cash flows were directed to noncore real estate ventures instead of paying off the buyout debt. Even with its sizable cash flows, the company could not service its high debt load and fell into bankruptcy where it was "rescued" by its Japanese franchisee Seven and I Holdings Corp.

- *Analyzing historical cash flows.* Although historical cash flows are used to project future cash flows, the past may be an imperfect guide to the future. Market conditions change, and the future business environment may be less favorable than what the company's historical data reflect. The lenders must make a judgment as to whether the past will be a reliable indicator of what the future will hold. Lenders and borrowers usually construct cash flow projections based on restrictive budgets and new cost structures. Such budget planning takes place for both secured and unsecured LBOs, but it is even more critical for cash flow LBOs. These budgets may include lower research and development expenditures and labor costs. The target attempts to find areas where costs may be cut—at least temporarily. These cost savings may be used to meet the loan payments on the LBO debt. The importance of cash flows to LBOs was underscored by a study by Lehn and Poulsen.[29] They showed that buyout premiums were positively related to the firm's free cash flow. That is, the market is willing to pay higher premiums for greater cash flow protection.

- *Stable and experienced management.* Stability is often judged by the length of time management is in place. Lenders feel more secure when management is experienced; that is, if management has been with the firm for a reasonable period of time, it may imply that there is a greater likelihood that management will stay on after the deal is completed. Creditors often judge the ability of management to handle an LBO by the cash flows that were generated by the firms they managed in the past. If their prior management experience was with firms that had significant liquidity problems, lenders will be much more cautious about participating in the buyout.

- *Room for significant cost reductions.* Assuming additional debt to finance an LBO usually imposes additional financial pressures on the target, these pressures may be alleviated somewhat if the target can significantly cut costs in some areas, such as fewer employees, reduced capital expenditures, elimination of redundant facilities, and tighter controls on operating expenses. Lichtenberg and Siegel showed that LBO employee cutbacks were concentrated at the administrative levels of employment, with an average administrative workforce reduction of 16%, while there tended to be minimal cutbacks at the manufacturing level.[30]

- *Equity interest of owners.* The collateral value of assets provides downside risk protection to lenders. The equity investment of the managers or buyers and outside parties also acts as a cushion to protect lenders. The greater the equity cushion, the more likely secured lenders will not have to liquidate the assets. The greater the managers' equity investment, the more likely they will stay with the firm if the going gets tough. Leveraged buyout lenders in the 1990s demanded a much greater equity cushion than they did for the heavy debt deals they financed in the mid-1980s. As conditions improved in the 2000s, however, lending terms became more liberal.

- *Separable, noncore businesses.* If the LBO candidate owns noncore businesses that can be sold off to quickly pay down a significant part of the firm's post-LBO debt, the deal may be easier to finance. This may be important for both secured and unsecured LBOs. Problems may occur when debt is incurred based on an unrealistic sales price for noncore divisions. The inability to sell components of the firm on a timely basis, at

---

[29] Kenneth Lehn and Annette Poulsen, "Free Cash Flow and Stockholder Gains in Going Private Transactions," *Journal of Finance* 44, no. 3 (July 1989): 771–778.

[30] Frank Lichtenberg and Donald Siegel, "The Effects of Takeovers on Employment and Wages of Central Office and Other Personnel," *Journal of Law and Economics* 33, no. 2 (October 1990): 383–408.

prices similar to those expected by investment bankers, was one of the main factors that caused the bankruptcy of the Campeau Corporation in 1989. Deals that are dependent on the large-scale sell-off of most of the firm's businesses are referred to as *breakup LBOs*.

Types of LBO Risk

LBOs present a variety of risk. The risk of an LBO may be broken down into two main categories: business risk and interest rate risk.

Business risk refers to the risk that the firm going private will not generate sufficient earnings to meet the interest payments and other current obligations of the firm. This risk category takes into account factors such as cyclical downturns in the economy and competitive factors within the industry, such as greater price and nonprice competition. Firms that have very cyclical sales or companies that are in very competitive industries tend not to be good LBO candidates.

Interest rate risk is the risk that interest rates will rise, thus increasing the firm's current obligations. This is important to firms that have more variable rate debt. Interest rate increases could force a firm into bankruptcy even when it experienced greater than anticipated demand and held nonfinancial costs within reasonable bounds. The level of interest rates at the time of the LBO may be a guide to the probability that rates will rise in the future. For example, if interest rates are low at the time of the buyout, interest rate increases may be more likely than if interest rates are at peak levels.

RETURNS TO STOCKHOLDERS FROM LBOS

One well known early study was conducted by DeAngelo, DeAngelo, and Rice analyzed the gains to both stockholders and management from MBOs of 72 companies that proposed to go private between 1973 and 1980.[31] We have already noted that the premiums paid for their sample was 56%, which was higher than the premium data we have shown for more recent years. They concluded that managers are willing to offer a premium. In the 2000s, however, private equity firms came to dominate the buyout market, and they are known to be more careful buyers.

Their research found that an average change in shareholder wealth around the announcement of the deal was 22%. Over a longer time period around the announcement, the total shareholder wealth change was approximately 30%. Consistent with the results of the research for M&As generally, the announcement of the bid being withdrawn caused shareholder wealth to decline by 9%.

A study by Travlos and Cornett shows a statistically significant negative correlation between abnormal returns to shareholders and the P/E ratio of the firm relative to

---

[31] Harry DeAngelo, Linda DeAngelo, and Eugene Rice, "Going Private: Minority Freezeouts and Stockholder Wealth," *Journal of Law and Economics* 27, no. 2 (October 1984): 367–402. Similar results are found in Lourentius Marais, Katherine Schipper, and Abbie Smith, "Wealth Effects of Going Private on Senior Securities," *Journal of Financial Economics* 23, no. 1 (June 1989): 155–191.

the industry.[32] This implies that the lower the P/E ratio, compared with similar firms, the greater probability that the firm is poorly managed. Travlos and Cornett interpret the low P/E ratios as reflecting greater room for improvement through changes such as the reduction of agency costs. Some of these efficiency gains may then be realized by going private. These gains become the source of the buyout premium.

Modern LBOs Compared to Early LBOs

The collapse of many of the LBOs of the fourth merger wave led dealmakers to be more conservative in creating the financial structures of their deals. This was confirmed by the aforementioned study of 192 buyouts over the years 1990–2006 by Guo, Hotchkiss and Song. They found that, consistent with some of the findings we have already discussed, modern deals were more conservatively priced and less levered than the deals of the fourth merger wave. They also found median and risk-adjusted returns to pre- (post-) buyout capital are 72.5% (40.9%).[33] They defined the returns to capital as follows:

$$\text{Nominal Return to Capital} = \frac{\sum \text{Interim Payments to Capital} + \text{Terminal Value}}{\text{Capital}} - 1$$

$$(8.3)$$

Where the interim payments are the post-buyout payments made to the debt and equity capital providers. The terminal value is the amount received at the outcome date. Capital refers to the value of the equity and debt either prior to the buyout, which is used to compute returns to pre-buyout capital, as well as the butout price which is used to compute returns to post-buyout capital.

Guo et al also found that the LBOs in their sample showed operating performance at least equal to, and sometime higher, than a benchmark group of firms they selected.

RETURNS TO STOCKHOLDERS FROM *DIVISIONAL* BUYOUTS

As we have already noted, MBOs are deals where a management group buys a division from the parent company. Many of these transactions have been criticized for not being "arm's-length" deals. Managers of the parent company are often accused of giving preferential treatment to a management bid. The parent company may forsake the auction process and accept management's offer without soliciting other higher offers. One way to see if these transactions are truly in shareholders' interests would be to look at their shareholder wealth effects.

In 1989, Hite and Vetsuypens conducted a study designed to show whether divisional buyouts had adverse effects on the wealth of parent stockholders.[34]

[32] Nicholas G. Travlos and M. M. Cornett, "Going Private Buyouts and Determinants of Shareholder Returns," *Journal of Accounting, Auditing and Finance* 8, no. 1 (Winter 1993): 1–25.

[33] Shourun Guo, Edith S. Hotchkiss, and Weihong Song, "Do Buyouts (Still) Create Value," *Journal of Finance* 66, no. 2, (2011): 479–517.

[34] Galen L. Hite and Michael R. Vetsuypens, "Management Buyouts of Divisions and Stockholder Wealth," *Journal of Finance* 44, no. 4 (September 1989): 953–970.

Many researchers believe that divisional buyouts may present opportunities for efficiency-related gains as the division becomes removed from the parent company's layers of bureaucracy. This may be a source of value to the managers of the buying group but does not negate the often-cited possibility that a fair price, such as that which might be derived from an auction, was not paid for the division.

Hite and Vetsuypens failed to find any evidence of a reduction in shareholder wealth following divisional buyouts by management. Their results show small, but statistically significant, wealth gains for a two-day period surrounding the buyout announcement. They interpret these results as indicating that division buyouts result in a more efficient allocation of assets. The existence of small wealth gains indicates that shareholders in the parent company shared in some of these gains.

Post-LBO Firm Performance

A number of studies showed substantial operating performance improvements after management buyouts that occurred in the 1980s. Some of the early research on this issue included Kaplan as well as Lichtenberg and Siegel studies which both found improvements in financial performance following the management buyouts.[35] Later research also presented similar findings. For example, Guo, Hotchkiss, and Song analyzed a sample of 192 leveraged buyouts that were completed during the period 1990–2006.[36] Not only did they find that the deals were less levered than their 1980s predecessors, but also they also found that operating performance of the firms that were taken private was at least as good, and sometimes better, than matched industry companies. They attribute the performance gains to the large positive returns these deals yielded their investors. For example, Gao et al. found an 11% increase in EBITDA/sales relative to comparable firms.

The positive results on LBO performance were not just restricted to U.S. LBOs. Various research studies have arrived at similar findings for LBOs in different European countries such as Great Britain, France, and Sweden.

The impressive improvements in returns found by researchers such as Gao et al. raised questions in the minds of some researchers who wondered whether the fact that the companies that were studied were the only ones that had publicly available financial statements made them a biased sample. The companies that have publicly available financial statements could have sold public debt or undergone a subsequent transaction, such as an IPO, which required disclosure of such data.

Cohn, Mills, and Towery analyzed a subsample of 71 companies that underwent an LBO that had both tax returns and financial statements available to be studied. Consistent with the prior research, they found that these firms did indeed show substantial improvements in financial performance. For example, they found a 9% improvement in mean return on sales over a two-year period after the buyouts.

Cohn et al. then focused on a broader sample of 317 companies taken private in an LBO, including the 71 that had both tax return and financial statements available,

---

[35] Kaplan, "Effects of Management Buyouts," and Frank Lichtenberg and Donald Siegel, "The Effects of Takeovers on Employment and Wages of Central Office and Other Personnel," Columbia Graduate School Working Paper #FB-89-05, 1989.

[36] Shourun Guo, Edith S. Hotchkiss, and Weihong Song, "Do Buyouts (Still) Create Value," *Journal of Finance* 66, no. 2 (April 2011): 479–517.

and others that had on only tax return data available.[37] They found little evidence that there are any meaningful performance improvements for this larger sample. This implies that those companies that had publicly available financial statements may have been the ones that performed the best, which allowed them to issue public debt or even go public again. Others may not have performed as well and may not have been able to pursue such transactions.

The conclusion of the Cohn et al. research is that the positive view of LBOs that has prevailed in the world of M&A research for many years may have been overly sanguine. LBOs may enrich dealmakers and private equity investors and managers of these private equity firms, but they may not have any positive effect on the companies themselves.

Employment Effects

One of the goals of LBO dealmakers, such as private equity buyers, is to lower the costs of the acquired entity, which usually has to incur significantly higher debt service costs after the deal. Such cost reduction strategies could include reductions in employment levels. Various early studies have examined this issue and found that while employment levels do not necessarily decline after an LBO, they do not rise as much as other companies in the same industry.[38] A recent large sample study conducted by Davis et al. has shed considerable light on this issue. They analyzed 3,200 target companies over the period 1980–2005.[39] They found a somewhat small 1% decline in employment levels over a two-year period following the buyout. However, their analysis delved deeper into the natural process of job creation and destruction at bought-out companies. The firms could reduce employment levels at some establishments they own that they decide are not operating efficiently. They also may open new establishments, and with these openings new workers are hired by the bought-out companies. Thus the net employment effects they found naturally include layoffs but also new hiring. Together this process resulted in only a 1% overall decline in employment levels. However, they did find that the average earnings per workers at continuing establishments declined 2.4% over the two-year postbuyout period. Buyouts may bring about some declines in worker earnings as the dealmakers seek to lower costs, but the net effect on the total number of workers may feature a somewhat modest decline.

Efficiency Gains and Unsuccessful Buyouts

We have discussed how certain researchers have documented various efficiency gains associated with buyouts. They point to the buyout process and the changes in the companies that are normally associated with the buyouts as being the source of the gains.

[37] Jonathan B. Cohn, Lillian F. Mills and Erin M. Towery, "The Evolution of Capital Structure and Operating Performance After Leveraged Buyouts: Evidence from U.S. Corporate Tax Returns," *Journal of Financial Economics* *111*, no. 2, (2014): 469–494.
[38] Kaplan, "Effects of Management Buyouts," and Frank Lichtenberg and Donald Siegel, "The Effects of Leveraged Buyouts on Productivity and Related Aspects of Firm Behavior," *Journal of Financial Economics* 27, no. 1 (1990): 165–194.
[39] Steven Davis, John Haltiwanger, Kyle Handley, Ron Jarmin, Josh Lerner, and Javier Miranda, "Private Equity Jobs and Productivity," NBER Working Paper 19458, September 2013.

Another way to look at this issue would be to compare companies that successfully completed their buyouts with those that did not. Do the ones that did not get to complete their buyouts experience similar efficiency gains? Ofek analyzed a sample of 120 unsuccessful management buyouts over the period 1983–1988.[40] Consistent with the efficiency-enhancing theory of buyouts, he found that the unsuccessful group did not experience efficiency gains. He also found higher management turnover, underscoring the board's displeasure with their lack of success.

Reverse LBOs

A reverse LBO occurs when a company goes private in an LBO only to be taken public again at a later date. This may be done if the buyers who take the company private believe that it is undervalued, perhaps because of poor management. They may buy the firm and institute various changes, such as replacing senior management and other forms of restructuring. If the new management converts the company into a more profitable private enterprise, it may be able to go through the initial public-offer process again.

The opportunity to conduct a successful reverse LBO is greater when the going-private transaction takes place when the stock market is down and the public offering occurs in a bull market.[41] This may make the assets of the LBO candidate undervalued in a poor market and possibly overvalued in the bull market. This reasoning, however, implies that the seller is somewhat naive and does not realize the impact of the short-term market fluctuation.

Reverse LBO Research

Muscarella and Vetsuypens reviewed 72 reverse LBOs that went public since 1983 and underwent a buyout.[42] Their study presents a favorable picture of the postbuyout performance of these firms. They found that the ownership structure tended to be concentrated, with management retaining a substantial fraction of the equity. Using traditional accounting measures of performance and financial condition, they found improvements in profitability that were the result of cost reductions as opposed to increased revenues. These results were more dramatic for divisional LBOs than for full firm buyouts. Reductions in capital expenditures were one of the more significant sources of efficiency gains, but reduction in staffing was not. Even though the firms increased their leverage to finance the buyout, management took steps to reduce debt after the buyout. These results imply that the postbuyout firms are in better condition than their prebuyout predecessors. It is not surprising, therefore, that shareholders pay more when the firms go public for the second time compared with the price the company sold for in the LBO. One question arises, however: If the management group is essentially the same before and after the buyout, why did management not enact these increased efficiencies as part of the fiduciary responsibilities for shareholders when

---

[40] Eli Ofek, "Efficiency Gains in Unsuccessful Management Buyouts," *Journal of Finance* 49, no. 2 (June 1994): 637–654.

[41] Leslie Wayne, "Reverse LBOs Bring Riches," *New York Times*, April 23, 1987, D1.

[42] Chris J. Muscarella and Michael R. Vetsuypens, "Efficiency and Organizational Structure: A Study of Reverse LBOs," *Journal of Finance* 45, no. 5 (December 1990): 1389–1414.

they were running the prebuyout company? This criticism may be less relevant for divisional buyouts, in which management may be able to take broader actions because they are not part of a larger bureaucratic structure of a parent company. It is also less relevant for many of the private equity–conducted buyouts as the new private equity owners seek to make whatever changes are necessary, including managerial changes, to increase the value of their investment and resell the acquisition.

Holthausen and Larcker analyzed the postbuyout accounting and stock-price performance of 90 companies that engaged in reverse LBOs from 1983 to 1988.[43] They found that these companies outperformed their industries over the four years following the initial public offering. In addition, they noted that reverse LBOs also increased capital expenditures and working capital levels following the offering. They also noted that when the ownership structure became less concentrated in the hand of managers, firm performance declined.

A much larger sample of 526 reverse LBOs over the period 1981–2003 was analyzed by Cao and Lerner.[44] They compared the performance of reverse LBOs over three to five years with that of initial public offerings (IPOs). They found that reverse LBOs performed as well as the market overall and comparable to other IPOs. However, "quick flips," where a private equity firm sells the investment after holding it for a short period such as one year, tended to underperform.

LBO Regulation and Disclosure: SEC Rule 13e-3

SEC Rule 13e-3, which attempts to regulate some of the problems of management self-dealing associated with going private, is an amendment to the Securities Exchange Act of 1934. The rule governs repurchases in going-private transactions, and it applies to share repurchases that result in fewer than 300 shareholders or when the previously public company would no longer be listed on public stock exchanges or would no longer be quoted in an interdealer quotation system. The rule requires that the firm going private file a Schedule TO. In Chapter 3 we have already discussed the items that are required to be revealed in this filing. With respect to MBOs, however, the filing must contain information about the alternatives to MBOs that were considered as well as the position of the outside directors.

Leveraged Buyouts, the Position of Other Debt Holders, and Wealth Transfers

One area of interest for many critics in recent years has been the potential impact of the assumption of high amounts of LBO debt, and the associated issuance of junk bonds, on the value of the investment of current bondholders. The fact that bondholders are not part of the approval process has attracted much attention. The additional debt increases the fixed payments that the firm has to make after the buyout. In doing so, it increases the likelihood that the firm will be unable to meet these payments and be forced into receivership.

---

[43] Robert W. Holthausen and David F. Larcker, "The Financial Performance of Reverse Leveraged Buyouts," *Journal of Financial Economics* 42, no. 3 (November 1996): 293–332.
[44] Jerry Cao and Josh Lerner, "The Performance of Reverse Leveraged Buyouts," *Journal of Financial Economics* 91, no. 2 (February 2009): 139–157.

This problem came to the fore in the RJR Nabisco buyout of November 1988. The value of current bonds dropped sharply after the announcement of the LBO. Some bonds fell as much as 15 points, or $150 for each $1,000 face-value amount, in the week the buyout was announced. Although the losses incurred by bondholders drew widespread attention in the RJR Nabisco buyout, bondholders have recognized it as a problem for some time. When the R. H. Macy and Company $3.6-billion buyout proposal was announced in 1985, the stock price rose $16 per share, whereas the price of Macy notes fell more than three points.

Investors who are holding bonds in a corporation that is involved in an LBO see the value and rating of their bonds deteriorate rapidly following the LBO announcement. This has alienated bondholders, particularly institutional investors. For example, Metropolitan Life saw its $340 million worth of A-rated RJR bonds downgraded to a junk bond rating for a $40 million loss. Metropolitan Life Insurance Company sued Nabisco in a New York State court. Metropolitan's suit alleged that a small group of Nabisco's management sought to enrich themselves at the expense of bondholders who had invested capital in Nabisco in good faith. Opponents of the bondholders contended that the bondholders were seeking to control the operations and decisions of the corporation in a manner that should be reserved only for stockholders. They thought that if bondholders wanted such control, they should have taken the risk of buying stock, not the relatively lower-risk bonds.

On May 31, 1989, a federal judge ruled that an "implied covenant" *did not* exist between the corporation and the RJR Nabisco bondholders, which would prevent the corporation from engaging in actions, such as an LBO, that would dramatically lower the value of the bonds. The court ruled that, to be binding, such agreements had to be in writing.

 ## EMPIRICAL RESEARCH ON WEALTH TRANSFER EFFECTS

There has been much public outcry in the media regarding the losses that bondholders have incurred after going-private transactions. Such media coverage implies that there is a general wealth transfer effect from bondholders to equity holders in these transactions. A study by Lehn and Poulsen failed to confirm the existence of such an effect.[45] They found no decrease in value of preferred stock and bonds associated with LBOs. This result, however, was to some extent contradicted by Travlos and Cornett.[46] Although their analysis did reveal a decline in the value of bonds and preferred stock following the announcement of going-private proposals, the decline they reported was relatively small.

The limited research in this area fails to provide support for a large wealth transfer effect. The empirical research indicates that if such an effect exists, it is not very significant.

---

[45] Ken Lehn and Annette Poulsen, "Leveraged Buyouts: Wealth Created or Wealth Distributed," in M. Weidenbaum and K. Chilton, eds., *Public Policy towards Corporate Takeovers* (New Brunswick, NJ: Transaction, 1988).
[46] Nicholas Travlos and M. M. Cornett, "Going Private Buyouts and Determinants of Shareholder Returns," *Journal of Accounting, Auditing and Finance* 8, no. 1 (Winter 1993): 1–25.

PROTECTION FOR CREDITORS

After the unfavorable federal court decision in the Metropolitan Life Insurance case, bond purchasers began to demand greater protection against the financial losses resulting from event risk. In response, they received from bond issuers agreements that would allow them to get back their full principal in the event of a buyout that would lower the value of their debt holdings. The covenants are usually triggered by actions such as the purchase of a block of stock by a hostile bidder or other actions such as a management-led buyout. In return for the added protection, bond buyers pay a somewhat higher interest rate, which is dependent on the issuer's financial condition. The rate may be structured to the magnitude of the rating change.

Much of the protection provided by the covenant agreements is in the form of a *poison put*, allowing the bondholders to sell the bonds back to the issuer at an agreed-upon price. Poison puts had also been used as a form of "shark repellent"—that is, companies would issue poison puts as a means of creating a financial obstacle to hostile bidders. However, as we moved into the late 1990s and early 2000s, these protections became less in demand. The fact that the mega-LBO has been around for some time, along with the high volume of LBOs we have seen worldwide, means that these events are already internalized in risk premiums that are built into corporate bonds.

Research by Billet, Jiang, and Lie showed that protective covenant agreements provide value to bondholders.[47] In a sample of 407 LBOs over the period of 1980–2006, they found that bondholders who lacked covenant protection experienced significantly negative −6.76% shareholder wealth effects around the announcement of LBOs, compared to a positive 2.3% for bonds that have protection.

INTRA-INDUSTRY EFFECTS OF BUYOUTS

In Chapter 4 we discuss the effects on the stock prices of competitors from horizontal mergers. Slovin, Sushka, and Bendeck analyzed 128 buyout bids over the period 1980–1988.[48] Of these, 78 were from managers and 50 were from outsiders. They noted that while target returns were significantly higher when the bids came from buyout firms, this had no impact on rivals. Slovin et al. found that bids resulted in positive valuation effects for rivals and that these effects were not that different in outsiders or management bids. They concluded that these positive valuation effects were due to new information about the industry and firms in it were being created by the buyout, and the price paid to target shareholders.

---

[47] Matthew T. Billet, Zhan Jiang, and Erik Lee, "The Effect of Change-in-Control Covenants on Takeovers: Evidence from Leveraged Buyouts," *Journal of Corporate Finance* 16, no. 1 (2010): 1–15.
[48] Myron B. Slovin, Marie E. Sushka, and Yvette M. Bendeck, "The Intra-industry Effects of Going Private Transactions," *Journal of Finance* 46, no. 4 (September 1991): 1537–1550.

CHAPTER NINE

The Private Equity Market

THIS CHAPTER CONTINUES THE discussion of going-private transactions by first focusing on the role of private equity firms. Private equity firms have played a major role in the takeover market during the past quarter of a century. Particularly in the mid-2000s, these firms were able to attract large amounts of capital and very aggressively pursued *mergers and acquisitions* (M&As). Their ability to raise capital has greatly increased in recent years. We will see that at times, rather than competing with each other, many private equity firms have decided to become partners in deals. This has greatly enhanced the size of transactions they can pursue while also lowering the exposure of each fund to a particular deal.

 ## HISTORY OF THE PRIVATE EQUITY AND LBO BUSINESS

The modern private equity business is not that old a business. We have had highly leveraged transactions for some time, so using large amounts of debt to buy businesses is not a novel concept. As we discussed in Chapter 8, Henry Ford did a highly leveraged transaction to regain control of his company in 1919. This was long before the words *leveraged buyout* and *private equity* even came into the vernacular of finance.

The first leveraged buyout took place in 1955 when McLean Industries, run by Malcolm McLean, acquired the Pan-American Steamship Company and the Waterman Steamship Company. He financed these acquisitions with the proceeds of his sale of his trucking company, McLean Trucking (regulations at the time prohibited a trucking company from owning a steamship company), and through bank debt and the issuance of preferred stock. However, he was able to use the cash and assets of the target companies to help pay down the buyout debt.

In the 1960s and 1970s other dealmakers learned from McLean and formed their own investment firms to do similar types of buyouts. In the 1960s and 1970s some high-profile dealmakers, such as Warren Buffett (Berkshire Hathaway) and Victor Posner (DWG Corporation), used similar leveraged financing structures. They were followed some years later by Boone Pickens (Mesa Petroleum) and Saul Steinberg (Reliance Insurance).

In the 1970s a few bankers at Bear Stearns also did leveraged deals. Two of them, Henry Kravis and Jerome Kohlberg, left Bear Stearns to form their own firm—Kohlberg Kravis and Roberts (KKR). KKR formalized the model of the LBO firm—a type of business that later became known as private equity. The success of KKR has attracted many competitors and led to a segment of the financial services industry we know today as the private equity business.

 ## PRIVATE EQUITY MARKET

During the period 2003–2007 private equity firms provided a substantial part of the fuel for the M&A boom that occurred during that period. This is very apparent in Figure 9.1.

The private equity market is a collection of funds that have raised capital by soliciting investments from various large investors where the funds will be invested in equity positions in companies. When these investments acquire 100% of the outstanding equity of a public company, we have a going-private transaction. When the equity is acquired through the use of some of the investment capital of the private equity fund but mainly borrowed funds, we tend to call such a deal a *leveraged buyout* (LBO). The fact that such deals are very common investments for private equity funds has led some to call these funds LBO funds. Private equity funds may make other investments, such as providing venture capital to nascent businesses. Funds established for this purpose are sometimes called venture capital funds. These investments might exclusively use the fund's capital and not necessarily use borrowed funds. Having such an equity investment, however,

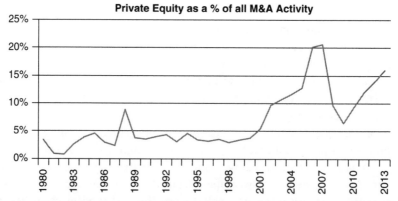

FIGURE 9.1 Private Equity as a Percentage of All M&A Activity. *Source:* Thomson Financial Securities Data, January 20, 2014.

may enable the target company itself to have improved access to debt markets after it secures the equity investment from the private equity fund. The fund might take a minority or a majority position in the company. Usually venture capital investments contain incentives, such as stock options, that enable the investor who assumes the risk to enjoy greater profits if the business turns out to be successful. However, there are many important differences between private equity funds and venture capital funds. We will discuss these shortly.

Private equity funds seek out investments that are undervalued. These could be whole companies that are not trading at values commensurate with what the fund managers think is possible. They could also be divisions of companies that want to sell the units due to a change in strategy or a need for cash. This was the case in 2002, for example, when the international liquor conglomerate Diageo, the marketer of brands such as Smirnoff vodka, Guinness beer, and Cuervo tequila, finally came to the realization that there probably was not a lot of synergy between the liquor brands just mentioned and the burgers and fries that were sold at its Burger King division. The Texas Pacific Group and Goldman Sachs Group purchased Burger King from Diageo in 2002 for $1.5 billion.

Private equity funds raise capital ex ante and then seek investments over the life of the fund. Their investment time frame theoretically provides them with certain advantages in weak economies where capital is less plentiful. By using previously committed capital, private equity funds can invest in projects and companies with high potential returns that find it difficult to raise capital in a weak market.[1] It is ironic that in recent years the pressure from activist hedge fund managers can force some corporate managements to not adopt a long-term perspective but instead sacrifice the future for short term returns.

In general, private equity fund managers raise capital from a variety of institutional investors. They typically charge their investors "2 and 20." This refers to 2% of invested capital and 20% of profits. The 20% of profits is referred to as "carried interest." We will discuss the various sources of income that private equity firms earn a little later in this chapter.

Private Equity Funds Compared to Venture Capital Funds

It is useful to compare private equity funds with venture capital funds as they really are both users of private equity. Both are organized as limited partnerships, with the general partner making the investment decisions. However, there are several very significant differences between the two.

Venture funds often make investments in new companies that may have limited revenues. The companies they invest in are often startups. Private equity firms seek out more established companies that have lengthy revenue, if not a profit, history.

It is not unusual to see several venture funds invest together in a *syndicated* manner. While this can also occur in private equity deals (as we will discuss later), it is much less common. In addition, in the venture capital business we may have

---

[1] Ulf Axelson, Per Stromberg, and Michael S. Wiesbach, "Why Are Buyouts Levered? The Financial Structure of Private Equity Funds," *Journal of Finance* 64, no. 4 (August 2009): 1549–1582.

several rounds of funding as a company goes through stages in its development and passes specific milestones. In a private equity acquisition, the fund typically acquires a company, holds the business for a period of time, and then sells it off—hopefully at a profit.

The investment horizon for venture funds can be shorter, and additional capital is provided only if the company meets the aforementioned milestones. If the company fails to achieve these goals, such as progress in development of a certain technology or progress in the development of a specific pharmaceutical product, the venture capitalist may simply walk away.

It is common with venture capital investments that the business needs multiple rounds of funding over its life. However, most private equity acquisitions are self-funding and are able to maintain themselves through their own self-generated cash flows.

There is usually much more uncertainty about the success of companies venture capitalists invest in. Roughly one-half of all venture capital–funded companies fail. This is why some research studies have showed that the *alpha* generated by venture capital investments can be high.[2] Researchers in this area also clearly understand that selection bias, including the fact that the returns of companies that may have ceased to exist, may give their results an upward bias.[3] However, when researchers such as John Cochrane of the University of Chicago took steps to attenuate this bias, the mean arithmetic returns were much lower (698% to 59%—not a typo) and the arithmetic alpha is 32% (down from 462%).

Unlike venture capital investments, a business failure of a private equity acquired business is much less common. It happens—sometimes on a huge scale. TPG lost all its investment in Washington Mutual, GMAC, and in the disastrous buyout of TXU Corp., in which TPG partnered with KKR and Goldman Sachs to acquire the company for $45 billion. That deal was the biggest LBO in history and ended up in bankruptcy under its mountain of LBO debt. However, while such private equity busts receive many headlines, they are not all that common. This is due to the fact that the companies that they invest in tend to have similar risk characteristics to the market overall. This was underscored by Susan Woodward, who found that private equity investments had an average beta of 0.86—meaning they are less risky than the market.[4] She contrasted this with a beta for venture capital investments of 2.0.

Seller versus Private Equity Fund Valuations and Negotiations

In order for private equity firms to generate an acceptable return for their investors, they need to be able to purchase target companies at prices that allow them to achieve a particular hurdle rate. When private equity firms believe that a target has been poorly managed, there may be a greater gap between the value that the private equity firm

[2] John Cochrane, "The Risk and Return of Venture Capital," *Journal of Financial Economics* 75, no. 1 (2005): 3–52.

[3] Susan E. Woodward, "Measuring Risk and Performance for Private Equity," Sandhill Econometrics, August 11, 2004.

[4] Ibid.

believes it can readily achieve through the installation of a new management team and the enactment of certain necessary changes in company operations, and the current value of the target based on its unadjusted future cash flows. This gap may provide the basis for some flexibility in negotiations and allow for an agreed-on price. However, when the target has been reasonably well-managed and both are aware of the risk-adjusted present value of the company's cash flows, there is less room to provide the seller with the full value of the company while allowing private equity buyers an opportunity to generate a good return on their investment. An example of this occurred in 2006 when the Salt Lake City–based Huntsman Corp., a $13 billion industrial company, broke off negotiations with private equity firm Apollo Management LP. Huntsman, which lost money in 2005, because it could not come to terms with Apollo at a price that the private equity firm believed made sense. The same result occurred in late 2005 when the grocery-store chain Albertsons could not initially agree on terms with a group of private equity buyers. This led the bidders to back away from Albertsons, and later that year a deal was struck with an investment group to sell the company for a revised price of $10.97 billion. Sellers who are seeking to offer their companies to private equity firms have to be willing to accept a price that will allow these firms some room to generate a return with another sale of the business in a few years. While they are certainly not immune from making valuation mistakes, private equity buyers tend to be careful not to overpay, as their gains mainly come from the difference between their purchase price and an eventual resale price, plus any monies extracted from the company prior to that resale.

Deals Outside Auctions and Proprietary Deals

Private equity firms are often times approached by dealmakers, such as investment bankers, who may represent a potential seller who is looking for a clean and smooth sale and is not interested in a very public auction process. These bankers may represent that they have a *proprietary deal* that the private equity buyer may be interested in. However, when the potential seller is a public company, this deal may only be temporarily a proprietary one, as Revlon duties may soon kick in. Private equity firms tend to be quite knowledgeable about M&A law and the times when an auction may be required. Nonetheless, occasionally, such as when a founder who holds considerable equity in the company wants to sell in a quick and smooth transaction, such deals may be more appealing to private equity firms. However, deals outside of auctions tend to be the clear minority. It is also important to recall, as we already discussed, how there can be a competitive bidding process occurring even prior to a public announcement of the potential sale of a company and the start of a more formal auction.

Private versus Public Deals

When one thinks about the private equity business, the stereotypical deal has been the large-scale, going-private transaction involving a public target. That is still an important part of the private equity business, but the more common transactions are private deals. These involve acquisitions from founders of businesses, other sponsors, or venture capital–sponsored firms. This trend has grown significantly over the past decade.

The increasing prevalence of private sellers, especially closely held founders, has provided private equity buyers with increased risk. Part of the reason for that is that many of these deals include a *survival clause*, which may indicate that the representations made by the seller (representations that the buyer may have used to come up with a purchase price the seller accepted) may survive for only a limited time after the closing period. Such clauses may be more normal in acquisitions of public companies that have operated under the U.S. securities laws and the penalties imposed for false financial disclosure during the life of the company. However, in acquisitions of private companies a whole host of concerns about the reliability of the data in the seller's financials may arise. We discuss this further in Chapter 15 when we discuss the differences in valuing private versus public companies.

Survivability clauses became an ever greater concern for buyers in 2011 when the Delaware Chancery Court ruled that the survival clause served as a kind of statute of limitations on the ability of the buyer to pursue breach of contract claims.[5] Other states, such as New York as well as California, however, have not agreed with Delaware's view regarding whether such clauses can be so limiting.[6]

Private equity buyers have dealt with this change by securing *representations and warranties insurance*. Such insurance used to be very customized and was time-consuming to secure. Now with the newfound demand from private deals, brokers of such insurance, such as Marsh McLennan, are well aware of the characteristics of these policies that buyers want and have become more comfortable creating and pricing them. In addition, the insurance companies that these brokers work with, such as AIG, Concord, Allied World, and Ambridge, have paid out claims so buyers of policies are more comfortable with the belief that, if they have a problem and need to rely on their insurance, it likely will pay. For larger policies, such as those in the $100 million range, buyers may need to syndicate the policy and involve multiple insurance carriers to bind the level of insurance they believe they need.

While clauses like survival clauses are newer to many U.S. private equity buyers, they are really fairly common in Europe. In Europe, management, which may have some equity in the deal, may bear this responsibility. In the United States as well, though, when managers realize that after the deal goes through they will have a new employer, they may on their own make certain relevant disclosures or may tone down overly aggressively representations made by the seller so that they are not left with a set of very unhappy bosses.

Another trend is that representatives of private sellers are including in agreements with private equity buyers more significant *reverse breakup fees*. This can create an incentive to make sure the buyer pushes its bankers to provide the needed debt capital to complete the deal. Later in this chapter we will discuss the rising activism and involvement of limited partners. LPs invest in private equity funds to get deals done that will maximize their return. It is very uncomfortable for private equity firms to have to inform their LPs that they are cutting a check to a seller using the equity in the fund and not

---

[5] In *GRT, Inc. v. Marathon GTF Tech., Ltd.*, 2011 Del. Ch. LEXIS 99 (July 11, 2011).
[6] *Hurlbut v. Christiano*, 405 N.Y.S. 2d. 871, 873 (App. Div., 4th Dep't, 1978).

only will the LPs not make a return on that capital, but also they will never even get it back. Both the general partners and their limited partners know this now requires much more superior performance from the rest of their investments to offset this loss. Therefore, large reverse breakup fees provide great incentives for private equity firms to get deals done and not have to be in such an awkward position with their LPs.

Leading Private Equity Firms

A private equity firm may raise capital to build several different funds. Based on investors' participation in the fund, they will receive a proportion of the return that the fund enjoyed, less the management fees for running the fund. Table 9.1 lists some of the leading private equity funds and their net revenues and share of the market.

Structure of a Private Equity Fund

Private equity funds are usually established as limited partnerships run by a general partner (GP), the private equity firm, and a number of investors or limited partners (LPs). In large funds there may be as many as 30 or 40 different LPs. The general and limited partners enter into agreements when the fund is formed. These agreements provide for how the partners are going to profit from the investments that the funds make. Sometimes some LPs are able to negotiate MFNs, "most favored nation" agreements, with the fund. These MFNs may provide certain investors with special rights or information. Sometimes they are used to get larger monetary commitments or to get an initial investment to "kick start" the capital raising process.

Private equity funds may tie up their investor's capital for an extended time period, such as 10 years, which is the typical lifetime of a fund. However, the agreements usually require them to invest the capital within three to five years. That time period is

TABLE 9.1 Leading Private Equity Firms by Funds Raised

Firm	5-Year Fundraising Total ($mil)
The Carlyle Group	30,650
Kohlberg Kravis Roberts	27,182
The Blackstone Group	24,640
Apollo Global Management	22,298
TPG	18,783
CVC Capital Partners	18,082
General Atlantic	16,600
Ares Management	14,114
Clayton Dubilier & Rice	13,505
Advent International	13,228

Source: Private Equity International's 2014 PEI 300.

referred to as the *investment period*. As a result of the Great Recession and weak economy that followed, several large private equity firms struggled to find acceptable investments. This became an issue for many private equity firms, such as TPG and the Carlyle Group, which raised large sums in 2006 and 2007 but which had billions of uncommitted capital in 2010 when the M&A business was weak.

Compensation of Private Equity GPs

The general partners of a private equity fund earn fixed income, which is independent of the performance of the fund, and variable income, which is a function of that performance. *Management fees*, which are fixed, are paid from what is called *committed capital*, which is the funds provided by the limited partners. Committed capital is composed of *lifetime fees* and *investment capital*. Management fee agreements between the GP and the LPs can vary. They could be a fixed percentage over the life of the fund, or, more commonly, it could decline over that time period. The fees themselves are calculated by applying the relevant percentage to some base, which could be committed capital or some alternative, such as net invested capital, which is defined as invested capital, the capital that has already been invested, less the cost basis of investments that have been disposed of.

Variable Fees: Carried Interest

In addition to fixed management fees, GPs earn income from several variable or performance-based sources. Principal among these is the controversial carried interest, which, simply stated, is earned from gains on the transactions conducted by the GP. How GPs can make income from this source varies as a function of the agreement with the LPs. For example, it could be that the GP does not earn any of this type of income until the LPs have received back their capital. This amount could be higher if a *hurdle rate* was agreed to. This is a threshold rate of return—let's say 6%—that is applied to the committed capital. If, for example, we assume that the LPs committed $250 million to the fund, and proceeds from exited investments totaled $300 million, then the LPs would receive not only their $250 million back but also 6% of that amount, $15 million, before a percentage of the remaining gains, $35 million ($300 million–$265 million), would be paid to the GP.

The percentage of the applicable profits that is used to calculate the GPs earnings is called the *carry level*. A common carry level is 20%. We often hear that GPs are paid based upon 2/20. The 2 would be the fixed percentage, and the 20 would be the variable component based upon the 20% carry level.

Sometimes GPs are allowed to take some profits early, and this is determined by what is called the *carry timing*. However, if later performance does not allow the LPs to receive back their capital and possibly an amount based upon the hurdle rate, then the LPs may be able to get back some of these early paid profits if the original agreements between the GP and the LPs included *clawback provisions*.

Variable Fees: Monitoring and Transactions Fees

Monitoring and *transaction fees* make up the remainder of the variable income the GPs receive. The monitoring is done by the GPs, which oversee the operations and performance of the companies they have acquired. These fees are usually shared with the LPs, who receive the bulk of the fees (often 80%). These fees are usually based upon some multiple of a financial performance measure, such as EBITDA.

GPs may charge a transaction fee for each transaction they complete. This can be structured so that there is a total transaction fee and part of the total is shared with the LPs.

Changing Market Conditions and Preferences of LPs

When the economy and the market turned down in the Great Recession and the weak recovery that followed, IRRs (internal rates of return) from investments declined dramatically. In the private equity heyday of 2005–2007, some of these returns were in the 20% range. Years later they fell to less than 10%.

When returns were in the 20% range, LPs often were quite pleased and there was little to complain about. Many of the large private equity funds were in excess of $10 billion in size and would pursue all kinds of diverse deals that could generate the sought returns. When returns fell in the years 2008–2011, LPs began to reevaluate the private equity component of their overall portfolio. This led many to consider only focused private equity funds that may, for example, concentrate on a particular industry rather than the ones that were broad, "anything-and-everything" funds. Sometimes this led the LPs to invest in smaller private equity funds as focused funds tend to be smaller than broad, unfocused funds. As an example, a few years ago KKR had a huge $18 billion fund. More recently, though, they have many smaller but still good-sized funds, such as its Asia fund, that are more focused. So while KKR's flagship fund may be smaller, all KKR funds together are still comparable to the private equity heyday.

This trend toward more focused funds is really part of the overall evolution of the private equity industry in general. If one considers the genesis of the private equity industry to be the fourth merger wave LBO funds, we can see why it is still evolving.

Recent years such as 2013 and 2014 were very good for private equity firms. When the economy does well and the market is strong, it creates a fertile environment for private equity firms to sell previously acquired investments at attractive prices. When this occurs the LPs realize good returns, and the pressure on the GPs declines. LPs are then more open to a broad array of investment ideas from GPs, and also the LPs tend to be less vigilant on monitoring the fees that GPs charge.

LP "Activism" and the Evolving the Private Equity Business

Investors in private equity funds, the so-called LPs, used to be relatively passive investors who invested their capital and waited for the seemingly automatic high returns. The strong equity markets enabled private equity managers, the general partners, to more easily be able to meet the expectations of the clients—the LPs. This all changed when the economy and market turned down. Now private equity managers have to work harder for their returns and they find themselves under closer scrutiny from the LPs. The LPs want more detailed explanations and want to know more about how a transaction will generate good returns; they want to be updated on the progress toward this goal. This is particularly true of government pension fund LPs and may be a bit less true for university endowment LPs. Government pension funds are the leading providers of capital to private equity funds (see Table 9.2).

While LPs are more active than they used to be, this is relative as in the past they were almost totally inactive. Part of that activism is requiring private equity firms to eliminate some of the charges that had tended in the past to slip past nonattentive LPs. As we have noted, when the market is strong and LPs realize good returns, such as in 2013–2014, LPs tend to be less vigilant in monitoring fees and expenses charged by GPs. This is unfortunate as LPs, such as pension funds, owe an obligation to the employees they represent to receive the highest returns they can and to prevent GPs from siphoning off monies through fees the LPs should not have agreed to pay if they read and negotiated the investment agreements more closely. This is an issue that the Securities and Exchange Commission has been focusing on more.

The situation began to change in 2014 when some pension funds demanded better explanations and justifications from private equity funds they had invested in regarding the fees and expenses they were charged. This came at a time when the SEC was taking a closer look at the private equity business. The Dodd-Frank legislation passed in 2010 required that private equity firms with more than $150 million in assets had to register with the SEC. This registration process started in 2012. It allowed the SEC to more closely examine the private equity business, and it began to express concerns about the nature of its practices and the way fee and expenses are allocation to LPs.

TABLE 9.2 Top 10 Pension Funds by Dollars Invested in Private Equity

		Amount Invested ($ billion)	Percent of Fund's Total
1	California Public Employees' Retirement System (Calpers)	$32.3	10.7%
2	California State Teachers' Retirement System (CalStrs)	$21.9	11.5%
3	Washington State Investment Board	$16.2	15.5%
4	Oregon Public Employees' Retirement System	$14.4	16.3%
5	Teacher Retirement System of Texas	$14.4	11.6%
6	New York State and Local Retirement System	$14.1	7.9%
7	State of Wisconsin Investment Board	$10.0	10.3%
8	Pennsylvania Public School Employees' Retirement System	$9.2	17.3%
9	Michigan Public School Employees' Retirement System	$8.4	18.2%
10	Ohio Public Employees' Retirement System	$8.2	9.2%

Source: Private Equity Growth Capital Council, October 2014 Report.

Some LPs wanted to hire an independent advisor to look over the various fees the funds had charged. Naturally, several funds resisted as they were used to the lucrative world where they passed on charges to LPs who never questioned them. Remember, the LPs are investing other people's money and if they do not get the best return for them, they will likely not be personally affected. The GPs, however, stand to personally gain from the more of the return they can extract for themselves. Some funds also demanded that the terms of the GPs compensation agreements be kept secret. Some GPs stated that if the terms were revealed, they would not accept future investments from certain LPs. It seems now that finally LPs are waking up and taking a more aggressive stance towards some GPs.

Expansion and Diversification of Large Private Equity Firms

On the sponsor side, another trend that has been noticeable is the expansion and diversification of large private equity firms outside of traditional pure private equity investments. Many, such as Blackstone, have really become global asset managers. Some have sought to emphasize this in their capital raising and have moved away from the use of the term private equity and prefer *alternative asset managers*.

Another obvious trend has been global expansion outside of what was the traditional bailiwick of private equity firms, the United States and Europe, and into growth areas of Asia and Latin and South America. As an example of this trend, as of 2014 TPG has as many offices in China (four) as it does in the United States. This global expansion was brought on by the fact that private equity funds struggled to find fruitful investments when the Great Recession consumed the United States, and then as the U.S. economy slowly recovered, Europe went into its sovereign debt crisis. If large private equity firms were going to meet investor return expectations, it became imperative to go where the growth is.

Private Equity Fund Partnerships and "Club Deals"

Private equity funds may acquire stock in a target company individually or they may combine with other private equity firms to acquire a target. These types of deals are sometimes referred to as *club deals* or *consortium* deals. The combinations enable them to spread out the risk. This may be necessary as many funds require that no more than a certain percentage, such as 10%, of a fund's assets be invested in any particular investment. For 100% acquisition, a $10 billion fund, a large private equity firm by any standards, would then be limited to acquisitions no larger than $1 billion if it chose not to utilize debt to complete the transactions. For this reason it may choose to join forces with other private equity firms when it is attempting to complete a large acquisition. As an example, in March 2005, Silver Lake Partners completed the second-largest LBO up to that time when it combined with six other private equity firms to acquire Sunguard Data Systems for $10.8 billion. The other private equity firms that participated in the takeover were the Blackstone Group, Kohlberg Kravis & Roberts, Texas Pacific Group, Goldman Sachs Partners, and Providence Equity Partners.

Private equity firms have become so involved in takeovers that they find themselves forming competing groups or partnerships and bidding against each other for takeover targets. This was the case in August 2005, when Kohlberg Kravis & Roberts (KKR) joined forces with Silverlake Partners to acquire Agilent Technologies Inc.'s semiconductor products business for $2.6 billion. This company was spun off by Hewlett-Packard in 1999 as part of a focusing strategy. Agilent itself was pursuing a focusing strategy in 2005 when it decided to try to sell its chip unit and lighting business. The company's CEO, William Sullivan, stated that Agilent, being a diversified company, was "trading at a 25% to 35% discount to" its peers.[7] He believed that giving the company increased focus through sell-offs such as this would lower the discount that the market was applying to his company. KKR and Silverlake won the contest in which they were bidding against two other buyout groups: one that featured Bain Capital and Warburg Pincus and another that had Texas Pacific Group, CVC Partners, and Francisco Partners as participants.

Some have argued that the club deals tend to lower the pool of potential demanders for target companies, thereby lowering the prices that targets receive in the market. This was the finding of a study by Officer, Ozbas, and Sensoy.[8] They found that target shareholders receive 10% less of pre-bid value and 40% lower premiums! They conclude with concerns that private equity buyers may be colluding to lower prices they pay for targets.

The Officer et al. results were not consistent with other results, such as those of Boone and Mulherin, who failed to find lower target prices.[9] They analyzed a sample of 870 publicly traded targets over the period 2003–2007. They attributed their results, in part, to changes in the market such as the increased use of go-shop provisions and the availability of stapled financing—the latter of which could eliminate some of the benefits club deals may have over single buyers.

Club or consortium deals have become less popular in recent years. Private equity firms have learned that when they do not have complete control, as they usually do when they acquire the target by themselves, dealing with other owners can make the transaction and the management and subsequent sale more complicated. Differing views on how the company should be managed and the appropriate time and way to seek an exit have made more private equity firms bypass this option.

SIMMONS BEDDING COMPANY

The fate of the Simmons Bedding company is not one that the private equity industry can be proud of. In 2003 the company was acquired by Thomas H. Lee Partners of Boston. Simmons was originally founded in Wisconsin with headquarters in Atlanta, had been in existence for 133 years before it had to file Chapter 11 in

---

[7] Pui-Wing Tam, "Agilent Unveils Broad Restructuring," *Wall Street Journal*, August 16, 2005, B8.
[8] Micah Officer, Oguzhan Ozbas, and Berk A. Sensoy, "Club Deals in Leveraged Buyouts," *Journal of Financial Economics* 98, no. 2 (November 2010): 214–240.
[9] Audra Boone and Harold Mulherin, "Do Private Equity Consortiums Facilitate Collusion in Takeover Bidding," *Journal of Corporate Finance* 17, no. 5 (December 2011): 1475–1495.

2009. It boasted such leading industry products as the Simmons Beautyrest mattress. However storied its products were, the company could not sustain the bloated debt load that different private equity buyers had imposed on it over the years. During its ownership of Simmons, Thomas Lee caused the company to take on debt for a total of $375 million, which more than repaid Thomas Lee's cash investment in the initial buyout.

The mattress business is cyclical and tends to suffer when the economy turns down. Like other companies that private equity buyers had loaded up with debt to finance their dividend cash extractions, Simmons could not service the debt. Instead of the debt proceeds providing cash to operations or being invested in a way to make the company more productive, debt used for dividend recapitalizations helps only the private equity buyers, not the company itself. In the case of Simmons, the company could not afford to be a cash cow for its owners and still stay out of bankruptcy when the economy inevitably turned down.

Private Equity Business Model

While some of the leading names in finance work in this industry and often earn incredibly lucrative compensation, the business model is a relatively simple one. The first step in the process for private equity buyers is to have contacts with investors and sales skills that will enable them to convince institutional investors to invest a portion of their capital into one of their private equity funds. The next step is to find undervalued targets. Here they can be indirectly aided by poor management in the target company, perhaps facilitated by weak corporate governance, where the managers may have run the company in a manner that suppressed its potential. Once an acceptable target is found, and an acquisition price agreed to, the GPs secure the debt capital using relationships they have with various banks. The recent expansionary monetary policy for the Federal Reserve helped funds to acquire this capital at very low rates.

Private equity buyers use the cheap debt to buy undervalued targets. It helps if the targets do not already have significant debt, as the buyers may want to have the target acquire more debt, which they can use to pay themselves a "dividend." As we discussed, they oversee the acquired company, which is run by its own management, and charge the monitoring fees for this oversight.

An ideal environment for private equity firms is one where the market is rising. This allows them to buy at one price, and then a few years later, maybe even earlier, they will sell the target in an elevated market at a higher price than what they paid.

The next step in the process is to conduct this business in a good economy with a rising market. Consistent with the saying that a rising tide carries with it all ships, private equity buyers hope that the rising market will uplift the value of their now debt-laden target. Once they perceive an opportune moment they "flip" the target, higher debt and all, onto a buyer. The high leverage they used to finance the deal—and in the 2000s this was done at low costs—magnifies their returns on the relatively small equity investment they made.

When the market is rising, such as in 2013–2014, and the cost of debt is low with an ample supply of capital available, the results can be favorable for the private equity industry. On the surface the dealmakers may seem like wizards (and they expect out-of-this-world compensation for their wizardry), but the steps in the process are quite simple.

Alternative Private Equity Exit Strategies

There are several ways a private equity buyer can exit from an investment. One is through a sale to a corporate buyer that sees the acquisition as a complement to its overall business strategy. These buyers are sometimes referred to as *strategic buyers*. Such buyers have been traditionally the mainstay of private equity exits. However, when the economy is weak, as it was during the Great Recession of 2008–2009 and the weak recovery that followed, these buyers can be more difficult to find. During such periods companies are not looking to expand and aggressively pursue their strategic growth plan as they become more risk-averse when they see their sales growth and overall economic growth are weak. However, as the U.S. economy began to grow more steadily in 2012–2014, and U.S. corporate treasuries became flush with cash, strategic buyers returned, albeit cautiously, to the M&A market.

Another exit strategy is a *sponsor-to-sponsor* deal, where one private equity firm sells a prior acquisition to another private equity firm. These deals can be popular in a market where there is abundant private equity capital in funds seeking deals, while there are also other private equity firms looking to generate returns from prior acquisitions.

Still another exit strategy is a *public offering*. Here the private equity firm sponsors a public offering in the stock it owns in its prior acquisition. The viability of this avenue is very much dependent on the vitality of the equities markets and the IPO market in particular. In 2013, offerings by private equity firms were roughly half of all IPOs (see Figure 9.2).

Dividend Recapitalizations

Private equity firms generate returns from their portfolio companies in more ways than just cashing out the investment when it is sold. In recent years we are seeing private equity firms engaging in "dividend recapitalizations." This is when private equity firms have companies they have acquired take on more debt, such as through issuing bonds and using the proceeds to pay a dividend to the fund investors. This was the case in September 2004, when KKR had PanAmSat issue $250 million in notes that were used to pay the investors who bought the firm just one month prior for $4.3 billion. In the aforementioned purchase of Burger King by private equity investors, the buyers paid themselves a $400 million special dividend in 2006, which Burger King financed through the assumption of approximately $350 million in debt. In May 2006 Burger King did a $425 million IPO, which offset the substantial debt the company had taken on to pay the dividend. The combination of the dividend and their share of the private

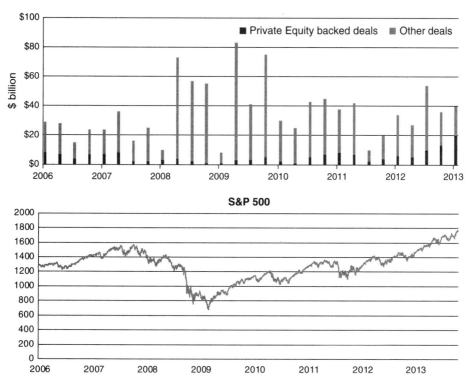

FIGURE 9.2 S&P 500 Graph and Double Bar Chart on SEO and Private Equity Component. *Source*: Dealogic (secondary offerings); WSJ Market Data Group (S&P 500).

equity proceeds were reported to eventually provide the private equity investors with a 115% return on their three-year-plus investment![10]

Debt Financing and Use of "Covenant-Lite" Loans

During the heyday of the private equity era, 2003–2007, private equity firms were able to negotiate very favorable conditions with the lender, banks that they had relationships with and to which they brought a lot of business. In addition, many banks felt confident based upon the very good economic environment and their own inability to understand how a business cycle works. Part of these favorable conditions involved the granting of covenant-lite loans, which feature a lack of restrictive covenants that require certain financial performance, such as the maintenance of specific financial ratios. The loan agreements could even be so liberal that they may forgive in advance certain violations of the agreement by the borrower. In exchange, they may allow the GP to "cure" transgressions by adding more equity to the target.

---

[10] Maxwell Murphy, "Private Investors in Burger King to Get Dividend," *Wall Street Journal*, February 4–5, 2006, B4.

While lenders were quite flexible during the 2003–2007 private equity boom times, they became much more restrictive when the economy collapsed after the subprime crisis.

Bridge Financing

In the context of private equity transactions, bridge financing is capital that is provided to allow the GP to complete the deal while they wait for long-term financing to be worked out. To do this the private equity firm secures a commitment from an investment bank. Ideally, the private equity GP and the bank hope the bridge financing will not be necessary as they will be able to syndicate a bank credit facility or simply float an offering of junk bonds. We will discuss junk bonds later in this chapter.

Bridge financing is riskier than longer-term financing that is associated with a closed deal. For this reason, private equity firms try to avoid using it.

Once the debt availability has been agreed to, the private equity firm is in a position to make a commitment to the seller. Part of this commitment is the equity they will put into the deal. Sometimes if the private equity firm does not have immediate access to the total amount of equity capital needed to complete the deal, they may go to a bank and ask it to temporarily provide the additional needed equity—called *bridge equity*. Obviously, the recipient has to pay the bank the necessary fees to make this equity capital available. Once the bank makes the commitment, then a commitment for the total acquisition amount can be made to the seller.

Impact of Delaware General Corporation Law Rule 251h

Private equity buyers have long been in a disadvantageous position relative to strategic buyers when it comes to tender offers. Private equity buyers faced the risk that the deal would or would not be approved by selling stockholders in a closing-out second-step transaction. Private equity firms have to secure bridge financing without the benefit of the assets of the target for collateral support as they do not get such access and support until the deal is completed. Such bridge financing can be expensive, and this caused many private equity firms to avoid the tender offer.

Rule 251h allowed buyers which receive a simple majority of a target's shares in a tender offer to quickly close rather than to wait for a shareholder vote. The rule improved the competitive landscape for financial buyers, such as private equity firms, or strategic buyers which are using debt financing compared to strategic buyers which may be using their own cash or stock.

Rule 251h, which became effective on August 1, 2013, reduces the burden of a second-step short-form merger if several conditions are met:

- The target has more than 2,000 holders.
- The merger agreement expressly provides that it will be governed by 251h.
- The buyer does a tender offer for any and all shares that would normally have a vote on the merger.
- After the tender offer the buyer has a majority of the shares of the target.

- As of the time that the board approved the merger there were no other interested shareholders.
- The buyer of the shares offers to merge with or into the target.
- The outstanding shares not purchased in the tender offer received the same consideration as the shares that were purchased.

Computing Private Equity Internal Rates of Return

As we will discuss shortly, some researchers have an issue with how returns of private equity funds are computed. However, it is useful to initially note how internal rates of returns for private equity funds are computed. First, using the Guidance Statement on Private Equity established by the CFA Institute, Equation 9.1 depicts an annualized internal rate of return:[11]

$$V_E = \left[V_B X \left(1 + r_{IRR} \right)^{\frac{TD}{365}} \right] + \sum_{i=1}^{I} \left[CF_i X \left(1 + r_{IRR} \right)^{\frac{t_i}{365}} \right], \tag{9.1}$$

where

V_B = value of the investment at the beginning of the measurement period
V_E = value of the investment at the end of the measurement period
CF_i = cash flow i (positive values for inflows and negative values for outflows)
i = number of cash flows $(1, 2, \ldots, I)$ during the measurement period
r_{IRR} = annualized internal rate of return
t_i = number of calendar days from the day when the cash flow i occurred to the end of the measurement period
TD = total number of calendar days within the measurement period

Sometimes, however, it may be useful to also see a nonannualized version, such as when an investment covers only part of a year and there is no guarantee that proceeds from a given investment could be reinvested at the same rate for the remainder of the period. When that is an issue, we look to a nonannualized version such as that shown here.

The same CFA Institute standards show the computation of a nonannualized version – since inception internal rate of return (SI-IRR) as follows:

$$R_{IRR} = \left[\left(1 + r_{IRR} \right)^{\frac{TD}{365}} \right] - 1, \tag{9.2}$$

where

R_{IRR} = nonannualized internal rate of return
r_{IRR} = annualized internal rate of return
TD = total number of calendar days within the measurement period

---

[11] "Guidance Statement on Private Equity," CFA Institute, 2010, www.gipsstandards.org.

The foregoing calculations seem very straightforward, yet very interesting issues arise when researchers actually go about dealing with the data and using it to do the requisite computations. For example, how do we handle investments that have not been exited as of the end of the study period? Do we simply accept values provided by the private equity fund regarding what they should be worth? What if these investments were of an age when they should have been liquidated, and they have not been cash flow–positive for some time? Do we still accept the fund's representations or should the researchers simply write them off and make them zero?

Characteristics of Private Equity Returns

The data shown in Figure 9.3 imply that private equity returns do not outperform the market. This was confirmed by Kaplan and Schoar, who examined the LBO fund and venture capital fund returns of private equity firms.[12] They found that gross of fees, both LBO and venture capital fund returns, exceeded the S&P 500. However, when fees were also considered, the superior performance of these funds disappeared. One has to remember that low-cost investment vehicles, such as exchange-traded funds as well as regular mutual funds, enable investors to earn the rate of the return of the market at a relatively low cost. Therefore, private equity funds have to do substantially better than the market to justify their comparatively higher fees. There is not much evidence to support these fees.

One characteristic of investment performance that has attracted much attention over the years has been the *persistence* of returns of mutual fund managers. This refers to the likelihood that above-average returns in one period are associated with above-average returns in later periods. Mutual fund managers have not been able to

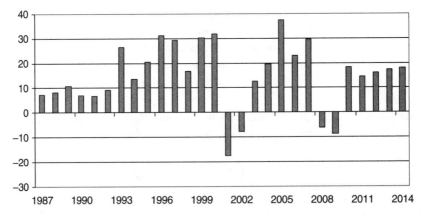

FIGURE 9.3 Cambridge Associates Private Equity Index. *Source:* Cambridge Associates Private Equity Index, www.cambridgeassociates.com/indexes/docs/PE%20Benchmark.pdf.

---

[12] Steven N. Kaplan and Antoinette Schoar, "Returns, Persistence and Capital Flows," *Journal of Finance* 60, no. 4 (August 2005): 1791–1823.

demonstrate much persistence.[13] However, Kaplan and Schoar do find persistence in performance for general managers of one fund and others that they establish. They did so using a regression analysis that sought to determine if the coefficient β in equation 9.3 was statistically significant and positive.

$$P_{iN} = \alpha + \beta P_{iN-1} + \varepsilon_{iN} \tag{9.3}$$

where

P_{iN} = performance of fund N, which is managed by private equity firm i
P_{iN-1} = performance of fund N – 1, which is managed by private equity firm i

Glode and Green theorize that the findings of persistence by researchers may be due to the fact that private equity managers do not have to submit to the significant disclosure requirements imposed on mutual fund managers, and they have a better chance of maintaining the secrecy of their investment strategies that may have enabled them to achieve above-average returns.[14]

Another relevant issue is whether the persistence is long-term. Chung regressed P_{iN} on P_{iN-2} and found a weaker relationship.[15] That is, Chung found performance persistent for the first follow on fund but not subsequent ones. This implies that if persistence exists it may be short-lived. This research also suggests an answer to the question of why private equity GPs don't charge even higher fees if their performance is so consistently wonderful. The answer Chung suggests is that it may not be so wonderful in the longer term.

Another issue for LPs is whether the persistence performance of some private equity funds and specific managers is "investable." Investable persistence reflects the ability of LPs to identify superior PE firms and managers. If LPs can't do that, then the existence of persistence is not as valuable. Korteweg and Sorensen analyzed a large sample of 1,924 funds raised during the period 1969–2001 and managed by 891 firms.[16] Their sample included buyout funds and venture capital funds. While they did find a significant amount of even long-term persistence, they found that past performance was quite "noisy" and also that luck clearly played an important role. Thus, the ability of LPs to identify the persistent performance of some funds was limited. This was particularly true for venture capital funds.

Kaplan and Schoar also examined capital flows into private equity funds. As expected, fund flows are positively related to fund performance—both on the fund and industry level. However, they found that higher industry performance seems to enable

---

[13] Mark M. Carhart, Jennifer N. Carpenter, Anthony W. Lynch, and David K. Musto," *Review of Financial Studies* 15, no. 5 (Winter 2002): 1439–1463.

[14] Vincent Glode and Richard Green, "Information Spillovers and Performance in Private Equity Partnerships," *Journal of Financial Economics* 101, no. 1 (July 2011): 1–17.

[15] Ji-Woong Chung, "Performance Persistence in Private Equity Funds," Ohio State University Working Paper, 2010.

[16] Arthur Korteweg and Morten Sorensen, "Skill and Luck in Private Equity Performance," Stanford University Working Paper 179, February 2014.

more funds to be formed, but many of the funds do not perform as well in the future. That is, better industry performance seems to allow less-skilled managers to form new funds that do not exhibit the same performance as those that enabled the industry to grow and allowed them to attract capital. Many of these newly formed funds then go out of existence.

The Kaplan and Schoar research examined data that did not include the recent economic downturn. The returns of private equity firms were much lower during this period. Stowell has shown that of the 287 U.S. companies with assets over $1 million or revenues over $10 million that filed for bankruptcy protection in 2008, 71 or just under 25% were then or before then owned by private equity firms.[17] If returns for the years 2008 and 2009 were considered, the track record of private equity investments would seem much less favorable. However, consistent with Kaplan and Schoar, even in this period the returns are somewhat comparable to the market. The fact that private equity buyers tend to load the targets up with debt means that they are more susceptible to downturns than the typical acquired company.

Phalippou and Gottschalg took a fresh look at the calculations that resulted in some semi-impressive returns for the private equity industry.[18] They used an expanded version of the data set utilized by Kaplan and Schoar. However, they changed the way that residual values were treated. Kaplan and Schoar accepted the residual values of unexited investments as of the sample study period put forward by private equity firms and, therefore, treated them as positive cash inflows. It was generally thought this would not have a significant impact for mature funds. However, Phalippou and Gottschalg pointed out that these investments had reached their normal liquidation date and most of the time were not generating positive cash flows for some time prior to that. They contend that such values should be written off. When they are written off, the average fund's Profitability Index declines by 7%! Based upon these and other computational adjustments, they found that the average fund's performance *underperformed* the S&P 500 by 3% after taking fees into account, even though gross of fees they outperformed this index by 3%.

Board Interlocks and Likelihood of Targets to Receive Private Equity Bids

In Chapter 13 we will discuss the impact that interlocked boards have on corporate governance. However, using a sample of all U.S. publicity traded companies over the years 2000–2007, Stuart and Yim found that when a company had directors that had previous positive experience in receiving private equity bids while at other companies, such firms were more 42% likely to receive offers from private equity firms.[19] When the

---

[17] David P. Stowell, *An Introduction to Investment Banking, Hedge Funds and Private Equity* (Burlington, MA: Academic Press, 2010), 327.

[18] Ludovic Phalippou and Oliver Gottschalg, "The Performance of Private Equity Funds," *Review of Financial Studies* 22, no. 4 (April 2009): 1747–1776.

[19] Toby Stuart and Soojin Yim, "Board Interlocks and the Propensity to Be Targeted in Private Equity Transactions," *Journal of Financial Economics* 97, no. 1 (July 2010): 174–189.

directors had negative experiences with private equity in the past, what they termed the "PE Interlock Effect" largely disappeared. They concluded that board members and the social networks they bring to the board influence which companies become takeover targets.

SECONDARY MARKET FOR PRIVATE EQUITY INVESTMENTS

For some time there has been a relatively inactive market for private equity investments. Transactions in this market have come in several forms. An LP could adjust its portfolio by using this market to get out of certain private equity investments. Part of such a sale could be not only the investment but also any remaining financial commitments that were expected to be made by the LP. The buyers of these investments could be institutions and hedge funds. The extent to which the LP can enter into such a sale is governed by the investment agreement, which may require the approval of the GP in order for it to be completed. If the potential seller is a large investor, especially one who has made other investments with the GP and with whom the GP wants to continue to work, this approval may not be difficult to get. The sale can be relatively seamless, and the partnership can continue to function undisturbed by a switch of LPs.

In 2014 the secondary market took a step forward when KKR allowed investors to sell portions of their stakes in buyout funds through a private market managed by the Nasdaq OMX Group. Institutional investors, such as pension funds, could use this marketplace to sell some of their private equity investments to other investors, including smaller investors. Prior to this development, smaller investors who wanted to invest in private equity could buy shares in the few private equity companies that had gone public. These include the Blackstone Group and Carlyle. However, these are shares in the private equity companies themselves as opposed to investments in specific private equity funds, which had been the exclusive domain of large institutions.

The new market is in its development phase, but the plans are for it to be open to, presumably, sophisticated investors with a minimum purchase requirement in the tens of thousands of dollars. The market should make private equity investments more liquid, which would logically make capital raising even easier.

CHAPTER TEN

The Junk Bond and the Leveraged Loan Market and Stapled Financing

JUNK BONDS, ALSO CALLED high-yield bonds, are debt securities that have ratings below investment grade. For rating agencies such as Standard & Poor's, this is a rating of BB or worse. The junk bond market is another financing source that can be used to finance takeovers—especially leveraged takeovers. It played a very important role in the fourth merger wave, but its importance has diminished in the years that followed.

 ## HISTORY OF THE JUNK BOND MARKET

Contrary to what some believe, junk bonds were not a creation of the fourth merger wave. They went by the term *low-grade bonds* for decades. In the 1930s and 1940s, they were called "fallen angels." In the 1960s, some of the lower-grade debt that was issued to help finance conglomerate acquisitions was referred to as "Chinese paper." Financier Meshulam Riklis, chief executive officer (CEO) of Rapid American Corporation, stated that the term *junk bonds* first originated in a conversation he had with Michael Milken, the former head of Drexel Burnham Lambert's junk bond operation. Riklis claimed that when Milken surveyed some of the bonds that Riklis had issued, he exclaimed, "Rik, these are junk!"[1] In the 1920s and 1930s, approximately 17% of all new corporate bond offerings were low-grade/high-yield bonds. A broader range of firms used these securities to finance their growth. The ranks of the high-yield bonds swelled during the 1930s as the Great Depression took its toll on many of America's companies. In 1928, 13% of all outstanding corporate bonds were low-grade bonds; in 1940, this percentage had risen to

---

[1] Connie Bruck, *The Predators' Ball* (New York: Simon & Schuster, 1988), 39.

42%.[2] Many of the bonds had entered the low-grade class through downgradings from rating agencies. (The rating process is discussed later in this chapter.) As the economy fell deeper and deeper into the depression and firms suffered the impact of declining demand for their goods and services, their ability to service the payments on their outstanding bonds was called into question. This led to a downgrading of the debt. As the overall level of economic demand fell, the revenues of some firms declined so much that they could no longer service the interest and principal payments on the outstanding bonds. As a result, the default rate on these bonds rose to 10%. Investors became disappointed by the rising default rate in a category of securities that they believed was generally low-risk. These investors were previously attracted to the bond market by investment characteristics such as dependability of income coupled with low risk of default. As the risk of default rose, low-grade bonds became unpopular.

By the 1940s, the low-grade bond market started to decline as old issues were retired or the issuing corporations entered into some form of bankruptcy. The declining popularity of the low-grade bond market made new issues difficult to market. Between 1944 and 1965, high-yield bonds accounted for only 6.5% of total corporate bond issues. This percentage declined even further as the 1970s began; by the beginning of the decade only 4% of all corporate bonds were low-grade bonds. The low-grade/high-yield bond market's declining popularity preempted access to one form of debt financing to certain groups of borrowers. Many corporations that would have preferred to issue long-term bonds were now forced to borrow from banks in the form of term loans that were generally of shorter maturity than 20- and 30-year corporate bonds. Those that could not borrow from a bank on acceptable terms were forced to forsake expansion or to issue more equity, which had the adverse effect of diluting the shares of ownership for outstanding equity holders. In addition, the rate of return on equity is generally higher than debt. Therefore, equity is a more costly source of capital.

The high-yield/low-grade market began to change in the late 1970s. Lehman Brothers, an investment bank that was itself acquired in the 1980s by Shearson, underwrote a series of new issues of high-yield corporate debt. These bonds were offered by Ling-Temco-Vought (LTV) ($75 million), Zapata Corporation ($75 million), Fuqua Industries ($60 million), and Pan American World Airways ($53 million).[3] This was followed by the entrance of a relatively smaller investment bank, Drexel Burnham Lambert, which started to underwrite issues of low-grade/high-yield debt on a larger scale. The first such issue that Drexel underwrote was a $30-million issue of bonds on Texas International Inc. in April 1977.[4]

Drexel Burnham Lambert's role in the development was the key to the growth of the low-grade/high-yield bond market. It served as a market maker for junk bonds, as they had begun to be called, which was crucial to the dramatic growth of the market.

---

[2] Kevin J. Perry, "The Growing Role of Junk Bonds," *Journal of Applied Corporate Finance* 1, no. 1 (Spring 1988): 37–45.

[3] Ibid., 44.

[4] Harlan D. Platt, *The First Junk Bond* (Armonk, NY: M. E. Sharpe, 1994), xiii.

By 1982, junk bond issuance had grown to $2 billion per year. Just three years later, in 1985, this total had risen to $14.1 billion and then jumped to $31.9 billion in the following year. This was the highest level the market reached in the fourth merger wave. It maintained similar levels until it collapsed in the second half of 1989. After falling to $1.4 billion in 1990, the market rebounded in 1992 and rose to new heights in the first half of the 1990s. Although the market thrived in the 1990s, it took a different form from being a major source of merger and LBO financing, which accounted for its growth in the fourth merger wave.

Why the Junk Bond Market Grew

The junk bond market experienced dramatic and rapid growth in the 1980s, although when compared to the decades that followed, this growth would seem modest (see Figure 10.1).

The fourth wave growth occurred for several reasons. Some of these factors are as follows:

- *Privately placed bonds.* Prior to the late 1970s, high-yield bonds were privately placed with institutional investors. These bonds tended to have unique indenture contracts with varying restrictive covenants that varied based on what different buyers negotiated. This lack of standardized contracts made them difficult to market. Even more fundamentally, they were not registered with the SEC and could not be publicly traded. This made them somewhat illiquid. Later, investment bankers such as Drexel Burnham Lambert would recognize this as an opportunity.
- *Development of market makers.* A major factor leading to the growth of this market was the existence of an active market maker—an entity that serves as an agent of

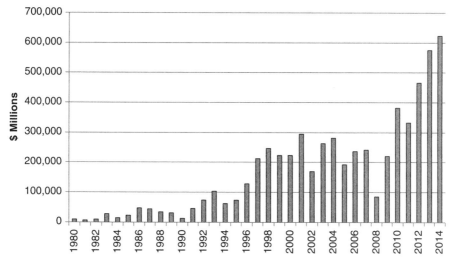

FIGURE 10.1 Growth of the Junk Bond Market 1980–2014. *Source*: Thomson Financial Securities Data, March 6, 2015.

liquidity in facilitating sales between buyers and sellers. Drexel Burnham Lambert became a very active market maker in the junk bond market. Drexel's growth in the 1980s was attributable largely to its involvement in the junk bond market. Therefore, the firm went to great lengths to ensure the growth and vitality of the market.

▪   *Changing risk perceptions.* Another factor has been the changing risk perceptions of investors toward junk bonds. Investors began to believe that the risks associated with junk bond investments were less than what they once believed. The altered risk perceptions came as a result of active promotion of this financing vehicle by interested parties such as Drexel Burnham Lambert and through academic research. Certain research studies examined the riskiness of junk bonds and reported that the risk of default was far less than was popularly believed. Some of these findings would later be challenged by other studies.

▪   *Deregulation.* A more relaxed regulatory climate enabled the junk bond market to attract investment capital from traditionally conservative institutional investors, such as pension funds and thrift institutions. The 1974 Employee Retirement Income Security Act, and its subsequent interpretations, allowed managers to invest in a broader range of assets, including riskier securities, as long as the portfolio was sufficiently diversified. The Garn–St. Germain Act of 1982 allowed thrift institutions to invest in business loans and corporate bonds. While most thrifts did not invest in corporate bonds, some amassed large portfolios of these securities.

▪   *Merger demand.* Yet another factor was the expansion of the field of M&As. As the targets of M&As as well as LBOs became increasingly larger, the demand for capital to fund these purchases grew. Investors increasingly relied on the junk bond market to provide a large part of this funding. In fact, research has showed that over half of the junk bonds issued in the fourth merger wave were M&A-related.

Historical Role of Drexel Burnham Lambert

Drexel Burnham Lambert was one of the first investment banks to underwrite new-issue junk bonds and was unique in its efforts to promote the junk bond market as an attractive investment alternative. These efforts were spearheaded by the former manager of Drexel's Beverly Hills office, Michael Milken. Drexel's unique role as a market maker became most apparent in 1986, when bondholders accused Morgan Stanley of failing to make a market for the junk bonds of People Express, which it had previously underwritten. When the price of the bonds fell significantly, Morgan Stanley was reported to have done little to support them.

Morgan Stanley's reported passive stance contrasts strongly with Drexel's aggressive market making in the 1980s. As a result of its involvement in the junk bond market, Drexel progressed from a second-tier investment banking firm to a major first-tier firm. The firm's dominance in the junk bond field during the 1980s made Drexel second only to Salomon Brothers as an underwriting firm.

Drexel made a market for the junk bonds it had underwritten by cultivating a number of buyers who could be depended on to purchase a new offering of junk bonds. The network of buyers for new issues often consisted of previous issuers whose junk bonds were underwritten by Drexel Burnham Lambert. Drexel and Michael Milken used this network to guarantee a demand for new issues of junk bonds. This guarantee often came in the form of a *commitment letter*, indicating that the buyer would buy a specific amount of a given issue of junk bonds when they were issued. The commitment fees that the investor might receive were usually less than 1% (i.e., three-quarters of 1%) of the total capital committed. In riskier deals, however, it ranged as high as 2%.

Drexel commanded a dominant 57% of the total market share of new public issues of junk bonds in 1983 and 40% to 50% from 1984 through the beginning of 1987, when its market share began to steadily decline. This was mainly the result of the energetic efforts of other large investment banks—especially Goldman Sachs, Merrill Lynch, First Boston, and Morgan Stanley—to capture part of the lucrative junk bond market. They increased their junk bond resources by expanding their trading, research, and sales staffs. The investment apparently paid off; by the late 1980s each of these banks had captured a significant part of the new public issue junk bond market. Drexel's dominant role in the junk bond market appeared to loosen in 1989 after Milken's indictment. Some firms, hesitant to do business with Drexel, turned to other underwriters. Drexel's end came ingloriously with its Chapter 11 filing in February 1990.

Investment Bankers and Highly Confident Letters

As the size and complexity of the financing packages associated with the deals of the fourth merger wave increased, the need to demonstrate an ability to raise the requisite capital became more important, particularly for bidders who were significantly smaller than their targets. This process was facilitated by the use of a Highly Confident Letter, in which the bidder's investment bank states that, based on market conditions and its analysis of the deal, it is highly confident that it can raise the necessary capital to complete the deal. This letter is often attached to tender offer filing documents.

The genesis of the Highly Confident Letter can be traced to Carl Icahn's $4.5 billion bid for Phillips Petroleum in 1985. Icahn's investment banker, Drexel Burnham Lambert, issued a Highly Confident Letter in which it stated, "We are highly confident we can arrange the financing."[5] The letter gave Icahn instant credibility and was a major contributing factor in his success in selling the shares he had acquired back to Phillips without testing the strength of Drexel's letter. Thereafter the Highly Confident Letter became an important part of the takeover business.

Icahn later used the Highly Confident Letter as an essential part of his "takeover tool kit." Armed with the letter and the resulting increased credibility produced by this investment banker's ability to marshal the vast financial resources of the then-strong junk bond market, Icahn had to be taken more seriously. Targets responded to threats from hostile bidders armed with their letters with offers of greenmail.

Investment Banks and Liquidity of Junk Bond Investments

As noted previously, investment banks, led by the trailblazing role of Drexel Burnham Lambert in the 1980s, served as a market maker for junk bonds. In doing so, they

---

[5] Moira Johnston, *Takeover* (New York: Penguin, 1987), 147.

became buyers when holders wanted to sell and sellers when investors wanted to buy. This gave the market liquidity it otherwise would not have had. The enhanced liquidity lowered the risk of these investments and made them more marketable. Another way in which investment banks enhanced the liquidity of these investments was to work with troubled issuers when they appeared to be in danger of defaulting. At one time, Drexel prided itself that issues underwritten by Drexel did not default. Drexel would go to great lengths to ensure that these troubled issuers would not be technically declared in default. Sometimes the default might be prevented by the issuance of a new offering that would be exchanged for the troubled outstanding issue. In cases of more serious liquidity problems, very different types of bonds might be offered in exchange for the bonds that investors were holding. Such bonds might not pay cash interest payments for a period of time while the issuer took steps to improve its financial condition. One version of such securities is *PIK*, or *payment-in-kind* securities. These bonds do not make cash payments for an initial period, which might range from 3 to 10 years. These bonds came under sharp criticism as the junk bond market began to falter in the late 1980s and investors were being presented with the alternative of exchanging their interest-paying bonds that were about to default for other bonds that would not pay cash interest payments for an extended period of time. Given the poor prospects that security holders with an inferior position in the bankruptcy liquidation hierarchy have, many bondholders reluctantly accepted the exchanges.

Junk Bond Refinancing and Bridge Loans

When companies do a cash acquisition, they need the up-front capital to pay the target company shareholders for their shares. They may plan on using high-yield bonds to finance the deal, but the seller might not want to exchange its shares for the high-yield bonds the buyer would issue. To solve this problem the buyer then can enlist the services of its investment banker, who raises the short-term financing the buyer needs. This financing can come in the form of a bridge loan from the bank. This loan can then be "refinanced" at a later date through an issuance of high-yield bonds.

Collapse of the Junk Bond Market in the Late 1980s

In spite of its rapid growth in the mid-1980s, the junk bond market collapsed at the end of that decade. Certain major events rocked the junk bond market in the 1980s. They include the bankruptcy of the LTV Corporation and Integrated Resources, and the legal problems of Michael Milken and his investment bank, Drexel Burnham Lambert. These events are discussed in the following sections.

LTV Bankruptcy

The resiliency of the junk bond market was called into question in 1986, when the LTV Corporation defaulted on the high-yield bonds it had issued. The LTV bankruptcy was the largest corporate bankruptcy at that time and represented 56% of the total debt defaulting in 1986.[6] Ma, Rao, and Peterson showed that this event caused a temporary six-month revision in the market's probabilities for default, as reflected by the risk-premium yields on junk bonds. This effect proved transitory, and the market more than fully rebounded afterward. The Ma study indicates that the junk bond market was at that time quite resilient and more than capable of withstanding the shock of a major default.

Financing Failures of 1989

In addition to the bankruptcy of LTV, the junk market was jolted by other critical events. While the LTV bankruptcy was not related to M&As, the failures of other junk bond issuers were directly related to overpriced and overleveraged deals. Large offerings by issuers, such as Campeau Corporation, swelled the market with increased supply. In the first half of 1989, $20 billion worth of junk bonds was offered, compared with $9.2 billion for the same period in 1988. Issuers had to offer higher and higher rates to attract investors to buy the risky securities. Campeau Corporation's offering of junk bonds in 1988, led by the investment bank First Boston Corporation, was poorly received, even though it provided 16% coupon payments on 12-year bonds and 17.75% coupons on 16-year bonds. In October 1988, First Boston had to withdraw a $1.15 billion junk-bond offering as investor demand for the debt-laden concern's securities failed to materialize. The investment bank responded with a $750-million offering that provided higher yields. However, demand was very weak. For example, junk bonds issued by Resorts International, Tracor, and Interco declined significantly during this year. The lack of a strong, reliable secondary market made it even more difficult to offer new high-yield bonds. This downturn was a contributing factor in the unraveling of the financing for the buyout of United Airlines in October 1989. Even when reputable issuers, such as Ohio Mattress—maker of Sealy and Stearns & Foster mattresses—offered 15% interest rates for a proposed $475 million issue in 1989, the market refused to respond. This event became known as the "burning mattress."

Default of Integrated Resources

Integrated Resources, a company built on junk bonds and the most prominent buyer of junk bonds among insurance companies, defaulted in June 1989 and filed for bankruptcy in early 1990. This sent shock waves through the ranks of institutional investors who had helped fuel the growth of the junk bond market.

Bankruptcy of Drexel Burnham Lambert

In its heyday in 1986, Drexel reported pretax annual profits of $1 billion. Only two years later, in late 1988, it pleaded guilty to criminal charges and paid more than $40 million in fines. In 1989, Drexel showed a loss of $40 million.

---

[6] Christopher K. Ma, Ramesh P. Rao, and Richard L. Peterson, "The Resiliency of the High-Yield Bond Market," *Journal of Finance* 44, no. 4 (September 1989): 1085–1097.

The immediate cause of Drexel's Chapter 11 bankruptcy filing was a liquidity crisis resulting from the firm's inability to pay short-term loans and commercial paper financing that came due. Securities firms generally rely on short-term capital to finance their securities holdings. Drexel had been the issuer of more than $700 million in commercial paper.[7] When the commercial paper market contracted in 1989, Drexel was forced to pay off more than $575 million, which could not be refinanced through the issues of new commercial paper. Closing the commercial paper market effectively wiped out Drexel's liquidity. With the prior collapse of the junk bond market, Drexel could not seek long-term financing as a substitute. The firm had no recourse but to file for Chapter 11 protection.

Banking Regulation

The savings and loan difficulties of this period led to a regulatory backlash against those institutions that invested heavily in junk bonds. Many of these institutions did so to avoid the disintermediation that came from having to compete for deposits that were leaving savings and loans (S&Ls) in favor of other higher-yielding investments. In order to be able to pay higher rates to depositors, S&Ls often invested in high-yield bonds. When the Financial Institutions Reform, Recovery, and Enforcement Act was passed in 1989, banks were forced to mark their junk bond holdings to market values. Many were forced to sell off their junk bond investments into a market in which demand was weak and supply was increasing. This further weakened the junk bond market.

Role of Junk Bond Research in the Growth of the Market in the Fourth Wave

Various studies on junk bonds have been performed that seem to indicate these securities are not as risky as some investors perceive, and may provide returns in excess of the risk they have. One such study was done by W. Braddock Hickman's National Bureau of Economic Research, which was published in 1958.[8] One of Hickman's main conclusions was that noninvestment-grade bonds showed higher returns than investment-grade bonds, even after taking into account default losses. The time period of his study was from 1900 to 1943. These results were challenged by Fraine and Mills, who pointed out that factors such as interest rate fluctuations may have biased Hickman's results.[9] Although Hickman's pro–junk bond results have been widely cited by the securities industry, the contradictory findings of Fraine and Mills failed to receive similar attention. Indeed, Michael Milken used Hickman's findings to market high-yield bonds to conservative institutional investors.

The existence of the Hickman research notwithstanding, high-yield bonds remained a difficult sale until the late 1970s. Institutional investors were reluctant to

---

[7] Affidavit filed by Frederick H. Joseph in Drexel Bankruptcy Filing, printed by the *New York Times*, February 15, 1990, D5.

[8] W. B. Hickman, *Corporate Bond Quality and Investor Experience* (Princeton, NJ: Princeton University Press, 1958), 195.

[9] Harold G. Fraine and Robert H. Mills, "The Effects of Defaults and Credit Deterioration on Yields of Corporate Bonds," *Journal of Finance* 16, no. 3 (September 1961): 423–434.

add to their portfolio securities that they considered unduly risky. This attitude started to change with the publication of another major research study that seemed to lend support to the Hickman findings. A study by Altman and Namacher seemed to provide evidence that the default rates of low-rated firms were much lower than was believed.[10] The Altman and Namacher study showed that the average default rate for junk bonds was 2.1%, which was not significantly higher than the default rate on investment-grade securities, which was almost 0%. The Altman and Namacher study revealed that as the time of default approaches, the rating declines. They observed that 13 of 130 (10%) were rated as investment-grade one year before default, whereas only 4 out of 130 (3%) received such a rating six months before default.[11] This implies that the bond rating can be used as a reliable indicator of the likelihood of default.

The Altman and Namacher study had been one of the dominant pieces of research on the default risk of junk bonds. Their results and those of other studies of that era implied that the marketplace is inefficient and pays a return in excess of the risk on these securities.[12] However, the results were affected by the fact that Altman's default measure, the dollar value of bonds in default divided by the total dollar value of high-yield bonds in the market, was very much affected by the rapid growth of this market in the mid-1980s, which to some extent masked the default rate. Bonds that may be risky may not manifest this risk until they have "aged" for a period of time. The Altman and Namacher study did not follow the bonds over their life to see how their risk profile changed as the bonds aged.

A study by Asquith, Mullins, and Wolff considered the aging effect of junk bonds.[13] He and his co-researchers followed the junk bonds that were issued in 1977 and 1978 until 1986. In doing so, they offset the impact of the rapidly growing junk bond market that affected the Altman and Namacher results. Their study also commented on the role that exchanges played in understating the true junk bond default rate. When junk bond issuers were in danger of defaulting, investment banks such as Drexel Burnham Lambert sometimes would offer bondholders an exchange of new bonds that might not pay interest right away but that might offer higher interest in the future. Other exchanges involved non-dividend-paying (at least not paying dividends at that time) stock. Bondholders often reluctantly accepted such exchanges, as the alternative of default was less attractive.

The Asquith study also considered the adverse impact that the call-in of bonds had. Many firms that issued junk bonds with relatively higher interest rates took advantage of the decline in interest rates after they were issued. Many junk bonds have call protection for a limited period of time; during that period the bonds may not be called in. At the end of that period the bonds may be called in, as a result of which the bondholders may be

---

[10] Edward I. Altman and Scott A. Namacher, *The Default Rate Experience on High-Yield Corporate Debt* (New York: Morgan Stanley, 1985).

[11] Ibid.

[12] Mark I. Weinstein, "A Curmudgeon View of Junk Bonds," *Journal of Portfolio Management* 13, no. 3 (Spring 1987): 76–80.

[13] Paul Asquith, David W. Mullins, Eric Wolff, "Original Issue High Yield Bonds: Aging Analysis of Defaults, Exchanges and Calls," *Journal of Finance*, 44 (4), September 1989, 923–952.

TABLE 10.1 Cumulative Junk Bond Default Rate in Asquith Study

	Total Issued		Total Defaulted		Cumulative % of Total Default	
Issue Year	Number	Amount ($ mil)	Number	Amount ($ mil)	Number	Amount (mil $)
1977	26	908	6	308	23.08	33.92
1978	51	1,442	17	494	33.33	34.26
1979	41	1,263	12	312	29.27	24.70

deprived of a rate of return superior to other rates available in the market. Asquith and his co-researchers reported that 23 to 43% of the bonds issued from 1977 to 1982 were called by November 1, 1988. These calls were a result of the decline in interest rates that started in 1982.

The Asquith study defined defaults to be either a declaration of default by the bond trustee, a bankruptcy filing by the issuer, or the assignment of a D rating by Standard & Poor's. If the bonds were exchanged for other securities that eventually defaulted, this was also considered a default of the original issue. This study showed that, as expected, default rates were higher for "older" issues. For example, bonds issued in 1977 had a cumulative default rate of 33.92%, whereas bonds issued in 1978 had a cumulative default rate equal to 34.26% (Table 10.1).

Junk Bond Defaults and Aging

The Asquith study also measured the relationship between defaults and aging. As noted, it showed that default rates were low in the early years after the issuance of a junk bond. They found, for example, that for 7 of the 10 issue years covered by their study, there were no defaults in the first year. Seven years after issue, however, defaults rose to between 17% and 26%. By years 11 and 12, the default rates increased to greater than one-third for the two relevant issue years, 1977 and 1978. Altman, however, disputes the relationship between aging and defaults and fails to find a discernible pattern that would support this relationship.[14]

The Asquith study raises serious questions regarding the riskiness of junk bonds. It contradicts the Altman and Namacher findings, which downplay the riskiness of junk bonds. However, later research by Altman supports the aging factor. For example, Altman and Kishore show that low-rated bonds are less likely to default in the first year of their life, but that this probability rises significantly by the third year.[15]

---

[14] Edward Altman, "Setting the Record Straight on Junk Bonds: A Review of the Research on Default Rates and Returns," *Journal of Applied Corporate Finance* 3, no. 21 (Summer 1990): 82–95. Also in Patrick A. Gaughan, ed., *Readings in Mergers and Acquisitions* (Cambridge: Basil Blackwell, 1994), 185–200.

[15] Edward Altman and Vellore Kishore, "Report on Defaults and Returns on High-Yield Bonds: Analysis through 1997," Working Paper, New York University Salomon Center, December 1997.

Changing Role of Junk Bond Financing in Takeovers and Corporate Finance

The growth of the junk bond market in the 1980s added a highly combustible fuel to the fires of the fourth merger wave. As described previously, one of the first hostile takeover attempts financed by junk bonds was the attempted bid for Gulf Oil Co. by the celebrated raider T. Boone Pickens. Pickens was president of a relatively small company, Mesa Petroleum. A small oil company by Seven Sisters standards, Mesa was not a serious threat. When Pickens arranged a $2 billion commitment from Drexel Burnham Lambert, as set forth in a Highly Confident Letter, the smaller oil company gained instant credibility. The monies were ultimately to be raised by an offering of junk bonds. The access to such large amounts of financing instantly made Mesa a credible threat. Gulf took the offer seriously and finally agreed to be bought out by a white knight—Chevron. This $13.3 billion deal was the largest U.S. merger at that time, and it enabled Chevron/Gulf to become the largest U.S. refiner. In 2001, Chevron would merge with Texaco, forming one of the largest oil companies in the world.

Junk bond financing was particularly important for bidders that lacked the internal capital and access to traditional financing sources, such as bank loans. The use of junk bond financing to finance acquisitions grew dramatically in 1988 but then collapsed in the years that followed.

The collapse of the junk bond market in the late 1980s contributed to the end of the fourth merger wave. There were other major factors, such as the slowdown of the economy along with the overall decline of the stock market. Many of the companies that utilized high-yield bonds to finance highly leveraged takeovers ended up defaulting in the 1990s. When the economy began to recover in the early 1990s and companies began to again consider the benefits of rapid growth that M&As provide, many vowed they would never overleverage themselves. Many companies initially indicated that deals have a sound financial structure with more equity and less reliance on debt. Therefore, when the fifth merger wave ensued, high-yield bonds played a much less significant role.

Following the fourth merger wave the M&A market relied much less on junk bond financing. However, the original issue high-yield bond market became a permanent part of the world of corporate finance. Companies that had been shut out of the bond market could now offer a higher yield and access the bond market. In addition, bank lending became more flexible as private equity buyers helped fuel the demand for loans by banks to borrowers, which would be much more heavily levered customers than what banks would normally lend to. Thus, the leveraged loan market became another financing alternative for acquirers to consider.

Junk Bond Financing of M&As in the 2000s

Junk bonds remain an important source of financing for M&As. They are used in conjunction with other sources of debt financing including leverage loans. The demand for junk bond financing varies with both the strength of the M&A market as well as the risk preferences of investors. Being a more high risk security, investors may shy away from this area of finance when market conditions weaken and investors become more risk adverse. However, when rates decline, as they did in the wake of the subprime crisis when central banks engaged in expansionary monetary policy which drove down rates, investors may chase yields and move more capital into the junk bond market. Such conditions can make implementing junk bond financing of M&As easier to complete as the demand for these bonds may be higher.

LEVERAGED LOAN MARKET

One of the reasons why the original issue junk bond market grew was that there was a demand for an alternative to bank loans. It is ironic, therefore, that in the 2000s leveraged loans have often replaced junk bond financing as the preferred debt financing source used to complete deals.

Leveraged loans are loans to speculative grade borrowers. These are usually borrowers who already have a significant amount of debt or who are now taking on a high amount of debt relative to equity capital. These loans are usually *syndicated loans* that are loans with a single set of terms but that have multiple lenders with each supply part of the overall debt capital.

Loans can be characterized as leveraged loans due to their higher rate, such as LIBOR + 150 basis points. They also can be rated, and the rating system is similar to that of junk bonds, with leveraged loans having a rating of BB or lower being considered part of the leveraged loan market.

This market is not a new one but has existed for some time (see Figure 10.2). However, like many financial markets it has evolved over time. This is especially true for the role that leveraged loans play in the M&A business. Syndicated loans grew significantly in the 1970s as Western commercial banks made large loans to developing countries, especially to Latin and South American companies. When there were significant defaults in these loans, the syndicated loans market shifted to corporate

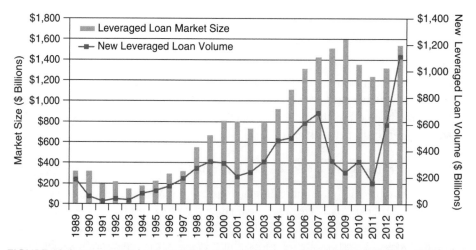

FIGURE 10.2   Leveraged Loan Market Size ($ Billions). *Source*: Credit Suisse, LPC.

America and became an important source of financing for M&As in the fourth merger wave. However, lenders were again "burned" by large defaults by borrowers such as Federated Stores and Ames. The economic slowdown at the end of the 1980s and the recession of 1990–1991 caused this market to slow down. However, as the economy rebounded in the mid-1990s, leveraged loans again became an important source of financing for M&As.

As Figure 10.3 shows, the M&A-related leveraged loan market grew exponentially in the sixth merger wave, particularly based upon demand from private equity buyers. However, the market collapsed after the subprime crisis and the related default of Lehman Brothers. As the M&A market slowly recovered in the years that followed, so too did the leveraged loan market.

Leveraged loans have certain advantages over junk bonds for acquirers. Junk bonds are public market securities and bring with them all the drawbacks that an issuance of public market bonds has. In addition, as we will discuss ahead, leverage loans may be somewhat less risky for investors compared to junk bonds.

One major difference between the leveraged loan market that now exists compared with the past is that there are now more sources of lending, such as hedge funds. These funds provide financing for loans such as second-lien debt. This debt is senior debt that has a secondary claim on assets after debt that is held by banks.

Commercial banks may assume loans with the knowledge that they can syndicate the debt to hedge funds. These loans may have a higher claim on the assets of the ultimate borrower and thus offer a lower rate relative to junk bonds, which is attractive to borrowers. Because this market grew significantly in the mid-2000s, there is an abundant supply of capital that commercial banks know they can tap into to offload the risks of these loans. The availability of this capital makes the loans relatively liquid, which encourages banks to lend. In turn, this has caused this supply of debt financing to grow—and often surpass—junk bonds as the preferred debt financing source.

M&As and LBOs constitute a very significant percentage of the overall leveraged loan market. This percentage, however, varies with the volume of deals.

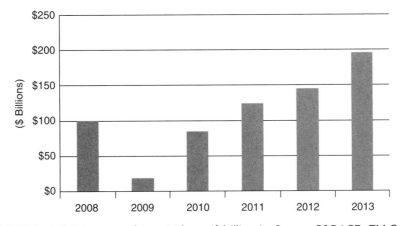

FIGURE 10.3 M&A Leveraged Loan Volume ($ billions). *Source:* S&P LCD, TM Capital.

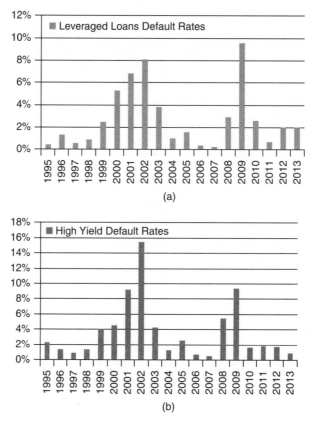

FIGURE 10.4   (a) Leveraged Loans Default Rates and (b) High-Yield Default Rates. *Source*: Credit Suisse, LPC.

Default, Recovery, and Loss Rates: Leveraged Loans versus Junk Bonds

Both junk bonds and leveraged loans have comparable default rates. As would be expected, these default rates are very sensitive to economic conditions. The leverage loan default rate was less than 1% in 2007 but rose to greater than 10% by 2009. The default rate steadily declined after 2009, and by 2011–2012 it was similar to presubprime crisis levels (see Figure 10.4).

While the default rate of junk bonds and leverage loans is somewhat similar, the *recovery rate* can be greater for leveraged loans. This lowers the risk of leveraged loans, giving them an advantage over junk bonds.

Expansion of Banks Originating Leveraged Loans

Commercial banks have discovered that by syndicating leveraged loans to buyers of debt, such as hedge funds, they can quickly take the debt off their balance sheet while originating the loans and generating good income from this service. In the early 2000s, in the

United States only a few large commercial banks accounted for the bulk of the leveraged loan business. These included banks such as Bank of America and Wells Fargo. However, the rest of the banking industry has responded to the profits with measured risks that are available in this business. This came at a time when hedge funds were eager to participate in this lending. As a result, the number of large commercial bank lenders in this area of finance has significantly increased.

Dealmakers in the mid-2000s noticed that they could not always count on a positive reception from the high-yield bond market, whereas the response was often more favorable in the leveraged loan market. In addition, in the mid-2000s, the junk bond market might ask rates in the 12% to 14% range, while the leveraged loan market might quote a rate that is in the range of 200 to 300 basis points above LIBOR. However, when markets perceive higher risk levels, such as when the subprime crisis took hold, rates can rise sharply. It is ironic that when overall rates fell in response to the Federal Reserve's expansionary monetary policy in 2008–2009, risk premiums on leveraged loans rose. More importantly, however, many lenders withdrew from the market and were reluctant to make these loans even when the rate included a significant risk premium.

In 1999, regulations that previously limited the ability of banks to underwrite securities were relaxed. This allowed commercial banks to enter underwriting markets, such as the junk bond business. Once given the opportunity to enter this arena, commercial banks moved in aggressively and grabbed market share. As of 2005, the leader in this business was the securities units of Bank of America, with approximately 12% of the total market.[16] They were followed by JPMorgan Chase and Citigroup Inc. These banks are also leaders in the leveraged loan market; these are loans made to noninvestment-grade borrowers. These loans play an important role in the LBO business as borrowers may look to both sources of debt to complete leveraged takeovers.

Recent Trends in Regulation of the Leveraged Loan Market

In the wake of the subprime crisis the Federal Reserve had been concerned about the leverage loan market. However, deal volume slowed dramatically during the Great Recession, and this was less of a concern. However, deal volume began to pick up in the years that followed and with it a more aggressive expansion of the leveraged loan market. In 2013 the Federal Reserve and the Comptroller of the Currency issued guidance that sought to deter the financing of very highly leveraged deals. The regulator's reasoning is that if the economy faltered, highly leveraged companies would be extra vulnerable to failure.

The guidance indicated that banks should avoid funding deals that left the companies with debt that was more than six times EBITDA. The guidance also discouraged repayment time periods that were excessively long.

---

[16] Tom Sullivan, "Big Commercial Banks Are Junk Bond Giants: Units of Bank of America, J.P. Morgan Rise to the Top of the Underwriting Ranks," *Wall Street Journal*, July 14, 2005, C4.

STAPLED FINANCING

Another innovation in the M&A market is the use by buyers of *stapled financing*. When a buyer is considering a purchase of a target, one element of uncertainty is the financing that will be needed to complete the deal. Such uncertainty could cause a buyer to pass on a given transaction. In order to maximize the chances of a favorable bid, the investment banks of some targets sometimes offer prearranged financing with specific agreed-on terms. Stapled financing is a prearranged financing package made available to bidders by the *target's* financing advisor.

Stapled financing became popular during and right after the 2001 recession that followed the downturn in securities markets. The economic contraction made access to capital markets more problematic and helped cool off deal volume. Investment banks, seeking to make deals easier for sellers and buyers, began to prearrange the financing that would be necessary to purchase the target. This became an additional service that they offered that enhanced the total fees they realized from deals. While stapled financing was an innovation brought about to deal with weakness in capital markets, it has grown significantly as the markets improved in the 2000s.

Morgan Stanley claims that it is the first investment bank to provide such a complete package. One of the first deals in which Morgan Stanley used these financing packages involved the auction of Dresser Industries, which was a unit of Halliburton Co. Dresser makes engineering equipment used in the petroleum industry. Morgan Stanley got together with CSFB and was able to arrange the sale of the unit to two private equity buyers, First Reserve Corp. and Odyssey Investment Partners LLC, for $1.3 billion.[17] Of this total, $820 million came from a loan package that the two investment banks arranged in advance.

Stapled financing can help facilitate an auction, which tends to result in greater sale prices. By making the financing easier, a potentially greater number of buyers may pursue a given deal. For this reason it may be advantageous for sellers to utilize the services of investment bankers and advisors that also have a strong financing capability.

The terms of the stapled financing package may not always be the best for the buyer. The investment banks offering the stapled financing are making the deal easier to finance and seek a fee for this service. However, shrewd buyers, such as private equity firms that normally have good access to other financing providers, can "shop the loan" to other banks so that they assure themselves they are getting the best terms.

As with other areas of M&A, stapled financing is not without its potential conflicts. Seeking the returns from financing, investment banks may have an incentive to push deals through that may not be in the seller's interests. Sellers need to be aware of their own value so that they do the deal that is in the best interests of their shareholders. Admittedly, they utilize the services of an investment advisor to help them with this process. However, when that advisor is also the stapled financing provider, the seller has to be mindful of the advisor's other interests.

---

[17] Vyvyan Tenorio, "A Permanent Staple? Stapled Financing," *The Deal* (May 1–7, 2006): 36.

Stapled Financing Potential Conflicts: *Del Monte* Decision

The potential conflicts involved with stapled financing got significant attention in the Del Monte shareholder lawsuit in which the Delaware Chancery Court issued a preliminary injunction enjoining a shareholder vote on a proposed 2010 $5.3 billion leveraged buyout of the company by a consortium of three private equity buyers.[18] The court was concerned that the board was not sufficiently active in the sales process and perhaps the sell-side financial advisor had too much incentive to see the deal with the private equity advisor go through so as to reap the financial rewards from the financing fees. In fact, the court stated that the seller's financial advisor had "secretly and selfishly manipulated the sale process to engineer a transaction that would permit Barclays to obtain lucrative buy-side financing fees." The court also prevented the enforcement of no-shop provisions and termination fees, which could impede a true auction. The lawsuit was settled in October 2011 by Barclays Capital agreeing to pay $89 million.[19]

In spite of concern about conflicts, having a stapled financing commitment in place can greatly reduce the financing-related uncertainties for both buyers and sellers, but it is not foolproof. If markets suddenly shift, such as when the subprime crisis took hold, lenders may simply choose to not honor the agreement or provide the financing. Buyers and sellers are then left to resort to litigation to try to remedy the situation. This is a time-consuming, expensive, and uncertain route to take.

---

[18] *In re Del Monte Foods Co. S'holders Litig*, 25 A. 3d 813 (Del. Ch. Feb 14, 2011).
[19] Steven J. Daniels and Faiz Ahmad, "Stapled Financing and Delaware's Del Monte Decision: Private Equity Buyer Beware?" Skadden, Arps, Slate, Meagher & Flom LLP, Global Reference Guide 2012, Private Equity and Venture Capital.

PART FOUR

IV

Corporate Restructuring

CHAPTER ELEVEN

Corporate Restructuring

ALTHOUGH THE FIELD OF mergers and acquisitions (M&As) tends to focus on corporate expansion, companies often have to contract and downsize their operations. This need may arise because a division of the company is performing poorly or simply because it no longer fits into the firm's plans. Restructuring may also be necessary to undo a previous merger or acquisition that was unsuccessful. While we see that many sell-offs are motivated by financial pressures brought on by a combination of high leverage and weak economic demand, we also see that the volume of sell-offs increases when overall deal volume increases. As such, sell-off deal volume tends to follow the ups and down of the economy just like M&As follow the overall pattern of economic fluctuations. This is the case not only in the United States but also in Asia and Europe.

In this chapter, the different types of corporate contraction are considered, and a decision-making methodology for reaching the divestiture decision is developed. The methods used to value acquisition targets are also used by companies to determine whether a particular component of the firm is worth retaining. Both the divesting and the acquiring firms commonly go through a similar type of analysis as they view the transaction from opposite sides. Even though the methods are similar, the two parties may come up with different values because they use different assumptions or have different needs.

This chapter considers the shareholder wealth effects of several forms of corporate restructuring. Corporate contraction may have positive stock price effects when the divested component fails to yield a value to the corporation that is commensurate with its market value. In such instances the corporation may be able to enhance the value of shareholder investments by pursuing a policy of corporate restructuring.

Corporate restructuring can take several different forms: divestitures, equity carve-outs, spin-offs, split-offs, exchange offer, and split-ups. A *divestiture* is a sale of a portion of the firm to an outside party. The selling firm is usually paid in cash, marketable securities, or a combination of the two. An *equity carve-out* is a variation of a divestiture that involves the sale of an equity interest in a subsidiary to outsiders. The sale may not necessarily leave the parent company in control of the subsidiary. The new equity gives the investors shares of ownership in the portion of the selling company that is being divested. In an equity carve-out, a new legal entity is created with a stockholder base that may be different from that of the parent selling company. The divested company has a different management team and is run as a separate firm.

A new legal entity is also created in a standard *spin-off*. Once again, new shares are issued, but here they are distributed to stockholders on a pro rata basis. As a result of the proportional distribution of shares, the stockholder base in the new company is the same as that of the old company. Although the stockholders are initially the same, the spun-off firm has its own management and is run as a separate company. Another difference between a spin-off and a divestiture is that a divestiture involves an infusion of funds into the parent corporation, whereas a spin-off normally does not provide the parent with a cash infusion. In an *exchange offer*, also called a *split-off*, new shares in a subsidiary are issued and shareholders in the parent company are given the option to either hold on to their shares or exchange these shares for an equity interest in the new publicly held subsidiary. This type of transaction is somewhat similar to a spin-off in that new shares are issued that represent an equity interest in a subsidiary that is separated from the parent. It is different from a spin-off, however, in that in order the get the newly issued shares, parent company shareholders have to part with their shares. For example, in 2013 Pfizer offered its shareholders the opportunity to exchange their shares for the shares of its spun-off animal health subsidiary, Zoetis. Shareholders were offered $107.52 worth of Zoetis shares for each $100 of Pfizer shares. The additional $7.52 in Zoetis shares gave them an incentive to exchange. While the parent company loses the contribution to profits of the entity that is separated from the parent company, total shares outstanding of the parent company are reduced which may offset the losses of profits in earnings per share.

In a *split-up*, the entire firm is broken up into a series of spin-offs. The end result of this process is that the parent company no longer exists, leaving only the newly formed companies. The stockholders in the companies may be different because stockholders exchange their shares in the parent company for shares in one or more of the units that are spun off.

Sometimes companies do a combination of more than one of these methods of separation. For example, in February 1999, General Motors (GM) did an equity carve-out of just over 17% of its auto products subsidiary, Delphi Automotive Systems. Three months later the remainder of the company was spun off, with GM shareholders receiving 0.7 shares of Delphi for each share of GM that they owned. With these transactions GM believed it was exiting the auto parts business. However, the labor agreements GM had with the United Auto Workers left GM with some responsibility for the burdensome wage and benefit payments to Delphi workers. This was problematic when Delphi was forced to file for bankruptcy in 2005.

RJR NABISCO RESTRUCTURING

RJR Nabisco announced in 1999 that it was engaging in a dramatic restructuring that would involve divestitures and spin-offs. The parent company, RJR Nabisco Holdings Corp., decided to sell R. J. Reynolds International to Japan Tobacco for almost $8 billion. The tobacco business, long known for impressive cash flows, was already run as separate domestic and international entities. R. J. Reynolds Tobacco, the domestic unit, was then spun off. Part of the reason for the deal was the problems that the domestic tobacco unit had as it faced an ongoing onslaught of litigation in the United States. In addition, the unit was losing market share to a stronger rival—Philip Morris. The U.S. tobacco market is a declining market, and R. J. Reynolds was losing market share in a market that was itself shrinking. In addition, although the tobacco business generates steady cash flow, the litigation liabilities loomed large over the company. The international tobacco unit showed more promise, but this promise would have been difficult to realize with the international business tied to the U.S. unit. As part of the restructuring plan, 80% of the food business, Nabisco Holdings Corp., would be owned by Nabisco Group Holdings. The food business was improving, and the company was hoping that the increased focus brought about by the restructuring would enable the company to capitalize on the momentum it was establishing in improving the food business.

Following the restructuring, the stock price of the independent R. J. Reynolds tobacco unit faltered, only to rebound in 2000. The declines in market share began to stabilize at the 24% level, but then deteriorated again due to aggressive discounters, especially those that were not affected by the Master Settlement Agreements, which impose huge cash flow penalties on the four major U.S. cigarette manufacturers as a result of their legal settlement with the states.

In 2004, R. J. Reynolds, the number-two U.S. cigarette manufacturer, merged with Brown and Williamson, the then number-three-ranked company in the industry. The combined company is now called Reynolds American. The fact that this merger was unopposed by the Federal Trade Commission (FTC) underscores the weakness of these two firms. The merger of these two companies, both of which have similar problems in the form of a high volume of litigation and erosion of market share from aggressive discounters, allowed R. J. Reynolds to expand its position in the tobacco business at a time when the sale of its food business to Kraft allowed it to be more focused, while allowing Kraft to become even more of a major presence in the international food business. In 2014 Reynolds approached number three ranked Lorrilard with a merger proposal.

DIVESTITURES

Most sell-offs are simple divestitures. Companies pursue other forms of sell-offs, such as a spin-off or an equity carve-out, to achieve other objectives in addition to getting rid of a particular division. These objectives may be to make the transaction tax-free, which may call for a spin-off.

The most common form of divestiture involves the sale of a division of the parent company to another firm. The process is a form of contraction for the selling company but a means of expansion for the purchasing corporation. The number of divestitures that took place between 1985 and 2014 is listed in Table 11.1.

TABLE 11.1 U.S., European, and Asian Divestitures: 1985–2014

	U.S.			Europe			Asia		
Year	Value ($ mil)	# of Deals	Avg.	Value ($ mil)	# of Deals	Avg.	Value ($ mil)	# of Deals	Avg.
1985	67,038	1,091	61.4	3,305	111	29.8	368	19	19.4
1986	96,610	1,533	63.0	14,974	213	70.3	1,013	39	26.0
1987	101,034	1,305	77.4	18,227	429	42.5	6,530	80	81.6
1988	144,246	1,834	78.7	39,578	893	44.3	12,811	150	85.4
1989	137,228	2,626	52.3	62,535	1,172	53.4	14,500	165	87.9
1990	93,096	2,727	34.1	87,475	1,884	46.4	21,256	313	67.9
1991	69,368	2,654	26.1	73,335	3,953	18.6	13,095	497	26.3
1992	85,295	2,457	34.7	68,210	4,107	16.6	12,913	372	34.7
1993	95,181	2,719	35.0	71,474	3,652	19.6	18,950	683	27.7
1994	153,816	2,956	52.0	66,608	3,279	20.3	17,489	670	26.1
1995	255,077	3,365	75.8	96,620	3,861	25.0	36,384	896	40.6
1996	197,086	3,572	55.2	117,702	3,543	33.2	34,509	948	36.4
1997	342,465	3,612	94.8	175,643	3,498	50.2	52,531	1,011	52.0
1998	283,879	3,686	77.0	216,644	3,466	62.5	47,152	1,503	31.4
1999	385,672	3,297	117.0	314,786	4,592	68.6	64,275	1,435	44.8
2000	357,639	3,107	115.1	375,948	5,243	71.7	94,667	1,625	58.3
2001	364,067	2,822	129.0	219,682	4,421	49.7	75,669	1,641	46.1
2002	180,267	2,765	65.2	220,321	3,415	64.5	63,055	1,917	32.9
2003	235,879	3,125	75.5	214,214	3,992	53.7	59,949	2,390	25.1
2004	267,621	2,946	90.8	281,805	3,615	78.0	69,483	2,834	24.5
2005	370,990	3,102	119.6	409,292	3,953	103.5	96,927	2,691	36.0
2006	468,432	3,391	138.1	532,066	4,277	124.4	119,048	2,733	43.6
2007	598,958	3,406	175.9	753,323	4,590	164.1	197,192	3,300	59.8
2008	345,004	3,021	114.2	377,574	4,305	87.7	165,032	3,461	47.7
2009	262,243	2,847	92.1	218,049	4,707	46.3	164,025	3,712	44.2
2010	292,223	2,638	110.8	338,033	5,658	59.7	292,583	3,709	78.9
2011	468,728	2,801	167.3	306,906	5,800	52.9	176,594	3,569	49.5
2012	374,703	2,940	127.5	373,972	5,152	72.6	193,196	3,439	56.2
2013	343,882	2,915	118.0	304,046	4,860	62.6	244,041	3,397	71.8
2014	537,192	3,118	172.3	467,072	5,355	87.2	322,006	3,911	82.3

Source: Thomson Financial Securities Data, March 6, 2015.

Historical Trends

In the late 1960s, during the third merger wave, the number of divestitures and sell-offs was relatively small as a percentage of the total number of transactions. Companies were engaging in major expansions at this time, widely using the acquisition of other firms to increase the acquiring company's stock price. This expansion came to an abrupt end following changes in the tax laws and other regulatory measures, along with the stock market decline. Companies then began to reconsider some of the acquisitions that had proven to be poor combinations—a need intensified by the 1974–1975 recession. Under the pressure of weaker economic demand, firms were forced to sell off divisions to raise funds and improve cash flow. International competition also pressured some of the 1960s conglomerates to become more efficient by selling off prior acquisitions that were not competitive in a world market.

This reversal of the acquisition trend was visible as early as 1971, when divestitures jumped to 42% of total transactions. The trend peaked in 1975, a period of economic recession, when the number of divestitures constituted 54% of all transactions. They remained between 35% and 40% throughout the 1980s. In the fifth merger wave, however, the number of divestitures rose again as downsizing and refocusing became prominent business strategies. When overall deal volume weakened at the end of that wave, divestiture volume also slowed, only to rebound again in the 2000s, when M&A activity resumed.

Many divestitures are the result of sell-offs of previous acquisitions. The relationship between acquisitions and subsequent divestitures is shown in Figure 11.1. The belief that many divestitures are the undoing of previous acquisitions is seen in the leading trend in the acquisitions curve relative to the divestiture curve. The intense period of

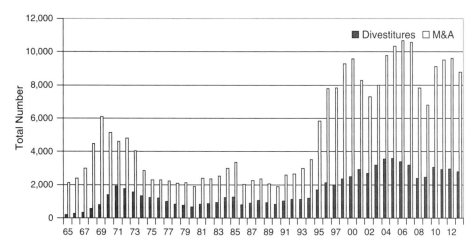

FIGURE 11.1 U.S. Mergers and Acquisitions versus Divestitures: 1965–2013.
Source: Mergerstat Review, 1994–1998, 2014.

merger activity of the late 1960s is reflected in a pronounced peak at this time, followed by a peak in the divestiture curve in the early 1970s. The stock market performance seemed to play a determining role in the volume of divestitures. Linn and Rozeff used regression analysis to show that in years when the stock market fell, such as 1966, 1969, and 1973–1974, the rate of divestiture fell below what one would have predicted given the previous merger rates. When the market performed well (periods that usually correspond to when the economy is doing well), the number of divestitures increased.[1] This research is also consistent with the rising stock market and increased number of divestitures of the 1990s. Figure 11.1 shows that when M&A activity slowed in the late 1980s, the pace of spin-offs and divestitures increased. However, as the fifth merger wave accelerated in the 1990s, the number of sell-offs continued to increase, although as a percentage of total transactions they declined.

Many critics of some corporate acquisitions use the record of the divestitures following poor acquisitions as evidence of ill-conceived expansion planning. These criticisms, which we hear often today, have been voiced for many years. For example, using a sample of 33 companies during the period 1950–1986, Porter showed that these firms divested 53% of the acquisitions that brought the acquiring companies into new industries.[2] Based on this evidence, he concludes that the corporate acquisition record is "dismal." These results were somewhat supported by Ravenscraft and Scherer, who found that 33% of acquisitions made during the 1960s and 1970s were later divested.[3] The track record of many more recent acquisitions also leaves something to be desired.[4]

Global Divestiture Trends

There is a strong similarity among the variations in the volume of divestitures in the United States, Europe, and Asia. However, the value of total divestitures in Europe and Asia rose more sharply in the second half of the fifth merger wave than they did in the United States. All three series declined when the economy turned down in 2000–2001; however, they began to increase again in 2003—especially in Europe (see Figure 11.2a, b, and c). As of the end of 2008, the total value of divestitures in Europe was somewhat greater than in the United States, while deal total and average deal value in Asia was much lower. Deal volume in all three regions fell in 2008 as a result of the fallout from the subprime crisis, which made financing for acquisitions of divested assets more difficult to access. Also, most companies were not looking to expand during this period by acquiring units of other companies, as such companies were more often than not in retrenchment mode.

---

[1] Scott C. Linn and Michael S. Rozeff, "The Corporate Selloff," *Midland Corporate Finance Journal* 2, no. 2 (Summer 1994): 17–26.

[2] Michael Porter, "From Competitive Advantage to Corporate Strategy," *Harvard Business Review* 65, no. 3 (May/June 1987): 43–59.

[3] David Ravenscraft and Frederic Scherer, *Mergers, Selloffs and Economic Efficiency* (Washington, DC: Brookings Institution, 1987).

[4] Patrick A. Gaughan, *Mergers: What Can Go Wrong and How to Prevent It* (Hoboken, NJ: John Wiley & Sons, 2005).

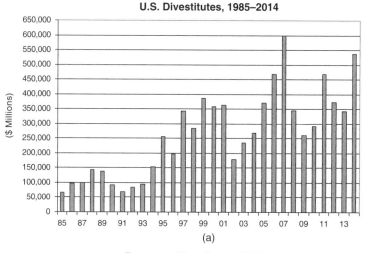

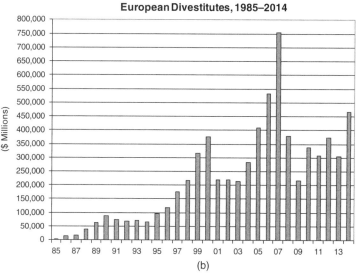

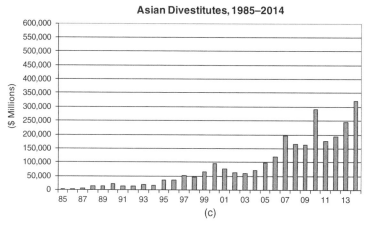

FIGURE 11.2 Divestitures, 1985–2014: (a) United States, (b) Europe, and (c) Asia.
Source: Thomson Financial Securities Data, March 6, 2015.

Divestiture Likelihood and Prior Acquisitions

Kaplan and Weisbach analyzed 271 large acquisitions completed between 1971 and 1982.[5] A total of 43.9%, or 119, of these acquisitions were divested by 1982. The divested entities were held for an average of seven years. Kaplan and Weisbach investigated the pattern of the divestitures in a search for a common motive for some of the sell-offs. They found that diversifying acquisitions are four times more likely to be divested than nondiversifying acquisitions. This result supports other evidence, discussed in Chapter 4, that questions the benefits of acquisition programs. The motives for divestitures, which are discussed in subsequent sections, are summarized in Table 11.2.

Involuntary versus Voluntary Divestitures

A divestiture may be either voluntary or involuntary. An involuntary divestiture may occur when a company receives an unfavorable review by the Justice Department or the Federal Trade Commission (FTC), requiring the company to divest itself of a particular division. For example, in June 1987, in a 4-to-1 vote, the Interstate Commerce Commission (ICC) ruled that the merger of the Santa Fe and Southern Pacific railway systems might reduce competition. Santa Fe had merged with Southern Pacific in 1983 in one of the biggest mergers in railway history. The combined railway was operated together while awaiting an antitrust analysis and ruling from the ICC, which had antitrust jurisdiction for this type of merger. After the ruling, the ICC required Santa Fe–Southern Pacific to submit a divestiture plan within 90 days. The adverse ruling had a depressing effect on Santa Fe's stock price and made the firm a target of a bid by the Henley Group.

TABLE 11.2 Reasons for Divestitures

Reason	Number of Divestitures
Change of focus or corporate strategy	43
Unit unprofitable or mistake	22
Sale to finance acquisition or leveraged restructuring	29
Antitrust	2
Need cash	3
To defend against takeover	1
Good price	3
Divestitures with reasons	103

Source: Steven N. Kaplan and Michael N. Weisbach, "The Success of Acquisitions: Evidence from Divestitures," *Journal of Finance* 47, no. 1 (March 1992):107–138.

---

[5] Steven N. Kaplan and Michael N. Weisbach, "The Success of Acquisitions: Evidence from Divestitures," *Journal of Finance* 47, no. 1 (March 1992): 107–138.

Reasons for Voluntary Divestitures

Poor Strategic Fit of Division

Voluntary divestitures are more common than involuntary divestitures and are motivated by a variety of reasons. For example, the parent company may want to move out of a particular line of business that it feels no longer fits into its overall strategic plans. This decision can be difficult if the unit is generating good financial performance. However, if a company maps out a clear overall strategic direction in which it wants to move and if a unit does not mesh well with those plans, a divestiture may make good sense. If the unit has been performing well, it may generate significant divestiture proceeds that the company can invest in pursuing its overall strategic goals.

Reverse Synergy

One motive that is often ascribed to M&As is synergy. As described in Chapter 4, synergy refers to the additional gains that may be derived when two forms combine. When synergy exists, the combined entity is worth more than the sum of the parts valued separately. In other words, $2 + 2 = 5$. *Reverse synergy* means that the parts are worth more separately than they are within the parent company's corporate structure. In other words, $4 - 1 = 5$. In such cases, an outside bidder might be able to pay more for a division than what the division is worth to the parent company. For instance, a large parent company is not able to operate a division profitably, whereas a smaller firm, or even the division by itself, might operate more efficiently and therefore earn a higher rate of return.

REFOCUSING THROUGH SALES OF COMPONENTS OF PRIOR ACQUISITIONS—THE CASE OF TAITTINGER

When a company acquires a diversified target, it is often the case that it has some business units that are more appealing than others. This was the case in 2005, when Starwood Capital Group, a real estate company, acquired Taittinger for $3.45 billion. Taittinger is the sixth-largest champagne company in that industry. Starwood is known for its diverse hotel properties in an industry that it knows well. However, Taittinger, through its Concorde Group, owned approximately 70 upscale hotels in Europe, such as the Hotel de Crillon in Paris and Hotel Lutetia, as well as the second-largest budget hotel chain on the continent—the Envergure Group. These assets were the main appeal of Taittinger to Starwood. In addition to champagne and hotels, Taittinger also owned the famous Baccarat crystal brand. Like a number of other diversified European companies, such as LVMH, the combinations within the corporate entity are only loosely related. This makes them more easily separable.

(continued)

(*continued*)

The Greenwich-based Starwood is run by Barry S. Sternlicht, a shrewd real estate investor/hotel operator. He founded Starwood in 1995, and in a few years he acquired the Westin hotel chain along with ITT (what was left of that conglomerate), which owned the Sheraton and St. Regis chains. He acquired Taittinger knowing that he would be acquiring real estate assets that he felt were quite valuable. He also knew that while he did not want his company in the champagne or crystal business, the brands he was acquiring would command a good value in the market as they were among the leaders in their respective fields. Taittinger, the third oldest champagne house, was founded in 1734 and since 1931 has been controlled by the Taittinger family. This is another example of large European corporations controlled by family interests.

A good example of reverse synergy occurred in the late 1980s when the Allegis Corporation was forced to sell off its previously acquired companies, Hertz Rent A Car and the Weston and Hilton International hotel chains. Allegis had paid a high price for these acquisitions based on the belief that the synergistic benefits of combining the travel industry companies with United Airlines, its main asset, would more than justify the high prices. When the synergistic benefits failed to materialize, the stock price fell, setting the stage for a hostile bid from the New York investment firm Coniston Partners. Coniston made a bid based on its analysis that the separate parts of Allegis were worth more than the combined entity.

Poor Performance

Companies may want to divest divisions simply because they are not sufficiently profitable. A nonprofitable unit may be diluting the performance of the overall company. Such poorly performing divisions can be a financial drain on the overall company. The performance may be judged by an inability to pay a rate of return that exceeds the parent company's *hurdle rate*—the minimum return threshold that a company will use to evaluate projects or the performance of parts of the overall company. A typical hurdle rate could be the firm's cost of capital.

An example of this occurred in 2014 when Proctor & Gamble, the world's largest maker of consumer products, announced that it would initiate a program to sell off up to 100 of its brands. This would leave the company with approximately 70–80 brands. These 70–80 brands generate about 95% of the company's profitability. The company had been under pressure from activist William Ackman, who contended that the Cincinnati-based company, founded by William Proctor and James Gamble in 1837, badly needed to cut costs and get rid of weaker-performing brands. The company had been built up into an international consumer products colossus through both organic growth as well as significant acquisitions, such as the 1957 acquisition of the Charmin Paper Mills. In the 1990s it acquired MaxFactor and Old Spice. In 2001 it acquired

Clairol from Bristol Myers Squibb, and in 2005 it acquired Gillette. The problem the company had is that it had too many brands that did not generate financial results in line with market expectations. Thus the company needed to slim down and increase its focus.

Capital Market Factors

A divestiture may also take place because the postdivestiture firm, as well as the divested division, has greater access to capital markets. The combined corporate structure may be more difficult for investors to categorize. Certain providers of capital might be looking to invest in steel companies but not in pharmaceutical firms. Other investors might seek to invest capital in pharmaceutical companies but may think that the steel industry is too cyclical and has low growth potential. These two groups of investors might not want to invest in a combined steel and pharmaceutical company, but each group might separately invest in a stand-alone steel or pharmaceutical firm. Divestitures might provide greater access to capital markets for the two firms as separate companies than as a combined corporation.

ALTRIA'S SALE OF MILLER BREWING

Altria is the former Philip Morris. For many years the company operated in three main areas: tobacco, food, and beer (they had a small presence in the finance business). Philip Morris is the leading cigarette company in the world and had a U.S. market share in the 50% range. Its brand Marlboro is one of the leading brand names in the world. Philip Morris's tobacco business is divided into two parts: Philip Morris USA and Philip Morris International. The U.S. business is distinctly different from its international business. First, the U.S. business has been the target of over a thousand lawsuits. Second, U.S. tobacco consumption, on a unit basis, has declined at approximately a 2% annual rate for many years. However, the international tobacco business has been quite robust.

While Miller was the second-largest U.S. brewer, it lagged behind the Budweiser and Busch brands of market leader Anheuser Busch. The beer business in the United States is highly competitive and requires major marketing expenditures to build and expand a brand. Despite their best efforts, Miller failed to make the desired contribution to company profits to warrant Altria staying in this business. In July 2002, the company decided to sell Miller to South African Brewers (SAB) in a deal that valued the company at $5.5 billion. SAB assumed $2 billion of Miller's debt while issuing shares to Philip Morris, which would own a little over a third of the combined SAB/Miller.

SAB was, at the time of the Miller acquisition, the fourth-largest brewer in the world. The deal vaulted SAB into the number-two position in the international beer market. We have seen in Chapter 4 that that the number-one and number-two positions often confer advantages that smaller rivals have difficulty matching. In addition, SAB, which also marketed Pilsner Urquell, now had a major brand in

(continued)

(continued)

the U.S. market. SAB also planned to use its international clout to help advance the Miller brand in and outside of the United States. This deal was part of SAB's growth through acquisition strategy in which the company expanded into a variety of markets in Eastern Europe and Asia. It also acquired a major international brand in the Italian Pironi Group.

In the years following the Miller transaction, the global beer industry consolidated. SAB kept pace with this process by acquiring brewers in Australia, China, and India, as well as in South America and Poland. In 2007 it entered a joint venture with Coors to combine the two company's U.S. operations. InBev, the global industry leader, responded in 2008 by acquiring the largest American beer company, Anheuser Busch, for $52 billion.

Similarly, divestitures may create companies in which investors would like to invest but that do not exist in the marketplace. Such companies are sometimes referred to as *pure plays*. Many analysts argue that the market is incomplete and that there is a demand for certain types of firms that is not matched by a supply of securities in the market. The sale of those parts of the parent company that become pure plays helps complete the market.

The separation of divisions facilitates clearer identification and market segmentation for the investment community. For corporate divisions that need capital to grow, the ability to attract new investment funds may be enhanced if the company is an independent entity. Here, investors contemplating putting funds into a company can more easily project the future returns when the business is a defined and separate unit as opposed to being housed with a corporate shell that has very different growth prospects.

WESTERN UNION 2006 SPIN-OFF BY FIRST DATA CORP

In 2006, First Data Corp decided to spin off its Western Union unit rather than keep it housed with the overall First Data corporate umbrella. First Data, which itself was spun off by American Express in 1992, is a credit card processor. These are companies that process and keep track of credit card charges and provide other related services, such as sending out credit cards to consumers. Over the 2004–2005 time period, First Data's core business suffered significantly as rivals, such as Total Services Systems, aggressively attacked its market share. While its overall financial performance was weak, one bright spot it had was its money transfer business—Western Union. While the credit card processor business was deteriorating, Western Union's business was booming.

It is ironic that Western Union is such a high-growth business, as it was founded in 1851. It began as a communications company and built the first trans-Atlantic telegraph. While so many of the companies founded at that time have long gone by the wayside, Western Union continues to adapt to a changing marketplace and is thriving. It is now the largest money transfer company in the world, with annual revenues of $4 billion. The company does 275 million transactions per year, using 271,000 agencies throughout Asia, Europe, Latin America, and the United States.[a] It has been able to fuel its growth through a broad international expansion strategy. However, much of the great progress Western Union was making was difficult to see when housed within a mundane credit card processing business. The logical conclusion was to release Western Union in a tax-free spin-off to First Data Corp. shareholders and let them realize the benefits of Western Union's anticipated continued success.

[a] Eric Dash, "Western Union, Growing Faster Than Its Parent, Is to Be Spun Off," *New York Times*, January 27, 2006, C3.

Cash Flow Needs

A company may sell off even a well-performing unit if it encounters pressing cash flow needs and if the unit is not essential to its corporate strategy. A sell-off may produce the immediate benefits of an infusion of cash from the sale. The selling firm is selling a long-term asset, which generated a certain cash flow per period, in exchange for a larger payment in the short run. Companies that are under financial duress are often forced to sell off valuable assets to enhance cash flows. Beset with the threat of bankruptcy in the early 1980s, Chrysler Corporation was forced to sell off its prized tank division in an effort to stave off bankruptcy. International Harvester (now known as Navistar) sold its profitable Solar Turbines International Division to Caterpillar Tractor Company Inc. to realize the immediate proceeds of $505 million. These funds were used to cut Harvester's short-term debt in half.

Cash flow factors also motivated the aforementioned sales of Hertz by Ford in 2005 (see case study ahead) as well as the sale by GM of 51% of GMAC in 2006. These divisions were profitable and commanded good prices in the marketplace, while bringing much-needed cash that these two auto companies used to offset sizable operating losses.

FORD MOTOR COMPANY SELLS OFF HERTZ

In the 2000s, both Ford and General Motors (GM) steadily lost market shares to foreign competitors such as Toyota and Honda. These competitors were not hamstrung by the burdensome labor agreements that Ford and GM were forced to deal with. This allowed Toyota and Honda to establish manufacturing plants in the United States and pay laborers a fraction of the costs that Ford and GM were forced to pay. In addition, both companies face huge "legacy" costs of future pension and health care costs for retired employees. When sales of previously hot vehicles, such as SUVs, turned down as consumer tastes changed, both companies began to incur large losses.

(continued)

(*continued*)

In prior years both Ford and GM had vertically integrated. They built up large suppliers that they eventually spun off as Visteon and Delphi. The union liabilities, however, forced Ford to take back Visteon while GM still maintained responsibilities for Delphi labor costs. As its position began to worsen, Ford was forced to sell off its forward vertical integration unit—Hertz. Hertz is one of the market leaders in the U.S. car rental market. Even though Hertz is a leading car rental company, Ford's sales to Hertz did not generate high profits, as car rental companies typically buy using large volume discounts that provide low profits for auto manufacturers. The benefit of the high-volume purchases, however, while not very profitable, allowed auto manufacturers to maintain market share and keep their plants operating at a high capacity. This was necessary as Ford and GM were forced to make payments to union workers even when they did not need all their capacity. The union compensation commitments to employees became mainly fixed costs for Ford and GM, while these same costs were more variable for foreign auto companies, such as Toyota and Honda.

In 2005, Ford decided to sell off Hertz to a consortium of private equity firms, including Clayton Dublier & Rice, Carlyle Group, and Merrill Lynch Global Private Equity. The sale of Hertz, which was reported to have an enterprise value of $15 billion, brought a cash infusion into Ford. The benefits of this additional cash provided Ford some respite from financial pressures while it worked on a major restructuring to restore the company to profitability. The strategy began to bear fruit by 2010 when Ford returned to profitability.

Abandoning the Core Business

The sale of a company's core business is a less common reason for a sell-off. An example of the sale of a core business was the 1987 sale by Greyhound of its bus business. The sale of a core business is often motivated by management's desire to leave an area that it believes has matured and presents few growth opportunities. The firm usually has already diversified into other more profitable areas, and the sale of the core business may help finance the expansion of these more productive activities. Another example of this was Boise Cascade's decision to sell off its paper manufacturing production business and become an office products retailer through its prior acquisition, OfficeMax. OfficeMax was acquired by Boise Cascade in 2003 for $1.15 billion as part of a vertical integration strategy, as Boise Cascade makes paper products that are ultimately sold through retailers such as OfficeMax. However, over time the paper production business became less attractive while the retail distribution business gained in appeal.

DIVESTITURE AND SPIN-OFF PROCESS

Each divestiture is unique and takes place in a different sequence of events. A generalized six-step process is briefly described here.

Step 1. Divestiture or Spin-Off Decision. The management of the parent company must decide whether a divestiture is the appropriate course of action. This decision can be made only after a thorough financial analysis of the various alternatives has been completed. The method of conducting the financial analysis for a divestiture or spin-off is discussed later in this chapter.

Step 2. Formulation of a Restructuring Plan. A restructuring or reorganization plan must be formulated, and an agreement between the parent and the subsidiary may be negotiated. This plan is necessary in the case of a spin-off that will feature a continuing relationship between the parent and the subsidiary. The plan should cover such details as the disposition of the subsidiary's assets and liabilities. The plan should include details such as the formation of a divestiture team including members of management from a cross-section of corporate functions, including human resources, legal, accounting, and finance.[6] The work of this group can be quite varied, including activities such as negotiating with buyers or handling the various human resources issues that may arise when employees may be transferred to another company or when they may even be terminated. The larger the unit being divested, the more managerial resources tend to be invested in the planning and implementation process.

In cases in which the subsidiary is to keep certain of its assets while others are to be transferred back to the parent company, the plan may provide a detailed breakdown of the asset disposition. Other issues, such as the retention of employees and the funding of their pension and, possibly, health care liabilities may need to be addressed.

Step 3. Selling the Business. In the case of a divestiture a buyer must be found. This is often done using the services of an investment banker, which may facilitate the process. The seller and its banker will identify possible buyers and market the company to them. They will usually prepare a confidential memorandum featuring a large amount of relevant information buyers would be interested in. Once interest is received, a negotiating process may ensue. In the case where multiple offers are received, the most advantageous one will be selected.

Step 4. Approval of the Plan by Shareholders. The extent to which approval of the plan is necessary depends on the significance of the transaction and the relevant state laws. In cases such as a spin-off of a major division of the parent company, stockholder approval may be required. If so, the plan is submitted to the stockholders at a stockholders' meeting, which may be the normally scheduled shareholders' meeting or a special meeting called to consider only this issue. A proxy statement requesting approval of the spin-off is also sent to stockholders. The materials submitted to stockholders may address other issues related to the meeting, such as the amendment of the articles of incorporation.

---

[6] William J. Gole and Paul J. Hilger, *Corporate Divestitures: A Mergers and Acquisitions Best Practices Guide* (Hoboken, NJ: John Wiley & Sons, 2008), 10–22.

Step 5. Registration of Shares. If the transaction requires the issuance of shares, then this stock must be registered with the Securities and Exchange Commission (SEC). As part of the normal registration process, a prospectus, which is part of the registration statement, must be produced. The prospectus must be distributed to all shareholders who receive stock in the spun-off entity.

Step 6. Completion of the Deal. After these preliminary steps have been taken, the deal may be consummated. Consideration is exchanged, and the division is separated from the parent company according to a prearranged timetable.

MARKET LIQUIDITY AND THE DECISION TO DIVEST A UNIT

Various factors can motivate a company to sell a unit. One of the most obvious is poor performance of that business. One would think that this would be the most fundamental and obvious factor. Surprisingly, research by Schlingemann, Stulz, and Walking, however, shows that market liquidity is actually more important.[7] In an analysis of 168 divesting companies over the years 1979–1994, they found that companies in industries that were more liquid were more likely to be divested. In a liquid market, sellers will have a better opportunity to receive the full value, if not an even higher value, for their asset than in markets that are less liquid. Schlingemann et al. measured liquidity by the volume of assets that were being sold in a given time period. So when firms want to divest an unrelated segment as part of a focus enhancement program, those that can sell in liquid markets will be more likely to do so, whereas those that face less liquid market may hold on to a unit until market liquidity improves.

ROUND-TRIP WEALTH EFFECTS

When a company announces an acquisition, in many cases the market response is negative. The research we have just reviewed indicates that when a company announces a sell-off, perhaps a prior acquisition, the market response is often positive. This raises the question, what is the net, round-trip effect? Marquette and Williams analyzed 79 acquisitions and 69 spin-offs over the period 1980 to 1988.[8] They examined the shareholder wealth effects of both the acquisition and subsequent spin-offs of the acquired entity. They tried to determine if paired acquisitions and sell-offs, what they called "flips," drawing on real estate terminology, generate on average positive or negative values. If the value was positive, then we might conclude that M&A has a positive impact even if the acquired entity is subsequently sold off. However, their results really did not indicate a positive or negative effect—mainly a neutral response. While they did

[7] Frederik P. Schlingemann, Rene M. Stulz, and Ralph A. Walking, "Divestitures and the Liquidity of the Market for Corporate Assets," *Journal of Financial Economics* 64, no. 1 (April 2002): 117–144.

[8] Christopher J. Marquette and Thomas Williams, "Takeover-Divestiture Combinations and Shareholder Wealth," *Applied Financial Economics* 17, no. 7 (April 2007): 577–586.

find negative effects for acquisitions and positive ones for sell-offs, the combined effects were not statistically significant. There was, however, an interesting exception. When the target was a research and development (R&D)–intensive business, and where there is evidence that the parent may have supplied capital to fuel the target's R&D needs, the net effect was positive. Hypothetically, we could imagine this type of effect when a huge capital-filled conglomerate, such as GE, acquires a growing R&D–intensive business. Here the parent can accelerate the target's growth. If the target does not fit into the parent's long-term plans, then it could possibly be sold off at a higher value in part based upon the parent's capital contributions during its ownership of the target. Here we can make a more convincing argument for the benefits of financial synergy.

 ## WEALTH EFFECTS OF SELL-OFFS

A major motivating factor for divestitures and spin-offs is the belief that reverse synergy may exist. Divestitures, spin-offs, and equity carve-outs are basically a downsizing of the parent firm. Therefore, the smaller firm must be economically more viable by itself than as a part of its parent company. Several research studies have analyzed the impact of spin-offs by examining the effect on the stock prices of both the parent company and the spun-off entity. This effect is then compared with a market index to determine whether the stocks experience extranormal performance that cannot be explained by market movements alone. Spin-offs are a unique opportunity to analyze the effects of the separation because a market exists for both the stock of the parent company and the spun-off entity.

The research in the field of sell-offs, whether they are divestitures, spin-offs, or other forms of asset sales, such as equity carve-outs, presents a picture of clear benefits for shareholders.

Price Effects of Voluntary Sell-Offs

While there is a larger body of research on the shareholder wealth effects of sell-offs on the selling company, there is a good enough number of studies on the impact on buyers to also draw meaningful conclusions. Let us first focus on the effects on sellers.

Effects of Sellers

Table 11.3 shows an increase in stockholder wealth resulting from corporate sell-offs has a weighted average abnormal shareholder return of 1.2%. This is derived from a large number of studies over a long time period—1963–2005. The equity market clearly concludes that the voluntary selling of a division is a positive development that will result in an increase in the value of the firm's stock.

There are good intuitive explanations for the positive market reaction to sell-offs. If a company is selling a unit, it often may be because it is no longer a good strategic fit. Perhaps it was a diversification acquired in a prior acquisition. It could be that the company was a drain on the overall performance of the business. This was the

TABLE 11.3 Average Seller Abnormal Returns from Voluntary Sell-Offs

Study	Average Abnormal Returns (%)	Period Sampled	Sample Size
Alexander, Benson, and Kampmeyer (1984)	0.3%	1964–1973	53
Linn and Roself (1984)	1.6%		77
Rosenfeld (1984)	2.3%	1963–1981	62
Jain (1985)	0.5%	1976–1978	1,062
Klein (1986)	1.1%	1970–1979	202
Hite, Owens, and Rogers (1987)	1.5%	1963–1981	114
Hirschey and Zaima (1989)	1.6%	1975–1982	170
Hirschey, Slovin, and Zaima (1990)	1.5%	1975–1982	75
Afshar, Taffer, and Sudarsanam (1992)	0.7%	1985–1986	178
Sicherman and Pettway (1992)	0.9%	1980–1987	278
John and Ofek (1995)	1.5%	1986–1988	258
Lang, Poulsen, and Stulz (1995)	1.4%	1984–1989	93
Loh, Bezjak, and Toms (1995)	1.5%	1980–1987	59
Slovin, Sushka, and Ferraro (1995)	1.7%	1980–1991	179
Hanson and Song (2000)	0.6%	1981–1995	326
Mulherin and Boone (2000)	2.6%	1990–1999	139
Clubb and Stouraitis (2002)	1.1%	1984–1994	187
Dittmar and Shivdasani (2003)	3.4%	1983–1994	188
Kiymaz (2006)	3.2%	1989–2002	205
Benou, Madura, and Ngo (2008)	0.9%	1981–2001	1,812
Cao, Owen, and Yawson (2008)	1.3%	1992–2003	668
Francoeur and Niyubahwe (2009)	0.6%	1990–2000	167
Ataullah, Davidson, and Le (2010)	2%	1992–2005	195
Owen, Shi, and Yawson (2010)	1.6%	1997–2005	797
Sample-size weighted seller average	1.2%	1963–2005	7,544

Source: Reproduced with Permission from B. Espen Eckbo and Karin S. Thorburn, "Corporate Restructuring," *Foundations and Trends in Finance* 7, no. 3 (Hanover, MA: Now Publishers Inc., 2013): 159–288.

case when GE, which for a period of time profited handsomely from its expansion into financial operations, was badly burned in the subprime crisis. In the years that followed, the company began to reduce its reliance on financial earnings through sales of assets, such as its retail lending business. This move appealed to shareholders who see GE as more of an industrial company and worry about exposure to financial-type businesses.

Clearly one of the benefits of sell-offs is to enable the seller to be more focused—presumably in areas it excels in. We will revisit the increased focus explanation a little later in this chapter in the context of sell-offs through spin-offs.

TABLE 11.4 Average Buyer Stock Price Effects of Voluntary Sell-Offs

Study	Average Abnormal Returns (%)	Period Sampled	Sample Size
Jain (1985)	0.5%	1976–1978	304
Hite, Owers, and Rogers (1987)	0.6%	1963–1981	105
Sicherman and Pettway (1992)	0.5%	1980–1987	278
Datta and Iksandar-Datta (1995)	0%	1982–1990	63
John and Ofek (1995)	0.4%	1976–1988	167
Hanson and Song (2000)	0.5%	1963–1995	326
Kiymaz (2006)	0.8%	1989–2002	185
Benou, Madua, and Ngo (2008)	2.3%	1981–2001	872
Sample-size weighted Buyer average	1.2%	1963–2002	2,300

Source: Reproduced with Permission from B. Espen Eckbo and Karin S. Thorburn, "Corporate Restructuring," *Foundations and Trends in Finance* 7, no. 3 (Hanover, MA: Now Publishers Inc., 2013): 159–288.

Effect of Buyers

While the market is often not keen on acquisitions, it is more positive when it comes to acquiring a unit of another company. Table 11.4 shows that the average abnormal return to buyers is also 1.2%. However, a closer examination of Table 11.4 reveals that the weighted average of 1.2% is significantly influenced by the Benou et al. study, which showed a 2.3% return.[9] Most of the other studies showed returns between 0% and 1%. Nonetheless, the market seems to be somewhat positive about acquisitions of units of other companies. There is an intuitive explanation for both the seller and buyer effects. As we have noted, for the seller it may involve getting rid of a unit that is no longer a good strategic fit. However, what kind of company may be in the market for purchasing such a unit? Often it is a company that is already in that very business. For the buyer this may be a good complementary fit and an extension of a business that they already had some success in. In such instances it would be reasonable to have a positive market response for the seller and the buyer.

Corporate Governance and Sell-Offs

Managers may be reluctant to sell off a unit—especially if they played a role in its acquisition. The sell-off ends up being an admission of a mistake, which is something that many managers are reluctant to do. Owen, Shi, and Yawson analyzed a sample of 797 divestitures over the years 1997–2005.[10] Consistent with other related research, they

---

[9] Georgina Benou, Jeff Madura, and Thanh Ngo, Wealth Creation from High Tech Divestitures, *Quarterly Review of Economics*, 48 (3) August 2008, 505–519.

[10] Sian Owen, Liting Shi, and Alfred Yawson, "Divestitures, Wealth Effects and Corporate Governance," *Accounting and Finance* 50, no. 2 (June 2010): 389–415.

found that divestitures created wealth. However, their most significant contribution to the research literature was to determine the role that corporate governance played in the divestiture decision and the magnitude of the positive wealth effect.

They found that companies with more independent boards and large blockholders had greater positive shareholder wealth effects. Their research implies that the decision to divest needs more than the obvious recognition of poor performance on a unit or a poor fit of that unit within the overall company. It seems that management often needs some pressure from independent directors and large equityholders to be sufficiently motivated to "do the right thing." In the United States this pressure has often come from hedge funds that acquire significant blocks of stock in undervalued companies, with their goal being to force value-increasing corporate restructuring. However, in many continental European companies, controlling shareholders may be less responsive to the concerns of smaller shareholders who oppose the acquisition strategies the companies have pursued and who would want to pursue sell-offs that could release value to the shareholders.

MANAGERIAL OWNERSHIP AND SELL-OFF GAINS

Many companies have used various incentives to try to deal with the agency problems and align the interests of management and shareholders. One of the main compensation tools is stock options that make managers also owners. This does not eliminate the agency problems as managers still may get the bulk of their compensation from nonequity-based sources, such as salary and perks. Hansen and Song analyzed a sample of 152 divestitures.[11] They found that not only did sellers enjoy positive shareholder wealth effects but also these effects were positively related to the equity ownership of managers and directors. This is an intuitive result as it shows that when managers and directors are playing with their own money, they are less likely to hang on to losers.

ACTIVISTS AND SELL-OFFS

One trend that has been relatively prominent in recent years has been the aggressiveness of activists. These are typically hedge funds that monitor and analyze companies, especially diverse companies, with a mind toward seeing if structural changes could improve shareholder return. For example, in 2011 William Ackman and his Pershing Square fund acquired an 11% stake in the conglomerate Fortune Brands. Fortune Brands was an odd mix of businesses that included the fourth-largest liquor company in the world, the Titleist line of golf products, and a home and security business that included well-known brands such as Moen, Master Locks, Simonton Windows, and Therma Tru Doors. The combination of liquor, golf products, and home products is hard to explain. As a result of Ackman's pressure, Fortune sold off the Titleist and Footjoy businesses to a group of foreign investors.

---

[11] Robert Hansen and Moon H. Song, "Managerial Ownership, Board Structure and the Division of Gains in Divestitures," *Journal of Corporate Finance* 6, no. 1 (March 2000): 55–70.

Activists analyze the public filings of diverse companies and will try to ascertain if some of the divisions show low margins. If that is the case, then the overall margin of the company can be improved by a sale of the lower-margin businesses. From an activist perspective, it may also be convenient if the overall company's performance is less than spectacular. Other disgruntled investors may then be very receptive to a quick solution of a sell-off of a lower margin business—a "solution" that management may have a hard time explaining why they did not pursue without external pressure.

Spin-Offs

In a spin-off the parent company gives shares in the business it is getting rid of to share-holders in accordance with their ownership interest in the parent company. A spin-off is an alternative to an outright divestiture, where the company sells the unit and receives cash or other consideration.

The spun-off entity then becomes a separate business that is independent of the parent company. Shareholders of the parent are also shareholders of the spun-off business, but the two companies usually operate independently. There is a pro rata distribution to the parent company's shareholders, which is usually done through a dividend. Because the spin-off is done through the payment of a *dividend*, the courts usually regard dividend payments as part of the normal responsibilities of the board of directors; thus share-holder approval is usually not required unless the amount of assets being spun off is substantially the bulk of the company's assets.

Later in this chapter we will contrast spin-offs with equity carve-outs. For now we can point out that in a spin-off the shareholders involved in the transaction may stay the same as the original company, whereas with a carve-out a new set of shareholders are established. However, there are other variations that can be pursued, such as a *sponsored spin-off*. In a sponsored spin-off an outside party acquires an interest in spun-off entity. Often this is done by giving the sponsor an incentive in the form of a discount on the price of the shares.

The debt of the overall company is allocated between the remaining parent company and the spun-off entity. Usually this is done in relation to the respective posttransaction sizes of the respective businesses. If the company has warrants and convertible debt out-standing, the conversion ratio may have to be adjusted as the stock price of a company may adjust downward in cases of more significant spin-offs. Shareholders may directly gain by maintaining their shares in the parent company but also receiving shares in the spun-off entity. Without some additional consideration, warrant and convertible debt holders may not realize gains. Therefore, these factors have to be taken into account when structuring the deal.

Spin-offs are usually easier to implement and also less expensive compared to equity carve-outs. For example, one study found that carve-outs are also about four times as expensive to implement as spin-offs.[12] Spin-offs are also much less time-consuming to implement than equity carve-outs.

---

[12] Roni Michaely and Wayne H. Shaw, "The Choice of Going Public: Spinoffs vs. Carve Outs," *Financial Management* 24, no. 3 (Autumn 1995): 5–21.

If the business that is being spun off is well integrated into the parent company, then there will usually be much more work that needs to be done creating a distinct and separate business that will be spun off. If, however, the business was a prior acquisition that was not well integrated into the parent company, then the job may be easier.

Trends in Spin-Offs

Spin-off dollar volume is quite variable, but it somewhat follows M&A volume. Like M&A, spin-off volume in the United States fell after the subprime crisis but spiked up sharply in 2011, only to fall off again. There was a similar postsubprime crisis fall-off in Europe that was preceded by a large spike in 2007. In Asia there was also a large spike in 2007 that was followed by a sharp fall-off and more of a rebound in the years that followed what took place in Europe (see Figures 11.3a, b, and c and Table 11.5).

Tax Treatment of Spin-Offs

One of the major advantages of a spin-off over an outright divestiture is that the spin-off may qualify for tax-free treatment. This can be done if the transaction meets certain Internal Revenue Code requirements (Sections 354 and 355). These rules can be complex, which is why tax attorneys are an integral part of the M&A team in most deals but especially spin-offs. Among the requirements to qualify for tax-free treatment is that the parent company must own at least 80% of the shares of the unit being spun off. In addition, the parent company must not have acquired control of the unit less than five years ago. The transactions must also satisfy the business purpose test. That is, it should not be done only as a means of avoiding taxes. If, for example, the seller can convincingly assert it is doing the deal to increase its focus and depart a business that is no longer a good strategic fit, then this should be acceptable. The added benefit then is tax-free treatment. However, the business purpose does not have to be the sole purpose—only part of the reason for the spin-off.

Shareholder Wealth Effects of Spin-Offs

Not surprisingly, the market likes spin-offs. These transactions accomplish many of the same objectives of divestitures but without the possible adverse tax effects. Table 11.6 shows that the average abnormal return derived from a large number of research studies over the period 1962–2007 is 3.3%.

Shareholder Wealth Effects of Spin-Offs: Parent and Subsidiary Effects Evidence

Cusatis, Miles, and Woolridge examined the common stock returns of both spin-offs and their former parent companies.[13] Unlike some prior research studies, which mainly examined the shareholder returns leading up to and including the announcement of the spin-off, the study by Cusatis et al. tracked the companies after the spin-off to determine what the more long-term wealth effects were. These researchers examined 815 distributions of stock in spun-off firms from 1965 to 1988.

---

[13] Patrick J. Cusatis, James A. Miles, and J. Randall Woolridge, "Restructuring through Spinoffs—The Stock Market Evidence," *Journal of Financial Economics* 33, no. 3 (June 1993): 293–311.

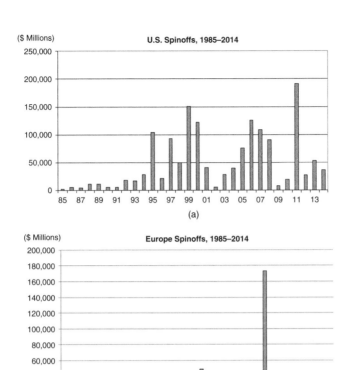

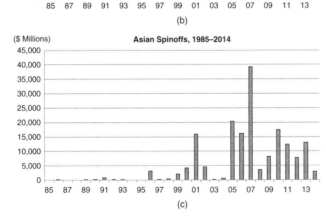

FIGURE 11.3 Spin-Offs, 1985–2014: (a) United States, (b) Europe, and (c) Asia.
Source: Thomson Financial Securities Data, March 6, 2015.

The Cusatis et al. research presents a very favorable picture of the postevent performance of spin-offs. Both spin-offs and their parent companies showed positive abnormal returns over a period that ranged between 6 months before and 36 months after the stock distribution date. Another interesting finding of Cusatis et al. was that both the spin-off and the parent company *were more active in takeovers* than the control group of comparable firms. This takeover activity may help explain some of the positive

TABLE 11.5 Spin-Offs in the United States, Europe, and Asia: 1985–2014

Year	United States Value ($ mil)	# of Deals	Avg.	Europe Value ($ mil)	# of Deals	Avg.	Asia Value ($ mil)	# of Deals	Avg.
1985	1,861	27	68.9	—	—	—	—	—	—
1986	5,309	39	136.1	—	—	—	256	3	85.5
1987	4,516	31	145.7	0	2	0.0	0	6	0.0
1988	10,646	51	208.7	0	7	0.0	0	1	0.0
1989	10,881	46	236.5	3,906	9	434.0	120	4	30.0
1990	5,734	57	100.6	6,227	12	518.9	304	1	303.6
1991	4,851	25	194.0	1,231	14	87.9	818	5	163.6
1992	17,698	55	321.8	7,024	10	702.4	34	4	8.6
1993	16,584	52	318.9	1,726	10	172.6	30	8	3.8
1994	28,100	44	638.6	8	6	1.3	0	4	0.0
1995	103,619	71	1,459.4	5,677	11	516.1	0	6	0.0
1996	20,827	85	245.0	21,720	25	868.8	3,176	12	264.6
1997	93,181	81	1,150.4	18,722	19	985.4	121	7	17.2
1998	50,062	74	676.5	23,240	38	611.6	395	4	98.6
1999	150,992	72	2,097.1	17,091	35	488.3	2,173	6	362.2
2000	122,344	94	1,301.5	49,004	61	803.3	4,166	21	198.4
2001	40,490	41	987.6	18,242	33	552.8	15,967	38	420.2
2002	4,929	48	102.7	6,425	8	803.1	4,727	50	94.5
2003	27,497	53	518.8	28,864	32	902.0	187	45	4.1
2004	39,110	50	782.2	14,809	40	370.2	732	32	22.9
2005	75,734	58	1,305.8	27,843	45	618.7	20,392	33	617.9
2006	125,425	54	2,322.7	28,446	51	557.8	16,092	62	259.5
2007	108,768	88	1,236.0	173,075	69	2,508.3	39,272	85	462.0
2008	90,279	80	1,128.5	23,065	37	623.4	3,519	60	58.6
2009	7,082	57	124.2	11,487	16	717.9	8,257	96	86.0
2010	19,355	49	395.0	41,721	28	1,490.0	17,373	83	209.3
2011	189,429	74	2,559.8	9,987	50	199.7	12,368	61	202.8
2012	23,027	52	442.8	3,179	26	122.3	7,766	55	141.2
2013	4,954	76	65.2	10,754	33	325.9	13,061	52	251.2
2014	36,282	81	447.9	13,282	34	390.7	2,959	47	63.0

Source: Thomson Financial Securities Data, March 6, 2015.

shareholder wealth effects. When the firms that were involved in takeovers were removed from the sample, the returns were still positive but not statistically different from zero. This suggests that spin-offs and their parent company are more likely to be involved in takeovers, and when they are, they enable their shareholders to realize takeover premiums.

TABLE 11.6   Abnormal Returns from Spin-Offs Announcements

Study	Average Abnormal Returns (%)	Period Sampled	Sample Size
Miles and Rosenfeld (1983)	3.3%	1963–1980	55
Hite and Owers (1983)	3.3%	1963–1981	123
Schipper and Smith (1983)	2.8%	1963–1981	93
Rosenfeld (1984)	5.6%	1969–1981	35
Vijh (1994)	2.9%	1964–1990	113
Allen, Lummer, McConnell, and Reed (1995)	2.1%	1962–1991	94
Slovin, Sushka, and Ferraro (1995)	1.3%	1980–1991	37
Daley, Mehrotra, and Sivakumar (1997)	3.4%	1975–1991	85
Best, Best, and Agapos (1998)	3.4%	1979–1993	72
Desai and Jain (1999)	3.8%	1975–1991	144
Krishnaswami and Subramaniam (1999)	3.1%	1979–1993	118
Mulherin and Boone (2000)	4.5%	1990–1999	106
Gertner, Powers, and Scharstein (2002)	3.9%	1982–1996	160
Wruck and Wruck (2002)	3.6%	1985–1995	172
Burch and Nanda (2003)	3.7%	1979–1996	106
Maxwell and Rao (2003)	3.6%	1976–1997	80
Seoungpil and Denis (2004)	4%	1981–1988	150
Veld and Veld-Merkoulova (2004)	1.7%	1987–2000	156
McNeil and Moore (2005)	3.5%	1980–1996	153
Qian and Sudarsanam (2007)	4.8%	1987–2005	157
Veld and Veld-Merkoulova (2008)	3.1%	1995–2002	91
Chemmanur, Jordan, Liu, and Wu (2010)	2.2%	1990–2000	139
Harris and Madura (2011)	2.5%	1984–2007	472
Jain, Kini, and Shenoy (2011)	4.9%	1986–2005	46
Sample-size weighted average	3.3%	1962–2007	2,957

Source: Reproduced with permission from B. Espen Eckbo and Karin S. Thorburn, "Corporate Restructuring," *Foundations and Trends in Finance* 7, no. 3 (Hanover, MA: Now Publishers Inc., 2013): 159–288.

AT&T BREAKUP: ONE OF THE MORE FAMOUS SPIN-OFFS

AT&T has undergone several restructurings in its history. Before AT&T broke up in 1984, it dominated the local and long-distance telecommunications business in the United States. With an eye on more exciting industries, such as the computer

(continued)

(*continued*)

business, AT&T parted ways with its "boring" local operating companies. These businesses were spun off into seven regional operating companies: Ameritech, Bell Atlantic, BellSouth, Nynex, Pacific Telesis, Southwestern Bell, and U.S. West. Several of these "Baby Bells" later merged, such as Nynex and Bell Atlantic, which combined to form Verizon, which would eventually become one of the largest telecommunications companies in the United States. AT&T shareholders received 1 share in each of these regional companies for every 10 shares they held in AT&T. They also still owned 10 shares in the new AT&T, which would prove to be a company that would engage in some of the more notable merger failures in merger history. Indeed, the surviving AT&T would eventually be acquired by one of its progeny—Southwestern Bell.

The AT&T that emerged from the spin-off had the unenviable track record of conducting some of the worst mergers in history. AT&T proved to be a company that had difficulty learning from its mistakes and would proceed to initiate ever larger merger blunders. The spin-off of the operating companies allowed AT&T to enter the computer industry, as an antimonopoly consent decree had prohibited it from using revenues from its telecommunications businesses to finance competitive ventures into other industries. When AT&T was unsuccessful with its computer business, it acquired NCR in a hostile acquisition and greatly overpaid after it encountered resistance from the target. Cultural rifts created further problems, and AT&T eventually broke itself up into three parts.

Recovering from wounds received in the fourth merger wave, a new management team decided to outdo their predecessors in the merger flop business. AT&T's management envied the growth and profitability of its progeny, such as Verizon. It wished to be able to offer local phone services. Unfortunately, while it was once in this business, it had given it all away in the fourth merger wave so as to be able to enter the computer business, in which it failed. The fifth-wave version of AT&T wanted to gain access to local phone markets and believed that two cable targets, MediaOne and TCI, would enable it to accomplish this. It also wanted to be a one-stop shop, offering long distance, mobile, and local telecommunications plus cable for its customers. Readers know to be wary when management is offering customers a one-stop shop. AT&T announced that it was paying approximately $100 billion for its two cable acquisitions. After it bought the companies (rushing the sellers through without doing its own proper due diligence), it discovered that the acquired local cable lines could not support telecommunications services without a major capital infusion. Once again, AT&T blundered in the M&A area—with each blunder being larger than the last one. Not long after the deals, AT&T announced it was breaking itself up—again. It is ironic that after this latest M&A debacle and breakup, AT&T was acquired in November 2005 by one of the companies it had previously spun off—SBC. SBC then assumed the AT&T name.

SHAREHOLDER WEALTH EFFECTS OF SPIN-OFFS: U.S. VERSUS EUROPE

Much of the research literature of the shareholder wealth effects of sell-offs, and spin-offs in particular, focuses on U.S. companies and markets. Boreiko and Murgia analyzed 97 European spin-offs.[14] They found that in Europe, spin-offs were often triggered by what they called "governance earthquakes," such as the appointment of a new CEO or a threat of a takeover. Indeed, Shimizu and Hitt analyzed a sample of U.S. divestitures and also found that the appointment of a new CEO increased the probability of a unit being divested.[15]

Corporate spin-offs have been more common in England than in continental Europe, although they are becoming more frequent in continental Europe. The typical ownership structure in Europe is more concentrated than it is in England or the United States.[16] This puts continental European shareholders, other than those large controlling equityholders who are often family-related, in a less influential position than their British counterparts.

Like much of the research on U.S. spin-offs, Boreiko and Murgia's European sample showed positive shareholder wealth effects for spin-off announcements. Also consistent with U.S. findings, they found higher (5.7%) effects for focus-enhancing spin-offs than for non-focus-enhancing deals (3.3%). However, they did not find operating performance improvements at parent companies after the spin-off, but they did find such effects for the spun-off entity. The spun-off firms that had the greatest improvements were not ones that enabled the parent to be more focused but typically were internally grown units. This contrasts with research on U.S. spin-offs, which tended to show performance improvements only for focus-enhancing deals.

Wealth Effects of Voluntary Defensive Sell-Offs

We discussed in previous sections the positive wealth effects of voluntary sell-offs. There is some evidence that when these voluntary sell-offs are used as an antitakeover defense, positive effects may not exist. Loh, Bezjak, and Toms found positive shareholder wealth effects to voluntary sell-offs that are consistent with the other research that has been discussed.[17] However, they found that this positive response was not present when companies used sell-offs as an antitakeover defense.

In a sample of 59 firms from 1980 to 1987, 13 of which featured takeover speculation, Loh, Bezjak, and Toms found cumulative average abnormal return equal to 1.5% over a one-day period up to the sell-off date. However, when they divided their sample into two subsamples—those with and without takeover speculation—the 13 firms that were the targets of takeover speculation failed to show any significant changes in shareholder wealth. These results suggest that when firms engage in sell-offs to prevent themselves from being taken over, the market treats the transactions differently and does not consider it a positive change.

---

[14] Dmitri Boreiko and Maurizio Murgia, "Which Spinoffs Generate Value and Performance Improvements," unpublished working paper.

[15] Katsuhiko Shimizu and Michael A. Hitt, "What Constrains or Facilitates Divestitures of Formerly Acquired Firms? The Effects of Organizational Inertia," *Journal of Management* 31, no. 1 (February 2005): 50–72.

[16] Mara Faccio and Larry Lang, "The Ultimate Ownership of Western European Corporations," *Journal of Financial Economics* 65, no. 3 (September 2002): 365–395.

[17] Charmen Loh, Jennifer Russell Bezjak, and Harrison Toms, "Voluntary Corporate Divestitures as Antitakeover Mechanisms," *Financial Review* 30, no. 1 (February 1995): 41–60.

Wealth Effects of Involuntary Sell-Offs

Most research studies on the effects of sell-offs on stockholder wealth conclude that sell-offs increase the wealth of parent company stockholders and that the market is somewhat efficient in anticipating the event. Therefore, the stock price reaction occurs in advance of the actual sell-off date. The wealth-increasing effects of a sell-off of an unwanted or poorly performing subsidiary should be different from those of a parent company being forced to divest itself of a profitable division. This was the case when Santa Fe–Southern Pacific received its unfavorable ruling requiring it to divest itself of the Southern Pacific Railway. As noted previously, the stock price declined and Santa Fe became a takeover target.

In 1981, Kudla and McInish conducted a case study of the effects of the required spin-off of the Louisiana-Pacific Corporation by Georgia-Pacific, the parent company.[18] The spin-off was required by the Federal Trade Commission (FTC), which concluded that the acquisition of 16 companies in the southern part of the United States, which accounted for a total of 673, 000 acres of pine trees, would result in an anticompetitive concentration in the plywood industry. Using cumulative residuals to adjust for market effects, Kudla and McInish showed that the price of Georgia-Pacific stock had been declining before the formal filing of the FTC complaint. Louisiana-Pacific was spun off in 1972. However, this downward movement ended with the spin-off, after which the stock price rebounded. Although the stock price rebound was significant, the cumulative residuals did not fully recover to the start of the 1971 level, even as late as March 1974.

A study by Miles and Rosenfeld showed that the wealth of bondholders declined after the spin-off even while the wealth of stockholders increased.[19] This was believed to be attributed to the lower cash flows after the spin-off and the resulting increase in risk to bondholders. Kudla and McInish attempted to measure the risk effects of the involuntary Louisiana-Pacific spin-off by examining the betas of Georgia-Pacific before and after the spin-off. The betas would then reflect any change in the systematic or undiversifiable risk associated with Georgia-Pacific stock. Kudla and McInish found a large, statistically significant increase in the betas of Georgia-Pacific after the spin-off. They attributed this increase to the market's perception that Georgia-Pacific incurred a decrease in monopoly power after the spin-off and that this caused the firm to be riskier.

The finance research community seems to have reached a consensus that a divestiture that is forced by government mandate, as opposed to a voluntary sell-off, will have an adverse effect on the divesting firm's stock price. Ellert's review of 205 defendants in antitrust merger lawsuits showed a 21.86% decline in the value of the equity of these firms during the month the complaint was filed.[20] The issue that the Kudla and McInish study addresses is the timing of that impact and the reversal of the declining trend.

---

[18] Ronald Kudla and Thomas McInish, "The Microeconomic Consequences of an Involuntary Corporate Spin-Off," *Sloan Management Review* 22, no. 4 (1981): 41–46.

[19] James A. Miles and James D. Rosenfeld, "The Effect of Voluntary Spinoff Announcements on Shareholder Wealth," Journal *of Finance*, 38, 1983, 1597–1606.

[20] James C. Ellert, "Mergers, Antitrust Law Enforcement and the Behavior of Stock Prices," *Journal of Finance* 31, no. 2 (May 1976): 715–732.

If the antitrust enforcement is effective in reducing the selling firm's monopoly power, this should be reflected in an *increase* in the value of the equity of that firm's competitors. Unfortunately, the antitrust authorities can find little support for their actions in the stock prices of the competitors of divesting firms.[21] The value of the equity of competitors of divesting firms failed to show a significant positive response to mandated sell-offs.

Corporate Focus and Spin-Offs

One of the benefits a company can derive through a sell-off is to become more focused. This is particularly true for companies that have become diversified and suffer from having their shares trade at the diversification discount. This is not to imply that all diversified companies trade at such a discount. For example, for many years GE, a highly diversified industrial conglomerate, was the darling of the market, and its CEO, Jack Welsh, was one of the world's most popular CEOs. This all changed when the company moved heavily into financial services, which bore great fruit for the company until the company was taken by the subprime crisis. Following the overexposure to financial services the company began to refocus on more industrial businesses.

We now discuss focus-related benefits in the context of spin-offs. However, while many of the studies use spin-offs to demonstrate focus-related benefits, they also apply to other types of sell-offs, such as divestitures or equity carve-outs.

Dale, Mehrotra, and Sivakumar conducted a study of 85 spin-offs over the period 1975 and 1991, in which they examined the relationship between spin-offs and corporate focus by comparing the performance of spin-off firms when the parent company and the spun-off entity were in two different Standard Industrial Classification (SIC) codes (cross-industry spin-offs) relative to instances in which both were in the same SIC code (own industry spin-offs).[22] They found improvements in various measures of performance, such as the return on assets, for cross-industry spin-offs but not for own-industry deals. They conclude that cross-industry spin-offs create value only when they result in an increase in corporate focus. They attribute the performance improvements to companies removing unrelated businesses, allowing managers to concentrate their efforts on the core business and removing the distraction of noncore entities.

Are all types of increased focus transactions the same? One study by Dasilas and Leventi shed light on which types of focus-increasing spin-offs had the greatest positive shareholder wealth effects.[23] They compared spin-offs that increased industrial focus with those that increased geographical focus. They found that spin-offs that increased industrial focus generated positive shareholder wealth effects, while those that increased

---

[21] Robert Stillman, "Examining Antitrust Policy towards Horizontal Mergers," *Journal of Financial Economics* 11, no. 1–4 (April 1983): 225–240; and Bjorn E. Eckbo, "Horizontal Mergers, Collusion and Stockholder Wealth," *Journal of Financial Economics* 11, no. 1–4 (April 1983): 241–273.

[22] Lane Daley, Vikas Mehrotra, and Ranjini Sivakumar, "Corporate Focus and Value Creation: Evidence from Spinoffs," *Journal of Financial Economics* 45, no. 2 (August 1997): 257–281.

[23] Apostolos Dasilas and Stergios Leventi, "Wealth Effects and Operating Performance of Spin-Offs: International Evidence," working paper, International Hellinic University, Greece, 2010.

geographical focus did not. In addition, the positive market response to increases in industrial focus was greater for U.S. spin-offs than it was for European deals.

Corporate Split-Ups

Sometimes companies can pursue a diversification strategy and the market supports it through higher equity values. This can often happen when we are in a bull market and the rising tide is carrying with it all ships—if not carrying them equally. However, while the market may be sometimes slow to catch on to the failings of a given conglomerate's "strategy," it eventually may change its view of the multiple combinations that make up the company. When this happens, the company's management will be under pressure to make significant changes, and this often means sell-offs of not an outright split-up. AT&T and ITT did this each more than once. However, there are several other examples, including Cendant, Sara Lee, and Tyco. The goal is to separate the businesses so that there is greater focus and the enterprise becomes more manageable. With a more focused business, the market can better understand the overall strategy. This may allow the company to appeal to investors who are seeking investments in a specific sector.

CENDANT: SPLIT-UP OF A CONGLOMERATE

In October 2005, the board of directors announced that it had approved a proposal to split up Cendant, an $18 billion conglomerate that had been built through a series of acquisitions over many years. The Cendant of 2005 included the real estate companies Century 21 and Coldwell Banker; car rental businesses Avis, the second-largest car rental company in the United States, and Budget; hotel chains Days Inn, Ramada, and Super 8; and travel companies Orbitz, Cheaptickets.com, and Galileo International (an international network of travel agents). The company merged with CUC International in 1997, and that deal was a disaster due to the bogus financials of CUC. CUC proved to be one of the bigger financial frauds in history. While the stock price took a difficult short-term hit due to this problem, it recovered due to the fact that the upper management of Cendant, including its CEO Henry Silverman, was not involved in this fraud and worked hard to correct the problem. However, over the years 2003–2005, while the market steadily grew, Cendant stock was weak and even declined (see Figure A). Management finally came to the resolution that the market did not understand or like the confusing combination of companies housed within the Cendant corporate structure.

In 2004, Cendant recognized that its conglomerate structure was a problem. It tried to take some steps to correct it while not really admitting that the whole overall structure was problematic. Toward that end, the company parted ways with its mortgage business, PHH Corp., the Jackson Hewitt Tax Services business, and Wright Express, which is a fleet management company. PHH Corp. was spun off while Cendant did an equity carve-out of its Jackson Hewitt unit. Jackson Hewitt is an example of a business, tax preparation, that is pretty far removed from the other travel-related businesses housed within Cendant. Its combination with Cendant's other businesses made little sense. The market liked these deals, as the stock performance of the carved-out businesses exceeded that of Cendant.

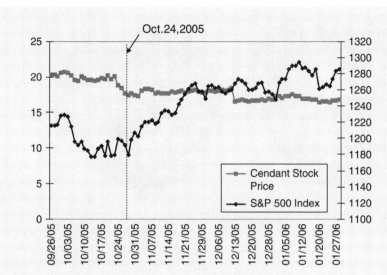

FIGURE A Cendant Stock Price versus S&P 500 Index. *Source*: Yahoo! Finance.

Before approving the split-up, Cendant's board considered other options, such as leveraged recapitalization and more sales of other business units.[a] However, the board finally decided that halfway measures would not fix the problem and that the market wanted more focused businesses, not the combination that CEO Silverman had put together. The combination may have worked well for Silverman and his personal goals, but not for investors.

The four new businesses formed from the split-up are:

1. Travel
2. Car rental
3. Hospitality/hotels
4. Real estate

When we look at the preceding combinations, one can see that the first three have a common travel connection, so one could theorize that there might be synergistic benefits. However, all one has to do is to look back at other attempts to combine such travel businesses, such as what United Airlines tried to do, to discover that extracting synergies from such combinations would be hard. However, one lesson we are always aware of in M&As is that managers and investors have short memories and tend to repeatedly make the same mistakes.

[a] Ryan Chittum, "Cendant to Split into Four Firms," *Wall Street Journal*, October 24, 2005, A3.

 EQUITY CARVE-OUTS

An equity carve-out is a public offering of a partial interest in a wholly owned subsidiary, although the seller could, theoretically, sell as much as the entire 100% in the offering. Usually, however, that is not the case and only a partial interest is sold. Most of

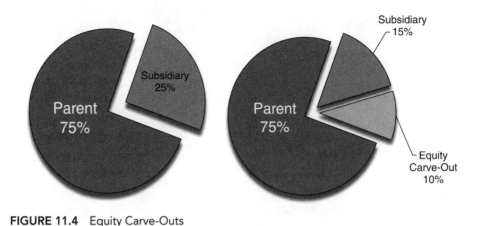

FIGURE 11.4 Equity Carve-Outs

the time the seller retains control of the unit, although the carve-out may be the first step in selling off the entire business. By retaining a high percentage of the shares of the subsidiary, one that is equal to or greater than 80%, the parent retains the right to do a tax-free spin-off in the future. Thus equity carves are often two step transactions (see Figure 11.4)

By retaining at least 50% the parent can consolidate the businesses for tax purposes. Allen and McConnell found that on average parents retained just under 70% of their carved-out unit's shares, while Vijh found parents retained almost three-quarters of the unit's shares.[24]

Equity carve-outs are often linked to some subsequent event. For example, a parent company may first do an equity carve-out where it sells some of the shares it owns in a subsidiary but may follow that translation by a spin-off of the remaining shares to its own shareholders. By issuing some equity the seller establishes a market value for the unit, which may be used in the eventual total separation of the business from the parent. Thus the carve-out can enable the parent to "test the waters" for the market's appetite for the unit's shares. If this does not look promising, it may simply require the unit's shares—thus cancelling the "sale."

The shares can be sold by the unit itself, or the parent can sell the shares. If the parent sells the shares, this is called a secondary offering. If the subsidiary does the selling, it is referred to as a primary issuance. The primary offering has no tax consequences, but a secondary offering could result in capital gains taxes for the parent. This is why most equity carve-outs are primary issues. When the unit sells the shares, it receives the proceeds. This gives rise to a decision about what to do with the proceeds. One option is to leave them with the unit. Another is to pay them to the parent—but in a way that will not have adverse tax effects. One way to do that is to have the unit issue a note or debt obligation to the parent as a dividend prior to the carve-out. When

[24] Jeffrey W. Allen and John J. McConnell, "Equity Carve Outs and Managerial Discretion," *Journal of Finance* 53 (1998): 163–186; and Anand Vijh, "The Positive Announcement Period Returns of Equity Carveouts: Asymmetric Information or Divesture Gains?," *Journal of Business* 75 (2002): 153–190.

the unit receives the share proceeds, it can pay off the note. Many firms look to equity carve-outs as a means of reducing their exposure to a business that they believe is no longer a good strategic fit or that has higher risk than what it prefers. For example, American Express bought the brokerage firm Shearson in 1981. It later acquired the investment bank Lehman Brothers to form Shearson Lehman. This is a riskier line of business than American Express's traditional credit card operations. American Express later decided that, although it liked the synergy that came with being a diversified financial services company, it wanted to reduce its exposure to the risks of the securities business. In 1987, Amexco, its holding company, sold off a 39% interest in Shearson Lehman. This proved to be fortuitous because the sale preceded the stock market crash, an event that securities firms still had not recovered from by the end of the 1980s. The company would later completely undo these acquisitions. American Express would further streamline its business in 2005, when it spun off its personal finance unit, which became Ameriprise Financial Inc. This is yet another example of a related business that appeared to have valuable synergies but that in reality did not.

One of the benefits of a partial interest carve-out is that it establishes a market for the shares of the subsidiary. Hulbert analyzed a sample of 172 carve-outs and found that most of the time the carve-out is a "temporary event."[25] By this he means that the carved-out entity often does not stay independent. This happened roughly half of the time. Twenty percent of the time the unit's shares were bought back by the parent, and sixteen percent of the time the unit was acquired by another company.

Shareholder Wealth of Equity Carve-Outs

As with divestitures and spin-offs, equity carve-out announcements yield positive average abnormal returns. Drawing on a number of studies that considered a total of 1,251 carve-outs during 1965–2007, Eckbo and Thornburn found returns equal to 1.8% (see Table 11.7). The explanation for these positive effects is similar to that of other forms of sell-offs. The difference is the method by which the parent company accomplishes the sell-off.

Characteristics of Equity Carve-Out Firms: Post Carve-Out Performance

Eric Powers analyzed 181 equity carve-outs to try to determine the motives for the transactions.[26] Were the deals motivated by a desire of the parent to try to realize increased efficiencies or were they trying to unload an overvalued unit? He found that the carved-out companies' financial performance, as measured by return on assets, peaked at issue (17.2%) and then subsequently *declined*. He also found that other measures, such as capital expenditures, profit margin, and sales growth, also declined. He then compared this performance to that of the industries they were in

---

[25] Heather M. Hulbert, "Equity Carve-Outs and Changes in Corporate Control," *Journal of Applied Business Research* 19, no. 1: 2003, 29–40.

[26] Eric Powers, "Deciphering the Motives for Equity Carve Outs," *Journal of Financial Research* 26 (Spring 2003): 31–50.

TABLE 11.7 Average Abnormal Returns for Equity Carve-Out Announcements

Study	Average Abnormal Returns (%)	Period Sampled	Sample Size
Schipper and Smith (1986)	1.8%	1965–1983	76
Klein, Rosenfeld, and Beranek (1991)	2.7%	1966–1983	52
Slovin, Sushka, and Ferrrao (1995)	1.2%	1980–1991	32
Allen and McConnell (1998)	2.1%	1978–1993	186
Vijh (1999, 2002)	1.9%	1980–1997	336
Mulherin and Boone (2000)	2.3%	1990–1999	125
Hulburt (2003)	1.6%	1981–1994	172
Wagner (2004)	1.7%	1984–2002	71
Jain, Kini, and Shenoy (2011)	1.6%	1986–2005	65
Sun and Shu (2011)	0.5%	1994–2007	136
Sample-size weighted average	1.8%	1965–2007	1,251

Source: Reproduced with permission from B. Espen Eckbo and Karin S. Thorburn, "Corporate Restructuring," *Foundations and Trends in Finance* 7, no. 3 (Hanover, MA: Now Publishers Inc., 2013): 159–288.

and the parent companies. He found that the carved-out subsidiaries performed better than the industry peers. As we will discuss a little later when we review the work of Allan and McConnell, the comparative industry finding is not consistent with some other research.

Powers found that the parent companies had fairly consistent performance (10.5% per year) and did not decline after the carve-out. Thus he found that at the time of the transaction the subsidiaries that were carved-out subsidiaries performed better than the parent.

Powers also found the parent companies sold a higher percentage of the units' shares to the market when the financial performance of that business was worse. That is, "the more the parent sells, the worse the carve out subsidiary performs in the future."[27] He also found an inverse relationship between the liquidity of the parent and the percentage of shares sold. It seems the parent companies trade ownership in the subsidiary for cash—especially when their liquidity is low. While Powers found that carved-out companies' performance declined after they were separated from the parent, other studies using different samples found just the opposite. For example, Hulbert, Miles, and Woolridge found improvements in both the parent and the subsidiary relative to their industry peers.[28]

---

[27] Ibid., 48.

[28] Heather Hulbert, James A. Miles, and J. Randall Woolridge, "Value Creation from Equity Carve Outs," *Financial Management* 31 (2002): 83–100.

TABLE 11.8   Comparison of Pre-Carve-Out Firms with Industry Peers

Performance Measure	Pre-Carve-Out Firms	Industry Peers
EBDIT/Interest	2.29	5.42
Long-term debt/Total assets	0.260	0.220
Total debt/Total assets	0.331	0.285
EBDIT/Sales	0.070	0.103

Source: Jeffrey Allen and John J. McConnell, "Equity Carve-Outs and Managerial Discretion," *Journal of Finance* 53, no. 1 (February 1998): 163–186.

Characteristics of Equity Carve-Out Firms and the Disposition of Carve-Out Proceeds

Allen and McConnell conducted a study of the financial characteristics of firms that undertook equity carve-outs. They analyzed 188 carve-outs between 1978 and 1993.[29] They found that carved-out subsidiaries tended to have poorer operating performance and higher leverage than their industry counterparts. As Table 11.8 shows, pre-carve-out firms have lower interest coverage and higher ratios of long-term debt and total debt to total assets. They also have lower ratios of EBDIT (earnings before depreciation, interest, and taxes) to sales and total assets. Allen and McConnell also traced the use of the carve-out proceeds. They found that when the funds were used to pay down debt, the company showed an average excess return of +6.63%, whereas when the funds were retained for investment purposes, the company experienced a −0.01% return. Thus, they showed that the market's reaction to the carve-outs depended on what the company used the funds for.

Equity Carve-Outs versus Public Offerings

An equity carve-out, as opposed to a spin-off, brings in new capital to the parent company. Because the acquisition of capital is obviously a motivating factor for this type of sell-off, we must investigate why the equity carve-out option may be chosen over a public offering of stock. Katherine Schipper and Abbie Smith conducted a study of equity carve-outs that examined the share price reactions to 76 carve-out announcements. They compared these reactions with previous studies documenting the stock price reactions to public equity offerings.[30] Previous studies have shown that the announcement of seasoned equity offerings results in an abnormal stock return of between 22% and 23% in the periods around the equity offering.[31] In contrast to other equity financing arrangements, Schipper and Smith found that equity carve-outs

---

[29] Allen and McConnell, "Equity Carve Outs and Managerial Discretion."

[30] Katherine Schipper and Abbie Smith, "A Comparison of Equity Carve-Outs and Seasonized Equity Offerings," *Journal of Financial Economics* 15, no. 1–2 (January/February 1986): 153–186.

[31] For a review of some of this literature and additional research showing that the effects of stock offerings are more negative for industrial firms than for public utilities, see Ronald W. Masulis and Ashok N. Korwar, "Seasonized Equity Offerings," *Journal of Financial Economics* 15, no. 11 (January/February 1986): 91–118.

increase shareholder wealth. Schipper and Smith found that the shareholders of the parent firms experienced average gains of 1.8%. They compared this positive stock price effect with a 23% shareholder loss for a subset of parent firms that engaged in public offerings of common stock or debt.

Schipper and Smith propose that the positive stock price reactions are due to a combination of effects, including better and more defined information available about both the parent and the subsidiary. This is clear to those who have attempted to evaluate the subsidiaries of a publicly held company. The annual reports and other publicly available documents may be very brief and yield little of the data necessary to value the components of a company. When the subsidiary becomes a stand-alone public company, it publishes more detailed information about its operations because its activities are its only line of business, as opposed to merely being a part of a larger parent company.

Schipper and Smith also point out other possible factors responsible for the positive stock price reaction to equity carve-outs, such as the restructuring and asset management that tend to be associated with equity carve-outs. In addition, divisions may be consolidated into a more efficient form, and managers may work with new compensation incentives. The combination of these and other changes may make the subsidiary a more viable entity as a separate public company. The market's perception of this value may be a source of a premium for the selling company. The parent company, no longer encumbered by a subsidiary that it could not manage as well as another owner might, becomes more valuable when it converts this asset into cash, which it can, it is hoped, invest in more productive areas.

Equity Carve-Outs versus Spin-Offs

There are a number of important differences between spin-offs and equity carve-outs. A carve-out results in a new set of shareholders, whereas the same shareholders hold stock in the spun-off entity as in the parent company. There are positive cash flow effects in carve-outs, but spin-offs do not result in initial changes in parent company cash flows. Carve-outs are more expensive to implement and are subject to greater securities law disclosure requirements.

In a study of 91 *master limited partnerships* (MLPs) that were created between 1981 and 1989, Michaely and Shaw found that, for their sample, riskier and more highly leveraged firms chose to go the spin-off route rather than to opt for a carve-out.[32] They show in their study that bigger, less leveraged, and more profitable firms chose the carve-out option. They conclude that the equity carve-out versus spin-off decision is determined by access to capital markets. Those companies that have better access—that is, more desirable firms in better financial condition—will choose to market themselves to public markets and enjoy the positive cash flow effects of an equity carve-out. Less desirable firms will be forced to choose the spin-off route. It should be noted that although it may seem that the Michaely and Shaw results contradict those of Allen and McConnell reported earlier, this is not the case. The Allen and McConnell results show

---

[32] Roni Michaely and Wayne H. Shaw, "The Choice of Going Public: Spinoffs vs. Carve Outs," *Financial Management* 24, no. 3 (Autumn 1995): 5–21.

a comparison of carved-out firms with industry peers, whereas the Michaely and Shaw study compares firms that did carve-outs with those that did spin-offs.

The Michaely and Shaw findings were supported by a study by Johnson, Klein, and Thibodeaux.[33] In their study of 126 spin-offs, they found that companies doing the spin-offs were more highly leveraged and had lower asset growth than their industry peers. They also helped shed light on the reasons for the positive stock market responses to spin-offs. They found that following the spin-offs there were gains in the cash flow margin on sales and asset growth for both the parent company and the spun-off firm.

These studies clearly do not explain all spin-off versus equity carve-out decisions. They do not address, for example, the large spin-offs of 1995, such as the ITT and AT&T transactions. However, these research results provide much useful insight into other types of transactions.

VOLUNTARY LIQUIDATIONS OR BUST-UPS

Voluntary liquidations, or bust-ups, are the most extreme form of corporate restructuring. Corporate liquidations are more often associated with bankruptcy. A company may be liquidated in bankruptcy when all parties concerned recognize that the continuation of the firm in a reorganized form will not enhance its value. The outlook, however, is not as negative for voluntary liquidations. In a voluntary liquidation, the general criterion applied is as follows: If the market value of the firm's assets significantly exceeds the value of the firm's equity, a liquidation may need to be seriously considered. This is not to imply that liquidation should be an alternative in instances of a temporary downturn of the firm's stock. The liquidation option becomes viable only when the firm's stock has been depressed for an extended time or the business is simply not viable going into the future. Even businesses with established name brands could possibly not be viable in the marketplace. For example, as part of its restructuring, General Motors concluded that such historically well-known brands as Pontiac, Saturn, and Saab had to be simply discontinued. GM tried unsuccessfully to sell Saab but could not find a buyer in a global marketplace that featured great overcapacity.

For whole companies, as opposed to divisions or brands within a company, the liquidation option becomes even more likely when the stock prices of other firms in the same industry are not also depressed. In addition, low price-earnings (P/E) ratios may sometimes point to a need to consider the liquidation option. Managers are often reluctant to consider such a drastic step, which would result in their loss of position. They may prefer to sell the entire firm to a single acquirer rather than pursue liquidation. Stockholders sometimes try to force management's hand by threatening a proxy battle to decide the issue.

Voluntary liquidations may be contrasted with divestitures. A divestiture is generally a single transaction in which a certain part of the firm is sold, whereas a voluntary liquidation is a series of transactions in which all the firm's assets are sold in separate parcels. Tax motives may make a liquidation more attractive than a divestiture.

---

[33] Shane Johnson, Daniel Klein, and Verne Thibodeaux, "The Effects of Spinoffs on Corporate Investment and Performances," *Journal of Financial Research* 19, no. 2 (Summer 1996): 293–307.

Divestitures may be subject to capital gains taxes, whereas voluntary liquidations may often be structured to receive more preferential tax treatment.

Shareholder Wealth Effects of Voluntary Bust-Ups

Skantz and Marchesini's study of liquidation announcements made by 37 firms from 1970 to 1982 showed an average excess return of 21.4% during the month of the announcement.[34] Hite, Owers, and Rogers found similar positive shareholder wealth effects during the month of the announcement of voluntary liquidations made by the 49 firms in their sample, which covered the years 1966 to 1975.[35] They showed a positive abnormal return in the announcement month equal to 13.62%. Almost half the firms in their sample had been the object of a bid for control within two years of the announcement of the liquidation plan. These bids included a wide range of actions, including leveraged buyouts (LBOs), tender offers, and proxy contests. Moreover, more than 80% of the firms in their sample showed positive abnormal returns. This suggests that the stock market agreed that continued operation of the firm under its prior operating policy will reduce shareholder wealth.

The positive stock market reaction was affirmed by two other studies. Kim and Schatzberg found a 14% positive return for 73 liquidating firms during a three-day period associated with the liquidation announcement.[36] They revealed that a 3% return was added when shareholders confirmed the transaction. Kim and Schatzberg failed to detect any significant wealth effect, either positive or negative, for the shareholders of the acquiring firms. In a study of 61 publicly traded firms that completed voluntary liquidations between 1970 and 1991, Erwin and McConnell found that voluntary liquidations were associated with an even higher average excess stock return of 20%.[37] They also confirmed the intuitive expectation that firms that decide to voluntarily liquidate face limited growth prospects. The liquidation decision is the rational one because it releases financial resources to be applied to higher-yielding alternatives. As suggested previously, these research studies imply that the stock market often agrees that the continued operation of the firm under its prior operating policy will reduce shareholder wealth. This is not surprising because most firms that are considering liquidation are suffering serious problems. Liquidation then releases the firm's assets to other companies that might be able to realize a higher return on them.

 TRACKING STOCKS

In the 1990s, companies began to issue *tracking stocks* as alternatives to sell-offs. A tracking or targeted stock is an equity issue that represents an interest in the earnings of a

[34] Terrence Skantz and Roberto Marchesini, "The Effect of Voluntary Corporate Liquidation on Shareholder Wealth," *Journal of Financial Research* 10 (Spring 1987): 65–75.

[35] Gailen Hite, James Owers, and Ronald Rogers, "The Market for Interfirm Asset Sales: Partial Selloffs and Total Liquidations," *Journal of Financial Economics* 18, no. 2 (June 1987): 229–252.

[36] E. Han Kim and John Schatzberg, "Voluntary Corporate Liquidations," *Journal of Financial Economics* 19, no. 2 (December 1987): 311–328.

[37] Gayle R. Erwin and John J. McConnell, "To Live or Die? An Empirical Analysis of Piecemeal Voluntary Liquidations," *Journal of Corporate Finance* 3, no. 4 (December 1997): 325–354.

division of a company. It also is sometimes called *letter stock* or *alphabet stock*. Sometimes when a company acquires other firms but the market prices of the combined entity sell at a discount, the company may try to boost the stock by allowing one or more divisions to trade separately as tracking stocks. AT&T did this with its AT&T Wireless segment.

Tracking stocks were first created in 1984, when General Motors (GM) acquired Electronic Data Systems (EDS). Ross Perot, the colorful CEO of EDS, was concerned that employees, who owned significant shareholdings in the company, would be less motivated if they received shares in slow-growth GM in exchange for their fast-growing shares in EDS. As a solution, they issued Class E shares, which tracked the performance of the EDS division of GM. General Motors also used this mechanism in 1985 when it issued Class H shares, which followed the performance of its Hughes Aircraft division.

Tracking stocks have also been used as a defense measure when a company is confronted with a large and somewhat hostile shareholder. This was the case in 1991 in the next use of a tracking stock, when Carl Icahn, a holder of 13% of USX, demanded that the company spin off the steel division of the company, which owned U.S. Steel and Marathon Oil. As an alternative and less drastic step, the company issued a tracking stock for its steel and oil divisions.

One of the major differences between tracking stocks and sell-offs is that a separate legal entity is created in a sell-off. With a tracking stock, the shareholder has a legal interest in the earnings of a division, but that division remains part of the overall company. Holders of targeted stock usually still retain their voting rights in the overall company. In some instances, however, such as in the USX case, these voting rights may be adjusted based on the market valuation of the targeted shares.

Tracking stocks do not represent an ownership interest in the assets of the entity being tracked. This may make one wonder why the company does not simply do a spin-off that would give holders shares that have such an interest. However, it may be the case that the transaction would not qualify for tax-free treatment, and this would eliminate one of the advantages of a spin-off.

After the issuance of the tracking stock, the parent company still has legal control of the assets and the division and is a consolidated entity. The parent has the voting rights of the tracking shares.

A tracking stock can be issued by a parent company in a couple of ways. One way is to issue the shares to its shareholders as a dividend. However, it is more common for the parent to simply have a public offering of the shares and receive cash in exchange. Once these shares become listed with an exchange, it then has to have its own audited financial statements and it does its own filings with the SEC. It does all of this while still being part of the parent company and under its control. Since the shares were really an offering of the parent company's shares (since it owns the unit), there are no tax consequences.

As with announcements of sell-offs, the market tends to react positively to announcements of tracking stocks. D'Souza and Jacob found a statistically significant 3.61% stock price reaction within a three-day window of an announcement of proposed tracking stock issues.[38] D'Souza and Jacob tried to determine whether the creation of

---

[38] Julia D'Souza and John Jacob, "Why Firms Issue Targeted Stock," *Journal of Financial Economics* 56, no. 3 (June 2000): 459–483.

tracking stocks achieves some of the same benefits that a company would receive if it were a totally independent entity. They examined the correlation between the returns of the tracking stock and the overall firm, as well as the correlation between the returns of the tracking stock and similar firms in the tracking stock's industry. They found a greater correlation between parent firms and tracking stock returns than the returns between the tracking stocks and their industry counterparts. That is, they found that the "firm effect" was greater than the "industry effect." They postulate that the firm effect exists because of all the shared resources and liabilities that exist between the division and the parent company. Clearly, a tracking stock is an intermediate step between being totally independent and staying within the parent company.

The findings of positive announcement effects for tracking stocks are consistent with other studies, such as those of Billet and Vijh, Chemmanur and Paeglis, Elder and Westra, and Harper and Madura.[39] These studies report positive announcement period returns in the 2% to 3% range. However, given the limited number of issues of tracking stocks, the available data cause us to be cautious about conclusions compared to other types of restructurings, such as divestitures or spin-offs.

The evidence of the long-run performance of tracking shares is a "mixed bag." Chemmanur and Paeglis found that the shares of the 19 parent companies that issued tracking shares underperformed over a three-year post-issuance period relative to industry peers.[40] This contrasted to the out-performance of the subsidiary relative to its peers. Billett and Vijh examined 29 completed tracking stock restructurings over the period 1984–1999.[41] They found that shareholders of tracking stocks experienced significant post-issue wealth losses. Shareholders of the parent company experienced insignificant returns, although they incurred negative returns for the year prior to the tracking stock restructuring announcement. These negative preannouncement returns are not surprising as the issuance of a tracking stock is usually an attempted partial solution to poor performance of the parent. The negative preannouncement returns also contrast sharply with those of spin-offs and equity carve-outs.

MASTER LIMITED PARTNERSHIPS AND SELL-OFFS

Master limited partnerships (MLPs) are limited partnerships in which the shares are publicly traded. A limited partnership consists of a general partner and one or more limited partners. The general partner runs the business and bears unlimited liability. This

---

[39] M. T. Billet and A. M. Vijh, "The Wealth Effects of Tracking Stock Restructurings," *Journal of Financial Research*, 27, 2004, 559–583; J. Elder, P. K. Jain, J. C. Kim, "Do Tracking Stocks Reduce Information Asymmetries?" *Journal of Financial Research*, 28, 2005, 197–213; J. Elder and P. Westra, "The Reaction of Security prices to Tracking Stock Announcements," *Journal of Economics and Finance*, 24, 2000, 36–55; J. T. Harper and Jeff Madura, "Sources of Hidden value and Risk Within Tracking Stock," *Financial Management*, 31, 2002, 91–109.

[40] Thomas J. Chemmanur and Imantis Paeglis, "Why Issue Tracking Stock? Insights from a Comparison with Spinoffs and Carve-outs," *Journal of Applied Corporate Finance* 14, no. 2 (2001): 102–144.

[41] Matthew T. Billett, and Anand M. Vijh, "The Wealth Effects of Tracking Stock Restructurings," *Journal of Financial Research* 27, no. 4 (December 2004): 559–583.

is one of the major disadvantages of this form of business organization compared with a corporation. In a corporation, the owners—the stockholders—are insulated from the company's liabilities. The limited partners in the MLP, however, do not incur the liability exposure of the general partner.

The key advantage of the MLP is its elimination of the corporate layer of taxation. Stockholders in a corporation are taxed twice on their investments: first at the corporate level and then, with distributions in the form of dividends, at the individual level. MLPs are not taxed as a separate business entity, and the returns to the business flow through to the owners just as they do in other partnerships. This advantage was strengthened by the 1986 Tax Reform Act, which lowered the highest personal income tax bracket to 28% (which is less than the top corporate rate of 34%). This advantage was reduced when the tax law was changed in later years to raise the rate charged in the upper tax bracket.

Corporations have used MLPs to redistribute assets so that their returns are not subject to double taxation. In a rollout MLP, corporations may transfer assets or divisions in separate MLPs. Stockholders in the corporation are then given units of ownership in the MLP while maintaining their shares in the corporation. The income distributed by the MLP is not subject to double taxation.

MLPs may be involved in either spin-offs or equity carve-outs. In a spin-off, assets are directly transferred from the parent company to the MLP. Parent company shareholders receive MLP units on a pro rata basis. In an equity carve-out, the MLP raises cash through a public offering. This cash is then used to purchase assets of the division of the parent company that is being sold off.

MLPs have been popular in the petroleum industry. Oil companies have distributed oil and gas assets into MLPs, allowing the returns to flow through directly to stockholders without double taxation. Initially, startup businesses may also be structured as MLPs. The MLP may be run by a general partner, who receives an income from managing the business. The general partner may or may not own a unit in the MLP. Capital is raised through an initial sale of MLP units to investors.

MLPs are generally held by individuals as opposed to corporations, which are predominantly owned by institutional investors. This trend may be explained by observing several differences between corporations and MLPs. Limited partners in MLPs do not have control, which is an attribute that institutions are starting to value more. Moreover, corporate shareholders are normally taxed on their MLP income, as opposed to the exclusion they would qualify for if they were receiving dividends from another corporation. In addition, even institutions that are normally tax-exempt may have their MLP income taxed. For these reasons, MLPs are not very attractive to institutions.

While the MLP structure can provide attractive benefits for investors, it is not a business structure that allows the entity to take all the same steps that a traditional corporation would to grow in the long term. This is a restricting structure that provides clear financial benefits. This is why in 2014 Kinder Morgan announced that it was acquiring three of its related MLPs and wrapping them all into its larger C corporation. The deal was very large—in the $70 billion range. The resulting structure is much simpler as prior to that there were four different equity securities related to the overall business.

ITT: DISSOLUTION OF THE QUINTESSENTIAL CONGLOMERATE

On June 13, 1995, the ITT Corporation announced that it would split the giant conglomerate that was constructed during the third merger wave through the acquisition of many dissimilar businesses throughout the world. The transaction was one of the largest of its kind in history. It involved the creation of three separate public companies, each with its own board of directors and each listed on the New York Stock Exchange. Holders of ITT stock received one share of stock in each of the new companies.

The breakup of ITT, once known as the International Telephone and Telegraph Company, was an endorsement of the belief that the sum of the parts of the company, as stand-alone entities, was worth more than the value of them combined under the ITT umbrella. It was difficult to find many commonalities or synergies in ITT's diverse business interests; that is, it is a stretch to say that casinos and hockey teams have much in common with casualty insurance or the hotel business.

One of the clear benefits of splitting the company up was better access to capital.

"We just think that having these three companies acting and operating and being evaluated in their own business environment will provide investors, analysts and those who deploy debt a simpler, more clear way to evaluate us," said the chairman, president, and chief executive of ITT, Rand V. Araskog.[a,b]

The $25 billion conglomerate that was built by Harold Geneen was split into three companies: an insurance company, ITT Hartford; an industrial products firm, ITT Industries; and a casino, hotel, and sports company, ITT Corporation. During the 1960s and 1970s, ITT had acquired more than 250 companies, including Avis Rent A Car, Continental Baking Company, Canteen, Rayonier, Sheraton Hotels, Hartford Insurance Company, and others. ITT sold what was originally its core business in 1986. At that time, it sold its telecommunications operations to Alcatel Alsthom (CGE France).

The three new companies each included divisions that shared common elements for which there might be some synergies. For example, many of the managerial skills and administrative systems necessary to run a hotel are somewhat similar to those of casinos. Within the new ITT Corporation, Sheraton and Ciga hotels were combined. Also included in this company was the Madison Square Garden (MSG) sports arena, along with two of the major users of the arena, the New York Knickerbockers and the New York Rangers. In addition, the company had a partnership arrangement with Cablevision System Corporation—the New York cable television company that offers the MSG cable programming that televises the games of these teams. In 1997, ITT sold Madison Square Garden and its interests in the sports teams to Cablevision.

The breakup of ITT was typical of the transactions that took place in the mid-1990s, when the pressure to increase efficiency rather than pursue convoluted acquisitions strategies was the way of the day. Whereas the third and fourth merger waves featured many questionable acquisitions, the early to mid-1990s featured more strategic acquisitions, in addition to the unraveling of many of the poorly conceived deals of earlier periods.

[a] Stephanie Storm, "ITT, the Quintessential Conglomerate, Plans to Split Up," *New York Times*, June 14, 1995, D1.

[b] ITT Company press release, June 13, 1995.

CHAPTER TWELVE

Restructuring in Bankruptcy

A S NOTED, MERGER AND acquisition (M&A) volume tends to move with the ups and downs of the economy. When we have a strong economic expansion, the likelihood that we may have a merger wave is higher. For example, this was the case in both the fourth and fifth merger waves. When we have an economic downturn, M&A volume tends to decline. It is in such downturns that we tend to see more bankruptcies.

In an economic downturn, revenues often weaken while costs may be slower to decline. In addition, companies may have increased their debt levels during the expansion, which can leave them in a vulnerable position during a recession. In the years 2003–2007, corporate and household leverage rose to new heights. Many companies could not service their higher debt levels when the economy turned down in 2008, and we entered the Great Recession. The natural result of the combination of a slow economy and high leverage is increased bankruptcies.

In addition to being a drastic step that companies take when they become insolvent, bankruptcy can also be a creative corporate finance tool. Reorganization through the bankruptcy process can in certain instances provide unique benefits that are unattainable through other means. This chapter explores the different forms of bankruptcy in the United States and discusses the circumstances in which a company would use either of the two broad forms of corporate bankruptcy that are available under U.S. law: Chapter 7 and Chapter 11. Chapter 7, liquidation, is appropriate for more severely distressed companies. Chapter 11, reorganization, however, is the more flexible corporate finance tool that allows a company to continue to operate while it explores other forms of restructuring. In addition, Chapter 11 allows the management of a bankrupt company to stay in control while the company pursues reorganization.

TYPES OF BUSINESS FAILURE

Clearly, bankruptcy is a drastic step that is pursued only when other more favorable options are unavailable. A bankruptcy filing is an admission that a company has in some way failed to achieve certain goals. The term *business failure* is somewhat ambiguous and has different meanings, depending on the context and the users. There are two main forms of business failure: economic failure and financial failure. Each has a very different meaning.

The word *bankruptcy* actually comes from a combination of two Latin words: *bankus*, which means bank, and *ruptus*, which means broken. Some have traced these words to a tradition in Italy in the 1800s, when Italian merchants did business on benches. If one of their businesses failed, their benches would be broken by other merchants as a way of letting the failed business know it was no longer welcome in the area.

Economic Failure

Of the two broad types of business failure, economic failure is the more ambiguous. For example, economic failure could mean that the firm is generating losses—that is, revenues are less than costs. However, depending on the users and the context, economic failure could also mean that the rate of return on investment is less than the cost of capital. It could also mean that the actual returns earned by a firm are less than those that were forecast. These uses of the term are very different and cover situations in which a company could be unprofitable, as well as cases in which the company is profitable but not as profitable as was expected.

Financial Failure

Financial failure is less ambiguous than economic failure. Financial failure means that a company cannot meet its current obligations as they come due. The company does not have sufficient liquidity to satisfy its current liabilities. This may occur even when the company has a positive net worth, with the value of its assets exceeding its liabilities.

Costs of Financial Distress

Financial distress is a condition where a company has difficulty meeting its promises to creditors. This condition tends to bring with it certain costs that may include direct costs, such as legal and accounting fees, as well as indirect costs that can come from the market's reaction to a company that may not honor its commitments to securities holders.

Andrade and Kaplan conducted a study of 31 distressed, highly leveraged transactions (HLTs) consisting of management buyouts (MBOs) and leveraged recapitalizations.[1] They focused on firms that were financially but not economically

---

[1] Gregor Andrade and Steven N. Kaplan, "How Costly Is Financial (Not Economic) Distress? Evidence from Highly Leveraged Transactions That Became Distressed," *Journal of Finance* 53, no. 5 (October 1998): 1443–1493.

distressed. They traced the causes of the distress to a pre- versus post-HLT leverage, as measured by the median ratio of book value of debt to total capital, 0.21 versus 0.91, and median ratios of earnings before interest, tax, depreciation, and amortization (EBITDA) interest coverage of 7.95 versus 1.16. Their analysis points to the higher leverage as the cause of the financial distress. They then compared the value of the company over a period of two months before the HLT until the resolution of the distress. The resolution was defined as the date they either exited Chapter 11, were sold, issued new equity, or were liquidated. They conclude that the changes brought about by the HLTs and the subsequent distress result in an *increase* in value. It is important to note that their conclusions are relevant only to financial distress, not to economic distress.

George and Hwang examined the relationship between distress costs and capital structure in a large sample of companies over the period of 1966–2003.[2] Their analysis results in a very intuitive finding—firms with high distress costs tend to have lower leverage (so as to try to avoid default) and have lower probabilities of default. However, the operating performance of low-leverage firms deteriorates much more rapidly when in financial distress since these firms are much more sensitive to financial distress. Presumably, knowing their vulnerability to distressed situations, the companies adjust their capital structure to employ less leverage so that they avoid being in distress.

CAUSES OF BUSINESS FAILURE

Dun & Bradstreet conducted a study of the causes of business failure. They found that the three most common factors, in order of frequency, were economic factors, such as weakness in the industry; financial factors, such as insufficient capitalization; and weaknesses in managerial experience, such as insufficient managerial knowledge (see Table 12.1). The last factor highlights the role of management skills in preventing bankruptcy and is one reason workout specialists focus so strongly on managerial skills when they are working on a company turnaround.

Dun & Bradstreet also analyzed the average ages of the businesses that failed (see Table 12.2). They found only 10.7% of the failures were in business for one year or less. Just under one-third of the companies were in business for three years or less, whereas 44.3% existed for up to five years.

Causes of Financial Distress following Leveraged Recapitalizations

Financial distress and bankruptcy have been linked to many of the highly leveraged deals that took place in the 1980s. As discussed in Chapter 8, leveraged buyouts (LBOs) became popular during this period, along with the use of leveraged recapitalization as

---

[2] Thomas J. George and Chuan-Yang Hwang, "A Resolution of the Distress Risk and Leverage Puzzles in the Cross Section of Stock Returns," *Journal of Financial Economics* 96, no. 1 (April 2010): 56–79.

TABLE 12.1 Causes of Business Failure

Underlying Causes	Percentage (%)*
Economic factors (e.g., industry weakness, insufficient profits)	41.0
Financial factors (e.g., heavy operating expenses, insufficient capital)	32.5
Experience factors (e.g., lack of business knowledge, lack of line experience, lack of managerial experience)	20.6
Neglect (e.g., poor work habits, business conflicts)	2.5
Fraud	1.2
Disaster	1.1
Strategy factors (e.g., receivable difficulties, overexpansion)	<u>1.1</u>
	100.0

*Results are based on primary reason for failure.
Source: The Dun & Bradstreet Corporation, Economic Analysis Department, March 1991.

TABLE 12.2 Failure by Age of Business

Number of Years in Business	Percentage (%)
One year or less	10.7
Two years	10.1
Three years	<u>8.7</u>
Total three years or less	29.5
Four years	7.8
Five years	<u>7.0</u>
Total five years or less	44.3
Total six to ten years	23.9
Total over ten years	<u>31.8</u>
	100.0

Source: Dun & Bradstreet Corporation, *Business Failure Record*, 1997.

an antitakeover defense. Denis and Denis conducted a study of 29 leveraged recapitalizations that took place between 1984 and 1988.[3] They define leveraged recapitalizations as transactions that use proceeds from new debt obligations to make a payout to shareholders. Their results show that 31% of the firms that completed leveraged recapitalizations encountered financial distress. This is contrary to what had been hypothesized by other researchers, such as Kaplan and Stein, who had asserted that failures of leveraged transactions were due to overpricing and poor financial structure. Denis and Denis conclude that although these factors are important, the 1990–1991 recession and the

---

[3] David J. Denis and Diane K. Denis, "Causes of Financial Distress following Leveraged Recapitalizations," *Journal of Financial Economics* 37 (1995): 129–157.

regulatory factors were the reason some leveraged recapitalizations failed and others did not.[4] They did find that distressed firms had similar but somewhat higher debt levels and lower interest coverage. However, distressed firms required more postdeal cash than nondistressed firms. For example, the cash needs of distressed firms required them to sell an average of 6.3% of their assets, whereas nondistressed firms would have had to sell only 3.6% of their assets. Distressed firms also had to achieve greater postdeal performance improvements. For example, in order to meet the postdeal debt service, distressed firms would have had to have a median increase in operating income of 41.8%, compared with 18.9% for nondistressed firms.

Given the reliance on postdeal asset sales, regulatory changes and the recession of 1990–1991 played a key role in the failure of the leveraged recapitalizations. These regulatory factors were related to the collapse of the junk bond market in the late 1980s. Following the difficulties of this market, certain financial institutions were forced to sell off their junk bond holdings, which hurt the ability of potential junk bond issuers to sell new bonds. This, in turn, limited the resources available to buyers of assets of companies that engaged in leveraged recapitalizations.

The limited resources lower the values that leveraged recap firms could realize from asset sales. Many of these firms overestimated the prices they would receive for assets, such as divisions. This error was partially related to not being able to anticipate the dramatic changes that occurred in the junk bond market. The difficulties of the market for assets were compounded by the recession of 1990–1991, which made performance improvement more difficult to achieve.

When an economy turns down, as it did in the 2008–2009 recession, debt pressures become more pronounced as cash flows may weaken. In addition, downturns are a poor environment in which to conduct asset sales to pay down debt.

Asset Restructuring

One way a company can to try to deal with financial distress is to sell off assets to generate cash, which can be used to pay down debt or alleviate cash flow pressures. In this section we discuss asset sales prior to a bankruptcy filing. Later in this chapter we discuss assets sales while in Chapter 11.

Lang, Poulsen, and Stulz found that asset sales often follow a period of poor stock market performance.[5] As we discussed in Chapter 11, these assets sales are often followed by increases in the seller's stock price. This is an intuitive result. A weak stock price *may* reflect that the company is not using its assets to its maximal benefit and/or that these assets may be more valued by other firms. Selling the assets coverts them into cash, which can either be returned to shareholders through a dividend or stock repurchase, used to pay down debt, or reinvested in the company (hopefully not into other assets that also will generate a weak return).

---

[4] Steven Kaplan and Jeremy Stein, "The Evolution of Buyout Pricing and the Financial Structure of the 1980s," *Quarterly Journal of Economics* 108, no. 2 (May 1993): 313–357.
[5] Larry Lang, Annette Poulsen, and Rene M. Stulz, "Asset Sales, Firm Performance, and the Agency Costs of Managerial Discretion," *Journal of Financial Economics* 37, no. 1 (1995): 3–37.

Brown, James, and Mooradian failed to detect a stock uplifting effect in their study of 62 distressed companies.[6] While one might think that it is a good idea for financially distressed firms to use the proceeds from asset sales to pay down debt, the results from Brown et al.'s analysis of those 62 companies showed that the announcement returns for those companies were lower than for the distressed companies that did not use the monies to pay down debt. In addition, they found that the greater the proportion of short-term debt in their total liabilities, the greater the probability that the proceeds would be paid out to creditors. The authors conclude that the asset sale and subsequent creditor payout decision could be the result of pressure applied by the creditors. The failure of the equity markets to respond favorably is understandable as the value of the assets is going to creditors and not for the benefit of stockholders. So stockholders lose both the assets and the proceeds, although they may benefit from the overall leverage of the company being lower.

Research by Asquith, Gertner, and Scharfstein studied junk bond issuers that got into financial distress.[7] Only 3 of the 21 companies in their sample that sold off more than 20% of their assets had to file bankruptcy. These firms were able to use asset sales as a mean of avoiding a bankruptcy filing. They also found that companies in an industry that was distressed had trouble selling assets. This empirical observation was expected by Shleifer and Vishny, who concluded that when an industry is distressed, assets may sell at fire sale discounts.[8] The importance of industry conditions for asset sale prices was also supported by research by Maksimovic and Phillips in their study of the sales of assets by manufacturing firms.[9] In addition, the more specialized the assets are, the less useful they are to those outside the distressed industry and the greater the expected fire sale discount.

Asset Fire Sales: Case of the Airline Industry

Pulvino analyzed fire sales in the airline industry, an industry that has had more than its share of bankruptcies, including multiple bankruptcies by the same carriers. He looked at sales of aircraft by companies that were in Chapter 11 or Chapter 7. He found that the prices the bankrupt companies received were significantly lower than nondistressed airlines that sold aircraft. In addition, his research failed to find any difference in the fire sale discounts between those firms that were in Chapter 7 or Chapter 11. Clearly, the airline industry is interesting as the assets are specialized and cannot be readily sold to firms outside the industry. While specific airlines could have unique problems that are not shared by others, the airline industry is quite cyclical as well as very sensitive to fuel prices. Therefore, it is not unusual to see a strong economic downturn or a sharp

---

[6] David T. Brown, Christopher M. James, and Robert M. Mooradian, "Asset Sales by Financially Distressed Firms," *Journal of Corporate Finance* 1, no. 2 (1994): 233–257.

[7] Paul Asquith, Robert Gertner, and David Scharfstein, "Anatomy of Financial Distress: An Examination of Junk Bond Issuers," *Quarterly Journal of Economics* 109, no. 3 (1994): 625–658.

[8] Andrei Shleifer and Robert W. Vishny, "Liquidation Values and Debt Capacity," *Journal of Finance* 47, no. 4 (September 1992): 1343–1366.

[9] Vojislav Maksimovic, and Gordon Phillips, "Asset Efficiency and Reallocation Decisions of Bankrupt Firms," *Journal of Finance* 53, no. 5 (October 1998): 1495–1532.

rise in fuel costs cause widespread distress among many airlines. Those that are in the best financial condition with the least leverage may be able to survive the tumult. Those that are not in good condition or find themselves unable to service high debt levels when they experience weak revenues or higher fuel charges may have to resort to downsizing through assets sales. The problem they may experience is that the most likely buyers probably are also experiencing weakened revenues and are not in the market to expand their fleet. This may lead the seller having to sell to financial institutions specializing in this industry, and they may seek to drive a hard bargain with the distressed seller. Indeed, this is what Shleifer and Vishny envisioned with their model wherein pools of outside money would seek to acquire assets at significant discounts and sell them at a later time at higher prices.

Even when the whole industry is not in the doldrums, distressed firms may be forced to still sell assets at fire sale prices. This was the case when Peoples Express overexpanded and also when Eastern Airlines fought a battle with its unions. Peoples Express, which had too quickly gone from a small regional carrier to being a national, and even international, airline, was forced to sell to Texas Air's subsidiary Continental Airlines. Eastern was a high-cost airline that was acquired by union-busting cost-cutter Frank Lorenzo, who had an all-out battle with machinists, and then their supporters, the pilots and flight attendants unions. He lost this battle and was forced to sell off parts of the airline to Continental but at fire-sale prices and eventually had to file for bankruptcy. Ironically, the employees were not really winners either as when the airline shut down operations, it laid off thousands of employees.

LEHMAN BROTHERS: BIGGEST BANKRUPTCY IN HISTORY

The subprime crisis, and the ensuing global recession that followed, took its toll on businesses across the world. The financial services sector was one of the major causes of the downturn. As a result of the financial crisis, three of the five largest independent U.S. investment banks no longer existed as vibrant and independent institutions. Along the way Bear Stearns was acquired by JPMorgan Chase and Merrill Lynch was acquired by Bank of America. These two acquisitions were facilitated by the assistance of the federal government. However, in the case of Lehman Brothers, no assistance was forthcoming.

The fact that an investment bank that existed for over 100 years could so quickly fail is surprising. While there are many reasons for the failure, clearly at the top of the list is managerial failures. Many financial institutions invested heavily in real estate and mortgage-related investments. Many of the public wrongly believe that the leaders of Wall Street's top financial institutions are astute investors and buy at good prices and sell at the right time. However, in the case of Lehman, as well as many of the larger financial institutions, including some that were favored by the government, such as Goldman Sachs, this was far from the case.

(continued)

(continued)

Lehman, run by its CEO Dick Fuld, a man who has been reported as out of touch with his managers and in-house experts, led the company into assuming tremendous leverage while making massive investments in various aspects of the real estate market. For example, Lehman had acquired mortgage issuer Aurora Loan Services and helped transform it into one of the larger players in the Alt A mortgage market, which is the market for loans that require little or no documentation. They also acquired another aggressive mortgage issuer by the name of BNC. Fuld also oversaw the acquisition of very expensive real estate, not buying at good prices but at the peak of the market in 2007! These were not astute investors who learned a great deal from their decades of experience in the investment world. Rather, they were "me too" followers, lacking any imagination or ability to see an extreme bubble while they sat at the top of it. Lehman was not alone in this incompetence, as Stanley O'Neil led Merrill Lynch down the road to failure while also extracting great compensation from the company.

Lehman employed extreme leverage but, like most investment banks, relied on short-term financing in the commercial paper market to finance its long-term investments at the peak of the market and was financed by extreme leverage. While one would think that normally a board of directors would be vigilant and try to keep management from making such foolish blunders, this board lacked the skill set and diligent efforts to properly monitor management.

When the mortgage market turned down, a number of aggressive investors began to short Lehman's stock. As its stock price fell, the market woke up to Lehman's many investment errors. Fuld probably could have sold the company for some positive value early in the process, but he added to his errors by refusing to accept Lehman's fate and get the best deal for shareholders. The result is that Lehman Brothers no longer exists, although parts of its business are now owned by Barclay's, which has profited by Lehman's management's poor judgment.[a]

[a] Lawrence G. McDonald and Patrick Robinson, *A Colossal Failure of Common Sense: The Inside Story of the Collapse of Lehman Brothers* (New York: Crown Books, 2009).

 BANKRUPTCY TRENDS

When an economy slows, revenue growth weakens at many companies. This puts many companies under financial pressure—especially those that had assumed higher debt burdens. In a robust economy many companies assume leverage to facilitate growth, such as to finance M&As. Too often management is short-sighted and believes that the "good times" will continue and they will be able to service the higher debt loads. Even though recessions are a fact of life in the world economy, too often management is surprised when a recession arrives and their revenue growth slows.

Figure 12.1 shows that when economic growth picked up between 2005 and 2006, total US bankruptcies fell sharply. Figure 12.2 shows a similar trend for Chapter 11 filings, although the falloff is less dramatic. However, as the economy began to

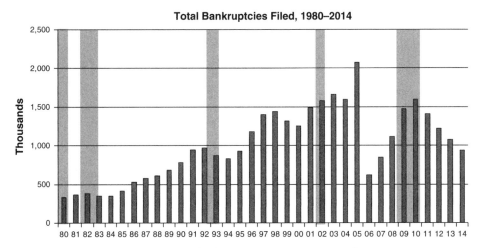

FIGURE 12.1 Total Bankruptcies Filed, 1980–2014. *Source*: BankruptcyData.com, New Generation Research, Administrative Office of the United States Courts.

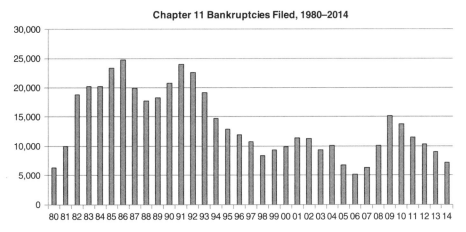

FIGURE 12.2 Chapter 11 Bankruptcies Filed, 1980–2014. *Source*: BankruptcyData.com, New Generation Research, Administrative Office of the U.S. Courts.

slow in 2007 and eventually go into a recession in 2008–2009, total bankruptcies and Chapter 11 filings rose. This is also seen in Figure 12.3, which shows a dramatic rise in the total assets of companies that filed for bankruptcy in 2008. This intuitive procyclical trend in these filings is confirmed by other research.[10]

---

[10] Lance Bachmier, Patrick Gaughan, and Norman Swanson, "The Volume of Federal Litigation and the Macroeconomy," *International Review of Law & Economics* 242, no. 2 (June 2004): 191–208.

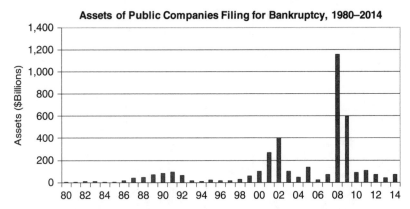

FIGURE 12.3 Assets of public companies filing for bankruptcy, 1980–2014.
Source: BankruptcyData.com, A Division of New Generation Research, Inc.

Fraud-Related Bankruptcies

Table 12.1 shows the causes of bankruptcy based on research by Dun & Bradstreet prior to the huge bankruptcies that occurred at the end of the fifth merger wave. This research shows that only 1.2% of the time is fraud the cause of bankruptcy. This changed in a big way in the 2000s. The two largest U.S. bankruptcies are WorldCom and Enron. Both corporate giants were brought down by management fraud. The list of the largest bankruptcies also includes a number of other fraud-related collapses, including Adelphia and Refco (see Table 12.3). These bankruptcies have led to changes in laws such as the Sarbanes-Oxley Act. While Enron's bankruptcy is not related to M&A, WorldCom's failed merger strategy and the company's inability to achieve organic growth were closely related to its ultimate demise.

Fraud-related bankruptcies were not a U.S.-exclusive phenomenon. In December 2003, the Italian food group Parmalat Finanziaria SpA announced that it would file for bankruptcy protection. This bankruptcy shocked the European corporate world when it was revealed that a fraud of this magnitude could take place in a company that was an international household name.

Comment on Largest Bankruptcies Data

Table 12.3 lists the largest bankruptcies by asset size without an adjustment for inflation. If such an adjustment was made, and all asset values were presented in same year terms, the list would be somewhat similar, but some famous earlier bankruptcies would appear on it. For example, the bankruptcy filing by Penn Central in 1970 listed assets at that time of $6.85 billion. However, this value would equal approximately $43 billion in 2015 dollars.

TABLE 12.3 Largest U.S. Public Bankruptcies

Company	Assets in $ mil.	Date Filed
Lehman Brothers Holdings Inc.	$691,063	9/15/2008
Washington Mutual, Inc.	327,913	9/26/2008
WorldCom, Inc.	103,914	7/21/2002
General Motors Corporation	91,047	6/1/2009
CIT Group Inc.	80,448	11/1/2009
Enron Corp.	65,503	12/2/2001
Conseco, Inc.	61,392	12/17/2002
Energy Future Holdings Corp.	40,970	4/29/2014
MF Global Holdings Ltd.	40,541	10/31/2011
Chrysler LLC	39,300	4/30/2009
Thornburg Mortgage, Inc.	36,521	5/1/2009
Pacific Gas & Electric Company	36,152	4/6/2001
Texaco, Inc.	34,940	4/12/1987
Financial Corp. of America	33,864	9/9/1988
Refco Inc.	33,333	10/17/2005
IndyMac Bancorp, Inc.	32,734	7/31/2008
Global Crossing, Ltd.	30,185	1/28/2002
Bank of New England Corp.	29,773	1/7/1991
General Growth Properties, Inc.	29,557	4/16/2009
Lyondell Chemical Company	27,392	1/6/2009

Source: BankruptcyData.com, a division of New Generation Research Inc.

REFCO BANKRUPTCY CAUSED BY FRAUD

Refco was a futures-trading firm that provided execution and clearing services for exchange-traded derivatives. The company also served as a prime broker in the fixed income and foreign exchange markets. It did business with different hedge funds and various investment companies. At its peak it employed over 2,000 employees and had over 200,000 customer accounts.

In 2004, 57% of Refco was acquired in a leveraged buyout (LBO) by the private equity (IPO) firm Thomas Lee Partners. This transaction was followed by an initial public offering in 2005. The proceeds of the sale went to several purposes, including cashing out equity positions of pre-IPO shareholders as well as retiring debt and paying pre-IPO shareholders dividends. However, just two months after the IPO, the company announced to the markets the existence of a previously undisclosed

(continued)

(*continued*)

receivable from an affiliated entity controlled by one Philip Bennett, the pre-LBO CEO. However, this receivable had been previously disguised as an obligation from an unaffiliated third party. This was done through a fraudulent scheme that used various "round-trip loans," where monies were lent to a third party to make payments and create the illusion that the receivable was collectable. The total principal amount of these loans was $6.25 billion. Rather than reduce the receivable, as the loans were designed to appear to do, they actually increased it, as interest, which accumulated to approximately $1.2 billion, was added to the principal. Following the disclosure, an investigation was conducted and payment from Mr. Bennett and the affiliated entity he controlled was demanded, but no such payment was made. The disclosure led to a "run on the bank" and billions left customer accounts. The stock collapsed from $28.56 on October 7, 2005, to $0.65 on October 18, 2005.

Refco was composed of some regulated and some unregulated businesses. The regulated entities had cash reserves to handle the withdrawal requests, but the unregulated ones did not. This left the company with no choice but to file for Chapter 11 bankruptcy protection on October 17, 2005. However, it was no longer a viable business, and on November 25, 2006, it filed a petition for relief under Chapter 7 of the bankruptcy code. Refco would become one of the largest bankruptcies in U.S. history.

U.S. BANKRUPTCY LAWS

The Bankruptcy Act of 1978 (the Bankruptcy Code) is the main bankruptcy law of the United States. It organized bankruptcy laws under eight odd-numbered chapters (see Table 12.4).

Changes in the U.S. Bankruptcy Laws

Bankruptcy laws vary across countries. The United States and France have laws that are somewhat favorable to bankrupt companies and their managers. Other countries,

TABLE 12.4 Prepackaged Bankruptcy Filings: 1995–2001

Chapter	Subject
1	General provisions and definitions
3	Case administration
5	Creditors, debtors, and estates
7	Liquidation
9	Bankruptcies of municipalities
11	Reorganization
13	Bankruptcies of individuals
15	U.S. trustees system

such as Great Britain, Canada, and Sweden, take a harsher stance toward the bankrupt companies and provide for fewer restructuring opportunities.

For many years bankruptcy in the United States was governed by the Bankruptcy Act of 1978. This law was enhanced in 1984 with the Bankruptcy Amendments and Federal Judgeship Act, which established the jurisdiction of the bankruptcy court as a unit of the district courts. This law was in response to a Supreme Court ruling that challenged the jurisdiction of bankruptcy courts. The 1984 law also made it more difficult to immediately void labor contracts in bankruptcy. This was in response to a Supreme Court ruling in the Wilson Foods case, in which the court decided that companies could abrogate existing labor contracts as soon as they filed for bankruptcy. The revised law, which was passed partly because of labor union pressure, requires that a company try to work out a labor agreement before going to the bankruptcy courts. If the sincerity of the efforts of the parties is an issue, a bankruptcy court will decide whether each party acted in good faith and under compliance with the law.

The Bankruptcy Reform Act of 1994 enhanced the powers of the bankruptcy courts. The act gave these courts the right to issue orders that they deem necessary or appropriate to carry out the provisions of the Bankruptcy Code. In October 2005, the Bankruptcy Abuse Prevention and Consumer Protection Act was focused mainly on personal bankruptcy and causes such as credit card abuse. However, the law did contain some changes affecting Chapter 11 filings. We will discuss the rules that relate to the length of what is known as the exclusivity period later in this chapter. Other changes related to corporate bankruptcy involved limits on retention bonuses paid to management. Managers receiving such bonuses must prove they have a bona fide job offer at or near the retention bonus. Such a bonus cannot be greater than 10 times the average incentives paid to retain nonmanagers.

Another change brought about by the 2005 law is the requirement that the debtor in position has seven months after the filing to accept or reject leases. This is an important requirement for retailers. It forces them to make a long-term commitment even though the full reorganization plan may not be finalized and approved. Still another change brought about by the new law is the requirement that the debtor in position pay in full for all goods it received 20 days prior to bankruptcy. This eliminates some of the benefits of doing a Chapter 11 filing but it also prevent supplies from being cut off for companies that are rumored to be filing Chapter 11.

 ## REORGANIZATION VERSUS LIQUIDATION

The purpose of the reorganization section of the Bankruptcy Code is to allow a *reorganization plan* to be developed that will allow the company to continue to operate. This plan will contain the changes in the company that its designers believe are necessary to convert it to a profitable entity. If a plan to allow the profitable operation of the business cannot be formulated, the company may have to be liquidated, with its assets sold and the proceeds used to satisfy the company's liabilities.

WILBUR ROSS: FINDING VALUE IN TROUBLED BUSINESSES

Certain investors excel at finding valuable opportunities in troubled businesses. Wilbur Ross, a former restructuring advisor at Rothschild, is a leader in the turnaround field. He quickly earned a reputation as a sought-after leader in turnarounds. He formed his own Manhattan-based private equity firm, W. L. Ross & Co., which makes equity investments in firms in dire need of restructuring. The steel industry in the United States had been troubled since the 1980s, when some of its larger companies proved to be unable to compete internationally due to their burdensome labor cost structure combined with inefficient plants, which caused them to lose market share to rivals from countries such as Japan and South Korea. Ross recognized an opportunity when he entered the steel industry in 2002 by buying a Cleveland steel mill for $325 million. He continued to buy steel companies and combined them into an entity called International Steel Group (ISG). He then took this company public and sold to it Lakshmi Mittal of Mittal Steel 10 months later at an attractive 42% premium.[a] With the addition of ISG, Mittal became the largest steel company in the world. Ross's business acumen is underscored by a comparison of the $2.165 billion he paid for the five steel companies that made up ISG—LTV Corp., Bethlehem Steel, Acme Metals, Weirton Steel, and Georgetown Steel—and the $5.1 billion that Mittal paid for them.[b]

Ross also successfully acquired troubled textile businesses. He skillfully acquired Burlington's debt at deeply discounted prices after the textile maker filed for bankruptcy. In 2001, he ended up acquiring the company in bankruptcy for $614 million.

Following up on his success in the steel and textile industries, Ross then set his sights on the troubled auto suppliers industry. This sector has a lot in common with steel and textiles. Each has a high-cost labor force that has difficulty competing in an increasingly international market that has many lower-cost competitors. In 2005, Ross formed the International Auto Components Group (IAC), which set about acquiring various different international auto suppliers, such as the European operations of Collins and Aikman Corp.

[a] Heather Timmons, "Mergers Show Steel Industry Is Still Worthy of Big Deals," *New York Times*, October 24, 2004, 1.
[b] Ibid.

 REORGANIZATION PROCESS

Although the Chapter 11 process varies somewhat depending on the particular circumstances of the bankruptcy, most Chapter 11 bankruptcies have certain important common characteristics. These are highlighted next.

Bankruptcy Petition and Filing

The reorganization process starts with the filing of a bankruptcy *petition for relief* with the bankruptcy court. In the petition, the debtor lists its creditors and security holders.

Standard financial statements, including an income statement and balance sheet, are also included. The court then sets a date when the creditors may file their *proofs of claim*. The company then attempts to put together a reorganization plan while it continues its operations. Contrary to what a layperson might think, there is no financial test that is performed by the court at this time to determine whether the debtor is truly financially insolvent.

The petition is usually filed in the federal district in which the debtor has its home office. After the petition is filed, a case number is assigned, a court file is opened, and a bankruptcy judge is assigned to the case.

Filing Location

A troubled company can file a bankruptcy petition in one of 94 regional bankruptcy courts. The most common locations where bankruptcy cases are filed are Delaware and the Southern District of New York. Unlike the decision of where to incorporate, corporations are supposed to file in a district either where they have their headquarters or where they have a substantial percentage of their operations. Even though bankruptcy laws are federal laws as opposed to state laws, companies can choose to file their cases in specific local venues within the federal court system. There is some evidence that companies that have reorganized in Delaware have a tendency to refile Chapter 11 in Delaware later on.[11] Others have concluded that there is insufficient evidence that such a displayed preference for Delaware results in any losses for debtors.[12]

LoPucki and Whitford conducted a study of 43 large public firms that were in financial distress.[13] They did find evidence that the companies engaged in "forum shopping," which refers to the phenomenon that companies may file in a location in which they really do not have a substantial physical presence. This is done when they believe that the courts in the most reasonable location, such as where their corporate headquarters is located or where they have most of their facilities, would be more hostile to their proposals and plans, such as requests for extensions of the exclusivity period, than some other locations. This can be discerned from the experience of bankruptcy counsel in these various jurisdictions.

Debtor in Possession

After the bankruptcy filing, the bankrupt company is referred to as the *debtor in possession*. This is a new legal entity; however, for all practical purposes, it usually is the same company with the same management and the same employees. From the creditors' point of view, this is one of the problems of the bankruptcy process; that is, the same management that led the company into its financial troubles usually is still running the business while a reorganization plan is being developed.

---

[11] Theodore Eisenberg and Lynn M. LoPucki, "Shopping for Judges: An Empirical Analysis of Venue Choice in Large Chapter 11 Reorganizations," *Cornell Law Review* 84, no. 4 (May 1999): 967.

[12] David A. Skeel, "What's So Bad about Delaware?" *Vanderbilt Law Review* 54 (March 2001): 309–329.

[13] Lynn M. LoPucki and William C. Whitford, "Venue Choice and Forum Shopping in the Bankruptcy Reorganization of Large Publicly Held Companies," *Wisconsin Law Review* 1 (1991): 11–63.

If the creditors strongly oppose the management of the debtor staying in control of the business, they may petition the court and ask that a trustee and examiner be appointed. If concerns exist about fraudulent actions or incompetence of the debtor's directors or management, the court may agree. A trustee is charged with overseeing the operations of the company while it is in bankruptcy. An examiner may be appointed to investigate specific issues. If the court denies a request for a trustee, an examiner is usually appointed.

Automatic Stay

When the petition is accepted by the court, an automatic stay is granted. This is one of the main benefits the debtor receives in the Chapter 11 process. During the automatic stay, a halt is placed on any prepetition legal proceedings as well as on the enforcement of any prefiling judgment. Creditors are unable to pursue a lien on the debtor's assets or to collect money from the debtor. Parties seeking relief from the stay may petition the court and request a hearing. If the creditors can convince the court that the assets that are being used as collateral for obligations due them are not necessary for the continued operation of the company, or the debtor has no equity interest in the assets, they may be able to get relief from the stay.

Time Line in the Reorganization Process

Table 12.5 shows some of the key events and dates in the Chapter 11 process. Within 10 days of filing the Chapter 11 bankruptcy petition, the debtor is required to file a schedule of assets and liabilities with the court. This schedule must include the name and address of each creditor. The next important date is the *bar date*, which is the date when those creditors who have disputed or contingent claims must file a *proof of claim*. A proof of claim is a written statement that sets forth what is owed by the debtor to the particular creditor. Failure to file by the bar date may result in the forfeiture of the claim. It is automatically assumed, however, that other claimholders have filed a proof of claim. Following the bar date, the next important dates are those associated with the filing and approval of the reorganization plan.

TABLE 12.5 Time Line of Key Events and Dates in a Chapter 11 Reorganization

1. Filing of the Chapter 11 petition
2. Filing a schedule of assets and liabilities
3. Bar date
4. Filing a reorganization plan and disclosure statement
5. Hearing on the disclosure statement
6. Voting on the plan
7. Plan confirmation hearing
8. Effective date of plan/distribution of new claims under the plan

Duration of the Chapter 11 Process

According to New Generation Research Inc., over the period 1982–2004 the average duration of a Chapter 11 filing was 16.4 months. In more recent years, however, this time period has been getting somewhat shorter. For example, over the period 1996–2000 the average duration was 14 months.

Use of Secured Creditors' Collateral

The Chapter 11 process allows for the use of the secured creditors' collateral by the debtor in possession. Creditors are barred from seizing assets while the stay is in effect. This does not mean that the debtor has free use of the property. The debtor must make some accommodation to the creditors, such as periodic payments (i.e., monthly), for continued use of the assets.

Duties of the Debtor in Possession

After the filing of the petition, the court establishes certain schedules that feature various reporting requirements. For example, the debtor has to file monthly financial statements 15 days after the end of each calendar month. In addition to the court rules as set forth in the federal law, each federal district may have additional reporting requirements. For example, the Southern District of New York has local rules that relate to further reporting requirements and the opening of bank accounts.

Stakeholder Committees

The Bankruptcy Code provides for various committees to be formed to represent the interests of different claimholders before the court. The committees are usually composed of the seven largest members of a given class who are interested in serving on the committee. These committees have the power to hire their own attorneys and other professionals to assist them. These expenses of these professionals are paid for by the debtor-in-possession. A committee to represent the interests of unsecured creditors is almost always appointed. Other committees, such as an equityholders committee, may also get formed. The ultimate decision about which committees are formed is made by the Executive Office of the Trustees or the court.

A creditors' meeting is usually held within 20 to 40 days of the bankruptcy filing. The meeting is called by the U.S. trustee and is usually held at his office. The debtor and its principal officers must be present at this meeting. All creditors may attend this meeting and may ask the debtor specific questions that are of concern to them.

Along with the U.S. trustee, the creditors' committee monitors the actions of the debtor, ensuring that it does not do anything that would adversely affect the creditors' interests. The creditors' committee may retain counsel, accountants, and other financial experts to represent the creditors' interests during the reorganization process. The fees of professionals are borne by the debtor.

The bigger the bankruptcy, the more likely it is that there may be more committees, such as an equityholders' committee, or different types of creditors' committees, such as a bondholders' committee, representing the various forms of debt that might exist. One example of a megabankruptcy that had several committees was the bankruptcy of the Campeau Corporation, which featured the bankruptcy of Campeau's two major sub-units, Federated Department Stores Inc. and Allied Stores Corp. In this proceeding, there were several committees, including a bondholders' committee and two trade creditors' committees. The court attempted to appoint a cross section of similarly situated credi-tors on each committee. In smaller bankruptcies, creditors may have little interest in the committees. In the Campeau bankruptcy, the office of U.S. trustee Conrad J. Morgenstern was flooded with bondholders who were interested in serving on the committee.

Debtor's Actions and Its Supervision

The debtor may continue to operate the business during the reorganization process. The law requires that the debtor obtain the approval of the bankruptcy court before it takes any extraordinary action that is not part of the normal business operations, such as selling assets or property.

Technically, the supervision of the debtor is the responsibility of the judge and the creditors. They may acquire resources, such as legal and accounting or other financial expert assistance, to help them. Practically, neither the judge nor the creditors usually have the resources or time to closely supervise the debtor. Even if the debtor does some-thing that the creditors do not approve of, the debtor may be able to convince the judge that some actions are necessary for the survival of the company; that is, if the court does not allow the debtor to take these actions, the company may go under. Thus, the judge is put in the difficult position of making this decision with limited information. If the judge rules against the debtor and is wrong, he risks the company's going out of business and all the duress and employee suffering this might cause. For this reason, the debtor is usu-ally granted significant leeway and will be opposed only when its proposed actions are clearly objectionable.

Exclusivity Period

After the filing of the bankruptcy petition and the granting of the automatic stay, only the debtor has the right to file a reorganization plan. This period, which is initially 120 days, is known as the *exclusivity period*. It is rare, however, particularly in larger bankruptcies, to have the plan submitted during that time frame. It is common for the debtor to ask for one or more extensions. Extensions are granted only for cause, but they are not difficult to obtain. However, the Bankruptcy Abuse Prevention and Consumer Protection Act of 2005 placed an absolute limit of 18 months on the exclusivity period.

Obtaining Postpetition Credit

One of the problems a near-bankrupt company has is difficulty obtaining credit. If trade creditors are concerned that a company may become bankrupt, they may cut off all additional credit. For companies that are dependent on such credit to survive, this may mean that a bankruptcy filing is accelerated. In fact, if a company may be on the verge of bankruptcy, its vendors may decline to offer them normal credit terms and may insist on cash on delivery. For example, this was the case in 2008 for Linens & Things, which found it had to pay cash to vendors who normally offered them 30 to 60 days to pay. When this happens it elevates a company's cash needs at a time when it is actually less liquid than normal. This can accelerate the path to a bankruptcy filing.

Sometimes the bankruptcy of one company can create liquidity problems for other companies. For example, when Montgomery Ward filed for bankruptcy in 1997, suppliers became concerned about other companies and preemptively cut off shipments and required cash payments.

To assist bankrupt companies in acquiring essential credit, the code has given post-petition creditors an elevated priority in the bankruptcy process. This type of lending is referred to as debtor-in-possession, or DIP, financing. DIP lenders have an elevated priority over prepetition claims. It is ironic that creditors may be unwilling to extend credit unless the debtor files for bankruptcy so that the creditor can obtain the elevated priority.

A company that seeks such postbankruptcy financing has to file a motion with the bankruptcy court seeking permission to do so. It is not unusual to see companies file such motions at the time they do their Chapter 11 filing or shortly thereafter. Section 364 of the Bankruptcy Code provides that such loans have *super-seniority* status and have a priority over other secured creditors. Thus, while creditors might not want to lend to the company on an unsecured basis, the fact that the debtor-in-possession may possess significant assets with a high collateral value, combined with the super seniority status, may give them confidence that their loans will be repaid. Various financial institutions specialize in DIP financing.

Credit Conditions and Length of Time in Bankruptcy

The management of cash-strapped companies that have significant assets that can be used as collateral may find the reorganization process comfortable and not have incentive to move the process along. Prepetition creditors, however, would have a different view as they see the claims fall in value as new creditors' interests are placed ahead of theirs. In weak credit markets that process may work very differently. For example, in the wake of the subprime crisis, credit availability declined sharply. This created more liquidity issues for bankrupt companies—even those that had significant assets that normally could be used as collateral. This, in turn, caused bankruptcy stays to become shorter and for the increased use of prepackaged bankruptcies (discussed later in this chapter).

Reorganization Plan

The reorganization plan, which is part of a larger document called the *disclosure statement*, looks like a prospectus. For larger bankruptcies, it is a long document that contains the plans for the turnaround of the company. The plan is submitted to all the creditors and equityholders' committees. The plan is approved when each class of creditor and equity holder approves it. Approval is granted if one-half in number and two-thirds in dollar amount of a given class approve the plan. Once the plan is approved, the dissenters are bound by the details of the plan.

Sometimes, to avoid slowdowns that may be caused by lawsuits filed by dissatisfied junior creditors, senior creditors may provide a monetary allocation to junior creditors. This is sometimes referred to as *gifting*.

A confirmation hearing follows the attainment of the approval of the plan. A notice of the hearing in published in publications like the *Wall Street Journal*. The hearing is not intended to be a pro forma proceeding, even if the vote is unanimous. The presiding judge must make a determination that the plan meets the standards set forth by the Bankruptcy Code. After the plan is confirmed, the debtor is discharged of all prepetition claims and other claims up to the date of the confirmation hearing. This does not mean that the reorganized company is a debt-free entity. It simply means that it has new obligations that are different from the prior obligations. Ideally, the postconfirmation capital structure is one that will allow the company to remain sufficiently liquid to meet its new obligations and generate a profit.

Cramdown

The plan may be made binding on all classes of security holders, even if they all do not approve it. This is known as a *cramdown*. The judge may conduct a cramdown if at least one class of creditors approves the plan and the "crammed down" class is not being treated unfairly. In this context, *unfairly* means that no class with inferior claims in the bankruptcy hierarchy is receiving compensation without the higher-up class being paid 100% of its claims. This order of claims is known as the *absolute priority rule*, which states that claims must be settled in full before any junior claims can receive any compensation.

The concept of a cramdown comes from the concern by lawmakers that a small group of creditors could block the approval of a plan to the detriment of the majority of the creditors.[14] By giving the court the ability to cram down a plan, the law reduces the potential for a holdout problem.

Fairness and Feasibility of the Plan

The reorganization plan must be both fair and feasible. Fairness refers to the satisfaction of claims in order of priority, as discussed in the previous section. Feasibility refers to the probability that the postconfirmation company has a reasonable chance of survival. The plan must provide for certain essential features, such as adequate working capital and a reasonable capital structure that does not contain too much debt. Projected revenues must be sufficient to adequately cover the fixed charges associated with the postconfirmation liabilities and other operating expenses.

Partial Satisfaction of Prepetition Claims

The plan will provide a new capital structure that, it is hoped, will be one that the company can adequately service. This will typically feature payment of less than the full amount that was due the claimholders. For example, in the classic bankruptcy of

---

[14] Rosemary E. Williams and Daniel P. Jakala, *Bankruptcy Practice Handbook* (Deerfield, IL: Callaghan & Company, 1990), 11–54.

the Penn Central Railroad, the bankruptcy process lasted eight years and produced a confirmed plan that gave holders of secured bonds 10% of their claims in cash. The cash was generated by the sale of assets. The remaining 90% was satisfied by 30% each in new mortgage bonds, preferred stock, and common stock. This provided Penn Central with a lower amount of financial leverage because the secured bond debt was 10% discharged by the cash payment, and 60% was converted to preferred and common equity.

BENEFITS OF THE CHAPTER 11 PROCESS FOR THE DEBTOR

The U.S. Bankruptcy Code provides great benefits to debtors, some of which are listed in Table 12.6. The debtor is left in charge of the business and allowed to operate relatively free of close control. This has led some to be critical of what they perceive as a process that overly favors the debtor at the expense of the creditors' interests. The law, however, seeks to rehabilitate the debtor so that it may become a viable business and a productive member of the business community.

Company Size and Chapter 11 Benefits

The fact that debtors enjoy unique benefits while operating under the protection of the bankruptcy process is clear. Smaller companies, however, may not enjoy the same benefits that the process bestows on larger counterparts. A study by Turnaround Management Associates showed that the probability of surviving the Chapter 11 process is directly related to the size of the company.[15] Figure 12.4 shows that 69% of the larger

TABLE 12.6   Benefits of Chapter 11 for Debtors

- The ability to restrain creditors from seizing the debtor's property or canceling beneficial contracts and to stay judicial actions against the debtor
- The ability to continue to operate the business effectively without interference from creditors
- The ability to borrow money by granting liens on debtor's assets equal to or superior to the liens of the existing creditors
- The ability to avoid certain transfers that occurred before the filing of the bankruptcy petition
- The cessation of interest accrual on debts that were unsecured as of the filing date
- The ability to propose and negotiate a single plan with all of the debtor's creditors
- The power to bind dissenting creditors to a reorganization plan that meets the Bankruptcy Code standard
- The receipt of a discharge by the bankruptcy court of all prepetition claims treated under the reorganization plan

Source: William A. Slaughter and Linda G. Worton, "Workout or Bankruptcy?" in Dominic DiNapoli, Sanford C. Sigoloff, and Robert F. Cushman, eds., *Workouts and Turnarounds* (Homewood, IL.: Business One Irwin, 1991), 72–96.

---

[15] *Wall Street Journal*, July 14, 1988, 29.

Chapter 11 Filings: How Firms Fared

In 1987, 17,142 companies sought protection from creditors under Chapter 11 of the Federal Bankruptcy Code. A breakdown by annual revenue of firm:

Of those firms, 6,722 are still in business under the same ownership. A breakdown of the success cases, by revenue of firm:

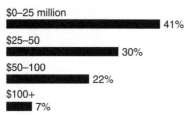
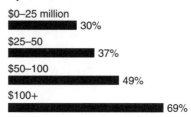

$0–25 million — 41%
$25–50 — 30%
$50–100 — 22%
$100+ — 7%

$0–25 million — 30%
$25–50 — 37%
$50–100 — 49%
$100+ — 69%

Source: Turnaround Management Association

FIGURE 12.4   How Chapter 11 Firms Fared by Company Size

companies, those with revenues in excess of $100 million, survived the process and were viable afterward, whereas only 30% of the smaller firms, those with revenues under $25 million, were able to do so.

The reason for the size differential in survival rates is that larger companies are in a better position to handle the additional unique demands placed on a Chapter 11 debtor. For example, the bankruptcy process is very demanding on management time. Before the bankruptcy, management presumably was devoting all its time to managing the business, and the business still was not successful. Now management has to devote its time to managing the business and dealing with the time demands that the bankruptcy litigation imposes. This task may be more difficult for smaller companies, where management is not as deep as in larger firms.

Although the additional expenses of the bankruptcy process may be relatively small compared with a larger company's revenue base, such expenses may be an additional burden that a smaller business cannot handle. For example, Lawrence A. Weiss reports that direct costs average 3.1% of the book value of the debt, plus the market value of the equity.[16] Professional fees may be very high—particularly in larger bankruptcies. For example, in the Johns Manville bankruptcy, professional fees were almost $200 million.[17] For a small firm with a thin capitalization, percentages may be much higher than the average reported by Weiss. For these reasons, Chapter 11 may be an excellent choice for some large companies but may not be a good idea for smaller businesses.

---

[16] Lawrence A. Weiss, "Bankruptcy Resolution: Direct Costs and Violation of Priority of Claims," *Journal of Financial Economics* 27, no. 2 (October 1990): 285–314.

[17] William A. Slaughter and Linda G. Worton, "Workout or Bankruptcy?" in Dominic DiNapoli, Sanford C. Sigoloff, and Robert F. Cushman, eds., *Workouts and Turnarounds* (Homewood, IL: Business One Irwin, 1991), 87.

Projections Done in Chapter 11

Before emerging from Chapter 11, a company is required to put forward certain financial and operational projections as part of its reorganization plan. These projections include balance sheets, income statements, and cash flow statements. Michel, Shaked, and McHugh followed 35 Chapter 11 companies from 1989 to 1995.[18] They found that these projections were frequently overstated—sometimes significantly so. For example, they found that actual sales generally lagged projected sales in the first year after emerging from Chapter 11. In some cases the overstatement was as much as 20%.

CASE STUDY: MULTIPLE CHAPTER 11 FILINGS: LEVITZ FURNITURE

The Chapter 11 bankruptcy process is one in which a company can seek to address specific flaws, such as burdensome debt levels and a flawed capital structure. Often this is sufficient to turn the company around and enable it to be a viable business. However, sometimes the company simply has a flawed business model and there are limitations to what can be accomplished through reorganization. An example is Levitz Furniture, which in November 2007 filed for Chapter 11 reorganization for the third time in a 10-year period. The company was a marketer of less expensive and lower-quality furniture. It went public in 1968 and private in an LBO in 1985, only to do a reverse LBO in 1993. Rather than use the going-public proceeds to reduce debt, it used some of them to do acquisitions.

Levitz first filed Chapter 11 in September 1997. It then merged with Seaman's Furniture, which was a comparable company and which had itself filed for bankruptcy reorganization in the early 1990s. Combining two ill companies does not necessarily create one healthy one. The expanded Levitz then emerged from Chapter 11 in 2001, which was a very weak economic period. It did not do well in the ensuing years and had to file Chapter 11 again in 2005—a much better economic period. It later emerged from Chapter 11 only to file for a third time in November 2007 as the economy started to weaken. This time the company was liquidated and its absence from the market created an expansion opportunity for competitors such as Raymour and Flanigan. Levitz's repeated visits to Chapter 11 are instructive regarding the limits of Chapter 11 reorganization. Reorganization cannot correct a flawed business model, and sometimes it is simply better to liquidate the business rather than have return visits to the bankruptcy court.

Post–Chapter 11 Performance

The Chapter 11 reorganization process is designed to transform the distressed company into one that is financially viable. How successful is the reorganization process? Edith

---

[18] Allen Michel, Isreal Shaked, and Christopher McHugh, "After Bankruptcy: Can Ugly Ducklings Turn into Swans?" *Financial Analysts Journal* 54, no. 3 (May/June 1998): 31–40.

Hotchkiss analyzed the postbankruptcy performance of a sample of 806 bankrupt companies. Of these 197 emerged from Chapter 11 as public companies, while others experienced "other outcomes," such as emerging as a private company, merging with another firm, or being liquidated.[19] The results were not all that impressive.

Hotchkiss also found 40% of the firms experienced operating losses over the three years following their Chapter 11 emergence. Roughly one-third either fell back into bankruptcy or had to privately restructure their debt. Hotchkiss's research shows that many firms left Chapter 11 even though they were really not viable companies. The bankruptcy process is designed to facilitate corporate rehabilitation, but perhaps it contains a bias that overly favors the debtor in possession. The court is supposed to approve Chapter 11 reorganization plans only if there is a reasonable basis to believe that the reorganized company can be viable. Too often, though, this is not the case.

Maksimovic and Phillips analyzed the productivity of plants owned by companies emerging from Chapter 11.[20] They found that the plants retained by companies after Chapter 11 had lower productivity as opposed to ones that were sold off. They concluded that bankrupt companies had a tendency to retain their least productive assets. However, this may be because the more productive assets were more marketable and, if there is sufficient demand in the industry, and if the industry as a whole is not depressed, then the better assets may be the more marketable ones. Companies that need to increase their liquidity may need to sell off some of their better assets. This does not bode well for the postbankruptcy performance.

Management and Postbankruptcy Performance

Hotchkiss also looked at changes in the management structure of the postbankrupt companies. Not surprisingly, she found that there was a strong relationship between poor postbankruptcy performance and retaining prebankruptcy management. Retaining the managers that helped lead the company into bankruptcy greatly increases the likelihood that the company will continue to do poorly. This is a lesson for creditors to keep in mind when evaluating reorganization plans.

While the postbankruptcy managers often lead the company on to continued poor performance, they often receive lower compensation for their managerial efforts. Gilson and Vetsuypens analyzed the compensation of managers in 77 publicly traded firms that filed for bankruptcy or privately restructured their debt over the period 1981–1987.[21] Approximately one-third of the CEOs were replaced, and those managers who retained their position often had to accept a substantial cut in their salary and bonus. When these

[19] Edith S. Hotchkiss, "Post-Bankruptcy Performance and Management Turnover," *Journal of Finance* 50, no. 1 (March 1995): 3–89.
[20] Vojislav. Maksimovic and Gordon M. Phillips, "Asset Efficiency and the Reallocation Decisions of Bankrupt Firms," *Journal of Finance*, 53 (5), 1998, 1495–1532.
[21] Stuart Gilson and Michael R. Vetsuypens, "CEO Compensation in Financially Distressed Firms: Empirical Analysis," *Journal of Finance* 48, no. 2 (June 1993): 425–458.

managers were replaced by internal hires, they were paid roughly one-third less. However, when the hire was an outside manager, they were paid approximately one-third more, although a lot of their compensation was from stock options. Recruiting for a bankrupt company is naturally a harder sell.

PREPACKAGED BANKRUPTCY

A new type of bankruptcy emerged in the late 1980s. By 1993, it accounted for one-fifth of all distressed restructurings. During the 1990s, prepackaged bankruptcies accounted for 9.2% of all bankruptcies, while in 2000 they equaled 6.8% of all bankruptcies in that year. Table 12.7 shows some of the larger prepackaged bankruptcies.

In a prepackaged bankruptcy, the firm negotiates the reorganization plan with its creditors before an actual Chapter 11 filing. Ideally, the debtor would like to have solicited and received an understanding with the creditors that the plan would be approved after the filing. In a prepackaged bankruptcy, the parties try to have the terms of the reorganization plan approved in advance. This is different from the typical Chapter 11 reorganization process, which may feature a time-consuming and expensive plan development and approval process in which the terms and conditions of the plan are agreed to only after a painstaking negotiation process.

The first major prepackaged bankruptcy was the Crystal Oil Company, an oil and natural gas exploration company located in Louisiana.[22] The total time between the bankruptcy filing in 1986 and the company's emergence was only three months. During this time the company negotiated a new capital structure in which it reduced its total indebtedness from $277 million to $129 million.[23] As is typical of such debt restructurings, the creditors received other securities, such as equity and convertible debt and warrants, in exchange for the reduction in the original debt.

Benefits of Prepackaged Bankruptcy

The completion of the bankruptcy process is usually dramatically shorter in a prepackaged bankruptcy than in the typical Chapter 11 process. Both time and financial resources are saved. This is of great benefit to the distressed debtor, who would prefer to conserve financial resources and spend as little time as possible in the suspended Chapter 11 state.[24] In addition, a prepackaged bankruptcy reduces the holdout problem associated with voluntary nonbankruptcy agreements. In such agreements, the debtor often needs to receive the approval of all the creditors. This is difficult when there are many creditors, particularly many small creditors. One of the ways a voluntary agreement is accomplished is to pay all the small creditors 100% of what they are

---

[22] John J. McConnell, "The Economics of Prepackaged Bankruptcy," *Journal of Applied Corporate Finance* 4, no. 2 (September 1991): 93–97.

[23] Ibid.

[24] Critics of the Chapter 11 debtor benefits would disagree. They would contend that some Chapter 11 companies prefer the benefits that protection of the Bankruptcy Code gives them and try to exploit these advantages over their creditors for as long as possible. Therefore, they are not in a hurry to leave the Chapter 11 protection.

TABLE 12.7 Largest Prepackaged Bankruptcy Filings

Company Name	Bankruptcy Start Date	Assets	Industry	Effective Date	Outcome Notes
CIT Group Inc.	11/01/2009	$80,448,900,000	Banking & Finance	12/10/2009	Emerged—Public (CIT)
Charter Communications, Inc.	03/27/2009	$13,882,000,000	Telecommunications	12/01/2009	Emerged—Public (CCMM)
Home Holdings, Inc.	01/15/1998	$7,593,000,000	Insurance		Reorganized
Station Casinos, Inc.	07/28/2009	$5,831,636,000	Hotel & Gaming	06/17/2011	Emerged—Private; n/k/a Station Casinos LLC
Southland Corp., (The)	10/24/1990	$3,438,760,000	Retail	03/05/1991	Reorganized
Dex One Corporation (2013)	03/17/2013	$2,835,418,000	Publishing	04/30/2013	Emerged—Public (DXM)
Houghton Mifflin Harcourt Publishing Co.	05/21/2012	$2,680,000,000	Publishing	06/22/2012	Emerged—Private
MGM Holdings Inc. (Metro-Goldwyn-Mayer Inc.)	11/03/2010	$2,673,772,000	Entertainment	12/21/2010	Emerged—Private
Masonite Corporation	03/16/2009	$2,660,052,000	Manufacturing	06/09/2009	Emerged—Public (MASWF)
Trans World Airlines, Inc. (1995)	06/30/1995	$2,495,210,000	Aviation	08/23/1995	Emerged—Public (TWA)

Source: BankruptcyData.com, a division of New Generation Research Inc.

owed and pay the main creditors, who hold the bulk of the debt, an agreed-upon lower amount.

It was noted previously that approval of a Chapter 11 reorganization plan requires creditors' approval equal to one-half in number and two-thirds in dollar amount. With the imminent threat of a Chapter 11 filing, creditors know that after the filing is made, these voting percentages, as opposed to unanimity, will apply. Therefore, if the threat of a Chapter 11 filing is real, the postbankruptcy voting threshold will become the operative one during the prepackaged negotiation process.

Prevoted versus Postvoted Prepacks

The voting approval for the prepackaged bankruptcy may take place before or after the plan is filed. In a "prevoted prepack" the results of the voting process are filed with the bankruptcy petition and reorganization plan. In a "postvoted prepack" the voting process is overseen by the bankruptcy court after the Chapter 11 filing. In a study of 49 prepackaged bankruptcies, Tashjian, Lease, and McConnell found that prevoted prepacks spend less time in bankruptcy court but devote more time to prefiling negotiations.[25] Prevoted prepacks also had lower direct costs as a fraction of assets and had higher recovery rates for nonequity obligations.

Tax Advantages of Prepackaged Bankruptcy

A prepackaged bankruptcy may also provide tax benefits because net operating losses are treated differently in a workout than in a bankruptcy. For example, if a company enters into a voluntary negotiated agreement with debtholders whereby debtholders exchange their debt for equity and the original equityholders now own less than 50% of the company, the company may lose its right to claim net operating losses in its tax filings. The forfeiture of these tax-loss carryforwards may have adverse future cash flow consequences. In bankruptcy, however, if the court rules that the firm was insolvent, as defined by a negative net asset value, the right to claim loss carryforwards may be preserved. Betker estimates that the present value of future taxes saved by restructuring through a prepackaged bankruptcy, as opposed to a workout, is equal to 3% of total assets.[26]

If a debtor company reaches a voluntary agreement whereby creditors agree to cancel a certain percentage of the debt—say, one-third—this amount is treated as income for tax purposes, thus creating a tax liability. A similar debt restructuring in bankruptcy, however, does not create such a tax liability.[27]

---

[25] Elizabeth Tashjian, Ronald Lease, and John J. McConnell, "Prepacks: An Empirical Analysis of Prepackaged Bankruptcies," *Journal of Financial Economics* 40, no. 10 (January 1996): 135–162.

[26] Brian Betker, "An Empirical Examination of Prepackaged Bankruptcy," *Financial Management* 24, no. 1 (Spring 1995): 3–18.

[27] John J. McConnell, "The Economics of Prepackaged Bankruptcy," *Journal of Applied Corporate Finance* 4, no. 2 (September 1991): 93–97.

CIT GROUP INC.'S PREPACKAGED BANKRUPTCY

The November 1, 2009, bankruptcy of financing company CIT was one of the biggest corporate bankruptcies and was the largest prepackaged bankruptcy. It also served as a model for how quickly the prepackaged bankruptcy process can work. Most financial firms do not survive the bankruptcy process and are either merged into other companies or are liquidated. This was not the case with CIT. After receiving overwhelming support from its bondholders, CIT emerged from bankruptcy just 40 days after filing. The postbankruptcy company came out with a new capital structure that lowered its burdensome debt by $10.5 billion. These bondholders agreed to exchange their debt for other debt with a later maturity and almost all of the stock in the reorganized company.

CIT, a company founded in 1908, provides financing, such as factoring, for a variety of small and medium-sized businesses. When the subprime crisis took hold, the company found its access to credit markets was cut off. It was given $2.3 billion in financial support from the government, but that was not enough to stave off bankruptcy. The government (and taxpayers in particular) did not fare well in the bankruptcy process since it was given preferred stock, which was wiped out in the reorganization plan. The company also became a bank holding company, which is a step other financial institutions took to be able to get access to some of the sources of liquidity that large banks have access to.

Like many other companies that have found themselves in bankruptcy, CIT's woes can be largely attributed to a failed acquisition/expansion strategy. CEO Jeffrey Peek led the company to pursue a diversification strategy into subprime mortgages and student loan lending. He sought to move CIT into higher-return businesses and followed the crowd into mortgages and student loans. For example, he acquired Education Lending Group, a student loan consolidation company, for a 24% premium. Profits were more than $1 billion in 2006—well above their 2003 levels—when Peek joined the company. When the subprime market collapse took hold in 2007, however, CIT posted a $111 million loss. This is yet another example of a new CEO who was not content to manage the core business he had taken over, commercial lending, and sought to diversify and move the firm into higher return–higher risk areas. The diversification strategy was also flawed in light of the fact that the company continued to rely on short-term financing from the commercial paper market but increasingly moved into longer-term lending. Once the commercial paper market collapsed, one of CIT's main sources of capital dried up. The firm left its core competency and shareholders paid the price for this strategic failure.

Ironically, in February 2010 the postbankruptcy CIT chose John Thain as its CEO. This was interesting in light of Thain's role as CEO of Merrill Lynch during Bank of America's troublesome acquisition of Merrill. In the years that followed, CIT was back to using M&A to expand. In 2014 it acquired the closely held Southern California bank One West for $3.4 billion.

WORKOUTS

When a debtor is experiencing financial difficulties, the creditors and the debtor have to decide if they can work out a private solution to their problems or seek a court-supervised outcome. One of the impediments to a private solution is *information asymmetry*. Creditors usually know much less about the debtor's true financial condition and ability to pay and restructure itself than the debtor. When these asymmetries are quite substantial in the eyes of the creditors, they may prefer the formal court process.[28] A *workout* refers to a negotiated agreement between the debtors and their creditors outside the bankruptcy process. The debtor may try to extend the payment terms, which is called *extension*, or convince creditors to agree to accept a lesser amount than they are owed, which is called *composition*. A workout differs from a prepackaged bankruptcy in that in a workout the debtor either has already violated the terms of the debt agreements or is about to. In a workout, the debtor tries to convince creditors that they would be financially better off with the new terms of a workout agreement than with the terms of a formal bankruptcy.

Benefits of Workouts

The main benefits of workouts are cost savings and flexibility.[29] Workout agreements generally cost less for both the debtor and the creditors in terms of the resources the participants need to devote to the agreement process. In addition, participants in a workout are not burdened by the rules and regulations of Chapter 11 of the Bankruptcy Code. They are free to create their own rules as long as the parties agree to them. They also avoid the public scrutiny, such as from opening accounting records to the public, that occurs in a bankruptcy filing. Workouts may also help the debtor avoid any business disruption and loss of employees and overall morale that might occur in a bankruptcy. With these benefits come certain risks. The key risk is the holdout problem discussed previously. If this problem cannot be circumvented, a bankruptcy filing may be the only viable alternative.

Recognizing Better Workout Candidates

Depending on the particular financial circumstances of the company and the personal makeup of the parties involved, a negotiated private settlement outside the bankruptcy process may or may not be possible. Gilson, John, and Lang analyzed 169 debt restructurings from 1978 to 1987 and found that a little over one-half of them were able to successfully restructure their debt.[30] The roughly 50–50 split between those that could restructure their debt and those that had to file for bankruptcy was also found by Franks

---

[28] Robert M. Mooradian, "The Effect of Bankruptcy Protection on Investment: Chapter 11 as a Screening Device," *Journal of Finance* 49, no. 4 (September 1994): 1403–1430.

[29] William A. Slaughter and Linda G. Worton, "Workout or Bankruptcy?" in Dominic DiNapoli, Sanford C. Sigoloff, and Robert F. Cushman, eds., *Workouts and Turnarounds* (Homewood, IL.: Business One Irwin, 1991), 72–96.

[30] Stuart C. Gilson, Kose John, and Larry H. P. Lang, "Troubled Debt Restructurings: An Empirical Study of Private Reorganization of Firms in Default," *Journal of Financial Economics* 27, no. 2 (October 1990): 315–354.

and Tourous, who studied 161 companies that experienced debt downgrades to CCC or below (S&P ratings).[31]

Gilson, John, and Lang found that the financially distressed firms that had a higher percentage of their assets as intangible and that owed less of their debt to banks were more likely to be able to restructure their liabilities. This is not surprising as banks tend to be less willing to accept reductions in principal payments, although they may be willing to waive covenants.[32] They also found that distressed firms that had more public debt outstanding found the road to restructuring more challenging and less fruitful.

Gertner and Scharfstein discuss the various conflicts that can arise when there are multiple creditors.[33] This can be the case, for example, when there are a very large number of bondholders. Getting such a large group of public investors to agree on a specific workout strategy may not be practical. This problem is compounded by the fact that the Trustee Indenture Act of 1939, another of the various post–Great Depression securities laws that were passed, requires that for changes in interest rates or principal amounts, there must be unanimous approval of the security holders. If one or more groups of bondholders agree to accept a lower rate or principal payment, holdouts may be able to require that they receive the full original interest and principal payments. This may then mean that the large group voluntarily agrees to accept less, while a small number of holdouts get full payment. Chapter 11, with its ability to bind creditors to an agreement upon attaining majority vote, was designed to be able to deal with the holdout problem.

Hotchkiss, John, Mooradian, and Thorburn have opined on the reasons for a decline in the percentage of distressed firms that are able to successfully utilize out-of-court restructurings.[34] One of the reasons they cited was court decisions that made debt restructurings outside of bankruptcy more difficult. In addition, they point to the rise of prepackaged bankruptcy as an alternative that many distressed firms find more appealing.

There is evidence that the market prefers workouts over a bankruptcy filing. Chatterjee, Dhillon, and Ramírez found that the stock returns of companies that announced workouts were less negative than those of companies that went the Chapter 11 route.[35] To understand this, however, one needs to consider that creditors, including bondholders, and stockholders may, at times, have very different interests. Stockholders may be quite eager to see a debt restructuring as that may lower their interest payments and/or the total debt of the company. However, the world of Chapter 11 may not be that kind to equityholders. Thus stockholders may be quite happy when creditors agree to steps that

---

[31] Julian Franks and Walter Torous, "A Comparison of Financial Recontracting in Distressed Exchanges and Chapter 11 Reorganizations," *Journal of Financial Economics*, 35 (3), June 1994, 349–370.

[32] Paul Asquith, Robert H. Gertner, and David Scharfstein, "Anatomy of Financial Distress: An Examination of Junk-Bond Issuers," *Quarterly Journal of Economics* 109, no. 3 (1994): 625–658.

[33] Robert H. Gertner and David Scharfstein, "A Theory of Workouts and the Effects of Reorganization Law," *Journal of Finance* 46, no. 4 (September 1991): 1189–1222.

[34] Edith Hotchkiss, Kose John, Robert Mooradian, and Karin S. Thorburn, "Bankruptcy and the Resolution of Financial Distress," in B. E. Eckbo, ed., *Handbook of Corporate Finance: Empirical Corporate Finance*, vol. 2. (Amsterdam: Elsevier/North-Holland, 2008), 235–289.

[35] Sris Chatterjee, Upinder S. Dhillon, and Gabriel G. Ramírez, "Resolution of Financial Distress: Debt Restructurings via Chapter 11, Prepackaged Bankruptcies, and Workouts," *Financial Management* 25, no. 1 (Spring 1996): 5–18.

may keep the company out of Chapter 11—especially when creditors "pick up the tab" for this benefit they bestow on equityholders.

Evidence on the Role of Transactions Costs in Voluntary Restructuring versus Chapter 11 Decision

Gilson analyzed 108 publicly traded companies between 1980 and 1989 that either restructured their debt out of court (57 companies) or reorganized under Chapter 11 (51 companies).[36] He found that the firms that attempt voluntary restructuring outside Chapter 11 were less able to reduce their leverage compared with Chapter 11 firms. He traced the problem to higher transactions costs of voluntary restructuring. Examples of these costs include the credit holdout problem, which makes it difficult to get all creditors to participate in the agreement. This problem is greater for holders of smaller claims, who have an incentive to hold up transactions until they receive preferential treatment. Although a small number of such creditors may not be as much of a problem, the situation becomes very difficult if there are numerous creditors with similar motivations. Other difficulties of voluntary restructuring include the fact that creditors may be less willing to exchange their debt for equity when managers of the company have a significant informational advantage over them. This disadvantage renders creditors less able to assess the value of the equity they would receive in exchange for their debt claims. One additional factor is that institutional holders of debt may simply prefer debt to equity and may not want to voluntarily become an equity holder. These issues become moot when the process moves into Chapter 11 and the position of the debtor improves.

Acquisitions of Companies in Bankruptcy

Bidders sometimes can find attractive acquisition opportunities in companies that are in Chapter 11. The question arises, under what circumstances does an outright sale of the debtor in possession in Chapter 11 create more value than the emergence of the firm from Chapter 11 as a restructured company? There is compelling evidence that companies that are sold in bankruptcy sell at a significant discount compared to comparable companies not in Chapter 11. For example, Hotchkiss and Mooradian analyzed a sample of 55 transactions, of which 18 had multiple bidders, and found that bankruptcy targets sold at a 45% discount compared to comparable, nonbankrupt company sales.[37] Clearly, for the buyers the acquisitions allowed them to acquire businesses at very good prices. However, in their pursuit of an answer to whether sales in Chapter 11 create economic value, they went on to follow the postacquisition performance of the acquired bankrupt firms. They found that the postacquisition performance of the acquired firms was better than the firms that emerged from Chapter 11. They traced these gains to costs and headcount reductions. These postacquisition findings were also associated with positive and significant abnormal returns for the bidder around the time of the acquisition

---

[36] Stuart Gilson, "Transactions Costs and Capital Structure Choice: Evidence from Financially Distressed Firms," *Journal of Finance* 52, no. 1 (March 1997): 161–196.

[37] Edith S. Hotchkiss and Robert M. Mooradian, "Acquisitions as a Means of Restructuring Firms in Chapter 11," *Journal of Financial Intermediation* 7, no. 3 (July 1998): 240–262.

announcement.[38] Hotchkiss and Mooradian conclude that acquisitions of companies in Chapter 11 tend to result in an economically efficient allocation of assets.

In light of the interesting findings it is useful to probe further into the characteristics of the Hotchkiss and Mooradian sample of bankrupt company sales. They found that the size of the target was on average 25.8% of the size of the buyer as measured total assets and 30.2% in terms of sales. This is consistent with research on acquisitions in general.[39] In addition, like Clark and Ofek, Hotchkiss and Mooradian found that acquirers of bankrupt firms were often in the same industry. This makes sense as an acquisition of bankrupt companies seems risky but among competitors who know the industry and the target, you would expect buyers to know what they are getting.

Reorganization versus Going Concern Sales

Companies involved in a bankruptcy have to determine whether a sale of the entire company or an exit from bankruptcy as a reorganized business will yield the greatest return. LoPucki and Doherty conducted an empirical study in which they compared returns from going concern sales and reorganizations over the period of 2000–2004.[40] They found that returns were significantly greater with reorganizations. Going concern "fire sales" generated reduced values due to a variety of reasons, including illiquidity of the market. The values that are realized in going concern sales are affected by the state of the M&A market, with stronger markets bringing higher values. However, bankrupt companies are at a significant disadvantage when trying to receive high values for their companies. Reorganized companies get to try to realize values over an extended period of time, as opposed to sales that occur so close to the recent failure of the company.

Asset Sales during Chapter 11

A company in Chapter 11 can sell assets, and even substantially all of its assets, via one of two paths. One is through Section 363 of the U.S. Bankruptcy Code, and the other is as part of the reorganization plan. In order to do a Section 363 sale, the company must first receive an offer and then take the bid to the court for its approval. While bankruptcy courts do not enforce Revlon-like duties for these sales, they want to see some efforts by the seller to get the best prices for the assets, such as through some marketing, not an auction, process. A hearing is held, and the judge must formally approve the sale.

Hotchkiss and Mooradian found that about a third of the companies in their sample had multiple bidders. They also found a comparable presence of multiple bidders for sales through reorganization. Research on discounts from nondistressed values for companies in Chapter 11 yield similar findings as the research we discussed for asset sales by distressed companies that had not filed Chapter 11.

---

[38] Once again, the ability of the market to often correctly anticipate a longer-term financial outcome continues to be a theme in M&A research.

[39] See, for example, Kent Clark and Eli Ofek, "Mergers as a Means of Restructurings Distressed Firms: An Empirical Investigation," *Journal of Financial and Quantitative Analysis* 29, no. 4 (December 1994): 541–565.

[40] Lynn M. LoPucki and Joseph W. Doherty, "Bankruptcy Fire Sales," *Michigan Law Review* 106, no. 1 (2007): 1–60.

In addition to the sale of the entire bankrupt company, such companies can try to ease their cash flow pressures and reduce their debt burden through asset sales. Shleifer and Vishny examined the factors that affected liquidation costs for firms in financial distress.[41] They found that sale prices of assets were lower when the entire industry was in distress. When this is the case, other firms in the industry may not be in a position to bid for the bankrupt firm's assets, thus lowering the overall demand for them. If the assets are more fungible, however, such as being useful to others outside the industry, this may offset lower intra-industry demand.

SUNBEAM: BANKRUPTCY FOLLOWING A FAILED ACQUISITION PROGRAM

Companies that pursue acquisitions that fail, especially those that incur significant debt to finance the deals, run the risk of going bankrupt. This is one of the extreme penalties that the market imposes for a poor acquisition strategy. Such a fate befell Sunbeam Corp. when it had to file for Chapter 11 bankruptcy protection in the Southern District of New York in February 2001. The company, which marketed Sunbeam appliances, First Alert smoke alarms, and Coleman camping gear, showed negative net worth on its bankruptcy petition, listing assets of $2.96 billion and liabilities of $3.2 billion. The company could not handle the burden of $2.5 billion in debt that it had accumulated, partially from unsuccessful acquisitions.

One of the main sources of financial pressure was a $1.7 billion bank loan that the company had entered into in 1998 to finance three acquisitions. In these deals Sunbeam acquired the Coleman Company, maker of sleeping bags and other camping equipment; Signature Brands, owner of the Mr. Coffee brand; and the First Alert company. The disparate nature of these acquisitions should have presented red flags to investors. The loan was provided by Morgan Stanley Dean Witter, First Union Corp., and the Bank of America. It was then discovered that Sunbeam, led by turnaround artist Albert Dunlop, known as "Chainsaw Al," fresh from his turnaround of the Scott Paper Company, inflated sales by overselling retailers goods they did not want so as to increase short-term revenues.

Sunbeam emerged from Chapter 11 in 2002 as a closely held business under the name American Household Inc. The company's reorganization plan provided for its debt to be converted into equity. American Household was itself acquired in 2005 by the Rye, New York–based Jarden Corporation for $745.6 million in cash plus the assumption of $100 million in debt.[a]

[a] Terry Brennan, "Sunbeam Files for Chapter 11," *Daily Deal*, February 7, 2001, 2.

Companies that have been in bankruptcy have a different risk profile, and many potential acquirers may want to avoid them. We have seen that takeover prices are often maximized when there is an auction process. This is why such bankruptcy sales may

---

[41] Andrei Shleifer and Robert W. Vishny, "Liquidation Values and Debt Capacity," *Journal of Finance* 47, no. 4 (September 1992): 1343–1366.

feature *stalking horse bidders*. These are bidders who come forward and make the first bid. In doing so, they establish a floor value and get the bidding process going. Often such stalking horse bidders receive protections in the form of compensation if they are outbid.

LAMPERT ACQUIRES BANKRUPT KMART AND THEN ACQUIRES SEARS

The acquisition of Kmart by Eddie Lampert and his hedge fund, ESL Investments, is a classic example of how acquisition opportunities can arise in the bankruptcy process. Kmart was the third-largest retailer in the United States, after Walmart and Target. It had over 1,500 stores and 16 distribution centers. Lampert was able to acquire the large but troubled retailer for less than $1 billion. Lampert used the bankruptcy process to become the largest shareholder in the company. He did this by purchasing the company's busted bonds and bank debt and then using the leverage of this position as a creditor to become a controlling equityholder in the company. As Kmart's troubles became widely discussed in the media, Lampert was able to purchase this debt at attractive prices. The company emerged from bankruptcy in May 2003 with Lampert in charge.

Kmart traces its roots back to the S. S. Kresge variety store chain, which was founded in 1899. The first Kmart store was opened in 1962 as a unit of Kresge. At the end of the 1970s, Kmart dwarfed Walmart. However, since then Walmart used aggressive pricing and wise inventory management to steadily attack Kmart's market shares all across the United States. The battle culminated with Kmart's strategic blunder of getting into a price war with Walmart, using what Kmart called a "Blue Light Always" promotion. Walmart is a very lean retailer and enjoys significant cost advantages over Kmart. This was a battle that Kmart, with its cost structure, could not win. In January 2002, Kmart had no choice but to file for Chapter 11.

Lampert was able to transform Kmart's troubles into an acquisition opportunity for him. Prior to Kmart, Lampert had become an approximately 27% shareholder in AutoZone. He used this position to pressure management into making changes that would enhance the value of his and other shareholders' investment. He leveraged his large stock holdings in the company to get a seat on the board and replace the CEO with one more to his own liking (a former executive at Goldman Sachs, a firm at which Lampert once worked).

Eddie Lampert showed the influence that a dominant creditor can have on the effectiveness and speed of the reorganization process. When he saw that the resources of the company were being drained by inefficient activities, such as paying bankruptcy professionals (reportedly between $10 million and $12 million per month) who may not have an interest in seeing the payment stream end soon, he stepped in and confronted management. Lampert forced the company to exit Chapter 11—a state in which it was becoming too comfortable. He was not as interested in management's reorganization plan since he had his own strategy for the company's future. Once again, we see the role that large blockholders can play in pushing companies in the right direction.

In March 2005 Lampert completed a $12 billion merger of Kmart and retail giant Sears. Sears was a storied retailer that was founded in 1893 by Richard Sears (see "Sears—A Failed Diversification Strategy," Chapter 4). At the time of the deal, Home

Depot had risen to become the second-largest retailer behind Walmart. Both Kmart and Sears experienced declining revenues and profitability while losing market share to competitors such as Walmart. Kmart could not handle this competitive market and fell into bankruptcy. Sears, while certainly not bankrupt, had seen its affinity for malls lead to a steady decline in sales as U.S. consumers increasingly made purchases outside of these suburban malls. Lampert had amassed a significant stock position in Sears and used this holding as leverage to merge the two companies in the hopes of creating one sound business. Unfortunately for Lampert, these hopes did not materialize into reality.

By 2014 Sears Holdings, the combined Sears and Kmart entity, had gone through four CEOs after the merger, and none of them were able to halt the steady decline of the merged retailer. Lampert's track record was one of aggressively cutting costs and using the lower cost structure to generate returns. This did not work out well at Sears Holdings. In addition, competitors, such as Target, used Lampert's track record to invest more aggressively in capital expenditures so as to improve their appearance, knowing that such investment was what many of the aging Sears stores needed but Lambert would not do (see Figure A). This caused the differences in appearance between the Sears Holdings stores and its competitors to be even more dramatic.

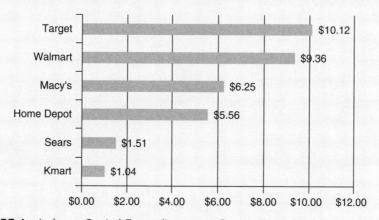

FIGURE A Industry Capital Expenditures per Square Foot, 2012

Sears Holdings has deteriorated steadily since the buyout. Revenues peaked in 2006 and have fallen precipitously. The company closed stores, but profits fell steadily and have been negative since 2011 (see Figure B). The company's liquidity has steadily deteriorated, and the outlook is not promising in spite of the ownership of quality brands, such as Kenmore, Craftsman, and Land's End. It is clear that simplistic cost cutting is a poor business strategy and not one that will best such successful retailers as Walmart.

(*continued*)

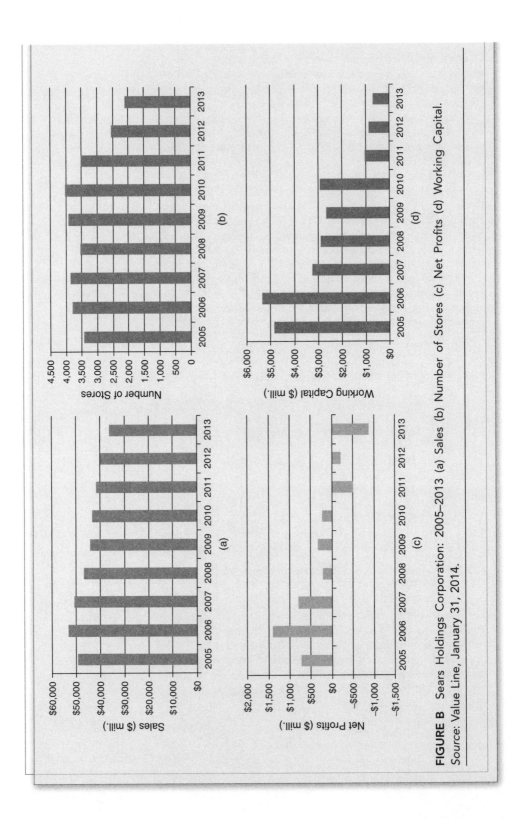

FIGURE B Sears Holdings Corporation: 2005–2013 (a) Sales (b) Number of Stores (c) Net Profits (d) Working Capital.
Source: Value Line, January 31, 2014.

CORPORATE CONTROL AND DEFAULT

When a firm defaults, it typically loses control, which is passed to its creditors. Creditors may then acquire seats on the defaulting firm's board of directors and may even require that there be a change in management. Creditors may also receive an ownership position in the debtor in exchange for other consideration, such as a reduction in the amount owed. Gilson analyzed a sample of 111 publicly held companies that experienced significant financial distress between 1979 and 1985.[42] Of this sample, 61 filed for Chapter 11 and 50 restructured their debt privately. He found that banks received an average of 36% of the distressed firm's stock. Gilson found that only 46% and 43% of the predistress directors and chief executive officers (CEOs), respectively, remained in place two years later, when they had either emerged from bankruptcy or reached a negotiated restructuring agreement. It is interesting that directors who resign from distressed boards serve less often than other directors on other boards. As might be expected, very few of the distressed firms were involved in acquisition-related activity during this period.

Leveraged Buyouts and Bankruptcy Proceedings

If a company that has undergone an LBO files for Chapter 11 protection, pre-LBO creditors may try to argue that the transaction was improper and that their potential losses are a result of a deal that allowed shareholders to gain a premium while leaving the firm with insufficient capital to meet its normal postdeal obligations. Creditors may seek to recapture the distribution that the company made to shareholders, alleging that it violated state corporation laws. Under Delaware law, for example, companies are prohibited from repurchasing their shares if their capital is, or will be, impaired as a result of the transaction. In addition to remedies under state law, the creditors may also try to argue that the transaction was a fraudulent transfer of assets and in violation of the U.S. Bankruptcy Code. The company may argue that the business was solvent after the deal and at that time had a reasonable expectation of sufficient future cash flows. As support for its position, it may produce a *solvency opinion* from a firm that analyzed the company's financial condition at the time of the deal and attested to its solvency as well as to the sufficiency of its cash flows.

 LIQUIDATION

Liquidation is a distressed firm's most drastic alternative, and it is usually pursued only when voluntary agreement and reorganization cannot be successfully implemented.

---

[42] Stuart C. Gilson, "Bankruptcy, Boards, Banks, and Blockholders: Evidence on Changes in Corporate Ownership and Control When Firms Default," *Journal of Financial Economics* 27, no. 2 (October 1990): 355–388.

In a liquidation, the company's assets are sold and the proceeds are used to satisfy claims. The sales are made pursuant to the regulations that are set forth under Chapter 7 of the Bankruptcy Code.

When a company files under Chapter 7 the court appoints a trustee to oversee the sale of the company's assets. The trustee may then hire a firm that specializes in such liquidation sales.

The priority of satisfaction of claims is made pursuant to the *absolute priority rule*, which is set forth as follows:

- Secured creditors (If the amount owed exceeds the proceeds from the sale of the asset, the remainder becomes an unsecured claim.)
- Bankruptcy administrative costs
- Postpetition bankruptcy expenses
- Wages of workers owed for three months before the filing (limit $2,000 per employee)
- Employee benefit plan contributions owed for six months before the filing (limit $2,000 per employee)
- Unsecured customer deposits (limit $900)
- Federal, state, and local taxes
- Unfunded pension liabilities (Limit is 30% book value of preferred and common equity; any remainder becomes an unsecured claim.)
- Unsecured claims
- Preferred stockholders (up to the par value of their stock)
- Common stockholders

Deviations from the Absolute Priority Rule

Chapter 11 does not explicitly require that the absolute priority rule be followed. Creditors sometimes willingly make concessions in exchange for benefits in the form of a quicker bankruptcy process, which wastes fewer of the bankrupt company's resources on the process itself. For a number of years deviations from the absolute priority rule had begun to become more common. This led some to conclude that creditors were losing control in favor of management and equityholders. However, more recent research seems to indicate that this trend may be reversing. Bharath, Panchalegesan, and Werner found significant differences in the frequency of absolute priority deviations when they compared the 1980s with the 1990s and 2000s.[43] In the 2000s the frequency of deviation was significantly lower than in prior years. They also highlighted the role of *key employee retention plans*, in which creditors agree to provide bonuses for management for them to stay and to work with them to move the bankruptcy process along.

---

[43] Sreedhar Bharath, Venky Panchalegesan, and Ingrid Werner, "The Changing Nature of Chapter 11," October 2007, working paper.

Involuntary Bankruptcy Petitions

Sometimes creditors may try to initiate an involuntary bankruptcy filing under Chapter 7. For example, a creditor may seek to have its obligations satisfied through the sale of the debtor's assets. Oftentimes, however, a debtor company is able to convince the bankruptcy court to convert the case to a Chapter 11 reorganization proceeding. In cases where the court is not convinced that the debtor will be an appropriate candidate for reorganization, the court may deny the debtor's request to seek reorganization.

 ## INVESTING IN THE SECURITIES OF DISTRESSED COMPANIES

Investing in the securities of distressed companies may offer great profit potential, but only if the buyer is willing to assume significant risks. Distressed securities are defined as the bonds or stocks of companies that have defaulted on their debt obligations or have filed for Chapter 11. The market for these securities grew significantly in the late 1980s through the 1990s. In the early 1970s, it was uncommon to find quotes for the securities of bankrupt firms.[44] This changed in the 1980s, when such quotes were common. Investment firms dedicated to the distressed securities field began to actively manage distressed securities portfolios.

Hedge funds have long focused on the distressed securities market for undervalued opportunities. We have already seen how Eddie Lampert was able to use this market as a way of conducting a major acquisition at an attractive price. The business is fraught with risks, as securities holders could easily see their investment collapse if the debtor's business deteriorates and is liquidated. Holders of distressed securities try to use the bankruptcy process to convert their discounted bonds and other debt into more valuable investments. They often are able to garner a significant equity stake in a reorganized company that hopefully will have a capital structure that they can live with.

Returns on Distressed Debt Securities

Returns on distressed debt securities have a unique profile. Hradsky and Long found that returns start to become negative approximately 18 months before default as the market internalizes information on the weak condition of the issuer.[45] These returns start to turn sharply negative five months before default and bottom out at approximately −40% around five months after default (Figure 12.5). If investors were to buy after default, returns would equal 7.5% over the two-year postdefault period.

---

[44] Dale Morse and Wayne Shaw, "Investing in Bankrupt Companies," *Journal of Finance* 43, no. 5 (December 1988): 1193–1206.

[45] Gregory Hradsky and Robert Long, "High Yield Default Losses and the Return Performance of Bankrupt Debt," *Financial Analysts Journal* 45, no. 4 (July/August 1989): 38–49.

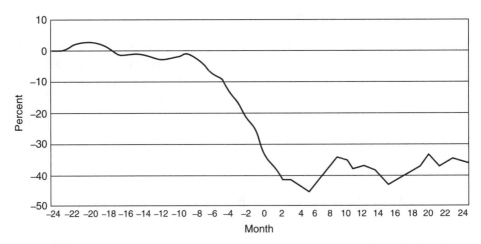

FIGURE 12.5 Distressed Securities Returns. *Source*: Gregory Hradsky and Robert Long, "High-Yield Default Losses and the Return Performance of Bankrupt Debt," *Financial Analysts Journal* 45, no. 4 (July/August 1989): 46.

Altman created an index of defaulted debt securities covering the period January 1987 through July 1990.[46] He found that while returns were highly variable, they had an average annual rate of return over this period of 10%. This exceeded the high-yield index return for the same period, which was equal to 6.7%. One must be careful drawing long-term conclusions from this short analysis period. However, there is some evidence to support the high-return but high-risk attributes of distressed debt securities.

Altman also analyzed the correlation of the returns on debt securities with those on other major categories of investments. Portfolio theory shows that if there is a low correlation between returns on distressed securities and other potential investment portfolio components, these securities may provide diversification benefits. He found a lower-than-expected correlation, 0.56, between the returns on distressed debt securities and high-yield bonds.

Control Opportunities Using Distressed Debt Securities

One of the typical changes that a reorganized company undergoes in the Chapter 11 process is to have its capital structure altered, with some debt being replaced by equity and some, possibly all, prepetition equity disappearing. Debtholders may become equityholders. When these debt securities become a path to equity, they are sometimes referred to as *fulcrum securities*. Buyers of distressed debt securities may actually be seeking to obtain an equity stake in the distressed company when they purchase the debt securities. This has helped fuel the market for *claims trading*. Investors in Chapter 11 companies may buy the claims themselves or purchase components of the bankrupt company as the firm seeks to finance its turnaround or *fund its reorganization plan*.

---

[46] Edward I. Altman, "Investing in Distressed Securities," in Dominic DiNapoli, Sanford C. Sigoloff, and Robert F. Cushman, eds., *Workouts and Turnarounds* (Homewood, IL: Business Irwin One, 1991), 663–685.

The more aggressive of these opportunistic investors are sometimes referred to as *bankruptcy sharks* or *vultures*. They purchase the debt of bankrupt companies with a goal of taking control of the company. The strategy may yield high returns to those who are able to aggressively participate in the reorganization negotiation process to acquire the desired control. Although the securities may be purchased relatively inexpensively, the outcome of the negotiation process, which may be quite lengthy, is very uncertain. For this reason, this type of takeover strategy is particularly risky.

Claims trading provides potential benefits not just for the vultures but also for creditors who find themselves with a higher risk investment than what their risk profile would prefer. For them this can be a good exit strategy as they transfer the risk and potential return to those investors who are better suited to deal with it.

Hotchkiss and Mooradian analyzed a sample of 288 firms that defaulted on public debt.[47] Of these, they narrowed their focus to 172 firms that were the targets of vulture investors. They found that the vulture investors were very active in the distressed companies. Approximately a quarter of the time they joined the board of directors, and a little less than 10% of the time they became chairman or CEO. In 16% of the cases they acquired control through the purchase of claims including bank debt. They found post-bankruptcy performance improvements after the vulture investors joined the boards or became CEO or chairman.

CAMPEAU BANKRUPTCY

In January 1988, Campeau Corporation launched a takeover of Federated Stores. The company had a market value of $4.25 billion, with $2.93 billion being equity and $1.33 billion being debt. The purchase price was double the market value of the company ($8.17 billion). The deal was a highly leveraged transaction, with 97% of the total value financed by debt.

In the beginning of 1990, after two years of troubled operations in which the company failed to refinance its takeover debt and bridge loans through the issuance of junk bonds, Campeau filed for Chapter 11 reorganization. Campeau's management of Federated Stores was poor. Under Campeau's reign the company suffered through a difficult Christmas season in 1990, and was also affected by the overall downturn in the economy as the country moved into a recession. In the period between the acquisition and the bankruptcy filing, EBITDA declined. The board of directors took away all operating responsibility from Robert Campeau. The company had excess inventories and had to lower prices in an effort to sell off these inventories while paying down the debt.

During bankruptcy, a management team composed of new CEO Allen Questrom, President James Zimmerman, and CFO Ronald Tysoe increased operating efficiency and raised capital through asset sales while managing to keep most of the management team of this large department store chain intact. They sold

(continued)

[47] Edith Hotchkiss and Robert Mooradian, "Vulture Investors and the Market for Distressed Firms," *Journal of Financial Economics* 43 (1997): 401–432.

(continued)

TABLE A Market-Adjusted and Nominal Values[a] of Federated Department Stores (A) Post-Campeau, Post-Chapter 11, (B) Pre-Campeau, and (C) Purchase Price Paid by Campeau Corporation

	Market-adjusted December 1987	Market-adjusted February 1992	Nominal
(A) Post Campeau, post-Chapter 11 Federated market value			
Asset sales[b]	3.77	7.31	4.04
Interim cash flows	0.79	1.52	1.29
Less direct costs of bankruptcy[c]	(0.14)	(0.27)	(0.27)
Value remaining assets	1.41	2.75	2.75
Total	5.85	11.31	7.81
(B) Pre-Campeau Federated market value[d]	4.25	8.25	4.25
(C) Price paid by Campeau for Federated[e]	7.67	14.89	8.17

Note: Post-Campeau, post-Chapter 11 value of Federated equals the sum of asset sales, interim cash flows, and the value of remaining Federated assets. All sales are in billions of dollars.
[a]Market-adjusted values in December 1987 equal the actual values discounted from the month in which they occur to December 31, 1987, by the actual return on the S&P 500. If invested in the S&P 500 on January 1, 1988, the market-adjusted value would equal the actual value in the month the cash flow occurs. The market-adjusted values in February 1992 equal the actual values adjusted from the month in which they occur to February 1992, by the actual return on the S&P 500 over that period.
[b]Asset sales are the value of the divisions sold by Federated from May 1988 to February 1989. These values are detailed in Kaplan (1989).
[c]Interim cash flow equals EBITDA, less capital expenditures, less the increase in net working capital, plus the proceeds from asset sales, less tax paid.
[d]Pre-Campeau Federated market value on December 31, 1987, equals the sum of the market value of Federated debt.
[e]Purchase price paid by Campeau is the sum of the market value paid for all equity and the fees paid in May 1988 and the book value of Federated debt outstanding on January 30, 1988.

off or closed unprofitable stores, streamlined operations, and remodeled stores that needed improvement. Kaplan concludes that the Chapter 11 process worked remarkably well.[a] The process was not costly in terms of a deterioration of value. He compared the value of the postbankrupt company with the preacquisition value. He measured the postbankruptcy value of Federated, net of bankruptcy costs and inclusive of interim cash flows earned during bankruptcy. As Table A shows, the value of the company increased with the acquisition, from a preacquisition market value of $4.25 billion to the $8.17 billion value Campeau paid. Using the preceding definition of value, Kaplan computed a $7.81 billion value before an adjustment for market fluctuations. After taking into account market fluctuations, he arrived at a substantially higher value ($11.31 billion).

Kaplan's analysis shows that a leveraged acquisition may increase value even if the company proves not to have sufficient cash flows to service its debt. Campeau's inability to service its debt led to its Chapter 11 filing. However, the Chapter 11 process did not result in a deterioration in value of the bankrupt company. Kaplan does not imply that this is the rule. Rather, he uses the Campeau Chapter 11 reorganization to illustrate that if the process is handled correctly, Chapter 11 does not necessarily result in a loss of company value.

[a] Steven N. Kaplan, "Campeau's Acquisition of Federated Stores," *Journal of Financial Economics* 35, no. 1 (February 1994): 123–136.

Role of Vulture Investors and the Market for Control of Distressed Firms

Hotchkiss and Mooradian analyzed the role of vulture investors in the governance of 288 firms that defaulted on their debt between 1980 and 1993.[48] Contrary to the reputation that such investors have, Hotchkiss and Mooradian's research found that they had a positive effect on the postdebt operating performance. They found that postrestructuring operating performance is improved relative to the predefault level when the vulture investor becomes CEO or in some way gains control of the company. They attribute this improved performance to enhanced managerial discipline. It is interesting that they also found that a greater percentage of vulture firms were reorganized under Chapter 11 (70.3% for vulture firms versus 39% for nonvulture firms), indicating that these investors seek the benefits of the Chapter 11 process more than management.

---

[48] Edith S. Hotchkiss and Robert M. Mooradian, "Vulture Investors and the Market for Control of Distressed Firms," *Journal of Financial Economics* 43, no. 3 (March 1997): 401–432.

CHAPTER THIRTEEN

13

Corporate Governance

 STRUCTURE OF CORPORATIONS AND THEIR GOVERNANCE

Corporations are one of three general forms of business organizations: sole proprietorships, partnerships, and corporations. Corporations trace their roots back many centuries as a business form that was designed to encourage the investment of capital into potentially risky ventures, such as oceangoing trade, that were subject to major risks (e.g., bad weather or theft from pirates). Some of the earliest corporate charters were the Muscovy Company in 1555, the Spanish Company in 1577, and the Dutch East India Company in 1601.[1]

Corporations provide an incentive for shareholders to invest by limiting their exposure to their investment in the entity. Normally the personal assets are shielded from exposure to litigation. This is different from sole proprietorships and partnerships, where the owners' personal assets are at risk. However, in recent years alternatives to simple partnerships have been formed that limit the exposure and liability of partners. The most common form of business is the corporate form, and this percentage accounts for the vast majority of the dollar value of businesses.

While limited liability is a benefit, shareholders in corporations face the problem that they have to select others to represent their interests. This is usually done by an election of a board of directors by shareholders. These directors in turn select managers who run the company on a day-to-day basis (see Figure 13.1).

---

[1] Jack Beatty, "Of Huge and Greatness," in Jack Beatty, ed., *Colossus* (New York: Broadway Books, 2001), 6.

477

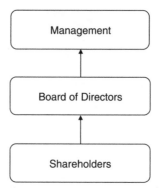

FIGURE 13.1 Flowchart: Management, Directors, and Shareholders

Corporate Democracy

Corporate democracy is different from the democratic process that one learns about in political science. Elections for directors are not commonly contested. Most of the time shareholders, while the true owners of the company, have only two choices when they receive their ballots for election of directors: vote to approve the slate or throw away their ballots and withhold their vote. Occasionally the withholding of votes has been used to voice displeasure with the board and management. This was the case in March 2004 when a large percentage of Disney's shareholders withheld their support of Michael Eisner, CEO of Disney. This led to the eventual departure of the highly paid Eisner.

In recent years there has been a movement away from plurality voting system to majority voting. Under such a system directors could get elected even if they won few votes as long as they got more than anyone else. However, shareholder activists, such as the proxy advisory firm Institutional Shareholder Services (ISS), have pressured corporations to make sure directors are supported by a majority of shareholders. Directors who are not—that is, they fail to have a majority of their shareholders vote for them—now oftentimes find themselves under pressure to step down.

Under the corporate law of most states, boards are given great latitude to run the company as they see fit. Sometimes boards totally ignore majority shareholder votes. For example, companies such as the REIT Vornado Realty Trust have ignored majority votes by shareholders that requested that board members be reelected each year by a majority of the shareholders. Vornado has been able to get away with plurality voting, although such governance practices are becoming an endangered species.

Shareholder Voting Approval by Bidders

Throughout this book we have discussed the problem of bidders doing questionable M&As which do not benefit their shareholders. In the U.S. this problem is compounded by the fact that shareholder voting rights are limited to the election of directors and approving certain corporate by law changes. Stock exchange rules, such as those of the New York Stock Exchange, do provide for securing shareholder approval of acquisitions which require the issuance of 20% or more of the bidder's shares. However, if a U.S. bidder's management and board wants to avoid shareholder approval, they can do so by making sure they use all cash or at least less than 20% of its shares.

Hsieh and Wang analyzed a sample of 2,205 bids from 1995 through 2005.[2] They found that deals done with without shareholder approval had lower synergistic gains and underperformed in the long run. These results imply that a shareholder approval requirement could result in better deals for bidder shareholders.

Becht, Polo, and Rossi looked to international comparisons to shed further light of the value of shareholder approval in M&As.[3] In the United Kingdom, listing rules require that for deals where the target is significant in size (25%) compared to the bidder, called Class I transactions, bidder shareholder approval must be secured. In an analysis of a large sample of UK transactions over the period 1992–2010, they found that Class I transactions almost never fail to secure approval. This is because Class I deals which seem to be attracting bidder shareholder opposition typically get withdrawn before an actual shareholder vote. They further found that Class I transaction showed 8% announcement period returns compared to Class II deals, which do not require approval and which showed announcement period losses. Once again, this research supports the notion that shareholder approval of significant deals, regardless of whether they are paid for by stock or cash, benefit bidder shareholders.

Corporate Governance and Equity Prices

It is intuitive to believe that companies that exhibit better corporate governance realize a gain in their market value compared to companies that lack such a system. However, over the years some companies have instituted various restrictions on shareholder rights partly in response to the increases in hostile takeovers and proxy fights that occurred starting in the fourth merger wave of the 1980s. Gompers, Ishii, and Metrick developed a *governance index*, which reflects the various measures that some companies put in place to restrict shareholders' rights.[4] They then grouped the companies with the poorest corporate governance system into a "dictatorship portfolio" and the ones with the best into a "democracy portfolio." Over the period 1990–1999 the democracy portfolio outperformed the dictatorship portfolio by 8.5% per year! This research provides empirical support for the notion that shareholders are better off with better corporate governance. We will come back to this study later in the chapter.

Early Corporate Governance Activists

In Chapter 7 we discussed the rising role of hedge fund activists. However, it is useful to look back and recall that some of the early activists were funds like the California Public

---

[2] Jim. Hsieh and Quinghai Wang, "Shareholder Voting Rights in Mergers and Acquisitions," Georgia Institute of Teechnology Working Paper,

[3] Marco Becht, Andrea Polo and Stefano Rossi, "Does Mandatory Shareholder Voting Prevent Wealth Destruction in Corporate Acquisitions," paper presented at the American Finance Association annual meetings, 2015.

[4] Paul Gompers, Joy Ishii, and Andrew Metrick, "Corporate Governance and Equity Prices," *Quarterly Journal of Economics* 118, no. 1 (February 2003): 107–155.

Employees Retirement System (CalPERS) and TIAA. These large pension funds arrived at the belief that if the companies in their portfolio had better corporate governance, their stock price performance would be better and this would uplift the fund's returns. Some funds, such as CalPERS, went so far as to create list of companies that needed to improve their governance. In 2010 CalPERS dropped its "name-and-shame" Focus List but still actively engaged with underperforming companies in its portfolio.

The list clearly had value. However, a study by Wilshire Associates seemed to support private contacts as opposed to the public shaming approach. Wilshire followed 155 companies over the years 1999–2008 and found that the 96 companies that were privately contacted outperformed the 59 companies that were on the Focus List. An updated study by Wilshire examined the performance of companies engaged by CalPERS over the period 1999–2012.[5] Wilshire found that in the three years prior to being engaged by CalPERS, the engaged companies trailed the Russell 1000 by an average of 38% and also trailed the Russell sector indices by 35%. However, in the first five years after the engagement date these companies exceeded the Russell 1000 by 13.7% and their sector Russell indices by 13.7% and 12.1%, respectively.

Agency Costs

In smaller companies, shareholders may also choose the managers of the company. In this case, there is less of a concern that the managers will take actions that are not in the best interests of shareholders. In large companies, however, shareholders hold a relatively small percentage of the total shares outstanding. When shareholders own a portfolio of assets, with their equity positions in any given company constituting a relatively small percentage of their total assets, they do not have a big incentive to oversee the operations of the company. In addition, even if they wanted to, as the shareholders' percentage of total shares outstanding declines, shareholders have less ability to influence the operations of the company—even if they wanted to devote time to doing so. For this reason, shareholders must trust that managers will really run the business in a manner that maximizes shareholder wealth. One of the concerns that shareholders have is that managers will pursue their own personal goals and will not run the company in a manner that will maximize shareholder wealth. If managers do pursue policies that shareholders oppose, their relatively small shareholdings often do not allow them to take actions to effectively oppose management. Shareholders have to put their trust in the board of directors and hope that they will look after their collective interests when they monitor management. This is the essence of the board's fiduciary duties. When directors are insufficiently diligent and do not require managers to act in shareholders' interests, they violate their fiduciary duties.

The topic of agency costs was popular in the 1970s and 1980s. Yet it is ironic that it remains in the forefront as we go through the 2000s. This seems to be a function of human nature and the inability of some to put their ethical obligations ahead of their own personal ambitions. A directorship is not a full-time position, and directors pursue

---

[5] Andrew Junkin, "Update on the CalPERS Effect on Targeted Company Share Prices," September 24, 2014, Wilshire Associates.

other work, including possibly serving on other boards. One survey of directors reported that on average there were 5.6 board meetings per year and that they devoted an average of 19 hours per month to board issues.[6] The challenge of board members is to make sure that the time they allocate to monitoring managers is sufficient to allow them to ensure that management runs the company in a way that maximizes shareholder wealth.

Since directors are not generally monitoring the company on a daily basis, they use periodic updates from management and monitor their performance as reflected in various financial statements, such as quarterly reports. Even with such reporting, there is opportunity for the managers, the agents of the shareholders, to pursue their own self-interest at the expense of shareholders. When this occurs, the owners of the company are said to incur agency costs. Shareholders will never be able to eliminate agency costs, and they will always exist at some level. The goal is to limit them to some minimal or acceptable level. One of the solutions that has been used to try to control agency costs is to create incentives for managers to act in the interests of shareholders. This is sometimes done by giving management shares or stock options that would enable them to profit when shareholder values increase, thereby aligning the interests of both managers and shareholders.[7] According to a 2006 annual survey of CEO compensation done by Mercer Consulting, 192 of the CEOs cashed in options in 2005 that had a median value of $3,493,400.[8] Occasionally, the value of the grants rises to much greater heights. In 2005, the CEO of Capital One cashed in options equal to $249.27 million.[9] Another of the more extreme cases of profiting from exercising options was Disney's Michael Eisner, who in 1997 exercised over $500 million in options in Disney.

For a while, option grants were touted as the solution to the agency costs problem. However, with the various highly publicized accounting scandals of the late 1990s and 2000s, many have questioned the large offerings of stock options. Option grants are given by the board with the details of the grant being handled by the board's compensation committee. At some companies there have been questions about the timing of the option grants, which sometimes come too close to upward movements in the stock price to be coincidental. In addition, some companies have given option grant recipients the right to select the date when options are granted. Normally options do not vest for a period of time, such as a year or more, and have an exercise price of the closing stock price on the day the grant is given. Therefore, the date that the options are officially granted can make a big difference in their value. This whole issue has come under increased scrutiny in recent years.

As a result of concerns about the appropriateness of some option grants to managers, this method of reducing agency costs has become somewhat less popular. To some extent, this solution became more of a problem than the problem it was designed to solve.

---

[6] "What Do Directors Think" Study: 2003, *Corporate Board Member*, July 2003.
[7] Michael Jensen and W. H. Meckling, "The Theory of the Firm: Managerial Behavior, Agency Costs and Ownership Structure," *Journal of Financial Economics* 3 (1976): 305–360.
[8] Joann Lublin, "Adding It All Up," *Wall Street Journal*, April 10, 2006, R1.
[9] Ibid.

Dual Classifications and Agency Costs

In Chapter 5 we discussed how dual classifications can concentrate shareholder voting power in the hands of certain parties such as insiders. In an analysis of a large sample of 503 dual class companies over the period 1995–2003, Masulis, Wang, and Xie found that shareholder wealth declines as the divergence between insider voting rights and cash flow rights increases.[10] In addition, as this divergence increases, CEO compensation rises and the propensity to pursue value-destroying M&As grows. Their research confirmed the intuitive result that dual classifications increase agency costs.

CEO Compensation and Agency Costs

The recent accounting scandals have attracted even more attention to what was already a major source of concern—the high compensation of the CEOs of U.S. companies. At the extreme upper end is Oracle's CEO Larry Ellison, who the *Wall Street Journal* reported in July 2010 to have earned over $1.8 billion over the years 1999–2009, topping IAC's CEO Barry Diller, who earned a paltry $1.14 billion over the years 2000–2009. More recently, Charif Souki, CEO of Cheniere Energy, earned $142 million in 2013. To put that absurd compensation level in perspective, that amount was more than half of Cheniere's total annual revenue in 2013. Even worse, the company lost almost a half a billion dollars in 2013. Shareholders were so outraged that they filed a lawsuit, and the company had to cancel its annual meeting.

Many questioned whether these CEOs really were generating value for shareholders consistent with the high compensation they withdrew from these firms. The compensation of U.S. CEOs seems particularly high when compared with their counterparts in Europe and Asia. The difference in these compensation levels can be readily seen in data compiled by the Hay Group in a study commissioned by the *Wall Street Journal*, which shows that in 2013 the median CEO compensation at 300 large U.S. companies was approximately $11.4 million, of which two-thirds was a function of performance.[11] The large percentage of the total that incentives pay accounts for can be a concern, as it is often not fully transparent. In fact, some argue that this lack of transparency may be by design in an effort to disguise upper management extracting unjustified gains or "rents" from shareholders.[12]

According to the Institute for Policy Studies, senior executives of European companies earned only about a third of what their U.S. counterparts earned.[13] Another survey by Towers Perrin (now Towers Watson) found that the average U.S. CEO earned about twice as much as his or her British counterpart.[14] Part of the reason for this is that

---

[10] Ronald M. Masulis, Cong Wang, and Fei Xie, "Agency Problems at Dual Classification Companies," *Journal of Finance* 64, no. 4 (August 2009): 1697–1727.

[11] *Wall Street Journal*/Hay Group 2012 CEO Compensation Survey, May 2014.

[12] Lucian Arye Bebchuk, Jesse M. Fried, and David Walker, "Managerial Power and Rent Extraction in the Design of Executive Compensation," *University of Chicago Law Review* 69 (2002): 751–846.

[13] "Executive Excess 2007: The Staggering Social Cost of U.S. Business Leadership," Institute for Policy Studies, August 29, 2007.

[14] Joanna L. Ossinger, "Poorer Relations: When It Comes to CEO Pay, Why Are the British So Different?" *Wall Street Journal*, April 10, 2006, R6.

corporate reforms were adopted in Britain that required that shareholders vote annually on executive compensation. When we consider that institutional investors wield significant power at some British corporations, it is not hard to understand why executive compensation seems under better control in that nation.

The differences between the compensation levels of U.S. CEOs and their counterparts in other parts of the world cannot be explained by cost-of-living factors. The fact that the U.S. economy is the richest in the world still does not explain these large compensation differences, as the gap in the CEO compensation is far in excess of the relative differences in the size of the economies. Moreover, although a larger economy may have more large corporations than a smaller economy, other reasons must be found for the fact that at comparably sized companies across different countries, the U.S. CEO earns a far greater compensation. Given that U.S. CEOs have become accustomed to earning the highest compensation in the world by international standards, U.S. shareholders have a right to expect superior performance in exchange. Indeed, if it could be shown that U.S. CEOs generated increased shareholder value commensurate with their higher compensation level, shareholders would not have cause to complain. It is only when the value of their investment does not benefit from the high pay that they give their CEOs that shareholders have reason to be upset.

CEO Compensation and Shareholder Returns

When determining CEO compensation, one obvious question that arises is, do companies that pay their CEOs more generate greater return for their shareholders? If the answer is yes, then maybe the CEOs are worth their higher compensation. Recent research, however, fails to find support for this assertion. In analyzing a large sample of the firms included in the S&P Execucomp database covering the period 1994–2006, Cooper, Gulen, and Rau found that firms in the highest decile ranking of executive compensation earned significant negative excess returns![15] In fact, their results showed that for each dollar that was paid to CEOs their shareholders *lost* $100. They also found that these higher-paying firms generated stock returns that trailed their peers by over 12 percentage points!

Other research has come to a similar conclusion but approaches the problem differently. Bebchuk, Cremers, and Peyer looked at the "CEO slice"—the percentage of total compensation of the top five managers in companies that goes to the CEO.[16] In analyzing a sample of more than 2,000 companies, they found that the CEO pay slice, which was approximately 35%, was negatively related to firm value as reflected by industry-adjusted Tobin q values.

Management Perks, Agency Costs, and Firm Value

Management perks have clear direct costs that are measurable, but there is some evidence that indicates that such expenses may have costs well beyond these direct

[15] Michael Cooper, Huseyin Gulen, and P. Raghavendra Rau, "Performance for Pay? The Relationship between CEO Incentive Compensation and Future Stock Price Performance," Working Paper, 2014. .
[16] Lucian A. Bebchuk, Martijn Cremers, and Urs Peyer, "The CEO Pay Slice," Project Syndicate, January 2010.

costs. A study by Yermack looked at certain high-profile perks, such as use of corporate aircraft, and showed that companies that disclosed such managerial perks tended to underperform annual market benchmarks by 4%.[17] His study analyzed 237 large corporations over the years 1993–2002. The magnitude of the aggregate dollar underperformance was significantly greater than the actual monetary costs of the specific perks. One explanation is that the market takes the revelation of the perks as an indication of corporate waste and management that may not be running the company in a manner that will maximize shareholder value. Clearly, for large corporations, corporate aircraft may be more efficient than scheduled airlines. It is unlikely that investors disagree. However, they are concerned not with necessary corporate transportation but with signs that might be indicative of symptomatic waste and a lack of concern about management's fiduciary obligations. This was alleged to be the case at the Arkansas-based Acxiom Corp., which became the target of a 2006 proxy battle led by its largest shareholder, ValueAct Capital. ValueAct alleged that Acxiom's CEO spent millions of the company's money to sponsor NASCAR cars and trucks.[18] He then had the company lease a Falcon jet that he repeatedly used to fly back and forth to NASCAR events.

CEO Compensation and Board Characteristics

If U.S. shareholders often do not receive sufficient benefits from the higher compensation they pay their CEOs, then this raises questions regarding how effective the corporate governance process is in controlling the financial benefits that CEOs seem to be extracting from the company without a comparable gain for shareholders. A study by Core, Holthausen, and Larker provides some insight into the relationship between CEO compensation and the makeup of boards.[19] They examined 205 large corporations over a three-year period in 14 different industries. They related the different levels of CEO compensation to different characteristics of boards.

   In their analysis, Core et al. assumed that larger boards were less effective and more susceptible to CEO influence.[20] This conclusion is intuitive, as at a larger board each director constitutes a smaller percentage of the total board and commands a smaller percentage of the total votes needed to approve board decisions. Additionally, Core et al. also looked at the percentage of outside directors on boards as well as the number of "gray" directors. These were directors who receive other compensation or benefits beyond the director payment that directors receive for serving on the board. In addition, the study's authors also assumed that if the director was appointed to the board after the CEO was in place, then the CEO played a role in that decision. Their analysis also highlighted interlocked directors, as those directors may be weaker from a corporate governance perspective (interlocked boards will be discussed in greater detail later in this chapter).

---

[17] David Yermack, Corporate Jets, CEO Perquisites and Inferior Shareholder Returns," *Journal of Financial Economics*, 80, 2006, 211–242.

[18] Gretchen Morgenson, "Gentlemen, Start Your Proxy Fight," *New York Times*, May 14, 2006, 3.1.

[19] John E. Core, Robert W. Holtausen, and David Larker, "Corporate Governance, Chief Executive Officer Compensation, and Firm Performance," *Journal of Financial Economics* 51, no. 3 (March 1999): 371–406.

[20] David Yermack, "Higher Market Valuation of Companies with a Small Board of Directors," *Journal of Financial Economics* 40, no. 2 (February 1996): 185–211.

They also assigned a negative value to CEOs being older (over 70) and being on too many other boards.

Core et al.'s findings are consistent with human nature. Their research showed an inverse relationship between CEO compensation and the percentage of outside directors on the board. They also found that CEO compensation was positively related to board size as well as to the number of members of the board who were appointed by the CEO.

CEO compensation was also greater for the directors who were gray, over age 69, or who served on three or more boards. There was also an inverse relationship between CEO compensation and the size of the shareholdings of the CEO. In addition, they found that CEO compensation was lower when there were external blockholders who owned 5% or more of the outstanding shares. These external blockholders had sufficient power to try to keep the CEO's pursuit of higher personal compensation in check. The lower the size of the holdings of the largest shareholders, the less likely they would have the power, or the incentive, to hold the CEO in check. Earlier in this book we saw the important role large blockholders can play in preventing value-reducing deals.

CEO Compensation and Peer Group Benchmarking

CEO compensation is usually determined by a subcommittee of the board of directors. Often this is done by selecting a peer group of CEOs of companies that in the committee's view are sufficiently comparable to be included in the comparison. Recent SEC proxy disclosure rules require that the peer group be disclosed. Research by Bizjak, Lemmon, and Nguyen provides support for the contention that the peer group is opportunistically selected to derive a higher compensation level for the CEO.[21] Their research shows that S&P 500 companies appear to select peers that are similar or smaller than their company in an apparent effort to justify the compensation of the CEO, whereas non–S&P 500 companies appear to select peers that are larger in an apparent effort to support higher compensation levels.

Another factor that needs to be considered is an effort by boards to try to hire above-average CEOs who then may logically command above-average compensation. However, if most firms pursue this practice, we end up with an upward spiral of compensation levels with the lower half of the distribution continually being adjusted to be consistent with levels in the upper half.[22] It is interesting to note that insofar as this practice may be prevalent in the United States, there is less evidence that it is pursued in Europe, where there seems to be more concern about keeping upper management compensation at controlled levels.

CEO Compensation, Incentives, and the Role of Luck

In response to concerns that guaranteeing CEO compensation would not provide sufficient incentives to guarantee good performance and shareholder returns, boards have

---

[21] John Bizjak, Michael Lemmon, and Thanh Nguyen, "Are All CEOs above Average? An Empirical Analysis of Compensation Peer Groups and Pay Design," *Journal of Financial Economics* 100, no. 3 (June 2011): 538–555.
[22] Rachel Hayes and Scott Schaefer, "CEO Pay and the Lake Wobegon Effect," *Journal of Financial Economics* 94, no. 2 (November 2009): 280–290.

developed more incentive-based compensation, such as stock options. For a while this seemed to address the incentive problem, but then the backdating of options scandal called that solution into question.[23] Research has shown that companies that are better governed charge CEOs more for their options than those that lack such good governance.[24] In addition, when incentives are based on factors that are heavily influenced by luck, such as when profits at oil companies rise as a function of the higher price of oil rather than good management, the compensation system is questionable. Research has shown that better-governed firms reduce the role of luck. Bertrand and Mullainathan showed that when the equity base includes a large shareholder, pay for luck is much less.[25] Smaller boards also reduce the role of luck in CEO compensation.

Superstar CEOs: Are They Worth It?

Many large corporations have sought out "superstar CEOs" to whom they give high compensation. Malmendier and Tate analyzed the performance of CEOs who were awarded this status in the form of relatively high compensation, awards, and press coverage.[26] They found such CEOs underperform compared to their prior performance as well as the performance of their peers. Their compensation rose significantly on attainment of the superstar status, but their performance declined. In fact, they showed that such CEOs spent a disproportionate amount of time doing other activities, such as attending public and private events as well as writing books—work from which the company may derive little benefit. Their peers who may not have had as many of these opportunities presumably devoted more of their time to running the company, which may explain why they outperformed the superstars. One of the lessons of this research is that hiring a superstar and paying the high price tag may not be in the company's best interest. The company may be better served by hiring an executive who will work smart and hard for good but not outlandish pay.

 GOLDEN PARACHUTES

Golden parachutes are special compensation agreements that the company provides to upper management. The word *golden* is used because of the lucrative compensation that executives covered by these agreements receive. Although companies typically maintain that they adopt such agreements for reasons other than the prevention of takeovers, they may have some antitakeover effects. These effects may occur whether the parachutes are used in a preventative or an active manner. They may be used in

---

[23] Randall Heron and Erik Lee, "Does Backdating Explain the Stock Price Pattern around Executive Stock Option Grants?" *Journal of Financial Economics* 83 (2007): 271–295.

[24] Marianne Bertrand and Sendhil Mullainathan, "Do CEOs Set Their Pay? The Ones without Principals Do," National Bureau of Economic Research, Working Paper No. 7604, 2000.

[25] Marianne Bertrand and Sendhil Mullainathan, "Are CEOs Rewarded for Luck? The Ones without Principals Are," *Quarterly Journal of Economics* 116, no. 3 (August 2001): 901–932.

[26] Ulrike Malmendier and Geoffrey Tate, "Superstar CEOs," *Quarterly Journal of Economics* 12, no. 4 (November 2009): 1593–1638.

advance of a hostile bid to make the target less desirable, but they may also be used in the midst of a takeover battle. It should be kept in mind, particularly for large takeovers, that the golden parachute payments are a small percentage of the total purchase price. This implies that the antitakeover effects of these benefits may be relatively small. Many CEOs of corporations believe that golden parachutes are a vital course of action in a takeover contest. One problem corporations face during a takeover battle is that of retaining management employees. When a takeover has been made, a corporation's management is often besieged by calls from recruiters. Managers who are insecure about their positions are quick to consider other attractive offers. Without a golden parachute agreement, the managers might be forced to litigate to realize certain compensation in the event that they were terminated following a change in control. Therefore, some corporations adopt golden parachutes to alleviate their employees' concerns about job security. Jensen contended that properly constructed golden parachutes should result in management possessing sufficient incentives to negotiate higher takeover premiums for shareholders.[27] On the other hand, the ability of target managers to negotiate their own special arrangements at the posttakeover company while at the same time negotiating the acquisition price may present an inherent conflict that may mitigate some of the positive effects of golden parachutes.

Shareholder Wealth Effects of Golden Parachute Agreements

A study by Lambert and Larcker provides some support for Jensen's view. They found that stock prices rose 3% when companies announced the adoption of golden parachutes.[28] Other studies have provided a basis for the market's positive stock price response. In a sample of 146 firms that adopted golden parachutes between 1975 and 1988, Machlin, Choe, and Miles found that the number of multiple takeover offers was significantly greater for firms that possessed golden parachute agreements than for those firms without such agreements.[29] They also found a positive relationship between the size of the golden parachute agreement and the magnitude of the takeover premium. Other research has found negative shareholder wealth effects following the adoption of golden parachute agreements, but these results were not statistically significant.[30]

Some studies find that the shareholder wealth effects of golden parachutes are dependent on when they are adopted. Hall has found that the effects are negative if they are adopted when a firm is in play but are neutral when that is not the case.[31]

---

[27] Michael Jensen, "Takeovers: Causes and Consequences," in Patrick A. Gaughan, ed., *Readings in Mergers and Acquisitions* (Oxford: Basil Blackwell, 1994), 15–43.

[28] Richard A. Lambert and David F. Larcker, "Golden Parachutes, Executive Decision Making and Shareholder Wealth," *Journal of Accounting Economics* 7, no. 1–3 (April 1985): 179–203.

[29] Judith Machlin, Hyuk Choe, and James Miles, "The Effects of Golden Parachutes on Takeover Activity," *Journal of Law and Economics* 36, no. 2 (1993): 861–876.

[30] Pamela L. Hall and Dwight C. Anderson, "The Effect of Golden Parachutes on Shareholder Wealth and Takeover Probabilities," *Journal of Business Finance and Accounting* 23, no. 3 (April 1997): 445–463, and Damian J. Mogavero and Michael F. Toyne, "The Impact of Golden Parachutes on Fortune 500 Stock Returns: A Reexamination of the Evidence," *Quarterly Journal of Business and Economics* 34, no. 4 (1995): 30–38.

[31] Pamela L. Hall, "An Examination of Stock Returns to Firms Adopting Golden Parachutes under Certain Conditions," *American Business Review* 16, no. 1 (January 1998): 123–130.

Some studies show that the adoption of golden parachutes increases the likelihood that the company will be a takeover target.[32] However, Schnitzer has shown that this effect is less likely when the management team is efficient.[33]

Mechanics of Golden Parachutes

A typical golden parachute agreement provides for lump-sum payments to certain senior management on either voluntary or involuntary termination of their employment. This agreement is usually effective if termination occurs within one year after the change in control. The agreements between the employee and the corporation may have a fixed term or may be an *evergreen* agreement, in which the term is one year but is automatically extended for an additional year if there is not a change in control during a given year. Monies to fund golden parachutes are sometimes put aside in separate accounts referred to as *rabbi trusts*. Rabbi trusts provide assurance to the employee that the monies will be there for the payment of the parachutes.

The amount of compensation is usually determined by the employee's annual compensation and years of service. For example, the agreement could provide for the terminated employee to receive some multiple of a recent year's annual salary, possibly also including incentive and bonuses, for a certain number of years.

Golden parachutes are usually triggered by some predetermined ownership of stock by an outside entity. Lambert and Larcker found that the trigger control percentage of stocks acquired by a bidder was an average 26.6% for the firms they studied.[34] However, some corporations have control trigger percentages below 10%—well below the Lambert and Larker sample average. Lambert and Larker also showed that the participants in golden parachute plans are narrowly defined. In their sample, golden parachute agreements covered only 9.7% of the executives. These agreements are extended to executives who do not have employment contracts. They are effective even if the managers leave the corporations voluntarily after a change in control.

Golden parachutes are not usually applied broadly. One unusual exception is what are known as *silver parachutes*, compensation agreements given to most employees in the firm, including lower-level employees. The most common type of silver parachute is a one-year severance pay agreement.

Single versus Golden Trigger Parachutes

Golden parachutes can be *single trigger* or *double trigger*. A single trigger parachutes kick in when there is a change in control. A double trigger parachute is one where there has to be both a change in control and a termination to be effective. Single trigger parachutes have been criticized as the parachute itself was designed to help employees who may lose their job after their company is acquired. However, they can provide the employee with a windfall if the company is acquired and they choose to voluntarily leave. This may even

---

[32] Jeffrey A. Born, Emery A. Trahan, and Hugo J. Faria, "Golden Parachutes, Incentive Aligners, Management Entrenchers, or Takeover Bids Signals?" *Journal of Financial Research* 16, no. 4 (Winter 1993) 299–308.

[33] M. Schnitzer, "Breach of Trust in Takeovers and the Optimal Corporate Charter," *Journal of Industrial Economics* 43, no. 3 (1995): 229–260.

[34] Richard A. Lambert and David F. Larcker, "Golden Parachutes, Executive Decision Making and Shareholder Wealth," *Journal of Accounting Economics* 7, no. 1–3 (April 1985): 179–203.

create an incentive for the employees to bring about a change in control that may not be in shareholders' interests. This has led to the replacement of single trigger parachutes with double trigger ones or none at all.

Legality of Golden Parachutes

Golden parachutes have been challenged in court by stockholders who contend that these agreements violate directors' and management's fiduciary responsibilities. The problem arises because golden parachutes generally do not have to be approved by a stockholder vote before implementation. The courts have held that the actions of directors in enacting golden parachute agreements were within their purview under the business judgment rule.[35] As discussed in Chapter 3, this rule holds that management's actions are valid as long as they are enacted while management is acting in the stockholders' best interests. The fact that management's actions may not maximize stockholder wealth, in retrospect, is irrelevant according to this rule.

Courts have generally refused to distinguish between golden parachute agreements and other types of executive compensation arrangements.[36] Part of the reason courts have not been persuaded by the self-dealing argument of golden parachute critics is because the agreements are typically approved by a compensation committee of the board of directors, which should be dominated by disinterested directors and not those who would expect to profit from the parachutes.[37] When the golden parachute agreements are triggered by the manager's own actions, however, courts have invalidated them or at least granted a preliminary injunction against their use.[38]

Criticism of Golden Parachutes

Some shareholder rights activists believe that golden parachutes are a burden on both the corporation and the stockholders. Some critics cite moral hazard concerns, and golden parachutes could be considered a form of self-dealing on the part of management and one of the more flagrant abuses of the modern takeover era. The magnitude of these compensation packages, they state, is clearly excessive. Critics contend that managers of companies that were poorly managed and have experienced a declining stock price end up being rewarded for that mismanagement. The golden parachute that was given to Michael Bergerac, former chairman of Revlon Corporation, after his resignation at the end of the unsuccessful defense against corporate raider Ronald Perelman was estimated to have provided Bergerac with a compensation package in excess of $35 million. This package included stock options worth $15 million. This is not an isolated situation. While these excessive payments raised eyebrows at the time, as we moved into the fifth merger wave and the years that followed the problem only got worse.

---

[35] *Buckhorn Inc. v. Ropak Corp.*, 656 F. Supp. 209 (S.D. Ohio), aff'd by summary order 815 F.2d 76 (6th Cir. 1987).

[36] *Royal Crown Cos. v. McMahon*, 359 S.E. 2d 379 (Ga. Ct. App. 1987), cert. denied (Ga. September 8, 1987).

[37] *E. Tate & Lyle PLC v. Staley Continental, Inc.*, Fed. Sec. L. Rep. 93, 764 (Del. Ch. CCH 93, 764) (Del. Ch. May 9, 1988); *Nomad Acquisition Corp. v. Damon Corp.*, CCH Fed. Sec. L. Rep. 94, 040 (Del. Ch. September 16, 1988).

[38] John C. Coffee, "Shareholders versus Managers: The Strain in the Corporate Web, " in John Coffee, Louis Lowenstein, and Susan Rose Ackerman, eds., *Knights, Raiders, and Targets* (New York: Oxford University Press, 1988), 71–134.

The excessiveness of golden parachute agreements has given rise to the term *golden handcuffs*, which reflects the belief that golden parachutes serve only to entrench management at the expense of stockholders. This belies their role as an antitakeover device. If the compensation package is very large, some raiders might be put off from making a bid for the company. As noted previously, although a large golden parachute agreement may be a mild deterrent, it is not considered an effective antitakeover tool. In conjunction with other, stronger devices, however, these agreements may have some role as a deterrent.

The tax treatment of golden parachutes can be complex. However, Congress, in the tax reform acts of 1984 and 1986, imposed penalties on golden parachute payments. These penalties feature the payment of a nondeductible 20% tax, to be paid by the employee, for "excessive" golden parachute payments. Generally, the excess is defined as the amount greater than a typical annual compensation. In addition, the employer corporations are denied tax deductions for excessive golden parachutes. Excessive is defined as being three times the average salary of the employee in the previous five-year period.

 ## CEO SEVERANCE PAYMENTS

Boards are not just generous with shareholder money when it comes to paying takeover premiums; they are generally generous when it comes to paying CEOs with other people's—shareholders'—money. Some CEOs have received huge payouts following the sale of their companies. For example, in 2005, James Kilts, CEO of Gillette, received $165 million following the sale of his company to Procter & Gamble Co. Another example was the $102 million that Bruce Hammonds was reported to have received in connection with MBNA's acquisition by Bank of America, and the $92 million that Pete Correll was reported to have received in connection with the 2005 sale of his company, Georgia Pacific, to Koch Industries. Even companies known for poor performance still have similar payouts for their CEOs when they are finally sold. For example, AT&T CEO David Dorman is reported to have received $55 million in connection with the sale of his company to SBC Communications.

Goldman and Huang conducted an empirical analysis of every CEO who left his position in an S&P 500 company over the years 1993 to 2007.[39] They measured the excess severance pay for departing CEOs and defined excess as the amount beyond what the company contractually agreed to pay as severance in the CEO employment contract. As shocking as it sounds, excess CEO pay was an average of $8 million, which was over 240% of the CEO's annual compensation. They found that for the CEO who left voluntarily, weak corporate governance was positively associated with the size of the excess severance pay. This is no surprise. For CEOs who were forced out, however, they believed the data showed that a desire to protect shareholders' interests and preserve an orderly transition was a more important explanatory factor than weak governance.

---

[39] Eitan Goldman and Peggy Huang, "Contractual versus Actual Severance Pay following CEO Turnover," working paper, March 2010.

REFORM OF EXCESSES OF GOLDEN PARACHUTES AND SEVERANCE PAYMENTS

For a long time it seemed that management and compliant directors have been able to adopt excessive severance payments and golden parachutes easily, and shareholders have been able to do little to oppose such giveways of shareholder wealth. However, in recent years there has been more shareholder pressure to halt these outright abuses. Part of that process was the SEC Rules implemented in 2011, which required companies to allow shareholders to vote on executive compensation at least once every three years. As part of these regulations shareholders have the right to also vote on the frequency of these "say on pay" votes, as well as to vote on golden parachutes when they are presented with a transaction such as a merger. The votes are only advisory in nature and not binding on the company. However, companies are required to report the results of the "say on pay" and "say on frequency" votes through a special 8K filing within four business days after their shareholder meeting or other meeting that addressed this issue. In addition, the rules also require more detailed and clear disclosure of the golden parachute payments in connection with any change of control transactions.

As a result of these rules, along with increasing focus on these payments, we are starting to see smaller severance payments and fewer "gross ups." Gross ups are perks that require the corporation to pay the taxes on company benefits so that the executive enjoys the full payment without it being reduced for taxes. Clearly, this is a benefit that rank-and-file, blue-collar employees who are paid far lower amounts of money do not get to enjoy.

We are also seeing fewer instances of executives receiving golden parachute payments even if they keep their jobs after a merger. These payments were designed to provide some compensation to executives who lose their jobs as a result of a merger, but they have been more widely applied to cover even executives who do not get fired. Many consider this an abuse of shareholders' interests.

Another area of reform has been the treatment of management stock options, which often automatically vest after an M&A. This early vesting can provide significant early compensation to executives, giving them an additional incentive, along with handsome severance payments and parachutes, to approve a deal at a price that may not necessarily be optimal for shareholders. There has been pressure to not give executives such early vesting rights as part of their stock-based compensation.

MANAGERIAL COMPENSATION, MERGERS, AND TAKEOVERS

Managers often personally gain from M&As. That is, many CEOs and other senior management have employment agreements that provide them with large payouts upon changes of control. Sometimes such agreements are called golden parachutes. An example of such payouts is the change of control provisions in Caesar's Entertainment's CEO Wallace R. Barr's employment agreement, which has been reported to provide total compensation of almost $20 million in accelerated options and stock awards.[40] In early July 2004, Harrah's announced that it would acquire Caesar's for $5.2 billion. Usually shareholders do not have a lot to say against such large payouts. In theory, target shareholders may stand to gain from the premiums offered by a bidder. However, target management may stand to lose their positions and their compensation if there is a change in control and the bidder replaces them. Employment agreements that provide financial benefits for managers who pursue changes in control that may result in the termination of their positions may help shareholders receive a wealth-increasing control premium. However, it may not always work in the way outlined in the theory. Sometimes managers may promote deals that will create a situation where they receive the payout even if the deals are not the best move for shareholders at the time. This seemed to be the position of the California Public Employees Retirement System (CalPERS) when it voted against the 2004 merger of two health care companies—Anthem Inc. and WellPoint Health Networks. Total executive compensation from the change of control provisions equaled approximately $200 million. Leonard Schaeffer, WellPoint's CEO, alone was to receive $47 million in various severance agreements. The deal was eventually completed in November 2004 at a $20.88 billion value.

The issue is important due to the pivotal role that a target CEO may play in negotiating his or her own postmerger position and compensation. While it probably shouldn't be part of the premerger negotiating process, it is well known that it is. As an example, it has been reported that the breakdown of the merger negotiations in the fourth merger wave between American Home Products (later called Wyeth and in 2009 merged with Pfizer) and Monsanto was the result of neither CEO being willing to relinquish control of the merged company to the other.[41] These issues should be secondary to the impact the deal would have on shareholder wealth. CEOs should consider the impact on shareholders well before the impact on their own careers. Placing their careers and positions ahead of shareholders' interests is a violation of their fiduciary obligations to shareholders. However, to deny that this occurs in practice is to be naive. This is one of many areas that need to be addressed in corporate governance reform as it relates to M&As. Hartzell, Ofek, and Yermack analyzed 311 primarily friendly transactions over the period 1995–1997.[42] They found that target CEOs enjoyed mean wealth increases between $8 million and $11 million. The bulk of these financial gains came from increases in stock and options as well as from golden parachute payments. Some CEOs even receive last-minute increases in their golden parachute agreements—presumably in exchange for promoting the deal. They also found that about one-half of the CEOs became officers in the buying entity, although their departure rates over the three years following the merger were very high. Even for these exits, however, the former target CEO received enhanced compensation.

---

[40] Gretchen Morgenson, "No Wonder CEOs Love Those Mergers," *New York Times,* July 18, 2004, Sec. 3, 1.

[41] Thomas M. Burton and Elyse Tanouye, "Another Drug Industry Megamerger Goes Bust," *Wall Street Journal,* October 13, 1998, B1.

[42] Jay Hartzell, Eli Ofek, and David Yermack, "What's in It for Me? CEOs Whose Firms Are Acquired," *Review of Financial Studies* 17, no. 1 (2004): 37–61.

The Hartzell et al. study also showed that, in deals where target CEOs enjoyed extraordinary personal treatment, shareholders received lower acquisition premiums. This creates the disquieting concern that target CEOs are trading premium for their shareholders in exchange for their own personal enrichment.

One of the potential limiting factors that hinders unscrupulous managers from expanding their own compensation beyond what would be prudent is the threat of takeovers. Managers who extract excessive benefits from their own companies or who pursue a strategy that enriches themselves, as opposed to shareholders, may create an opportunity for an outside bidder to acquire the company in a hostile takeover and correct this inefficiency. Agrawal and Knoeber examined a sample of 450 corporations and looked at the compensation of their CEOs.[43] They divided their sample into two subgroups, where the CEO either was or was not protected by an employment agreement or golden parachute that would provide him with protection from removal by a hostile bidder. The bidder could remove the CEO following an acquisition, but the CEO's short-term compensation might not be affected that much. Their results showed what they referred to as a *competition effect*. This occurs when managers receive lower compensation when there is a greater threat of takeover. They also found what they termed a *risk effect*—that managers tend to demand more compensation when they are employed by companies that are more likely to be takeover targets.

Clearly takeovers are an event that managers are mindful of and that may keep them honest.

CEO COMPENSATION AND POWER

Common sense tells us that if CEOs have greater power, many will use it to increase their own compensation. Research seems to support this assumption. One study by Cyert, Kang, and Kumar considered a sample of 1,648 small and large companies. The average CEO in their study was 55 years of age, and had served in that position for an average of eight years.[44] They found that in 70% of the cases the CEO was also the board chairman. In addition, they noted that equity ownership of the largest shareholder and the board was negatively correlated with CEO compensation. This is consistent with the findings of the Core, Holthausen, and Larcker study, wherein they noted that CEO compensation was lower when there were large equity blockholders.[45] Interestingly, Cyert et al. found that equity ownership of the members of the board was more important in keeping CEO compensation under control than the size of the board or the percentage of outside directors. When board members have their own capital at risk, they seem to do a better job of monitoring the CEO and reviewing how much of the potential profits of the

[43] Anup Agrawal and Charles R. Knoeber, "Managerial Compensation and the Threat of Takeover," *Journal of Financial Economics* 47 (1998): 219–239.

[44] Richard M. Cyert, Sok-Hyon Kang, and Pravenn Kumar, "Corporate Governance, Takeovers and Top-Management Compensation: Theory and Evidence," *Management Science* 48, no. 4 (April 2002): 453–469.

[45] John E. Core, Robert Holthausen, and David Larcker, "Corporate Governance, Chief Executive Compensation, and Firm Performance," *Journal of Financial Economics*, 51, 1999, 371–406.

business the CEO extracts in the form of compensation. Once again, these findings are quite intuitive.

There is another force that can help keep CEOs in check and that is the takeover market. Bertrand and Mullainathan found that when a company is allowed to install anti-takeover defenses that insulate the company from takeovers, CEO compensation tends to be higher.[46] Therefore, there are both internal and external forces that monitor the CEO and ensure that he runs the company in a manner consistent with shareholders' goals. The process is far from perfect, but research seems to imply that it often works in a somewhat satisfactory manner, although it can benefit from improvement.

CEO Overconfidence and Takeovers

In Chapter 4 we discussed the hubris hypothesis and how hubris-filled executives have a greater tendency to pay higher takeover premiums. Malmendier and Tate analyzed the role of CEO overconfidence in the tendency for CEOs to engage in M&As.[47] They measured CEO overconfidence, using factors such as the tendency for CEOs to hold options in their company's stock until their expiration, thereby exhibiting bullishness about the company's prospects and their ability to create stock gains. In analyzing a sample of large companies covering the period 1980–1994, they found that overconfident CEOs were more likely to conduct acquisitions and, in particular, more likely to pursue value-destroying deals. As part of this value-destruction process they found that overconfident CEOs were more likely to pursue diversifying deals, which abundant research has shown tends to destroy value for acquiring company shareholders. They also do not find that the relationship between overconfidence and acquisitiveness varies with CEO tenure, implying that for overconfident CEOs it is a function of their position and their personal hubris.

Are Overconfident CEOs Good for Anything?

There is convincing research support for the notion that overconfidence can lead to value-destroying M&As. This gives rise to a question: Are overconfident CEOs good for anything? The answer may be *yes*. Hirshleifer, Low, and Teoh analyzed a large sample of 2,577 CEOs covering 9,807 firm years drawn from the time period 1993 to 2003.[48] They found that overconfident CEOs are more likely to pursue risky projects and, in general, are better innovators. They tend to invest more in research and development and their companies tend to apply for and receive more patents. In addition, the returns of their companies tend to be more volatile. So for risk-seeking investors, overconfident CEOs may be "just the ticket."

---

[46] M. Bertrand and S. Mullainathan, "Is There Discretion in Wage Setting? A Test Using Takeover Legislation," *Rand Journal of Economics* 30 (1999): 535–554.

[47] Ulrike Malmendier and Geoffrey Tate, "Who Makes Acquisitions? CEO Overconfidence and the Market's Reaction," *Journal of Financial Economics* 89 (2008): 2043. Note that prior research had shown that optimal investment decisions suggest that CEOs should sell their options prior to expiration, as failing to do so would result in their assuming too much company-specific risk.

[48] David Hirshleifer, Angie Low, and Siew Hong Teoh, "Are Overconfident CEOs Better Innovators?" *Journal of Finance* 67, no. 4 (2012): 1457–1498.

HEWLETT-PACKARD–COMPAQ MERGER: SHAREHOLDERS LOSE, CEOS GAIN

In February 2005, the board of Hewlett-Packard (HP) announced that it had terminated the employment of its colorful CEO, Carly Fiorina. Fiorina, formerly of AT&T and Lucent, had orchestrated the $25 billion stock-financed merger between Compaq and HP in September 2001. This merger was strongly opposed by leading shareholders, such as Walter Hewlett, son of the company's founder. Fiorina barely won shareholder approval of the deal. When we look back on the merger, we see that the concerns of the market and opposing shareholders were well founded. The gains that she projected when the operations of the rival computer makers were combined never materialized. While revenues at HP rose steadily over her tenure, profitability had been weak. Fiorina caused the company to move even more deeply into the PC business, which it had not been able to manage profitably, unlike its rival Dell.

She was not content to focus on HP's more successful business segments, such as printers. Instead she expanded into areas where it would command a larger market share—but not make a meaningful contribution to shareholder value. In merging with Compaq, HP was adding a company that had similar troubles. Compaq itself was the product of a prior merger between Compaq and Digital Equipment. However, the PC business is very unusual in that it exists in a deflationary market, with industry competitors often having to reduce prices of their products while their costs are rising. This is a very difficult environment in which to be successful. It is noteworthy that the founder of the PC, IBM, sold its PC business in 2005 to Chinese computer manufacturer Lenovo.

The acquisitive Fiorina was replaced by Mark Hurd, who immediately changed the focus at HP from doing megadeals to being a lower-costs company and emphasizing the company's strength in areas such as printers. It is too early to tell how successful this very reasonable strategy is, but early results show promise. Hurd separated the printer and PC businesses and focused on dealing with the PC unit's problems. He has cut costs and managed to purchase components, such as chips, cheaper by playing chipmakers AMD and Intel against each other. He has also developed better relationships with retailers, while Dell has started to suffer from its lack of a retail distribution system.

It is ironic that while shareholders suffered under Fiorina's reign, she profited handsomely from her five-year stint at the company. At the time of her dismissal, it was estimated that she would enjoy a severance package in excess of $20 million. In addition, Michael Capellas, the former CEO of Compaq, who served as president of the postmerger HP, received in excess of $15 million when he left, even though he was with the combined entity for only a relatively short period. The merger was the most significant action that Fiorina orchestrated at HP, and it was a clear failure. When CEOs receive great rewards for eroding shareholder value, there are few incentives for them to pursue different strategies. One solution would be to tie CEO compensation to the achievement of specific targets. If a CEO very aggressively pushes a major merger in which the success is predicated on the achievement of certain measurable performance targets, then let the board agree only if the CEO's

(continued)

(*continued*)

compensation and bonuses are also tied to the achievement of those targets. This should be particularly true for deals that face strong opposition, as this one did. If the CEO does not agree to performance-based compensation tied to such major corporate gambles, then maybe the likelihood of these goals being achieved is questionable.

After some major acquisition blunders, such as the acquisitions of EDS and Autonomy, HP finally decided to undo the empire different CEOs, such as Ms. Fiorina, had assembled. In 2014 CEO Meg Whitman decided to break the company in two parts. Certainly, HP has had an acquisition history no company can be proud of.

COMPENSATION CHARACTERISTICS OF BOARDS THAT ARE MORE LIKELY TO KEEP AGENCY COSTS IN CHECK

We can use the findings of the Core et al. study to highlight some of the characteristics of boards that will be in a better position to keep agency costs in control. These characteristics are as follows:

- Fewer or no gray directors
- Fewer inside board members
- Fewer interlocked directorships
- Board members who were selected with minimal CEO influence
- Board members who serve on fewer boards
- Boards that are not too large

These desirable board characteristics are supported by other research beyond the Core et al. study. In the following section we will focus on specific board characteristics in greater detail and look at other research that sheds light on their impact on shareholder wealth.

ROLE OF THE BOARD OF DIRECTORS

The board of directors is charged with the role of monitoring management, and the CEO in particular, to try to ensure that the company is run in a manner that will maximize shareholder wealth. We have discussed how sometimes CEOs are able to pursue a strategy that facilitates their own personal goals, which may not be consistent with those of shareholders. We will now explore the role of the board of directors and why the board's oversight process may not always function properly.

Multiple Board Appointments and Busy Directors

It is not unusual for a director of one corporation to sit on the boards of one or more other companies. Such directors are referred to as "busy directors." Being asked to serve on multiple boards can be construed to be a sign of a good reputation. However, being on too many boards may cause the director to be spread too thin and the oversight may suffer as a result. Fich and Shivdasani have shown that companies that have over half of the outside directors sitting on three or more boards have lower financial performance as reflected by lower market-to-book ratios and weaker corporate governance in general.[49] While it is an intuitive conclusion, this result has been contradicted by other research that failed to find such lower market-to-book ratios.[50] However, research has shown that when CEOs receive excessive compensation, their boards are more likely to have busy outside directors.[51]

Interlocking Boards

In an interlocked board, directors sit on each other's boards. In one variant of this, the CEO of one company may sit on the board of another firm that has its CEO sitting on his board. One can only imagine that this cozy situation will not result in closer CEO oversight. Once again, this is what one would expect based on human nature. This expectation is supported by research findings, such as those of Hallock, who analyzed a dataset of 9,804 director seats covering 7,519 individuals and 700 large U.S. companies.[52] He found that 20% of the companies in his sample were interlocked. He defined interlocked to be where any current or retired employee of one company sat on another company's board where the same situation was the case for the other company. He found that approximately 8% of CEOs are reciprocally interlocked with another CEO.

In addition to quantifying the frequency of interlocked boards, Hallock's study also provided other interesting results. He noted that in his sample, interlocked companies tended to be larger than noninterlocked firms. In addition, CEOs of interlocked companies tended to earn significantly higher compensation. This implies that CEOs stand to gain when their boards are interlocked. In his study he controlled for firm characteristics, such as firm size, and found that pay gap could not account for all of the difference.

Other research has shown that interlocked boards are less likely to occur when more of a CEO's compensation comes from stock options as opposed to salary. They are also less likely when boards are more active and meet more frequently. Research seems to show that interlocking boards are not desirable. CEOs are highly sought after as directors. Fahlenbrach, Low, and Stulz analyzed 26,231 board appointments at 5,400 firms over the period 1989–2002 in an effort to discern why CEOs are so in demand as directors.[53] They found some positive stock responses to appointments of CEO as outside

---

[49] Eliezer M. Fich and Anil Shivdasani, "Are Busy Boards Effective Monitors?" *Journal of Finance* 61 (2004): 689–724.

[50] Stephen Ferris, Murali Jagannathan, and Adam Prichard, "Too Busy to Mind the Business? Monitoring by Directors with Multiple Board Appointments," *Journal of Finance* 58 (2003): 1087–1111.

[51] John E. Core, Robert W. Holtausen, and David Larker, "Corporate Governance, Chief Executive Officer Compensation, and Firm Performance," *Journal of Financial Economics* 51, no. 3 (March 1999): 371–406.

[52] Kevin Hallock, "Reciprocally Interlocked Boards of Directors and Executive Compensation," *Journal of Financial and Quantitative Analysis* 32, no. 3 (September 1997): 331–344.

[53] Rudiger Fahlenbrach, Angie Low, and Rene M. Stulz, "Why Do Firms Appoint CEOs as Outside Directors," *Journal of Financial Economics*, 97, 2010, 12–32.

directors—especially to the appointment of the first CEO to come on the board. However, they failed to find any significant effects of these appointments on company performance or even on corporate decision making, including CEO compensation and decisions on M&A strategy.

Independence of Directors

Boards have two groups of directors: inside and outside board members. Inside board members are also management employees of the company. These board members may include the CEO, as well as certain other senior members of management whose input may be useful in board deliberations. A 2009 survey conducted by *Corporate Board Member* found that the average number of inside directors is 1.41, down from 2.7 in its 2003 survey, while the average number of outside directors is 6.95, down from 7.2, giving an average size of a board of 8.36 directors.[54] This same survey found that 52.7% of the time the chairperson was an insider. Certain rules require a certain percentage of outside directors be on a company's board. For example, the New York Stock Exchange (NYSE) requires that a majority of directors be independent for companies listed on this exchange.

Research findings provide convincing support for the belief that the more outside directors are on the board, the more likely the board will make decisions that are in shareholders' interests. This body of research also indicates that shareholders will realize greater gains if their companies are taken over when their boards contain more outside directors.[55] Another study by Rosenstein and Wyatt noted that stock prices of companies tend to increase when an outside director is added to a board.[56] The market has indicated a clear preference for outside control of the board, and it usually is concerned when boards fall under the control of management.

It is reasonable to conclude that boards in which insiders have limited influence will be able to make tough decisions involving managers and their performance. Such boards are more likely to be able to make a change in upper management when current managers fail to generate the performance that shareholders may be expecting. This was readily apparent in the removal of Robert Stempel from the CEO position at General Motors (GM) in 1992. In this managerial change, John Smale led the board of GM. Smale held great stature in the corporate world from his years of being CEO of Procter & Gamble. When he asserted that GM would benefit from a change at the helm, his recommendation was taken very seriously. This theme was also apparent in other prominent CEO overthrows. For example, Robert Morrow, CEO of Amoco, led the ouster of Paul Lego of Westinghouse. The same was the case when James Burke, former CEO of Johnson & Johnson, led the overthrow of IBM CEO John Akers. Each of these situations has some important common characteristics. In each case the situation called for a change at the

[54] "What Directors Think: Research Study," *Corporate Board Member*/Pricewaterhouse Coopers Survey, 2009.

[55] James Cooter, Anil Shivdasni, and Marc Zenner, "Do Independent Directors Enhance Target Shareholder Wealth during Tender Offers?" *Journal of Financial Economics* 43 (1997): 195–218.

[56] Stuart Rosenstein and Jeffrey Wyatt, "Outside Directors, Board Independence, and Shareholder Wealth," *Journal of Financial Economics* 26 (1990): 175–192.

wheel. In all of these removals of high-profile CEOs, the company was lagging behind where it should have been, and the position of CEO was a prominent one that was very much in the public eye. In these situations the markets had been critical of the company's performance and thus indirectly, if not directly, of the performance of the CEO. The market and the media put pressure on the board to take decisive action and make changes at the helm. In each instance the board members, and chairman in particular, were prominent corporate figures.

When decisive action is needed and where the performance of management needs to be critically reviewed, outside boards will be in a better position to implement such an objective review. However, we have to understand that there are good reasons why boards have certain managers on them. These management board members can provide useful insight into the performance of the company that other, outside directors may lack. However, we would not want a board composed solely of such directors. Indeed, much can be said for a mixed board composed not just of insider and outside directors but also of outside directors of diverse backgrounds who can bring a wide range of expertise and experience to the management monitoring process. Outsiders, and especially some prominent outside directors, can play a key role when action such as removal of an incumbent CEO is needed.

A study by Weisbach showed that boards with a greater percentage of outside directors were more likely to discipline their CEO for performing poorly than those where insiders played a more prominent role.[57] Inside-dominated boards may simply be too close to the CEO and may be reluctant to make decisions that may have adverse effects on their comanagers. Outside board member directors are often less close to the CEO and can react more objectively. However, exceptions to this are interlocking directorships that may have outsiders with reciprocal relationships on each other's boards. These interlocking board members should not be considered in the same light as other outside directors.

Splitting CEO and Chairperson Positions

In the United States it is not unusual to see that the CEO is also the chairman of the board. This is very different from the United Kingdom, where this practice is much less common. This has given rise to concern in the U.S. that when the CEO is also the chairperson there are insufficient checks and balances, as the CEO may also dominate the board. In response to these concerns, more companies have split the two positions. Research from Russell Reynolds Associates showed that as of 2011 44% of the S&P500 have separate individuals in the CEO and chair positions.[58] This was a significant increase over the percentage from 2001 which was 21%. The percentage is higher for NASDAQ companies which was 65% in 2011. While these percentages have risen they are still well below those which prevail in Europe. For example, 90% of the FTSE100 companies have these positions separated.

---

[57] Michael Weisbach, "Outside Directors and CEO Turnover," *Journal of Financial Economics* 37 (1988): 159–188.

[58] Charles Tribbett, "Splitting the CEO and Chairman Roles—Yes or No?," *The Corporate Board*, Russell Reynolds Associates, November/December 2012.

Board Size

Over the years boards have gotten smaller. In its 34th Annual Survey of Boards of Directors, the Korn Ferry Institute found that the average board consists of 10 directors compared to 1973, the first year of their board survey, when one-fifth of the boards had between 16 and 25 directors.[59]

The size of a board plays an important role in how effectively it may oversee management. In a larger board, each board member may wield less influence, and this may shift the balance of power to the CEO in a way that may reduce shareholder wealth. There is evidence to support this proposition, but the relationship between board size and firm value is not that simple.

Yermack attempted to determine if there was a relationship between the market valuation of companies and board size. He analyzed a sample of 452 large U.S. corporations over the period 1984–1991. The average board size for his sample was 12 directors.[60] Yermack found that there was an inverse relationship between market value, as measured by Tobin's q, and the size of the board of directors (see Figure 13.2). Smaller boards were associated with higher market values, and larger boards tended to be associated with lower valuations. The higher valuations often come from relatively smaller boards that have fewer than 10 members. He also looked at other performance measures, such as operating efficiency and profitability measures, and found that they were also inversely associated with board size. He also found that smaller boards were more likely to replace a CEO following a period of poor performance. In addition, Yermack found some evidence that CEO compensation was more closely linked to performance, especially poor performance, when boards are smaller. Based on these results, boards need to be kept to a certain size beyond which efficiency and ability to carry out their corporate governance functions seem to deteriorate. CEOs may personally benefit in the form of higher compensation when boards are larger, but shareholders may suffer.

It is generally believed that smaller and more independent boards work best. However, Coles, Daniel, and Naveen have shown that optimal board size varies by type of firm.[61] They find that more complex firms, firms that have greater advising requirements, have larger boards and a greater percentage of outside directors. They found that for complex firms Tobin q values increase with board size. There is also evidence that firms with larger boards have less volatile stock returns and accounting returns on assets.[62]

Kini, Kracaw, and Mian found that board size tended to shrink after tender offers for firms that were not performing well.[63] This implies that disciplinary takeovers, or at

[59] 34th Annual Board of Directors Survey, Korn Ferry Institute (2007).

[60] David Yermack, "Higher Market Valuation of Companies with a Small Board of Directors," *Journal of Financial Economics* 40 (1996): 185–211.

[61] Jeffrey Coles, Naveen D. Daniel, and Lalitha Naveen, "Boards: Does One Size Fit All?" *Journal of Financial Economics* 87 (2008): 329–356.

[62] Shijun Cheng, "Board Size and the Variability of Corporate Performance," *Journal of Financial Economics* 87 (2008): 157–176.

[63] Omesh Kini, William Kracaw, and Shehzad Mian, "Corporate Takeovers, Firm Performance and Board Composition," *Journal of Corporate Finance* 1 (1995): 383–412.

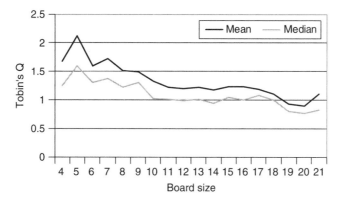

FIGURE 13.2 Board Size and Tobin's q: Sample Means and Medians.
Sample means and medians of Tobin's q for different sizes of boards of directors. The sample consists of 3,438 annual observations for 452 firms between 1984 and 1991. Companies are included in the sample if they are ranked by *Forbes* magazine as one of the 500 largest U.S. public corporations at least four times during the eight-year sample period. Utility and financial companies are excluded. Data for board size is gathered from proxy statements filed by companies near the start of each fiscal year. Tobin's q is estimated at the end of each fiscal year as Market value of assets/Replacement cost of assets. The estimation of q follows the q_{PW} specification of Perfect and Wiles (1994), which is described more fully in the text.
Source: D. Yermack, "Higher Market Valuation of Companies with a Small Board of Directors," *Journal of Financial Economics* 40 (1996): 185–211.

least the threat of such takeovers, tend to reduce the size of boards to that which the market believes may be more effective. When companies receive such hostile bids, they may be good buys for the bidder, which sees the company as relatively cheap when its market value is compared with the bidder's perception of its intrinsic value. The company may respond by taking various actions that will make it become less vulnerable to a takeover. The Kini et al. study implies that among these actions may be reductions in the board size.

Cornelli and Karakas analyzed how private equity firms and management govern the companies they have taken private in LBOs and MBOs.[64] They found that the post-LBO company that was once public but is then private has a smaller board and few outside directors. In addition, board size tended to decline over time after the buyout. In management buyouts the board consists of managers. Companies that had a larger number of outside directors prior to the buyout were taken by these researchers to be ones that might have presented more managerial challenges. Such companies tended to have a larger presence of private equity sponsors on the board than companies with more insiders on the board prior to the buyout.

---

[64] Francesca Cornelli and Oguzhan Karakas, "Private Equity and Corporate Governance: Do LBOs Have More Effective Boards?" in J. Lerner and A. Gurung (eds.), *The Global Impact of Private Equity Report 2008: Globalization of Alternative Investments*, Working Papers Volume 1 (Davos, Switzerland: World Economic Forum, 2008), 65–84.

Director Characteristics

Boards have gotten more diverse over time. The Korn Ferry Survey reported that 85% of the boards they reviewed had at least one woman on the board compared to 10% in 1973. However, only 15% of all directors are female.[65] This is significantly higher than some European countries, such as Germany (5%) and France (8%), but well below countries such as Norway (39%) and Sweden (22%).[66] Adams and Ferreira found that some aspects of corporate governance improve when female representation on boards increases.[67] Female directors have better attendance than their male counterparts, and male attendance actually improves after the appointment of female directors. They also found that CEO turnover was more sensitive to the market performance of the company's stock and that directors receive more equity-based compensation in boards that were more gender-diverse.

There is evidence that good directors, ones whom the market reacts positively to when appointed, are often CEOs of other companies. In a study of Fortune 1000 firms Eliezer Fich found that not only was this generally the case but also it was particularly true for companies with greater growth opportunities.[68] There is also evidence that companies tend to appoint directors who are overly sympathetic to management. Cohen, Frazzini, and Malloy analyzed a database of former sell-side analysts who were subsequently appointed to boards they previously covered.[69] The analysts who became board members were far more likely to issue strong buy recommendations when they were covering the companies than their peers. However, the relative recommendations were poor. These findings support the belief that companies have a tendency to hire directors who are supportive of management and who are more cheerleaders than objective critics.

Companies that are more reliant on government work or work that can be influenced by lobbying tend to hire directors who have significant political or regulatory experience. There is evidence that directors tend to direct the companies whose boards they sit on to utilize services of their field. For example, Gunber, Malmendier, and Tate showed that when more commercial bankers were on the board, companies increased the size of their loans, whereas when investment bankers were more present on the board, companies utilized more outside financing.[70]

---

[65] 2009 Catalyst Census: Fortune 500 Women Board Directors.

[66] "Board Composition: Turning a Complex Issue into a Strategic Asset," Russell Reynolds Associates' Series, Issue 1, 2009.

[67] Renee Adams and Daniel Ferreira, "Women in the Boardroom and Their Impact on Governance," *Journal of Financial Economics* 94 (2009): 291–309.

[68] Eliezer Fich, "Are Some Outside Directors Better Than Others? Evidence from Director Appointments by Fortune 1000 Firms," *Journal of Business* 78, no. 5 (2005): 1943–1972.

[69] Lauren Cohen, Andrea Frazzini, and Christopher Mallor, "Hiring Cheerleaders: Board Appointments of Independent Directors," NBER Working Paper No. 14232, August 2008.

[70] Burak Gunber, Ulrike Malmendier, and Geoffrey Tate, "Financial Expertise of Directors," *Journal of Financial Economics* 88, no. 2 (2008): 323–354.

Director Compensation

The average board of director compensation for the companies in the S&P 500 index was $251,000.[71] As expected, this compensation varies with company size, with larger companies paying higher fees. When directors sit on committees that present greater time demands, their compensation is usually higher. However, a Korn Ferry Directors Survey showed that directors devote an average of 250 to 300 hours a year to their oversight duties. Using an average of 275 hours, this translates to an hourly rate of $913.

In the 1990s, while director retainer fees and meeting compensation remained relatively stable, stock option compensation grew significantly. In a study of over 200 firms from the Fortune 1000 that offered stock option compensation to directors, Fich and Shivdasani found that such compensation was more likely when boards were dominated by outside directors and when institutional equity ownership was high.[72] They also found that such plans were more likely to occur in high-growth companies.

Prestige of Directorships and Allocation of Director's Time

Due to the fact that some directors may sit on multiple boards, the question arises of how they allocate their time across the different boards. Masculis and Mobbs analyzed a large sample of 86,330 director years for 17,525 outside directors over the years 1997–2006.[73] They found that the reputation of a company was a key determinant n the allocation of director's time. They found that directors spend more time working on boards whose companies are larger and more prestigious compared to less prestigious assignments. When the prestige of an assignment rises due to external factors affecting the company, the directors allocate more of their time to that firm. When a firm declines, such as when it has a significant falloff in revenues or profitability, the directors may devote less time and may even resign. Thus reputational incentives are a key element in determining whether individuals accept and devote significant time to certain directorships. Once again, basic human nature can be a great guide to understanding human behavior.

Role of Social Ties in M&A Returns

In business and in life, sometimes it matters more who you know than what you know. Social connections can play a major role in career success. How about M&A returns? In an analysis of 539 acquisitions over the period 1999 and 2007 Ishii and Xuan showed that social ties between the directors and senior managers of acquiring and target firms

---

[71] Jeff Green and Hideki Suzuki, "Board of Director Compensation Hits Record $251,000 for 250 Hours," www.bloomberg.com/news/print/2013-05-30/board-director-pay-hits-record-251-000-… 6/9/2014.

[72] Eliezer Fich and Anil Shivdasani, "The Impact of Stock Option Compensation for Outside Directors on Firm Value," *Journal of Business* 78, no. 6 (2005): 2229–2254.

[73] Ronald Masculis and Shawn Mobbs, "Independent Director Incentives: Where Do Talented Directors Spend Their Limited Time and Energy," *Journal of Financial Economics* 111, no. 2 (February 2014): 406–429.

had a significant negative effect on acquirer returns and those of the combined entity.[74] These ties, though, did increase the likelihood that the target's CEO and more of the target's directors stayed on after the deal.

COCA-COLA'S PROPOSED ACQUISITION OF QUAKER OATS*

While it seems that many boards simply rubber-stamp M&As proposed by their CEOs, some boards have the foresight and the courage to stand up to the CEO and question proposed deals. This was the case when a $15.75 billion offer for Quaker Oats was proposed to Coca-Cola Company's board of directors in November 2001. Quaker Oats had a certain appeal to Coca-Cola because it included its popular Gatorade line, which might fit in well with Coke's other soft drink products. Gatorade commands more than 80% of the sports drink market, whereas Coke's own Powerade brand accounted for just over 10% of that market. The whole sports drink business had grown significantly; Powerade had a distant second position to the leader Gatorade, and Coke was having great difficulty gaining ground on the leader. Acquiring Gatorade through an acquisition of Quaker Oats could have been a quick solution to this problem. However, the acquisition also presented a problem because Coke most likely would have been forced by antitrust regulators to divest Powerade in order to have the deal approved.

Coke was not the first bidder for Quaker Oats. On November 1, 2000, Pepsi made an initial offer for Quaker following negotiations between Robert Enrico, Pepsi's CEO, and Robert Morrison, Quaker's CEO. However, after Quaker could not get Pepsi to agree on improved terms, including a stock collar provision, negotiations between Pepsi and Quaker broke down. Quaker was then in play, and other potential bidders, such as Coke and French food giant Group Danone, expressed interest in the U.S. food company. Both companies made competing bids, which featured improved terms over Pepsi's bid, yet Pepsi held fast and declined to exceed its prior offer. Coke's CEO assured Quaker Oats that he had been keeping his board apprised of the bid's progress, and had asked and received agreement from Quaker to exclusively negotiate with just Coke. Coke's CEO, Douglas Daft, however, did not count on the negative response of the market to the deal (see Figure A).[a] The board, however, was mindful of the market, and after a long meeting on November 21, 2000, they forced Daft to go back to Quaker Oats and inform them that Coke was pulling out of the negotiations. The market loved this, and the stock price immediately rose. Pepsi eventually acquired Quaker Oats in August 2001 for $13 billion.

There were some clear problems with the deal that Coke's board obviously paid attention to. As already noted, the market did not like the proposed acquisition, and it voiced its displeasure by dropping its valuation of Coke's stock. In the years before the Coke bid, the company had experienced problems with other failed acquisitions, and the spotlight was on its merger strategy. Right at the start, management faced an uphill battle. Another problem with the deal was that the acquisition would

---

[74] Joy Ishii and Yuhai Xuan, "Acquirer-Target Social Ties and Merger Outcomes," *Journal of Financial Economics* 112 (2014): 344–363.

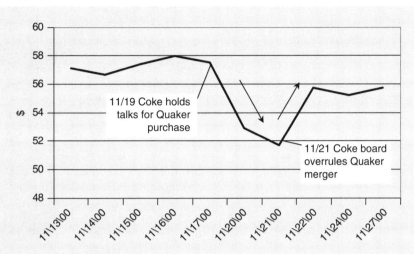

FIGURE A Coca-Cola Stock Price Response to Quaker Oats Bid. *Source*: Yahoo! Finance, http://finance.yahoo.com.

require Coke to be able to effectively manage the components of Quaker Oats' business that were outside of Coke's soft- and sports-drink business lines. These were Quaker's food brands, which included Captain Crunch cereals, Rice-A-Roni, and Aunt Jemima pancakes, as well as other snack products, such as rice cakes and granola bars. Some of Quaker's brands were impressive, but they were a little far afield from Coke's core business. Another problem with the deal was its defensive nature. Coke's bid was in response to Pepsi's original offer. Such defensive responses are not the best motive for a merger or acquisition.

One of the reasons why the Coke board stood up to this proposal lies in the nature of its board and their relationship with the CEO. Coke had a CEO, Roberto Goizueta, who was highly acclaimed. Unfortunately, after many successful years at the helm of the soft drink giant, Goizueta passed away in October 1997 at a relatively young age. He was succeeded by Douglas Ivester, who resigned at the end of 1999 and was replaced by Douglas Daft, who was well thought of but could not draw on the track record of success that Goizueta enjoyed. Perhaps if Goizueta had brought this deal to the board, they might have considered it more seriously. Nonetheless, there is little reason to believe that they would have ultimately approved it no matter who brought the deal because they considered it generally flawed.

Coke's board featured some leading business figures, including the renowned Warren Buffett, who is considered by many to be one of the market's shrewdest investors, as well as a new CEO who was looking to make a name for himself. This board, however, would have none of it. In 2006, Buffett announced he would step down from Coke's board, creating a void that would be hard to fill.

The board of directors is one of the last lines of defense against poorly conceived merger strategies. In order for it to work with maximum effectiveness, the board needs to be knowledgeable and strong-willed. However, it is not enough that a board be composed of individuals who are strong-willed and capable of standing

(continued)

> *(continued)*
>
> up to the management leaders of the company. Knowledge of the industry and the company's operations is also essential to being an effective director. Management, who runs the company on a day-to-day basis, should have a distinct advantage over board members who are engaged full-time in other activities, such as running their own companies, and have not invested nearly as much time as management in studying the company. However, there is a certain minimum level of knowledge that the board must have in order for it to function properly. When considering the commitment of billions of dollars in merger costs, the board needs to get whatever resources it needs to be able to effectively evaluate management's proposals. If this means retaining outside consultants to study the proposal in depth, then this should be done. This is sometimes difficult to do because the proposals may be time-sensitive and require a quick response. Nonetheless, the board must apply all of the necessary resources to reach an enlightened and impartial decision. The bigger the deal, the more work and research the board needs to do. However, in the case of Coke's offer for Quaker Oats, the board's studied response was clear and strong. In properly exercising their fiduciary responsibilities, they saved shareholders from a possibly costly acquisition.
>
> *Source: Patrick A. Gaughan, *Mergers: What Can Go Wrong and How to Prevent It* (Hoboken, NJ: John Wiley & Sons, 2005), 237–239.
>
> a Pepsi's Bid for Quaker Oats (B), Harvard Business School, 9-801-459, August 5, 2002.

REGULATORY STANDARDS FOR DIRECTORS

Both the SEC and the NYSE have enacted what are called "bright line" standards for defining director independence. They were conceptualized in the wake of Enron, and it took some time before they eventually came to affect public companies. The new rules require that a majority of directors and board members sitting on key board committees must be independent. They have certain specific tests that when applied bar certain people from being considered independent. For example, directors who have received more than $100,000 from a company over the prior three years may not be considered independent (the SEC limit is $60,000).[75] The NYSE has gone beyond such tests and focuses on more broadly defined "material" relationships that may be more subtle than what can be defined under direct compensation. However, even if a relationship is determined to be immaterial, the company still needs to provide shareholders with an explanation of why it believes it is immaterial so that shareholders can make their own judgment about the relationship.

---

[75] The compensation of family members is included in this total.

ANTITAKEOVER MEASURES AND BOARD CHARACTERISTICS

Do companies adopt antitakeover defenses to avoid the disciplinary pressure of the takeover market? Are certain types of boards more likely to adopt such defenses?

A study by Brickley, Terry, and Coles found that board compensation affected the likelihood that a company would adopt a poison pill defense.[76] The Brickley et al. study analyzed the role that the composition of the board might play in any negative reaction the market might have to the adoption of poison pills by 247 companies over the period 1984–1986. This was a period where prior research had shown that the negative market reaction to poison pills was the greatest. They found a statistically significant positive relation between the stock market's reaction to the adoption of poison pills and the percentage of the board accounted for by outside directors. The market's reaction was positive when the board was dominated by outsiders and negative when it was dominated by insider board members. This implies that the market tended to believe that when an outside-dominated board adopted a strong antitakeover defense like a poison pill, they did so to advance shareholder wealth. However, when an insider-dominated board took the same action, the market seemed to believe that they were doing this to entrench managers and insulate them from the disciplinary forces of the takeover market. The market was also saying that it believes that outside directors represent shareholder interests better than insider directors.

Masculis, Wang, and Xie looked at the impact of corporate governance on acquirer returns.[77] They found that companies that had several antitakeover defenses in place had significantly lower returns when they announced takeovers of other companies. This research lends support to the view that the market casts a dim eye on an acquisition strategy that is put forward by management that is insulated from market forces by antitakeover measures. The market may believe, with justification, that such managers are more likely to engage in value-destroying empire building.

[76] James A. Brickley, Jeffrey L. Terry, and Rory L. Coles, "Outside Directors and the Adoption of Poison Pills," *Journal of Financial Economics* 35 (1994): 371–390.
[77] Ronald W. Masculis, Cong Wang, and Fei Xie, "Corporate Governance and Acquirer Returns," *Journal of Finance* 62, no. 4 (August 2007): 1851–1889.

HOLLINGER INTERNATIONAL[*]

The 2004 probe of Hollinger International into what it referred to as a "corporate kleptocracy" was released at the end of summer 2004. The report, issued by a special committee of the Hollinger board of directors, found that the company's CEO, Conrad Black, and ex-president, David Radler, "siphoned off more than $400 million through aggressive looting of the publishing company."[a] Hollinger International is a publishing company that publishes various newspapers, including the *Chicago Sun-Times* and the *Jerusalem Post*. Black controlled Hollinger through a holding company he owned, Ravelston, which owned 78% of the stock of a Canadian company, Hollinger Inc., which in turn owned 68% of the voting shares in Hollinger International. Through his control of a 68% interest in Hollinger International, Black was able to effectively influence the board of directors.

One astounding finding of the report was that the total cash taken equaled "95.2% of Hollinger's entire adjusted net income during the period 1997–2003!"[b] The probe of the activities of Hollinger's CEO and ex-president was headed by former SEC chairman Richard Breeden and was filed with the federal courts and the SEC. Black and Radler engaged in lavish spending that included $24,950 for summer drinks, $3,530 for silverware for their corporate jet, which they put to regular personal use, thousands of dollars for handbags, tickets for the theater and opera, as well as very generous donations made by the company to charities and establishments favored by Black and his wife, columnist Barbara Black. The couple threw lavish dinner parties for friends, including Henry Kissinger, who was, coincidentally, on the board of directors. Birthday parties for Mrs. Black were thrown at the company's expense. One such party for 80 guests cost the company $42,870. Other examples of looting of the company were a 10-day vacation to Bora Bora at a cost of $250,000 and refurbishing work on Black's Rolls-Royce, which cost $90,000.[c] Black and Radler took compensation from the company in several ways, including $218 million in management fees that they derived over the period of 1997–2003. Management fees were paid to Ravelston, while Hollinger International also paid "noncompete" fees to other entities controlled by Ravelston. In addition, Hollinger sold newspaper businesses to entities controlled by Lord Black and his associates for below market values. These included the sale of the *Mammouth Times*, in Mammouth Lakes, California, which went for "$1 when there was a competing bid of $1.25 million."[d]

The report called the board and the audit committee's monitoring of payments such as these management fees "inept." The board of directors included some very prominent names in international diplomacy. Among its members was former secretary of state Henry Kissinger, as well as former assistant secretary of defense in the Reagan administration Richard Perle, and James Thompson, former governor of Illinois, who headed the company's audit committee. While such political figures may be world-renowned, it is not clear what special expertise they brought to the board of directors of a publishing company. Clearly, if one wanted to talk foreign affairs at a board meeting, this was probably a board that could have an enlightening discussion on such topics. If it was corporate oversight you were looking for, the track record of these directors was dismal at best. The report of the special committee particularly singled out Perle for "repeatedly breaching his fiduciary duties as a member of the executive committee of the board, by authorizing unfair related party transactions that enabled Black and Radler to evade disclosure to the audit committee. The report calls on Perle to return $3 million in compensation he received from the company."[e]

Hollinger's use of former political figures as directors of the corporation is not unusual. However, it is not clear what specialized expertise they bring to overseeing a corporation. Many have worked in the public sector much if not all of their careers, isolated from the pressures of running an organization to turn a profit. Often their leading expertise is to market themselves to the public to gain votes.

Hollinger's board also included friends and family members. For example, Lord Black's wife, Barbara Amiel Black, was on the board, along with family friend Marie-Josee Kravis, the wife of financier Henry Kravis of Kohlberg, Kravis & Roberts. Clearly, Black pushed the appointment of directors to an extreme. This became possible because Black controlled the votes required to place individuals on the board. The hand-picked board appeared to have been kept in the dark, as Black could keep them, but they did not go to any great lengths to remove themselves from any clouds that he surrounded them with. They were being taken care of very well by Black and Hollinger and did not seem to want to rock the boat. The following passage from the *Wall Street Journal* that describes one Hollinger board meeting is instructive of the atmosphere in Hollinger's board room:

> Gathered around a mahogany table in a boardroom high above Manhattan's Park Avenue, eight directors of the newspaper publisher, owner of the Chicago Sun-Times and the Jerusalem Post, dined on grilled tuna and chicken served on royal blue Bernardaud china, according to two attendees. Marie-Josee Kravis, wife of financier Henry Kravis, chatted about world affairs with Lord Black and A. Alfred Taubman, then chairman of Sotheby's. Turning to business, the board rapidly approved a series of transactions, according to the minutes and a report later commissioned by Hollinger. The board awarded a private company, controlled by Lord Black, $38 million in "management fees" as part of a move by Lord Black's team to essentially outsource the company's management to itself. It agreed to sell two profitable community newspapers to another private company controlled by Lord Black and Hollinger executives for $1 apiece. The board also gave Lord Black and his colleagues a cut of profits from a Hollinger Internet unit. Finally, the directors gave themselves a raise. The meeting lasted about an hour and a half, according to minutes and two directors who were present.[f]

One lesson we can learn from the Hollinger scandal is that a board should not be too close to the CEO, and definitely should not be picked by the CEO. The board needs to be somewhat at arm's length from those whom they will be monitoring. If they are indebted to the CEO, then how objective will they be in pursuing the interests of shareholders? This lesson, however, flies in the face of the recent trend of activist hedge fund managers who seek to place their own hand-picked members on target boards who would, presumably, represent their interests of the hedge fund and not necessarily other shareholders.

*Source: Patrick A. Gaughan, *Mergers: What Can Go Wrong and How to Prevent It* (Hoboken, NJ: John Wiley & Sons, 2005), 225–227.

(*continued*)

(*continued*)

[a] Mark Heinzl and Christopher J. Chipello, "Report Slams Hollinger's Black for Corporate Kleptocracy," *Wall Street Journal*, September 1, 2004, 1.

[b] Ibid.

[c] Geraldine Fabricant, "Hollinger Files Stinging Report on Ex-Officials," *New York Times*, September 1, 2004, 1.

[d] Ibid.

[e] Mark Heinzl and Christopher J. Chipello, "Report Slams Hollinger's Black for Corporate Kleptocracy," *Wall Street Journal*, September 1, 2004, 1.

[f] Robert Frank and Elena Cherney, "Lord Black's Board: A-List Cast Played Acquiescent Role," *Wall Street Journal*, September 27, 2004, 1.

DISCIPLINARY TAKEOVERS, COMPANY PERFORMANCE, CEOS, AND BOARDS

The board of directors, as fiduciaries of shareholders, monitor the performance of the company and management, including the CEO. This is the internal process we have referred to earlier. When this process fails to yield acceptable results, external forces may come into play. This is often done through disciplinary takeovers of poorly performing companies. Kini, Kracaw, and Mian analyzed a sample of 244 tender offers and looked at the effects that these hostile bids had on CEO and director turnover.[78] They found an inverse relationship between posttakeover CEO turnover and pretakeover performance. Companies that yielded poor performance prior to the takeover were more likely to have their CEO replaced. However, this finding was not substantiated in certain situations. It was the case when the companies had insider-dominated boards but not the case when the boards were dominated by outside directors. This finding seems to imply that when the board was composed mainly of outsiders, the problem was not the CEO; otherwise, the outsiders on the board would have already changed the CEO.

The Kini, Kracaw, and Mian study also found that board composition tended to be changed following disciplinary takeovers. Boards that were previously dominated by insiders were changed and the number of insiders reduced. This implies that the bidders identified the composition of the board, and the large number of insiders, as a potential source of problems the company may have had. In making these changes, the takeover market altered board composition. However, this is an expensive way of making such changes.

There is some evidence that the effect of disciplinary takeovers is greatest in more active takeover markets. Mikkelson and Partch found a greater rate of CEO, president, and board chair turnover for companies that were performing poorly in an active takeover market relative to a less active takeover market.[79] Specifically, they found that

---

[78] Omesh Kini, William Kracaw, and Shehzad Mian, "Corporate Takeovers, Firm Performance and Board Composition," *Journal of Corporate Finance* 1 (1995): 383–412.

[79] Wayne H. Mikkelson and M. Megan Partch, "The Decline of Takeovers and Disciplinary Managerial Turnover," *Journal of Financial Economics* 44 (1997): 205–228.

33% of the companies in the "poor performer" sample experienced complete turnover of the CEO, president, and board chair during the 1984–1986 time period, which were years within the fourth merger wave. This was almost double the 17% rate they found for comparable performing companies during the less active 1989–1993 time period. Takeovers can serve an important role in eliminating poor managers. It is important to note that this can take place even if the company is not taken over. Directors are aware of the intensity of the takeover market and some will act before the company actually receives an unwanted bid. However, this study implies that they may monitor and change the CEO more aggressively in an active takeover market. This has been confirmed by other research that shows that management turnover is greater when companies are actually taken over.[80] The threat of a takeover alone can bring about turnover of top management.[81] This implies that active takeover markets can be good for corporate governance. Conversely, it also implies that a sluggish takeover market may not be best for shareholders interested in improving corporate governance.

 ## MERGER STRATEGY AND CORPORATE GOVERNANCE

Having discussed corporate governance in this chapter, we will focus on the relationship between corporate governance and merger strategy. We will try to determine whether better corporate governance means that companies will carry out more or fewer deals. How does the quality of corporate governance affect the types of deals that are done and the shareholders' returns that these transactions generate? These are the issues that we will focus on for the rest of this chapter.

 ## CEO COMPENSATION AND M&A PROGRAMS

Larger companies have higher revenues and greater assets, and they also have higher costs. Part of these costs is management compensation and CEO compensation in particular. Therefore, one of the ways CEOs of companies can get paid more is to run larger companies. They can do that by finding a position managing a large company or by converting their current corporation into a larger one through M&A. It is this latter motive, and the link between CEO compensation and M&A programs, that we want to explore.

Hallock and Torok examined the compensation packages of more than 2,300 CEOs of publicly traded companies of various different sizes. They found out that for every 1% increase in company size, CEO compensation went up by one-third of 1%.[82] Stated alternatively, for every 10% increase in company size, CEO compensation increases by approximately 3%. Another study of the largest 1,000 U.S. companies by Steven Hall & Partners showed that the median 2005 CEO compensation at the top 27 companies in

[80] K. J. Martin and J. J. McConnell, "Corporate Performance, Corporate Takeovers, and Management Turnover," *Journal of Finance* 46 (1991) 671–687.

[81] David J. Denis and Diane K. Denis, "Ownership Structure and Top Management Turnover," *Journal of Financial Economics* 45 (1997): 193–222.

[82] Kevin F. Hallock, "The Relationship between Company Size and CEO Pay," *Workspan*, February 2011.

their sample, $16.8 million, was five times greater than the $3.2 million median compensation of the CEOs at the smallest quintile.[83] Thus, CEOs have a great incentive to use M&A to make their companies bigger and their paycheck larger. It is up to the boards to make sure that CEOs are pursuing M&A programs for the financial gain of the shareholders and not just for their own personal gain.

 ## DO BOARDS REWARD CEOS FOR INITIATING ACQUISITIONS AND MERGERS?

It is well known that many deals do not fare well; one wonders why boards are so willing to approve M&A proposals. Ironically, there is even evidence that boards actually encourage CEOs to pursue such deals. A study was conducted by Grinstein and Hribar of 327 large M&As that occurred during the fifth merger wave period, 1993–1999.[84] They examined proxy statements that broke down CEO compensation into individual components, with an eye toward identifying which companies attributed part of the CEO's compensation to his ability to complete M&As. They found that in 39% of cases they considered, the compensation committee cited completion of a deal as the reason they provided certain compensation. In other instances companies awarded bonuses following deals even though they did not specify that the bonuses were for deals. This implies that the real percentage of boards that gave bonuses for mergers was even higher than the 39% that overtly cited this as a reason.

Consistent with much other research in M&A, Grinstein and Hribar noted that bidder announcement period returns were negative for the companies included in their sample. However, they found that the negative reaction was greatest in cases when the CEOs had the greatest corporate power as reflected by the CEO also being head of the board of directors. The market often seems to not only dislike acquisitions but also really dislike deals done by CEOs whose power is less constrained by the board of directors. The market seems to prefer more power limitations on the CEO and will penalize companies less for doing acquisitions when they know that there is a group of directors who are potentially capable of preventing the CEO from doing deals that might not be in the best interest of the company. Whether the board actually does this is another issue.

Grinstein and Hribar found not only that the market reacted more negatively to deals done by CEOs with more power, but also that managers of companies who had more power got higher bonuses and tended to do bigger deals. Their power was less checked and they seemed to personally gain from this situation—at the expense of shareholders.

Another study also found that companies that were active in M&A paid higher compensation to their managers. Schmidt and Fowler analyzed a sample of 127 companies, of which 41 were bidders that used tender offers to make acquisitions, 51 were

[83] "By the Numbers: Dramatic Differences in CEO Pay by Company Size, Steven Hall & Partners Survey Shows," *BusinessWire*, November 3, 2006.
[84] Yaniv Grinstein and Paul Hribar, "CEO Compensation and Incentives: Evidence from M&A Bonuses," *Journal of Financial Economics* 73, no. 1 (July 2004): 119–143.

nontender offer acquirers, and 35 were control firms.[85] They found that both bidders and acquirers showed higher managerial compensation than the control group.

These studies show that boards tend to pay managers of companies that are active in M&A greater compensation. When one considers the questionable track record of many M&As, we have to conclude that boards need to rethink such M&A-based incentives.

CEO COMPENSATION AND DIVERSIFICATION STRATEGIES

In Chapter 4 we saw that diversification strategies generally cause the shareholders of companies pursuing such strategies to lose value. There are some examples of diversified companies, such as GE, who generated significant gains for shareholders. In addition, we have also discussed in Chapter 4 the fact that not all diversifications are the same, with related diversifications yielding better performance than unrelated diversifying deals. In spite of the dubious track record of diversifications, it is surprising to see that companies pay their CEOs a diversification premium—meaning that research has shown the CEOs of diversified companies earn on average 13% more than CEOs of companies that operate in only one line of business. We have already noted that Malmendier and Tate found that overconfident CEOs are more likely to pursue value-destroying deals and, in particular, diversification strategies.[86] There is some evidence that eventually diversification strategies lead to lower CEO compensation, but the process of correcting the CEO compensation level seems to be slow.[87] Boards seem to be slow to stop diversification deals recommended by CEOs and penalize them after the fact in the form of lower compensation.

AGENCY COSTS AND DIVERSIFICATION STRATEGIES

Agency costs may help explain the tendency of some CEOs and their companies to engage in diversifying M&As. Management may be pursuing a merger strategy that generates gains for themselves, even though such a strategy may not be the one that is in the best interest of shareholders. That is, the agents of the owners, the managers, derive private benefits that are greater than their own private costs from doing these deals. Diversifying deals may provide managers greater prestige and what economists call "psychic income." They may also generate other direct monetary gains, such as higher compensation that is paid to management of larger companies. Denis, Denis, and Sarin analyzed a sample of 933 firms starting in 1984.[88] They examined the degree of ownership held by managers and related this to the tendency of managers with different

[85] Dennis R. Schmidt and Karen L. Fowler, "Post-Acquisitions Financial Performance and Executive Compensation," *Strategic Management Journal* 11, no. 7 (November/December 1990): 559–569.

[86] Ulrike Malmendier and Geoffrey Tate, "Who Makes Acquisitions? CEO Overconfidence and the Market's Reaction," *Journal of Financial Economics* 89 (2008): 20–43.

[87] Nancy L. Rose and Andrea Shepard, "Firm Diversification and CEO Compensation: Managerial Ability or Executive Entrenchment," *Rand Journal of Economics* 28, no. 3 (Autumn 1997): 489–514.

[88] David J. Denis, Diane K. Denis, and Atulya Sarin, "Agency Problems, Equity Ownership and Corporate Diversification," *Journal of Finance* 52, no. 1 (March 1997): 135–160.

percentages of equity ownership to engage in diversifying deals, which research has shown often tend to reduce shareholder value. They found that diversification, moving the company into other business segments, was more likely to reduce shareholder values when CEO ownership was lower (e.g., less than 5% of the outstanding shares). Such deals, however, had a mild positive effect when the CEO's ownership shares were greater than 5%. Similar effects were found when they looked at the combined share percentages owned by overall management. They also found that there was a strong relation between decreases in diversification and external control threats. Almost one in five of the decreases in diversification, such as selling off diversified divisions, was preceded by a takeover bid. In other words, decreases in diversification were associated with market pressure. This implies that often management may not be willing to sell off prior acquisitions that reduced shareholder value until they were faced with an outside bidder that may be taking advantage of reduced stock values relative to the underlying value of the divisions if they were sold separately on the market. If the diversification strategy reduced value, it made the company vulnerable to a takeover, and when the takeover threats materialized, management financially responded by refocusing.

The agency costs hypothesis can partially explain the tendency of some companies to engage in diversifying deals. This hypothesis is also consistent with the reaction of management to outside threats. However, we do not have to rely just on outside market forces to limit these costs. Boards are in a good position to prevent deals that will reduce shareholder value. Directors need to be aware of the track record of certain types of deals and make sure that management and the CEO do not get to complete them. They also need to be aware of the company's own track record of deals. Some companies, such as AT&T and Daimler, have a very poor M&A track record. Boards of such companies need to be especially wary.

 ## INTERESTS OF DIRECTORS AND M&AS

Directors are fiduciaries for shareholders, and as such they have the responsibility to oversee the management and direction of the company so that the goals of shareholder wealth maximization are pursued. However, it would be naive for us to ignore the fact that directors are human and also consider what is in their own interests. How are directors affected by takeovers? Directors of target companies are usually not retained after the takeover by a company. The bidding company already has a board of directors, and there is usually no place or need for the target's directors. Therefore, the target directors know that the takeover will normally bring an end to their directorships. This may or may not be an important issue to them—depending on their own personal circumstances.

The personal, adverse financial impact on a target director as a result of approving a merger or hostile takeover has been documented in a study by Harford, who considered 1,091 directors of Fortune 1000 companies over the period 1988–1991.[89] As expected,

---

[89] Jarrad Harford, "Takeover Bids and Target Director Incentives: The Impact of a Bid on Director's Wealth and Board Seats," *Journal of Financial Economics* 69, no. 1 (July 2003): 51–83.

he remarked that directors of target companies were rarely retained after the merger or acquisition. However, what was especially interesting was the fact that such directors were less likely to get another director's post in the future. This is the case for both inside and outside directors. Harford also found that directors of poorly performing companies whose companies were, nonetheless, able to be acquired do not seem to suffer a reduced frequency of future directorships. Conversely, directors of poorly performing companies that mounted antitakeover defenses that successfully prevented takeovers were less likely to be directors of companies in the future. These findings are remarkable as they imply that the market for directors seems to be pretty efficient in weeding out those directors who may place their own interests ahead of those of shareholders.

Investment Bankers and Directors

Sometimes companies ask investment bankers to serve on their boards. Such individuals can bring a wealth of experience to a board, although they may also bring with them some conflicts, which we will discuss shortly. With respect to takeovers, however, Huang, Jiang, Lie, and Yang found that having investment bankers (IBs) on the board may yield various financial benefits.[90] In an analysis of 41,393 firm-year observations over the period 1998–2008 they found a positive relation between having IBs on the board and the probability of doing M&A. They also found that when such companies do M&As they get 0.8% higher abnormal announcement period returns. This effect was higher the larger the deal. Huang et al. then went on to try to determine the source of the higher returns. They found that acquirers with IBs on their boards tended to pay lower takeover premiums in deals involving larger companies. They also paid lower advisory fees. Last but not least, they found that these IB-director companies tended to have better operating performance than companies without IB directors. The study makes a good case for companies, especially ones that are considering being active in M&A, having investment bankers on the board.

While Huang et al.'s research paints IB directors in a very favorable light, other research does not. Guner, Malmendier, and Tate assembled a large dataset of 32,943 "director-years" covering the period 1998–2001.[91] They found that when commercial bankers (CBs) join boards, the companies utilized more external capital. This increase did not turn out to be fruitful as they showed that it involved companies with good credit, and therefore a good ability to borrow, but, unfortunately, the firms had poor investment opportunities. They also noticed that companies seem to ask CBs to join boards when they want to borrow more and the CBs tend to leave the boards sometime after the financing.

When investment bankers joined the boards, the companies did more bond offerings and engaged in poorer acquisitions. Guner et al. compared M&A announced returns over a relatively long window of 36 months before and after the announcement. They

---

[90] Qianqian Huang, Feng Jiang, Erik Lie, and Ke Yang "The role of investment banker directors in M&A: Can experts help?" *Journal of Financial Economics* 112, No. 2 (May 2014): 269–286.
[91] A. Burak Guner, Ulrike Malmendier, and Geoffrey Tate, "Financial Expertise of Directors," *Journal of Financial Economics* 88 (2008): 323–354.

found firms with IBs showed clearly negative returns following the announcement, while those without IBs showed the opposite. Thus, it seems the effects of IBs will vary on a case-by-cases basis, which may explain the different results from these studies, which used different samples.

MANAGERIAL COMPENSATION AND FIRM SIZE

It has long been postulated by economists that managers run companies in a manner that is more consistent with revenue maximization than profit maximization.[92] This is based on the purported relationship between managerial compensation and firm size. The optimal firm size may be less than that which would maximize revenues. The reason why researchers theorize that management would want to have a larger than optimal company is the positive relationship between firm size and managerial compensation. Senior management of larger companies tends to earn more than their smaller corporate counterparts.[93] Lambert, Larcker, and Weigelt have shown that this positive association exists for most major levels of management:

- Corporate CEO: the manager with the greatest authority in the company
- Group CEO: a manager who has authority for various different subgroups within the overall corporation
- Subgroup CEO: senior manager of one of the individual subgroups
- Divisional CEO: senior manager of a division or corporate unit
- Plant manager: senior manager of a cost center[94]

The Lambert et al. results for these broad categories of management may help explain why there may not be as much managerial resistance to the recommendations of very senior management who advocate transactions that result in greater corporate size but not necessarily greater profitability. Their findings are not unique to this field of research. In general, research in this area tends to show that there is a good relationship between company size and executive compensation but a poor one between compensation and corporate performance.[95]

CORPORATE CONTROL DECISIONS AND THEIR SHAREHOLDER WEALTH EFFECTS

Does the nature of management's compensation agreements affect the likelihood that managers will pursue M&As? If this is the case, then does the market react differently when these deals are pursued by managers who receive a significant percentage of their

---

[92] William Baumol, *Business Behavior: Value and Growth* (New York: McMillan, 1959), 46.

[93] Sidney Finkelstein and Donald Hambrick, "Chief Executive Compensation: A Study of the Intersection of Markets and Political Processes," *Strategic Management Journal* 10 (1989): 121–134.

[94] Richard A. Lambert, David F. Larcker, and Keith Weigelt, "How Sensitive Is Executive Compensation to Organizational Size?" *Strategic Management Journal* 12, no. 5 (July 1991): 395–402.

[95] Henry L. Tosi and Luis R. Gomez-Mejia, "The Decoupling of CEO Pay and Performance: An Agency Theory Perspective," *Administrative Science Quarterly* 34 (1989): 169–189.

compensation from equity-based components? Dutta, Dutta, and Raman analyzed a sample of 1,719 acquisitions made by U.S. companies over the period 1993–1998.[96] This was a period of large increases in stock option–based compensation for senior executives. Therefore, it is an excellent time period to test market reactions as a function of the extent to which the managers pursing the deals will gain in a similar manner to shareholders. If the deals are value-reducing to shareholders, then managers would stand to personally lose from such deals. They found that companies with managers having high equity-based compensation tended to receive positive stock market responses to the announcement of their acquisitions, while those with lower equity-based manager compensation tended to receive negative reactions. The market seemed to assume that given the financial impact that these deals would have on the equity holdings of managers, they would not pursue them if they were not wealth-enhancing for shareholders.

Dutta et al. also looked at the size of the takeover premium paid by acquiring firms. When managers had their own wealth at risk, due to the impact that a premium may have on their equity-based compensation, were the premiums they offered different? Interestingly, they found that companies with higher equity-based compensation tended to pay lower premiums. Once again, when managers are playing with their own money, to some extent, they are more frugal with exchanging premiums, whereas when they are playing with "house money"—shareholder wealth—they will tend to be more generous and more liberally give away corporate wealth. Dutta et al. also found that high equity-based compensation managers tended to acquire targets with higher growth opportunities than their lower equity-based counterparts did. That is, they tended to acquire companies with a greater likelihood of generating equity-based gains for both themselves and shareholders. Moreover, they found that lower equity-based compensation managers/companies significantly underperformed their higher equity-based counterparts.

The Dutta et al. study implies that if management's interests are aligned with shareholders', they tend to do better deals and pay less. It also seems to be reasonable to assume that such managers may try harder to pursue value-increasing deals. The market is aware of this and reacts more positively when such managers announce deals but penalizes acquiring shareholders when they, and their board of directors, allow managers to push deals when they do not have their own compensation at risk.

Moeller analyzed the *target* takeover premiums for a sample of 373 deals over the period of 1990–1999.[97] Consistent with the general conclusions from Dutta et al., but now applied to the target as opposed to the bidder, Moeller found that targets that are highly controlled by certain shareholders received lower takeover premiums. On the other hand, targets that had more outside directors and outside blockholders tended to receive higher premiums. He found that targets with entrenched CEOs received lower premiums. It is important to note, however, that these results precede the period when

---

[96] Sanip Dutta, Mai Iskandar-Dutta, and Kartik Raman, "Executive Compensation and Corporate Acquisition Decisions," *Journal of Finance* 56, no. 6 (December 2001): 2299–2336.

[97] Thomas Moeller, "Let's Make a Deal! How Shareholder Control Impacts Merger Payoffs," *Journal of Financial Economics* 76, no. 1 (April 2005): 167–190.

activist hedge funds became a more significant factor in the takeover market. It is reasonable to conclude that such findings *may* not apply to cases where they amass stock in a target and seek to have the target sold to the highest bidder.

 ## DOES BETTER CORPORATE GOVERNANCE INCREASE FIRM VALUE?

We have already answered the foregoing question in a piecemeal fashion by looking at specific governance issues, such as director independence, and noted that research finds a clear linkage between better governance and firm value. Many of these studies use short-term-oriented event studies to ascertain the effects of specific governance elements. We have already discussed how such studies can be quite telling when it comes to determining long-term effects. However, the previously discussed study by Gomers, Ishii, and Metrick used a governance index (G) to test the shareholder wealth effects of a collection of governance factors.[98] They created their index using 24 corporate governance measures for 1,500 large companies over the 1990s. The data were culled from the Investor Responsibility Research Center's database of corporate charter provisions. Among these are antigreenmail and classified board provision, poison pills, golden parachutes, and many others. They found that corporate governance was closely related to value of firms as measured by Tobin's q. The way they constructed their index, lower G values were indicative of better governance. Not only did lower G values result in higher qs, but also the relationship got significantly stronger as the researchers traced their sample over the 1990s. They found that at the beginning of the decade, a one-point increase in G was associated with a 2.2% decrease in q values. By the end of the 1990s, a one-point increase in G was associated with an 11.4% decrease in q values. This implies that not only is corporate governance inextricably linked to firm values but also the relationship has become stronger over time.

Masulis, Wang, and Xie analyzed a large sample of 3,333 competed acquisitions over the period of 1990–2003. They found that companies that had more antitakeover measures in place were more likely to conduct value-destroying acquisitions.[99] They concluded that these results support the hypothesis that managers of companies with more antitakeover defenses in place tend to indulge in empire building since they are more insulated from the pressures of the market for corporate control that otherwise might force them to be more "honest."

In another approach to measuring the relationship between corporate governance and equity returns, the Corporate Library compiled three hypothetical portfolios that had different degrees of strict corporate governance.[100] They compared these greater

[98] Paul Gomers, Joy Ishii, and Andrew Metrick, "Corporate Governance and Equity Prices," *Quarterly Journal of Economics* 118, no. 1 (February 2003): 107–155.

[99] Ronald Masulis, Cong Wang, and Fei Xie, "Corporate Governance and Acquirer Returns," *Journal of Finance* 62, no. 4 (August 2007): 1851–1875.

[100] Kimberly Gladman, "The Corporate Library's Governance Ratings and Equity Returns," Corporate Library, Portland, Maine, 2010.

corporate governance portfolios with the market as measured by the Russell 1000. Over the study period, July 2003–January 2010, the various corporate governance portfolios outperformed the market, with the portfolio with the strictest governance yielding an additional 74 basis points on an industry-weighted basis relative to the market.

CORPORATE GOVERNANCE AND COMPETITION

Theoretically, in highly competitive markets, "managerial slack" will result in lower returns and competitive forces will bring about changes to move a company toward more optimal performance. However, we all know that markets are far from perfect. Indeed, Federal Reserve chairman Alan Greenspan believed that market forces would pressure financial institutions to act in their own long-term best interests, and this belief in market forces and a *laissez faire* approach to financial regulation clearly backfired, leading to the recent subprime crisis. Giroud and Mueller analyzed the role of industry competition and corporate governance by examining the impact of the adoption of business combination laws on operating performance of companies after the passage of these laws.[101] They found that operating performance declined in noncompetitive industries but not in competitive ones. They noted that input costs, wages, and overhead all increased after the passage of these laws in noncompetitive industries but not in competitive ones. Interestingly, the market seems to correctly anticipate the true effects. When the passage of the laws was announced, share values of the companies in noncompetitive industries declined, while that was not the case in competitive ones.

EXECUTIVE COMPENSATION AND POSTACQUISITION PERFORMANCE

Is the compensation of senior management affected by the success or failure of acquisition programs? For companies that pursue large-volume acquisition programs, with M&As being an integral part of their growth strategy, linking managerial compensation to the success of those deals makes good sense. Schmidt and Fowler analyzed a sample of 127 companies, of which 41 were bidders that used tender offers to make acquisitions, 51 were nontender offer acquirers, and 35 were control firms.[102] Consistent with research previously discussed, bidder companies, those that would more likely be involved in initiating hostile takeovers, showed a significant decrease in postacquisition shareholder returns. This was not the case for acquirers who did not use tender offers, as well as for the control group. Also interesting from a corporate governance perspective was that both bidders and acquirers showed higher managerial compensation than the control group. Takeovers pay "dividends" for management in the form of higher compensation, even though they may generate losses for shareholders of those companies

---

[101] Xavier Giroud and Holger M. Mueller, "Does Corporate Governance Matter in Competitive Industries?" *Journal of Financial Economics* 95, no. 3 (March 2010): 312–331.
[102] Dennis R. Schmidt and Karen L. Fowler, "Post-Acquisitions Financial Performance and Executive Compensation," *Strategic Management Journal* 11, no. 7 (November/December 1990): 559–569.

that use tender offers and hostile takeovers to pursue the acquisition strategy. Takeovers may enhance the personal wealth of managers, but they may not be in the interests of shareholders. It is for this reason that boards have to be extra diligent when overseeing managers who may be acquisition-minded. There is greater risk of shareholder losses and managers, in effect, gaining at shareholder expense. For this reason, the board needs to make extra sure the deals will truly maximize shareholder wealth and not just provide financial and psychic income for managers.

 ## MERGERS OF EQUALS AND CORPORATE GOVERNANCE

In mergers of equals, two companies combine in a friendly deal that is the product of extensive negotiations between the management teams of both companies and especially between the CEOs of both firms. Research shows that bidders (normally the larger of the two companies) do better in mergers of equals, while targets do worse when compared with more traditional M&As. This was the case in a study by Wulf, who showed that bidder shareholders enjoyed more of the gains in these types of takeovers.[103] She pointed to the negotiation process between the management and directors of the respective companies as being an important factor that explains why mergers-of-equals deals have different relative financial effects for target and bidder shareholders.[104] Wulf found that the abnormal returns that target shareholders received were lower when target directors received equal or even greater control of the combined entity! This result raises corporate governance concerns. Are target directors, fiduciaries for target shareholders, trading off returns for their shareholders just so they can gain positions in and control of the combined entity? We have to also acknowledge that such positions come with compensation that is important to these directors. If it were not important they would be serving for free, and that is not consistent with the way the corporate world is overseen.

Another very interesting finding of the Wulf study, and one that has important ramifications for corporate governance, is that shared corporate governance was more common for larger and more poorly performing target companies and ones that were in industries that were undergoing restructuring. CEOs of target companies that may not have been doing well or that are in industries that are consolidating may pursue mergers of equals so as to prevent a bid that might not provide them with any continued control. They may see a friendly merger-of-equals deal as their best option, even though it may be self-serving and not in the best interests of shareholders.

---

[103] Julie Wulf, "Do CEOs in Mergers Trade Power for Premiums? Evidence from Mergers of Equals," *Journal of Law, Economics and Organization* 20, no. 1 (Spring 2004): 60–101.
[104] Ibid.

WORLDCOM: GOOD MERGER PLAN GONE OUT OF CONTROL*

WorldCom is an excellent example of a good M&A idea that was pushed too far and ended up killing the company that was built through such mergers. Mergers enabled the company to grow to a size where it could compete effectively with the largest telecommunications companies in the U.S. market. At one time WorldCom was one of the better M&A success stories. However, this great story of corporate growth all came to a crashing end.

WorldCom's M&A History

WorldCom traces its roots to a small telecommunications reseller called LDDS. The telecom resale business grew in the wake of the breakup of AT&T, which allowed other companies to come in and compete with the venerable telecom giant. At that time, AT&T offered price breaks for bulk buying of minutes on the AT&T long-distance network. Companies, including many small firms, would commit to buying bulk minutes from AT&T and then passing along some of the discount that they would receive to customers they would solicit. These customers would be able to receive lower rates than they might get on their own. As a result, a whole industry of resellers grew. However, such companies were limited in the profit opportunities they would enjoy as they would have to incur switching and access costs at both the origination and end of a call. The reseller industry eventually grew into subgroups, switchless and switch resellers, as some of the resellers purchased their own switches so that they could avoid some of the costs they would incur going to and from the long-distance network. The industry grew through M&As, and one of the companies that used this method to grow was a Mississippi-based reseller—LDDS Communications. The head of that company was Bernie Ebbers, who was far from being a major figure in the deal-making business.

The idea for what would become WorldCom can be traced back to 1983, when Ebbers and a few friends met at a diner in Hattiesburg, Mississippi, to discuss the concept of forming a long-distance company now that the breakup of AT&T was moving toward reality. Ebbers was initially an investor in the business, but he took the reins when the company began to perform poorly. Within six months he took this losing operation and moved it to profitability. In doing so he showed that he had the management skills to run a small business efficiently. Years later he would demonstrate that these same management skills could not be translated to a multibillion-dollar telecommunications business. Ebbers would show that he could very effectively build a large company through M&As. However, when it came to running such an enterprise profitably, he failed.

The business went on to grow, and in 1989 it went public through an acquisition with the already public Advantage Companies. As a result of this deal, LDDS now had operations in 11 different states—mainly in the South and Midwest of the United States. The next major step in LDDS's history was a 1993 three-way deal in which LDDS would merge with Metromedia Communications and Resurgens Communications Group. Each of these companies was a full-service

(continued)

(*continued*)

long-distance firm. Ebbers had established momentum in his growth-through-M&As strategy, and he would not be slowed. LDDS was still a small company compared with giants such as AT&T and MCI. However, there was no denying the company's meteoric growth path. Ebbers continued on this path when on the last day of 1994 he completed the acquisition of IDB Communications Corp., and on January 5, 1995, the acquisition of the WilTel Network Services took place. The IDB deal moved LDDS more clearly into the international telecommunications market as that company had more than 200 operating agreements in foreign countries. WilTel operated a national digital fiber-optic network and was one of only four companies in the United States to do so. Using this network, LDDS would be able to transfer some of its traffic and save outside network costs. With these deals LDDS then changed its name to WorldCom, as it considered itself a major U.S. telecommunications company but also a presence in the world telecom market. M&A had now helped the company continue with its exponential growth, as shown in Figures A through C.

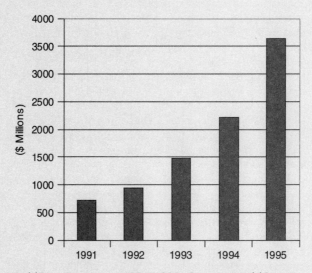

FIGURE A WorldCom Revenues: 1991–1995. *Source*: WorldCom Annual Report.

In December 1996, WorldCom completed its first megamerger when it merged with MFS Communications in a deal that was valued at approximately $14 billion. This deal brought several valuable capabilities to WorldCom. For one, MFS had various local networks throughout the United States as well as in Europe. For another, the deal brought with it UUNet, which was a major Internet service provider, thus expanding the package of services that WorldCom could offer customers. However, Ebbers was not content to sit on his laurels. He was determined to make WorldCom an industry leader. He continued in 1997 to seek out other merger partners to help him fulfill this dream.

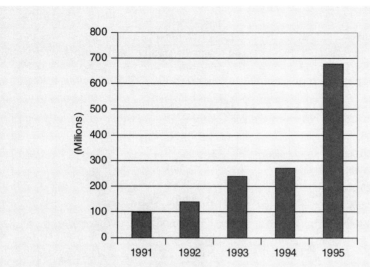

FIGURE B   WorldCom Operating Income. *Source*: WorldCom Annual Report.

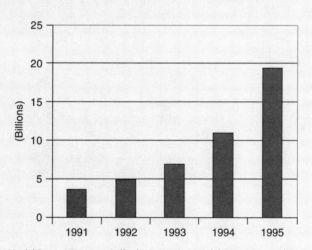

FIGURE C   WorldCom Minutes Billed. *Source*: WorldCom Annual Report.

At the beginning of 1998, WorldCom completed three more deals. They were the mergers with BrooksFiber, a company in the local exchange business, Compuserve, and ANS Communications Inc. Compuserve was acquired from H&R Block. This sale by H&R Block was the undoing of a failed prior deal as H&R did not derive significant benefits from its ownership of Compuserve. However, in the fall of 1998, WorldCom announced a deal that would vault the company to a leadership position in the world telecommunications business. In September 1998, WorldCom merged with MCI in a transaction valued at $40 billion. By 1999, the company would have revenues of over $37 billion—with the growth coming from M&As as opposed to

(*continued*)

(continued)

organic processes. As rapidly as the company was growing in the early 1990s, the end of the decade made that progress seem modest (see Figure D). However, while the revenue growth over the period 1995–1998 was impressive, profits were not, although they appeared to move in the right direction in 1999 (see Figure E).

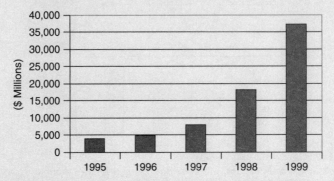

FIGURE D   WorldCom Revenues, 1995–1999. *Source*: WorldCom Annual Report, 2000.

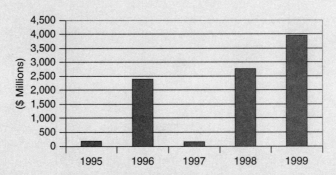

FIGURE E   WorldCom Net Income, 1995–1999. *Source*: WorldCom Annual Report, 2000.

The MCI deal put WorldCom on a new level. However, Ebbers was not satisfied to stay put. His expertise was doing deals, and he sought out even more deals. He reached an agreement to acquire Sprint in a $155 billion stock transaction. However, right away antitrust concerns began to materialize. The market was skeptical that the Justice Department would approve the acquisition, and this skepticism proved warranted as in July 2000 the Justice Department stopped the deal. By this time, however, the stock had already begun the slide from which it would never recover until the company had to file for bankruptcy. Amazingly, Ebbers kept right on doing deals. In July 2001, WorldCom announced that it was acquiring Intermedia Communications.

While Ebbers seemed to keep trying to grow the company through deals virtually right up to the end of his tenure with the company, an irreversible slide had now begun (see Figure F). The Securities and Exchange Commission (SEC), fresh from dealing with major accounting frauds, such as Enron and Adelphia, now began an investigation into WorldCom's accounting practices. It questioned the company's revenue recognition and other accounting practices. It appeared that many of the revenues and profits that the company was booking were fictitious. Ebbers was forced to resign from the company on April 30, 2002. The demise of WorldCom resulted in the largest corporate bankruptcy in history. From this bankruptcy a new company, now called only MCI, would emerge (see Figure G).

What Went Wrong with WorldCom's Strategy?

This is a very broad question. However, we can provide a short answer and say the company and its CEO followed an excellent growth-through-mergers strategy. Probably all the way through the MCI deal, the strategy was working, although even then some questions began to arise. Ebbers was great at doing deals and building up his company to be a leading player in the world telecommunications business. The telecommunications industry has natural economies of scale that can be exploited through growth. His performance at achieving growth through mergers has to rank up there with leaders in U.S. business history. So where did it all go wrong? It went wrong in several ways. The obvious one was the accounting manipulations and other alleged improprieties. However, from a strategy perspective, the problem was that Ebbers and the company could not turn off the M&A acquisition binge. This really was what Ebbers was good at. However, he also proved that he was not good at managing a large company on a day-to-day basis. Reports of him micromanaging minutiae at company headquarters are quite amusing, as the following passage relates:

> It was billed as a strategy meeting not to miss. WorldCom, Inc. senior executives from around the globe gathered two months ago at the telecom giant's headquarters in Clinton, Miss. They had to come to hear CEO Bernard J. Ebbers reveal his grand vision for rescuing a company mired in debt, sluggish growth, and rising controversy about its accounting practices. What executives heard instead was their boss thundering about the theft of coffee in the company's break room.
>
> How did Ebbers know? Because he had matched brewing filters with bags, and at the end of the month, filters outnumbered bags. Henceforth, Ebbers commanded, his executives would follow a checklist of priorities now referred to as Bernie's seven points of light. They would count coffee bags, make sure no lights were left on at the end of the day, and save cooling costs in the summer by turning the thermostat up four degrees, say three former and current executives. "Bernie is running a $40 billion company as if it were still his own mom and pop business," says one WorldCom exec who attended the meeting. "He doesn't know how to grow the company, just save pennies."[a]

(*continued*)

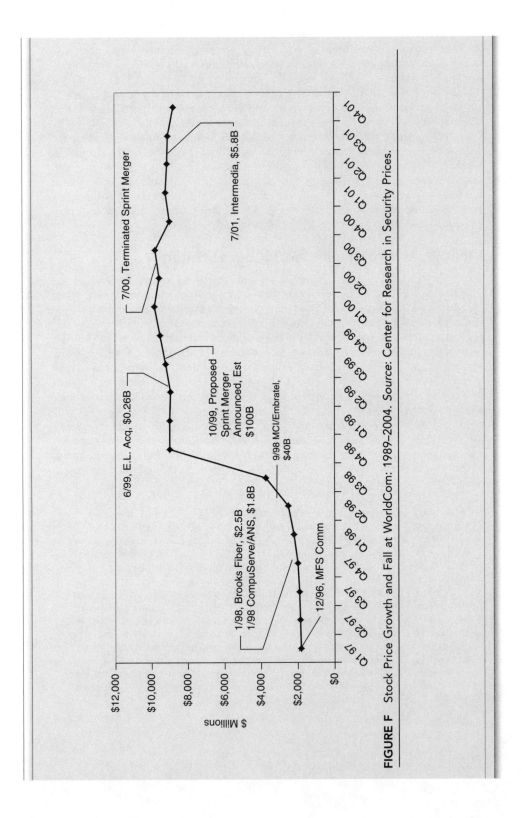

FIGURE F Stock Price Growth and Fall at WorldCom: 1989–2004. Source: Center for Research in Security Prices.

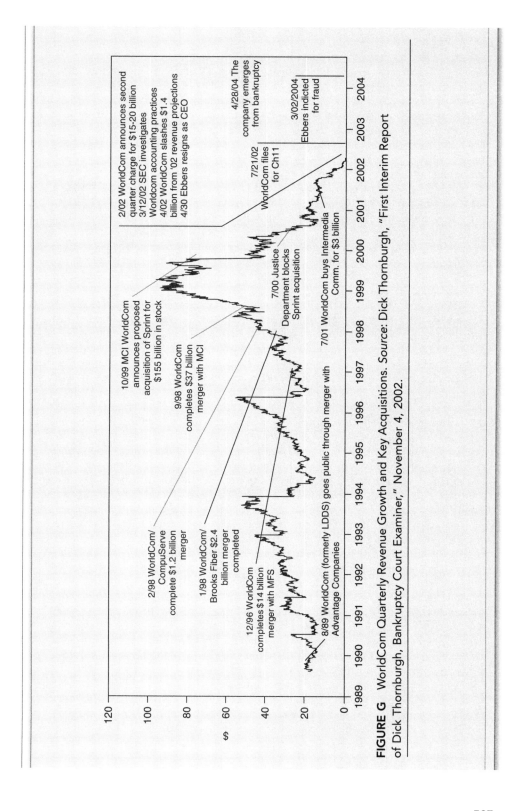

FIGURE G WorldCom Quarterly Revenue Growth and Key Acquisitions. *Source:* Dick Thornburgh, "First Interim Report of Dick Thornburgh, Bankruptcy Court Examiner," November 4, 2002.

(continued)

Other reports state that Ebbers installed video cameras outside company facilities to record the length of employee smoking breaks. Still other reports talk about his approving expenditures above $5,000 and of personally reviewing all press releases the company would issue. Running a large company was not what Ebbers was good at. The skills that one needs to run a small company, or to do creative and aggressive deals, are not the same skills that one needs to manage a multibillion-dollar company. Indeed, with the exception of his grand-scale deal making, Ebbers gave all the signs of being a small-company CEO. Managing a business as though it were a small, closely held enterprise also contributed to his personal woes. Prior to his resignation from the company, Ebbers borrowed $366 million from the company to bail him out when personal loans he had taken had come due and he would have had to sell some of his WorldCom shares at a time when the price was not favorable. It is not unusual for CEOs of closely held companies to cause the company to function for their own personal benefit. However, when a company is mainly owned by public shareholders, it has to be run for the shareholders' benefit, and it is no longer the founding shareholder/CEO's personal fiefdom.

Ebbers and his management also did a poor job of managing the capital structure of the telecom giant. The company had assumed significant amounts of debt that had by 2002 risen to $30 billion. In that year interest payments were $172 million but were scheduled to rise dramatically to $1.7 billion in 2003 and $2.6 billion in 2004.[b] In addition, investment bankers were reporting that the company had negative cash flow in 2001. This was not a time to have a major increase in debt service pressures when the company's market shares and cash flows were under pressure. The company had over a billion in cash on hand and had a line of credit with banks of up to $8 billion. However, credit lines regularly come up for renewal, and a bank will reexamine a company's liquidity position at such times. WorldCom was heading for a liquidity crisis, and dealmaker Ebbers had no answer. The wrong man was at the wheel, and he kept the company on course for disaster.

When it is clear that the company has gotten all it is going to get out of a growth-through-M&A strategy, and the company is at an efficient size, then the deal-making process needs to be, at least temporarily, turned off. At that point organic growth needs to be the focus, not more deals. The board let shareholders down by not stopping Ebbers and putting in place someone else to run the business. Ebbers was allowed to run the company right into bankruptcy. The outcome is a sad one, as the growth Ebbers achieved was so impressive, but many will now know him only for allegations of improprieties and the bankruptcy of the company. Who knows what would have happened had the board been vigilant and asked him to step aside before they got close to bankruptcy? Would a good manager have been able to maintain and grow the business Ebbers built?

One factor that helped allow Bernie to stand unopposed was the fact that there was no major blockholder who would stand up and insist that the board of directors better represent shareholders' interests. These failures can be contrasted with a notable corporate governance success from many years gone by. The case is GM, which was run by a CEO who shared many of the same positive and negative traits of Bernie Ebbers. GM was built by the great dealmaker Willie Durant. His great skill, like Ebbers's, was doing deals and combining companies. Also like Ebbers, he was not good at managing and could not create a management structure at GM that would maintain profitability in the face of frantic deal making. Unlike Ebbers, Durant knew he had some shortcomings in managing, and he convinced the great Walter

Chrysler to postpone his plans to start his own company and to run GM instead. However, Chrysler could not endure Durant's disruptive and chaotic deal making and left to form his own very successful auto company.

Fortunately for GM, it had an outspoken large shareholder, Pierre DuPont, who insisted on making sure that the company would be profitable—not just ever larger. DuPont became convinced that Durant had outlived his usefulness and that his constant deal making had to stop. He had a showdown with Durant in 1916. By then GM was the second-largest auto company in the United States but was a financially troubled concern. DuPont insisted that Durant resign, and he replaced him with the great manager Albert Sloan (after whom the Sloan school at MIT is named). Ironically, Durant built one of the largest companies in the world but died a poor man.

Lessons of the WorldCom Strategy

- Deal-making CEOs need to be controlled by the board. There will come a time that deal making may need to be paused and possibly stopped. Acquisitive CEOs need to be held in check. They also need to demonstrate that they can run a company and do something other than acquisitions.
- Deal making and managing are two different skills. Some managers are capable of doing both. Some are better at one than the other. Boards need to put in place the right people with the right skills. Having a dealmaker in place greatly increases the likelihood that deals will be made. If that is not what is needed, then get someone else in the leadership position.

[*]*Source*: Patrick A. Gaughan, *Mergers: What Can Go Wrong and How to Prevent It* (Hoboken, NJ: John Wiley & Sons, 2005), 237–239.

[a] Charles Haddad and Steve Rosenbush, "Woe Is WorldCom," *BusinessWeek*, May 6, 2002, 86.
[b] Ibid.

CHAPTER FOURTEEN

Joint Ventures and Strategic Alliances

A S WE HAVE SEEN, a merger with, or an acquisition of, another company can be a costly endeavor but may provide great gains for the companies pursing the deal. It may also be the case, however, that many of the gains that the participants hoped to achieve could be realized without having to do a merger or an acquisition. It may be possible that these gains can be achieved with a joint venture or a strategic alliance. In this chapter we will explore these two options as alternatives to mergers and acquisitions (M&As). We will consider their respective benefits and costs and then compare these to M&As. We will see that in certain instances, companies are better off with an alliance or joint venture; but in other cases such deals will not achieve a company's goals, and it will have to focus on M&As.

As with our discussions of M&As, we will review the shareholder wealth effects of both joint ventures and strategic alliances. We will see that the studies of the market's initial reaction, like those of M&As, can provide great insight into whether a deal will ultimately be beneficial.

CONTRACTUAL AGREEMENTS

Even before discussing joint ventures and strategic alliances, we should first consider a simpler alternative to an alliance or joint venture—a contractual agreement between the parties. If the goals of the relationship are specific and can be readily set forth in an enforceable contract between the parties, then this may be the least costly and most efficient solution. As an example, consider a company that is concerned about sources of supply and is contemplating an acquisition of a supplier to lower the risk of availability of inputs for its production process. It is possible that these risk-lowering benefits could be achieved by a long-term contractual agreement between the company and a supplier. The company may not need to create a strategic alliance or a joint venture to get a supplier to commit to providing specific products and services. However, when the products in question are not readily available and require a specific development commitment on the part of the supplier, a contract may or may not suffice. If the process is even more complicated and involves the parties exchanging valuable and proprietary information as well as a buyer providing funding for the supplier to engage in a long-term and uncertain development process, such as what often occurs between biotechnology and pharmaceutical firms, then a contract may not be enough and either a strategic alliance or a joint venture may be needed, if not an outright merger or acquisition. We would expect to have a contractual agreement with a strategic alliance or joint venture, but most contracts between businesses are not strategic alliances or joint ventures. Thus, strategic alliances and joint ventures involve agreements that go beyond the usual contractual relationships with businesses. They are more complicated and require more detailed roles and commitments between the parties.

 COMPARING STRATEGIC ALLIANCES AND JOINT VENTURES WITH MERGERS AND ACQUISITIONS

Strategic alliances feature less involvement between the alliance partners than joint ventures, which in turn are also a lesser commitment than a merger or acquisition. In terms of investment of capital, control, and the cost of reversal, Figure 14.1 shows that strategic alliance is the lowest on this scale, followed by joint venture and then M&A.

 JOINT VENTURES

In a joint venture, two or more companies combine certain assets and work toward jointly achieving a business objective. Usually the time period of this combination is defined and limited in duration. This is another difference between joint ventures and M&As because the latter involves an indefinite period unless it is a specialized deal where

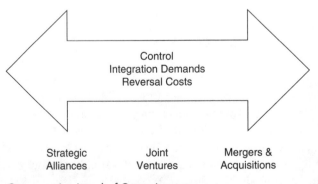

FIGURE 14.1 Comparative Level of Commitment

a company is acquired with the planned goal of selling it within a limited time period. There are many recent examples of private equity firms buying public companies, taking them private with the goal of improving the business, and then putting them up for sale at a higher price than they paid. However, in this chapter we consider very different types of transactions.

The companies involved in a joint venture maintain their own separate business operations and continue to exist apart as they did before the joint venture. This venture is then formally created as a business entity, such as a separate corporation or partnership. A formal agreement among the venture participants sets forth the extent to which they each will exercise control over the venture's activities and will participate in the entity's profits or losses. Presumably this will be a road map that each can follow to assess the venture's progress toward achieving its goals.

Joint ventures can be used for a wide variety of business purposes. Perhaps two companies have specialized resources that when combined can be used to create or market a specific product. For example, one could be a traditional pharmaceutical manufacturer, while the other might be a biotechnology firm. The pharmaceutical company may want to utilize the research and development (R&D) resources of the biotech business to develop a particular drug for the treatment of some ailment. If this is the goal, buying the biotech business, which may be involved in many other areas in which the drug manufacturers are not interested, may be an expensive way of gaining the research capability it needs to develop the drug. The drug manufacturers may have in place a widespread marketing network that would be able to rapidly capture market share when the product is eventually developed. In this case, both parties bring resources to the table and, for this one particular venture, each can gain from the other's resources. The solution may be a joint venture in which the two businesses come together for this one activity and may not necessarily do anything else together in the future. Of course, if this venture works out well, they might pursue other joint efforts.

Joint ventures may be a way for two potential merger partners to assess how well they work together. Cultural differences between two companies may become apparent when they are involved in a joint venture or strategic alliance. If these differences are problematic, the business dealing usually can be curtailed at lower costs in a joint venture or strategic alliance compared with a merger or acquisition that may erode shareholder value.

Motives for Joint Ventures

If we consider that a merger or acquisition is a combining of the resources of two different companies, then a joint venture is a different process that, to some extent, may achieve the same goals. The motives for joint ventures are varied, but the following list provides a few examples that often occur:

- *Enhance research and development capabilities.* A company, such as a pharmaceutical company, may enter into a joint venture with another business that has some specific capability that it needs to further its R&D process. On the other hand, the R&D capability may be so important that a company may want to "lock it up" and do an outright acquisition.

- *Gain access to key supplies.* Two or more companies may form a joint venture so they can have a better source of supplies for their production process. Such supplies could range from joint exploration for oil by petroleum companies to joint training programs for workers.
- *Enhance distribution systems.* Two companies may enter into a joint venture agreement that will enable one or both of them to have an enhanced distribution network for their products. One company could be a manufacturer of a product but lacks a distribution system, including an established sales force, that the other possesses.
- *Gain access to a foreign market.* International joint ventures may enable companies that operate in different countries to work together to achieve gains in one or more countries. Such international joint ventures are common in the automobile industry. An example occurred in April 2007 when Renault launched a joint venture with the conglomerate Mahindra and Mahindra (M&M). The two agreed to work together to build an automobile plant to make cars for the rapidly growing Indian auto market. Renault was an "old hand" at joint ventures, having done others with companies such as Japanese automaker Nissan Motors. However, this joint venture would prove challenging for Renault. Initial sales projections were at 2,500 cars per month; however, by the end of 2009 the companies were up to only 500 per month, resulting in a money-losing effort. Even with the expertise of a local manufacturer, the venture did not get the specifications correct. For example, the venture's "Logan" car was made a little too long, which put it into a higher tax bracket for buyers. In 2010 Renault agreed to walk away from the venture and M&M took it over.

Regulation and Joint Ventures

Simply because two companies form a joint venture instead of doing a formal merger or acquisition they are not exempted from some of the same regulatory scrutiny they might face if they merged or if one was acquired by the other. This is definitely the case for antitrust laws. The anticompetitive provisions of the Sherman Act and the Clayton Act can be also applied to joint ventures, where the effect of the venture on the market is to reduce competition. The cases of the Justice Department or the Federal Trade Commission challenging joint ventures are less common than their challenges of M&As. However, in theory the same laws look at the business combination and its impact on the degree of competition in the market. Keep in mind that when a company enters into a joint venture or a strategic alliance, it cannot be doing so to circumvent antitrust laws, and those laws still apply. Another point to remember is that if the antitrust authorities find a venture to be anticompetitive, it usually can be terminated at a lower cost than a merger or acquisition of a business that has been fully integrated into the parent company.

Shareholder Wealth Effects of Joint Ventures

In several sections of this book we have examined the shareholder wealth effects of corporation combinations. It was found that the market responses to acquisition announcements are often not positive, and target shareholders often do not do well. When target shareholders receive their premium, assuming it is not in stock and they do not hold those shares for an extended period, they have measurable gains. In light of these M&A shareholder wealth effects, the logical question that arises is, "How do shareholders do in joint ventures?"

McConnell and Nantell did a study of 136 joint ventures involving 210 U.S. companies over the period between 1972 and 1979.[1] The joint ventures were in a variety of industries, with the most common being real estate development (13%) and television and motion pictures (10%). The study was an announcement period, short-term-oriented study that compares with many of the event studies that have been conducted for M&A announcements. It is important to bear in mind, however, that when we say short-term-oriented, the market is adjusting to the announcement in the short term, such as during an event window of three days before and after a joint venture announcement, but this adjustment reflects the market's anticipation of the long-term effects of the benefits and costs of the venture. The reaction occurs in a short time period, but it is attempting to reflect or forecast long-term effects. This is different from a long-term study, which looks at the financial impact of an event after the fact, when we have had the benefit of the passage of a number of years.

The McConnell and Nantell study showed that shareholders in companies entering into joint ventures enjoyed announcement period returns of 0.73%. They found similar results when some of the industries, such as real estate, were removed from the sample. They also found that the gains were fairly evenly distributed across venture participants. When the authors tried to convert that seemingly small percentage return to a dollar amount, they found it corresponded to an average value of $4.8 million.

The McConnell and Nantell study supports the idea that, when considering the shareholder wealth effects, joint ventures are a viable alternative to a merger or an acquisition. Whether they may accomplish what a company wants to achieve with an M&A is going to be determined on a case-by-case basis. However, while they also vary depending on the circumstances, one cannot argue that joint ventures lack some of the aggregate positive shareholder wealth effects that M&As provide. One thing that a joint venture will not provide, and for acquirers this is a good thing, is a large buyout premium for target shareholders. Without that premium, the opportunities for management to make bad decisions by overpaying may be more limited. They may still be able to negotiate poor terms for their own companies, but the opportunities for large financial losses *may* be more limited.

The McConnell and Nantell findings of positive shareholder wealth effects for joint ventures were supported by the research of Woolridge and Snow, who analyzed a sample of 767 announcements of strategic investment decisions involving 248 companies operating in 102 industries.[2] These strategic investment decisions included joint ventures as well as R&D projects and major capital investments. Their methodology featured an examination of the stock market reaction to the announcement of

[1] John J. McConnell and Timothy J. Nantell, "Corporate Combinations and Common Stock Returns: The Case of Joint Ventures," *Journal of Finance* 40, no. 2 (June 1985): 519–536.

[2] J. Randall Woolridge and Charles C. Snow, "Stock Market Reaction to Strategic Investment Decisions," *Strategic Management Journal* 11, no. 5 (September 1990): 353–363.

these decisions. In general they found positive stock market responses to these various announcements. When the sample was divided into subsamples for the different types of announcements, they were able to determine that the shareholder wealth effects were positive for joint venture announcements. These results are consistent with the McConnell and Nantell findings.

Shareholder Wealth Effects by Type of Venture

While the McConnell and Nantell study looked at the shareholder wealth effects by type of industry, it did not differentiate these effects by type of venture. Johnson and Houston analyzed a sample of 191 joint ventures over the period of 1991–1995.[3] They divided their sample into vertical joint ventures (55%) and horizontal joint ventures (45%). They defined *vertical joint ventures* as transactions between buyers and suppliers. *Horizontal joint ventures* are transactions between companies that are in the same general line of business and that may use the products from the venture to sell to their own customers or to create an output that can be sold to the same group. The results showed average positive gains from joint ventures equal to 1.67%. For horizontal joint ventures, it appears that the gains are shared by the venture participants. The average returns for vertical joint ventures were somewhat higher — 2.67%. However, what was particularly interesting when they looked at the vertical sample was that the gains did not accrue to both parties. Suppliers gained an average of 5%, with 70% of the returns being positive, while buyers received an average return of only 0.32%, which was not statistically significant and of which only 53% of the returns were even positive. For vertical joint ventures, the biggest winners were suppliers, who were able to capture the bulk of the gains, while the market did not see major benefits for buyers.

Johnson and Houston recognized that when two companies entered into a joint venture, especially a vertical venture that showed greater gains, the venture participants could have entered into a contract as opposed to a joint venture. Why did they choose the venture alternative? Johnson and Houston analyzed a sample of announcements of contracts and also found positive shareholder wealth effects with such announcements. However, they found that companies enter into joint ventures, as opposed to contracts, when transaction costs are high. They describe some of these transaction costs as "hold-up hazards." This could occur, for example, if a supplier had to make buyer-specific investments, such as investments in certain machinery and capital goods needed to produce the buyer-specific products. Although a contract may provide some temporary protection to the supplier over the contract period, once this period is over, the supplier may be vulnerable unless this capital equipment could be redeployed to another buyer. For these types of transactions, Johnson and Houston saw benefits for joint ventures that mere contracts could not provide.

Relatedness and Size

Consistent with the research on M&As that showed deals involving related companies yield better returns than deals with companies that were not related, Koh and

---

[3] Shane Johnson and Mark Houston, "A Reexamination of the Motives and Gains in Joint Ventures," *Journal of Financial and Quantitative Analysis* 35, no. 1 (March 2000): 67–85.

Venkatraman found that the positive shareholder wealth effects from joint venture announcements were greater for deals involving companies that were more related to each other.[4] In addition, they found that the smaller joint venture partner benefits more than the larger one. This is a logical conclusion because for the smaller partner the venture affects more of their business than the larger company, which may be involved in more diverse areas outside the venture's activities.

Restructuring and Joint Ventures

Sometimes a company may be able to pursue restructuring or a sell-off through the use of a joint venture. Consider a company that wants to divest itself of a division but is having difficulty finding a suitable buyer for 100% of the company that would provide a sufficient value to make the company sell off the division. One alternative would be to sell off part of the company and in effect run the division as a jointly owned entity. If the goal of the company doing the partial sale is really to be able to do a 100% sale, it may negotiate terms with the partial buyer, whereby that buyer would be able to purchase the remaining shares in the division at some point in the future based on the occurrence of certain events. Such events might be the division achieving certain performance goals. If this occurs, the seller would, in stages, have found its buyer. That buyer is able to utilize the capabilities of the business unit without, at least initially, having to do a 100% acquisition. If it buys control of the target, it may be able to enter into whatever agreement it needs while saving on the costs of a 100% acquisition. If it finds that the relationship is rewarding, it may then want to be a 100% shareholder and not have to share in the ownership of the company. The seller may also be able to add terms to the original agreement that state that if certain targets are met, the buyer is bound to complete the purchase and buy the remaining shares as of some date.

Potential Problems with Joint Ventures

Many potential problems can arise with joint ventures. They are certainly not a cure for all of the ills of M&As. This is obvious from the fact that we continue to do so many M&As, and if joint ventures were the solution, we would see more of them instead of M&As. The potential problems with joint ventures are as varied as the types of ventures. They may fail because the venture partners do not work well together. There may be disagreements between the participants, which may get in the way of accomplishing the venture's goals. The venture may require participants to share intellectual property or other proprietary knowledge, and they may be reluctant to do so, or one venture partner may be using such information in a way that was not intended by the other venture participant. The participants may not see themselves as fully committed as they might if the activities of the venture were part of the overall business. This lack of full commitment may prevent the venture from achieving its goals. Other problems may be that the venture simply does not accomplish what it set out to accomplish. We will see that many of these same problems can occur with strategic alliances as well.

---

[4] Jeongsuk Koh and N. Venkatraman, "Joint Venture Formations and Stock Market Reactions: An Assessment of the Information Technology Sector," *Academy of Management Journal* 34, no. 4 (December 1991): 869–892.

STRATEGIC ALLIANCES

Strategic alliances are less formal associations between companies compared with joint ventures. In a joint venture, a separate entity is often created, whereas in a strategic alliance the agreement and the relationship are less formal. We can define strategic alliances as collaborative efforts by two or more companies in which each company maintains its own independence. Such alliances are strategic when they are formed to facilitate the achievement of the company's strategic goals.

Strategic alliances are common in various different industries, including the pharmaceutical, airline, and computer industries. Airlines that serve different geographic markets often form alliances or airline partner agreements. Under such agreements, they remain separate airlines but share routes. This enables them to be able to keep a customer who wants to fly beyond the range of a given airline's routes. Each airline alliance partner can market the entire route, and the same flights may be marketed under different flight numbers for each partner. With such alliances, the various partners may be able to provide customers with a global network. In addition, as various companies in an industry form such alliances, this puts pressure on competitors to follow suit so they are not at a disadvantage because of a smaller network.

Enhancing R&D is a major reason why companies form strategic alliances. Robinson reports a National Science Foundation study that indicated that 1 company in 10 that was involved in R&D financed such work outside of the company.[5] Robinson and Stuart also report a survey from the Pharmaceutical Research and Manufacturers of America, which suggested that approximately "25% of the $26 billion in U.S.-based, industrially financed, pharmaceutical R&D that occurred in 2000 took place in over 700 collaborative agreements with outside organizations."[6] An example of such an agreement is the alliance between Novartis, a Swiss-based pharmaceutical company, and Vertex, a biotechnology research company, whereby Novartis made various payments, including an initial payment of $600 million and additional payments of $200,000 staggered over six years, in exchange for the rights to market various pharmaceutical products. With such agreements, pharmaceutical companies can gain access to technology provided by biotech firms that may not be available to the drug companies. As technological change accelerates in the pharmaceutical industry, the methods of developing drugs also change. In recent years, the way in which pharmaceutical companies create new drugs has changed, and many of these companies have lacked some of the capabilities and expertise to conduct more modern research. Drug manufacturers need access to research capabilities that biotech companies have and that they may not be able to develop quickly in the time frame they need to stay competitive with other drug companies, which may have such capabilities in-house or through other alliances with biotech companies.

---

[5] David Robinson, "Strategic Alliances and the Boundaries of the Firm," *Review of Financial Studies* 21, no. 2 (March 2008): 649–681.
[6] David Robinson and Toby Stuart, "Financial Contracting in Biotech Strategic Alliances," *Journal of Law and Economics* 50, no. 3 (August 2007): 559–596.

Governance of Strategic Alliances

When a company acquires another company, the governance process is hierarchical in the sense that the acquirer pays for and receives the right to control the target. It governs the target—hopefully in a manner that facilities growth of the wealth of the acquirer's shareholders. The governance of strategic alliances is bilateral and is determined by the agreement the alliance partners enter into as well as by factors such as the nonlegal commitment of the alliance partners to make the alliance succeed. In entering into such an agreement, the alliance participants seek to lower some of the various costs that might exist if they had a looser arrangement. This does not mean that they will not have opportunities for strategic behavior. Depending on the type of alliance entered into, a significant degree of trust may be needed between the partners. If the success of the alliance requires that they share confidential information, then the parties must be confident that this valuable intellectual property will not be used inappropriately. If this proves to be a concern, it may inhibit the success of the alliance because the parties may be reluctant to share what needs to be shared in order to have complete success.

There has been much discussion in the economic and financial literature on the assignment of control rights in joint ventures.[7] This assignment is important in alliances involving the development of new technologies. Aghion and Nobel prize winner Triole point out that two factors should govern the allocation of control rights.

1. The degree to which there may be an underinvestment of either party that could have an adverse effect on the success of the alliance.
2. The relative bargaining parties of the two partners.

We can add another factor as follows:

3. The extent to which one party may engage in opportunistic behavior, which can have an adverse effect on the outcomes.

Lerner and Merges describe a case study involving pharmaceutical company Eli Lilly and the Repligen Corporation, a biotechnology company. They worked together on a project involving monoclonal antibody treatments of inflammation:

> In the negotiations there were three areas where control rights were in dispute. The first was the management of clinical trials: which drugs would be pursued and when. A second was the control over the marketing strategy, an area in which Lilly had extensive experience and Repligen only a slight acquaintance. Finally, both parties wished to undertake the process of development and ultimate manufacturing of the drug. Repligen, in fact, had recently acquired a cell culture facility and the key personnel that went with it.

---

[7] Phillipe Aghion and Jean Triole, "The Management of Innovation," *Quarterly Journal of Economics* 109, no. 4 (November 1994): 1185–1209.

The final agreement appeared to assign control rights to the parties with the greatest discretion to behave opportunistically. Repligen was allowed a great deal of flexibility in developing the lead product candidate (where it had the greatest experience), but tangential product development activities would only be supported when precise milestones were reached. Lilly was assigned control over all aspects of marketing; while Repligen was assigned all manufacturing control rights, unless it encountered severe difficulties with regulators.[8]

Lerner and Merges did an empirical study of 200 contracts/alliances between biotechnology companies and sponsoring firms. They found results that were consistent with the previous case study they described in their paper. They found that, in general, control rights were assigned to the smaller alliance partner as an increasing function of their financial health. It seems that in the drug development industry, it may be optimal for control rights to be assigned to the smaller company, but the limiting factor may be its own financial condition. Smaller companies that are in better financial condition are in a stronger bargaining position and also are less risky alliance partners. Larger pharmaceutical companies may be less able to force their terms on a financially sound smaller biotech company. They also may have more confidence in a financially sound but smaller biotech company and may worry less about its being able to do what it agreed to do.

Alliance Knowledge Flows: Benefits and Risks

One of the reasons why companies enter into strategic alliances is to jointly benefit from specific knowledge resources of one of the partners. Often it is a situation where a smaller partner possesses specific knowledge and expertise that is valued by a larger company that may have the resources to transform this knowledge into profitable global sales. The expectation that alliances actually do lead to knowledge transfers between alliance partners is supported by empirical research. Gomes-Casseres, Hagedoorn, and Jaffe found a greater incidence of citations of another company's patents by alliance partners who were applying for their own patents.[9] They found these citations, their measure of knowledge transfer, to be greater the more alliances the companies had and to be less when they appeared to be "one-shot" deals.

One of the risks that smaller alliance partners face when dealing with a larger company is that the larger company may seek to take advantage of the knowledge it is receiving and may not fully share in the gains. One partner may use the knowledge to compete with the other in its own markets. If this is done in an unlawful manner, the smaller company is faced with having to pursue its rights in court, which can be difficult and costly. However, the sale of equity interests may reduce those risks as it lowers the entry incentive.[10]

---

[8] Josh Lerner and Robert P. Merges, "The Control of Strategic Alliances: An Empirical Analysis of Biotechnology Collaborations," NBER Working Paper No. 6014, April 1997.

[9] Benjamin Gomes-Casseres, John Hagedoorn, and Adam B. Jaffe, "Do Alliances Promote Knowledge Transfers?" *Journal of Financial Economics* 80, no. 1 (April 2006): 5–33.

[10] Richmond D. Mathews, "Strategic Alliances, Equity Stakes and Entry Deterrence," *Journal of Financial Economics* 80, no. 1 (April 2006): 35–79.

Shareholder Wealth Effects of Strategic Alliances

Just as we have with joint ventures, we will look at the shareholder wealth effects of strategic alliances. Chan, Kensinger, Keown, and Martin looked at the shareholder wealth effects of 345 strategic alliances over the period of 1983–1992.[11] Almost one-half of their sample involved alliances for marketing and distribution purposes. For the overall group, they found positive abnormal returns equal to 0.64%. This is somewhat comparable to what was seen with the research of McConnell and Nantell for joint ventures. The Chan et al. study also found no evidence of significant transfers of wealth between alliance partners. This implies that there was no evidence that one partner was gaining at the expense of another. This result supports strategic alliances as an alternative to M&As—*in the limited circumstances where it is appropriate.*

Shareholder Wealth Effects by Type of Alliance

Chan et al. looked at how the shareholder wealth effects varied by type of alliance. They separated their sample into horizontal and nonhorizontal alliances. They defined horizontal alliances as those involving partners with the same three-digit SIC code. They found that horizontal alliances that involved the transfer of technology provided the highest cumulative abnormal return—3.54%. This may help explain why strategic alliances occur so often between technologically oriented companies. Nonhorizontal alliances that were done to enter a new market provided a positive but lower return—1.45%. Other nonhorizontal alliances failed to show significant returns. Another study conducted by Das, Sen, and Sengupta also looked at the types of alliances that might be successful, as reflected by their initial announcement shareholder wealth effects.[12] They were able to show how the announcement effects varied by type of alliance as well as by firm profitability and relative size of the alliance participants. They discovered that technological alliances were associated with greater announcement returns than marketing alliances. These are two of the more common types of alliances. In his research of 4,192 alliances, Hagedoorn has previously shown that, as expected, technological alliances were more common in high-growth sectors, whereas marketing alliances were more common in mature industries.[13] Das et al. also showed that the abnormal returns were negatively correlated with both the size of the alliance partners and their profitability. We see that the market is concluding that larger and more profitable partners will capture fewer of the gains from the alliance. Stated alternatively, the market sees greater benefits for smaller and less profitable businesses to partner with larger and more profitable companies. The smaller and less profitable companies seem to have more to gain from strategic alliances. This does not imply that the partnerships are not also good for larger companies. Given that they are bigger and

---

[11] Su Han Chan, John W. Kensinger, Arthur Keown, and John D. Martin, "Do Strategic Alliances Create Value?" *Journal of Financial Economics* 46, no. 2 (November 1997): 199–221.

[12] Somnath Das, Pradyot K. Sen, and Sanjit Sengupta, "Impact of Strategic Alliances on Firm Valuation," *Academy of Management Journal* 41, no. 1 (February 1988): 27–41.

[13] John Hagedoorn, "Understanding the Rationale of Strategic Technology Partnering: Interorganizational Modes of Cooperation and Sectoral Differences," *Strategic Management Journal* 14, no. 5 (July 1993): 371–385.

their profits are greater, it would be reasonable to expect that when such companies partner with smaller firms, they have less to gain because the impact of that alliance will have a smaller impact on the overall business of the larger company. That larger company may enter into several such alliances, and the aggregate effect of all of these alliances may make the difference less.

WYETH AND PROGENICS COLLABORATE ON DRUG DEVELOPMENT

In December 2005, Wyeth Corp. (formerly American Home Products and now merged with Pfizer) and Progenics announced that the two companies would collaborate on the development of a drug that would deal with the opioid-induced side effects of certain pain medications. Wyeth is a Madison, New Jersey–based pharmaceutical company that, like all other major drug companies, is seeking to expand its product line. Progenics Pharmaceuticals Inc. is a Tarrytown, New York–based biopharmaceutical company. It is well known that many opioid products that are used to treat pain, such as after major surgery, may have adverse gastrointestinal side effects. The two companies see this as a sizable market.

Progenics developed a product called methylnaltrexone (MNTX), which, with further refinement, could fill the void in this market. As part of their agreement, Wyeth agreed to provide Progenics with an up-front payment of $60 million and as much as $356.5 million based on Progenics achieving certain milestones in the development process. Wyeth also agreed to pay Progenics royalties on sales while also being responsible for further development and other commercialization costs. The companies were able to achieve Canadian and FDA approval of the drug, which is marketed under the name Relistor, in April 2008.

What Determines the Success of Strategic Alliances? Experience

What factors determine whether a strategic alliance is going to be a success? Which types of alliances are more likely to be successful and which will be more difficult to pull off? A study that focused on this issue was conducted by Kale, Dyer, and Singh.[14] They analyzed a sample of 78 companies that reported on 1,572 alliances that had been established for at least two years. As of the study date, approximately 12% of the alliances were already terminated. The researchers surveyed managers within the firm, who responded to questions designed to elicit responses on the degree of success of the alliances. They found that firms that had more experience with alliances were more likely to be successful in future alliances. This means that there is a learning curve, and companies do better at alliances the more they do them. This result is intuitive. They also found that companies that had a *dedicated alliance function*, such as a department and department

---

[14] Prashant Kale, Jeffrey H. Dyer, and Harbir Singh, "Alliance Capability, Stock Market Response and Long-Term Alliance Success: The Role of the Alliance Function," *Strategic Management Journal* 23, no. 8 (2002): 747–767.

head dedicated to overseeing alliances that the company entered into, were more likely to be successful with their alliances. An example would be companies that have a vice president or director of strategic alliances position. They found that Hewlett-Packard and Eli Lilly, for example, had such positions. It would also be reasonable to assume that if a given company established such a position, it would be more likely to engage in alliances than companies that did not have one. The reported success rate of companies with a dedicated alliance function was 68%, compared with a 50% rate for those without these positions. Interestingly, the market reacted more positively for alliance announcements for those companies that had such dedicated alliance functions (1.35% compared to 0.18%). The other interesting product of this research is that it shows a consistency between the initial market response and long-term results—in this case as applied to alliances. This is one of many pieces of evidence that allows us to take the results of studies of the short-term announcement effects for various events, such as mergers, acquisitions, joint ventures, and alliances, seriously because they seem to correlate well with long-term research results.

Strategic Alliances Followed by Joint Ventures and M&As

Strategic alliances can be a way for the alliance partners to test the relationship between the partners. The commitment level and costs are much lower than M&S and even joint ventures. If the alliance is not fruitful or if the cultures are not compatible, then the alliances are usually easy to terminate. However, if the parties are considering a more involved commitment, such as a merger, then an alliance may be a way to "test the waters." This was confirmed by Marciukaityte, Roskelley, and Wang's study of financial service alliances.[15] Consistent with other research, they found positive announcement effects to the formation of alliances. They also found that following the alliances there were improvements in operating performance relative to the industry. They also found that alliance partners were more likely to enter into joint ventures or M&A with each other than randomly selected firms. However, while these events were more likely ventures, M&As still occurred only with a relatively small percentage of the alliances (5%).

NISSAN-RENAULT STRATEGIC ALLIANCE

The Nissan-Renault strategic alliance is one that has survived the test of time after being formed in March 1999. Renault had previously been unsuccessful in pursing an alliance with Volvo. However, the company was undaunted by this failure and saw the opportunity to work with Nissan as potentially providing numerous benefits, including a significant presence in the all-important Asian markets. Nissan, however, was fighting for survival under a mountain of debt it had assumed. It had previously approached Chrysler, but the number-three U.S. carmaker declined the overture.

(continued)

---

[15] Dalia Marciukaityte, Kenneth Roskelley, and Hua Wang, "Strategic Alliances by Financial Services Firms," *Journal of Business Research* 62, no. 11 (November 2009): 1193–1199.

(*continued*)

Given Nissan's financial pressures, one of the most fundamental contributions of Renault was capital. It gave Nissan Motors $4.86 billion and $76.6 million to Nissan Diesel. In exchange, Renault received a 36.8% equity stake in Nissan Motors and a 22.5% stake in Nissan Diesel.[a] The agreement also allowed Renault to acquire additional equity in Nissan at a later date. In addition, the leadership of Carlos Ghosn, formerly of Renault and who became chief operating officer of the troubled Nissan, cannot be understated. Ghosn is one of the world's leading automobile executives, and his leadership was essential to the success of Nissan—a company that the world had doubts would survive. Nissan's managerial errors had caused it to assume a nonviable debt capital structure, and it needed to totally change the way it managed the company. Under Ghosn they were able to do this and grow.

Figure A shows that while Renault's sales have been basically flat since the alliance's formation, Nissan's sales have grown impressively. This is noteworthy, as Nissan continued to generate sales gains in weak economic years, such as 2008, when other automakers saw sales declines. It is also important to note that while Renault's sales have been flat, it profits from Nissan's gains through its sizable equity holding in the Japanese automaker.

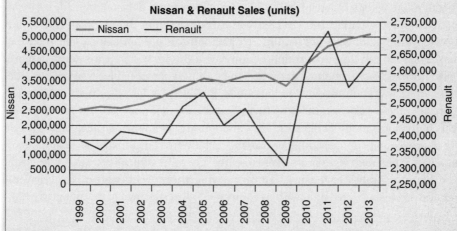

FIGURE A Nissan and Renault Sales. *Source*: Renault-Nissan Alliance press releases.

The two companies work in various ways to not only stimulate sales but also improve profitability. They formed RNPO, which handles common purchasing, to enhance the buying power of the two companies. In addition, each company has strong powertrain expertise—Renault for diesels and Nissan for gasoline. The alliance provided for each company to share this expertise with the other while each company maintained the uniqueness of its own car offerings. In addition, the alliance reduced the total number of engines they jointly used to eight through selecting the best that each company had to offer.

Renault also adopted many of the Nissan production techniques in its plants. They found that productivity improved 15% through the use of Nissan's manufacturing know-how. While prior to the alliance Nissan had several weaknesses, including its poor capital structure, it had excellent manufacturing expertise and its cars were well made. Through its association with Nissan, Renault was able to take advantage of this expertise. Each company was also able to use the manufacturing facilities of the other company, saving the costs of building new plants in foreign markets. For example, Renault's plants in Korea and Brazil make Nissan vehicles while Nissan assembles Renault vehicles in its Spanish, South American, and Mexican plants.

The benefits in growth and productivity for both companies better enabled them to withstand the overcapacity and weak demand conditions that prevailed in 2008–2009. Through the alliance they were able to implement numerous changes that made each more competitive while preserving the integrity of their own brands and corporate structures. The market still remains difficult and the alliance alone is not enough to enable them to succeed in trying times, but it gives each company advantages they lacked prior to forming the alliance. For example, the alliance markets several major auto brands, including not only Renault and Nissan but also Infiniti and Datsun. In addition, the companies try to enjoy economics of scale for capital-intensive research and development projects.

The alliance is structured through cross holdings of shares. Renault has a 43% (voting) stake in Nissan and Nissan owns 15% of Renault shares (nonvoting). In 2014 the alliance expanded through an agreement with Daimler to develop premium compact cars and manufacture them in Mexico, where Nissan already has production facilities. The plan is to market Infiniti as well as compact Mercedes cars for the Central American market. This venture in Mexico was the outcome of a 2010 agreement between Nissan/Renault and Daimler in which each agreed to own 3.1% of the other.

[a] Jean-Paul Susini, "The Determinants of Alliance Performance: Case Study of Renault and Nissan Alliance," *Economic Journal of Hokkaido University* 33 (2004–2007): 232–262.

CHAPTER FIFTEEN

Valuation

HE IMPORTANCE OF A systematic valuation process became more apparent for corporate America during the fourth merger wave, when many companies found themselves the targets of friendly or unfriendly offers. Even companies that had not been targets had to determine their proper value in the event that such a bid might materialize. To exercise due diligence, the board of directors must fully and properly evaluate an offer and compare this price with its own internal valuation of the firm. The need to perform this evaluation as diligently as possible was emphasized in the 1980 bid for the TransUnion Corporation by Jay Pritzker and the Marmon Corporation.

In September 1980, Jerome Van Gorkom, chairman and chief executive officer of TransUnion, suggested to Jay Pritzker that Pritzker make a $55-a-share merger bid for TransUnion, which would be merged with the Marmon Group, a company controlled by Pritzker. Van Gorkom called a board of directors meeting on September 20, 1980, on a one-day notice. Most of the directors had not been advised of the purpose of the meeting. The meeting featured a 20-minute presentation on the Pritzker bid and the terms of the offer. The offer allowed TransUnion to accept competing bids for 90 days. Some directors thought that the $55 offer would be considered only the beginning of the range of the value of the company. After a two-hour discussion, the directors agreed to the terms of the offer, and a merger agreement was executed.

The TransUnion directors were sued by the stockholders, who considered the offer inadequate. A Delaware court found that the decision to sell the company for $55 was not an informed business judgment:

The directors (1) did not adequately inform themselves as to Van Gorkom's role in forcing the "sale" of the Company and in the per share purchase price; (2) were uninformed as to the intrinsic value of the Company; and (3) given these circumstances, at a minimum, were grossly negligent in approving the "sale" of the Company upon two hours consideration, without prior notice, and without the exigency of a crisis or emergency.[1]

The court was also impressed with other deficiencies in the board of directors' decision-making process. Among them was the fact that the board did not even have a copy of the merger agreement to review at a meeting convened for the explicit purpose of deciding on the merger. The board members therefore did not read the amendments to the agreement, and they did not request an outside valuation study of the merger offer.[2] Based on these facts, the case seems to be one of clear negligence on the part of the directors. However, there is evidence that the directors had conducted an analysis of the value of the firm before the meeting in which they approved the offer. In fact, the directors had been monitoring the firm's financial condition for several years before the Pritzker bid. Their defense also included the following factors.

The directors' key defense was the "substantial" premium in Pritzker's $55 offer over Trans Union's market price of $38 per share. The merger price offered to the shareholders represented a premium of 62% over the average of the high and low prices at which Trans Union had traded in 1980, a premium of 48% over the last closing price, and a premium of 39% over the highest price at which the stock had traded at any time during the prior six years. They offered several other defenses as well. First, the market test period provided opportunity for other offers. Second, the board's collective experience was adequate to determine the reasonableness of the Pritzker offer. Third, their attorney, Brennan, advised them that they might be sued if they rejected the Pritzker proposal. Lastly, there was the stockholders' overwhelming vote approving the merger.[3]

The directors' defense clearly had some merit, as reflected in the opinions of the two dissenting justices, who saw adequate evidence that the directors had studied the value of TransUnion for an extended period of time before the directors' meeting and were in a position to determine whether the offer was inadequate.

The board of directors also considered the comments of Donald Romans, TransUnion's chief financial officer, who had stated that the $55 offer was at the beginning of the range within which an adequate value of TransUnion lay. Romans's analysis was prepared to determine whether TransUnion could service the necessary debt to fund the leveraged buyout (LBO) he was contemplating. The court had not, however, considered his analysis sufficient to approve a merger because it was not a valuation study. This ruling is significant because it affirms the need for a formal valuation analysis in all mergers, acquisitions, and LBOs. Ultimately, then, the *Smith v. Van Gorkom* decision is important because it set forth, under the business judgment rule,

---

[1] *Smith v. Van Gorkam*, 488 A.2d 858, 3 EXC 112 (Del. 1985).
[2] Stanley Foster Reed and Alexandra Reed Lajoux, *The Art of M&A: A Merger Acquisition Buyout Guide*, 2nd ed. (New York: John Wiley & Sons, 1995), 662–663.
[3] Arthur Fleisher, Geoffrey C. Hazard Jr., and Miriam Z. Klipper, *Board Games* (Boston: Little, Brown, 1988), 31–32.

the responsibilities of directors of public companies to have a thorough and complete valuation analysis conducted by an objective party, such as an investment bank or valuation firm. Following *Smith v. Van Gorkom*, even the more financially adept directors seek to get themselves off the hook by having an outside valuation firm or investment bank issue a "fairness opinion," expressing their belief that the offer is adequate. What is also significant about the *Smith v. Van Gorkom* decision was that the court was more impressed with the decision-making process that the directors engaged in than with the ultimate decision that they made. When compared with the usual standards to which merger offers are held, such as the size of the merger premium relative to recent or industry averages or what the offer price was relative to historical stock prices, the offer seemed to be a good one for shareholders. The soundness of the decision was not enough for the court, however, when it was the result of a process that the court found to be deficient.

In the wake of *Smith v. Van Gorkom* the demand for fairness opinions rose significantly. While such opinions may help get directors off the hook, they raise their own concerns. It is common that firms such as investment banks will issue fairness opinions involving transactions from which they stand to profit. This raises concerns of conflicts of interest. This is another area that M&A governance reform needs to address. In addition, fairness opinions really do not state that the price is the best value for the company. Rather they state merely that the price is "fair."

VALUATION METHODS: SCIENCE OR ART?

The methods and data considered in the valuation of businesses vary widely. In some respects, business valuation is as much an art as it is a science. It is exact and scientific in that there are standard methods and hard data to consider in the formulation of valuation. However, several different methods may be employed in a given evaluation. The methods may provide different business values and thus give the impression that the general methodology lacks systematic rigor.

The naive reader may infer that the valuation of businesses may be an overly subjective process. A closer examination of the methodology, however, reveals that objective valuations can be achieved. The variability of values is natural, given that we are considering the market for a business in which different participants may place varied values on the same business or collection of assets because the anticipated uses of these businesses or assets may be different in different hands.

In this chapter we will discuss the main methods of business valuation. We will consider the methods that are used to value both public and private companies. Many of the techniques used to value both types of companies are similar. For example, the selection of the discount rate and comparable multiples is clearly relevant to valuing both public and private companies. But some techniques, such as the marketability discount, may be more relevant to the valuation of closely held businesses.

MANAGING VALUE AS AN ANTITAKEOVER DEFENSE

The intensified takeover pressures that managers experienced in the fourth merger wave gave them a great incentive to increase the value of their firms so as to reduce their vulnerability to a takeover. Firms with a falling stock price but marketable assets are vulnerable to a takeover. Those with high liquid assets are even more vulnerable. Managers have found that adopting a management strategy that will boost the stock price makes the firm a more expensive target. With an increased stock price, raiders have trouble convincing stockholders that management is doing a bad job and that there are more value-enhancing ways to run the company.

An increase in stock price reduces the effectiveness of several takeover tactics. It makes a tender offer more difficult by raising the cost of control, and it decreases the effectiveness of a proxy fight because it is harder to garner the requisite number of votes from other shareholders when management has increased the value of their investment. Some supporters of takeovers maintain that the pressures placed on management have benefited shareholders by forcing management to take actions that maximize the value of their investment. The stock price has become a report card of management performance. Managers now have to regularly monitor the market's valuation of their actions. This marks a significant change in the way corporations were run in earlier years, when managers kept the stock price in mind but did not make it a factor in most of their major decisions. For this reason, among others, valuation has been placed in the forefront of corporation management.

 BENCHMARKS OF VALUE

The analysis presented in this chapter provides several different methods of valuing a company. Their accuracy can be tested through a basic sensibility check, which can be performed by comparing the resulting values with certain benchmarks that indicate the *floor value* of the company. The floor value is the normal minimum value that the company should command in the marketplace. Some of these benchmarks are described in the following sections.

Book Value

Book value is the per-share dollar value that would be received if the assets were liquidated for the values at which the assets are kept on the books, minus the monies that must be paid to liquidate the liabilities and preferred stock. Book value is sometimes also called shareholders' equity, net worth, or net asset value. Book value may not be an accurate measure of a company's market value. It merely reflects the values at which the assets are held on the books. If these historical balance sheet values are not consistent with the true value of the company's assets (including intangible assets, such as goodwill), book value will not be as relevant to the company's valuation.

One use of book value is to provide a floor value, with the true value of the company being some amount higher. The evaluator's role is to determine how much higher the true value of the company is. In some cases, however, the company may be worth less than the book value. Although this is not common, a company may have many uncertain liabilities, such as pending litigation, which may make its value less than the book value. Book value may also contain intangibles, such as goodwill, so it may also be useful to look at tangible book value, which excludes such components.

Sales prices of companies can be expressed as multiples of book values. These multiples tend to vary by industry. Depending on the current trends in the industry, there is a certain average value that can be used to gauge the current market price of potential targets. If firms in the industry are priced at a certain average value, such as selling at six times the book value, and the company in question is selling for only three times the book value, this might be an indicator of an undervalued situation.

Equity Value

Equity value means the value of an ownership interest in a business. In a corporation this value is usually represented by the value of its stock. If there is more than one call of stock, equity value is the combined value of these classes.

The book value of the equity, discussed above, reflects a value that is derived from the balance sheet as the difference between the book value of assets and the liabilities. The market value of equity reflects how the market values the shares of a corporation. This is also called market capitalization.

Enterprise Value

Enterprise value is the value of the entire business. It reflects the combined value of the claims of equityholders and debtholders. All types of equity, preferred and common, are included in equity value. When analysts think of the term enterprise value they are typically thinking of the market value of these equity claims. We will discuss how enterprise value is computed later in this chapter.

Liquidation Value

Liquidation value is another benchmark of the company's floor value. It is a measure of the per-share value that would be derived if the firm's assets were liquidated and all liabilities and preferred stock as well as liquidation costs were paid. This value may be different depending on whether the liquidation is being done under distressed conditions or if it is a more orderly liquidation. In a distressed liquidation assets may sell at "fire sale" prices.

Discounted Future Cash Flows or Net Present Value Approach

When the investment that is required to purchase the target firm is deducted from the discounted future cash flows or earnings, this amount becomes the net present value. This concept is similar to net present value calculations used for capital budgeting (equation 15.1). These techniques are covered in most corporate finance textbooks.

The discounted future cash flows approach to valuing a business is based on projecting the magnitude of the future monetary benefits that a business will generate. These annual benefits, which may be defined in terms of earnings or cash flows, are then discounted back to present value to determine the current value of the future benefits. Readers may be familiar with the discounting process from capital budgeting, where net present value (NPV) is used to determine whether a project is financially worth pursuing:

$$NPV = I_0 - \sum_{i=1}^{n} \frac{FB_i}{(1+r)} + \cdots = \frac{FB_n}{(1+r)^n} \tag{15.1}$$

where:

FB_i = future benefit in year i
r = discount rate
I_0 = investment at time 0

The future cash flows must be adjusted before constructing a projection so that the projected benefits are equal to the value that a buyer would derive. For example, adjustments such as the elimination of excessive officers' compensation must be made to the base that is used for the projection.

One of the key decisions in using the discounted cash flows (DCF) approach is to select the proper discount rate. This rate must be one that reflects the perceived level of risk in the target company. We will discuss the computation of discount rate a little later in this chapter.

When we use DCF to value a business, we do the valuation in a two-part process. Part one is to value the cash flows that have been specifically forecasted for a period over which the evaluator feels comfortable about the accuracy of the forecast (this is known as the discrete period). Typically this is five years in length. The second part of the process values the remaining cash flows as a perpetuity. The value of these remaining cash flows is sometimes referred to as *continuing or terminal value*. The longer the specific forecast period, the smaller the continuing value. The value of the business (BV) is equal to the sum of these amounts (equation 15.2):

$$BV = \text{Value derived from the specific forecast period}$$

$$+ \text{Value of remaining cash flows} \tag{15.2}$$

This value can then be computed as follows:

$$BV = \frac{FCF_1}{(1+r)} + \frac{FCF_2}{(1+r)^2} + \cdots + \frac{FCF_5}{(1+r)^5} + \frac{\frac{FCF_6}{(r-g)}}{(1+r)^5} \tag{15.3}$$

where:

BV = value of the business
FCF_i = free cash flows in the ith period
g = the growth rate in future cash flows after the fifth year

The numerators of all the fractions are free cash flows. Note that after the fifth year the values of all the future cash flows are measured by treating them as a perpetuity that is growing at a certain rate, g. This perpetuity or future stream of cash flows of indefinite length is valued using the process of capitalization. This process is explained subsequently because it is also used as a separate method of valuing businesses. However, the first step is to project free cash flows for the sixth year. This may be done by multiplying the fifth year's cash flows, FCF_5, by $(1 + g)$. The resulting value is then divided by the capitalization rate to obtain the present value of all cash flows from year 6 and thereafter. This is the value as of the beginning of year 6. We then compute the present value of that amount by dividing it by $(1 + r)^5$. This is the present value in year 0 of all future cash flows for year 6 and thereafter. This amount is sometimes referred to as the *residual*. It is then added to the other five present value amounts computed for the first five years to arrive at a value of the business.

Continuing or Terminal Value

The continuing value (CV) represents the value that the business could be expected to be sold for at the end of the specific forecast period. We have measured this value by treating it as a perpetuity and capitalizing the remaining cash flows, which we assumed were going to grow at a certain growth rate. Another way to arrive at the continuing value would be to apply an *exit multiple*. If we use an exit multiple for the continuing value, we need to make sure it is a multiple that we expect to apply during the exit period. For example, if a higher multiple is relevant as of the date of acquisition due to the company being in an initial high-growth phase of its life cycle, perhaps a lower multiple, consistent with mature firms in that industry, would be more relevant as an exit multiple.

It should be noted that when measuring the continuing value using the perpetuity calculation, the value that results is quite sensitive to the growth rate that is used. Different growth rate assumptions can change the resulting value significantly. As an example let us assume that the FCF at the end of the specific forecast period is $10 million and we are using an 11% discount rate. Applying a 6% growth rate results in:

$$CV_1 = \$10,000,000(1.06)/(0.11 - 0.06) = \$212,000,000 \qquad (15.4)$$

If we used a growth rate lower by one percentage point, 5%, the resulting value is:

$$CV_2 = \$10,000,000(1.05)/(0.11 - 0.05) = \$175,000,000 \qquad (15.5)$$

The increase of one percentage point in the growth rate, from 5% to 6%, increased the continuing value by 21% (remember this value still has to be discounted back to year 0 terms). This is why the assumptions about the continuing growth of the company after the end of the specific forecast period are important to the overall value of the company. As we will discuss in the Quaker Oats–Snapple case study, flawed growth rate assumptions can result in disastrous overpayment.

QUAKER OATS' ACQUISITION OF SNAPPLE

A classic example of overpaying was the acquisition of Snapple by Quaker Oats. In 1994, Quaker Oats had acquired Snapple for $1.7 billion. Just three years later, in March 1997, Quaker Oats announced that it was selling Snapple for $300 million to Triac Cos. Now *that* is value creation for you! The market reacted positively to this admission of an acquisition mistake when on March 27, 1997, Quaker Oats stock closed at $37.75—up 25 cents.

How did Quaker Oats, a well-known and established company with major consumer brands, make such a huge error? Clearly it overvalued Snapple and thought that its growth, which before the acquisition had been impressive, would continue. Snapple used its prior growth to demand a high premium, as it should have done. Quaker should have more realistically evaluated Snapple's growth prospects and used a more modest growth rate when it valued the company.

At the time that Quaker made its rich offer for Snapple, many analysts questioned it and thought that Quaker was overpaying. The word at the time was that Quaker might be overpaying by about as much as $1 billion. But Quaker was not buying Snapple in a vacuum, and it was already successful in the soft or recreational drinks business with its Gatorade line. Gatorade was and still is a successful beverage and has carved out its own niche in this business that is separate and distinct from giants such as Coke and Pepsi. To a large extent, Snapple had already done the same thing. However, with the familiarity it already had with the beverage business through its experience with Gatorade, Quaker Oats should have known better. It would be one thing for Quaker Oats to have had no experience with this business and make such a mistake. While that would not have made the misvaluation excusable, Quaker's experience in the sector makes the misvaluation even harder to explain.

Quaker Oats is an established company with a 100-year history in business. It has a diverse product line, which ranges from pancakes and cereals to juices and sports drinks. Quaker had already done well with its Gatorade acquisition. One author reported, however, that the success of this acquisition for Quaker's CEO, William Smithburg, was based on luck and impulsive decision making rather than shrewd acquisition planning.[a] He was reported to have bought this company based on "his taste buds" rather than a more serious market and valuation analysis. Regardless of his reasoning, however, the Gatorade purchase was a big success. The business cost Quaker $220 million, and it grew it into a $1 billion company. Based on this success, Quaker's board gave Smithburg more free rein for other acquisitions, and it was here that both he and the board made an error.

The Quaker Oats–Snapple debacle was compounded by the manner in which the deal was financed. In order to raise the capital to afford the Snapple acquisition, Quaker sold its "highly successful pet and bean divisions" to "raise $110 million of the $1.8 billion price tag."[b] It sacrificed a profitable, albeit boring, business to purchase an overpriced and mature business.

Triac was a company with its own acquisition history. It was run by Nelson Peltz and Peter May. Peltz was well known in the world of M&As, having led Triangle Industries, which was involved in some well-known leveraged transactions working with Drexel Burnham Lambert and Michael Milken in the fourth merger wave. Triangle grew from acquiring stakes in several can-making companies, consolidating them, and eventually selling them to a French company for $1.26 billion. More recently Peltz is known for his aggressive proxy fight for a presence on the board of Heinz Corp.

Quaker made more errors than just overpaying. After it bought Snapple, it changed its advertising and marketing campaign. Before its sale, Snapple used an odd set of advertisements that featured a Snapple employee named Wendy Kaufman. When Quaker bought Snapple, it changed this campaign to one that directly positioned Snapple behind Coke and Pepsi. This campaign, however, did little to help Snapple grow enough to justify its rich price.

Quaker also did not understand Snapple's distribution system, in which Snapple's distributors aggressively pursued unique deals to acquire shelf space. When the bureaucratic Quaker tried to get Snapple's distributors to convert some of their shelf space to Gatorade, there was little financial incentive for them to do so and they didn't.[c]

In 2000, Triac packaged together its beverage operations, which included RC Cola, Mistic, and Snapple, and sold them to Cadbury for $1 billion plus the assumption of $420 million of debt. This was a great deal for Triac when one considers that it invested only $75 million in equity for Snapple and borrowed the rest of the $300 million. The fact that Cadbury paid $1.4 billion for this business in 2000 is ironic in that it passed on the Snapple acquisition a few years earlier because it believed that the business was too troubled to justify a much lower price than what it eventually paid.[d]

Why did Quaker Oats overpay? One factor that is clear is that it believed there was more growth potential in the Snapple business than what was really there. To review the reasonableness of Quaker Oats' assessment of Snapple's growth potential, one can consider the distribution into the market that Snapple already enjoyed in 1997. Snapple had grown impressively before that year. It had a high growth rate to show potential buyers. Buyers, however, needed to assess whether that growth was sustainable. One way to do so would be to determine how many more food outlets Snapple could get into and how much more product it could sell at those that it had managed to get distribution into. Was it already in most of the food stores that it would be able to get into in the U.S. market? Could it really increase sales significantly at the outlets it was already in? If it was at a maturity position, in a noncarbonated beverage market that was growing significantly but where the growth was slowing, then this needed to be incorporated into the valuation model, using either a lower growth rate for a DCF model or a lower multiple for a comparable multiples model. That is, if historical growth rates were extrapolated, this would result in an overvaluation. Obviously, Quaker Oats was using inflated growth parameters when it significantly overpaid for Snapple.

[a] P. C. Nutt, "Averting Decision Debacles," *Technology Forecasting and Social Change* 71, no. 3 (2004): 239–265.

[b] Ibid., 245.

[c] Paul B. Carroll and Chunka Mui, *Billion Dollar Lessons* (New York: Portfolio Press, 2008), 27–28.

[d] Constance Hays, "Cadbury Schweppes to Buy Snapple Drinks Line," *New York Times*, September 19, 2000, C1.

Adjustments to DCF Enterprise Value

In computing enterprise value using DCF, we are implicitly including only those assets that contribute to the generation of free cash flows. If the company owns other assets that have a positive market value but that do not contribute to cash flow generation, then the value of these assets needs to be added to the enterprise value that has been computed using DCF. An example is real estate assets that are not involved in the operations of the business.

Arriving at Equity Value Using Enterprise Value

When we use DCF to arrive at enterprise value we compute the value of the equity by deducting the value of the liabilities from the total enterprise value. However, we may have to make other adjustments to the debt value that is found on the balance sheet. Two areas of sometimes significant liabilities that may not be on the balance sheet are unfunded pension liabilities and contingent liabilities.

Defining Free Cash Flows

Free cash flows are those cash flows, that are available to all capital providers, both equityholders as well as debtholders, after necessary deductions have been made for the capital expenditures (CE) that are needed to maintain the continuity of the cash flow stream in the future. These expenditures are made to replace capital that may have been depleted through the company's operating activities. While the term free cash flows (FCF) has been defined differently by some users, many also deduct any necessary changes in working capital (CWC) as well as cash taxes paid (CTP) (equation 15.6):

$$FCF = EBITDA - CE - CWC - CTP \qquad (15.6)$$

Free cash flow reflects the cash from a business that is available to make payments to shareholders and long-term debtholders. Therefore, it reflects the monies that generate value for these investors.

Accuracy of Discounted Cash Flows: Evidence from Highly Leveraged Transactions

Kaplan and Ruback conducted a study of 51 highly leveraged transactions (HLTs) between 1983 and 1989, in which they compared the market value of the transactions with the discounted values using cash flow forecasts in an effort to ascertain the accuracy of the forecasts relative to the actual purchase price.[4] Of the 51 transactions, 43 were management buyouts and 8 were recapitalizations. They found that the median estimates of the DCF were within 10% of the market values of the transactions.

---

[4] Steven N. Kaplan and Richard S. Ruback, "The Valuation of Cash Flow Forecasts: An Empirical Analysis," *Journal of Finance* 50, no. 4 (September 1995): 1059–1093.

It is interesting that they compared the accuracy of the DCF forecasts with that of other valuation methods, such as comparable multiples from transactions in similar industries. The results showed that the DCF valuation performed at least as well, if not better, than comparable methods. When they added the comparable data to their model, however, the explanatory power of the DCF estimates improved. This suggests that using information from *both* methods would result in better valuations than using just one.

The importance of the Kaplan and Ruback study is that it reinforces the superiority of DCF to other valuation methods while recognizing the value of other methods, such as comparables, in enhancing a valuation. It further affirms the validity of DCF methods as they are currently used in the valuation of public and closely held firms.

Choice of the Discount Rate

The choice of the appropriate discount rate to calculate the present value of the future projected cash flows requires that the riskiness of the target and the volatility of its cash flows be assessed. As is true of other forms of capital investment, an acquisition is a risky endeavor. We focus on the target's cash flows as they reflect the value of the investment that is about to be made by the acquirer. The discounting process gives us a means of internalizing our judgments about the risk of an acquisition within the discount rate.

If a project were judged to be without risk, the appropriate discount rate would be the rate offered on Treasury bills, which are short-term government securities with a maturity of up to one year. Treasury bonds, the longer-term version of U.S. government securities, may also have zero default risk, but they carry interest rate risk. Interest rate risk is the risk that interest rates may rise above the rate that the investor receives from the Treasury bond. Although the investor is guaranteed the predetermined interest payments, these interest payments will not necessarily be invested at the same rate of interest. If they are not, the investment's proceeds will not be compounded at the rate of interest offered on the Treasury bond.

The riskier the investment, the higher the discount rate that should be used; the higher the discount rate, the lower the present value of the projected cash flows. However, a firm methodology for matching the risk with the discount rate needs to be established.

Cost of Capital and the Discount Rate

One guide to selecting the proper discount rate is to consider the cost of capital. This measure is useful in capital budgeting because only one firm is involved. The cost of capital for a given company can be generally derived through:

$$CC = \sum_{i=1}^{n} w_i k_i \qquad (15.7)$$

where:

CC = the firm's cost of capital

w_i = the weight assigned to the particular k_i; this weight is the percentage of the total capital mix of the firm that this source of capital accounts for

k_i = the rate for this source of capital

Let us consider a simple example of a firm whose capital structure is composed of 50% debt and 50% equity. The weights for each source are 0.50. If the debt rate is 9% and the rate of return on equity is 15%, the cost of capital can be computed as follows:

$$CC = 0.50(0.09) + 0.50(0.15) + 0.045 + 0.075 = 0.12 \text{ or } 12\% \quad (15.8)$$

The target may have a very different risk profile than the acquirer. This is why the target's cost of capital may be more relevant to the computation of the discount rate than the acquirer's. This is then used as the discount rate for the firm when using DCF. As the analysis is expanded to make the cost of capital reflect the true capital costs of the firm, all the various components of the capital mix must be considered. Therefore, if the firm has preferred stock outstanding as well as different forms of debt, such as secured bonds, unsecured debentures, and bank loans, each needs to be considered separately in the new, expanded version of equation 15.8.

Cost of Debt

The after-tax debt rate reflects the true cost of debt, given the fact that debt is a tax-deductible expense. The after-tax rate of debt can be determined as follows:

$$k^t = k_d(1 - t) \quad (15.9)$$

where:

k^t = the after-tax cost of debt

k_d = the pretax cost of debt

t = the actual corporate tax rate for the firm

One question that often arises is what tax rate should be used to compute the after-tax cost of debt. Some analysts simply use the statutory corporate rate since there may be uncertainty as to what rate a given corporation may actually pay. However, it is important to note that many corporations may pay a different rate. John Graham has provided a methodology for how such rates can be determined.[5]

---

[5] John Graham, "Debt and the Marginal Tax Rate," *Journal of Financial Economics* 41, no. 1 (May 1996): 41–73; and John Graham, "Proxies for the Corporate Marginal Tax Rate," *Journal of Financial Economics* 42, no. 2 (October 1996): 187–221.

Cost of Preferred Stock

Because preferred stock dividends are usually fixed, preferred stock shares some of the characteristics of debt securities. Therefore, preferred stock is often considered a fixed-income security. The cost of preferred stock to the issuer can be determined by first focusing on the dividends that have to be paid each period relative to the proceeds derived by the issuer. These proceeds should be net of flotation costs. Let us consider a firm that has issued 8% preferred stock with a par value of $100. Let us further assume that flotation costs are 2.0% of the par value. This suggests a net of proceeds value of $98. The annual dividends are $8, or 8% of the $100 par value. (Dividends are annualized for simplicity.) The cost can be determined as follows:

$$\text{Cost of preferred stock} = D_p/P_n = \$8/\$98 = 8.16\% \qquad (15.10)$$

The consideration of flotation costs should also be applied to all publicly issued securities. For the sake of brevity, we consider only flotation costs for preferred stock.

Cost of Common Stock

Many rules determine the cost to the corporation of the common stock it has issued. One of the simplest methods is to calculate the historical rate of return on equity for the stock over a given time period. A 5- to 10-year historical period is often chosen. The time period selected would have to be placed in perspective by considering the corporation's growth to see whether it represents the company's current and expected condition.

If the company is a startup company with little available history, proxy firms should be used. Proxy firms are similar to the company being analyzed, but they have more historical rate of return data available. The rate of return on equity for proxy firms is used in place of the company being analyzed.

Another method that is sometimes employed is the beta risk measure, which is derived from the capital asset pricing model. This measure allows us to consider the riskiness of the company and to use this risk level to determine the appropriate rate of return on the company's equity. The beta can be derived from the following expression:

$$R_i = R_{RF} + \beta_i(R_M - R_{RF}) \qquad (15.11)$$

where:

R_i = the rate of return on equity for security i

R_{RF} = the risk-free rate; the Treasury bill rate is typically used as the risk-free rate of interest

β_i = the beta for security i

R_M = the rate of return for the market

$(R_M - R_{RF})$ = the market risk premium

Beta is derived from a regression analysis in which the variability of the market's return is compared with the variability of the security's return. From this analysis, a beta for the firm is computed, which can be used to weigh the risk premium. This weighed risk premium is then specific to the firm being analyzed. This method of measuring the cost of capital makes good conceptual sense but is not commonly used in daily merger analysis.

Betas can vary depending on how they are computed and the data that are relied upon in arriving at the value.[6] One can arrive at a different beta for the same security based upon various factors:

- The length of the time period used for the historical data inputted into the model
- The specific market index used
- The time periods or frequency used for the historical data
- The specific risk-free rate used[7]

The betas that are computed for various companies are sometimes referred to as *leveraged betas* since they reflect the capital structure of each company. Leveraged betas reflect two factors that influence systematic risk: business risk as well as financial risk that is a function of a company's capital structure. If an acquirer is less concerned about the target's capital structure because it can install its own capital structure following the acquisition, then a more useful measure may be an unleveraged beta. There are various formulas that can be used to compute an unleveraged beta. One of these is the Hamada formula, shown in equation 15.12.

$$B_u = \frac{B_L}{1 + (1 - t)\frac{W_d}{W_e}} \tag{15.12}$$

B_u = unleveraged beta

B_L = leveraged beta

t = tax rate for the company

W_d = percent debt in the capital structure

W_e = percent equity in the capital structure

The rate of return on equity can also be measured by directly projecting the dividend flow. This calculation is easy in the case of preferred stock because the dividends are generally fixed. Equation 15.13, derived from the Gordon model, demonstrates the relationship between the stock price and dividends.

$$P_s = D_i/(k_e - g) \tag{15.13}$$

---

[6] John Y. Campbell and Jainping Mei, "Where Do Betas Come From? Asset Price Dynamics and the Sources of Systematic Risk," *Review of Financial Studies* 6, no. 3 (1993): 567–592.

[7] Shannon Pratt and Roget J. Grabowski, *Cost of Capital: Applications and Examples* (Hoboken: NJ, 2008), 121.

where:

P_s = the price of the firm's stock

D_i = the dividend paid in period i (i.e., the next quarter)

k_e = the capitalization rate for this stock

g = the growth rate of dividends

We can manipulate the preceding equation to solve for k_e.

$$k_e = D_i/P_0 + g \qquad (15.14)$$

Consider the example of a firm whose common stock is currently selling for $40 per share. Annual dividends are $3, and the expected growth in dividends is 7% per year. (For simplicity's sake, dividends are considered annually, even though they may be paid quarterly.) The capitalization rate can be calculated as shown in equation 15.15.

$$k_e = \$3(1.07)/\$40 + 0.07 = 15\% \qquad (15.15)$$

The capitalization rate can be used as a measure of the firm's cost of equity capital.

A simple guideline in deriving the cost of equity is to consider that the rate of equity is generally 4% to 6% higher than the rate of debt. The rate of debt may be clear if the firm does not have many different types of debt. In this case, the debt rate is given, and 4% to 6% can simply be added to derive the rate for equity.

Another way to look at the appropriate rate on equity is to consider the long-term risk premium. This is the difference between the long-term average rate on risk-free T-bills and the rate on equities. Historically this has been between 6% and 7%. However, there has been much debate regarding whether the appropriate risk premium should be lower given what some see as one-time factors and institutional changes that would make the difference in return on these securities be less in the future than it has been in the past.[8]

Acquirer's Hurdle Rate

In discussing the cost of capital we have indicated that we would focus more on the target's costs of capital rather than the acquirer's. However, the buyer may also want to do the analysis using its own *hurdle rate*. This is the rate of return that it requires its investments generate. This in turn may be equal to the acquirer's own cost of capital. One problem that arises in using such a rate is that if the target's cash flows have a

---

[8] Jeremy J. Siegel, "The Shrinking Equity Premium," *Journal of Portfolio Management* 26, no. 1 (Fall 1999): 10–17; and Eugene Fama and Kenneth French, "The Equity Premium," *Journal of Finance* 57, no. 2 (April 2002): 637–659; as well as Ravi Jagannathan, Ellen R. McGrattan, and Anna Scherbina, "The Declining U.S. Equity Premium," *Federal Reserve Bank of Minneapolis Quarterly Review* 24, no. 4 (Fall 2000): 3–19.

higher volatility or risk than the acquirer's, the use of the hurdle rate may not fully capture all of the risk in the acquisition. However, this issue becomes somewhat moot if the two companies operate in the same industry and have a somewhat similar risk profile.

 ## HOW THE MARKET DETERMINES DISCOUNT RATES

As should now be clear, no set discount rate exists; many different interest rates are available to choose from. The overall market for capital consists of many submarkets. The rate within each market is determined by that market's supply and demand for capital. Markets are differentiated on the basis of risk level. For example, the market for debt capital contains many different gradations of debt that vary according to their risk level. The market for secured debt offers a lower rate of return than the market for unsecured debt. Within each of the secured and unsecured categories are other gradations, each of which has its own interest rate. The historical relationship between the broad categories of capital can be seen in Table 15.1.

Discount Rate and Risk

The greater the risk associated with a given earnings stream, the higher the discount rate that will be used. If the projected cash flow or income stream is considered highly likely, a lower discount rate should be used. For high-risk cash flow or income streams, a risk premium is added, which increases the discount rate. The use of a higher discount rate lowers the present value of each annual projected income amount.

TABLE 15.1 Rates of Return and Inflation: 1926–2013, 1984–2013, and 1994–2013

	1926–2013 Rate (%)	1984–2013 Rate (%)	1994–2013 Rate (%)
Inflation	3.0	2.8	2.4
Treasury bills	3.5	4.0	2.9
Long-term Treasury bonds	5.9	10.1	7.8
Long-term corporate bonds	6.3	9.8	7.5
Common stock of large corporations	12.0	12.6	11.1
Common stock of small corporations	16.9	13.4	14.3

Source: Morningstar Ibbotson SBBI 2014 Yearbook.

Cross-Border Acquisitions and Risk

Investing in foreign countries brings with it a new element that varies depending on the market. The acquirer may face the worry that the foreign government may take actions that will limit the ability of the acquirer to access the cash flows that are generated in the foreign market. These actions range from changing tax rates to imposing additional regulations to even nationalization of businesses. When governments are not stable, potential acquirers may not be able to predict what type of government will be in control over the life of the investment. An example of this occurred in 2012 when Argentina seized control of YPF, which was an affiliate of the Spanish energy company Respol. The seizure came after the company announced that its costly exploration efforts had finally paid off.[9]

Research on cross-border versus domestic acquisitions confirms what one's intuition would suggest—that cross-border deals may present some unique opportunities but they also bring with them unique risks that may even offset the returns. In analyzing a large sample of 4,430 acquisitions over the period 1985–1995, Moeller and Schlingemann found that U.S. acquirers experienced significantly lower equity and operating performance when they pursued cross-border deals compared to domestic acquisitions.[10] In addition, they found that stock returns responded negatively to global diversification. Other research, as well as this study, has confirmed that stock returns respond negatively to industry diversification.

Obviously some countries are riskier than others. This needs to be a factor that is incorporated into the discount rate. Markets that are in a state of transition, such as India and China, can be hard to predict. Investments in less stable markets will usually warrant a higher risk premium. Countries can increase the value of their businesses and attract more foreign capital by lowering their risk profile, thereby enabling businesses to better predict the cash flows they may expect to gain access to.

Changing Interest Rates and Acquisition Prices: Evidence from the Fifth Merger Wave

Lower interest rates tend to result in lower discount rates. Short-term fluctuations may not change the discount rate that one would use in a valuation, but changes in long-term rates that persist for an extended period of time should have an influence. Such was the case in the fifth merger wave, where interest rates fell and the average price of acquisitions rose. This is demonstrated in Figures 15.1a and 15.1b, which show that as the average yield on long-term Treasury bonds declined, the average

---

[9] Patrick A. Gaughan, *Maximizing Corporate Growth through Mergers and Acquisitions: A Strategic Growth Guide* (Hoboken, NJ: John Wiley & Sons, 2013), 204.

[10] Sara B. Moeller and Frederick P. Schlingemann, "Global Diversification and Bidder Gains: A Comparison between Cross-Border and Domestic Acquisitions," *Journal of Banking and Finance* 29, no. 3 (March 2005): 533–564.

Percent

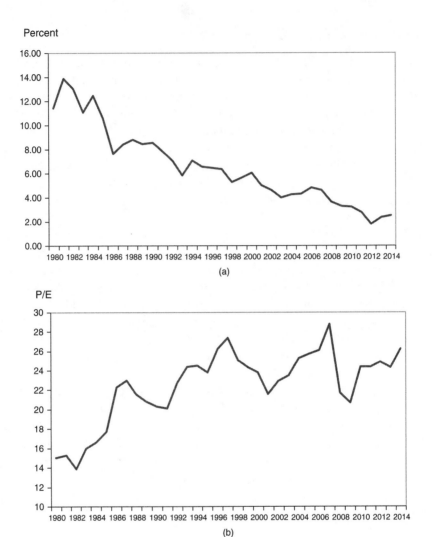

FIGURE 15.1 (a) Yield on Long-Term Treasuries and (b) Average Annual P/E Multiple. *Source*: Economic Report of the President, March 2014; *Mergerstat Review*, 1991 and 2014.

acquisition prices rose. Long-term Treasuries are used as a base on which a risk premium is applied to arrive at a risk-adjusted discount rate. When interest rates fall for an extended period of time, evaluators lower their discount rates, resulting in higher acquisition values. This is not to imply, however, that interest rates are the only factor determining acquisition prices. They are but one of several important factors that need to be considered.

APPLYING THE DISCOUNTED CASH FLOW METHOD OF BUSINESS VALUATION

This case study applies the discounted cash flow method of business valuation to a company that has $2.5 billion in sales in 2006. Sales are expected to grow at declining rates of growth over the next five years from 10% in 2007 to a maturity growth rate of 6% (*g*) after the fifth year. For the purposes of this simple example we define free cash flow as the difference between net operating income after tax (NOPAT) and new net capital expenditures:

$$\text{NOPAT} = \text{Earnings before Interest \& Taxes (EBIT)}(1 - \text{tax rate})$$

$$\text{FCF} = \text{NOPAT} - \text{New net capital expenditures}$$

The discount rate is taken to be the weighted average costs of capital for the company, which this case study assumes is 12% (*r*). The capitalization rate that is used to compute the terminal value of the company after year 5 is the difference between this rate and the long-term growth rate:

$$\text{WACC} = r = 12\% \text{ and } k = \text{Capitalization rate} = r - g = 12\% - 6\% = 6\%$$

The enterprise value of the company is the present value of its future projected cash flows. This value is computed as the sum of the present value of the individually projected cash flows for the first five years and the capitalized terminal value. This value is computed as follows:

$$\text{Terminal value} = \text{FCF}_6/(r - g)$$

It is important to remember that this terminal value is itself a year 5 value because it is the value of the company's cash flows that are projected to be received after year 5. Therefore, it must be brought to present value by dividing it by the PVIF applicable to year 5 or $1/(1.12)^5$:

$$\frac{\text{FCF}_1}{(1 + k)_1} + \frac{\text{FCF}_2}{(1 + k)_2} + \cdots + \frac{\text{FCF}_5}{(1 + k)_5} + \frac{\text{FCF}_6/(r - g)}{(1 + k)_5}$$

Assumptions

Sales growth: Growth at 10% per year declining by 5% and 6% thereafter
    Shares outstanding (mil): 40

(*continued*)

(continued)

TABLE A Using DCF to Compute Enterprise and Equity Values

	Years				
	1	2	3	4	5
Sales growth rate	10.0%	9.5%	9.0%	8.0%	7.0%
After-tax operating Margin	6.0%	6.0%	6.0%	6.0%	6.0%
Net op. cap. exp. %/sales	5.0%	5.0%	5.0%	5.0%	5.0%
Weighted average cost capital (WACC)	12.0%				
Long-run growth rate	6.0%				
Sales base level, 2006:	2,500				
Free Cash Flows (1–5)					
Sales (mil $)	2, 750.0	3, 011.3	3, 282.3	3, 544.8	3, 793.0
NOPAT	165.0	180.7	196.9	212.7	227.6
Net operating capital expenditures	137.5	150.6	164.1	177.2	189.6
Free cash flows (FCFs)	27.5	30.1	32.8	35.4	37.9
Present value of FCFs	24.6	24.0	23.4	22.5	21.5

Terminal Value Calculation		**Total Enterprise Value**	
Free cash flow year 6	40.2	Present value of FCF's (years 1–5)	116.0
Term. value of company in year 5	670.1	Present value company's terminal value	380.2
Present value of terminal value	380.2	Total enterprise value	496.2
		Deduct market value of debt & preferred	100.0
		Total value common equity	396.2
		Shares outstanding	40.0
		Price of share of stock	**9.9**

Source: Patrick A. Gaughan, *Measuring Business Interruption Losses and Other Commercial Damages*, 2nd ed. (Hoboken, NJ: John Wiley & Sons, 2009), 300–301. Case study developed by Professor Henry Fuentes of Economatrix Research Associates.

Real Options in Valuation

In the past decade the DCF analysis that is used in capital budgeting as well as in business valuation came under attack for its lack of flexibility. Capital investments normally carry with them various options or alternatives that may affect the value of the investment over their life. In the context of capital budgeting, these options, which allow for modification of the value of an investment over time, are referred to as *real options*.[11] Many options or alternatives are relevant to most capital investments, but some of the more common are the options to postpone or delay, to grow, or even to abandon an investment. In the context of M&As, the options could be postponing a proposed acquisition or selling off all of a division. Capital projects typically also feature many different growth options that allow a company to take steps and incur costs that may speed up or slow the growth of the cash flows from a proposed deal. In an acquisition context, this could involve a decision to invest capital in an acquired business in the hope that the target's growth can be increased.

In general, an option gives the holder the right to buy or sell an asset over a specific time period. Readers may be more familiar with *financial options*, such as calls and puts, which are traded on financial exchanges. *Real options* are those related to real assets as opposed to financial assets. They come in a wide variety, such as those related to property, equipment, intellectual property such as copyrights, licenses, and trademarks. In the context of M&A we are referring more to options related to capital investment decisions, including those related to whole businesses. This is why it is said that the M&A process carries with it embedded options that can come in a wide variety, such as the right to accelerate growth by combining businesses or terminating projects and selling off divisions.

Simply creating one projection of future cash flows without considering the many different options that can be pursued over the life of the investment or acquisition presents a limited picture of the wide range of alternatives that can occur or could be pursued. This limitation has long been considered by theoreticians and practitioners in the field of capital budgeting, and they have used various tools to try to augment simple net present value computations. Smith and Triantis argue that discounted cash flow models do not as easily capture the impact of potential M&A synergies that they assert can be better dealt with using a real options approach.[12]

In an effort to arrive at business values that explicitly incorporate the alternatives of various projected cash flows, researchers and practitioners applied models that are derived from the Nobel Prize–winning option pricing model (OPM) used to value financial options. While the analysis today has reached quite sophisticated levels, the original 1973 Black-Scholes option pricing model (see equations 15.16 through 15.18) can be

---

[11] For a good discussion of real options, see Richard A. Brealey and Stewart C. Myers, *Capital Investment and Valuation* (New York: McGraw Hill, 2003), 429–449.

[12] Kenneth W. Smith and Alexander J. Triantis, "The Value of Options in Strategic Acquisitions," in Lenos Trigeorgis, ed., *Real Options in Capital Investment: Models, Strategies and Applications* (Westport, CT: Praeger, 1995).

TABLE 15.2 Black-Scholes Call Option versus Business Real Option Parameters

Call Option Parameter	Symbol	Business Real Option Parameter
Underlying stock price	S	Present value of future cash flows
Exercise price	E or X	Investment
Volatility of the stock price	σ	Volatility of the cash flows
Risk-free rate	r	Risk-free rate
Time to option expiration	t	Time to end of relevant business period

successfully employed to show the real option approach. The model is still a mainstay in the valuation of options. For a call option:

$$C = SN(d_1) - Ee^{-rt}N(d_2) \tag{15.16}$$

$$d_1 = \frac{\ln(S/X) + rt}{\sigma\sqrt{t}} + \frac{1}{2}\sigma\sqrt{t} \tag{15.17}$$

$$d_2 = d_1 - \sigma\sqrt{t} \tag{15.18}$$

Table 15.2 shows the five parameters that are used in the typical Black-Scholes calculation and their equivalent if this model were applied to business valuation.

CASE STUDY: BIG PHARMA ACQUISITION OF BIOTECH USING REAL OPTIONS

Let us assume that Big Pharma Corp. (BPC) contemplates the acquisition of a medium-sized biotech company (BIOT) that conducts research in an area where BPC sees great potential. Let us further assume that it has certain patent-protected drugs (protection period assumed to be 15 years) that BPC expected to yield BIOT impressive cash flows and that DCF analysis shows that BIOT should have a value of $500 million given these projected cash flows and a weighted cost of capital (WACC) of 12%.

However, BIOT demands a price of $750 million. BIOT argues that its research into a specific new drug has a potential DCF value of $1 billion three years from now if an investment of $1.2 billion is made. The management of BPC is quite puzzled about why a seemingly negative NPV project in the future would give more value to BIOT. In fact, BPC responds to BIOT that this news may cause it to *lower*, not increase, its offer for BIOT. BIOT responds that the new drug DCF value has a standard deviation of 70% and claims that this gives the required value to the company as long as the three-year T-note has a yield of 5%. BIOT's CFO explains to BPC that this growth potential is analogous to a call option with a current value of the stock of $1 billion discounted for three periods at 12% (BIOT's WACC), which is approximately $712 million. He proceeds to use the call model (see equations 15.16–15.18) where S is $712 million, the exercise price E is $1.2 billion, the maturity of the option is three years, the risk-free rate is 5%, and the volatility is 70%.[a] Doing the computation with these inputs, the CFO obtains a value for the growth potential of BIOT of $253 million. Therefore, he maintains that the asking price of $750 million is more than justified. BPC is not yet convinced of all the arguments, but it is willing to take this valuation into consideration. After several rounds of discussions BPC agrees to offer $650 million for the company with contingency valuation rights of $100 million. This means that BPC will pay $100 million to the current shareholders of BIOT if in three years the new drug goes into production. The BPC CFO is quite pleased with how he structured the deal and thinks of himself as a clever financial engineer.

Across the ocean, La Grande Pharma (LGP) is looking at BIOT for its potential to develop the new drug. Given the sure stream of cash flow coming from existing patents and the potential of the new drug, it is prepared to make an offer of $650 million for the company. Well versed in their market, they know that BPC would still be interested in buying BIOT in three years mainly for the current drug for which they hold what LGP believes is a strong and defensible patent. LGP figures that BPC would pay about $455 million for the company, representing the remaining value over 12 years of the "annuity," which would value the company today at $500 million with a WACC of 12%.

LGP has a CFO quite versed in real option valuation (ROV) who recognizes that having the right to sell BIOT after three years is akin to having a put option (equation 15.19). He proceeds to value the put option with S, $650 million, an exercise price E of $455 million, and an overall volatility of the firm of about 50% (an average between the existing product and the much greater volatility for the new drug). The result is about $72 million. He is thinking that the total offer for BIOT could be as high as $720 million and makes an immediate offer to BIOT of $700 million (see equation below and 15.17 and 15.18).

$$P = Ee^{-rT}[1 - N(d_2)] - S[1 - N(d_1)] \tag{1}$$

where:

P = put premium

S = stock price

X = exercise price

T = time to expiration

r = the interest rate

Since the discounted value of the $100 million that BPC is willing to offer is today about $71 million, BIOT has now to decide if it likes the bird in hand ($700 million) or the one on the fence (about $720 million) along with the usual issues and other concerns that comes from an acquisition. This case study is provided by Professor Sorin Tuluca, Fairleigh Dickinson University.

[a] BPC finds this discussion curious but notes that BIOT's CFO was a former finance professor at a well-known academic institution, so it decided to "humor him."

Comparable Multiples

Comparable multiples are regularly used to value businesses. They are a quick and easy method to come up with a value for a company. Like DCF, they can be used to value both public and closely held businesses. There are three basic steps in using comparable multiple analysis: (1) selecting the appropriate comparable companies, (2) selecting the correct multiple, and then (3) applying it to the relevant earnings base. We will see that there are abundant areas for judgment and subjectivity in the selection of these two parameters.

Common multiples that are used are price-earnings multiples, so-called P/E ratios, price-to-book, enterprise value to EBITDA, price to revenues, and other combinations. Usually some normalized value of these measures is used, especially when the levels of the values fluctuate greatly. Once the multiple is derived, it is then applied to either the current year or an estimate of the next year's value of the base selected. Perhaps the most commonly cited multiple is the P/E ratio, which is the ratio of a company's stock price (P) divided by its earnings per share (EPS). When we multiply a derived P/E ratio by a target company's EPS, we get an estimated stock price. For example, let us say that we have analyzed 10 comparable companies and have found that the average P/E ratio is 17. We can then multiply this value by the target company's EPS, which we assume in this example is $3: $17 \times \$3 = \$41$. When the multiples are derived from an analysis of historical earnings, they are referred to as *trailing multiples*. When they are based on forecasts of future earnings, they are called *forward multiples*.

Other commonly used multiples are EBITDA multiples—sometimes called cash flow multiples because EBITDA is sometimes used as a proxy for cash flows. We usually obtain EBITDA multiples by dividing enterprise value, including the sum of equity and debt capital, by a given company's EBITDA level. This is done for our group of comparable companies to derive our average value. That value is then applied to the target company's EBITDA value to obtain its enterprise value. We then back out the debt of the target from this value to get the value of its equity.

Establishing Comparability

When we use comparable multiples, one obvious key issue is comparability. Are the comparable companies from which we derived the multiple truly similar to the target being valued? Are they more valuable or less valuable? If, for example, the company being valued is a troubled concern, then it may not be worth the same multiple of other, healthier companies in the same industry. The target's difficulties should be reflected not only in a lower earnings base but also in lower comparable multiples, which might reflect lower earnings growth in the future.

Comparable multiples are forward-looking measures. For example, a buyer may pay seven times EBITDA, not for access to the past EBITDA level, but for future cash flows. When the market establishes specific acquisition multiples for different companies that have been purchased in the industry, it is making a statement about the ability of those companies to generate future cash flows. When using such multiples, comparability is key. It is more than just saying that a company being acquired shares the same

Standard Industrial Classification (SIC) or North American Industry Classification System (NAICS) code and is in the same industry. It is a more specific examination of comparability. Finding multiples for companies in the same business as the target is a first step, not the final step, in the comparability process. Having established a range based on prior acquisitions and the multiples that were paid, the evaluator needs then to see how the target compares with those companies from which the average multiple was derived. If the target has many features that would enhance its future earning power, then perhaps a higher multiple should apply. It is likely that the buyer is aware of this and may be asking for such a multiple. If it is not, either the buyer is naive or this assessment of higher-than-average future earning power may be misguided.

The Delaware Chancery Court has held that there must be a reliable basis for establishing comparability.[13] One of the ways this can be done is through specific research. In *Global GT LP v. Golden Telecom* the court rejected the use of comparable multiples due to the fact that neither expert presented a reliable basis for establishing comparability and neither had detailed knowledge of the relevant industry and the companies in particular.

Dealing with Outliers

Users of industry multiples should know which companies entered into the computation of the average. It is useful to be aware of the degree of dispersion. It may be the case that many of the companies in the industry have multiples very different from the average. If one or two outliers have skewed the average, then we need to consider whether they should be eliminated. If the outliers are very different from the company being evaluated, then there may be a good case for eliminating the outliers from the computation of the average.

USE OF COMPARABLE MULTIPLES TO DETERMINE ENTERPRISE VALUE

Enterprise value is a broad measure that reflects the value of the capital, both debt and equity, that has been invested in the company. In this case study, we will measure enterprise value using comparable multiples derived from similar businesses that have been sold before the current valuation. As previously noted, comparable multiples are applied to specific performance measures. Some common performance measurements are as follows:

- EBITDA: earnings before interest, taxes, depreciation, and amortization
- EBIT: earnings before interest and taxes

(continued)

---

[13] *Global GT LP et al v. Golden Telecom Inc.*, Court of Chancery of Delaware, 2010 Del. Ch. Lexis 76, decided April 23, 2010.

(*continued*)

▪ Net income: earnings after interest and taxes
▪ Free cash flow: operational cash flow less capital expenditures

The example depicted in Figure A uses an EBITDA performance measurement. This is used as a base in Figure A, which shows how an enterprise value/EBITDA multiple may be computed.

Net Income	$2,000,000
Taxes	$700,000
Interest	$250,000
Depreciation and amortization	$150,000
EBITDA	$3,100,000
Equity acquisition price	$12,000,000
Interest bearing debt	$2,500,000
Total enterprise value	$14,500,000
Multiple	4.68

FIGURE A EBITDA Multiple

Figure A illustrates the relationship between total enterprise value ($14,500,000) and EBITDA ($3,100,000). The application of the multiple indicated to the EBITDA performance of a target company to be acquired will result in an estimate of total enterprise value. Equity value can then be determined by deducting interest-bearing debt from total enterprise value.

Figure B, however, shows how such a multiple can be derived from other comparable historical transactions.

	Court Company	Rotary Company	Bay Products	Western Manufacturing
Net Income	$748,125	$304,000	$776,000	$2,374,000
Taxes	$785,625	$110,000	$400,000	$1, 411 000
Interest	$48,750	$45,000	$182,000	$1,407,000
Depreciation/Amortization	$458,125	$233,000	$392,000	$3, 498,000
EBITDA	$2,040,625	$692,000	$1,750,000	$8,690,000
Equity Acquisition Price	$14,052,000	$4,600,000	$14,600,000	$54,300,000
Interest Bearing Debt	$498,000	$1,863,000	$2, 616,000	$15, 954,000
Total Enterprise Value	$14,550,000	$6,463,000	$17,216,000	$70,254,000
Multiple	7.13	9.34	9.84	8.08
Average EBITDA Multiple	8.601			
Weighted Average EBITDA Multiple	8.24			

FIGURE B OCI Inc., Summary of Acquisitions

An example of the application of comparable multiple valuation can be illustrated in the following case. We are attempting to determine the appropriate value of Wilson Company, which is being acquired by OCI Inc. OCI has made several acquisitions over the past years (see Figure B). Historically, OCI has paid between

7 and 10 times EBITDA, averaging 8.6 times on an unweighted basis or 8.24 times on a weighted basis, depending on the size of the transaction.

We can apply this multiple to the financial results of the Wilson Company, the target acquisition, to determine an approximate value to be assigned to the Wilson acquisition (see Figure C). It should be pointed out that the results of Wilson's historical financial performance should be adjusted for nonrecurring or unusual items, which are not anticipated in the future. The valuation results in an enterprise value of $33.2 million and an equity value, after deducting liabilities of approximately $9 million, of $24.2 million.

Net income	$1,539,000
Taxes	$928,000
Interest	$374,000
Depreciation and amortization	$1,194,000
EBITDA	$4,035,000
Average Multiple	8.24
Total enterprise value	$33,248,400
Interest bearing debt	$8,990,000
Total equity value	$24,258,400

FIGURE C Valuation of Wilson Company

Using P/E Multiples

P/E multiples are a very often cited measure of value. Like other multiples, such as EBITDA multiples, one needs to be aware of the subtleties. As noted before, we can have trailing or forward multiples. When using multiples to value a business, we need to make sure that they are applied to *permanent* income. This is income that excludes nonrecurring, one-time earnings. For example, gain from sales of assets may not be relevant to future performance and should be excluded. As discussed earlier, we also need to differentiate between trailing and forward multiples. In the context of P/E multiples, a *trailing multiple* would be a recent stock price divided by earnings in the last full accounting period, such as the last year. A *forward multiple* would be the current stock price divided by forecasted earnings. Such forecasts may be either projected by the evaluator or derived from a commercial source. However, for companies that have had stable earnings, constructing a forecast by applying the company's own historical earnings growth to the last year's earnings level may provide a usable forecasted value.

Keep in mind that multiples vary by industry. This is intuitive as industries vary in their expected earnings growth. Table 15.3 shows selected P/E acquisition multiples for different industries. We can see that there is a significant degree of cross-industry variation.

TABLE 15.3 Acquisition Multiples: Average P/E* by Industry

Industry	P/E
Agricultural Production	23.4
Comm. & Broadcasting	19.3
Financial Services	30.1
Manufacturing	29.1
Natural Resources	18.1
Other Services	23.8
Real Estate	36.0
Retail	29.6
Transportation	55.7
Utilities	25.5
Wholesale & Distribution	24.6
**All Industry Average 2009–2014	28.7

*Excludes P/E multiples less than 0 and greater than 100.
**Weighted Average
Source: *Mergerstat Review*, 2015.

MATTEL'S ACQUISITION OF THE LEARNING COMPANY: OVERPAYING THROUGH FLAWED DUE DILIGENCE AND POOR STRATEGY

The case of Mattel's acquisition of the Learning Company is a classic example of overpaying caused by poor due diligence and a flawed strategy. Mattel is a major player in the toy business and markets leading brand names, such as Barbie. The company grew into this leadership position partly through a series of strategic acquisitions. This included acquiring major toy companies, such as Tyco Toys and Fisher Price. These horizontal acquisitions of competitors expanded the company's product line while increasing its market share.

In 1997, a new executive took the helm at the toy company—Jill Barad. She quickly gained notoriety and became one of the better-known female executives in the United States. Her fame peaked when she appeared on the cover of *BusinessWeek*. After taking control of the toy company, she began to pursue her own acquisitions, and in 1999 committed the company to buy a very different type of business. Mattel paid $3.5 billion for the Learning Company, which was in the educational software business. The idea behind the strategy was that toys are becoming more computerized and the products that the Learning Company marketed were sold to a similar audience as Mattel's product line sold to. Skeptics were concerned that the similarities between the product lines of the two companies were hard to see. This was confirmed in 2000 when Mattel sold off the Learning Company for virtually nothing. The business had lost money for Mattel and, when overall poor performance forced the company to refocus, the company decided to cut its losses and part ways with the Learning Company.

VALUATION OF THE TARGET'S EQUITY

In conducting a valuation of a public company, the value of the debt is usually a fairly straightforward exercise. The valuation of the target's equity is the more challenging part of the process. For public companies, however, there is a market for the target's stock, and the values that a company's stock trades at in this market may be helpful in determining the value that should be paid for a target's equity in an acquisition. However, the bidder would not simply adopt the current price at the time an offer is being made. Several adjustments might have to be made. One would be a time variation adjustment that simply addresses the fact that the current price might not be representative of the long-term historical prices at which the stock traded. It could be that the market is in a temporary downturn. The bidder may want to use the temporarily low price, but it is unlikely that the seller would accept this. The difference between the near-term historical average price and the current price would provide some room for negotiations between the parties. In addition, the price of the stock at a moment in time does not reflect a control premium that normally accompanies acquisition offers.

 ## MARKETABILITY OF THE STOCK

The marketability of common stock varies considerably. The equity of publicly held companies that is traded on large organized exchanges, such as the New York Stock Exchange (NYSE), is generally considered quite liquid. However, more and more, much stock trading has left the NYSE, which at the start of the 2000s handled about 80% of all U.S. trading. By 2014 that percentage had fallen to about 20%. That share has been taken by other exchanges as well as private trading venues and "dark pools." The liquidity of stocks that trade in these other locations can vary significantly.

The market on which the security is traded is an important consideration in the valuation process. The broader the market and the greater the daily trading volume, the more liquid the security. This means that if you want to sell the stock, you have a better opportunity to sell a larger amount of stock without depressing the price significantly when it is actively traded on an organized exchange. If the stock is a seldom-traded security on the OTC market, however, the price quoted may be less reliable. The exact value of the stock may not be determinable until offers for the block have been made.

The "thinness" of the market is a major determinant of the liquidity of the security. Lack of liquidity is another element of risk that must be factored into the stock price. The liquidity or marketability risk can be factored into the risk premium that is used to value the projected cash flows.

Market thinness can be judged by looking at the number of *float shares*—the number of shares available for trading. Small companies on the OTC market may have only a small percentage of their shares traded, whereas most of the shares may be rarely traded. When the number of float shares is small compared with the total shares outstanding, the valuation provided by the market may not be very useful. Moreover, when the number of float shares is small, any sudden increase in trading volume can greatly affect the stock price. This is another element of risk that needs to be considered.

A related influence on the price a buyer may be willing to pay for a security is the concentration of securities in the hands of certain groups. The companies traded on the OTC market frequently have large blocks of stock concentrated in the hands of a small group of individuals. Some of these companies may be firms that have recently gone public and have large blocks of stock owned by family members. European companies, for example, tend to have a much higher percentage of shares held by large blockholders such as founding families. Such a concentration makes the likelihood of a successful takeover by an outside party less probable unless it is a friendly transaction. The greater the concentration of securities in the hands of parties opposed to a takeover, the more problematic and costly a takeover may be.

Data Reliability and Fraudulent Inaccuracies

Perhaps the worst scenario for acquirers is fraudulent misrepresentation of earnings. This was the case when Cendant Corp. reported in 1998 that its earnings were over-stated. As discussed in Chapter 10, Cendant was a franchisor of Ramada hotels, Cold-well Banker real estate, and Avis Rent A Car, and a marketer of membership clubs. It was formed with the December 1997 merger of HFS Inc. and CUC International Inc. The company was forced to report that CUC International deliberately inflated revenues and decreased expenses. Among the issues raised was the treatment of revenues from offered memberships for which customers may ask for a full refund. In its restated data, the company reported revenues reflecting a high 50% cancellation rate. Various esti-mates of the inflated profits ranged from $500 to $640 million. The deliberate falsifica-tion of financial statements is an acquisition nightmare scenario. Cendant survived this accounting debacle. It was a one-time event that the market understood and thought the company could overcome. The market was less sanguine about the company's diversifi-cation strategy, and the company eventually relented and agreed to break itself up into separate component companies.

Role of Arbitragers and Impact on Prices

When a company is rumored to be the object of a takeover, the target's stock becomes concentrated in the hands of risk arbitragers, which are institutions that gamble on the probability that a company will eventually be taken over. When this occurs, the holders of the shares, including the arbitragers, will receive a premium. As arbitragers accu-mulate stock, upward pressure is put on its price. As we discussed in Chapter 6, these arbitragers also sell shares of the target short, knowing that research shows the stock price of bidders often declines when acquisitions are announced.

The net effect of the arbitrage buying is to increase the price while also increasing the probability that the company will be taken over. As we have discussed in Chapter 6, the likelihood of a takeover is increased because now more shares will be concentrated in the hands of fewer investors, making large block purchases easier. In addition, given that arbitragers are simply looking to realize a good return on their investment as quickly as possible, they are very willing sellers if the price is right. A committed buyer, therefore, can be aided by risk arbitrage activities.

Valuation Effects of Mergers and Acquisitions

Numerous studies have considered the valuation effects of mergers and acquisitions. Many of these studies were done in the early 1980s. Their results, however, also apply to later time periods. Some more recent research, such as studies that consider the magnitude of returns over longer time periods as well as studies that look at the impact of the medium of exchange on returns, is discussed later in this chapter.[14]

Many of these research studies consider the impact of bids over a relatively short-term window, which may be several months before and after a bid. Proponents of the positive effects of mergers contend that it takes many years for the bidder's acquisition plans to come to fruition. Researchers, however, respond that the market has the long-term experience of many prior acquisitions and that it draws on this information when evaluating bids. In addition, it is difficult to conduct long-term studies that filter out the effects of a specific transaction from many events and other transactions that may occur over a longer time period. Nonetheless there are some that look at various financial measures over an extended time period after deals.

These studies on the valuation effects of M&As have five general conclusions:

1. **Target shareholders earn positive returns from merger agreements.** Several studies have shown that for friendly, negotiated bids, target common stockholders earn statistically significant positive abnormal returns.[15] The source of this return can be traced to the premiums that target shareholders receive.

2. **Target shareholders may earn even higher significant positive returns from tender offers.** Target common shareholders of hostile bids that are tender offers also receive statistically significant positive returns.[16] The hostile bidding process may create a competitive environment, which may increase the acquiring firm's bid and cause target shareholder returns to be even higher than what would have occurred in a friendly transaction.

3. **Target bondholders and preferred stockholders gain from takeovers.** Both target preferred stockholders and bondholders tend to gain from being acquired.[17]

---

[14] It is important to note that the fact that research studies may be dated several years earlier does not mean that their findings no longer apply. It is difficult to publish research that uses a similar methodology and reaches the same conclusions as studies published a decade earlier. Generally, only if their findings differ in some significant aspect will journal referees and editors accept a new version of prior research.

[15] Debra K. Dennis and John J. McConnell, "Corporate Mergers and Security Returns," *Journal of Financial Economics* 16, no. 2 (June 1986): 143–187; Paul Asquith, "Merger Bids, Uncertainty and Stockholder Returns, " *Journal of Financial Economics* 11, no. 1–4 (April 1983): 51–83; Paul Asquith and E. Han Kim, "The Impact of Merger Bids on Participating Firm's Security Holders, " *Journal of Finance* 37, no. 5 (December 1982): 1209–1228; and Peter Dodd, "Merger Proposals, Management Discretion and Shareholder Wealth," *Journal of Financial Economics* 8, no. 2 (June 1980): 105–138.

[16] Michael Bradley, Anand Desai, and E. Han Kim, "The Rationale behind Interfirm Tender Offers," *Journal of Financial Economics* 11, no. 1–4 (April 1983): 183–206.

[17] Debra K. Dennis and John J. McConnell, "Corporate Mergers and Security Returns," *Journal of Financial Economics* 16, no. 2 (June 1986): 143–187.

Given that bidders tend to be larger than targets, the addition of the bidder and its assets as another source of protection should lower the risk of preferred stocks and bonds, thus making them more valuable. Like the target common stockholder effects, this is an intuitive conclusion.

4. **Acquiring firm shareholders tend to earn zero or negative returns from mergers.** Acquiring firm stockholders tend not to do well when their companies engage in acquisitions (Note this is an average response but there are many examples of positive responses.). These effects are either statistically insignificant or somewhat negative. Presumably, this reflects the fact that markets are skeptical that the bidder can enjoy synergistic gains that more than offset the fact that it is paying a premium for the target. The fact that the bidder's stock response is small compared with that of the target is due to the fact that bidders tend to be larger than targets.

5. **Acquiring firm shareholders tend to earn low or no returns from tender offers.** Returns to acquiring firm shareholders following hostile bids are not impressive. There is some evidence that there may be a response that ranges from mildly positive to zero.

What Types of Acquiring Firms Tend to Perform the Poorest?

Given that acquiring firms often perform poorly in M&As, the question arises as to what types of firms do the worst and which do better. Rau and Vermaelen analyzed a sample of 3,169 mergers and 348 tender offers between 1980 and 1991.[18] They compared glamour firms, companies with low book-to-market ratios and high past earnings and cash flow growth, with value firms, companies with higher book-to-market ratios and poorer prior performance. The results of their research showed that glamour firms underperformed value companies. They attribute the relatively poorer performance of glamour firms to factors such as hubris. They also noted that glamour firms tended to more frequently pay with stock. This is understandable because their stock is more highly valued than that of so-called value firms.

 TAKEOVERS AND CONTROL PREMIUMS

When a company makes a bid for a target's stock, one way to assess the offer is to examine the magnitude of the control premium. There is a major difference between the price of a single share quoted on an organized exchange and the price of a 51% block of stock that will give the buyer effective control of the company. When a buyer buys a controlling interest in a target company, it receives a combined package of two "goods" in one: the investment features normally associated with ownership of a share of stock and the right to control and change the company's direction. Control allows the buyer to use the target's assets in a manner that will maximize the value of the acquirer's stock. This additional control characteristic commands its own price. Therefore, the buyer of a controlling block of stock must pay a control premium.

---

[18] P. Raghavendra Rau and Theo Vermaelen, "Glamor, Value and the Post-Acquisition Performance of Acquiring Firms," *Journal of Financial Economics* 49, no. 2 (August 1998): 223–253.

TABLE 15.4　Average Premium* by Industry, 2013

Industry	Premium
Agricultural production	45.6
Comm. & broadcasting	35.8
Financial services	50.4
Manufacturing	44.4
Natural resources	34.1
Other services	40.9
Real estate	15.0
Retail	48.0
Transportation	30.5
Utilities	36.5
Wholesale & distribution	31.8
**All industry average	37.5

*Excludes negative premiums
**Weighted average
Source: Mergerstat Review, 2014.

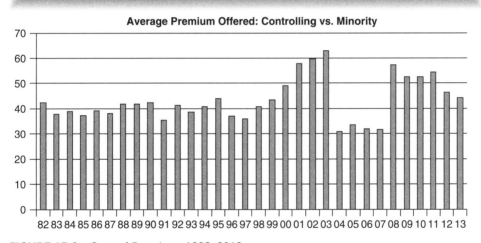

FIGURE 15.2　Control Premium: 1982–2013.
Note: Average percent premium for controlling interest, 1982–2013.
Source: Mergerstat Review, 1994 and 2014.

The comparative value of a controlling interest relative to a minority interest can be seen by examining the data in Table 15.4 and Figure 15.2. In each of the years shown (1982–2013), the controlling interest commanded a higher value, although, as with the P/Es shown in Table 15.3, there is a good deal of cross-industry variation.

The magnitude of acquisition premiums is often attributed to a combination of the bidder's estimate of the acquisition gains and the strength of the target's bargaining position. The acquisition gains may come from a variety of sources, including anticipated synergistic benefits derived from combining the bidder and the target, or the target being underpriced or poorly managed. The bidder's bargaining position may also be affected by several factors, including the presence of other bidders and the strength of the target's antitakeover defenses. Varaiya analyzed the role of these various factors in determining acquisition premiums in 77 deals between 1975 and 1980.[19] He found significant support for the role of competitive forces in the auction process and antitakeover measures in determining premiums but mixed results for the role of anticipated benefits.

Premiums and Mergers of Equals

Are premiums appropriate in mergers of equals? If the transaction is a combination of two companies of roughly similar size and when neither of the two is really acquiring the other, an argument can be made that there is no basis for a premium. The 1998 merger of GTE Corp. and Bell Atlantic (later Verizon) is a good example. If the transaction is considered an acquisition by Bell Atlantic, GTE shareholders were understandably disappointed when they received only 1.22 shares of Bell Atlantic for each share of their company, as GTE shares closed at $55.13 shortly after the deal was announced, whereas Bell Atlantic shares closed at $44.32. When one considers the fact that GTE had a higher P/E, a faster revenue growth rate, and a share price that was as high as $64, the offer was not impressive from GTE's point of view. GTE management, however, defended the deal as a "merger of equals." This view is consistent with the Delaware court's position that stock-for-stock mergers are not changes in control. Based on this legal view, a control premium may not be in order. The debate of whether a control premium is warranted came to a head in the wake of a lawsuit brought by Kirk Kerkorian and his Tracinda Corp., which was a large shareholder in Chrysler Corporation. The 1998 merger between Chrysler and Daimler Benz was termed at the time as a merger of equals.[20] However, particularly as the financial troubles at Chrysler became apparent, Daimler proved to be the dominant party. Chrysler executives were supplanted by Daimler managers, who took control of the former Chrysler operation. Kerkorian sued because he considered the deal a takeover and as such he and other shareholders were entitled to a takeover premium. The court, however, failed to agree with his position.

Mergers of Equals: Do Managers Trade Premium for Power?

One of the moral hazard problems that exists in merger negotiations, which is especially true for mergers of equals, is that at the time the CEO of the target is supposed to be negotiating the best deal for shareholders, he is also negotiating his own best compensation package and position in the combined company. Julie Wulf analyzed a sample of 53 mergers of equals over the period of 1991–1999.[21] She found that indeed CEOs

---

[19] Nikhil P. Varaiya, "Determinants of Premiums in Acquisition Transactions," *Managerial and Decision Economics* 8, no. 3 (September 1987): 175–184.

[20] See case study in Patrick A. Gaughan, *Mergers: What Can Go Wrong and How to Prevent It* (Hoboken, NJ: John Wiley & Sons, 2005), 306–316.

[21] Julie M. Wulf, "Do CEOs in Mergers Trade Power for Premium? Evidence from 'Mergers of Equals,'" *Journal of Law, Economics and Organization* 20, no. 1 (April 2004): 60–101.

do trade power for premium in such negotiations. These results were supported by a study by Hartzell, Ofek, and Yermack, who showed that, in deals where target CEOs enjoyed extraordinary personal treatment, shareholders received lower acquisition premiums.[22] This creates the disquieting concern that target CEOs are trading premium for their shareholders in exchange for their own personal enrichment.

Does the Market Value Control Independent of Takeovers?

Having cited the abundant evidence supporting the existence of a control premium in takeovers, we should determine whether control provides a premium in the absence of takeovers. In a study designed to measure the premium paid for control, Lease, McConnell, and Mikkelson sought to determine whether capital markets place a separate value on control.[23]

The Lease study examined the market prices of common stocks of 30 companies with classes of common stock that pay identical dividends but differ significantly in their voting rights. One group had substantially greater voting rights on issues related to the control of the firm, such as the election of directors. The two groups of securities provided the same opportunities for financial gain and differed only in their voting rights and the opportunities to control the company's future. Their results showed that for 26 firms that had no voting preferred stock outstanding, the superior voting common stock traded at a premium relative to the other classes of common stock. The average premium they found was 5.44%. It is important to remember that this is not inconsistent with the premiums cited previously because these other premiums are found in takeovers. This is expected, however, because the companies included in the Lease study were not involved in takeovers.

Four of the 30 firms considered in the study showed that the superior voting rights common stock traded at a discount relative to the other class of common stock. These firms differed from the other 26, however, in that they had a more complex capital structure that featured preferred stock with voting rights. Given the existence of this type of voting preferred stock, these four firms are not as comparable to the other 26 clear-cut cases. Another study that focused on specific industries, such as the banking industry, found control premiums in the range of 50% to 70%.[24]

Corporate Governance and Takeover Premiums

Does shareholder control in a target company affect the premiums such companies get in takeovers? One could theorize that a higher degree of control by certain shareholders, such as managers, should increase takeover premiums, as such shareholders would take the necessary actions to ensure that they receive the highest premium for their shares.

---

[22] Jay Hartzell, Eli Ofek, and David Yermack, "What's in It for Me? CEOs Whose Firms Are Acquired," *Review of Financial Studies* 17, no. 1 (2004): 37–61.

[23] Ronald C. Lease, John J. McConnell, and Wayne H. Mikkelson, "The Market Value of Control in Publicly Traded Corporations," *Journal of Financial Economics* 11, no. 1–4 (April 1983): 439–471.

[24] Larry G. Meeker and O. Maurice Joy, "Price Premiums for Controlling Shares of Closely Held Bank Stock," *Journal of Business* 53, no. 3 (July 1980): 297–314.

However, one could also anticipate that controlling shareholders could oppose takeovers so as to preserve their control and managerial positions.

Thomas Moeller found that in the 1980s, the period of the fourth merger wave, target shareholder control and takeover premiums were negatively related.[25] However, the relationship between these two variables was a positive one when we get to the 1990s and the fifth merger wave. He interprets his results to imply that direct shareholder control in the hands of large blockholders can have a positive effect on premiums, because such shareholders push to get the highest return for their investments. However, high shareholder control by managers, such as the CEO, can have the opposite effect on takeover premiums, as other factors, such as continuing in the position as the CEO, may carry more weight with the CEO.

Impact of Prices on Takeovers

Intuition and Economics 101 imply that if a given target's stock is priced lower by the market, its probability of being taken over is greater. Indeed, we have a large group of activist hedge funds that search for companies with valuable assets and possibly bad management where the stock price has fallen. They often accumulate shares in such companies and agitate for changes, such as the sale of the company. In light of this it has been difficult to reconcile various research studies that have failed to support the proposition that lower market valuations increase takeover probability.

Cremers, Nair, and John as well as Bates, Becher, and Lemmon found a negative, but statistically insignificant relationship between takeover probability and the Tobin's q of companies.[26] Companies which generate higher values with the assets they have may be less vulnerable to a takeover.

More recently Edmans, Goldstein, and Jiang have shed light on the complexity of the relationship between target stock prices and takeover probability.[27] They explained that the prices of potential targets are endogenous in the sense that when a stock price of an otherwise valuable company falls, the market recognizes that it is becoming a more attractive takeover target; this by itself may increase demand for the shares, thus offsetting some of the price decline. When we consider this, we then also have to recognize that managerial underperformance can have a significantly greater negative effect than what is apparent by merely looking at the company's stock prices, as some investors may have offset some of the negative impact that this underperformance had by buying the shares in anticipation of an eventual takeover. In other words, if management is

---

[25] Thomas Moeller, "Let's Make a Deal! How Shareholder Control Impacts Merger Payoffs," *Journal of Financial Economics* 76, no. 1 (2005): 167–190.

[26] Martijn Cremers, Vinay Nair, and Kose John, "Takeovers and the Cross Section of Returns," *Review of Financial Studies* 22 (2009): 1409–1445, and Thomas Bates, David Becher, and Michael Lemmon, "Board Classification and Managerial Entrenchment: Evidence from the Market for Corporate Control," *Journal of Financial Economics* 87 (2008): 656–677.

[27] Alex Edmans, Itay Goldstein, and Wei Jiang, "The Real Effects of Financial Markets," *Journal of Finance* 67, no. 3 (June 2012): 933–971.

underperforming, the weakness in the company's stock price will fail to reflect the full extent of that underperformance.

 ## VALUATION OF STOCK-FOR-STOCK EXCHANGES

In this section we will go through a basic discussion of valuation in stock-for-stock exchanges. Prior to beginning our discussion of valuation, we need to address some background issues.

Tax Incentives for Stock versus Cash Transactions

The tax laws provide that stock-for-stock exchanges may be treated as tax-free reorganizations.[28] This means the stock that target stockholders receive will *not* be taxed until the shares are sold. Target stockholders are thus able to postpone being taxed on the consideration that is received for the shares in the target company until the new shares in the acquirer are sold. One tax disadvantage of a reorganization is that the acquirer may not utilize other tax benefits that would be allowable if the transaction were not a reorganization, such as if it were financed by cash. If the transaction were not a reorganization, other tax advantages, such as the ability to step up the asset base or utilize unused tax credits that the target might possess, would be available. It is also possible to receive debt in exchange for the target's shares. For example, the target stockholders could receive debt as part of an installment sale of the target. In this case, the deferred payments are not taxed until they are actually received.[29] The seller can accumulate interest, tax-free, on the unreceived portions of the sale price.

Risk Effects: Stock versus Cash

In cash deals target shareholders immediately realize their gains, whereas acquiring firm shareholders assume the risk that the synergistic gains will offset the premiums paid and other costs of the acquisitions. In a stock deal the shareholders of both companies share the risk that the deal will be successful.

 ## SHAREHOLDER WEALTH EFFECTS AND METHODS OF PAYMENT

The choice of compensation paid by the acquirer to target shareholders can itself have important ramifications for the shareholders of both companies. We will see that these effects differ depending on whether we take a short- or long-term perspective.

---

[28] Alan J. Auerbach and David Reishus, "The Impact of Taxation on Mergers and Acquisitions," in Alan J. Auerbach, ed., *Mergers and Acquisitions* (Chicago: National Bureau of Economic Research, 1987), 69–85.

[29] Alan J. Auerbach and David Reishus, "Taxes and the Merger Decision," in John C. Coffee Jr., Louis Lowenstein, and Susan Rose Ackerman, eds., *Knights, Raiders, and Targets* (New York: Oxford University Press, 1988), 300–313.

Target Companies: Short-Term Effects of Method of Payment

Research studies show that the target company valuation effects are greater for cash offers than for stock offers. For example, using a sample of 204 deals, Huang and Walking find that cash offers are associated with substantially higher target returns before and after controlling for the type of acquisition and the amount of resistance.[30] They attribute the higher premiums of cash offers to tax effects. That is, they conclude that the higher premiums are required by shareholders who demand them because they will be forced to incur the costs associated with cash-financed acquisitions. Huang and Walking's finding regarding the higher premiums of cash offers has been confirmed by later research.[31] It is interesting that in a sample of 84 target firms and 123 bidding firms between 1980 and 1988, Sullivan, Johnson, and Hudson found that the higher returns associated with cash offers persisted even after offers were terminated. They interpret this as the market reevaluating firms that are targets of cash offers and placing a higher value on them as a result of the cash offer. When a bidder shows interest in a target, this tends to enhance the market's valuation of that company. It may also attract other bidders to make an offer. This is one of the reasons why bidders request that targets enter into no-shop agreements prior to their making an offer. They know that if they make an offer they may create additional value in the target, and they do not want the target to use the value the bidder created against the bidder by inviting other newly interested bidders to compete against the original offeror. New bidders who would be competing against an original cash offer will usually have to also respond with a cash bid as they might be at a competitive disadvantage if they offered securities (depending on the particular issuing company and securities offered).

Acquiring Companies: Short-Term Effects of Method of Payment

As noted previously, acquiring companies tend to show zero or negative returns in response to announcements of takeovers (with many exceptions). Chang analyzed the short-term announcement effects on acquiring firms that pursue takeovers of public and privately held companies while also considering how these effects differed for cash versus stock offers.[32]

Using a sample of 281 deals from 1981 to 1992, Chang found that abnormal returns were approximately zero and not statistically significant for cash takeovers of public companies, whereas returns were a positive and statistically significant 2.64% for stock offers. For private firm takeovers, returns were not statistically significant for cash offers but were a statistically significant −2.46% for stock deals. In conclusion, he found that for cash offers, returns were basically zero and did not vary depending on

---

[30] Yen-Sheng Huang and Ralph A. Walking, "Target Abnormal Returns Associated with Acquisition Announcements," *Journal of Financial Economics* 19, no. 2 (December 1987): 329–349.

[31] Michael J. Sullivan, Marlin R. H. Johnson, and Carl D. Hudson, "The Role of Medium of Exchange in Merger Offers: Examination of Terminated Merger Proposals," *Financial Management* 23, no. 3 (Autumn 1994): 51–62.

[32] Saeyoung Chang, "Takeovers of Privately Held Targets, Methods of Payment, and Bidder Returns," *Journal of Finance* 53, no. 2 (April 1998): 773–784.

whether the deal was a public or private acquisition. However, the positive stock price reaction to takeovers of private companies is in sharp contrast to the negative response for public company takeovers. One theory that explains this result is that there may be more monitoring when stock is given to a few owners of the closely held company. This greater monitoring may reduce adverse agency effects and increase value. When the market perceives this, it reacts with a positive stock price response. This conclusion is consistent with other related research on the influence of managerial holdings and those of institutional investors and other blockholders.

Acquiring Companies: Long-Term Effects of Method of Payment

The Chang finding of zero returns for cash offers was contradicted by Loughran and Vijh, who found positive abnormal long-term returns for cash acquisitions but negative abnormal return for stock deals.[33] A major difference between the two studies is that Loughran and Vijh viewed their results from a long-term perspective while Chang focused on short-term announcement effects.

Loughran and Vijh found that over the five-year period following acquisitions, stock deals averaged negative excess returns equal to −25%, whereas for cash tender offers the returns were an average abnormal return of a positive 61.7%! This is a sizable difference. Ghosh's research also provides some support for the long-term effects of the Loughran and Vijh study. He found that performance, as measured by total asset turnover, improved for cash acquisitions but performance measures such as cash flows declined for stock deals.[34] However, when he controlled for the size of the combined companies, which become larger after the deals, the performance difference of stock versus cash deals disappeared. In cash transactions, the firms were larger than those in the stock deal subsample. Ghosh attributes improvements to the larger size of the postacquisition cash deals compared with stock transactions, which involved relatively smaller combined companies.

Stock Mergers: Do Overvalued Acquirers Create Value for Their Shareholders?

The research we have discussed paints a negative picture of the shareholder wealth effects for acquiring firm shareholders. However, there are important exceptions to this. Shleifer and Vishny have pointed out there are incentives that overvalued companies have to use their equity to acquire valuable targets.[35] Probably the best example of this was the acquisition/merger of Time Warner by AOL, in which AOL was able to use its temporarily overvalued shares to basically acquire Time Warner and its valuable businesses. Savor and Lu explored this issue, which was challenging to research because

---

[33] Tim Loughran and Anand M. Vijh, "Do Long Term Shareholders Benefit from Corporate Acquisitions?" *Journal of Finance* 52, no. 5 (December 1997): 1765–1790.

[34] Aloke Ghosh, "Does Operating Performance Really Improve Following Corporate Acquisitions?" *Journal of Corporate Finance* 7, no. 2 (June 2001): 151–178.

[35] Andrei Shleifer and Robert Vishny, "Stock Market Driven Acquisitions," *Journal of Financial Economics* 70, no. 3 (December 2003): 295–311.

the greater the overvaluation the more likely an eventual correction.[36] However, the greater the overvaluation, the greater the incentive to merge. So rather than just look at deals that were actually completed, they also compared these deals to ones that failed to be completed and examined whether the stock price effects were more negative for the failed acquirers. Indeed they were. They found that abnormal returns for failed acquirers underperformed their successful counterparts by 13.6% one year out, 22.2% for a two-year horizon, and 31.2% for three years! The unsuccessful acquirers suffered weak abnormal returns after the bid collapsed as the market seemed to voice its recognition that the stock was overvalued and that the company lost an opportunity to use its temporarily overvalued "currency" to gain value through M&As.

Method of Payment and Managerial Ownership

When the shareholdings of a bidder are concentrated so that certain shareholders control a significant percentage of the shares and votes of the target, these holdings will be diluted if the bidder issues more shares to finance a bid.[37] Several studies have focused on verifying the extent to which the distribution of holdings is related to the use of stock financing of deals. In a study of 209 M&As in the early 1980s, Amihud, Lev, and Travlos found that the choice of stock versus cash was significantly and negatively related to the size of the shareholdings of managers and directors of the bidder.[38] Their results show that the higher the managerial stock equity ownership, the less likely a company will do stock offers. Ghosh and Ruland then extended this work to a sample of 212 M&As over the period 1981–1988.[39] They also found that managerial ownership of the bidder was negatively related to stock financing of deals. However, the research in this area does not find a linear relationship between stock financing and managerial ownership. Martin, researching a large sample of 846 public but also private acquisitions over the period 1978–1988, also confirmed the inverse relationship between stock financing and managerial ownership over *intermediate* ranges of ownership.[40] He found that this intermediate ownership range is between 5% and 25%. When acquiring firm management has low or high ownership percentages, managerial ownership is not related to stock financing. For low ownership, managers did not have much control to start off with, so a dilution of the level they had would not change their position significantly. Similarly, when management has a relatively high level of control, they may still be able to command significant control even after their holdings are somewhat diluted through the issuance of stock to effect an acquisition.

---

[36] Pavel G. Savor and Qi Lu, "Do Stock Mergers Create Value for Acquirers?" *Journal of Finance* 64, no. 3 (May 2009): 1061–1097.

[37] Rene M. Stulz, "Managerial Control of Voting Rights: Financing Policies and the Market for Corporate Control," *Journal of Financial Economics* 20, no. 1–2 (1988): 25–54.

[38] Yakov Amihud, Baruch Lev, and Nicholaos G. Travlos, "Corporate Control and the Choice of Investment Financing: The Case of Corporate Acquisitions," *Journal of Finance* 45, no. 2 (June 1990): 603–616.

[39] Aloke Ghosh and William Ruland, "Managerial Ownership, the Method of Payment for Acquisitions and Executive Job Retention," *Journal of Finance* 53, no. 2 (April 1998): 785–798.

[40] Kenneth Martin, "The Method of Payment in Corporate Acquisitions, Investment Opportunities and Managerial Ownership," *Journal of Finance* 51, no. 4 (September 1996): 1227–1246.

The Ghosh and Ruland study also considered the relationship between managerial ownership of the target and the form of payment in deals. They found that stock deals were positively related to the high managerial ownership for the target corporation. They also found that when managerial ownership was high and when the deal was a stock deal, target managers were more likely to stay in the employ of the company after the transaction. We will elaborate on this result a little later in this chapter. As it relates to this discussion, Ghosh and Ruland found that target managerial ownership was the more important factor in determining the form of consideration in bids. Thus it seems that when target management holds a significant percentage of the target's stock, they seem to influence the method of payment and demand shares, instead of cash, for their holdings. This implies that they are concerned about influencing control of the combined company, which in turn may better ensure their own employment in the future. When we consider that premiums are often higher in cash deals, target management seems to be considering control along with other factors, such as the tax treatment of the transaction, not just the immediate cash premium they might otherwise receive. Obviously, situations will differ. For some owners of closely held businesses, they may prefer cash as they seek to liquidate their investment and retire. Even in such situations, however, buyers may require that the prior owners stay involved and are able to only gradually cash out their investment.

Method of Payment, Managerial Ownership, and Executive Job Retention

Managers of acquiring companies who value control may want to avoid stock deals because such deals may dilute their control.[41] If this is the case, it may be reasonable to assume that the owners of target companies who value control may prefer stock instead of cash. As noted earlier, Ghosh and Ruland found a positive association between the likelihood of a stock financed acquisition and the managerial ownership of target firms. They also found that managers in target firms were more likely to retain their positions when they received stock as opposed to cash. When trying to understand this result, keep in mind that hostile deals are more likely to be financed with cash as opposed to stock. Cash has a clearly defined value and does not have the potential valuation and liquidity drawbacks that securities offers may have. In general, a sample of cash offers will tend to include more hostile deals than a comparable sample of stock-financed deals. However, hostile bidders will more likely remove target management than friendly bidders. When target management holds a significant number of shares, the bidder has to work to get them to accept the offer. This acceptance will more likely be given when the offer comes with features that meet these shareholders' wants. For target management this may mean staying in the employ of the company after the takeover. When they receive stock in the combined company for their shares, target managers are in a better position to help elect a board that would want to retain their services.

---

[41] Yakov Amihud, Baruch Lev, and Nicholas Travlos, "Corporate Control and the Choice of Investment Financing: The Case of Corporate Acquisitions," *Journal of Finance* 45, no. 2 (June 1990): 603–616.

Information Asymmetry, Payment Choice, and Announcement Bidder Performance

Corporate finance has put forward various hypotheses regarding the instances in which management will more likely use stock financing. The theory is that stock financing will more likely be used, as opposed to other financing alternatives such as borrowing, when the stock is overvalued.[42] Because management and directors have better information about the company's future profits and returns opportunities, they are in a better position to evaluate the market's attempt to value the company's expected profits and returns. When they find the market's assessment overoptimistic, they may be more inclined to issue what they consider to be overvalued shares. As applied to acquisitions, the theory assumes that the market is aware of the significance of management's announcement to use stock to finance a deal. Taking this as a negative signal that management believes the stock to be overvalued, the stock price of the bidder should weaken when the deal and its financing choice are announced. This theoretical conclusion is supported by Amihud, Lev, and Travlos, who found that the cases where there were negative bidder returns occurred when managerial ownership was low. The negative market response did not occur when managerial ownership was high. They assume the market is concluding that when managerial ownership is high, the deal is at least not value-reducing. When management has low ownership, the manager's interests may not be well aligned with shareholders and agency conflicts may increase. When companies with low managerial ownership issue stock to finance a deal, the market has less assurance that the deal will be in shareholders' interests and not one that will further management's own agenda.

Institutional Ownership, Blockholders, and Stock Financing

Managerial ownership is not the only factor affecting the use of stock in financing deals. Martin found that institutional holdings were also inversely related to the use of stock to finance deals. He found that companies that have more of their stock held by institutions tend to not use stock as much to finance their acquisitions. These institutions seem to act as a monitor on the willingness of management to liberally use stock to buy targets. Institutions, either directly or indirectly, seem to convey to management they do not want the company to issue more shares, thereby diluting their holdings, in order to acquire other companies. The empirical findings of Martin confirm what has been contended by those such as Jensen, who has opined that higher institutional ownership and blockholdings give these investors an incentive to engage in more close monitoring of management and corporate performance, which, given the incentives and rewards, would not be worthwhile for shareholders with relatively smaller holdings.[43]

---

[42] Stewart Myers and Nicholas S. Majluf, "Corporate Financing and Investment Decisions When Firms Have Information That Investors Do Not Have," *Journal of Financial Economics* 13, no. 2 (1984): 187–221.
[43] Michael C. Jensen, "Corporate Control and the Politics of Finance," *Journal of Applied Corporate Finance* 4, no. 2 (Summer 1991): 13–33.

Legal Issues in Stock-Financed Transactions

Buyers seeking to finance an acquisition through the use of securities must be mindful of the registration requirements of the Securities and Exchange Commission (SEC) that are set forth in the Securities Act of 1933. Sellers prefer registered securities that can be readily sold in the market. However, buyers may prefer to offer unregistered securities. One reason buyers may prefer unregistered securities is the cost of the registration process, which is expensive in terms of both professional fees and management time. The registration process may also require the buyer to make public information it may not want to reveal to other parties, such as competitors. In addition, the registration process may impose impediments on the buyer that may inhibit its ability to take certain actions lest they necessitate an amendment in the registration statement filed with the SEC.

It may be possible for the parties to negotiate an agreement that allows the buyer to take advantage of certain exemptions to the registration requirements. The buyer may try to qualify for an exemption on the grounds that the securities being offered to purchase the target company do not constitute a public offering. Although the attainment of this nonpublic offering exemption is often not a certainty, it may have a significant effect on the costs of the total transaction from the buyer's viewpoint, as well as on the value the seller places on the consideration being offered by the buyer.

 EXCHANGE RATIO

The exchange ratio is the number of the acquirer's shares that are offered for each share of the target. The number of shares offered depends on the valuation of the target by the acquirer. For example, in April 2006, Alcatel and Lucent announced a stock-for-stock merger in which each Lucent shareholder would receive 0.1952 of an Alcatel American depository share for each share of Lucent they owned.

To arrive at the exchange ratio both the acquirer and the target conduct a valuation of the target, and from this process the acquirer determines the maximum price it is willing to pay, while the target determines the minimum it is willing to accept. Within this range, the actual agreement price will depend on each party's other investment opportunities and relative bargaining abilities. Based on a valuation of the target, the acquirer determines the per-share price it is offering to pay. The exchange ratio is determined by dividing the per-share offer price by the market price of the acquirer's shares. Let us consider the example of United Communications, which has made an offer for Dynamic Entertainment (Table 15.5).

Let us assume that, based on its valuation of Dynamic, United Communications has determined that it is willing to offer $65 per share for Dynamic. This is a 30% premium above the premerger market price of Dynamic. In terms of United's shares, the $65 offer is equivalent to United's $65/$150 share.

$$\text{Exchange ratio} = \text{Offer price/Share price of acquirer}$$
$$= \$65/\$150 = 0.43 \ \text{shares}$$

TABLE 15.5 United Communications and Dynamic Entertainment: Comparative Financial Condition ($000)

	United Communications	Dynamic Entertainment
Present earnings	$50,000,000	$10,000,000
Shares outstanding	5,000,000	2,000,000
Earnings per share	10	5
Stock price	150	50
P/E ratio	15	10

Based on the preceding data, United Communications can calculate the total number of shares that it will have to offer to complete a bid for 100% of Dynamic Entertainment. Total shares that United Communications will have to issue:

$$= [(\text{Offer price})(\text{Total outstanding shares of target})]/\text{Price of acquirer}$$

$$= [(\$65)(2,000,000)]/\$150 = 866,666.67$$

Earnings per Share of the Surviving Company

Calculating the EPS of the surviving company reveals the impact of the merger on the acquirer's EPS:

$$\text{Combined earnings} = \$50,000,000 + \$10,000,000$$

$$\text{Total shares outstanding} = 5,000,000 + 866,666.67$$

United Communications' Impact on EPS—$65 Offer

Premerger EPS	Postmerger EPS
$10.00	10.23

United Communications will experience an increase in its EPS if the deal is completed. Let us see the impact on EPS if a higher price is offered for Dynamic Entertainment.

Let us assume that Dynamic Entertainment rejects the first offer of $65 per share. In addition, assume that this rejection is based partly on Dynamic's own internal analysis showing the value of Dynamic to be at least $75. Dynamic also believes that its value to United is well in excess of $75. Based on some hard bargaining, United brings a $90 offer to the table.

To see the impact on the surviving company's EPS, we will have to redo the preceding analysis, using this higher offer price:

$$\text{Exchange ratio} = \text{Offer price/Share price of acquirer}$$

$$= \$90/\$150 = 0.60 \text{ shares}$$

Total shares that United Communications will have to issue:

$$= [(\text{Offer price})(\text{Total outstanding shares of target})]/\text{Price of acquirer}$$

$$= [(\$90)(2,000,000)]/\$150 = 1,200,000$$

United Communications' Impact on EPS—$90 Offer

Premerger EPS	Postmerger EPS
$10.00	9.68

United Communications' EPS declined following the higher offer of $90. This is an example of dilution in EPS.

Criteria for Dilution in EPS

Dilution in EPS will occur any time the P/E ratio paid for the target exceeds the P/E ratio of the company doing the acquiring. The P/E ratio paid is calculated by dividing the EPS of the target into the per-share offer price. This is as follows:

$$\text{P/E ratio paid} = \$65/\$5 = \$13 \; < \; \$15$$

$$\text{Offer price} = \$65$$

In the case of the $65 offer, the P/E ratio paid was less than the P/E ratio of the acquirer, and there was no dilution in EPS. Figure 15.3 shows the variation in the P/E paid for public companies. It shows how these premiums rose in the fourth and fifth merger waves.

$$\text{Offer price} = \$90$$

$$\text{P/E ratio paid} = \$90/\$5 = \$18$$

In the case of the $90 offer, the P/E ratio paid was greater than the P/E ratio of the acquirer, and there was a dilution in EPS.

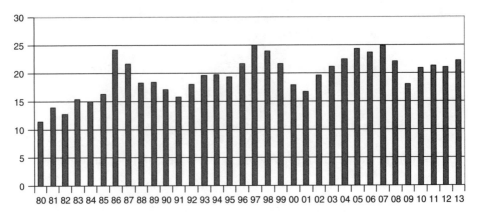

FIGURE 15.3 Median P/E Offered: 1980–2013. *Source: Mergerstat Review*, 1994, 1998, 2001, 2005, and 2014.

Highest Offer Price without Dilution in EPS

We can determine the maximum offer price that will not result in a dilution in EPS by solving for P' in the following expression:

$$\text{Maximum nondilution offer price}(P')$$

$$\$15 = P/\$5$$

$$P = \$75$$

Solving for P', we see that the maximum offer price that will not result in a dilution in EPS is $75. This does not mean that the acquirer will not offer a price in excess of $75 per share. A firm might be willing to incur an initial dilution in EPS to achieve certain benefits, such as synergies, that will result in an eventual increase in per share earnings. This can be seen in the trend in EPS in Table 15.6.

An examination of Table 15.6 reveals that although United Communications would incur an initial $0.32 dilution in EPS, United would quickly surpass its premerger EPS level. Let us assume that United had a historical 4% growth in EPS before the merger. In other words, United's rate of growth in EPS was equal only to the rate of inflation. Presumably, United was interested in Dynamic Entertainment in order to achieve a higher rate of growth. Let us also assume that a premerger analysis convinced United that it would be able to achieve a 5% rate of growth after it acquired Dynamic Entertainment.

Based on a 5% rate of growth, it is clear that United Communications would achieve a higher EPS level by the fourth year. A more precise estimate of the breakeven point can be determined as follows:

$$\$10(1.04)^t = \$9.68(1.05)^t \tag{15.19}$$

where t equals the breakeven time period.

TABLE 15.6 Earnings per Share with and without Merger: United Communications

Years	Without merger (4% growth) ($)	With merger (5% growth) ($)
0	10.00	9.68
1	10.40	10.16
2	10.82	10.67
3	11.25	11.21
4	11.70	11.77
5	12.17	12.35
6	12.66	12.97
7	13.16	13.62
8	13.69	14.30

Solving for t, we get:

$$\frac{\$10}{\$9.68} = \frac{(1.05)^t}{(1.04)^t}$$

$$0.033 = (1.05/1.04)^t$$

$$log(1.033) = t log(1.05/1.04)$$

$$0.01412 = (0.004156)$$

The firm may have a ceiling on the maximum amount of time it may be willing to wait until it breaks even with respect to EPS. If United Communications is willing to wait approximately 3.25 years to break even, it may agree to the merger at the higher price of $90. If United thinks that this is too long to wait, it may agree only at a lower price or it may look for other merger candidates.

Factors That Influence Initial Changes in Earnings per Share

The amount of change in EPS is a function of two main factors:

1. **Differential in P/E ratios.** Rule: The higher the P/E ratio of the acquirer relative to the target, the greater the increase in EPS of the acquirer.
2. **Relative size of the two firms as measured by earnings.** Rule: The larger the earnings of the target relative to the acquirer, the greater the increase in the acquirer's EPS.

The first factor has already been explained, but the role of the relative size of the two firms needs to be explored. For the sake of this discussion, let us assume that earnings are an acceptable measure of value. Because EPS is the ratio of earnings divided by the number of outstanding shares, the greater the addition to the earnings of the surviving

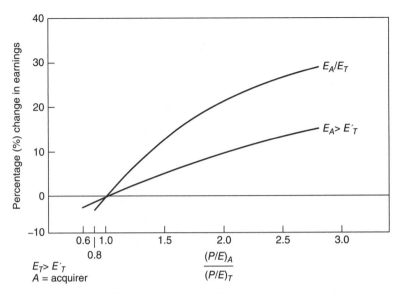

FIGURE 15.4 Combined Effect of P/E Ratio Differential and Relative Earnings

firm that is accounted for by the addition of the target's earnings, the greater the EPS of the surviving firm. This is a commonsense proposition.

We can combine the effect of both factors to say that the higher the P/E ratio of the acquirer relative to the target and the greater the earnings of the target relative to the acquirer, the greater the increase in the combined company's EPS. The opposite also follows. The combined effect of the P/E ratio differential and the relative earnings of the two firms can be seen in Figure 15.4.

Bootstrapping Earnings per Share

Bootstrapping EPS refers to the corporation's ability to increase its EPS through the purchase of other companies. These earnings were prevalent during the third merger wave of the late 1960s. During this time, the market was not efficient in its valuation of conglomerates. These conglomerates were able to experience an increase in EPS and stock prices simply by acquiring other firms.

In the case of United Communications' acquisition of Dynamic Entertainment, United issued 866,666.67 shares of stock based on a $65 offer price. This results in 5,866,667.67 total shares of United Communications outstanding (Table 15.7).

With the offer price of $65 per share, United Communications can offer Dynamic Entertainment a 30% premium above its premerger price of $50 and still experience an increase in EPS. If we assume that the market will apply the same EPS to United

TABLE 15.7 United Communications' Postmerger Financial Condition

Earnings	$60,000,000.00
Shares outstanding	5,866,666.67
EPS	10.23
P/E ratio	15.00
Stock price	153.45

before and after the merger, the stock price has to rise. This can be seen in the following expression:

$$P/E = P/EPS$$

$$15 = P/\$10.23$$

$$P = \$153.45 \qquad (15.20)$$

United Communications' postmerger stock price has risen to $153.45 as a result of bootstrapping EPS. Two conditions are necessary for bootstrapping EPS to occur:

1. *The P/E ratio must not decline following the merger.* This implies that the market must be willing to apply at least the premerger P/E ratio after the merger. If the market decides that the combined firm is not as valuable, per dollar of earnings, there may be a market correction and the P/E ratio may fall. In the third merger wave, the market was slow to reevaluate the growing conglomerates and apply a lower P/E ratio.
2. *The acquirer must have a higher P/E ratio than the target.* If these two conditions prevail, companies with higher P/E ratios can acquire companies with lower P/E ratios and experience growth in EPS. This gives the acquiring company an incentive to continue with further acquisitions and have even greater increase in EPS. The process will continue to work as long as the stock market continues to value the acquiring company with the same P/E ratio. This occurred during the late 1960s. The movement came to an end when the market corrected itself as it questioned many of the acquisitions that appeared to lack synergistic benefits.

Postmerger P/E Ratio

If the market is efficient, bootstrapping EPS is not possible. The postmerger P/E ratio will be a weighted average of the premerger P/E ratios. This can be calculated using the following expression:

$$\frac{P}{E_{A+B}} = \frac{(P_A \times S_A) + (P_B \times S_B)}{E_A + E_B} \qquad (15.21)$$

where

$\dfrac{P}{E_{A+B}}$ = the postmerger P/E ratio

P_A = the premerger stock price of Company A

P_B = the premerger stock price of Company B

S_A = the number of outstanding shares of Company A

S_B = the number of outstanding shares of Company B

E_A = the earnings of Company A

E_B = the earnings of Company B

Using the preceding expression, we can calculate United Communications' post-merger P/E ratio after the stock-for-stock acquisition of Dynamic Entertainment. We will calculate this ratio based on the $65 initial offer that required the issuance of 866,666.67 shares:

$$\frac{P}{E_{U+D}} = \frac{(P_U + S_U) + (P_D + S_U)}{E_U + E_D}$$

$$\frac{P}{E_{A+B}} = \frac{(\$150 \times 5,000,000) + (\$50 \times 2,000,000)}{50,000,000 + \$10,000,000}$$

$$= \frac{\$750,000,000 - \$100,000,000}{\$60,000,000} = \frac{\$850,000}{\$60,000} = 14.17 \quad (15.22)$$

Without the bootstrapping effect, the P/E ratio of the combined firm falls relative to United Communications' premerger P/E ratio. The resulting P/E ratio is a blended combination of United's P/E ratio (15) and Dynamic's lower P/E ratio (10).

AMERISOURCE: BERGEN BRUNSWIG STOCK-FOR-STOCK MERGER

In March 2001, two of the largest U.S. drug distributors announced a merger that would (assuming it was approved) result in a combined capitalization of approximately $5 billion. AmeriSource had $11.6 billion in revenues in 2000, while Bergen Brunswig generated almost $23 billion over the same time. Despite the big difference in size, as measured by revenues, AmeriSource was considered to be the acquirer. In 2000, AmeriSource generated net income of $99 million and Bergen lost $752 million. Bergen Brunswig's financial difficulties can be traced to problems with prior acquisitions.

Under the initially announced terms of the deal, AmeriSource shareholders would own 51% of the shares in the combined company. Each share of Bergen would be valued at 0.37 shares of the combined entity, while each share of common stock of AmeriSource would equal one share in the new firm. Before the deal, Bergen had 136.1 million fully diluted shares outstanding. Using the predeal closing stock price of AmeriSource of $44.48 and an exchange ratio of 0.37 shares in the combined company for each share of Bergen, the target is valued as follows:

Number of Bergen shares × Exchange ratio × Value of AmeriSource shares
$136.1 million shares × 0.37 × $44.48 = $2.44 billion = Value of Bergen
Number of AmeriSource shares × Predeal value of AmeriSource shares
$52.4 million shares × $44.48 = $2.33 billion
Approximate combined equity value = $5 billion
AmeriSource shareholder's percentage: 51%; Bergen shareholder's percentage: 49%

FIXED NUMBER OF SHARES VERSUS FIXED VALUE

A buyer in a stock-for-stock transaction can offer either a fixed number of shares in its company or a specific dollar value. When the number of shares is fixed, its value can vary as the stock price of the acquirer varies. The value the seller receives and the buyer provides then varies depending on movements in the bidder's stock price. A buyer, however, can simply offer a fixed value, and the actual number of shares may vary as the stock price of the acquirer varies. The uncertainty caused by a fixed number of shares can be reduced through a *collar agreement*. Such an agreement usually stipulates that if the stock price goes above or below a certain value, there will be an adjustment in the exchange ratio.

The collar agreement may tolerate small movements in the stock price without causing changes in the exchange ratio. A certain threshold is established beyond which the exchange ratio has to be adjusted. The existence of a collar agreement in a merger is usually a point of negotiation. It is more important if the stock of one or both of the participants tends to be volatile. If both firms are in the same industry, market movements in each stock might offset each other. However, many collar agreements allow the bidder to walk away from a deal if its stock price moves higher than the range for its stock set forth in the collar. This adds an element of uncertainty that is important for the parties to the transactions but also for risk arbitragers.

MERGER NEGOTIATIONS AND STOCK OFFERS: HALLIBURTON VS BAKER HUGHES

When a bidder makes a takeover offer, whether it be stock, cash, or both, targets will often try to negotiate for a better offer. In stock offers this translates to getting more shares of the bidder which really means more shares in a combined company. Sometimes these negotiations can go on for an extended period of time. During such a time period market conditions and the financial performance of the respective companies can change. A good example of this occurred towards the end of 2014 when Halliburton Co. offered $19 plus 1.05 of its shares for each share of Baker Hughes. This resulted in a value just under $35 billion. Baker Hughes wanted a better price and better terms such as a significant breakup fee. Negotiations between the two companies continued through the period when the third quarter financial results were reported. Unfortunately for Baker Hughes, its third quarter results were disappointing while Halliburton's exceeded street forecasts. This increased Halliburton's leverage and, while it did increase its offer, they did not have to go as far as Baker Hughes wanted and were able to reach an agreement with Baker Hughes, subject to approval from antitrust authorities, to acquire the company for roughly $35 billion using the same amount of cash but 1.12 Halliburton shares for each share of Baker Hughes.

INTERNATIONAL TAKEOVERS AND STOCK-FOR-STOCK TRANSACTIONS

One complication that can occur with international takeovers is that target company shareholders may not want to hold shares in the acquiring corporation. This often is the case for U.S. shareholders who receive shares in European corporations. Displaying a preference for U.S. stock, target company shareholders may sell their shares in the acquiring company. When these shares return to the acquiring company's market, they can cause its stock price to decline. Such a decline could effectively increase the costs of the acquisition for the bidder. This phenomenon is sometimes referred to as *domestic market flowback*.

DESIRABLE FINANCIAL CHARACTERISTICS OF TARGETS

Acquirers can use the following characteristics as financial screens:

- *Rapidly growing cash flows and earnings*. A pattern of rising cash flows and earnings is the most desirable characteristic. The future cash flows are the most direct benefit the buyer derives from an acquisition. Therefore, a rising historical trend in these values may be an indicator of higher levels in the future.
- *Low price relative to earnings*. A P/E that is low compared with its level over the past two to three years suggests that the company may be relatively inexpensive. A low P/E ratio is generally considered a desirable characteristic in a target. The lower the P/E ratio, the lower the price that will be paid to acquire the target's earning power. Because of market fluctuations, the P/E ratio of a firm or an industry category may go up and down. In addition, the market fluctuates up and down. A falling stock price that is not caused by a reduction in the potential target's earning power may present a temporary undervaluation and an acquisition opportunity. An acquirer can measure the extent of the undervaluation by comparing the P/E ratio with the previous level over the preceding three years. A low level can mean undervaluation due to changes in investor preferences, or it can reflect a change in the firm's ability to generate income in the future. The lowest value in three years is an indicator of

one of the two; it is the analyst's job to decide which one it is. (Although the prior discussion is framed in terms of a P/E ratio, it also applies to a pre–cash flow ratio.)

- *Market value less than book value.* Book value is a more reliable measure of value in certain industries. Industries that tend to have more liquid assets also tend to have more useful book values. Finance companies and banks are examples of firms that have a large percentage of liquid assets. Even in industries in which assets may be less liquid, such as in firms that have large real estate holdings, however, book value can be put to use as a floor value. This was the case in Campeau Corporation's acquisition of Federated Stores in 1988. Both firms had large real estate holdings and marketable divisions and store chains. The combined market value of these assets and the estimated market value of the divisions on a per-share basis made Federated a vulnerable target. In retrospect, the estimated value of the divisions proved to be greater than their market value when they were offered for sale.

- *High liquidity.* A target company's own liquidity can be used to help finance its own acquisitions. High liquidity ratios relative to industry averages are a reflection of this condition. The additional liquidity is even more applicable for debt-financed takeovers, where the liquidity of the target may be an important factor in the target's ability to pay for its own financing after the merger.

- *Low leverage.* Low leverage ratios, such as the debt ratio and debt-equity ratio, are desirable because this shows a lower level of risk as well as added debt capacity that can be used to finance the takeover. The more cyclical the industry, the more important it is to keep leverage within a manageable range.

Valuation of Private Businesses

Closely held businesses vary tremendously in size. Many think of closely held businesses as small businesses. This is not true. For example, the largest closely held company in the United States is Koch Industries. In November 2005, Koch acquired the publicly held Georgia Pacific for $13.2 billion. The deal gave the company total annual revenues of $80 billion, which enabled it to overtake Cargill as the largest closely held company in the United States. Large closely held companies are much more common in Europe. One example is Bertelsmann, the giant German media conglomerate controlled by the Mohn family since the 1800s. It has revenues in excess of $20 billion from a variety of sources, including broadcast and TV services, book and magazine publishing, and recorded music. Instead of traditional stock, the company has issued "profit participation certificates," which trade on the Frankfurt exchange. They allow investors to gain from Bertelsmann's profitability, while allowing the Mohn family and foundations it controls to retain controls of the media conglomerate. To raise capital the company completed Germany's largest IPO through a sale of 25.5 million shares in its RTL Group unit.

The valuation models that we have already discussed can be readily applied to value closely held businesses. However, certain adjustments may have to be made. These adjustments are warranted based on the differences between public and private companies.

A major difference between public and private business valuations centers on the availability and reliability of financial data.[44] Some of these differences are caused by the efforts of firms, particularly private businesses, to minimize taxable income. Another factor is the requirement that public firms disclose certain financial data in a specific manner, whereas private firms do not face such requirements.

Reported Taxable Income

Although current tax regulations mandate the same requirements with regard to the declaration of taxable income for both publicly and privately held companies, owners of closely held businesses take every opportunity to keep taxable income low and therefore have a lower tax obligation. Although public firms also want to minimize their taxes, privately held businesses have greater means available to do so than their public counterparts. Because of these efforts to minimize taxable income, private companies may issue financial data that is not a clear representation of their earning ability. This is usually not the case in public firms. Therefore, analysts may not be able to rely on the reported income of privately held firms to reflect their true profitability and earning power.

With regard to declaring income, public and private corporations have dramatically different objectives. Public corporations have several outside constraints that provide strong incentives to declare a higher taxable income. One of these constraints is the pressure applied by stockholders, the true "owners" of the corporation, to have a regular flow of dividends. Because dividends are paid out of taxable income, the public corporation's ability to minimize taxable income is limited.

Public Corporations and the Reporting of Income

Like their private counterparts, public corporations want to minimize taxes, but given their dividend obligations toward stockholders, public corporations have fewer opportunities to do so. They do not have as much ability to manipulate their reported income, primarily because of the accounting review requirements that the shareholder reporting process imposes on them.

In preparing financial statements, there are three levels of accounting reports: compilation, review, and audited statements. The compilation is the least rigorous of the three, whereas audited financial statements will result in a scrutiny of the financial data by an independent examination of the company's financial records. Public corporations are required to prepare audited financial statements for their annual reports. These audit requirements are enforced by the SEC, subject to the requirements of the Securities Exchange Act of 1934. The SEC does not accept a review or a compilation statement for a 10K report. A review is acceptable for a 10Q quarterly report (although for a public company this involves a more detailed review than for a closely held firm). However, a compilation is not acceptable for use in preparing either of these types of published financial reports. Because the reported income contained in published financial statements is subject to audit, the profit numbers tend to be more reliable than

---

[44] This section is drawn from Patrick A. Gaughan and Henry Fuentes, "Taxable Income and Lost Profits Litigation," *Journal of Forensic Economics* 4, no. 1 (Winter 1990): 55–64.

those that appear in the financial statements of private firms, which may or may not be audited. The lack of required audit scrutiny is one reason the reported profit levels may lack validity. The lack of an audit requirement allows private firms to manipulate their reported income levels to minimize taxable income. It is in this area that public and private corporations tend to have two very different agendas. Public firms may want to demonstrate higher reported profits to impress stockholders. Stockholders may become more impressed when these reported profits are translated into higher dividend payments or increased stock prices.

Private corporations are subject to neither the government's public disclosure requirements nor the constraints and pressures of public securities markets. Free to utilize every opportunity to show a smaller taxable income, they therefore have a lower tax bill. A private corporation can reduce taxable income in two ways. The first is to have lower reported revenues, and the second is to show higher costs. The first approach is more common for small businesses, particularly cash businesses, which sometimes show a smaller than actual level of reported income. This is occasionally done through deliberately inaccurate record keeping. In addition to being illegal, this practice creates obvious problems for the evaluators.

If there is a reason to believe that a company's revenues have been underreported, an estimate of the actual revenues may be reconstructed. This sometimes occurs in litigation involving minority stockholders who are suing for their share in a business. The actual revenue levels can be reconstructed from activity and volume measures, such as materials and inputs purchased, which can be translated into sales of final outputs.

The most common form of income manipulation for purposes of minimizing taxes is giving higher than normal compensation, benefits, and perquisites to officers. The entrepreneurs of closely held companies may withdraw a disproportionate amount of income from the company relative to total revenues. Furthermore, entrepreneurial owners may list a variety of extraordinary personal benefits on the corporation's books as expenses. Although these expenses may be legitimate tax deductions, they really are another form of compensation to the owner. Any measure of the closely held corporation's profitability that does not take into account these less overt forms of return to the owners will fall short of measuring the business's actual profitability. Evaluators of closely held businesses often have to *recast the income statement* to reflect the true earning power of the business. This may involve adding back, after an adjustment for tax effects, costs that are really a form of compensation for the owners.

Factors to Consider When Valuing Closely Held Businesses

One set of factors that is often cited in valuing private firms is Revenue Ruling 59–60. This ruling sets forth various factors that tax courts consider in a valuation of the stock of closely held businesses for gift and estate purposes. These factors are as follows:

- Nature and history of the business
- Condition of the economy and the industry
- Book value of the company and its financial condition
- Earnings capacity of the company

- Dividend-paying capacity
- Existence of goodwill or other intangibles
- Other sales of stock
- Prices of comparable stock

Evaluators of closely held businesses should be aware of the factors that are set forth in Revenue Ruling 59–60 because these are often-cited standards for the valuation of the stock of closely held companies. The inclusion of certain factors such as both earnings and dividend-paying capacity may be questionable because dividend-paying capacity presumably is a function of earnings capacity. In addition, closely held companies tend not to distribute earnings as dividends because dividends are not tax-deductible. Industry analysis and a macroeconomic and possibly regional economic analysis are important enough to be treated as separate components of the valuation process. Putting a lot of weight on book value, a measure that may not accurately reflect the value of the company, is questionable. Revenue Ruling 59–60 also fails to mention other benchmarks, such as liquidation value, which may be worth considering along with book value. Taking these issues into consideration, this revenue ruling is important to be aware of but should not be the exclusive list of factors that are considered.

Acquisition Multiples

The stock of public companies is marketable, whereas the stock of closely held companies generally lacks a broad market. For this reason, acquisition multiples of closely held companies are generally lower than those of public companies. Table 15.8 shows that the median P/E offered for public companies over the period 1995–2009 was 21.5, whereas the median P/E multiple for closely held companies was only 17.3. It is also noteworthy that as the economy slowed in 2008–2009 the median public P/E offered fell from 24.9 in 2007 to 18.1 in 2009, which is similar to the P/E offered for private companies.

Adjustments to Valuation Methods

We have noted that the same methods used to value public businesses can be applied to the valuation of closely held companies. In some ways it is easier to value a public company because there is a market that regularly values the equity of these companies. However, for private businesses there are various transactions databases that provide data on purchase prices of acquisitions and multiples that the companies sold for. They are organized by industry and size so that evaluators can get a list of comparable transactions and derive average multiples that can be applied to place a value on closely held businesses.

Since there is a much greater abundance of data on public companies than there is on closely held businesses, we may want to use multiples from market trading of public firms to value closely held businesses. That is, we may want to take an average industry P/E ratio and use it to value a closely held company. Before we do so we need to make certain adjustments before this value can be used. Various research studies have

TABLE 15.8 Median P/E* Offered: Public versus Private, 1995–2013

Year	Public P/E	Private P/E
1995	19.4	15.5
1996	21.7	17.7
1997	25.0	17.0
1998	24.0	16.0
1999	21.7	18.4
2000	18.0	16.0
2001	16.7	15.3
2002	19.7	16.6
2003	21.2	19.4
2004	22.6	19.0
2005	24.4	16.9
2006	23.7	21.4
2007	24.9	21.6
2008	22.1	10.6
2009	18.1	18.4
2010	20.9	9.3
2011	21.3	14.9
2012	21.1	18.5
2013	22.3	14.4
Average 1995–2013	21.5	16.7

*Excludes negative P/E multiples and P/E multiples larger than 100
Source: Mergerstat Review, 1998, 2005, 2010, and 2014

attempted to measure the *marketability discount* that should be applied to public stock prices and multiples to make them relevant to closely held companies. Many of them analyzed the difference between the prices that restricted (nontradable to the public on the market) shares trade for private sales and the market prices of those shares. Much of that research was initially done in the 1970s.[45] Later studies compared the prices that shares of closely held companies sold for prior to companies going public with IPO prices

---

[45] *Institutional Investor Study Report of the Securities and Exchange Commission* (Washington, DC: U.S. Government Printing Office), Document No. 93–64, March 10, 1971; Milton Gelman, "An Economist-Financial Analyst's Approach to Valuing Stock of a Closely Held Company," *Journal of Taxation* (June 1972); Robert E. Moroney, "Most Courts Overvalue Closely Held Stocks," *Taxes* 51, no. 3 (March 1973): 144–154; Robert R. Trout, "Estimation of the Discount Associated with the Transfer of Restricted Securities," *Taxes* 55 (June 1977): 381–385; and J. Michael Maher, "Discounts for Lack of Marketability for Closely Held Business Interests," *Taxes* 54, no. 9 (September 1976): 562–571.

after the company went public. Those studies were first done in the 1980s.[46] These various studies put forward a wide range of marketability discounts that supports a discount in the one-third range.

Minority Discounts

A second discount might also be needed, depending on the percentage of ownership the privately held stock position constitutes. This is because control is an additional valuable characteristic that a majority position possesses that is not present in a minority holding. A minority shareholder is often at the mercy of majority shareholders. The holder of a minority position can elect only a minority of the directors, and possibly none of the directors, depending on whether the corporation is incorporated in a state that allows cumulative voting. Majority shareholders and minority shareholders each possess proportionate rights to dividends distribution, but a majority shareholder possesses the right to control the actions of the corporations in addition to these dividend claims. This is an additional valuable characteristic, and an additional premium must be paid for it.

If the valuation of the closely held company was done using transaction data that featured the acquisition of control of the various companies considered, then these data need to be adjusted to eliminate the added value that entered into these data to eliminate the part of the multiple that accounted for control.[47]

A guide to the appropriate minority discount is the magnitude of the average control premium. Table 15.9 shows that the average control premium between 1980 and 2013 was 43.4%. This premium can be used to compute the appropriate minority discount using the formula in equation 15.23.

$$\text{Minority discount} = 1 - [1/(1 + \text{Average premium})] \qquad (15.23)$$

Using the average control premium of 42.8%, we get an implied minority discount of 30%.

Applying Marketability and Minority Discounts

Let us assume that a value of $50 per share has been computed for a 20% ownership position in a closely held firm. Assuming 33% marketability and minority discounts, the value of this stock position equals the following:

Unadjusted value $50/share
Less 33% marketability discount $33.50
Less 33% minority discount $22.45

---

[46] John D. Emory, "The Value of Marketability as Illustrated in Initial Public Offerings of Common Stock," *Business Valuation News* (September 1985): 21–24; and John D. Emory, "The Value of Marketability as Illustrated in Initial Public Offerings of Common Stock," *Business Valuation Review* (December 1986): 12–15.
[47] Shannon P. Pratt and Alina V. Niculita, *Valuing a Business*, 5th ed. (New York: McGraw Hill, 2008), 398–414.

TABLE 15.9 Average Control Premiums and Implied Discounts

Year	Average Control Premium Offer (%)	Implied Minority Discount (%)
1980	49.9	33.3
1981	48.0	32.4
1982	47.4	32.2
1983	37.7	27.4
1984	37.9	27.5
1985	37.1	27.1
1986	38.2	27.6
1987	38.3	27.7
1988	41.9	29.5
1989	41.0	29.1
1990	42.0	29.6
1991	35.1	26.0
1992	41.0	29.1
1993	38.7	27.9
1994	41.9	29.5
1995	44.7	30.9
1996	36.6	26.8
1997	35.7	26.3
1998	40.7	28.9
1999	43.3	30.2
2000	49.1	32.9
2001	58.0	36.7
2002	59.8	37.4
2003	63.0	38.7
2004	30.9	23.6
2005	33.6	25.1
2006	31.9	24.2
2007	31.6	24.0
2008	57.3	36.4
2009	52.4	34.4
2010	52.5	34.4
2011	54.3	35.2
2012	46.3	31.6
2013	44.2	30.7
Average	43.4	30.1

Source: *Mergerstat Review*, 2014

The $22.45-per-share value is the value of a nonmarketable minority position in this closely held business.

Valuation Research on Takeovers of Privately Held Companies

Although there is an abundance of published research on the valuation effects of takeovers of public companies, there is limited research for closely held businesses. This is because data are readily available on public companies, but they are much harder to come by for private firms. One study by Chang analyzed the stock price reaction of public bidding firms when they acquire private companies.[48] In a study of 281 merger proposals between 1981 and 1992, which did not include any tender offers, Chang found that bidding firms did not experience any abnormal returns for cash offers but did show positive abnormal returns for stock offers. The positive returns for stock offers contrast with some research on stock acquisitions of public companies that feature negative returns. Chang compared the stock offers with private equity placements because the closely held targets typically were owned by a small number of shareholders. These positive returns are consistent with the research on the returns to companies that issue stock in private placements.[49]

One possible explanation for the positive stock response for public acquirers is that there may be more monitoring when stock is given to a few owners of the closely held company. This greater monitoring may reduce adverse agency effects and increase value. When the market perceives this, it reacts with a positive stock price response.

Valuation Research on Takeovers by Privately Held Companies

Our discussions of corporate governance raised concerns that CEOs and boards were at times not sufficiently caring for the wealth of their shareholders. One test of this conducted by Bargeron, Schlingemann, Stulz, and Zutter analyzed a sample of 1,667 deals, of which 453 were acquisitions by private bidders.[50] They found that public shareholders received a 63% higher premium when the acquirer was a public company as opposed to a closely held firm. The difference between the private and public acquirer premiums was greatest when the share ownership by management in the public company was low. This confirms the intuitive proposition that people are more careful when they are spending their own money as opposed to someone else's, such as largely anonymous shareholders.

---

[48] Saeyoung Chang, "Takeovers of Privately Held Targets, Methods of Payment, and Bidder Returns," *Journal of Finance* 53, no. 2 (April 1998): 773–784.

[49] Michael Hertzel and Richard L. Smith, "Market Discounts and Shareholders Gains for Placing Private Equity," *Journal of Finance* 48, no. 2 (June 1993): 459–485.

[50] Leonce L. Bargeron, Frederik P. Schlingemann, Rene Stulz, and Chad Zutter, "Why Do Private Acquirers Pay So Little Compared to Public Acquirers, " *Journal of Financial Economics* 89, no. 3 (September 2008): 375–390.

CHAPTER SIXTEEN

Tax Issues in M&A

D EPENDING ON THE METHOD used to finance the transaction, certain mergers, acquisitions, and restructuring may be tax-free. Some firms may use their tax benefits as assets in establishing the correct price that they might command in the marketplace. For this reason, tax considerations are important as both the motivation for a transaction and the valuation of a company. Part of the tax benefits from a transaction may derive from tax synergy, whereby one of the firms involved in a merger may not be able to fully utilize its tax shields. When combined with the merger partner, however, the tax shields may offset income. Some of these gains may come from unused net operating losses, which may be used by a more profitable merger partner. Tax reform, however, has limited the ability of firms to sell these net operating losses through mergers.

Other sources of tax benefits in mergers may arise from a market value of depreciable assets, which is greater than the value at which these assets are kept on the target's books. The acquiring firm that is able to step up the basis of these assets in accordance with the purchase price may finally realize tax savings.

This chapter discusses the mechanics of realizing some of the tax benefits through mergers. It also reviews the research studies that attempt to determine the importance of tax effects as a motivating factor for mergers and leveraged buyouts (LBOs) and examines the different accounting treatments that may be applied to a merger or an acquisition. These methods, which are regulated by tax laws, affect the importance of taxes in the overall merger valuation. It will be seen that various reforms in tax laws have diminished the role that taxes play in mergers and acquisitions. However, taxes may still be an important consideration that both the seller and buyer must carefully weigh before completing a transaction. The importance of tax considerations in

M&As is underscored by the significant role tax attorneys play in deal making. That is, not just attorneys versed in securities and corporate law but also tax specialists are key members of the M&A team.

 ## FINANCIAL ACCOUNTING FOR M&AS

Until 2001, there were two alternative accounting treatments for mergers and acquisitions: pooling and the purchase method. The main difference between them is the value that the combined firm's balance sheet places on the assets of the acquired firm, as well as the depreciation allowances and charges against income following the merger. After much debate, however, the accounting profession eliminated pooling. All mergers must now be accounted for under the purchase method. In eliminating pooling, the United States came more into conformance with the accounting standards of most of the industrialized world.

Under the purchase method, the transaction is recorded at its fair market value. Fair market value is defined as the total amount paid for the acquisition, including related costs of the acquisition, such as legal and accounting fees, broker's commission, and the like. If the acquisition is consummated with stock, then the acquisition price is based on the fair market value of the stock.

Assets that are acquired are assigned part of the overall cost of the acquisition based on their fair market value as of the acquisition. Any excess value that cannot be allocated to specific assets is then assigned to *goodwill*. This goodwill value needs to be regularly revisited, and if the company determines that the value assigned to it is not accurate, then it needs to be adjusted. Goodwill can be amortized over 15 years (under certain circumstances this can be 10 years for certain closely held businesses).

Under the purchase method, the acquiring company is entitled to income of the acquired company only from the date of purchase. Prior retained earnings of the acquired company are not allowed to be brought forward to the consolidated entity.

 ## TAXABLE VERSUS TAX-FREE TRANSACTIONS

A merger or an acquisition may be either a taxable transaction or a tax-free transaction. The tax status of a transaction may affect the value of the transaction from the viewpoint of both the buyer and the seller. A tax-free transaction is known as a tax-free reorganization. The term *tax-free* is a misnomer because the tax is not eliminated but will be realized when a later taxable transaction occurs. So they are really only *tax-deferred*, not tax-free.

Rules of the U.S. Internal Revenue Service require that target shareholders immediately pay capital gains taxes on an all cash purchase of their shares. Sometimes a bidder may pay target shareholders an additional sum to offset the taxes they may have to pay. The extent to which this may occur depends on the relative bargaining power of the parties.

Deals involving stock may qualify for tax benefits. We will now discuss the circumstances in which this could occur.

Tax-Free Reorganizations

There are several different types of tax-free reorganizations. Each is discussed here.

Type A Reorganization

For a transaction to qualify as a tax-free reorganization, it must be structured in certain ways.[1] One way is a type A reorganization, which is considered a more flexible tax-free reorganization technique than some of the others that are discussed in the following sections. In contrast to a type B reorganization, a type A reorganization allows the buyer to use either voting stock or nonvoting stock, common stock or preferred stock, or even other securities. It also permits the buyer to use more cash in the total consideration because the law does not stipulate a maximum amount of cash that may be used. At least 50% of the consideration, however, must be stock in the acquiring corporation. In addition, in a type A reorganization, the acquiring corporation may choose not to purchase all the target's assets. For example, the deal could be structured to allow the target to sell off certain assets separately and exclude them from this transaction.

In cases in which at least 50% of the bidder's stock is used as the consideration, but other considerations are used, such as cash, debt, or nonequity securities, the transaction may be partially taxable. Capital gains taxes must be paid on those shares that were exchanged for nonequity consideration, whereas taxes are deferred for those shares that were exchanged for stock. Rights and warrants that are convertible into the bidding firm's equity securities are generally classified as taxable.[2]

A type A reorganization must fulfill the continuity of interests requirement. That is, the shareholders in the acquired company must receive enough stock in the acquiring firm that they have a continuing financial interest in the buyer.[3]

Type B Reorganization

A type B merger or reorganization requires that the acquiring corporation use mainly its own voting common stock as the consideration for purchase of the target corporation's common stock. Cash must constitute no more than 20% of the total consideration, and at least 80% of the target's stock must be paid for by voting stock in the acquirer. In this type of transaction, the acquiring corporation must buy at least 80% of the stock of the target, although the purchase of 100% is more common. Target company shareholders may not be given the option to opt for cash as opposed to stock, where the effect could

---

[1] For a good description of the tax-free reorganizations, see George Rodoff, "Tax Consequences to Shareholders in an Acquisitive Reorganization," in Steven James Lee and Robert Douglas Coleman, eds., *Handbook of Mergers, Acquisitions and Buyouts* (Englewood Cliffs, NJ: Prentice-Hall, 1981), 359–379.

[2] Cathy M. Niden, "Acquisition Premia: Further Evidence on the Effects of Payment Method and Acquisition Method," University of Notre Dame Working Paper, 1990.

[3] Joseph Morris, *Mergers and Acquisitions: Business Strategies for Accountants* (New York: John Wiley & Sons, 1995), 254–255.

be that less than 80% of stock could be used. The presentation of this option, even if at least 80% of stock is actually used, disallows the type B reorganization.

Following the purchase of the target's stock, the target becomes a subsidiary of the acquiring corporation. In both type A and type B reorganizations, the transactions are viewed, from a tax regulatory point of view, as merely a continuation of the original corporate entities in a reorganized form. Therefore, these transactions are not taxed because they are not considered true sales.

It is possible to have a *creeping type B reorganization*, in which the stock is purchased in several transactions over a period of time. To qualify as a type B reorganization, however, the stock purchases must be part of an overall plan to acquire the target company. The plan itself must be implemented over 12 months or less. In a creeping type B reorganization, only stock may be used as consideration. It is acceptable for the acquiring company to have bought some stock in the target with cash in the past as long as the purchases were not part of the acquisition plan.

Type C Reorganization

In a type C reorganization, the acquiring corporation must purchase 80% of the fair market value of the target's *assets*. Cash may be used only if at least 80% of the fair market value of the target's assets has been purchased using the voting stock of the acquiring corporation. As a result of the transaction, the target company usually must liquidate.

One advantage of a type C reorganization is that the acquiring company may not need to receive approval of its shareholders in such an asset purchase. Of course, target shareholders must approve this type of control transaction.

Type D Reorganization

There are two kinds of type D reorganizations. One type covers acquisitions, and the other covers restructuring. In an acquisitive type D reorganization, the acquiring company receives 80% of the stock in the target in exchange for voting stock in the acquiring company. Shareholders in the acquiring company become controlling shareholders in the target.

Divisive type D reorganizations cover spin-offs, split-ups, and split-offs. As discussed in Chapter 11, one or more corporations are formed in a spin-off, with the stock in the new companies being distributed to the original company shareholders according to some predetermined formula. In a split-off, a component of the original company is separated from the parent company, and shareholders in the original company may exchange their shares for shares in the new entity. In a split-up, the original company ceases to exist, and one or more new companies are formed from the original business.

There are some additional requirements that a divisive type D reorganization must fulfill to qualify as tax-free. For example, the distribution of shares must not be for the purpose of tax avoidance. Both the parent company and the spun-off entity must be in business for at least five years before the spin-off.

TAX CONSEQUENCES OF A STOCK-FOR-STOCK EXCHANGE

Target stockholders who receive the stock of the acquiring corporation in exchange for their common stock are not immediately taxed on the consideration they receive. Taxes must be paid only if the stock is eventually sold. Given the time value of money, this postponement of tax payments clearly has value. If cash is included in the transaction, this cash may be taxed to the extent that it represents a gain on the sale of stock.

Taxable Purchases of Stock

As noted, consideration other than stock, such as cash or debt securities, may result in a tax liability for the target shareholders. This tax liability applies only to a gain that might be realized from sale of the stock. If the stock is sold at a loss, no tax liability results.

Taxable Purchases of Assets

A tax liability may also result when the acquiring corporation purchases the assets of the target using consideration other than stock in the acquiring corporation. The potential tax liability is measured by comparing the purchase price of the assets with the adjusted basis of these assets.

Taxable versus Partially Taxable Transactions

A transaction may be partially taxable if the consideration is a combination of stock and cash. The stock consideration may not be taxed, but the cash is taxed. Therefore, the percentage of the transaction that is taxable depends on the relative percentages of stock and cash.

Tax Loss Carryforwards

A tax loss or tax credit carryover was a more important motive for mergers and acquisitions in prior years, such as the early 1980s, than it is today. In fact, at one time companies advertised the availability of such tax gains to motivate a sale. The Tax Code, however, has been changed to try to prevent such tax-motivated transactions.

The tax losses of target corporations can be used to offset a limited amount of the acquiring corporation's future income for a maximum of 15 years or until the tax loss is exhausted. Before 1981, the maximum period was five years. Only tax losses for the previous three years can be used to offset future income.

Tax loss carryforwards may motivate mergers and acquisitions in two ways. A company that has earned profits may find value in the tax losses of a target corporation that can be used to offset the income it plans to earn. Targets may demand that bidder compensate them for these benefits.[4] There is empirical evidence of this in studies which show that takeover premiums are higher in all cash bids compared to stock offers.

---

[4] Ron Gilson, Myron Scholes, and M. A. Wolfson, "Taxation and thr Dynamics of Corporate Control: The Uncertain Case for Tax Motivated Acquisitions," in John C. Coffee Jr., Louis Lowenstein, and Susan Rose Ackerman, eds., *Knights, Raiders and Targets* (New York: Oxford University Press, 1988.

Although tax benefits may be an important factor in determining whether a merger will take place, they may not be the sole motivating one. A merger may not be structured solely for tax purposes. The goal of the merger must be to maximize the profitability of the acquiring corporation.

An example of the gains that an acquirer may reap from merging with a target that has incurred past operating losses is the 2006 Alcatel SA–Lucent Technologies Inc. merger. When the telecom bubble burst in 2000, Lucent accumulated many billions of dollars of losses; while the company returned to profitability in 2003, it still did not use up all of its net operating loss tax credits. The size of these credits was reported to be as high as $3.5 billion.[5] The tax credits can be applied to U.S. profits by the merged company for many years. Alcatel also had net operating loss credits, and the merger with Lucent, a company that derives most of its business in the U.S. market, better enabled Alcatel to use its own credits. While this merger may have enabled Alcatel to receive tax benefits, it did not, however, result in a stronger company, as the combined entity still found the competitive landscape quite challenging.

Tax Loss Carryforward Research

A number of research studies have sought to estimate the present value of tax loss carryforwards. These tax benefits may be less than their face value, not only because of the time value of money but also because they might expire without being fully utilized. Estimates of these values have been developed by Auerbach and Poterba and by Altshuler and Auerbach.[6] These research studies indicate that the two offsetting factors of deferral and expiration reduce the tax benefits to half their face value.

 ## ASSET BASIS STEP-UP

Tax advantages may arise in an acquisition when a target corporation carries assets on its books with a basis for tax purposes that is a fraction of the assets' replacement cost or market value. These assets could be more valuable for tax purposes if they were owned by another corporation, which could increase their tax basis after the acquisition and gain additional depreciation benefits. The tax basis for the acquiring corporation is the cost or purchase price of the assets. The acquiring corporation may use this higher asset basis to shelter income.

The Tax Reform Act of 1986 reduced some tax benefits. Following its passage, the selling corporation incurs a greater tax liability on asset sales, which reduces the seller's incentive to participate in the transaction. Moreover, research seeking to find

---

[5] Jesse Drucker and Sara Silver, "Alcatel Stands to Reap Tax Benefit on Merger," *Wall Street Journal*, April 26, 2006, C3.
[6] Alan Auerbach and James Poterba, "Tax Loss Carry Forwards and Corporate Tax Incentives," in Martin Feldstein, ed., *The Effect of Taxation on Capital Accumulation* (Chicago: University of Chicago Press, 1987); and Roseanne Altshuler and Alan Auerbach, "The Importance of Tax Law Asymmetries: An Economic Analysis," National Bureau of Economic Research Working Paper No. 2279, National Bureau of Economic Research, Cambridge, MA, 1987.

the existence of *asset basis step-up* as a motivating factor for mergers and acquisitions before the Tax Reform Act of 1986 did not find asset basis step-up to be a significant motivating factor.[7]

CHANGES IN THE TAX LAWS

General Utilities Doctrine

Until its repeal with the Tax Reform Act of 1986, the General Utilities Doctrine allowed preferential treatment for "disincorporating" or liquidating corporations.[8] According to this doctrine, the sale of corporate assets and a liquidating distribution to shareholders were exempt from capital gains taxation. These distributions could occur, for example, following the acquisition of one corporation by another. The acquiring corporation could then sell off the assets of the acquired corporation and distribute the proceeds to shareholders without incurring capital gains tax liability to the corporation. These tax-free liquidating distributions could also occur without an acquisition, such as when a firm chose to sell off certain assets and distribute the proceeds to shareholders.

Assets sales were often structured by establishing separate subsidiary corporations. An acquired corporation could be purchased and its assets distributed into one or more subsidiaries. These subsidiaries would contain the assets that the acquiring corporation was not interested in keeping.[9] The assets that would be retained would be put into the parent corporation or into a separate subsidiary. The stock of the subsidiaries containing the unwanted assets could then be sold without incurring a significant tax liability. With the repeal of the General Utilities Doctrine, the gains or losses from an acquisition must be attributed to the acquiring corporation. The opportunities to avoid such tax liabilities were narrowed with the passage of the Tax Reform Act of 1986. They were further narrowed by the 1987 and 1988 tax acts.

Elimination of the Morris Trust

The Morris Trust is named after a 1966 tax court decision, *Commissioner v. Morris Trust*. This decision established certain variants of spin-offs as tax-free. Using a Morris Trust, a company could spin off component businesses that it did not want to keep. In a second set preplanned transaction, the spun-off business is merged into an acquirer's business in a tax-free stock transaction. The final result is that shareholders in the selling company end up with shares in both their own company and the company of the acquirer. Companies have creatively used these vehicles to borrow money through a subsidiary, spin it off, and later sell it while having the buyer agree to pay the loan. The selling parent

---

[7] Alan J. Auerbach and David Reishus, "The Impact of Taxation on Mergers and Acquisitions," in Alan J. Auerbach, ed., *Mergers and Acquisitions* (Chicago: National Bureau of Economic Research, University of Chicago Press, 1988), 69–88.

[8] General Utilities v. Helvering, 296 U.S. 200 (1935).

[9] George B. Pompan, "Federal Income Tax Considerations," in *Mergers and Acquisitions: Back-to-Basics Techniques for the 90s*, 2nd ed. (New York: John Wiley & Sons, 1994), 198–202.

company keeps the cash from the loan. The tax law was changed in 1997 to eliminate the tax-free status of a preplanned spin-off and subsequent sale, although if the deal is not preplanned it still may be tax-free.

Real Estate Investment Trusts

Real estate investment trusts (REITs) are publicly traded, passive investment vehicles that pay low or no federal taxes. The rebound of the real estate market in the mid-1990s enhanced the popularity of REITs. Their popularity rose to even greater heights in the speculative real estate bubble of the mid-2000s.

REITs consist of two entities in one: a management firm that manages real estate assets and an investment vehicle. Although they are supposed to be separate, their shares are paired and trade as one. Real estate investment trusts typically purchase property and rent it to a management firm. The management firm pays out its cash flow from properties to the investment vehicle, where it is treated as tax-free rent. Real estate investment trusts must distribute 95% of their earnings to shareholders, who then pay taxes on these monies at the individual level. Real estate assets such as hotels and shopping malls are often included in such investment vehicles. By combining them under the REIT umbrella, a real estate portfolio acquires tax benefits and liquidity. One of the more famous REITs is Starwood Hotels and Resorts Worldwide Inc. There has been much debate about reducing the tax benefits of REITs, but such discussions have not resulted in changes in the laws that relate to REITs.

Given that REITs are required to pay out 90% of their earnings, they are not considered good for companies that have good growth prospects. An example of the market's position on this came in April 1998, when Corrections Corporation of America, the nation's largest commercial operator of prisons, announced that it would merge into CCA Prison Realty Trust, which is a REIT that would be the surviving entity. In response to the announcement, the stock prices of both companies fell. Shareholders in Corrections Corporation of America were more interested in growth and believed that being in a REIT would limit growth prospects.

ROLE OF TAXES IN THE MERGER DECISION

If a deal is taxable to the selling shareholders, the benefits are reduced and the deal is less attractive compared to a tax-deferred transaction. This is why the tax experts working on the deal try to reduce the adverse tax ramifications of the deal. This is why research has showed that when the probability of a stock offer increases, measures such as the bidder's market-to-book ratio increase.[10]

There is an intuitive relationship between the premium a bidder offers and the tax ramifications of the acquisition. As we discussed earlier, if the deal will be taxable, the

---

[10] Willard Carelton, David Guilkey, Robert Harris, and John Stewart, "Empirical Analysis of the Role of Medium of Exchange in Mergers," *Journal of Finance* 38, no. 3 (June 1983): 813–826.

bidder may have to offer a higher premium. This was confirmed by research that shows that target announcement period returns were higher for taxable than nontaxable (remember really tax-deferred).[11] International M&A research shows similar findings. For example, Eckbo and Langhor found higher premiums for cash offers in France.[12]

Auerbach and Reishus examined a sample of 318 mergers and acquisitions that occurred between 1968 and 1983. Approximately two-thirds of these mergers were in the manufacturing sector, with the average acquiring firm approximately 10 times larger than the acquired company. They found that a significant percentage of the companies in their sample had various constraints on their ability to use their tax benefits. Nonetheless, many of the companies realized tax benefits as a result of merging. The average gain was 10.5% of the acquiring firm's market value.[13]

Scholes and Wolfson studied the number of mergers and acquisitions for various times, including the periods before 1981, between 1981 and 1986, and after 1986.[14] The 1981 Tax Act provided various tax incentives for mergers and other forms of restructuring. Some of these were eliminated in the tax reforms that were part of the 1986 Tax Act. They attribute part of the intensified level of merger activity to tax motives that were put in place with the 1981 act and eliminated by the 1986 act.

Hayn analyzed 640 successful acquisitions between 1970 and 1985.[15] In her sample she noted that 54% were taxable, 18% were partially taxable, and 28% were tax-free. There were 279 tender offers in her sample, and the majority of them (64%) were taxable. Mergers, however, varied in tax status. Of the 361 mergers in her sample, 39% were tax-free, whereas 46% were taxable and the remainder was partially taxable.

Hayn researched the role that the tax attributes of transactions played in determining abnormal returns for targets and acquirers. First, she noted that tax-free status is a prerequisite of certain deals. Targets that do not receive such a status may decline to continue with the deal and may look to other bidders who can structure the transaction so that such a status is attained. Specifically, she found that "potential tax benefits stemming from net operating loss carryforwards and unused tax credits positively affect announcement period returns of firms involved in tax-free acquisitions, and capital gains and the step-up in the acquired assets basis affects returns of firms involved in taxable acquisitions."[16]

---

[11] Yen Shen Huang and Ralph Walking, "Target Abnormal Returns Associated with Acquisition Announcements: Payment Method, Acquisition Form and Managerial Resistance," *Journal of Financial Economics* 19 (1987): 329–349; and Carla Hayn, "Tax Attributes as Determinants of Shareholder Gains in Corporate Acquisitions," *Journal of Financial Economics* 23 (1989): 121–153.

[12] Betton Eckbo and Herwig Langhor, "Information Disclosure, Method of Payment, and Takeover Premiums: Public and Private Tender Offers in France," *Journal of Financial Economics* 24 (1989): 363–403.

[13] Alan J. Auerbach and David Reishus, "Taxes and the Merger Decision," in John C. Coffee Jr., Louis Lowenstein, and Susan Rose Ackerman, eds., *Knights, Raiders and Targets* (New York: Oxford University Press, 1988), 300–313.

[14] Myron S. Scholes and Mark A. Wolfson, *Taxes and Business Strategy* (Englewood Cliffs, NJ: Prentice-Hall, 1992).

[15] Carla Hayn, "Tax Attributes as Determinants of Shareholder Gains in Corporate Acquisitions," *Journal of Financial Economics* 23 (1989): 121–153.

[16] Ibid., 148.

A study by Ayers, Lefanowicz, and Robinson looked at the impact of variations in the capital gains tax rates over time and the volume of M&A activity.[17] They compared transactions that were tax-free, stock-for-stock exchanges with other taxable transactions, such as cash for stock deals. In their study of acquisitions of publicly traded companies over the period of 1973–2001, they found a negative association between acquisition activity and the capital gains tax rate for individual investors. The results show that capital gains tax policy represented significant transactions costs that, in turn, decrease M&A activity during time periods when capital gains tax rates are relatively higher.

 ## ROLE OF TAXES IN THE CHOICE OF SELL-OFF METHOD

When management has determined that it will separate a unit from the company, one of the early decisions in that process is whether they are going to pursue a tax-free spin-off or a sale that may cause the company to incur tax costs. Maydew, Schipper, and Vincent analyzed 218 sales transactions and 52 nontaxable spin-offs.[18] The authors assumed that the sellers consider the trade-off between the tax costs of a sale and the acquisition premium they would derive from a sale, which would not be available in a tax-free spin-off. They attempted to estimate what the premium would be in tax-free transactions and reached the intuitive result that where attractive premiums could be achieved, the taxable sale is pursued, and when that is not the case, there is a higher probability of a tax-free spin-off.

 ## ORGANIZATIONAL FORM AND M&A PREMIUMS

Scholes, Erickson, Maydew, and Shevlin postulated that S corporations and other pass-through business entities, such as partnerships and limited liability companies, should sell to premiums that can be explained in part by tax factors.[19] This is because asset base step-up is available in acquisitions of S corporations but is usually not viable in the acquisitions of C corporations because the tax costs of the step-up usually are greater than the tax benefits. To test the hypothesis that there is a difference in premiums for acquisitions of S corporations compared to C corporations, Erickson and Wang analyzed 77 pairs of taxable stock acquisitions of S corporations and C corporations over the period between 1994–2000.[20] As expected, they found that all of the acquisitions of the S corporations in their sample were structured in a manner

[17] Benjamin C. Ayers, Craig E. Lefanowicz, and John R. Robinson, "Capital Gains Taxes and Acquisition Activity: Evidence of the Lock-In Effect," *Contemporary Accounting Research* 24, no. 2 (2007): 315–344.

[18] Edward L. Maydew, Katherine Schipper, and Linda Vincent, "The Impact of Taxes on the Choice of Divestiture Method," *Journal of Accounting and Economics* 28 (1999): 117–150.

[19] Myron S. Scholes, Merle M. Erickson, Edward L. Maydew, and Terrence J. Shevlin, *Taxes and Business Strategy*, 3rd ed. (Upper Saddle River, NJ: Prentice Hall, 2005).

[20] Merle M. Erickson and Shiing-wu Wang, "Tax Benefits as a Source of Merger Premiums in Acquisitions of Private Companies," *Accounting Review* 82, no. 2 (2007): 359–387.

that stepped up the tax basis of the acquired company's assets. In addition, they found that the acquisition multiples were higher for the S corporations compared to the C corporations. Thus, we see that organization form does influence takeovers.

CAPITAL STRUCTURE AND PROPENSITY TO ENGAGE IN ACQUISITIONS

Interest payments on debt are a tax-deductible expense, whereas dividend payments from equity ownership are not. The existence of a tax advantage for debt is an incentive to have greater use of debt, as opposed to equity, as the means of exchange in mergers and acquisitions.

The leverage argument suggests that the acquiring firm has a suboptimal debt-equity ratio and has not sufficiently used debt in its capital mix. The argument goes on to put forward mergers and acquisitions as a means whereby companies can achieve greater utilization of debt. An overly simplistic test of this hypothesis would be to look at the debt-equity ratios before and after various mergers and acquisitions. This test is considered overly simplistic because the acquiring corporation might retain earnings for one or more years before an acquisition in anticipation of the takeover. After the takeover, which might be financed with internal funds and borrowed capital, there would be a sudden increase in the debt-equity ratio. This jump in the debt-equity ratio may be offset by a gradual reduction over the years following the acquisition as the firm moves to a long-term debt-equity ratio that it considers optimal.

The tax deductibility of interest payments is not an incentive to merge; rather, it is an incentive to increase the potential acquiring firm's borrowing and alter its capital structure. This may be done in a much more cost-effective manner by issuing bonds or directly borrowing from a lender than through the costly process of engaging in an acquisition.

Auerbach and Reishus found that, contrary to popular belief, firms that merge more frequently do not borrow more than firms that have exhibited less tendency to merge.[21] They also discovered that the long-term debt-equity ratios of firms in their sample increased from 25.4% to only 26.7% after the mergers, which took place at a time when debt-equity ratios were increasing throughout the economy. The Auerbach and Reishus result may be less relevant to many of the private equity deals we saw in the 2000s. Many private equity firms acquire targets with unused debt capacity and engage in leveraged recapitalizations. In these deals, they acquire a target in a going-private transaction, increase its debt, and take some or all of the debt proceeds as a dividend. The acquired corporation then has a more levered capital structure that in turn provides tax benefits to the corporation at the expense of a higher risk profile. A somewhat similar situation is discussed in the following section when we describe Kaplan's research on the tax effects of management buyouts.

---

[21] Ibid., 80.

LEVERAGE AND DEAL STRUCTURE

In a study of 340 corporation acquisitions during the years 1985–1988, Erickson found that high tax rate acquirers were more likely to use debt to finance a transaction—a result that is quite intuitive.[22] In his study, the probability that an acquirer would use debt as opposed to equity was an increasing function of the acquirer's tax rates. He also found that the probability of a debt-financed taxable cash transaction was an increasing function of the acquirer's debt-to-equity ratio. This later result is somewhat inconsistent with the aforementioned findings of Auerbach and Reishus.

 TAXES AS A SOURCE OF VALUE IN MANAGEMENT BUYOUTS

Taxes have quite a different role in management buyouts (MBOs) than they have in mergers and acquisitions. Kaplan measured the value of tax benefits for 76 MBOs between 1980 and 1986.[23] In this sample of MBOs, the average premium was 42.3% above the market price two months before the initial announcement of the buyout. The median ratio of debt to total capital rose from 18.8% before the buyouts to 87.8% afterward. Kaplan found that the value of increased interest and depreciation deductions ranged between 21.0% and 142.6% of the premium paid to prebuyout shareholders. A regression analysis relating the total tax deductions generated by the buyout to the premium available to prebuyout shareholders suggested that total tax deductions are an important determining variable.

Leveraged Buyouts and Tax Revenues

Critics of LBOs contend that the tax deductibility of the debt used to finance these transactions causes a loss in tax revenues for the U.S. Treasury. These critics assert that, in effect, taxpayers are absorbing some of the financing costs of the LBOs. Jensen, Kaplan, and Stiglin, however, argue that LBOs result in *positive* tax revenues for the U.S. Treasury.[24] They cite factors such as the increased efficiency of post-LBO firms, which increases taxable income; tax payments on capital gains to shareholders; tax payments on the interest income; and capital gains taxes paid on post-LBO asset sales to support their position. Jensen and colleagues attempted to measure these factors for a typical LBO.

For a typical LBO of $500 million, Jensen et al. estimated that incremental tax revenues equal $226.9 million, with incremental tax losses equal to $116.9 million,

---

[22] Merle Erickson, "The Effects of Taxes on the Structure of Corporate Acquisitions," *Journal of Accounting Research* 86, no. 2 (Autumn 1998): 279–297.

[23] Steven Kaplan, "Management Buyouts: Evidence on Taxes as Source of Value," *Journal of Finance* 44, no. 3 (July 1989): 611–632.

[24] Michael C. Jensen, Steven Kaplan, and Laura Stiglin, "Effects of LBOs on Tax Revenues of the U.S. Treasury," *Tax Notes* 42, no. 6 (February 6, 1989): 727–733. Reprinted in *The Law of Mergers, Acquisitions, and Reorganizations*, Dale A. Oesterle, ed. (St. Paul, MN: West Publishing, 1991).

resulting in a net positive incremental tax revenue equal to $110 million. Scholes and Wolfson criticized some of the assumptions used by Jensen et al.[25] For example, they focused on the assumption that the LBO would cause an increased value of the company and its shares. They contend that it is reasonable that some of these gains would have occurred anyway. They also point out that some of the capital gains preceding the LBO would have resulted in capital gains for shareholders, some of whom would have sold their shares even without the LBO. These criticisms and others they point out would change the conclusions of the Jensen study. Scholes and Wolfson do not go so far as to say that their suggested refinements would have wiped out all the positive net incremental tax revenues noted by Jensen and colleagues. They simply state that the result would be different and probably lower, but that it remains an open and controversial issue.

Jensen et al.'s study takes a highly favorable view of LBOs and their expected benefits. As a result of the concerns pointed out by Scholes and Wolfson, as well as the overly positive view Jensen et al. take of the salutary effects of LBOs, we can conclude that the case has not been made that LBOs have a positive net effect on tax revenues. In fact, if anything, there probably is more concern that any effects may be negative.

MISCELLANEOUS TAX ISSUES

International Taxation and Cross-Border M&As

The parent-subsidiary structure of multinational companies that were created by cross-border M&As may give rise to potential additional costs that non–cross-border deals lack. By having a foreign subsidiary, the parent company may incur double taxation in the form of corporate taxes in the foreign country and then possible taxes on the repatriated dividend income in the home country. Recognizing this, some parent countries exempt the dividend income received from foreign subsidiaries. For example, this was the case when Germany exempted dividend income that could be received by Daimler from Chrysler, thus increasing the potential value of Chrysler to Daimler.[26] Huizinga and Voget have shown that countries that impose high rates of international double taxation are less likely to attract foreign parent companies.[27] This adverse effect on foreign investment is why many countries, especially European countries, have entered into bilateral treaties with each other to eliminate the double taxation. Indeed, the European Union adopted the EU Parent-Subsidiary Directive, which eliminated the taxation of intra-EU and intracompany dividend flows. Some countries, such as Great Britain, have lowered their corporate tax rates several times in recent years while the U.S., with its flawed political system, stubbornly maintains the high double taxation of corporate earnings. As we will discuss shortly, this has given an incentive for foreign bidders to target U.S. companies.

---

[25] Myron S. Scholes and Mark A. Wolfson, *Taxes and Business Strategy* (Englewood Cliffs, NJ: Prentice-Hall, 1992).

[26] We say potential, as in retrospect this was not a successful M&A.

[27] Harry Huizinga and Johannes Voget, "International Taxation and the Direction and Volume of Cross Border M&As," *Journal of Finance* 64, no. 3 (June 2009): 1217–1249.

Tax Inversions

In recent years U.S. companies have struggled to deal with the very high corporate tax rates in the U.S., which exceed those of other major industrial countries, including Japan and European nations. U.S. politicians have been unwilling to take steps to change the law lest these actions be used against them in their next election. The result is that multinational U.S. companies are unwilling to repatriate foreign subsidiary profits lest they be subject to the high U.S. tax rates. However, some have gone even further and have done mergers with foreign companies located in countries with lower tax rates. In such deals, the U.S. company may relocate its corporate headquarters to the other nation, and then it may be able to qualify for lower taxes. This then allows it full access to the non-U.S. accumulated profits it may have been holding. Under rules that were established in 2004 a U.S. company could do a tax inversion deal if its shareholders owned less than 80% of the combined company. Firms doing such deals have been accused of trying to inflate the value of the foreign company's share and to minimize the U.S. bidder share.

In 2014 and 2015 there were several tax inversion deals. For example, Medtronic acquired Ireland's Covidien PLC for $42.9 billion. U.S. pharmaceutical maker AbbVie tried to acquire Irish drug maker Shire, and Burger King merged with Canada's Tim Hortons.

To qualify for an inversion target, shareholders must receive at least 20% of the combined entity. If that is the case, then the acquirer may adopt the new homeland for tax purposes. While most stock-financed acquisitions do not have significant tax implications for acquiring firm shareholders, they do in inversion deals. The Internal Revenue Service holds that when a company moves abroad in a tax inversion deal, the buying company's shareholders must pay capital gains taxes.

In response to an uptick in the number of tax inversion deals, the Obama administration implemented new rules to limit the tax benefits of such deals. The new rules limit the ability of a U.S. company to use offshore cash to fund such deals. The rules also cracked down on manipulation of the respective merger partner values so as to stay under the 80% threshold. These rules forced the cancellation of some tax inversion deals including AbbVie's bid for Shire.

Tax Inversions and Cross Border M&As

With the crackdown is U.S. initiated tax inversion deals, the volume of these tax motived deals collapsed. However, the problem, the high U.S. corporate tax rates, remains thereby giving U.S. companies an incentive to come up with says of avoiding it. The new rules put in place in 2014, however, did not affect foreign acquisitions of U.S. companies. This gives foreign acquirers an advantage over U.S. acquires which may enable them to pay a higher premium and outbid U.S. acquirers. The foreign acquirer can try to apply its relatively lower tax rates after the acquisition. This occurred in 2015 when Salix Pharmaceuticals accepted a bid from Valient, a Canadian company that used to be a U.S. company but which did a 2010 inversion deal to become a Canadian firm. Other examples of such tax-related transactions were the recent acquisitions of several

U.S. companies by the Singaporean company Avago Technologies which has a single digit tax rate.

Taxes and Golden Parachutes

The Internal Revenue Code imposes a 20% excise tax on excess parachute payments. Deductions for such excess payments are not allowed. The excess amount of such compensation is defined as that amount that is greater than the compensation during a five-year base period. There are some exceptions, such as when it can be established that the payments were reasonable in relation to the specific services that were provided.

Taxes and Termination Fees

Termination fees paid by a winning bidder, such as the $1.8 billion paid by Pfizer to American Home Products (now Wyeth) after Pfizer's successful bid for Warner Lambert in 2000, may be tax-deductible. This arises out of a 1994 decision by a federal court in which monies paid to an unsuccessful white knight were found to be deductible if they were a separate transaction—that is, separate from the transaction that was eventually consummated.[28] The transactions are regarded as mutually exclusive if only one can be completed, which is normally the case when a buyer outbids a company that had already entered into a termination fee agreement with a target.[29]

Taxes and Greenmail

As noted in Chapter 5, penalties have been imposed on the receipt of greenmail payments. The Internal Revenue Service imposes a tax equal to 50% of the gain on such payments.

---

[28] *United States v. Federated Department Stores,* 171 Bankr (603 S. D. Ohio 1994).
[29] Robert Willens, "Guidant Eyes Tax Cut for Breakup Fee," *Daily Deal,* March 9, 2006, 5.

Glossary

Abnormal return   In event studies, the part of the return that is not predicted by factors such as the market.

Absolute priority rule   The hierarchy whereby claims are satisfied in corporate liquidation.

Acquisition   The purchase of an entire company or a controlling interest in a company.

Agency problem   The conflict of interest that exists between owners of firms (shareholders) and their agents (management).

Alphabet stock   *See* Tracking stock.

Antigreenmail amendment   A corporate charter amendment that prohibits targeted share purchases at a premium from an outside shareholder without the approval of nonparticipating shareholders.

Antitakeover amendment   Corporate charter amendment that is intended to make takeovers more difficult and/or expensive for an unwanted bidder.

Any-or-all tender offer   A tender offer for an unspecified number of shares in a target company.

Appraisal rights   The rights of shareholders to obtain an independent valuation of their shares to determine the appropriate value. Shareholders may pursue these rights in litigation.

Back-end rights plan   A type of poison pill antitakeover defense whereby shareholders are issued a rights dividend that is exercisable in the event that a hostile bidder purchases a certain number of shares. Upon the occurrence of that event, shareholders may then exchange their rights combined with their shares for a certain amount of cash and/or other securities equal to a value that is set by the target. In doing so, the target's board, in effect, establishes a minimum price for the company's stock.

Bear hug   An offer made directly to the board of directors of a target company, usually made to increase the pressure on the target with the threat that a tender offer may follow.

Beta   A risk measure derived from the capital asset pricing model. It quantifies the systematic risk of a security.

Bidder   The acquiring firm.

Blank check companies   Also called special purpose acquisition corporation (SPACS).

Blended price   The weighted average price that is set in a two-tiered tender offer.

Board out clause   An antitakeover provision that allows the board of directors to decide when a supermajority provision is effective.

Business judgment rule   The legal principle that assumes the board of directors is acting in the best interests of shareholders unless it can be clearly established that it is not. If that is established, the board would be in violation of its fiduciary duty to shareholders.

Bustup fees   The payments that the target gives the bidder if the target decides to cancel the transaction.

Bustup takeover   A takeover in which an acquisition is followed by the sale of certain, or even all, of the assets of the target company. This is sometimes done to pay down the debt used to finance a leveraged acquisition.

Capital asset pricing model   A financial model that computes a security's rate of return as a function of the risk-free rate and a market premium that is weighted by the security's beta.

Capital budgeting   A project analysis in which a project's receipts and outlays are valued over a project's life.

Cash flow LBO   Leveraged buyout in which the debt financing relies more on the expectation of projected cash flows than on the collateral protection of the target's assets.

Casual pass   When a bidder makes an informal overture to the management of the target expressing interest in an acquisition.

Celler-Kefauver Act   A 1950 amendment to the Clayton Act that modified Section 7 of that act to make the acquisition of assets, not just the stock, of a company an antitrust violation when the deal has anticompetitive results. This amendment also made "anticompetitive" vertical and conglomerate mergers an antitrust violation.

Chapter 7   The part of the bankruptcy law that provides for the liquidation of corporations.

Chapter 11   The part of the bankruptcy law that provides for the reorganization of a bankrupt company.

Chinese wall   The imaginary barrier separating the investment banking, arbitrage, and securities trading activities within a financial institution such as an investment bank.

Classified board   Also called a staggered board. An antitakeover measure that separates the firm's board of directors into different classes with different voting rights. The goal is to make acquisition of voting rights more difficult.

Clayton Act   A federal antitrust law passed in 1914. Section 7, which is most relevant to mergers and acquisitions, prohibits the acquisition of stock and assets of a company when the effect is to lessen competition.

Coercive tender offer   A tender offer that exerts pressure on target shareholders to tender early. This pressure may come in the form of preferential compensation for early tendering shareholders. Changes in securities laws have limited the effectiveness of such tender offers.

Coinsurance effect   Where cash flows of two combining companies are not perfectly correlated so that the volatility of the combined firm's cash flows exhibits less variability.

Collar agreement   Agreed-upon adjustments in the number of shares offered in a stock-for-stock exchange to account for fluctuations in stock prices before the completion of the deal.

Concentration ratios   Measures of the percentage of total industry revenues accounted for by a certain number of firms, usually the top four or eight.

Conglomerate   A combination of unrelated firms.

Cramdown   A situation that occurs when a reorganization plan is approved even when some classes of creditors do not approve it. At least one class of creditors needs to approve the plan for there to be a cramdown.

Cumulative abnormal return   The sum of daily abnormal returns over a certain period in an event study.

Cumulative voting rights   When shareholders have the right to pool their votes to concentrate them on the election of one or more directors rather than apply their votes to the election of all directors.

Dead hand provisions   Antitakeover measure that gives the power to redeem a poison pill to the directors who were on the target's board of directors before the takeover attempt.

Debtor in possession   A term used to refer to a bankrupt company in a Chapter 11 proceeding.

Deconglomerization   The process of taking apart a conglomerate through various sell-offs.

Dissident   A shareholder, or group of shareholders, who oppose current management and may try to use the proxy process to gain control of the company or to try to get the company to take certain actions, such as payment of certain dividends. Dissidents often try to have their representatives placed on the board of directors.

Diversification   In mergers and acquisitions, a term that refers to buying companies or assets outside the companies' current lines of business.

Divestiture   The sale of a component of the company, such as a division.

Dual classification   The creation of two classes of common stock, with the goal of concentrating more voting rights in the hands of management.

Economies of scale   The reduction of a company's average costs due to increasing output and spreading out fixed costs over higher output levels.

Economies of scope   The ability of a firm to utilize one set of inputs to provide a broader range of outputs or services.

Employee stock ownership plan (ESOP)   A type of pension plan in which the assets of the plan are the stock of the company.

Equity carve-out   The issuance of equity in a division or part of a parent company that then becomes a separate company.

ESOP   *See* Employee stock ownership plan.

Exclusivity period   The time period during the initial days after a Chapter 11 filing when only the debtor can put forward a reorganization plan. It is initially 120 days, but the time period is often extended.

Fair price provision   An antitakeover charter amendment that requires the payment of a certain minimum price for the shares of the target. It increases the bidder's cost of a takeover and makes coercive actions, such as two-tiered tender offers, less effective.

Fallen angel   A bond originally issued with an investment-grade rating that had its rating fall below the investment-grade level, BB or lower, into the junk bond category.

Flip-in poison pill plan   Shareholders are issued rights to acquire stock in the target at a significant discount, usually 50%.

Flip-over poison pill plan   The most commonly used poison pill antitakeover defense, in which shareholders are issued rights to purchase common stock in a bidding firm's company at a significant discount, usually 50%.

Free cash flow hypothesis   Theory put forward by Michael Jensen, which asserts that the assumption of debt used to finance leveraged takeovers will absorb discretionary cash flows and help eliminate the agency problem between management and shareholders. It is assumed that with the higher debt service obligations, management would apply the company's cash flows to activities that are in management's interest and not necessarily in shareholders' interests.

Front end-loaded tender offers   A tender offer in which the compensation of a first tier is superior to a later second tier. Such offers are designed to be coercive and cause shareholders to tender early.

General Utilities Doctrine   A component of the Tax Code that provided tax benefits for the sale of assets or liquidating distributions. It was repealed by the Tax Reform Act of 1986.

Go shop provision   When a seller agrees to seek out other potential offers in addition to one it is considering accepting.

Going private   When a public corporation becomes privately held. This is usually done through a leveraged buyout.

Golden parachute   Employment contract of upper management that provides a larger payout upon the occurrence of certain control transactions, such as a certain percentage share purchase by an outside entity or when there is a tender offer for a certain percentage of the company's shares.

Greenmail   The payment of a premium above current market price for the shares held by a certain shareholder, with the goal of eliminating that shareholder as a threat to the company's independence.

Hart-Scott-Rodino Antitrust Improvements Act of 1976   A law that requires a bidding company to file with the Federal Trade Commission and the Justice Department and receive antitrust approval from one of these entities before completing a takeover.

Herfindahl-Hirschman (HH) Index   The sum of the squares of the market shares of companies in a given industry. It is a measure of industry concentration and is more sensitive to the effects of mergers than simple market shares.

Highly Confident Letter   A letter issued by an investment bank indicating that it is confident that it can raise the necessary financing for a takeover.

High-yield bond   Another name for a junk bond.

Holding company   A company that owns the stock of other corporations. A holding company may not engage in actual operations of its own but merely manages various operating units that it owns an interest in.

Horizontal equity   A principle of equal treatment for all shareholders such as in tender offers. Front end-loaded tender offers violate this principle.

Horizontal integration   A merger of firms selling a similar product or service.

Hubris hypothesis   A theory by Richard Roll that asserts that managers in acquiring companies believe that their valuations of targets may be superior to the market. This hubris causes them to overpay and overestimate the gains from acquisitions.

Initial public offering (IPO)   The first offering of the common stock to the public by a closely held company.

In play   When the market believes that a company may be taken over. At this time, the stock becomes concentrated in the hands of arbitragers and the company becomes vulnerable to a takeover and the target of a bid.

Investment Company Act of 1940   One of several pieces of federal legislation passed after the October 1929 stock market crash and the Great Depression. This law regulated the activities and reporting requirements of investment companies, which are firms whose principal business is the trading and management of securities.

Joint venture   When companies jointly pursue a certain business activity.

Junk bond   High-yield bonds that receive a rating from Standard & Poor's (or other agency) of BB or below. Such bonds are riskier than investment-grade bonds, which have higher ratings.

LBO   See Leveraged buyout.

LBO funds   A pool of investment capital that invests in various leveraged buyouts seeking to realize the high returns potentially available in LBOs while lowering risk through diversification.

Letter stock   *See* Tracking stock.

Lerner Index   Developed by Abba Lerner, the index measures market power as the difference between price and marginal cost relative to price.

Leveraged buyout (LBO)   The purchase of a company that is financed primarily by debt. However, the term is more often applied to debt-financed going-private transactions.

Leveraged ESOP   An employee stock ownership plan in which the purchase of shares is financed by debt. The principal and interest payments may be tax-deductible.

Liquidation   The sale of all of a company's assets whereby the firm ceases to exist.

Lockup option   An option to buy certain valuable assets or stock in the target, which it issues to a friendly party. If the option limits the bidding process, it could be legally challenged.

Management buyout (MBO)   A going-private transaction in which the management of a company or division of a company takes the company or division private.

Management entrenchment hypothesis   Proposes that nonparticipating shareholders experience reduced wealth when management takes actions to deter attempts to take control of the corporation.

Marketability discount   A discount applied to the value of some securities, such as securities in closely held companies, based on their comparatively lower liquidity.

Market flowback   The depressing stock price effect in the domestic stock market of an acquirer when it purchases a foreign company using its own stock as consideration.

Market model   A method that is used in event studies. Regression analysis is used to compute the return that is attributable to market forces. It is used to compute "excess returns" that may be attributable to the occurrence of an event.

Market power   Although this term is used differently in different contexts, one definition used in an industrial organization is the ability to set and maintain price above competitive levels.

Master limited partnership (MLP)   A limited partnership whose shares are publicly traded. Its key advantage is that it eliminates the layer of corporate taxation because MLPs are taxed like partnerships, not corporations.

Mezzanine layer financing   Subordinated debt financing that is often used in leveraged buyouts. It is debt but also has equity-like characteristics in that the debt securities are often accompanied by "equity kickers."

Minority discount   A discount applied to the value of equity securities based on a lack of control.

MLP   *See* Master limited partnership.

Monopoly   An industry structure that is characterized by one seller.

Morris Trust   Using a Morris Trust, a company could spin off component businesses that it did not want to keep while in a second set, preplanned transaction the spun-off business is merged into an acquirer's business in a tax-free stock transaction. The end result is that shareholders in the selling company end up with shares in both their own company and that of the acquirer.

NASDAQ   National Association of Securities Dealers Automated Quotations. It is the trading system for the over-the-counter market.

Net operating loss carryover   Tax benefits that allow companies to use net operating losses in certain years to offset taxable income in other years.

Net present value (NPV)   A capital budgeting technique that combines the present value of cash inflows of a project with the present value of investment outlays.

No-shop provisions   Where a seller agrees not to solicit or enter into sale agreements with any other bidders.

Note purchase rights   Another name for back-end poison pill plans.

Oligopoly   Industry structure characterized by a small number of sellers (i.e., 3–12).

Pac-Man defense   One of the more extreme antitakeover defenses. It refers to a situation in which a target makes a counteroffer for the bidder.

Partial tender offer   A tender offer for less than all of a target's outstanding shares.

Perfect competition   An industry structure characterized by certain conditions, including many buyers and sellers, homogeneous products, perfect information, easy entry and exit, and no barriers to entry. The existence of these conditions implies that each seller is a price taker.

PIK debt securities   Bonds that may pay bondholders compensation in a form other than cash.

Poison pill   A right issued by a corporation as a preventative antitakeover defense. It allows right holders to purchase shares in either their own company or the combined target and bidder companies at a discount, usually 50%. This discount may make the takeover prohibitively expensive.

Poison put   A provision added to bond indenture contracts that allows bondholders to sell or "put" their bonds back to the issuing corporation at a predetermined exercise price. Poison puts became popular in the LBO era of the 1980s, when bond prices plummeted in response to the increased debt loads of post-LBO companies and the subsequent downgrading of the debt.

Preferred stock plans   Early version of poison pills that used preferred stock as opposed to rights.

Prepackaged bankruptcy   In a prepackaged bankruptcy, the debtor negotiates the reorganization plan with its creditors before an actual Chapter 11 filing.

Proxy contest   When a dissident shareholder, or group of shareholders, tries to take control of the board of directors or use the process to enact certain changes in the activities of the company.

Pure plays   Companies that operate within clearly defined market boundaries.

Rabbi trusts   Where monies to fund golden parachutes are sometimes put.

Real estate investment trusts (REITs)   Publicly traded, passive investment vehicles that pay little or no federal taxes.

Recapitalization plan   The alteration of the capital structure of a company that adds debt and may reduce equity. It often is used as an antitakeover device when a target uses it as an alternative offer to a hostile bid. It often involves assuming considerable debt and paying a superdividend to target shareholders.

Restructuring charges   Also referred to as big bath write-offs. In a merger context it refers to a company's taking large write-offs following an acquisition, which lowers current income but may carry the implication that future income may be higher.

Reverse LBO   Companies that go public after having gone private in an LBO.

Reverse merger   When a closely held company goes public by merging into a public shell company.

Reverse synergy $4 - 1 = 5$; where, following a sell-off, the remaining parts of a company are more valuable than the original parent business.

Revlon duties   Legal principle that actions, such as antitakeover measures, that promote a value-maximizing auction process are allowable whereas those that thwart it are not.

Roll-up acquisitions   An acquisition program that features multiple acquisitions of smaller companies by a larger consolidator.

Schedule 13D   The document that is required by the Williams Act to be filed with the SEC within 10 days of acquiring 5% or more of a public company's outstanding shares. This filing discloses certain information, including the purchaser's identity and intentions, as well as other related information, such as financing sources, in the case of a planned takeover.

Schedule 14D   The document that, pursuant to the Williams Act, must be filed with the SEC by the initiator of a tender offer. This filing discloses information about the identity of the bidder, specifics of the offer, and other relevant information, such as sources of financing and postacquisition plans.

Scorched-earth defense   An antitakeover defense that has such an adverse effect on the target that it renders it undesirable to bidders.

Securities Act of 1933   The first of the federal securities laws of the 1930s. It provided for the registration of publicly traded securities.

Securities Exchange Act of 1934   The federal law that established the Securities and Exchange Commission. It also added further regulations for securities markets. The law has been amended several times since its initial passage. One of the amendments that are relevant to mergers is the Williams Act of 1968.

Sell-off   A general term describing a sale of a part of a company. It also includes other more specific transactions, such as divestitures or spin-offs.

Shareholder interests hypothesis   It implies that stockholder wealth rises when management takes actions to prevent changes in control.

Shark repellent   Another name for an antitakeover defense.

Shelf registration rule   SEC Rule 415 that allows companies to register, in advance, shares they may want to offer in the future.

Sherman Act of 1890   The major piece of federal antitrust legislation. It contains two principal sections: Section 1 prohibits all contracts and combinations in restraint of trade; Section 2 prohibits monopolization and attempts at monopolization.

Special purpose acquisition corporation (SPAC)   Company that goes public and uses proceeds to buy a company to be determined.

Spin-off   A type of sell-off in which a parent company distributes shares on a pro rata basis to its shareholders. These new shares give shareholders ownership rights in a division or part of the parent company that is sold off.

Split-off   A type of sell-off in which shareholders of a parent company exchange their shares in the parent company for shares in the sold-off entity.

Split-up   When the parent company spins off all of its component parts and ceases to exist.

Staggered board   Also called a classified board. This is an antitakeover measure in which the election of directors is split in separate periods so that only a percentage of the total number of directors come up for election in a given year. It is designed to make taking control of the board of directors more difficult.

Stakeholder   Any entity that is affected by the actions of a company, which may include shareholders, management, workers, communities, consumers, and so on.

Standstill agreement   An agreement that a potential hostile bidder enters into with the target corporation whereby the bidder agrees, in exchange for some consideration, not to purchase more than an agreed-upon number of shares.

Strategic alliance   A more flexible alternative to a joint venture whereby certain companies agree to pursue certain common activities and interests.

Stock parking   The attempt to evade the disclosure requirements of securities law by keeping shares in names other than that of the true owner.

Street sweeps   Open-market purchases of a target's stock that are not tender offers and therefore are not subject to the requirements of the Williams Act.

Supermajority provision   A preventative antitakeover defense that amends the corporate charter to require a higher majority, such as two-thirds or even more, to approve certain transactions such as mergers.

Synergy $2 + 2 = 5$; a combination of businesses in which the combined entity is more valuable than the sum of the parts.

Targeted share repurchase   Refers to repurchase of stock of a large shareholder, such as a hostile bidder. It usually is done at a premium over market prices. This type of transaction is also referred to as greenmail.

Targeted stock   *See* Tracking stock.

Tax-free reorganizations Types of business combinations in which shareholders do not incur tax liabilities. There are four types—A, B, C, and D—which differ in various ways, including the amount of stock and/or cash that is offered.

Tender offer An offer made directly to shareholders. One of the more common ways hostile takeovers are implemented.

Tracking stock An issuance of equity that represents an interest in the earnings of a division of a company.

Two-tiered tender offer Tender offers in which the bidder offers a superior first-tier price for a maximum number of shares while it offers to acquire the remaining shares in the second tier at a lower price.

Unocal standard The legal principle that reasonable defensive measures that are consistent with the business judgment rule are legally acceptable.

Vertical merger A merger of companies that operate at different levels or stages of the production process in the same industry. For example, a company with large oil reserves buying a pipeline company for a gasoline retailer is an example of forward integration. A consumer electronics retail chain that buys a brand name manufacturer would be an example of backward integration.

Voting plans A variation on the poison pill defense theme. They allow preferred stockholders to have supervoting rights if a bidder acquires a certain percentage of the target's stock. They are designed to prevent a bidder from getting voting control of the target.

White knight A more acceptable buyer that a target of a hostile bid may approach.

White squire A friendly company or investor that purchases an interest in the target of a hostile bid. The target may do this to make a takeover more difficult.

Williams Act of 1968 An amendment of the Securities and Exchange Act of 1934 that regulates tender offers and other takeover-related actions, such as larger share purchases.

Winner's curse This is the ironic hypothesis that states that bidders who overestimate the value of a target will most likely win a contest. This is due to the fact that they will be more inclined to overpay and outbid rivals who more accurately value the target.

Workout A workout refers to a negotiated agreement between the debtors and its creditors outside the bankruptcy process.

Index

Page numbers followed by f and t refer to figures and tables, respectively.